BRIDGING THE GAP

College Reading

Seventh Edition

Brenda D. Smith

Emerita, Georgia State University

New York San Francisco Boston
London Toronto Sydney Tokyo Singapore Madrid
Mexico City Munich Paris Cape Town Hong Kong Montreal

To

My Mother and Father

Senior Acquisitions Editor	Steven Rigolosi
Development Manager	Janet Lanphier
Development Editor	Marion B. Castellucci
Technical Reviewer	Jackie Stahlecker
Marketing Manager	Melanie Craig
Supplements Editor	Donna Campion
Media Supplements Editor	Nancy Garcia
Electronic Page Makeup, Project Coordination, and Text Design	Pre-Press Company, Inc.
Senior Production Manager	Eric Jorgensen
Cover Designer/Manager	John Callahan
Photo Researcher	Photosearch, Inc.
Print Buyer	Lucy Hebard
Printer and Binder	RR Donnelley & Sons Company
Cover Printer	Lehigh Press, Inc.

Library of Congress Cataloging-in-Publication Data

Smith, Brenda D., 1944–
Bridging the gap : college reading / Brenda D. Smith.--7th ed.
p. cm.
Includes bibliographical references (p.) and index.
ISBN 0-321-08826-3 (student ed.)--ISBN 0-321-08827-1 (teacher's ed.)
1. Reading (Higher education) 2. Study skills. I. Title.
LB2395.3 .S64 2003
428.4'071'1--dc21 2001050461

Please visit our website at http://www.ablongman.com/smith

ISBN 0-321-08826-3 (Student edition)
ISBN 0-321-08827-1 (Instructor's annotated edition)

12345678910—DOC—05 04 03 02

Brief Contents

Detailed Contents

3 Reading and Study Strategies 79

4 Main Idea 125

5 Patterns of Organization 193

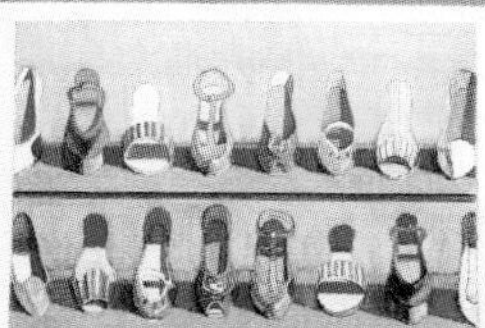

6 Organizing Textbook Information 247

7 Inference 291

8 Point of View 343

9 Critical Thinking 385

12 Test Taking 495

Preface

Success in college reading will be ultimately measured by a student's success in the academic courses required for graduation. The seventh edition of *Bridging the Gap* thus moves further than ever toward acquainting students with concepts in academic disciplines. In an exciting new feature called a **Concept Prep,** key concepts in several academic disciplines—psychology, computer science, art, anthropology, sociology, communications, life sciences, physical sciences, political science, allied health, business, economics, philosophy, and literature—are matched with the subjects of fifteen of the longer reading selections. These selected concepts, reflecting common knowledge that lies at the core of each academic area, are also an important part of the shared cultural heritage of educated thinkers. The purpose of this new feature is to develop schema and prior knowledge for students' later academic success. For example, the Concept Preps for psychology discuss people and ideas at the heart of every introductory psychology course, including Sigmund Freud's and Carl Jung's theories, Ivan Pavlov's discovery of and experiments with classical conditioning, and B. F. Skinner's behaviorism.

In addition to a separate chapter on vocabulary (Chapter 2), the new edition contains **Ten Weekly Vocabulary Lessons** that focus on linking and learning words through word parts or word families. Introducing more than 200 words, this feature represents a dramatic increase in the vocabulary-building activities offered in this textbook. To offer teaching flexibility and easy access for students, these lessons were placed in the appendix. The lessons can be assigned weekly, and student progress can be measured using the assessment quizzes in the Instructor's Manual. Also included in the appendix is a new ESL (English as a Second Language) section called **Making Sense of Figurative Language and Idioms**, which gives students practice with English similes, metaphors, and idioms. Finally, this edition includes more than 130 vocabulary words in context after the longer reading selections.

The seventh edition also contains separate chapters on main ideas (Chapter 4) and patterns of organization (Chapter 5), with additional models and practice exercises in both chapters. Practice exercises on transitional words are included, and the coverage of organizational patterns has been expanded. Instruction and practice on contrast, comparison, classification, addition, summary, location, and generalization and example patterns of organization have been added.

The **Contemporary Focus** features that were new in the last edition continue to connect textbook reading to real-world issues. The excerpts from recent magazine and newspaper articles have all been updated and are paired with the longer textbook reading selections. This edition contains twenty-two of these new introductory articles.

New **Search the Net** activities follow each longer textbook reading selection, and relevant URLs are suggested to help students launch a successful search. Since electronic reading skills are now essential for college students, the first Search the Net activity in Chapter 1 begins with an explanation of how to plan and conduct an effective Internet search. Subsequent activities pose questions that connect Internet exploration with the textbook topics in each longer reading selection.

The seventh edition contains fifteen new, longer reading selections. Many of these readings address international concerns and will challenge students to think critically about global issues.

The intent of this edition, as with previous editions, is to personally involve the reader, to build and enrich the knowledge networks for academic reading, to stimulate engaging class discussion, and to foster independent learning and thinking. I hope students enjoy learning from this colorful new edition.

Content and Organization

The seventh edition continues the tradition of previous editions by using actual college textbook material for teaching and practice. Designed for an upper-level course in college reading, each chapter introduces a new skill, provides short practice exercises to teach the skill, and then offers practice through longer textbook selections.

Presentation of skills in the text moves from the general to the specific. Initial chapters discuss active learning (Chapter 1), vocabulary (Chapter 2), study strategies (Chapter 3), main idea (Chapter 4), and patterns of organization (Chapter 5), while later chapters teach inference (Chapter 7), point of view (Chapter 8), critical thinking (Chapter 9), graphic illustrations (Chapter 10), rate flexibility (Chapter 11), and test-taking skills (Chapter 12). The reading and study skills discussions in the first portion of the book stress the need to construct the main idea of a passage and to select significant supporting details. Exercises encourage "engaged thinking" before reading, while reading, and after reading. Four different methods of organizing textbook information for later study are explained.

Special Features of the Seventh Edition

- **Concept Preps** in psychology, computer science, art, anthropology, sociology, communications, life sciences, physical sciences, political science, allied health, business, economics, philosophy, and literature explain key academic concepts and are matched with the subjects in most of the longer reading selections. These Concept Preps present common knowledge at the core of each academic area.
- **Ten Weekly Vocabulary Lessons** (Appendix 1) focus on linking and learning words through word parts or word families. These lessons, with more

than 200 words, are placed in the appendix for teaching flexibility and for easy student access.

- **Main Idea** and **Patterns of Organization** are presented in two separate chapters (Chapters 4 and 5) with expanded practice exercises. Transitional words are included, and the coverage of organizational patterns has also been expanded.
- **Making Sense of Figurative Language and Idioms** (Appendix 2) presents sixty idiomatic expressions that will be of particular value to ESL students.
- Twenty-two new **Contemporary Focus** articles linked to the longer textbook readings are included to stimulate cognitive connections and to promote group discussion. Each article is drawn from a popular source, such as a magazine or newspaper, to demonstrate the textbook reading's relevance to the "real world." **Contemporary Link** questions promote critical thinking by demonstrating the relevance of the introductory articles to the textbook selections that they accompany. A list of textbook readings, along with their accompanying Contemporary Focus features, follows the Preface.
- Twenty new **Search the Net** activities encourage students to amplify textbook study through Internet research. Instructions on how to use the Internet for research are presented in Chapter 1. A book-specific Longman website is also available: http://www.ablongman.com/smith.
- **Fifteen new longer reading selections** are included.
- A **Progress Chart** is located on the inside back cover so students can record their progress in understanding the longer reading selections.

Continuing Features

Other classroom-tested features of the book include the following:

- Actual **textbook selections** are used for practice exercises.
- **Many academic disciplines** are represented throughout, including psychology, history, economics, business, allied health, biology, sociology, art, nutrition, computer science, and literature.
- A broad range of **vocabulary development** topics and corresponding exercises is presented in Chapter 2. In addition, vocabulary exercises follow each of the longer textbook reading selections.
- **Reader's Tip** boxes give easy-to-access advice for readers, condensing strategies for improving reading into practical hints for quick reference.
- Each longer textbook selection has both **explicit and inferential questions**. Multiple-choice items are labeled as *main idea*, *inference*, or *detail questions*.
- Some selections include essay questions that elicit an organized **written response**.
- **Vocabulary is presented in context,** and vocabulary exercises are included in each chapter.

- Although skills build and overlap, **each chapter can be taught as a separate unit** to fit individual class or student needs.
- **Pages are perforated** so that students can tear out and hand in assignments.
- A **Reader's Journal** activity appears at the end of each chapter so that students can learn about themselves, reflect on their strengths and weaknesses, and monitor their progress as learners.
- Discussion and practice exercises on **barriers to critical thinking**—including cultural conditioning, self-deception, and oversimplification—appear throughout the book.
- Practice is offered in **identifying fallacies** in critical thinking and in **evaluating arguments.**

The Teaching and Learning Package

Each component of the teaching and learning package has been crafted to ensure that the course is a rewarding experience for both instructors and students.

The **Annotated Instructor's Edition** (0-321-08827-1) is an exact replica of the student edition but includes all answers printed directly on the fill-in lines provided in the text.

The **Instructor's Manual** (0-321-08828-X) contains overhead transparency masters and additional vocabulary and comprehension questions for each reading selection. The true-false, vocabulary, and comprehension quizzes can be used as prereading quizzes to stimulate interest or as evaluation quizzes after reading. Vocabulary-in-context exercises are also included to reinforce the words in the longer textbook selections. In addition, a true-false quiz is provided for each of the new Concept Prep sections. To receive an examination copy of the Instructor's Manual, please contact your Longman sales representative. You may also request an examination copy by calling 1-800-552-2499, or by sending your request via e-mail to exam@ablongman.com.

The **Test Bank** (0-321-08829-8) includes additional reading selections, chapter tests and vocabulary tests. To receive an examination copy of the Test Bank, please contact your Longman sales representative. You may also request an examination copy by calling 1-800-552-2499, or by e-mailing your request to exam@ablongman.com.

For a wealth of additional materials, including online chapter summaries, quizzes, and Internet activities, be sure to visit the *Bridging the Gap* **Companion Website** at http://www.ablongman.com/smith.

The Longman Basic Skills Package

In addition to the book-specific supplements discussed above, a series of other skills-based supplements is available for both instructors and students. All of these supplements are available either free or at greatly reduced prices.

Electronic and Online Offerings

Longman Reading Road Trip Multimedia Software, CD Version and Web Version. This innovative and exciting multimedia reading software is available either on CD-ROM format or on the Web. The package takes students on a tour of 15 cities and landmarks throughout the United States. Each of the 15 modules corresponds to a reading or study skill (for example, finding the main idea, understanding patterns of organization, and thinking critically). All modules contain a tour of the location, instruction and tutorial, exercises, interactive feedback, and mastery tests. To shrinkwrap the CD or the access code to the Website with this textbook, please consult your Longman sales representative.

Longman Vocabulary Website. For additional vocabulary-related resources, visit our free vocabulary Website at http://www.ablongman.com/vocabulary.

The Longman English Pages Website. Both students and instructors can visit our free content-rich Website for additional reading selections and writing exercises. From the Longman English pages, visitors can conduct a simulated Web search, learn how to write a resume and cover letter, or try their hand at poetry writing. Stop by and visit us at http://www.ablongman.com/englishpages.

The Longman Electronic Newsletter. Twice a month during the spring and fall, instructors who have subscribed receive a free copy of the Longman Developmental English Newsletter in their e-mailbox. Written by experienced classroom instructors, the newsletter offers teaching tips, classroom activities, book reviews, and more. To subscribe, visit the Longman Basic Skills Web site at http://www.ablongman.com/basicskills, or send an e-mail to BasicSkills@ablongman.com.

For Additional Reading and Reference

The Dictionary Deal. Two dictionaries can be shrinkwrapped with *Bridging the Gap* at a nominal fee. *The New American Webster Handy College Dictionary* is a paperback reference text with more than 100,000 entries. *Merriam Webster's Collegiate Dictionary*, tenth edition, is a hardback reference with a citation file of more than 14.5 million examples of English words drawn from actual use. For more information on how to shrinkwrap a dictionary with your text, please contact your Longman sales representative.

Penguin Quality Paperback Titles. A series of Penguin paperbacks is available at a significant discount when shrinkwrapped with any Longman Basic Skills title. Some titles available are Toni Morrison's *Beloved*, Julia Alvarez's *How the Garcia Girls Lost Their Accents*, Mark Twain's *Huckleberry Finn*, *Narrative of the Life of Frederick Douglass*, Harriet Beecher Stowe's *Uncle Tom's Cabin*, Dr. Martin Luther King, Jr.'s *Why We Can't Wait*, and plays by Shakespeare, Miller, and Albee. For a complete list of titles or more information, please contact your Longman sales consultant.

***The Pocket Reader* and *The Brief Pocket Reader,* First Edition.** These inexpensive volumes contains 80 and 50 readings, respectively. Each reading is brief (1–3 pages each). The readers are theme-based: writers on writing, nature, women and men, customs and habits, politics, rights and obligations, and coming of age. Also included is an alternate rhetorical table of contents. (0-321-07668-0)

The Longman Textbook Reader. This supplement, for use in developmental reading courses, offers five complete chapters from Addison-Wesley/Longman textbooks: computer science, biology, psychology, communications, and business. Each chapter includes additional comprehension quizzes, critical thinking questions, and group activities. Available FREE with the adoption of this Longman text. For information on how to bundle *The Longman Textbook Reader* with your text, please contact your Longman sales representative. Available in two formats: with answers and without answers.

***Newsweek* Alliance.** Instructors may choose to shrinkwrap a 12-week subscription to *Newsweek* with any Longman text. The price of the subscription is 57 cents per issue (a total of $6.84 for the subscription). Available with the subscription is a free "Interactive Guide to *Newsweek*"—a workbook for students who are using the text. In addition, Newsweek provides a wide variety of instructor supplements free to teachers, including maps, Skills Builders, and weekly quizzes. For more information on the Newsweek program, please contact your Longman sales representative.

For Instructors

Electronic Test Bank for Reading. (CD-ROM: 0-321-08179-X Print version: 0-321-08596-5) This electronic test bank offers more than 3,000 questions in all areas of reading, including vocabulary, main idea, supporting details, patterns of organization, language, critical thinking, analytical reasoning, inference, point of view, visual aids, and textbook reading. With this easy-to-use CD-ROM, instructors simply choose questions from the electronic test bank, then print out the completed test for distribution.

CLAST Test Package, Fourth Edition. (Reproducible sheets: 0-321-01950-4 Computerized IBM version: 0-321-01982-2 Computerized Mac version: 0-321-01983-0) These two 40-item objective tests evaluate students' readiness for the CLAST exams. Strategies for teaching CLAST preparedness are included. Free with any Longman English title.

TASP Test Package, Third Edition. (Reproducible sheets: 0-321-01959-8 Computerized IBM version: 0-321-01985-7 Computerized Mac version: 0-321-01984-9) These 12 practice pre-tests and post-tests assess the same reading and writing skills covered in the TASP examination. Free with any Longman English title.

***Teaching Online: Internet Research, Conversation, and Composition,* Second Edition.** (0-321-01957-1) Ideal for instructors who have never surfed the Net, this easy-to-follow guide offers basic definitions, numerous examples, and step-by-step information about finding and using Internet sources. Free to adopters.

[NEW] The Longman Guide to Classroom Management (0-321-09246-5) is the first in a series of monographs for developmental educators. Written by Joannis Flatley of St. Philip's College, it focuses on issues of classroom etiquette, providing guidance on dealing with unruly, unengaged, disruptive, or uncooperative students.

[NEW] The Longman Instructor Planner (0-321-09247-3) is an all-in-one resource for instructors. It includes monthly and weekly planning sheets, to-do lists, student contact forms, attendance rosters, a gradebook, an address/phone book, and a mini almanac. It is free upon request.

For Students

***Researching Online,* Sixth Edition.** (0-321-117733-6) A perfect companion for a new age, this indispensable new supplement helps students navigate the Internet. Adapted from *Teaching Online*, the instructor's Internet guide, *Researching Online* speaks directly to students, giving them detailed, step-by-step instructions for performing electronic searches. Available free when shrinkwrapped with this text.

Ten Practices of Highly Successful Students. (0-205-30769-8) This popular supplement helps students learn crucial study skills, offering concise tips for a successful career in college. Topics include time management, test-taking, reading critically, stress, and motivation.

***Thinking Through the Test,* by D. J. Henry.** This special workbook, prepared specially for students in Florida, offers ample skill and practice exercises to help student prep for the Florida State Exit Exam. To shrinkwrap this workbook free with your textbook, please contact your Longman sales representative. Available in two versions: with answers and without answers. Also available: Two laminated grids (one for reading, one for writing) that can serve as handy references for students preparing for the Florida State Exit Exam.

The Longman Reader's Journal, by Kathleen T. McWhorter. (0-321-08843-3) This reader's journal offers students a space to record their questions about, reactions to, and summaries of materials they've read. Also included is a personal vocabulary log, as well as ample space for free writing. For an examination copy, contact your Longman sales consultant.

The Longman Planner. (0-321-04573-4) This free planner helps students organize a busy life. Ask your Longman sales representative for an examination copy.

Acknowledgments

It has been a pleasure to work with my buddy and Basic Skills Editor, Steven Rigolosi. Steve has a creative idea every other minute. His discussions with teachers and his vision guided the new Concept Prep feature. Steve is very dedicated to identifying and meeting the needs of teachers and students.

I appreciate the opportunity to have worked with developmental editor Marion Castellucci. This is the first book that Marion and I have done together, and she has done an excellent job. She has been thoughtful, thorough, supportive, and prompt.

My two researchers, Donna Cassidy and Lisa Moore, have been invaluable helpers. Donna has worked diligently on vocabulary as well as on questions for the Instructor's Manual. Lisa located many of the Contemporary Focus articles and researched the Search the Net exercises. Both Donna and Lisa pushed themselves to deliver the best material possible for our teachers and students. Jackie Stahlecker of St. Philip's College served as technical reviewer. This book has benefited from the excellent contributions of all these individuals.

Again, I feel extremely privileged to have received advice from so many learned colleagues in the college reading profession. I am particularly grateful to Melinda Schomaker, Emily Johnson, and Maryann Errico of Georgia Perimeter College. This book is strengthened by their insightful, sincere, and constructive comments. I would also like to thank these knowledgeable and concerned instructors:

Edith Alderson, Joliet Junior College
Julia Beyeler, University of Akron–Wayne College
Helen R. Carr, San Antonio College
Jessica Carroll, Miami-Dade Community College
Dianne Cates, Central Piedmont Community College
Patricia Hill, Central Piedmont Community College
Marian Helms, College of Southern Idaho
Sylvia H. Holmes, Florence-Darlington Technical College
Susie Khirallah-Johnston, Tyler Junior College
Susan Pongratz, Thomas Nelson Community College
Dianne Ruggiero, Broward Community College
Susan K. Scott, Pensacola Junior College
Katie Smith, Riverside Community College

Brenda D. Smith
Atlanta, Georgia

An Overview of *Bridging the Gap*

The seventh edition of *Bridging the Gap* features paired readings at the end of most chapters, in many cases followed by a Concept Prep for a particular academic discipline. Each reading selection begins with a Contemporary Focus article drawn from a popular source, such as a newspaper or magazine, that demonstrates the relevance to the world beyond college of the textbook selection that follows. The Concept Prep provides background information about the subject area.

Discipline/Genre of Reading Selection	Textbook or Academic Selection	Accompanying Contemporary Focus Article	Accompanying Concept Prep
Chapter 1 Active Learning			
Computer Science	Security and Privacy for Computers and the Internet	Hackers Flaunt Dignitaries' Credit Card Data	Computer Science
Psychology	Critical-Period Hypothesis	Dolphin Saves Boy's Life	Psychology
Chapter 3 Reading and Study Strategies			
Communications	The Listening Process	Listening Skills Saves Time and Increases Effectiveness	Communications and Language
Sociology	Unity in Diversity	Make the Right Gesture on a Trip to Asia	Anthropology
Chapter 4 Main Idea			
Psychology	Monkey Love	Brain Research on Monkeys	Psychology
Art History	Why Write About Art?	A Blue Period for Art Buyers	Art
Sociology	Urbanization	Letter from Brazil	Sociology
Chapter 5 Patterns of Organization			
Economics	Slave Redemption in Sudan	In Sudan, Childhoods of Slavery	Economics
History	Women in History	Bush's Secret Weapon	History
Business	Expanding into the International Marketplace	Global Experience Through Study Abroad	Business

Discipline/Genre of Reading Selection	Textbook or Academic Selection	Accompanying Contemporary Focus Article	Accompanying Concept Prep
Chapter 6 Organizing Textbook Information			
Biology	Pregnancy and Birth	Blood Therapy	Life Science
Allied Health	Nutrition, Health, and Stress	Food and Stress	Health
Chapter 7 Inference			
Short Story	The Ant and the Grasshopper	A Short Course in Short-Short Fiction	Philosophy and Literature
Essay	Breakfast at the FDA Cafe	Dangerous Foods	
Narrative Nonfiction	Colin Powell	Leading People	Political Science
Chapter 8 Point of View			
Essay	Elderly Parents	50 Not So Nifty for Baby Boomers	
Business	Should Companies Stress English Only on the Job?	The Triumph of English	
Essay	Tracking the Werewolf	Ramseys Sue Ex-Cop	
Chapter 9 Critical Thinking			
Essay	The Importance of Being Beautiful	Why Looks Matter	
Editorial Essay	Students Led to Believe Opinions More Important than Knowledge	Practicing What He Preaches	
Editorial Essay	Marketing Fertility	The Ethics of Eggs	
Chapter 10 Graphic Illustrations			
Allied Health	Alcohol and Nutrition	Scouting a Dry Campus	Physical and Earth Sciences
Chapter 11 Rate Flexibility			
Allied Health	Passive Smoking		
Sociology	The Jaime Escalante Approach to Restructuring the Classroom		
History	American Lives: Bill Gates		

1

Active Learning

- What is active learning?
- How does the brain "pay attention"?
- Can you do two things at once?
- How can you improve your concentration?
- What are common internal and external distractors and cures?
- Why is your syllabus important?

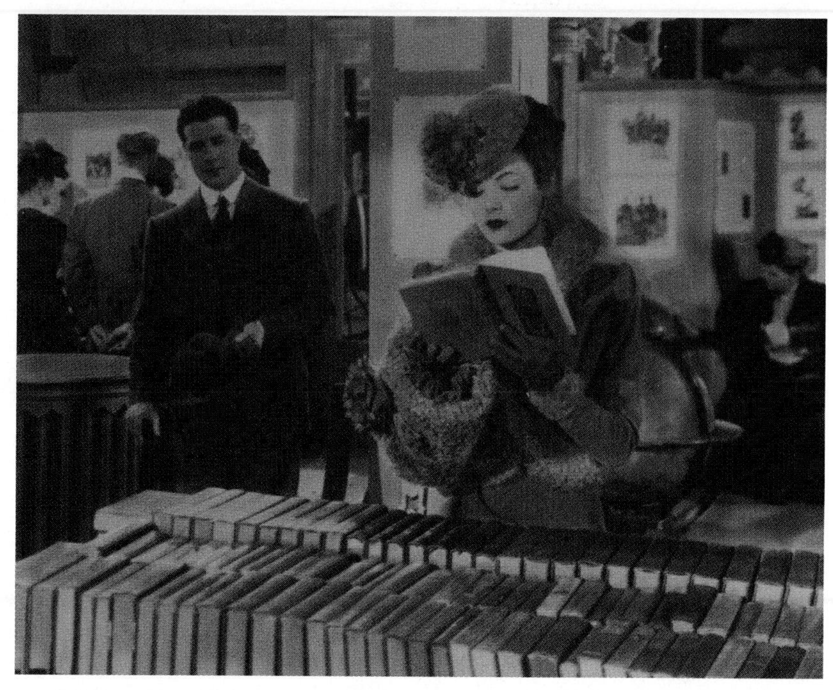

Colorized movie still from Heaven Can Wait, *1943. Photos12.com–Collection Cinéma.*

What Is Active Learning?

Rather than being a single task, active learning is a *project with multiple components.* You, your instructor, your textbook, and your fellow learners are all components in the project. All contribute to your ability to accumulate and interpret new information, to connect and arrange the information into your own unique knowledge networks, and to retain and recall that information. As an active learner, you are thoughtfully and intellectually involved in each of the components in the project of learning.

Active learning requires alertness, concentration, and attention to details beyond the pages of a textbook. Because it is a project, active learning also requires that you learn to manage yourself, manage the assignment or learning task, and manage others who can contribute to or detract from your success. In this chapter we will discuss many factors that contribute to your ability to become an effective active learner. First, however, let's consider what psychologists have to say about thinking and learning.

What Is Cognitive Psychology?

Cognitive psychology is the body of knowledge that describes how the mind works, or at least how experts think the mind works. Fortunately or unfortunately, the activity of the brain when concentrating, reading, and remembering cannot be observed directly. These cognitive processes are invisible, just as thinking and problem solving are also invisible.

Since so little is actually known about thinking, the ideas of cognitive psychologists are frequently described as *models* or designs of something else we understand. For the last thirty years, for example, the central processing unit of a computer has been a popular model for describing how the brain processes information. The human brain is more complex than a computer, but the analogy provides a comparison that can help us understand.

How Does the Brain Screen Messages?

Cognitive psychologists use the word **attention** to describe a student's uninterrupted mental focus. Thinking and learning, they say, begin with attention. During every minute of the day the brain is bombarded with millions of sensory messages. How does the brain decide which messages to pay attention to and which to overlook? At this moment, are you thinking about the temperature of the room, outdoor noises, or what you are reading? Since all of this information is available to you, how is your brain able to set priorities?

The brain relies on a dual command center to screen out one message and attend to another. According to a researcher at UCLA, receptor cells send millions of messages per minute to your brain.[1] Your reticular activating system (RAS), a network of cells at the top of the spinal cord that runs to the brain, tells the cortex in the brain not to bother with most of the sensory input. Your RAS knows that most sensory inputs do not need attention. For example, you are probably not aware at this moment of your back pressing against your chair or your clothes pulling on your body. Your RAS has decided not to clutter the brain with such irrelevant information unless there is an extreme problem, like your foot going to sleep because you are sitting on it.

The cortex can also make attention decisions. When you decide to concentrate your attention on a task, like reading your history assignment, your cortex tells your RAS not to bother it with trivial information. While you focus on learning, your RAS follows orders and "holds" the messages as if you were

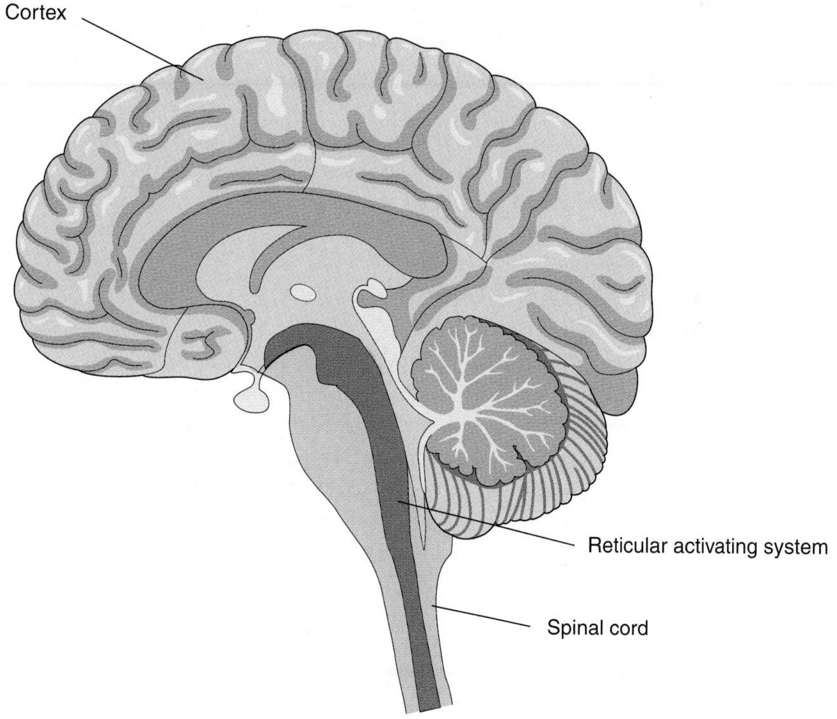

[1]H. W. Magoun, *The Waking Brain*, 2nd ed. (Springfield, IL: Charles C. Thomas, 1963).

on an important long-distance call. The cortex and the RAS cooperate in helping you block out distractions and concentrate on learning.

Is Divided Attention Effective?

Students often ask if it is possible to do two things at once, such as watching television and doing homework. Most psychologists agree that you can attend to only one thing at a time. An early researcher used a "switch model" to describe his belief, saying that attention operates like the on-off switch of a light fixture in that only one channel is "on" at a time.[2] The "cocktail party effect" illustrates this model. At a party with many available conversations within your listening range, you would probably attend to only one at a time. If your name were spoken in a nearby group, however, your attention would be diverted. You would probably "switch" your attention to the nearby group to seek more information on such a fascinating topic while only pretending to listen to the original conversation. According to this model, you would not be able to listen intently to both conversations at the same time.

Two later researchers conducted an experiment to test the effectiveness of divided attention.[3] They asked participants to watch two televised sports events with one superimposed over the other. When instructed to attend to only one of the games, they did an excellent job of screening out the other and answering questions accurately. When asked to attend to both games simultaneously, however, they made eight times more mistakes than when focusing on only one game. This research seems to confirm the old adage, "You can't do two things at once and do them well."

Can Tasks Become Automatic?

Can you walk and chew gum at the same time? Does every simple activity require your undivided attention? Many tasks—walking, tying shoelaces, and driving a car, for example—begin under controlled processing, which means that they are deliberate and require concentrated mental effort to learn. After much practice, however, such tasks become automatic. Driving a car is a learned behavior that researchers would say becomes an automatic process after thousands of hours of experience. You can probably drive, change radio stations, and talk at the same time. Driving no longer requires your full cognitive capacity unless conditions are hazardous. Similarly, a skilled athlete can dribble a basketball automatically while also attending to strategy and position. Attention is actually not divided because it can shift away from tasks that have become automatic.

---

[2]D. E. Broadbent, *Perception and Communication* (London: Pergamon Press, 1958).

[3]U. Neisser and R. Becklen, "Selective Looking: Attending to Visually Significant Events," *Cognitive Psychology* 7 (1975): 480–94.

Automatic Aspects of Reading

The idea of doing certain things automatically is especially significant in reading. As a first-grade reader, you had to concentrate on recognizing letters, words, and sentences, as well as trying to construct meaning. After years of practice and overlearning, much of the recognition aspect of reading has become automatic. You no longer stop laboriously to decode each word or each letter. For example, why can you look at the word *child* without processing the meaning? It is because you automatically think the meaning. Thus, you can focus your mental resources on understanding the *message* in which the word appears, rather than on understanding the word itself.

College textbooks often contain many unfamiliar words and complex concepts that are not automatically processed. Attention to the message can be interrupted by the need to attend to an individual unit of thought. Such breaks are to be expected in college reading because of the newness of the material. You can become caught in the dilemma of trying to do two things at once—that is, trying to figure out word meaning as well as trying to understand the message. When this happens, your attention shifts to defining and then returns to comprehending. After such a break, you can regain your concentration, and little harm is done if the breaks are infrequent. However, frequent breaks in this automatic aspect of reading can undermine your ability to concentrate on the message.

Cognitive Styles

Many psychologists believe that people develop a preference for a particular style or manner of learning at an early age and that these preferences affect concentration and learning. For example, some people learn easily by reading, but others benefit more readily from a demonstration or a diagram. Similarly, engineers like to work with details, whereas politicians prefer broad generalizations. Cognitive style theorists focus on strengths and assert that there is no right or wrong way. These researchers believe that instruction is best when it matches the learner's particular preference.

Although knowing your preferences may not affect how your classes are taught, such knowledge can improve your attitude about yourself as a learner and your ability to focus by enabling you to build on your strengths.

Cognitive Style Preferences. One popular personality inventory that can be used to determine individual cognitive style preferences is the Myers-Briggs Type Indicator (MBTI). Based on psychologist Carl Jung's theory of personality types, it measures personality traits in four categories. The results are used as indicators for learning styles, teaching styles, management styles, career planning, team building, organizational development, and even marriage counseling. The inventory must be administered by a licensed specialist and is frequently given to entering college freshmen. The following description of the four MBTI categories gives an idea of the kinds of issues that its proponents consider significant.

1. *Extroverted—introverted:* Extroverts prefer to talk with others and learn through experience, whereas introverts prefer to think alone about ideas.
2. *Sensing—intuitive:* Sensing types prefer working with concrete details and tend to be patient, practical, and realistic. Intuitive types like abstractions and are creative, impatient, and theory oriented.
3. *Thinking—feeling:* Thinking types tend to base decisions on objective criteria and logical principles. Feeling types are subjective and consider the impact of the decision on other people.
4. *Judging—perceiving:* Judging types are time-oriented and structured, whereas perceivers are spontaneous and flexible.

Another test that uses the same type indicators as the MBTI is the Keirsey Temperament Sorter II. This seventy-item online personality inventory issues an extensive printout, but experts do not consider it to have passed the same rigorous standards for validation and reliability as the Myers-Briggs. The Keirsey home page (http://www.keirsey.com) provides background information about the test. It begins with a brief questionnaire and then has a link to the longer Keirsey Temperament Sorter II.

Right- Versus Left-Brain Dominance. Another popular cognitive style theory is concerned with right- or left-brain dominance. Proponents of this theory believe that left-brain dominant people are analytical and logical and excel in verbal skills. Right-brain people, on the other hand, are intuitive, creative, and emotional, and tend to think in symbols. Albert Einstein, for example, said that he rarely thought in words, but that his concepts appeared in symbols and images.

Cognitive style theorists offer another way of looking at attention and learning by encouraging us to recognize and appreciate our strengths and differences. If you are "turned off" by an assignment, try to translate it into activities and ideas that are more compatible with your learning preferences. For example, if you prefer right-brain activities, use maps, charts, and drawings to help you concentrate while studying. Acknowledge your strengths and use them to enhance your concentration.

What Is Concentration?

Concentration is a skill that is developed through self-discipline and practice—not a mystical power, a hereditary gift, or an extra gene. It is a **habit** that requires time and effort to develop for consistent success. Athletes have it, surgeons have it, and successful college students must have it. *Concentration is essential for active learning.*

Concentration can be defined as the process of *paying attention*—that is, focusing full attention on the task at hand. Someone once said that the mark of a genius is the ability to concentrate completely on one thing at a time. This is easy if the task is fun and exciting, but it becomes more difficult when you are required to read something that is not very interesting to you. At this point your mind begins to wander, and the words on the page remain just words for the eyes to see rather than becoming meaningful thoughts to connect and remember.

Poor Concentration: Causes and Cures

The type of intense concentration that forces the RAS and cortex to close out the rest of the world is the state we would all like to achieve each time we sit down with a textbook. Too often, however, our attention becomes divided.

Students frequently ask, *How can I keep my mind on what I'm doing?* or they say, *I finished the assignment, but I don't understand a thing I read.* The solution is not a simple mental trick to fool the brain; rather, it involves a series of practical short- and long-range planning strategies targeted at reducing external and internal distractions.

External Distractions

External distractions are the temptations of the physical world that divert your attention away from your work. They are the people in the room, the noise in the background, the time of day, or your place for studying. To control these external distractions, you must create an environment that says, "Now this is the place and the time for me to get my work done."

Create a Place for Studying. Start by establishing your own private study cubicle; it may be in the library, on the dining room table, or in your bedroom. Wherever it is, choose a straight chair and face the wall. Get rid of gadgets, magazines, and other temptations that trigger the mind to think of *play.* Stay away from the bed because it triggers *sleep.* Spread out your papers, books, and other symbols of studying and create an atmosphere in which the visual stimuli signal *work.* Be consistent by trying to study in the same place at the same time.

Use a Pocket Calendar, Assignment Book, or Personal Digital Assistant. At the beginning of the quarter or semester, record dates for tests, term papers, and special projects on a calendar or personal digital assistant (PDA) that you can keep with you. Use the planner to organize all course assignments. A look at the calendar will remind you of the need for both short- and long-term planning. Assigned tests, papers, and projects will be due whether you are ready or not. Your first job is to devise a plan for getting ready.

Schedule Weekly Activities. Successful people do not let their time slip away; they manage time, rather than letting time manage them. Plan realistically and then follow your plan.

You can follow the model of a weekly activity chart shown here. Analyze your responsibilities and in the squares on the chart write your fixed activities—including class hours, work time, mealtime, and bedtime. Next, think about how much time you plan to spend studying and how much on recreation, and plug those into the chart. For studying, indicate the specific subject and exact place involved.

Weekly Activity Chart

Time	Monday	Tuesday	Wednesday	Thursday	Friday	Saturday	Sunday
7:00–8:00							
8:00–9:00							
9:00–10:00							
10:00–11:00							
11:00–12:00							
12:00–1:00							
1:00–2:00							
2:00–3:00							
3:00–4:00							
4:00–5:00							
5:00–6:00							
6:00–7:00							
7:00–8:00							
8:00–9:00							
9:00–10:00							
10:00–11:00							
11:00–12:00							

Make a fresh chart at the beginning of each week since responsibilities and assignments vary. Learn to estimate the time usually needed for typical assignments. Include time for a regular review of lecture notes.

Examinations require special planning. Many students do not realize how much time it takes to study for a major exam. Spread your studying out over several days and avoid last-minute cramming sessions late at night. Plan additional time for special projects and term papers to avoid deadline crises.

Plan Breaks. Even though it is not necessary to write this on the chart, remember that you need short breaks. Few students can study uninterrupted for two hours without becoming fatigued and losing concentration. Try the *50:10 ratio*—study hard for fifty minutes, take a ten-minute break, and then promptly go back to the books for another fifty minutes.

Internal Distractions

Internal distractions are the concerns that come repeatedly into your mind as you try to keep your attention focused on an assignment. Rather than the noise or the conversations in a room, they are the nagging worries or doubts in your mind that disrupt your work.

Unfortunately, students, just like everyone else, have to run errands, pick up laundry, make telephone calls, and pay bills. The world does not stop just because George has to read four chapters for a test in "Western Civ" by Wednesday. Consequently, when George sits down to read, he worries about getting an inspection sticker for his car or about picking up tickets for Saturday's ball game rather than concentrating completely on the assignment.

Make a List. For the most part, the interferences that pop into the mind and break reading concentration are minor concerns rather than major problems. To gain control over these mental disruptions, make a list of what is on your mind that is keeping you from concentrating on your studies. Jot down on a piece of paper each mental distraction and then analyze each to determine if immediate action is possible. If so, get up and take action. Make that phone call, write that letter, or finish that chore. Maybe it will take a few minutes or maybe half an hour, but the investment will have been worthwhile if the quality of your study time—your concentration power—has improved. Taking action is the first step in getting something off your mind.

For a big problem that you can't tackle immediately, ask yourself, "Is it worth the amount of brain time I'm dedicating to it?" Take a few minutes to think and make notes on possible solutions. Jotting down necessary future action and forming a plan of attack will help relieve the worry and clear the mind for studying.

Right now, list five things that are on your mind that you need to remember to do. Alan Lakein, a specialist in time management, calls this a **to-do list.** In his book, *How to Get Control of Your Time and Your Life,*[4] Lakein claims that successful business executives start each day with such a list. Rank the activities on your list in order of priority and then do the most important things first.

---

[4]A. Lakein, *How to Get Control of Your Time and Your Life* (New York: Signet, 1974).

To-Do List	Sample
1.	1. Get hair cut
2.	2. Do my book report
3.	3. Buy stamps
4.	4. Call power co.
5.	5. Pay phone bill

Increase Your Self-Confidence. Saying "I'll never pass this course" or "I can't get in the mood to study" is the first step to failure. Concentration requires self-confidence. If you didn't think you could do it, you would not be in a college class reading this book. Getting a college degree is not a short-term goal. Your enrollment indicates that you have made a commitment to a long-term goal. Ask yourself the question, "Who do I want to be in five years?" In the following space, describe how you view yourself, both professionally and personally, five years from now.

Five years from now I hope to be ________________________

____

____

____

Sometimes identifying the traits you admire in others can give you further insight into your own values and desires. Think about the traits you respect in others and your own definition of success. Answer the two questions that follow and consider how your responses mirror your own aspirations and goals.

Who is the person that you admire the most? ________________

Why do you admire this person? ________________________

____

____

____

Improve Your Self-Concept. Have faith in yourself and in your ability to be what you want to be. How many people do you know who have passed the particular course that is worrying you? Are they smarter than you? Probably not. Can you do as well as they did? Turn your negative feeling into a positive attitude. What are some of your positive traits? Are you a hard worker, an honest person, a loyal friend? Take a few minutes to pat yourself on the back.

Think about your good points and, in the following spaces, list five positive traits that you believe you possess.

Positive Traits

1. ______________________________
2. ______________________________
3. ______________________________
4. ______________________________
5. ______________________________

What have you already accomplished? Did you participate in athletics in high school, win any contests, or master any difficult skills? Recall your previous achievements, and in the following spaces, list three accomplishments that you view with pride.

Accomplishments

1. ______________________________
2. ______________________________
3. ______________________________

Reduce Anxiety. Have you ever heard people say, "I work better under pressure?" This statement contains a degree of truth. A small amount of tension can help you to force yourself to direct full attention on an immediate task. For example, concentrated study for an exam is usually more intense two nights before, rather than two weeks before, the test.

Yet too much anxiety can cause nervous tension and discomfort, which interfere with the ability to concentrate. Students operating under too much tension sometimes "freeze up" mentally and experience nervous physical reactions. The causes can range from fear of failure to lack of organization and preparation; the problem is not easily solved.

As an immediate, short-term response to tension, try muscle relaxation and visualization. For example, if you are reading a particularly difficult section in a chemistry book and are becoming frustrated to the point that you can no longer concentrate, stop your reading and take several deep breaths. Use your imagination to visualize a peaceful setting in which you are calm and relaxed. Imagine yourself rocking back and forth in a hammock or lying on a beach listening to the surf. Use the image you created and the deep breathing to help relax your muscles and regain control. Take several deep breaths and allow your body to release the tension so that you can resume reading and concentrate on your work.

As a long-term solution, nothing works better than success. Just as failure fuels tension, success tends to weaken it. Each successful experience helps to diminish feelings of inadequacy. Early success in a course can make a big psychological difference.

Spark an Interest. Approaching potentially dull material, like meeting reputedly dull people, can benefit from background work. Ask some questions, get some ideas, and do some thinking before starting to read. If the material was assigned, it must have merit, and finding it will make your job easier. Make a conscious effort to stimulate your curiosity before reading, even if in a contrived manner. Make yourself want to learn something. First look over the assigned reading for words or phrases that attract your attention, glance at the pictures, check the number of pages, and then ask yourself the following question: "What do I want to learn about this?"

With practice, this method of thinking before reading can create a spark of enthusiasm that will make the actual reading more purposeful and make concentration more direct and intense.

Set a Time Goal. An additional trick to spark your enthusiasm is to set a time goal. Study time is not infinite, and short-term goals create a self-imposed pressure to pay attention, speed up, and get the job done. After looking over the material, project the amount of time you will need to finish it. Estimate a reasonable completion time and then push yourself to meet the goal. The purpose of a time goal is not to "speed read" the assignment but rather to be realistic about the amount of time to spend on a task and to learn how to estimate future study time.

Reader's Tip

Improving Concentration

* Create an environment that says, "*Study.*"
* Use a calendar/assignment book/PDA for short- and long-term planning.
* Keep a daily to-do list.
* Visualize yourself as a successful graduate.
* Reduce anxiety by passing the first test.
* Set time goals for completing daily assignments.

Focusing on Successful Academic Behaviors

Good concentration geared toward college success involves more than the ability to comprehend reading assignments. College success demands concentrated study, self-discipline, and the demonstration of learning. If the "focused athlete" can be successful, so can the "focused student." Begin to evaluate and eliminate behaviors that waste your time and divert you from your goals.

Direct your energy toward activities that will enhance your chances for success. Adopt the following behaviors of successful students.

Attend Class. At the beginning of the quarter or semester, college professors distribute an outline of what they plan to cover during each class period. Although they may not always check class attendance, the organization of the daily course work assumes perfect attendance. College professors *expect* students to attend class, and they usually do not repeat lecture notes or give makeup lessons for those who are absent, although some post lecture notes on a course Website. Be responsible and set yourself up for success by coming to class. You paid for it!

Be on Time. Professors usually present an overview of the day's work at the beginning of each class, as well as answer questions and clarify assignments. Arriving late puts you at an immediate disadvantage. You are likely to miss important "class business" information. In addition, tardy students distract both the professor and other students. Put on a watch and get yourself moving.

Be Aware of Essential Class Sessions. Every class session is important, but the last class before a major test is the most critical of all. Usually students will ask questions about the exam that will stimulate your thinking. In reviewing, answering questions, and rushing to finish uncovered material, the professor will often drop important clues to exam items. Unless you are critically ill, take tests on time because makeups are usually more difficult. In addition, be in class when the exams are returned to hear the professor's description of an excellent answer.

Read Assignments Before Class. Activate your knowledge on the subject before class by reading homework assignments. The lecture and class discussion can thus be used to build your knowledge network rather than create it. Jot down several questions that you would like to ask the professor about the reading.

Review Lecture Notes Before Class. Always review your lecture notes before the next class period, preferably within twenty-four hours after the class. Review your notes during a break or when on the phone with a classmate. Fill in gaps and make notations to ask questions to resolve confusion.

Consider Using a Tape Recorder. If you are having difficulty concentrating, with the professor's permission tape-record the lecture. Take notes at the same time as you record, and you can review your notes while listening to the recording.

Pass the First Test. Stress interferes with concentration. Do yourself a favor and over-study for the first exam. Passing the first exam will help you avoid a lot of tension while studying for the second one.

Predict the Exam Questions. Never go to an exam without first predicting test items. Turn chapter titles, subheadings, and boldface print into questions, and then brainstorm the answers. Feeling prepared boosts self-confidence.

Network with Other Students. You are not in this alone; you have lots of potential buddies who can offer support. Collect the names, phone numbers, and e-mail addresses of two classmates who are willing to help you if you do not understand the homework, miss a day of class, or need help on an assignment. Be prepared to help your classmates in return for their support.

Classmate ____________________ Phone ______________ E-mail ____________________

Classmate ____________________ Phone ______________ E-mail ____________________

Form a Study Group. Research experiments involving college students have shown that study groups can be very effective. Studying with others is

Reader's Tip

Managing E-Mail Efficiently

* Always fill in an appropriate subject header to guide your reader.
* Don't recycle the same subject header over and over. Write a new one to get your reader's attention.
* Keep your message short and to the point. People are busy.
* Use correct grammar, spelling, and punctuation. Your message represents you.
* Use uppercase letters sparingly. They YELL, which is called flaming.
* In formal messages, avoid emoticons, combinations of keyboard characters that represent emotions, such as smilees :-).
* Use an autoreply if you are away for a week.
* If appropriate, save time by using the same message for several individual replies.
* Don't feel you have to reply to everything.
* If pressed for time, save your message as "new" and reply later.
* Delete unwanted advertisements without reading them.
* Do not reply to an entire group when an individual reply is more appropriate.
* Know your group before sending humor.
* If you are unsure about a group member, seek permission before forwarding a message. If sending humor, cut and paste as a new message rather than forwarding with many group member names.
* Monitor how much time you spend on e-mail.

not cheating; it is making a wise use of available resources. Many professors assist networking efforts by posting the class roll with e-mail addresses. A junior on the dean's list explained, "I e-mail my study buddy when I have a problem. One time I asked about an English paper because I couldn't think of my thesis. She asked what it was about. I told her and she wrote back, 'That's your thesis.' I just couldn't see it as clearly as she did." Use the Internet to create an academic support group to lighten your work load and boost your grades.

Learn from Other Student Papers. Talking about an excellent paper is one thing but actually reading one is another. In each discipline we need models of excellence. Find an "A" paper to read. Don't be shy. Ask the "A" students (who should be proud and flattered to share their brilliance) or ask the professor. Don't miss this important step in becoming a successful student.

Collaborate. When participating in group learning activities, set expectations for group study so that each member contributes, and try to keep the studying on target. As a group activity, ask several classmates to join you in discovering the resources that are available for students on your campus. First, brainstorm with the group to record answers that are known to be true. Next, divide responsibilities among group members to seek information to answer unknown items. Reconvene the group to complete the responses.

Exercise 1.1 Campus Facts

Form a collaborative study group to answer the following questions.

1. Where are the academic advisors located? ____________________

   ____

2. Where is the learning lab, and what kind of help is offered?____________

   ____

3. When does the college offer free study skills workshops? ____________

   ____

4. Where can you use a computer and check your e-mail? ____________

   ____

5. Where do you get an identification number for the Internet? __________

   ____

6. Where is your professor's office, and what are his or her phone number and e-mail address? ____________________________

   ____

7. What kind of financial aid is available, and where can you find this information?____________________________________

____

8. What services does the dean's office offer to students?

____

9. How late is the library open on weekends?

____

10. What free services does the counseling center offer?

____

Use the Syllabus. The syllabus is a general outline of the goals, objectives, and assignments for the entire course. The syllabus includes examination dates, course requirements, and an explanation of the grading system. Most professors distribute and explain the syllabus on the first day of class.

Ask questions to help you understand the "rules and regulations" in the syllabus. Keep it handy as a ready reference and use it as a plan for learning. Devise your own daily calendar for completing weekly reading and writing assignments.

The following is a syllabus for Psychology 101. Study the course syllabus and answer the questions that follow.

INTRODUCTION TO PSYCHOLOGY

Class: 9:00–10:00 a.m. daily
10-week quarter
Office hours: 10:00–12:00 daily

Dr. Julie Wakefield
Office: 718 Park Place
Telephone: 651-3361
E-mail: JuWake@ABC.edu

Required Texts

Psychology: An Introduction by Josh R. Gerow
Paperback: Select one book from the attached list for a report.

Course Content

The purpose of Psychology 101 is to overview the general areas of study in the field of psychology. An understanding of psychology gives valuable insights into your choices and behaviors and those of others. The course will also give you a foundation for later psychology courses.

Methods of Teaching

Thematic lectures will follow the topics listed in the textbook assignments. You are expected to read and master the factual material in the text as well as take careful notes in class. Tests will cover both class lectures and textbook readings.

Research Participation
All students are required to participate in one psychological experiment. Details and dates are listed on a separate handout.

Grading
Grades will be determined in the following manner:

Tests (4 tests at 15% each)	60%
Final exam	25%
Written report	10%
Research participation	5%

Tests
Tests will consist of both multiple-choice and identification items as well as two essay questions.

Important Dates
Test 1: 1/13
Test 2: 1/29
Test 3: 2/10
Test 4: 2/24
Written report: 3/5
Final exam: 3/16

Written Report
Your written report should answer one of three designated questions and reflect your reading of a book from the list. Each book is approximately 200 pages long. Your report should be at least eight typed pages. More information to follow.

Assignments
Week 1: Ch. 1 (pp. 1-37), Ch. 2 (pp. 41-75)

Week 2: Ch. 3 (pp. 79-116)
TEST 1: Chapters 1-3

Week 3: Ch. 4 (pp. 121-162), Ch. 5 (pp. 165-181)

Week 4: Ch. 5 (pp. 184-207), Ch. 6 (pp. 211-246)
TEST 2: Chapters 4-6

Week 5: Ch. 7 (pp. 253-288), Ch. 8 (pp. 293-339)

Week 6: Ch. 9 (pp. 345-393)
TEST 3: Chapters 7-9

Week 7: Ch. 10 (pp. 339-441), Ch. 11 (pp. 447-471)

Week 8: Ch. 11 (pp. 476-491), Ch. 12 (pp. 497-533)
TEST 4: Chapters 10-12

Week 9: Ch. 13 (pp. 539-577), Ch. 14 (pp. 581-598)
WRITTEN REPORT

Week 10: Ch. 14 (pp. 602-618), Ch. 15 (pp. 621-658)
FINAL EXAM: Chapters 1-15

Exercise 1.2

Review the Syllabus

Refer to the syllabus to answer the following items with *T* (true) or *F* (false).

_______ 1. Pop quizzes count for 5 percent of the final grade.
_______ 2. The written report is due more than a week before the final exam.
_______ 3. The professor is not in her office on Thursdays.
_______ 4. Each of the four tests covers two weeks of work.
_______ 5. Two books are required for the course.

Exercise 1.3

Review Your Own Course Syllabus

Examine your syllabus for this college reading course and answer the following questions.

1. How many weeks are in your quarter or semester?

   ____

2. When is your next test and how much does it count?

   ____

3. Will your next major exam have a multiple-choice or essay format?

   ____

4. What is the professor's policy about absences?

   ____

5. Which test or assignment constitutes the largest portion of your final grade?

   ____

   Explain. _______________

   ____

   ____

6. Do you have questions that have not been answered on your syllabus? Name two issues that you would like the professor to clarify.

   ____

   ____

   ____

   ____

   ____

Summary Points

- **What is active learning?**

  Active learning is your own intellectual involvement with the teacher, the textbook, and fellow learners in the process of aggressively accumulating, interpreting, assimilating, and retaining new information.

- **How does the brain "pay attention"?**

  Research indicates that the brain has two cooperating systems, the RAS and the cortex, that allow it to selectively attend to certain inputs and to block out others.

- **Can you do two things at once?**

  The ability to do several tasks at once depends on the amount of cognitive resources required for each.

- **What are common internal and external distractors?**

  External distractions are physical temptations that divert your attention. Internal distractions are mental wanderings that vie for your attention.

- **How can you improve your concentration?**

  Concentration requires self-confidence, self-discipline, persistence, and focus. You can manipulate your study area to remove external distractions. You can learn to control internal distractions by organizing your daily activities, planning for academic success, and striving to meet your goals for the completion of assignments.

- **What academic behaviors can lead to college success?**

  Adopt successful academic behaviors, including networking with other students and collaborating on assignments, to focus your energy and enhance your chances for success. Use your syllabus as a guide for learning.

- **Why is your syllabus important?**

  Your syllabus is the learning guide designed by the instructor to document the goals and requirements of the course.

Selection 1 COMPUTER SCIENCE

CONTEMPORARY FOCUS

New technology brings a sequence of challenges. First, it is "Please use it," and later it's "Let's not abuse it." How are you vulnerable to Internet crime and what can you do to protect yourself?

HACKERS FLAUNT DIGNITARIES' CREDIT CARD DATA

Atlanta Journal Constitution, February 6, 2001, p. D5

Computer hackers obtained credit card details and other personal information for hundreds of attendees of World Economic Forum meetings, which annually draw such notables as Madeleine Albright, Bill Gates and Yasser Arafat.

Anti-globalization protesters appeared to be behind the break-in. There was no indication the hackers used any of the information maliciously. Such acts, known as "hacktivism," are part of a relatively new way of combining hacking with political resistance.

The Zurich, Switzerland-based weekly publication *SonntagsZeitung* said its reporters had been shown 80,000 pages of information, including numbers of passports and personal cellular phones of many government and business leaders who have attended the annual gathering in Davos.

Kent Anderson, vice president of computer security with London-based Control Risks Group, said hacktivism has been on the rise in recent years. The early attacks were largely efforts to cripple Web sites for short periods, Anderson said, while hackers are now exposing credit cards and personal information.

Collaborative Activity

Collaborate on responses to the following questions:

- Have you used your credit card number to make a purchase on the Web?
- Are "hacktivists" engaged in legitimate political activities or in crimes?
- Who is harmed when hackers shut down a Website for a day?

Skill Development: Active Learning

Before reading the following selection, take a few minutes to analyze your active learning potential and answer the following questions.

1. **Physical Environment** Where are you and what time is it? ____________

   ____

   What are your external distractions? ______________________________

   ____

2. **Internal Distractions** What is popping into your mind and interfering with your concentration? ______________________

3. **Spark Interest** Glance at the selection and predict what it will cover. What about it will be of interest to you? ______________________

4. **Set Time Goals** How long will it take you to read the selection? ________ minutes. To answer the questions? ________ minutes.

Word Knowledge

What do you know about these words?

prying	caper	sinister	advent	miscreants
ply	defacing	unscrupulous	fraudulently	neophyte

Your instructor may give a true-false vocabulary review before or after reading.

Time Goal

Record your starting time for reading. ________:________

Security and Privacy for Computers and the Internet

From H. L. Capron, *Computers: Tools for an Information Age*, 6th ed.

There was a time when security and privacy issues related to computers were easily managed: You simply locked the computer room door. Those centralized days are, of course, long gone. Now, in theory, anyone can hook up to any computer from any location. In light of data communications access, the first issue is security. The vast files of computer stored information must be kept secure—safe from destruction, accidental damage, theft, and even espionage.

A second issue is privacy. Private data—salaries, medical information, Social Security numbers, bank balances, and much more—must be kept from prying eyes. The problems are many and the solutions are complex. The escalating expansion of the Internet has only heightened the existing problems and added new problems of its own.

Computer Crime

It was 5 o'clock in the morning, and 14-year-old Randy Miller was startled to see a man climbing in his bedroom window. "FBI," the man announced, "and that computer is mine." So ended the computer caper in San Diego where 23 teenagers, ages 13 to 17, had used their home computers to invade computer systems as far away as Massachusetts. The teenagers were hackers, people who attempt to gain access to computer systems illegally, usually from a personal computer, via a data communications network.

The term *hacker* used to mean a person with significant computer expertise, but the term has taken on the more sinister meaning with the advent of computer miscreants. In this case the hackers did not use the system to steal money or property. But they did create fictitious accounts and destroyed or changed some data files. The FBI's entry through the bedroom window was calculated: The agents figured that, given even a moment's warning, the teenagers were clever enough to alert each other via computer.

This story—except for the names—is true. Hackers ply their craft for a variety of reasons but most often to show off for their peers or to harass people they do not like. A favorite trick, for example, is to turn a rival's telephone into a pay phone, so that when his or her parents try to dial a number an operator interrupts to say, "Please deposit 25 cents." A hacker may have more sinister motives, such as getting computer services without paying for them or getting information to sell.

You will probably not be surprised to learn that hackers have invaded Websites. These vandals show up with what amounts to a digital spray can, defacing sites with taunting boasts, graffiti, and their own private jokes. Although the victims feel violated, the perpetrators view their activities as mere pranks. In reality, such activity is antisocial and can result in great expense.

Of all targets that hackers might choose, one would expect the venerable *New York Times* to be far down the list. But, no, the *Times*'s Website was seriously invaded. Hackers plastered messages across the screen, forcing the *Times* to shut down the site entirely.

The *Times* was not chosen randomly, however. The hackers, it seems, were displeased with articles in the newspaper about fellow hacker Kevin Mitnick, who had been convicted on a series of computer-related theft and forgery charges. (When arrested, he was in possession of over 10,000 credit-card numbers taken from a customer database of an Internet service provider site.) The messages placed on the *Times*'s site demanded his release. Mitnick, however, remains in prison.

The Internet is the new frontier of crime.
Source: Illustration on page 310, Computers: Tools for an Information Age, *6th ed. by H.L. Capron, ©2000. Reprinted by permission of Pearson Education, Inc., Upper Saddle River, NJ.*

Hackers and Other Miscreants

Hacking has long been thought the domain of teenagers with time on their hands. The pattern is changing, however. A recent government survey showed that the computer systems of over half of the largest U.S. corporations had been invaded, but not by teenagers. Most intruders were competitors attempting to steal proprietary information. Even more astounding, federal investigators told a U.S. Senate hearing that the U.S. Department of Defense computers are attacked more than 200,000 times per year. Most worrisome is the emerging computer attack abilities of other nations, which, in a worst-case scenario, could seriously degrade the nation's ability to deploy and sustain military forces.

Hackers ply their craft by surprisingly low-tech means. Using what is called social engineering, a tongue-in-cheek term for con artist actions, hackers simply persuade unsuspecting people to give away their passwords over the phone. Recognizing the problem, employers are educating their employees to be alert to such scams.

Hackers are only a small fraction of the security problems. The most serious losses are caused by electronic pickpockets who are usually a good deal older and not so harmless. Consider these examples:

- A brokerage clerk sat at his terminal in Denver and, with a few taps of the keys, transformed, 1,700 shares of his own stock, worth $1.50 per share, to the same number of shares in another company worth 10 times that much.
- A Seattle bank employee used her electronic fund transfer code to move certain bank funds to an account held by her boyfriend as a "joke"; both the money and the boyfriend disappeared.
- A keyboard operator in Oakland, California, changed some delivery addresses to divert several thousand dollars' worth of department store goods into the hands of accomplices.
- A ticket clerk at the Arizona Veteran's Memorial Coliseum issued full-price basketball tickets for admission and then used her computer to record the sales as half-price tickets and pocketed the difference.

These stories point out that computer crime is not always the flashy, front-page news about geniuses getting away with millions of dollars. These people were ordinary employees in ordinary businesses—committing computer crimes. In fact, computer crime is often just white-collar crime with a new medium. Every time an employee is trained on the computer at work, he or she also gains knowledge that—potentially—could be used to harm the company.

The Changing Face of Computer Crime

Computer crime once fell into a few simple categories, such as theft of software or destruction of data. The dramatically increased access to networks has changed the focus to damage that can be done by unscrupulous people with online access. The most frequently reported computer crimes fall into these categories:

- *Credit-card fraud.* Customer numbers are floating all over public and private networks, in varying states of protection. Some are captured and used fraudulently.

- *Data communications fraud.* This category covers a broad spectrum, including piggybacking on someone else's network, the use of an office network for personal purposes, and computer-directed diversion of funds.
- *Unauthorized access to computer files.* This general snooping category covers everything from accessing confidential employee records to the theft of trade secrets and product pricing structures.
- *Unlawful copying of copyrighted software.* Whether the casual sharing of copyrighted software among friends or assembly-line copying by organized crime, unlawful copying incurs major losses for software vendors.

Keeping a Secret

Employers wish that computer passwords were better-kept secrets. Here are some hints on password use.

- Do not name your password after your child or car or pet, an important date, or your phone number. Passwords that are easy to remember are also easy to crack. If a hacker can find out personal details about a victim, he or she can deduce a password from this information about 40 percent of the time.
- Make passwords as random as possible. Include both letters and numbers. The more characters the better. Embed at least one nonalphabetic character, and consider mixing uppercase and lowercase letters. Example: GO*TOP6.
- Keep your password in your head or in a safe. Astonishingly, an occasional thoughtless user will scribble the password on paper and stick it on the computer monitor where anyone can see it.
- Change your password often, at least once a month. In some installations, passwords are changed so seldom that they become known to many people, thus defeating the purpose.
- Do not fall for hacker phone scams—"social engineering"—to obtain your password. Typical ruses are callers posing as a neophyte employee ("Gosh, I'm so confused, could you talk me through it?"); a system expert ("We're checking a problem in the network that seems to be coming from your workstation. Could you please verify your password?"); a telephone company employee ("There seems to be a problem on your phone line"); or even an angry top manager ("This is outrageous! How do I get into these files anyway?").

Most people are naturally inclined to be helpful. Do not be inappropriately helpful. Keep in mind that you will be—at the very least—embarrassed if you are the source of information to a hacker who damages your company.

White-Hat Hackers

Faced with threats on every side, most network-laced companies have chosen a proactive stance. Rather than waiting for the hackers and snoops and thieves to show up, they hire professionals to beat them to it. Called *white-hat hackers* or tiger teams, or sometimes "intrusion testers" or "hackers for hire," these highly trained technical people are paid to try to break into a computer system before anyone else does.

Using the same kind of finesse and tricks a hacker might, white-hat hackers exploit the system weaknesses. Once such chinks are revealed, they can be protected. The hacker's first approach, typically, is to access the company's system from the Internet. The quality of security varies from company to company. Sometimes security is fairly tight; other times, as one hacker put it, "It's a cake-walk."

Sometimes companies will hire one company to establish security and then hire white-hat hackers to try to defeat it. The company may not even alert its own employees to the hacker activities, preferring to see whether the intrusions are detected and, if so, how employees react.

Time Goals

Record your finishing time: ______:______

Calculate your total reading time: ______

Rate your concentration as high ______ medium ______ or low ______.

Recall what you have read, and review what you have learned.

Your instructor may choose to give a true-false comprehension review.

Thinking About "Security and Privacy for Computers and the Internet"

Evaluate your own computer and Internet security and privacy issues. How are you vulnerable to hackers? List and explain four ways hackers could get information about you and cause harm.

Response Suggestion: Blend the text ideas with your own thoughts and form a list of four possible situations that could cause you harm. Explain and give examples of each.

Contemporary Link

What are the motivational differences between the scam artist hackers who engage in social engineering and the hackers who obtained information on the World Economic Forum attendees at Davos, Switzerland? What do the political resistance hackers hope to achieve?

Comprehension Questions

After reading the selection, answer the following questions with *a*, *b*, *c*, or *d*. In order to help you analyze your strengths and weaknesses, the question types are indicated.

Main Idea _________ 1. The best statement of the main idea is
a. security and privacy of computers and the Internet can be maintained by following a few simple rules of prevention.
b. millions of dollars are lost each year because of computer crimes by hackers and other miscreants.
c. computer crime is a growing and serious threat to the security and privacy of computers and the Internet.
d. in the future computers and the Internet will be protected by white-hat hackers who defeat intrusions.

Detail _________ 2. According to the passage, the FBI entered by the bedroom window of Randy Miller's house primarily because
a. they feared a personal attack if entering through the front door.
b. the teenagers were gathered in the bedroom.
c. they suspected that the computers at the U.S. Department of Defense had been invaded.
d. they wanted to secure the evidence before Miller could alert the other teenagers on his computer.

Detail _________ 3. According to the passage, changes in the pattern of hacking show a progressive movement from
a. espionage to graffiti.
b. teen pranks to corporate theft and espionage.
c. stealing proprietary information to turning a rival's phone into a pay phone.
d. electronically pickpocketing money from companies to spray painting Websites.

Detail _________ 4. In a social engineering scam, a password is obtained by
a. asking.
b. electronically entering the system.
c. figuring it out from family records.
d. reading it off a note on a computer.

Detail _________ 5. The term "white-collar crime" refers to
a. vandalism by teenagers.
b. theft by workers with office jobs.
c. spying for defense secrets by foreign agents.
d. defacing Websites with private jokes.

Inference _________ 6. The author implies that the motive for the hacker attack on the *New York Times* was
a. greed.
b. a teenage prank.
c. revenge.
d. to support Mitnick's imprisonment.

Inference

________ 7. The author implies all of the following about credit cards except that
a. some companies do not have sufficient protection of credit card information.
b. credit card numbers are housed in many places on the Internet.
c. money can be made from credit card fraud.
d. copyright theft is the first largest crime on the Internet and credit card theft is the second.

Detail

________ 8. According to the author's advice on keeping your password secure, you should
a. mix alphabetic and nonalphabetic characters.
b. change it no more than once a year.
c. use your phone number or family names.
d. write your password down and keep it in the office.

Detail

________ 9. White-hat hackers are hired by companies to
a. invade the computer security of a rival company.
b. find ways to infiltrate the computer security of the company that hired them.
c. locate and prosecute rival computer hackers.
d. train technical people to become computer hackers.

Inference

________ 10. The underlying reason for the author to present the four different examples of electronic pickpocketing is to
a. show four different ways ordinary people can commit computer crimes.
b. compare and contrast adult and teenage hackers.
c. show that people who commit computer crimes are usually detected and exposed.
d. calculate the revenue that companies lose through computer theft by employees.

Answer the following with *T* (true) or *F* (false).

Inference

________ 11. The author would be more likely to compare the old key to the computer room to your current password than to your computer's speed and power.

Inference

________ 12. The author implies that teenage hackers are not serious threats on the Internet and should not be prosecuted.

Inference

________ 13. The reader can conclude that companies always alert employees when white-hat hackers are hired.

Inference

________ 14. The reader can conclude that computer hacking that crosses state lines is a federal offense.

Inference

________ 15. The author implies that security and privacy issues will lead to a gradual decline of Internet popularity.

Vocabulary

According to the way the italicized word was used in the selection, select *a*, *b*, *c*, or *d* for the word or phrase that gives the best definition. The number in parentheses indicates the line of the passage in which the word is located.

_____ 1. "kept from *prying* eyes" (8)
a. dishonest
b. curious
c. disapproving
d. illegal

_____ 2. "ended the computer *caper*" (14)
a. illegal escapade
b. arrest
c. investigation
d. trail

_____ 3. "more *sinister* meaning" (20)
a. humorous
b. significant
c. relevant
d. evil

_____ 4. "with the *advent*" (20)
a. coming
b. violation
c. assault
d. domination

_____ 5. "computer *miscreants*" (21)
a. mistakes
b. investigators
c. villains
d. coming

_____ 6. "*ply* their craft" (26)
a. learn
b. perform
c. share
d. desire

_____ 7. "*defacing* sites" (34)
a. canceling
b. locating
c. monitoring
d. disfiguring

_____ 8. "by *unscrupulous* people" (84)
a. unethical
b. ignorant
c. knowledgeable
d. unknowing

_____ 9. "used *fraudulently*" (87)
a. frequently
b. occasionally
c. mysteriously
d. deceitfully

_____ 10. "as a *neophyte* employee" (114)
a. sneaky
b. beginner
c. disloyal
d. careless

Skill Development

Record your time for answering the questions: _____:_____

Calculate your total time for reading and answering the questions:

____

What changes would you make to enhance your concentration on the new selection? ____

____

Search the Net

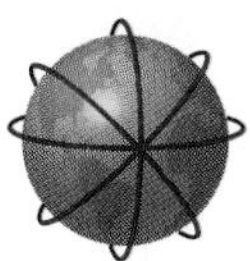

Each of the reading selections in this book will be followed by an Internet exercise to challenge your computer skills, research skills, and critical thinking skills. You will be asked to use the Internet, also known as the World Wide Web (WWW) or "Web," to research a question and find information at different Websites. Some of these sites will be suggested and others you may discover on your own. You will then blend or synthesize the new information with your own thoughts to produce a written response. These Internet exercises can be done individually or as group activities. To help you get started, read the following suggestions for successful Internet searches.

Secrets of a Successful Search

Searching for information on the Internet can be both rewarding and frustrating. The key to avoiding frustration, or at least reducing it to a bare minimum, is organization. Organization requires a plan, an ongoing search strategy, and good record keeping. A successful Internet search consists of the following five steps:

1. Make a plan.
2. Search and search again.
3. Read selectively.
4. Record as you go.
5. Consider the source.

1. Make a Plan

Locating information on the Web requires the use of a search engine such as Alta Vista, Excite, Google, Infoseek, or Lycos. Once you have selected a search engine, enter a search term or phrase, which may consist of one or more words, a phrase, or a name. The search engine will search the Internet for sites that contain your search term or phrase, count them, and display the first ten to twenty-five sites (called "hits") on the computer screen. Successful searches are dependent on which terms are chosen and how they are entered.

Experts recommend using a notebook to organize your search strategy. Using a two-column format, begin by writing down your general research topic and related questions. Next, jot down all of the key terms that you can think of that relate to your topic and create additional questions if necessary. At this beginning point, prior knowledge of the topic is extremely helpful. If your knowledge of the topic is limited, however, perform a quick search to select and read a few of the sites on the topic in order to become familiar with related terminology, names, and events.

Decide on a few key words that you believe will help you locate the information you want and use them as search terms. In your notebook, list each search term on the left side of the paper and allow room on the right side for

Sample Search Notebook Page

Research topic	Computer crimes
Research questions	How are computers used to commit crimes? How can someone prevent being the victim of a computer crime?
What I already know	Hacker—someone who attempts to gain access to computer systems illegally White-hat hacker—computer expert hired to find weaknesses in computer systems Data communications fraud—piggybacking on someone else's network; use of an office network for personal purposes; computer-directed diversion of funds Social engineering—hacker phone scams

Search Terms	**Notes and Websites**
■ *Computer crimes*	New government agency (http://www.cybercrime.gov/) International organization that fights Internet crimes http://www.web-police.org/) Database of fraudulent Internet activities (http://www.ScamWatch.com/) Internet law-enforcement site (http://www.ILETA.net/)
■ *Data communications fraud*	Provides extensive information on fraud-related resources (http://www.fraudvendors.com/)
■ *Preventing Internet crimes*	Overview of Internet crime, some information on preventing crime (http://www.digitalcentury.com/encyclo/update/crime.html)
■ *Internet privacy*	Guide to online privacy resources (http://epic.org/privacy/privacy_resources_faq.html) Information and links maintained by a college professor (http://www.osu.edu/units/law/swire1/pspriv.htm) Instant analysis of the privacy of one's Internet connection (http://www.Privacy.net/analyze/)
■ *Encryption*	Organization that studies Internet security issues (http://www.cert.org/) Computer Security Research Laboratory (http://www.cert.org/) Information on electronic privacy issues (http://www.epic.org/crypto/)

writing the locations of Websites and comments about the site. For example, if your research topic is computer crimes and prevention, your list of search terms may include computer hackers, Internet security, social engineering, and computer scams. A sample search notebook page is illustrated above.

Check with your college library on how to gain access to online databases containing online journals, collections, and other resources that can provide a wealth of information.

Reader's Tip

Popular College Databases

* Galileo
* Periodical abstracts
* Newspaper abstracts
* Lexis-Nexis Academic Universe
* MLA Bibliography
* ABI Inform
* Psyc FIRST
* Social Science abstracts
* ERIC
* MEDLINE

2. Search and Search Again

One of the most important tasks in conducting a successful search is to enter search terms that will produce the information that you want. Search terms that are too *wide* may bring thousands of hits. Some researchers suggest beginning with a *broad* search (a single term) and then narrowing the search, whereas others suggest beginning with a narrow search (multiple terms) and broadening it later. Both methods are acceptable, and you can experiment to discover which method works best for you. Be flexible in trying new terms and different combinations. In the previous example, searching for *prosecution, computer,* or *crimes* alone will bring a multitude of hits. Narrowing your search by typing in *prosecution for computer crimes* should produce sites more attuned to your research. Entering too many terms, however, may result in no hits or only limited information. Searches also provide additional terms to pursue.

Reader's Tip

Manipulating the Search

In our sample case, by entering *computer crimes* in the search term box, you will receive all sites that contain either *computer, crimes,* or *computer crimes.* Placing quotation marks around a phrase or the term—that is, *"computer crimes"*—will pull up only those sites containing the full term. Another way to find suitable sites is to add an AND, +, OR, or NOT in the phrase.

At some point you may need to find the home page of a particular company—for example, Harley-Davidson. If your search does not produce the home page of the company, try to guess or work out the company's Uniform Resource Locator (URL). Remember that a simple URL is composed of four or five parts. The first part is usually *http://. Http* is a protocol or mechanism used by browsers to communicate with Websites. The second part is *www* for the World Wide Web. The third part is usually the name or abbreviation of a company, product, or institution. The fourth part is the site's designation or type, such as http://www.cnn.com for the CNN News Corporation and http://www.whitehouse.gov for the White House.

The three-letter designation at the end of the URL, sometimes called the *domain*, depends on the type of site. For example, *gov* is for government, *org* is for organization, *com* is for commercial site, and *edu* is for education. Some URLs have a fifth part; they end in a two-letter code to signify a country. For example, *uk* means *United Kingdom* in the Website for the British monarchy, which is http://www.royal.gov.uk (see the diagram below).

3. Read Selectively

The amount of information on the Internet can be overwhelming. Rarely, however, is it desirable or practical to read all the available information on a subject. Read selectively to narrow the scope of your research. After entering a search term and receiving a list of possible sites, scan the list of hits to look for key words relating to your search needs. The sites that contain the most information are usually listed first. Some search engines, such as Excite and Infoseek, will place a percent value next to the site link indicating the likelihood that the information being sought is located at that site. In addition, a summary of the site may also be included.

After selecting a Website or link that appears to have the information you need, study the table of contents or outline and move around the site to determine its layout or structure. Check secondary links that look promising. Skim definitions, statements, quotes, and other text while asking yourself, "Is this the information I am looking for?" Web pages follow some uniform patterns, but styles vary because there are no requirements for a standard format. Most Websites, however, contain a title, subtitles, links, a table of contents, and an outline or introductory paragraph.

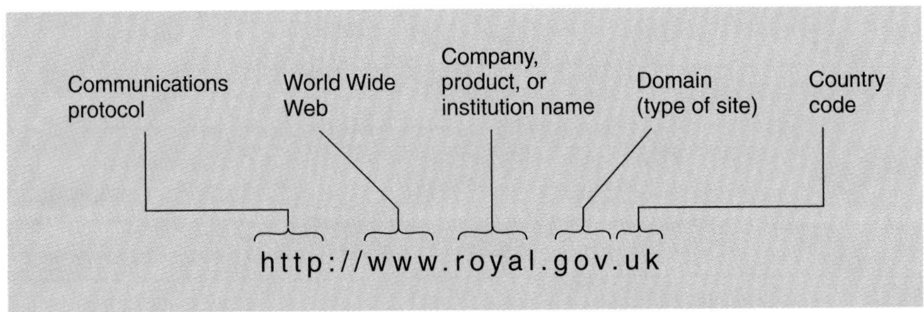

4. Record As You Go

As you discover sites, make sure to record them in your notebook. Once you have searched a term, check it off on your term list. You should also note the results of the search next to the term. This will help you avoid searching for the same term a second time. Include the site location (the URL), particularly if you would like to return to the site or include it as a reference. If you are trying to locate a specific URL, such as a Website listed in this textbook, do not be surprised if the URL has changed. Unfortunately, site locations may change without notice, thus making mastery of the steps in the search process even more important.

There are three ways of noting the site: (1) by recording the URL in your notebook next to the term, (2) by printing out the site material, since the URL is usually listed at the top of the printout, or (3) by bookmarking or saving a site so that you may return to it at a later date. If you are using a computer in a location that you may not again have access to, save your bookmarks on a disk.

5. Consider the Source

Information on the Internet, although abundant, may not be accurate. In 1998 a U.S. congressman saw an obituary for a prominent entertainer posted on the Web and announced the death to the Congress. As it turned out, the obituary had been posted by accident, and the entertainer, comedian Bob Hope, was quite alive and hitting golf balls at the time.

One of the best ways to avoid collecting poor data on the Internet is to use good judgment. In the case above, confirming the information would have avoided embarrassment for the congressman. In other instances, information posted on the Web can be misleading, unfounded, or based on personal opinions and beliefs rather than facts.

When reviewing information from a Website, ask yourself, "What person, company, or agency is providing the information?" and "Is this a reliable source?" Reliable information usually comes from reliable sources. Information gathered from sites such as news stations, libraries, city newspapers, and government databases is probably more reliable than that from obscure sites with no obvious signs of credibility. Finally, when you are doing a research paper, do not rely entirely on Internet sources. Use books, journals, and other reliable print sources as well.

Search the Net

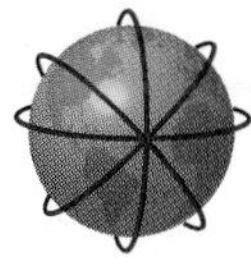

For your first activity, respond to the following items on computer crimes. Use the suggested Websites or conduct your own search. Remember that Websites change frequently without warning so your own Internet detective skills may be needed.

- Unfortunately, a popular computer crime is the creation and distribution of computer viruses via e-mail. List three different computer viruses, explain how each is spread, and describe the damage caused by each.

ScamBusters
http://www.cybercrime.org/

Virus Bulletin
http://www.virusbtn.com/

- Find information about two computer hackers. Describe what they did, how they did it, how they got caught, and how they were punished.

  Agent Steal
  http://www.agentsteal.com/

  KevinPoulsen
  http://www.kevinpoulsen.com/

  Organize your approach and use your own notebook to record information. In your response, list the Websites from which you took information as references.

Concept Prep

for Computer Science

Why learn concepts in different academic areas?

Your success in college reading will be measured by your ultimate success in the academic courses that you will take, such as psychology, history, sociology, and biology. The goal of this class is to prepare you to apply your skills in the courses required for your graduation so you will make good grades without struggling. In reality, both your skills and your knowledge interact to help you achieve that success.

As you will learn in Chapter 3, prior knowledge, or what you already know in a subject area, is a significant factor in your academic performance. Thus, in order to enhance your background knowledge and boost your success, key academic subject concepts are presented at the end of most of the longer reading selections in this textbook. Study these concepts and arm yourself with valuable knowledge for the courses ahead. The following concepts provide background in computer science.

What is the Internet?

The **Internet** is a collection of about 25,000 computer networks, owned by no one with no central headquarters. It is used globally for communication.

Who invented the Internet?

The Internet grew out of the **Cold War** of the 1950s, a period of icy relationships between the United States and communist countries. During this time, people feared a nuclear attack by the Soviet Union. The U.S. Department of Defense wanted to create a safe way to communicate in case a bomb wiped out all computing capabilities. The RAND Corporation worked with the government to design a message system that would rely on many computers scattered in different places around the world. No single computer would be in charge. Thus, if one computer failed, the others could carry messages by alternative routes. This system, established in 1969, was used by defense contractors and university researchers as well as the military. It was twenty-five years before the general public even knew it existed.

Tim Berners-Lee speaks at the Internet Caucus Speakers Series and explains the importance of keeping the Web universal as the technology moves forward.
AFP/Corbis

In 1990, **Tim Berners-Lee**, a Swiss physicist, thought his research would be easier if he could link quickly to his colleagues' computers around the world in links that he saw as a spider web. The home site he created is thus considered the birthplace of the World Wide Web. Lee was a key figure in popularizing the Internet.

What were the new business opportunities associated with computers and the Internet?

- **Steven Jobs** founded Apple Computer and popularized the personal computer (PC), making low-cost computing available to the general public.
- **Bill Gates** and his friend Paul Allen dropped out of college in 1975 to work on writing software (computer instructions) for a company in Albuquerque, New Mexico. They kept the rights to their work and formed their own company, called **Microsoft.** Later Gates and Allen secured an opportunity to write an operating system for IBM, a large computer manufacturer. The operating system, MS-DOS, launched their rise to fame and fortune.
- **Silicon Valley** is a high-tech, affluent region near San Francisco where the electronics computer industry is centered. The name refers to the element **silicon,** which is used in manufacturing computers.
- The **Ethernet** is a popular local area network that uses high-speed network cables.
- **Spamming** is mass advertising on the Internet through e-mail.
- **Dot-com entrepreneurs** are investors who take big risks to start Internet businesses.

Source: Adapted from H. L. Capron, *Computers: Tools for an Information Age,* 6th ed.

REVIEW QUESTIONS

After studying the material above, answer the following questions.

1. What is the Internet? ______________________________

2. Why did the Internet start? ______________________________

3. What did Tim Berners-Lee do for the Internet? ______________________________

4. What did Steven Jobs do? ______________________________

5. What did Bill Gates do? ______________________________

6. What is Silicon Valley? ______________________________

Your instructor may choose to give a true-false review of these computer science concepts.

Selection 2 PSYCHOLOGY

CONTEMPORARY FOCUS

Animals have instinctive behaviors that sometimes seem to take on human attributes. In response to many amazing rescue stories, some scientists assert that dolphins have an instinct to push floundering objects out of the water. Other scientists offer no explanation. What do you think? Is it instinct or heart?

DOLPHIN SAVES BOY'S LIFE

Daily Record, Scotland, August 30, 2000; from: http://www.crystalinks.com/dolphinnews.html.

A friendly dolphin has saved a teenage boy from drowning. Nonswimmer Davide Ceci, 14, was within minutes of death when dolphin Filippo came to his rescue. The friendly 61-stone creature has been a popular tourist attraction off Manfredonia in southeast Italy for two years. But now he is a local hero after saving Davide from the Adriatic when he fell from his father's boat.

While Emanuele Ceci was still unaware his son had fallen into the waves, Filippo was pushing him up out of the water to safety. Davide said: "When I realized it was Filippo pushing me, I grabbed on to him." The dolphin bore down on the boat and got close enough for Davide's father to grab his gasping son.

Davide's mother Signora Ceci said: "It is a hero, it seems impossible an animal could have done something like that, to feel the instinct to save a human life."

Filippo has lived in the waters off Manfredonia since he became separated from a visiting school of dolphins. Maritime researcher Dr. Giovanna Barbieri said: "Filippo seems not to have the slightest fear of humans. I'm not surprised he should have done such a wonderful thing as to save a human."

Collaborative Activity

Collaborate on responses to the following questions:

- What is an instinct?
- What other amazing rescue stories have you heard about animals? Were they acting instinctively?
- Where is the Adriatic?

Skill Development: Active Learning

Before reading the following selection, take a few minutes to analyze your active learning potential and answer the following questions.

1. **Physical Environment** Where are you and what time is it? ____________

____

What are your external distractions? ______________________________

____

____

____

2. **Internal Distractions** What is popping into your mind and interfering with your concentration? ______________________________

3. **Spark Interest** Glance at the selection and predict what it will cover. What about it will be of interest to you? ______________________________

4. **Set Time Goals** How long will it take you to read the selection? __________ minutes. To answer the questions? __________ minutes.

Word Knowledge

What do you know about these words?

hypothesis	incubator	genetic	instinctive	sustain
restrained	inseminate	disrupted	irreversible	coax

Your instructor may give a true-false vocabulary review before or after reading.

Time Goal

Record your starting time for reading. ______:______

CRITICAL-PERIOD HYPOTHESIS

From James V. McConnell, *Understanding Human Behavior*

There is some evidence that the best time for a child to learn a given skill is at the time the child's body is just mature enough to allow mastery of the behavior in question. This belief is often called the *critical-period hypothesis*—that is, the belief that an organism must have certain experiences at a *particular time* in its developmental sequence if it is to reach its mature state.

There are many studies from animal literature supporting the critical-period hypothesis. For instance, German scientist Konrad Lorenz discovered many years ago that birds, such as ducks and geese, will follow the first moving object they see after they are hatched. Usually the first thing they see is their mother, of course, who has been sitting on the eggs when they are hatched. However, Lorenz showed that if he took goose eggs away from the mother and hatched them in an incubator, the fresh-hatched *goslings* would follow him around instead.

Lorenz swims with the goslings who have imprinted on him.
Nina Leen/ TimePix

After the goslings had waddled along behind Lorenz for a few hours, they acted as if they thought he was their mother and that they were humans, not geese. When Lorenz returned the goslings to their real mother, they ignored her. Whenever Lorenz appeared, however, they became very excited and flocked to him for protection and affection. It was as if the visual image of the first object they saw moving had become so strongly *imprinted* on their consciousness that, forever after, that object was "mother."

During the past 20 years or so, scientists have spent a great deal of time studying *imprinting* as it now is called. The effect occurs in many but not in all types of birds, and it also seems to occur in mammals such as sheep and seals. Whether it occurs in humans is a matter for debate. Imprinting is very strong in ducks and geese, however, and they have most often been the subjects for study.

The urge to imprint typically reaches its strongest peak 16 to 24 hours after the baby goose is hatched. During this period, the baby bird has an innate tendency to follow anything that moves, and will chase after its mother (if she is around), or a human, a bouncing football or a brightly painted tin can that the experimenter dangles in front of the gosling. The more the baby bird struggles to follow after this moving object, the more strongly the young animal becomes imprinted to the object. Once the goose has been imprinted, this very special form of learning cannot easily be reversed. For example, the geese that first followed Lorenz could not readily be trained to follow their mother instead; indeed, when these geese were grown and sexually mature, they showed no romantic interest in other geese. Instead, they attempted to court and mate with humans.

If a goose is hatched in a dark incubator and is not allowed to see the world until two or three days later, imprinting often does not occur. At first it was thought that the "critical period" had passed and hence the bird could never become imprinted to anything. Now we know differently. The innate urge to follow moving objects does appear to reach a peak in geese 24 hours after they are hatched, but it does not decline thereafter. Rather, a second innate urge—that of fearing and avoiding new objects—begins to develop, and within 48 hours after hatching typically overwhelms the prior tendency the bird had to follow after anything that moves. To use a human term, the goose's *attitude* toward strange things is controlled by its genetic blueprint—at first it is attracted to, then it becomes afraid of, new objects in its environment. As we will see in a moment, these conflicting "attitudes" may explain much of the data on "critical periods" in both animals and humans.

How might these two apparently conflicting behavioral tendencies help a baby goose survive in its usual or natural environment?

In other experiments, baby chickens have been hatched and raised in the dark for the first several days of their lives. Chicks have an innate tendency to peck at small objects soon after they are hatched—an instinctive behavior pattern that helps them get food as soon as they are born. In the dark, of course, they cannot see grain lying on the ground and hence do not peck (they must be hand-fed in the dark during this period of time). Once brought into the light, these chicks do begin to peck, but they do so clumsily and ineffectively, as if their "critical period" for learning the pecking skill had passed. Birds such as robins and blue jays learn to fly at about the time their wings are mature enough to sustain flight (their parents often push them from the nest as a means of encouraging them to take off on their own). If these young birds are restrained and not allowed to fly until much later, their flight patterns are often clumsy and they do not usually gain the necessary skills to become good fliers.

The "Maternal Instinct" in Rats

Suppose we take a baby female rat from its mother at the moment of its birth and raise the rat pup "by bottle" until it is sexually mature. Since it has never seen other rats during its entire life (its eyes do not open until several days after birth), any sexual or maternal behavior that it shows will presumably be due to the natural unfolding of its genetic blueprint—and not due to learning or imitation. Now, suppose we inseminate this hand-raised female rat artificially—to make certain that she continues to have no contact with other rats. Will she build a nest for her babies before they are born, following the usual pattern of female rats, and will she clean and take care of them during and after the birth itself?

The answer to that question is yes—*if.* If, when the young female rat was growing up, there were objects such as sticks and sawdust and string and small blocks of wood in her cage, and which she played with. Then, when inseminated, the pregnant rat will use these "toys" to build a nest. If the rat grows up in a bare cage, she won't build a nest *even though we give her the materials to do so once she is impregnated.* If this same rat is forced to wear a stiff rubber collar around her neck when she is growing up—so that she cannot clean her sex organs, as rats normally do—she will not usually lick her newborn babies clean *even though we take off the rubber collar a day or so before she gives birth.* The genetic blueprint always operates best within a particular environmental setting. If an organism's early environment is abnormal or particularly unusual, later "innate" behavior patterns may be disrupted.

Overcoming the "Critical Period"

All of these examples may appear to support the "critical-period" hypothesis—that there is one time in an organism's life when it is best suited to learn a particular skill. These studies might also seem to violate the general rule that an organism can "catch up" if its development has been delayed. However, the truth is more complicated (as always) than it might seem from the experiments we have cited so far.

Baby geese will normally not imprint if we restrict their visual experiences for the first 48 hours of their lives—their fear of strange objects is by then too great. However, if we give the geese tranquilizing drugs to help overcome their fear, they can be imprinted a week or more after hatching. Once imprinting has taken place, it may seem to be irreversible. But we can occasionally get a bird imprinted on a human to accept a goose as its mother, if we coax it enough and give it massive rewards for approaching or following its natural mother. Chicks raised in darkness become clumsy eaters—but what do you think would happen if we gave them special training in how to peck, rather than simply leaving the matter to chance? Birds restrained in the nest too long apparently learn other ways of getting along and soon come to fear heights; what do you think would happen if we gave these birds tranquilizers and rewarded each tiny approximation to flapping their wings properly?

There is not much scientific evidence that human infants have the same types of "critical periods" that birds and rats do. By being born without strong innate behavior patterns (such as imprinting), we seem to be better able to adjust and survive in the wide variety of social environments human babies are born into. Like many other organisms, however, children do appear to have an inborn tendency to imitate the behavior of other organisms around them. A young rat will learn to press a lever in a Skinner box much faster if it is first allowed to watch an adult rat get food by pressing the lever. This learning is even quicker if the adult rat happens to be the young animal's mother. Different species of birds have characteristic songs or calls. A European thrush, for example, has a song pattern fairly similar to a thrush in the United States, but both sound quite different from blue jays. There are *local dialects* among songbirds, however, and these are learned through imitation. If a baby thrush is isolated from its parents and exposed to blue jay calls when it is very young, the thrush will sound a little like a blue jay but a lot like other thrushes when it grows up. And parrots, of course, pick up very human-sounding speech patterns if they are raised with humans rather than with other parrots.

Time Goals

Record your finishing time: ______:______ Calculate your total reading time: ______

Rate your concentration as high ______ medium ______ or low______.

Recall what you have read, and review what you have learned.

Your instructor may choose to give you a true-false comprehension review.

Thinking About "Critical-Period Hypothesis"

Provide proof that a critical period exists during which an organism must have certain experiences in order to reach its normal mature state.

Response Suggestion: Review the selection and number the experiments that provide proof of the hypothesis. Define the hypothesis and describe three to five supporting examples from the text.

Contemporary Link

After reading about the scientific studies to determine whether there is a critical time for instincts to develop in chicks, rats, and birds, what type of scientific study would you devise to determine if dolphins save drowning children out of love or instinct?

Comprehension Questions

After reading the selection, answer the following questions with *a, b, c,* or *d.*

Main Idea

_______ 1. The best statement of the main idea of this selection is
a. studies show that goslings can be imprinted on humans.
b. a particular few days of an animal's life can be a crucial time for developing long-lasting "natural" behavior.
c. imprinting seems to occur in mammals but is very strong in ducks and geese.
d. the "crucial period" of imprinting is important but can be overcome with drugs.

Detail

_______ 2. The critical-period hypothesis is the belief that
a. there is a "prime time" to develop certain skills.
b. most learning occurs during the first few days of life.
c. fear can inhibit early learning.
d. the "maternal instinct" is not innate but is learned.

Detail

_______ 3. In Lorenz's studies, after the goslings imprinted on him, they would do all of the following except
a. follow him around.
b. flock to him for protection.
c. return to their real mother for affection.
d. become excited when Lorenz appeared.

Detail

_______ 4. The author points out that in Lorenz's studies the early imprinting of geese with humans
a. was easily reversed with training.
b. caused the geese to be poor mothers.
c. later produced sexually abnormal behavior in the geese.
d. made it difficult for the goslings to learn to feed themselves.

Inference ________ 5. The author suggests that by 48 hours the innate urge to imprint in geese is
a. decreased significantly.
b. increased.
c. overwhelmed by the avoidance urge.
d. none of the above.

Inference ________ 6. In a small gosling's natural environment, the purpose of the avoidance urge that develops within 48 hours of hatching might primarily be to help it
a. learn only the behavior of its species.
b. follow only one mother.
c. escape its genetic blueprint.
d. stay away from predators.

Inference ________ 7. The author suggests that there is a critical period for developing all of the following except
a. desire to eat.
b. pecking.
c. flying.
d. cleaning the young.

Inference ________ 8. The studies with rats suggest that nest building and cleaning behavior are
a. totally innate behaviors.
b. totally learned behaviors.
c. a combination of innate and learned behaviors.
d. neither innate nor learned behaviors.

Detail ________ 9. Abnormal imprinting during the critical period can later be overcome by using all of the following except
a. tranquilizing drugs.
b. natural tendencies.
c. special training.
d. massive reward.

Inference ________ 10. Because humans do not seem to have strong innate behavior patterns, the author suggests that humans
a. are better able to adapt to changing environments.
b. have more difficulty learning early motor skills.
c. find adjustment to change more difficult than animals.
d. need more mothering than animals.

Answer the following with *T* (true) or *F* (false).

Detail ________ 11. The author states that whether imprinting occurs in humans is a matter of debate.

Inference ________ 12. The author implies that a goose can be imprinted on a painted tin can.

Inference ________ 13. In the author's opinion, studies show that organisms can catch up adequately without special training when skill development has been delayed past the critical period.

Inference ________ 14. If an abandoned bird egg is hatched and raised solely by a human, the author suggests that the bird will be abnormal.

Inference ________ 15. The author suggests that the urge to imitate is innate in both humans and animals.

Vocabulary

According to the way the italicized word was used in the selection, select *a*, *b*, *c*, or *d* for the word or phrase that gives the best definition. The number in parentheses indicates the line of the passage in which the word is located.

________ 1. "The critical-period *hypothesis*" (3)
a. association
b. tentative assumption
c. law
d. dilemma

________ 2. "in an *incubator*" (12)
a. cage
b. electric enlarger
c. nest
d. artificial hatching apparatus

________ 3. "its *genetic* blueprint" (48)
a. sexual
b. emotional
c. hereditary
d. earned

________ 4. "an *instinctive* behavior pattern" (54)
a. desirable
b. innate
c. early
d. newly acquired

________ 5. "to *sustain* flight" (61)
a. support
b. imitate
c. begin
d. imagine

________ 6. "birds are *restrained*" (62–63)
a. pressured
b. pushed
c. held back
d. attacked

________ 7. "suppose we *inseminate*" (71)
a. imprison
b. artificially impregnate
c. injure
d. frighten

________ 8. "may be *disrupted*" (87)
a. thrown into disorder
b. repeated
c. lost
d. destroyed

________ 9. "seem to be *irreversible*" (98)
a. temporary
b. changeable
c. frequent
d. permanent

________ 10. "*coax* it enough" (100)
a. encourage fondly
b. punish
c. feed
d. drill

Time Goals

Record your time for answering the questions: ______:______

Calculate your total time for reading and answering the questions: ______

What changes would you make to enhance your concentration on the new selection?

Search the Net

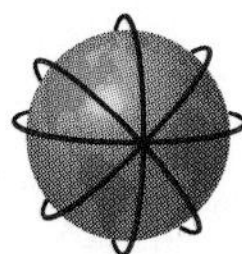

- Find autobiographical information on Konrad Lorenz. What experiences led to his interest in imprinting?

  Nobel E-Museum
  http://www.nobel.se/medicine/laureates/1973/lorenz-autobio.html

- How has the critical-period hypothesis been used to explain the acquisition of language skills? Conduct a search to find scientists who have studied this hypothesis as it relates to language. Explain one of the theories regarding language and the critical-period hypothesis.

  Lenneberg's (1967) Critical Period Hypothesis
  http://www.ucs.mun.ca/~emurphy/Frenchoverview/tsld001.htm

Sample Search Notebook Page

Research topic	Maternal instincts of birds
Research questions	What are some unusual maternal instincts of birds? How do these instincts aid in the survival of the species?
What I already know	Birds and other animals have some unusual instincts such as imprinting. Imprinting is the process where attachments are formed by young birds on the first social objects they encounter. Konrad Lorenz led the research on imprinting using goslings.

Search Terms	**Notes and Websites**
■ *Bird behavior*	Poor results—sites are related to pet bird behaviors
■ *Maternal instincts*	Only found instincts on cows, pigs, and sheep
■ *Bird instincts*	Host-parasite conflict (http://birding.miningco.com/library/weekly/aa060797.htm)
■ *Maternal instincts of birds*	Killdeer mother feigns broken wing (http://www.birdwatching.com/stories/killdeer.html) Personal report (http://www.newton.dep.anl.gov/natbltn/400-499/nb482.htm) Very brief description (http://www.baylink.org/wpc/killdeer.html)

Concept Prep for Psychology

What does psychology cover?

Psychology is the scientific study of behavior and the mind. Behavior is observed, studied, and measured with the ultimate goal of explaining why people act and think as they do. Special areas that you will study in psychology include the following:

Biological psychology: How do your genes, brain, and hormones affect your behavior?

Behavioral psychology: What stimulus in the environment triggers your response?

Cognitive psychology: How do you think and remember?

Humanistic psychology: Can you be anything you want to be? Do you control your destiny?

Developmental psychology: How do thoughts, desires, and actions differ in infancy, childhood, adolescence, adulthood, and old age?

Cross-cultural psychology: How do cultural differences affect your behavior and sense of self?

Author and psychoanalyst Sigmund Freud works at his desk in Vienna, Austria.
Topham/The Image Works

Why is Freud so important?

Sigmund Freud was a physician in Vienna, Austria, who formulated a theory of personality and a form of psychotherapy called **psychoanalysis**. Sigmund Freud emerged as a leader in modern psychology and wrote twenty-four books popularizing his theories. Freud died in 1939, and later psychologists questioned many of his ideas and criticized him because of his focus on sexual desires. Still, Freud has contributed many ideas to our culture and words to our vocabulary.

Freud's theories evolved from observing and treating patients who suffered ailments without any visible physical basis, but who responded favorably to hypnosis. He believed in treating their problems by tracing difficulties back to childhood experiences. Freud also believed in **dream interpretation,** a process in which the unconscious mind provides clues to psychological problems.

Freud's basic theories suggest that people are driven from early childhood by three principal unconscious forces: the **id** (an animal instinct and desire for pleasure), the **ego** (the sense of self that fights the id for reasonable compromises), and the **superego** (the social feeling of right and wrong and community values). Other terms that Freud established include **pleasure principle,** which refers to an instinctive need to satisfy the id regardless of the consequences; **libido,** which refers to sexual drive; and **egotism,** which refers to a sense of self-importance and conceit.

Other words we use today emerge from Freud's five stages of personality development: oral, anal, phallic, latency, and genital. An **oral personality** is fixated in the first stage of sucking and is satisfied by the pleasures of the mouth—for example, talking, smoking, eating, and chewing gum excessively. An **anal personality** is associated with the childhood period that involves bowel control and toilet training and as an adult is excessively focused on details and orderliness. Another term Freud popularized is ***Oedipus complex,*** which suggests that a young boy has a sexual desire for his mother. Finally, Freud was the originator of the **Freudian slip,** which is a misspoken word—such as *sex* for *six*—that reveals unconscious thoughts.

Who was Carl Jung?

Carl Jung was a Swiss psychologist who classified people as **introverts** (shy) or **extroverts** (outgoing). Jung was one of the original followers of Freud but later broke with him. Adding to Freud's theory of repressed personal experiences, Jung believed that we also inherit the memories and symbols of ancestors in an **inherited collective unconscious**. He believed this was exhibited in an inborn fear of snakes or spiders. Jung also developed theories about concrete and abstract learning stages. Many of his theories are used as a basis for the Myers-Briggs Type Indicator.

REVIEW QUESTIONS

Study the material and answer the following questions.

1. Using visual images on concept cards to improve memory of vocabulary words suggests what area of psychology? ______
2. Desiring a rocky road ice cream cone after passing a Baskin and Robbins store suggests what area of psychology? ______
3. Mapping physical activity in different areas of the brain as people read or listen to music suggests what area of psychology? ______
4. Attending a motivational seminar to become salesperson of the year suggests what area of psychology? ______
5. What is psychoanalysis? ______
6. What are the goals of the id, ego, and superego? ______
7. How does Freud relate dreams to reality? ______
8. Why did some psychologists break with Freud? ______
9. How do the theories of Jung and Freud differ? ______
10. What is Jung's inherited collective unconscious? ______

Your instructor may choose to give a true-false review of these psychology concepts.

READER'S JOURNAL

Name ______________________________ Date ______________

CHAPTER 1

To improve your skills, you must seriously reflect on the daily choices you make and your progress as a learner. Be your own best teacher by questioning your academic behaviors, your understanding of the material, and your academic performance. Take ownership of new ideas and strategies by finding a way to make them a part of you.

Many experts believe that writing is a mode of learning. In other words, writing about something helps a person understand it. With that purpose in mind, record a response to the following questions to communicate to yourself and your instructor. Learn about yourself through your journal writing. Use the perforations to tear the assignment out for your instructor.

1. Where have you decided to do most of your studying? Why?

   ____

2. If the telephone is a distraction, how are you managing your calls?

   ____

3. Which television programs do you plan to watch on a regular basis?

   ____

   ____

4. When and where do you tend to waste time? ______________

   ____

5. When do you write your to-do list for the day? ______________

   ____

6. Which classmates would you feel comfortable calling about an assignment?

   ____

7. Have some of your classmates been late for class? How were these tardy students put at a disadvantage? ______________

   ____

8. What two "success behaviors" have you observed in fellow classmates that you would like to copy? ______________

   ____

2

Vocabulary

- How do you remember new words?
- What are context clues?
- Why learn prefixes, roots, and suffixes?
- What will you find in a dictionary?
- What is a glossary?
- What is a thesaurus?
- What are analogies?
- What are acronyms?
- How are transitional words used?

Visa by *Stuart Davis, 1951. Oil on canvas, 40 × 52" (101.6 × 132.1 cm). The Museum of Modern Art, New York. Gift of Mrs. Gertrud A. Mellon. Photograph © 2003 The Museum of Modern Art, New York. © Estate of Stuart Davis/Licensed by VAGA, New York, NY.*

Remembering New Words

Have you ever made lists of unknown words that you wanted to remember? Did you dutifully write down the word, a colon, and a definition, and promise to review the list at night before going to bed? Did it work? Probably not! Memorization can be an effective cramming strategy, but it does not seem to produce long-term results. Recording only the word and definition does not establish the associations necessary for long-term memory. Think smart and use the clever techniques of memory experts to expand your vocabulary. The following suggestions can help you make new words into old friends.

Associate Words in Phrases. Never record a word in isolation. Think of the word and record it in a phrase that suggests its meaning. The phrase may be part of the sentence in which you first encountered the word, or it may be a vivid creation of your own imagination. Such a phrase provides a setting for the word and enriches the links to your long-term memory.

For example, the word *caravel* means a "small sailing ship." Record the word in a phrase that creates a memorable setting, like "a caravan of gliding caravels on the horizon of the sea."

Associate Words with Rhymes or Sounds. Link the sound of a new word with a rhyming word or phrase. The brain appreciates connections and patterns. For example, the word *hoard,* which means to accumulate or stockpile, can be linked with *stored* as in "He stored his hoard of Halloween candy in the closet."

Associate Words in Images. Expand the phrase chosen for learning the word into a vivid mental image. Create a situation or an episode for the word. Further, enrich your memory link by drawing a picture of your mental image.

For example, the word *candid* means frank and truthful. Imagine a friend asking your opinion on an unattractive outfit. A suggestive phrase for learning the word might be "My candid reply might have hurt her feelings."

Associate Words in Families. Words, like people, have families that share the same names. In the case of words, the names are called *prefixes, roots,* and *suffixes.* A basic knowledge of word parts can help you unlock the meaning to thousands of associated family members.

The prefix *ambi* means "both," as in the word *ambivert,* which means being both introverted and extroverted. Although this word is seldom used, it can be easily remembered because of its association with the other two more common words. A useful transfer occurs, however, when the knowledge of *ambi* is applied to new family members like *ambidextrous, ambiguous,* and *ambivalence.*

Seek Reinforcement. Look and listen for your new words. As suggested previously, you will probably discover that they are used more frequently than you ever thought. Notice them, welcome them, and congratulate yourself on your newfound wisdom.

Create Concept Cards. Many students use index cards for recording information on new words. As illustrated below, you write the word in a phrase on the front of the card, along with a notation of where the word was encountered. On the back of the card, write an appropriate definition, use the word in a new sentence, and draw an image illustrating the word. Review the cards to reinforce the words and quiz yourself.

Front

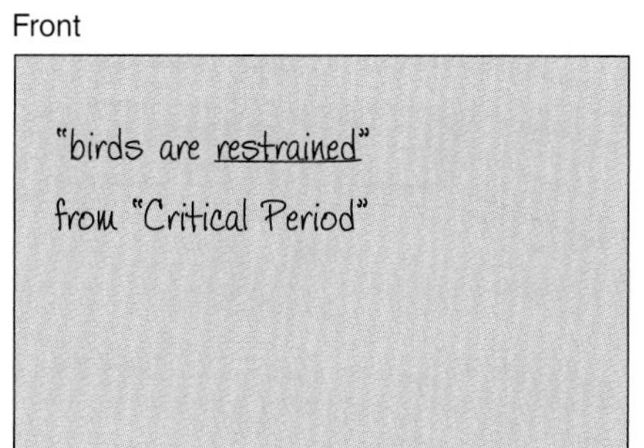

Back

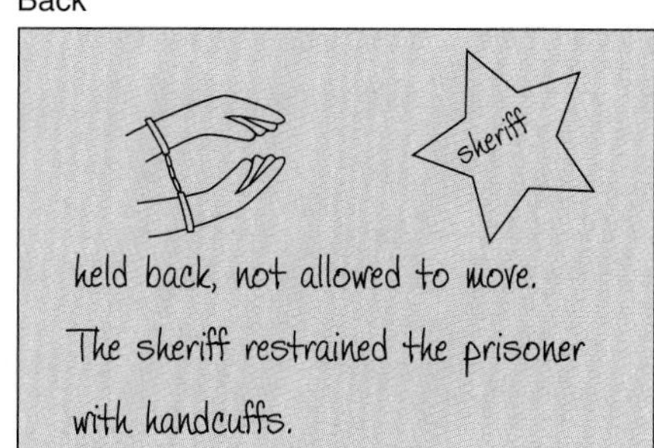

In *Vocabulary Cartoons*, a series of books by Sam, Max, and Bryan Burchers, humor is skillfully combined with the techniques of association to push the concept card to a new level. The idea for the books came from Bryan's inability to remember the definition of *aloof*. His father, Sam, asked Bryan for a rhyming word, and they developed the concept of the Burchers' cat, Snowball, being so aloof that she hid on the roof. Sam drew a cartoon to illustrate, and Bryan never forgot the definition.

The Burchers tested the power of their vocabulary cartoons on 500 Florida students by giving half the students words with definitions and cartoons and the other half words with definitions but no cartoons. They reported that the students who used the cartoons learned 72 percent more words than those without the cartoons. Keeping that level of success in mind, try adding rhymes and sound associations to your own concept cards. Notice in the illustration on page 52 how cleverly the Burchers use sound and images to form memory links for the words *irascible* and *curtail*.

Using Context Clues

Context clues are the most common method of unlocking the meaning of unknown words. The *context* of a word refers to the sentence or paragraph in which it appears. Readers use several types of context clues. In some cases, words are defined directly in the sentences in which they appear; in other instances, the

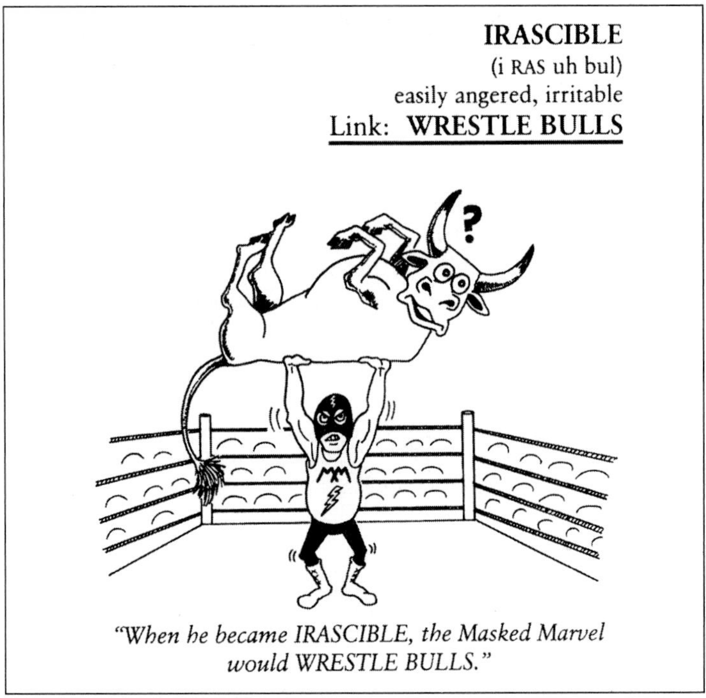

IRASCIBLE
(i RAS uh bul)
easily angered, irritable
Link: **WRESTLE BULLS**

"When he became IRASCIBLE, the Masked Marvel would WRESTLE BULLS."

CURTAIL
(ker TALE)
to truncate or abridge; to lessen, usually by cutting away from
Link: **CAT TAIL**

"Rex readies himself to CURTAIL the CAT'S TAIL."

Courtesy of New Monic Books, publisher of Vocabulary Cartoons SAT Word Power.

sentence offers clues or hints that enable the reader to arrive indirectly at the meaning of the word. The following are examples of how each type of clue can be used to figure out word meaning in textbooks.

Definition

Complex scientific material has a heavy load of specialized vocabulary. Fortunately, new words are often directly defined as they are introduced in the text. Do you know the meaning of *erythrocytes* and *oxyhemoglobin*? Read the following textbook sentence in which these two words appear, and then select the correct definition for each word.

EXAMPLE When oxygen diffuses into the blood in external respiration, most of it enters the red blood cells, or erythrocytes, and unites with the hemoglobin in these cells, forming a compound called oxyhemoglobin.

Willis H. Johnson et al., *Essentials of Biology*

________ *Erythrocytes* means
a. diffused oxygen.
b. red blood cells.
c. respiration process.

________ *Oxyhemoglobin* means
a. hemoglobin without oxygen.
b. dominant oxygen cells.
c. combination of oxygen and hemoglobin.

EXPLANATION The answers are *b* and *c*. Notice that the first word is used as a synonym to follow the words that define it, and the second is part of the explanation of the sentence.

Elaborating Details

In political science you will come across the term *confederation*. Keep reading and see if you can figure out the meaning from the hints in the following sentence.

EXAMPLE There is a third form of governmental structure, a *confederation*. The United States began as such, under the Articles of Confederation. In a confederation, the national government is weak and most or all the power is in the hands of its components, for example, the individual states. Today, confederations are rare except in international organizations such as the United Nations.

Robert Lineberry, *Government in America*

________ A *confederation* is a governmental structure with
a. strong federal power.
b. weak federal power.
c. weak state power.
d. equal federal and state power.

EXPLANATION The answer is *b* and can be figured out from the details in the third sentence.

Examples

In psychology you will frequently encounter a complicated word describing something you have often thought about but not named. Read the following sentence to find out what *psychokinesis* means.

EXAMPLE Another psychic phenomenon is *psychokinesis,* the ability to affect physical events without physical intervention. You can test your powers of psychokinesis by trying to influence the fall of dice from a mechanical shaker. Are you able to have the dice come up a certain number with a greater frequency than would occur by chance?

Douglas W. Matheson, *Introductory Psychology: The Modern View*

________ *Psychokinesis* means

a. extrasensory perception.
b. an influence on happenings without physical tampering.
c. physical intervention affecting physical change.

EXPLANATION The answer is *b*. Here the word is first directly defined in a complicated manner and then the definition is clarified by a simple example.

Comparison

Economics uses many complex concepts that are difficult to understand. The use of a familiar term in a comparison can help the reader relate to a new idea. Can you explain a *trade deficit?* The following comparison will help.

EXAMPLE When the United States imports more than it exports, we have a trade deficit rather than a trade balance or surplus. Similarly, a store manager who buys more than she sells will create a financial deficit for the company.

________ A *trade deficit* means that a nation

a. sells more than it buys.
b. buys more than it sells.
c. sells what it buys.

EXPLANATION The answer is *b*. The comparison explains the definition by creating a more understandable situation.

Contrast

Can you explain what *transsexuals* are and how they differ from *homosexuals?* The following sentences will give you some clues.

EXAMPLE

Transsexuals are people (usually males) who feel that they were born into the wrong body. They are not homosexuals in the usual sense. Most homosexuals are satisfied with their anatomy and think of themselves as appropriately male or female; they simply prefer members of their own sex. Transsexuals, in contrast, think of themselves as members of the opposite sex (often from early childhood) and may be so desperately unhappy with their physical appearance that they request hormonal and surgical treatment to change their genitals and secondary sex characteristics.

Rita Atkinson et al., *Introduction to Psychology*

_______ A *transsexual* is a person who thinks of himself/herself as a
a. homosexual.
b. heterosexual.
c. member of the opposite sex.
d. person without sex drive.

EXPLANATION The answer is *c*. By comparing homosexual and transsexual, the reader is better able to understand the latter and distinguish between the two.

Limitations of Context Clues

Although the clues in the sentence in which an unknown word appears are certainly helpful in deriving the meaning of a word, these clues will not always give a complete and accurate definition. To understand totally the meaning of a word, take some time after your reading is completed to look the word up in a glossary or a dictionary. Context clues operate just as the name suggests; they are hints and not necessarily complete definitions.

Exercise 2.1

The Power of Context Clues

How can context clues assist you in clarifying or unlocking the meaning of unknown words? For each of the following vocabulary items, make two responses. First, without reading the sentence containing the unknown word, select *a*, *b*, *c*, or *d* for the definition that you feel best fits each italicized word. Then, read the material in which the word is used in context and answer again. Compare your answers. Did reading the word in context help? Were you uncertain of any word as it appeared on the list, but then able to figure out the meaning after reading it in a sentence?

_________ 1. *usurped*
a. shortened
b. acknowledged
c. aggravated
d. seized

_________ Henry, to the end of his life, thought of himself as a pious and orthodox Catholic who had restored the independent authority of the Church of England *usurped* centuries before by the Bishop of Rome.

Shepard B. Clough et al., *A History of the Western World*

_________ 2. *assimilationist*
a. one who adopts the habits of a larger cultural group
b. a machinist
c. a typist
d. one who files correspondence

_________ When members of a minority group wish to give up what is distinctive about them and become just like the majority, they take an *assimilationist* position. An example is the Urban League.

Reece McGee et al., *Sociology: An Introduction*

_________ 3. *dyad*
a. star
b. two-member group
c. opposing factor
d. leader

_________ George Simmel was one of the first sociologists to suggest that the number of members in a group radically transforms its properties. He began with an analysis of what happens when a *dyad,* a two-member group, becomes a triad, a three-member group.

Ibid.

_________ 4. *hyperthermophiles*
a. animals
b. heat lovers
c. birds
d. winter plants

_________ Another group of archaea, the *hyperthermophiles,* thrive in very hot waters; some even live near deep-ocean vents where temperatures are above 100°C, the boiling point of water at sea level.

Neil Campbell et al., *Biology: Concepts & Connections,* 3rd ed.

_______ 5. *expropriated*
a. took from its owners
b. industrialized
c. approximated
d. increased in size

_______ Under a decree of September 1952, the government *expropriated* several hundred thousand acres from large landholders and redistributed this land among the peasants.

Jesse H. Wheeler, Jr., et al., *Regional Geography of the World*

_______ 6. *adherents*
a. children
b. followers
c. instigators
d. detractors

_______ One of the fundamental features of Hinduism has been the division of its *adherents* into the most elaborate caste system ever known.

Ibid.

_______ 7. *stimulus*
a. writing implement
b. distinguishing mark
c. something that incites action
d. result

_______ While we are sleeping, for example, we are hardly aware of what is happening around us, but we are aware to some degree. Any loud noise or other abrupt *stimulus* will almost certainly awaken us.

Gardner Lindzey et al., *Psychology*

_______ 8. *debilitating*
a. weakening
b. reinforcing
c. exciting
d. enjoyable

_______ However, anyone who has passed through several time zones while flying east or west knows how difficult it can be to change from one sleep schedule to another. This "jet lag" can be so *debilitating* that many corporations will not allow their executives to enter negotiations for at least two days after such a trip.

Ibid.

_______ 9. *autocratic*
a. automatic
b. democratic
c. self-starting
d. dictatorial

_______ *Autocratic* leadership can be extremely effective if the people wielding it have enough power to enforce their decisions and if their followers know that they have it. It is especially useful in military situations where speed of decision is critical. Among its disadvantages are the lack of objectivity and the disregard for opinions of subordinates.

David J. Rachman and Michael Mescon, *Business Today*

_______ 10. *ice page*
a. Web page that wiggles to center itself
b. Web page anchored to right of screen
c. Web page anchored to left of screen
d. Web page that flows to fit any size screen

_______ Ice, jello, and liquid are related terms describing three approaches to controlling content placement on a Web page. An *ice page* is one in which the primary content has a fixed width and is "frozen" to the left margin.

H. L. Capron, *Computers*, 6th ed.

Exercise 2.2 Context Clues in Academic Reading

Use the context clues of the sentence to write the meaning of each of the following italicized words.

1. Andrew was a thin old man despite his toughness, and soon he was in danger. Fortunately, friends formed a cordon and managed to *extricate* him through a rear door.

   John Garraty, *The American Nation*

   Extricate means _______________

2. But they were unfamiliar with the *regenerative* powers of the starfish. The central disk merely grows new arms, and a single arm can form a new animal.

   Robert Wallace, *Biology: The World of Life*

   Regenerative means _______________

3. To our delight, the *planarians* that had eaten educated victims learned much faster than did the worms that had consumed their untrained brethren.

Ibid.

Planarians are ______________________________

4. Belle Starr, the *moniker* of one Myra Belle Shirley, was immortalized as "the bandit queen," as pure in heart as Jesse James was socially conscious.

John Garraty, *The American Nation*

Moniker means ______________________________

5. Calamity Jane (Martha Cannary), later said to have been Wild Bill's *paramour*, wrote her own romantic autobiography in order to support a drinking problem.

Ibid.

A *paramour* is ______________________________

Multiple Meanings of a Word

Many words, particularly short ones, can be confusing because they have more than one meaning. The word *bank*, for example, can be used as a noun to refer to *a financial institution, the ground rising from a river,* or *a mass of clouds.* As a verb, *bank* can mean *to laterally incline an airplane, to accumulate,* or *to drive a billiard ball into a cushion.* Thus the meaning of the word depends on the sentence and paragraph in which the word is used. Be alert to context clues that indicate an unfamiliar use of a seemingly familiar word.

Exercise 2.3

Multiple Meanings

The boldface words in the following sentences have multiple meanings. Write the definition of each boldface word as it is used in the sentence.

1. The survivors tried to **band** together and form alliances. ______________
2. As a team player for IBM, she demonstrated **industry** and intelligence in accomplishing the goals. ______________________________
3. After being **canned** by the dot.com company, she looked for a new job marketing Verizon products. ______________________________
4. The accounting **firm** audited two health care companies on the New York Stock Exchange. ______________________________
5. The insect did not **light** long enough to be caught. ______________

Understanding the Structure of Words

What is the longest word in the English language and what does it mean? Maxwell Nurnberg and Morris Rosenblum in *How to Build a Better Vocabulary* (Prentice-Hall, 1949) say that at one time the longest word in *Webster's New International Dictionary* was

pneumonoultramicroscopicsilicovolcanokoniosis

Look at the word again and notice the smaller and more familiar word parts. Do you know enough of the smaller parts to figure out the meaning of the word? Nurnberg and Rosenblum unlock the meaning as follows:

pneumono:	pertaining to the lungs, as in *pneumon*ia
ultra:	beyond, as in *ultra*violet rays
micro:	small, as in *micro*scope
scopic:	from the root of Greek verb *skopein,* to view or look at
silico:	from the element *silicon,* found in quartz, flint, and sand
volcano:	the meaning of this is obvious
koni:	the principal root, from a Greek word for dust
osis:	a suffix indicating illness, as trichin*osis*

Now, putting the parts together again, we deduce that *pneumonoultramicroscopicsilicovolcanokoniosis* is a disease of the lungs caused by extremely small particles of volcanic ash and dust.

This dramatic example demonstrates how an extremely long and technical word can become more manageable by breaking it into smaller parts. The same is true for many of the smaller words that we use every day. A knowledge of word parts will help you unlock the meaning of literally thousands of words. One vocabulary expert identified a list of thirty prefixes, roots, and suffixes and claims that knowing these thirty word parts will help unlock the meaning of 14,000 words.

Words, like people, have families and, in some cases, an abundance of close relations. Clusters, or what might be called *word families,* are composed of words with the same base or root. For example, *bio* is a root meaning *life.* If you know that *biology* means *the study of life,* it becomes easy to figure out the definition of a word like *biochemistry.* Word parts form new words as follows:

prefix + root   root + suffix   prefix + root + suffix

Prefixes and suffixes are added to root words to change the meaning. A prefix is added to the beginning of a word and a suffix is added to the end. For example, the prefix *il* means *not.* When added to the word *legal,* the resulting word, *illegal*, becomes the opposite of the original. Suffixes can change the meaning or change the way the word can be used in a sentence. The suffix *cide* means to *kill*. When added to *frater*, which means *brother*, the resulting word, *fratricide*, means to *kill one's brother*. Adding *ity* or *ize* to *frater* changes both the meaning and the way the word can be used grammatically in a sentence.

EXAMPLE To demonstrate how prefixes, roots, and suffixes overlap and make families, start with the root *gamy*, meaning *marriage*, and ask some questions.

1. What is the state of having only one wife called? ____________________
   (*mono* means *one*)
2. What is a man who has two wives called? ____________________
   (*bi* means *two* and *ist* means *one who*)
3. What is a man who has many wives called? ____________________
   (*poly* means *many*)
4. What is a woman who has many husbands called? ____________________
   (*andro* means *man*)
5. What is a hater of marriage called? ____________________
   (*miso* means *hater of*)

EXPLANATION The answers are (1) monogamy, (2) bigamist, (3) polygamist, (4) polyandrist, and (5) misogamist. Note that in several of the *gamy* examples, the letters change slightly to accommodate language sounds. Such variations of a letter or two are typical when working with word parts. Letters are often dropped or added to maintain the rhythm of the language, but the meaning of the word part remains the same regardless of the change in spelling. For example, the prefix *con* means *with* or *together* as in *conduct*. This same prefix is used with variations in many other words:

cooperate *collection* *correlate* *communicate* *connect*

Thus, *con*, *co*, *col*, *cor*, and *com* are all forms of the prefix that means *with* or *together*.

Exercise 2.4

Word Families

Create your own word families from the word parts that are supplied. For each of the following definitions, supply a prefix, root, or suffix to make the appropriate word.

Prefix: *bi* means *two*

1. able to speak two languages: bi ____________
2. having two feet, like humans: bi ____________

3. representing two political parties: bi ____________
4. occurring at two-year intervals: bi ____________
5. having two lenses on one glass: bi ____________
6. cut into two parts: bi ____________
7. mathematics expression with two terms: bi ____________
8. instrument with two eyes: bi ____________
9. tooth with two points: bi ____________
10. coming twice a year: bi ____________

Root: *vert* means *to turn*

1. to change one's beliefs: ______vert
2. to go back to old ways again: ______vert
3. a car with a removable top: ______vert______
4. to change the direction of a stream: ______vert
5. activities intended to undermine or destroy: ______vers______
6. an outgoing, gregarious person: ______vert
7. a quiet, introspective, shy person ______vert
8. conditions that are turned against you; misfortune ______vers______
9. one who deviates from normal behavior, especially sexual: ______vert
10. one who is sometimes introspective and sometimes gregarious: ______ vert

Suffix: *ism* means *doctrine, condition,* or *characteristic*

1. addiction to alcoholic drink: ________ ism
2. a brave and courageous manner of acting: ________ ism
3. prejudice against a particular gender or sex: ________ ism
4. doctrine concerned only with fact and reality: ________ ism
5. system using terror to intimidate: ________ ism
6. writing someone's words as your own: ________ ism
7. driving out an evil spirit: ________ ism
8. purification to join the church: ________ ism
9. informal style of speech using slang: ________ ism
10. being obsessive or fanatical about something: ________ ism

Exercise 2.5 **Prefixes, Roots, and Suffixes**

Using the prefix, root, or suffix provided, write the words that best fit the following definitions.

1. *con* means *with*
   infectious or catching: con ___________
2. *sub* means *under*
   under the conscious level of the mind: sub ___________
3. *post* means *after*
   to delay or set back: post ___________
4. *vita* means life
   a pill to provide essential nutrients: vita ___________
5. *pel* means *drive* or *push*
   to push out of school: ___________ pel
6. *thermo* means *heat*
   device for regulating furnace heat: thermo ___________
7. *ven* means *come*
   a meeting for people to come together: ___________ ven ___________
8. *rupt* means *break* or *burst*
   a volcanic explosion: ___________ rupt ___________
9. *meter* means *measure*
   instrument to measure heat: ___________ meter
10. *naut* means *voyager*
    voyager in the sea: ___________ naut

Ten Weekly Vocabulary Lessons

Use the ten weekly vocabulary lessons in Appendix 1 at the end of this book to expand your vocabulary. Each lesson follows a structural approach and links words through shared prefixes, roots, and suffixes. The words are organized into different clusters or families to enhance memory, to organize your learning, and to emphasize that most new words are made up of familiar old parts. Strengthen your vocabulary by identifying your old friends in the new words. Then apply your knowledge of word parts to unlock and remember the meanings of the new words.

Your instructor may choose to introduce the words at the beginning of the week, assign review items for practice, and quiz your knowledge of the words at the end of the week. Learn more than 200 words through this easy word family approach.

Using a Dictionary

Do you have an excellent collegiate dictionary such as *Merriam-Webster's Collegiate Dictionary?* Every college student needs two dictionaries: a small one for class and a large one to keep at home. In class you may use a small paperback dictionary for quick spelling or word-meaning checks. The paperback is easy to carry but does not provide the depth of information needed for college study that is found in the larger collegiate editions. Good dictionaries not only contain the definitions of words, but also provide the following additional information for each word.

Guide Words. The two words at the top of each dictionary page are the first and last entries on the page. They help guide your search for a particular entry by indicating what is covered on that page.

In the sample below, *flagrante delicto* is the first entry on the page of the dictionary on which *flamingo* appears, and *flappy* is the last entry. Note that the pronunciation of the word *flamingo* is followed by part of speech *(n)*, plural spellings, and the origin of the word.

flagrante delicto • flappy

fla•min•go \flə-ˈmiŋ-(ˌ)gō\ *n, pl* **-gos** *also* **-goes** [obs. Sp *flamengo* (now *flamenco*), lit., Fleming, German (conventionally thought of as ruddy-complexioned)] (1565) : any of several large aquatic birds (family Phoenicopteridae) with long legs and neck, webbed feet, a broad lamellate bill resembling that of a duck but abruptly bent downward, and usu. rosy-white plumage with scarlet wing coverts and black wing quills

flamingo

\ə\ abut \$^{ə}$\ kitten, F table \ər\ further \a\ ash \ā\ ace \ä\ mop, mar
\au̇\ out \ch\ chin \e\ bet \ē\ easy \g\ go \i\ hit \ī\ ice \j\ job
\ŋ\ sing \ō\ go \ȯ\ law \ȯi\ boy \th\ thin \t̲h̲\ the \ü\ loot \u̇\ foot
\y\ yet \zh\ vision \ȧ, k̲, ^{n}, œ, œ̄, ᵫ, ᵫ̄, ^{y}\ *see* Guide to Pronunciation

Pronunciation. The boldface main entry divides the word into sounds, using a dot between each syllable. After the entry, letters and symbols show the pronunciation. A diacritical mark (ˊ) at the end of a syllable indicates stress on that syllable. A heavy mark means major stress; a lighter one shows minor stress.

As shown in the illustration above, a key explaining the symbols and letters appears at the bottom of the dictionary page. For example, a word like *ragweed* (ragˊ wēd) would be pronounced with a short *a* as in *ash* and a long *e* as in *easy.*

The *a* in *flamingo* sounds like the *a* in *abut,* and the final *o* has a long sound as in *go.* The stress is on the first syllable.

Part of Speech. The part of speech is indicated in an abbreviation for each meaning of a word. A single word, for example, may be a noun with one definition and a verb with another. The noun *flamingo* can be used as only one part of speech, but *sideline* can be both a noun and a verb (see the entry below).

[1]**side·line** \-ˌlīn\ *n* (1862) **1 :** a line at right angles to a goal line or end line and marking a side of a court or field of play for athletic games **2 a :** a line of goods sold in addition to one's principal line **b :** a business or activity pursued in addition to one's regular occupation **3 a :** the space immediately outside the lines along either side of an athletic field or court **b :** a sphere of little or no participation or activity — usu. used in pl.
[2]**sideline** *vt* (1943) **:** to put out of action **:** put on the sidelines

Spellings. Spellings are given for the plural of the word and for special forms. This is particularly useful in determining whether letters are added or dropped to form the new words. The plural of *flamingo* can be spelled correctly in two different ways. Both *flamingos* and *flamingoes* are acceptable.

Origin. For many entries, the foreign word and language from which the word was derived will appear after the pronunciation. For example, *L* stands for a Latin origin and G for Greek. A key for the many dictionary abbreviations usually appears at the beginning of the book.

The word *flamingo* has a rich history. It is Portuguese *(Pg)* and comes from the Spanish *(fr Sp)* word *flamenco.* It is derived ultimately from the Old Provençal *(fr OProv) flamenc,* from *flama* for *flame,* which comes from the Latin *(fr L)* word *flamma.*

Multiple Meanings. A single word can have many shades of meaning or several completely different meanings. Different meanings are numbered.

The word *flamingo* has only one meaning. The word *sideline,* however, has several, as shown in the entry above.

A sideline can be a business, a product, or a designated area. In addition, it can mean to move something out of the action.

Exercise 2.6 Using the Dictionary

Answer the following questions, using the page from *Merriam-Webster's Collegiate Dictionary* reproduced on page 66, with *T* (true) or *F* (false).

_________ 1. *Leicester* is a county in England, a breed of sheep, and a cheese.

_________ 2. A Hawaiian *lei* is a necklace of flowers.

_________ 3. The word *lemming* is derived from the Greek word *lemmus,* which means to drown.

664 legitimate • lenient

1 a : lawfully begotten; *specif* : born in wedlock **b** : having full filial rights and obligations by birth ⟨a ~ child⟩ **2** : being exactly as purposed : neither spurious nor false ⟨~ grievance⟩ ⟨a ~ practitioner⟩ **3 a** : accordant with law or with established legal forms and requirements ⟨a ~ government⟩ **b** : ruling by or based on the strict principle of hereditary right ⟨a ~ king⟩ **4** : conforming to recognized principles or accepted rules and standards ⟨~ advertising expenditure⟩ ⟨~ inference⟩ **5** : relating to plays acted by professional actors but not including revues, burlesque, or some forms of musical comedy ⟨the ~ theater⟩ *syn* see LAWFUL — **le·git·i·mate·ly** *adv*

²le·git·i·mate \-ˌmāt\ *vt* **-mat·ed; -mat·ing** (1531) : to make legitimate: **a** (1) : to give legal status or authorization to (2) : to show or affirm to be justified **b** : to put (a bastard) in the state of a legitimate child before the law by legal means — **le·git·i·ma·tion** \-ˌji-tə-ˈmā-shən\ *n* — **le·git·i·mat·or** \-ˈji-tə-ˌmā-tər\ *n*

le·git·i·ma·tize \li-ˈji-tə-mə-ˌtīz\ *vt* **-tized; -tiz·ing** (1791) : LEGITIMATE

le·git·i·mise *Brit var of* LEGITIMIZE

le·git·i·mism \li-ˈji-tə-ˌmi-zəm\ *n, often cap* (1877) : adherence to the principles of political legitimacy or to a person claiming legitimacy — **le·git·i·mist** \-mist\ *n, often cap* — **legitimist** *adj*

le·git·i·mize \-ˌmīz\ *vt* **-mized; -miz·ing** (1848) : LEGITIMATE — **le·git·i·mi·za·tion** \-ˌji-tə-mə-ˈzā-shən\ *n* — **le·git·i·miz·er** \-ˈji-tə-ˌmī-zər\ *n*

leg·man \ˈleg-ˌman *also* ˈlāg-\ *n* (1923) **1** : a reporter assigned usu. to gather information **2** : an assistant who performs various subordinate tasks (as gathering information or running errands)

leg–of–mut·ton *or* **leg–o'–mut·ton** \ˌle-gə(v)-ˈmə-tᵊn *also* ˌlāg-\ *adj* (1840) : having the approximately triangular shape or outline of a leg of mutton ⟨~ sleeve⟩ ⟨~ sail⟩

leg out *vt* (1965) : to make (as a base hit) by fast running

leg–pull \ˈleg-ˌpu̇l *also* ˈlāg-\ *n* [fr. the phrase *to pull one's leg*] (1915) : a humorous deception or hoax

leg·room \-ˌrüm, -ˌru̇m\ *n* (1926) : space in which to extend the legs while seated

le·gume \ˈle-ˌgyüm, li-ˈgyüm\ *n* [F *légume*, fr. L *legumin-, legumen* leguminous plant, fr. *legere* to gather — more at LEGEND] (1676) **1 a** : the fruit or seed of leguminous plants (as peas or beans) used for food **b** : a vegetable used for food **2** : any of a large family (Leguminosae syn. Fabaceae) of dicotyledonous herbs, shrubs, and trees having fruits that are legumes (sense 3) or loments, bearing nodules on the roots that contain nitrogen-fixing bacteria, and including important food and forage plants (as peas, beans, or clovers) **3** : a dry dehiscent one-celled fruit developed from a simple superior ovary and usu. dehiscing into two valves with the seeds attached to the ventral suture : POD

le·gu·mi·nous \li-ˈgyü-mə-nəs, le-\ *adj* (15c) **1** : of, relating to, or consisting of plants that are legumes **2** : resembling a legume

leg up *n* (1837) **1** : a helping hand : BOOST **2** : HEAD START

leg warmer *n* (1974) : a usu. knitted covering for the leg

leg·work \ˈleg-ˌwərk *also* ˈlāg-\ *n* (1891) : active physical work (as in gathering information) that forms the basis of more creative or mentally exacting work (as writing a book)

le·hua \lā-ˈhü-ə\ *n* [Hawaiian] (1888) : a common very showy chiefly Polynesian tree (*Metrosideros collinus*) of the myrtle family having bright red flowers and a hard wood; *also* : its flower

¹lei \ˈlā, ˈlā-ˌē\ *n* [Hawaiian] (1843) : a wreath or necklace usu. of flowers or leaves

²lei \ˈlā\ *pl of* LEU

Leices·ter \ˈles-tər\ *n* [*Leicester*, county in England] (1798) **1** : an individual of either of two English breeds of white-faced long-wool sheep raised esp. for mutton **2** : a hard usu. orange-colored cheese similar to cheddar

leish·man·ia \lēsh-ˈma-nē-ə\ *n* [NL, fr. Sir W. B. *Leishman* †1926 Brit. medical officer] (1914) : any of a genus (*Leishmania*) of flagellate protozoans that are parasitic in the tissues of vertebrates; *broadly* : an organism resembling the leishmanias that is included in the family (Trypanosomatidae) to which they belong — **leish·man·ial** \-nē-əl\ *adj*

leish·man·i·a·sis \ˌlēsh-mə-ˈnī-ə-səs\ *n* [NL] (1912) : infection with or disease caused by leishmanias

leis·ter \ˈlēs-tər\ *n* [of Scand origin; akin to ON *ljōstr* leister] (ca. 1534) : a spear armed with three or more barbed prongs for catching fish

lei·sure \ˈlē-zhər, ˈle-, ˈlā-\ *n* [ME *leiser*, fr. MF *leisir*, fr. *leisir* to be permitted, fr. L *licēre*] (14c) **1** : freedom provided by the cessation of activities; *esp* : time free from work or duties **2** : EASE, LEISURELINESS — **leisure** *adj* — **at leisure** *or* **at one's leisure** : in one's leisure time : at one's convenience ⟨read the book *at her leisure*⟩

lei·sured \-zhərd\ *adj* (1631) : having leisure : LEISURELY

¹lei·sure·ly \-zhər-lē\ *adv* (15c) : without haste : DELIBERATELY

²leisurely *adj* (1604) : characterized by leisure : UNHURRIED — **lei·sure·li·ness** *n*

leisure suit *n* (1975) : a suit consisting of a shirt jacket and matching trousers for informal wear

leit·mo·tiv *or* **leit·mo·tif** \ˈlīt-mō-ˌtēf\ *n* [G *Leitmotiv*, fr. *leiten* to lead + *Motiv* motive] (ca. 1876) **1** : an associated melodic phrase or figure that accompanies the reappearance of an idea, person, or situation esp. in a Wagnerian music drama **2** : a dominant recurring theme

¹lek \ˈlek\ *n* [Sw, short for *lekställe* mating ground, fr. *lek* mating, sport + *ställe* place] (1871) : an assembly area where animals (as the prairie chicken) carry on display and courtship behavior

²lek *n, pl* **leks** *or* **le·ke** \ˈle-kə\ *also* **lek** *or* **le·ku** \ˈle-(ˌ)kü\ [Alb] (1927) — see MONEY table

lek·var \ˈlek-ˌvär\ *n* [Hung *lekvár* jam] (ca. 1958) : a prune butter used as a pastry filling

le·man \ˈle-mən, ˈlē-\ *n* [ME *lefman, leman*, fr. *lef* lief] (13c) *archaic* : SWEETHEART, LOVER; *esp* : MISTRESS

¹lem·ma \ˈle-mə\ *n, pl* **lemmas** *or* **lem·ma·ta** \-mə-tə\ [L, fr. Gk *lēmma* thing taken, assumption, fr. *lambanein* to take — more at LATCH] (1570) **1** : an auxiliary proposition used in the demonstration of another proposition **2** : the argument or theme of a composition prefixed as a title or introduction; *also* : the heading or theme of a comment or note on a text **3** : a glossed word or phrase

²lemma *n* [Gk, husk, fr. *lepein* to peel — more at LEPER] (1906) : the lower of the two bracts enclosing the flower in the spikelet of grasses

lem·ming \ˈle-miŋ\ *n* [Norw] (1713) : any of various small short-tailed furry-footed rodents (as genera *Lemmus* and *Dicrostonyx*) of circumpolar distribution that are notable for the recurrent mass migrations of a European form (*L. lemmus*) which often continue into the sea where vast numbers are drowned — **lem·ming·like** \-ˌlīk\ *adj*

lem·nis·cate \lem-ˈnis-kət\ *n* [NL *lemniscata*, fr. fem. of L *lemniscatus* with hanging ribbons, fr. *lemniscus*] (ca. 1781) : a figure-eight shaped curve whose equation in polar coordinates is $\rho^2=a^2 \cos 2\theta$ or $\rho^2=a^2 \sin 2\theta$

lem·nis·cus \lem-ˈnis-kəs\ *n, pl* **-nis·ci** \-ˈnis-ˌkī, -ˌkē; -ˈni-ˌsī\ [NL, fr. L, ribbon, fr. Gk *lēmniskos*] (ca. 1905) : a band of fibers and esp. nerve fibers — **lem·nis·cal** \-kəl\ *adj*

¹lem·on \ˈle-mən\ *n* [ME *lymon*, fr. MF *limon*, fr. ML *limon-, limo*, fr. Ar *laymūn*] (15c) **1 a** : an acid fruit that is botanically a many-seeded pale yellow oblong berry and is produced by a small thorny tree (*Citrus limon*) **b** : a tree that bears lemons **2** : one (as an automobile) that is unsatisfactory or defective — **lem·ony** \ˈle-mə-nē\ *adj*

lemon 1: branch with fruit and flowers

²lemon *adj* (1598) **1** : of the color lemon yellow **2 a** : containing lemon **b** : having the flavor or scent of lemon

lem·on·ade \ˌle-mə-ˈnād\ *n* (1604) : a beverage of sweetened lemon juice mixed with water

lemon balm *n* (ca. 1888) : a bushy perennial Old World mint (*Melissa officinalis*) often cultivated for its fragrant lemon-flavored leaves

lem·on·grass \ˈle-mən-ˌgras\ *n* (1801) : a grass (*Cymbopogon citratus*) of robust habit that grows in tropical regions, is used as an herb, and is the source of an essential oil with an odor of lemon or verbena

lemon law *n* (1982) : a law offering car buyers relief (as by repair, replacement, or refund) for defects detected during a specified period after purchase

lemon shark *n* (1942) : a medium-sized requiem shark (*Negaprion brevirostris*) of the warm Atlantic that is yellowish brown to gray above with yellow or greenish sides

lemon sole *n* (1876) : any of several flatfishes and esp. flounders: as **a** : a bottom-dwelling flounder (*Microstomus kitt*) of the northeastern Atlantic that is an important food fish **b** : WINTER FLOUNDER

lemon yellow *n* (1807) : a brilliant greenish yellow color

lem·pi·ra \lem-ˈpir-ə\ *n* [AmerSp, fr. *Lempira*, 16th cent. Indian chief] (ca. 1934) — see MONEY table

le·mur \ˈlē-mər\ *n* [NL, fr. L *lemures*, pl., ghosts] (1795) : any of various arboreal chiefly nocturnal mammals that were formerly widespread but are now largely confined to Madagascar, are related to the monkeys but are usu. regarded as constituting a distinct superfamily (Lemuroidea), and usu. have a muzzle like a fox, large eyes, very soft woolly fur, and a long furry tail

lemur

le·mu·res \ˈle-mə-ˌrās, ˈlem-yə-ˌrēz\ *n pl* [L] (1555) : spirits of the unburied dead exorcised from homes in early Roman religious rites

lend \ˈlend\ *vb* **lent** \ˈlent\; **lend·ing** [ME *lenen, lenden*, fr. OE *lǣnan*, fr. *lǣn* loan — more at LOAN] *vt* (bef. 12c) **1 a** : to give for temporary use on condition that the same or its equivalent be returned **b** : to let out (money) for temporary use on condition of repayment with interest **2 a** : to give the assistance or support of : AFFORD, FURNISH ⟨a dispassionate and scholarly manner which ~s great force to his criticisms —*Times Lit. Supp.*⟩ **b** : to adapt or apply (oneself) readily : ACCOMMODATE ⟨a topic that ~s itself admirably to class discussion⟩ ~ *vi* : to make a loan *usage* see LOAN — **lend·able** \ˈlen-də-bəl\ *adj* — **lend·er** *n*

lending library *n* (1708) : a library from which materials are lent; *esp* : RENTAL LIBRARY

lend–lease \ˈlend-ˈlēs\ *n* [U.S. *Lend-Lease* Act (1941)] (1941) : the transfer of goods and services to an ally to aid in a common cause with payment made by a return of the original items or their use in the cause or by a similar transfer of other goods and services — **lend–lease** *vt*

length \ˈleŋ(k)th, ˈlen(t)th\ *n, pl* **lengths** \ˈleŋ(k)ths, ˈlen(t)ths, ˈleŋ(k)s\ [ME *lengthe*, fr. OE *lengthu*, fr. *lang* long] (bef. 12c) **1 a** : the longer or longest dimension of an object **b** : a measured distance or dimension ⟨10 feet in ~⟩ — see METRIC SYSTEM table, WEIGHT table **c** : the quality or state of being long **2 a** : duration or extent in time **b** : relative duration or stress of a sound **3 a** : distance or extent in space **b** : the length of something taken as a unit of measure ⟨his horse led by a ~⟩ **4** : the degree to which something (as a course of action or a line of thought) is carried — often used in pl. ⟨went to great ~s to learn the truth⟩ **5 a** : a long expanse or stretch **b** : a piece constituting or usable as part of a whole or of a connected series : SECTION ⟨a ~ of pipe⟩ **6** : a vertical dimension of an article of clothing — **at length 1** : FULLY, COMPREHENSIVELY **2** : at last : FINALLY

length·en \ˈleŋ(k)-thən, ˈlen(t)-\ *vb* **length·ened; length·en·ing** \ˈleŋ(k)th-niŋ, ˈlen(t)th-; ˈleŋ(k)-thə-, ˈlen(t)-\ *vt* (14c) : to make longer ~ *vi* : to grow longer *syn* see EXTEND — **length·en·er** \ˈleŋ(k)th-nər, ˈlen(t)th-; ˈleŋ(k)-thə-, ˈlen(t)-\ *n*

length·ways \ˈleŋ(k)th-ˌwāz, ˈlen(t)th-\ *adv* (1599) : LENGTHWISE

length·wise \-ˌwīz\ *adv* (ca. 1580) : in the direction of the length : LONGITUDINALLY — **lengthwise** *adj*

lengthy \ˈleŋ(k)-thē, ˈlen(t)-\ *adj* **length·i·er; -est** (1689) **1** : protracted excessively : OVERLONG **2** : EXTENDED, LONG — **length·i·ly** \-thə-lē\ *adv* — **length·i·ness** \-thē-nəs\ *n*

le·nience \ˈlē-nyən(t)s, -nē-ən(t)s\ *n* (1796) : LENIENCY

le·nien·cy \ˈlē-nē-ən(t)-sē, -nyən(t)-sē\ *n, pl* **-cies** (1780) **1** : the quality or state of being lenient **2** : a lenient disposition or practice *syn* see MERCY

le·nient \ˈlē-nē-ənt, -nyənt\ *adj* [L *lenient-, leniens*, prp. of *lenire* to soften, soothe, fr. *lenis* soft, mild; prob. akin to Lith *lėnas* tranquil — more

__________ 4. The word *leisurely* can be used as both an adverb and an adjective.

__________ 5. A *lemon* tree has both fruit and flowers.

__________ 6. The plural of *leman* is *lemen.*

__________ 7. One of the origins of *lemur* is the Latin word *lemures,* meaning *ghosts.*

__________ 8. The word *lemures* can be correctly pronounced in two different ways.

__________ 9. When the words *lend* and *lease* are used together to mean a transfer of goods, no hyphen is required.

__________ 10. The plural for *lemma* can be either *lemmas* or *lemmata.*

Word Origins

The study of word origins is called *etymology.* Not only is it fascinating to trace a word back to its earliest recorded appearance, but your knowledge of the word's origin can strengthen your memory for the word. For example, the word *narcissistic* means *egotistically in love with yourself.* Its origin is a Greek myth in which a beautiful youth named Narcissus falls in love with his own reflection; he is punished for his vanity by being turned into a flower. Thus the myth creates an intriguing image that can enhance your memory link for the word.

The amount of information on word origins varies with the type of dictionary. Because of its size, a small paperback dictionary such as the *American Heritage Dictionary* usually contains very little information on word origins, whereas a textbook-size edition of the *Merriam-Webster's Collegiate Dictionary* offers more. For the most information on word origins, visit the reference room in your college library and use an unabridged dictionary such as *Webster's Third New International Dictionary, Random House Dictionary of the English Language,* or *American Heritage Dictionary of the English Language.*

Exercise 2.7 Word Origins

Read the following dictionary entries and answer the questions about the words and their origins.

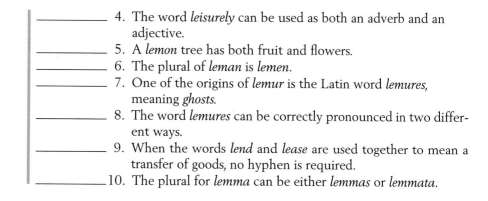

[1]**bribe** \\'brīb\\ *n* [ME, something stolen, fr. MF, bread given to a beggar] (15c) **1 :** money or favor given or promised in order to influence the judgment or conduct of a person in a position of trust **2 :** something that serves to induce or influence
[2]**bribe** *vb* **bribed; brib•ing** *vt* (1528) **:** to induce or influence by or as if by bribery **~** *vi* **:** to practice bribery — **brib•able** \\'brī-bə-bəl\\ *adj* —

By permission. From Merriam-Webster's Collegiate® Dictionary, Tenth Edition; *© 2001 by Merriam-Webster, Incorporated.*

1. *Bribe* means ______________________________

2. Explain the origin ______________________________

¹scape·goat \'skāp-ˌgōt\ *n* [¹*scape;* intended as trans. of Heb *'azāzēl* (prob. name of a demon), as if *'ēz 'ōzēl* goat that departs—Lev 16:8 (AV)] (1530) **1 :** a goat upon whose head are symbolically placed the sins of the people after which he is sent into the wilderness in the biblical ceremony for Yom Kippur **2 a :** one that bears the blame for others **b :** one that is the object of irrational hostility
²scapegoat *vt* (1943) **:** to make a scapegoat of — **scape·goat·ism** \-ˌgō-ˌti-zəm\ *n*

3. *Scapegoat* means ____________________________________

4. Explain the origin ____________________________________

mar·a·thon \'mar-ə-ˌthän\ *n, often attrib* [*Marathon,* Greece, site of a victory of Greeks over Persians in 490 B.C., the news of which was carried to Athens by a long-distance runner] (1896) **1 :** a long-distance race: **a :** a footrace run on an open course usu. of 26 miles 385 yards (42.2 kilometers) **b :** a race other than a footrace marked esp. by great length **2 a :** an endurance contest **b :** something (as an event, activity, or session) characterized by great length or concentrated effort

5. *Marathon* means ____________________________________

6. Explain the origin ____________________________________

____

om·buds·man \'äm-ˌbu̇dz-mən, 'ȯm-, -bədz-, -ˌman; äm-'bu̇dz-, ȯm-\ *n, pl* **-men** \-mən\ [Sw, lit., representative, fr. ON *umbothsmathr,* fr. *umboth* commission + *mathr* man] (1959) **1 :** a government official (as in Sweden or New Zealand) appointed to receive and investigate complaints made by individuals against abuses or capricious acts of public officials **2 :** one that investigates reported complaints (as from students or consumers), reports findings, and helps to achieve equitable settlements — **om·buds·man·ship** \-ˌship\ *n*

7. *Ombudsman* means ____________________________________

8. Explain the origin ____________________________________

____

van·dal \'van-dᵊl\ *n* [L *Vandalii* (pl.), of Gmc origin] (1555) **1** *cap* **:** a member of a Germanic people who lived in the area south of the Baltic between the Vistula and the Oder, overran Gaul, Spain, and northern Africa in the 4th and 5th centuries A.D., and in 455 sacked Rome **2 :** one who willfully or ignorantly destroys, damages, or defaces property belonging to another or to the public — **vandal** *adj, often cap* —

9. *Vandal* means ____________________________________

10. Explain the origin ____________________________________

Using a Glossary

When you begin studying a new subject area, like sociology or geology, the first shock is the vocabulary. Each subject seems to have a language, or jargon, of its own. For example, words like *sociocultural* or *socioeconomic* crop up again and again in a sociology text. In truth, these words are somewhat unique to the subject-matter area—they are *invented* words to describe sociological phenomena. The best explanation of such words and their relation to the subject area can usually be found in the textbook itself rather than in a dictionary. Often, textbooks have definitions displayed in the *margins* of a page, or more frequently, in a glossary of terms at the end of the book or at the end of a chapter. The glossary defines the words as they are used in the textbook.

Notice the following examples from the glossary of a psychology textbook. The terms using "learning" are part of the jargon of psychology and would probably not be found in the dictionary.

latent learning Hidden learning that is not demonstrated in performance until that performance is reinforced.

learned helplessness A condition in which a subject does not attempt to escape from a painful or noxious situation after learning in a previous, similar situation that escape is not possible.

learning A relatively permanent change in behavior that occurs as the result of practice or experience.

learning set An acquired strategy for learning or problem solving; learning to learn.

Exercise 2.8

Using Your Glossary

Turn to the glossary at the end of this book for help in defining the following terms. Write a definition for each in your own words.

1. schema ______________________________

____

2. bias ______________________________

____

3. context clues ______________________________

____

4. metacognition ______________________________

____

5. inference ______________________________

____

Using a Thesaurus

The first thesaurus was compiled by Dr. Peter Mark Roget, an English physician, who collected lists of synonyms as a hobby. The book, called *Roget's Thesaurus,* focuses mainly on suggested synonyms for commonly used words, but it also includes antonyms. Since its publication in 1852, the book has been updated many times, and Roget's thesaurus has been copied by others.

A thesaurus is a writer's tool. It is not a dictionary, and it does not include all words. Use a thesaurus to add variety to your writing and avoid repetitious wording. For example, if you find yourself repeating the word *guilt* in a research paper in sociology, consult a thesaurus for substitutes. *Roget's 21st Century Thesaurus* suggests synonyms such as *delinquency, fault, misconduct, shame,* or *transgression.*

guilt [*n*] ***blame; bad conscience over responsibility*** **answerability, blameworthiness, contrition, crime, criminality, culpability, delinquency, dereliction, disgrace, dishonor, error, failing, fault, indiscretion, infamy, iniquity, lapse, liability, malefaction, malfeasance, malpractice, misbehavior, misconduct, misstep, offense, onus, peccability, penitence, regret, remorse, responsibility, self-condemnation, self-reproach, shame, sin, sinfulness, slip, solecism, stigma, transgression, wickedness, wrong;** SEE CONCEPTS ***101,532,***

At the end of the entry, inclusion of the words SEE CONCEPTS (printed in capitals and followed by numbers) indicates that you can find additional synonyms under these numbers at the end of the book.

Most word-processing programs have an electronic thesaurus. Usually it is located near the spell check or in the "tools" pull-down menu. Use your cursor to highlight (select) the word for which you want alternatives, and then click on the thesaurus. Consider the context of your sentence in choosing from the array of words that appear. A thesaurus in book form will offer more choices than the one offered by your word-processing program.

Exercise 2.9 Thesaurus

Use the entries on page 71 for *edge* in *Roget's 21st Century Thesaurus* to select an alternative word that fits the meaning of *edge* in the sentences.

1. On the tenth hole the least experienced golfer took the *edge* with a long putt. ________
2. The new software company is on the *edge* of bankruptcy. ________
3. Disruptive children can reach the *edge* of a parent's patience. ________
4. The decorator wanted to *edge* the blue fabric with a yellow one. ________
5. The baseball player's face was shaded by the *edge* of his hat. ________

edge [*n1*] *border, outline*
bend, berm, bound, boundary, brim, brink, butt, circumference, contour, corner, crook, crust, curb, end, extremity, frame, fringe, frontier, hem, hook, ledge, limb, limit, line, lip, margin, molding, mouth, outskirt, peak, perimeter, periphery, point, portal, rim, ring, shore, side, skirt, split, strand, term, threshold, tip, trimming, turn, verge; SEE CONCEPTS ***484,513***
edge [*n2*] *advantage*
allowance, ascendancy, bulge, dominance, draw, handicap, head start, lead, odds, start, superiority, upper hand*, vantage; SEE CONCEPT ***712***
edge [*v1*] *border, trim*
bind, bound, decorate, fringe, hem, margin, outline, rim, shape, skirt, surround, verge; SEE CONCEPTS ***751,758***
edge [*v2*] *defeat narrowly*
creep, ease, inch, infiltrate, nose out*, sidle, slip by, slip past, squeeze by*, squeeze past*, steal, worm*; SEE CONCEPT ***95***
edge [*v3*] *sharpen*
file, grind, hone, polish, sharpen, strop, whet; SEE CONCEPTS ***137,250***

Using Analogies

Analogies are comparisons that measure not only your word knowledge, but your ability to see relationships. They can be difficult, frustrating, and challenging. Use logical thinking and problem-solving skills first to pinpoint the initial relationship and then to establish a similar relationship with two other words.

Exercise 2.10 Analogies

Study the analogies that follow to establish the relationship of the first two words. Record that relationship, using the categories outlined on page 72. Then choose the word that duplicates that relationship to finish the analogy.

1. *Trash* is to *refuse* as *soil* is to ________.

   Relationship __________
   a. earthworms
   b. dirt
   c. minerals
   d. growing

2. *Cappuccino* is to *coffee* as *jazz* is to ________

   Relationship __________
   a. singer
   b. opera
   c. rock
   d. music

Reader's Tip

Categories of Analogy Relationships

* **Synonyms:** Similar in meaning

  Find is to *locate* as *hope* is to *wish.*

* **Antonyms:** Opposite in meaning

  Accept is to *reject* as *rude* is to *polite.*

* **Function, use, or purpose:** Identifies what something does; watch for the object (noun) and then the action (verb)

  Pool is to *swim* as *blanket* is to *warm.*

* **Classification:** Identifies the larger group association

  Sandal is to *shoe* as *sourdough* is to *bread.*

* **Characteristics and descriptions:** Shows qualities or traits

  Nocturnal is to *raccoon* as *humid* is to *rainforest.*

* **Degree:** Shows variations of intensity

  Fear is to *terror* as *dislike* is to *hate.*

* **Part to whole:** Shows the larger group

  Page is to *book* as *caboose* is to *train.*

* **Cause and effect:** Shows the reason (cause) and result (effect)

  Study is to *graduation* as *caffeine* is to *insomnia.*

3. *Fork* is to *eat* as *television* is to ________

   Relationship ____________
   a. video
   b. actor
   c. entertain
   d. produce

4. *Smart* is to *genius* as *rigid* is to ________

   Relationship ____________
   a. steel
   b. comedy
   c. angle
   d. focus

5. *Recklessness* is to *accident* as *laziness* is to ________

   Relationship ______________

   a. work
   b. money
   c. failure
   d. ability

Easily Confused Words

Pairs or groups of words may cause confusion because they sound exactly alike or almost alike, but are spelled and used differently. *Stationary* and *stationery* are examples of such words. You ride a stationary bike to work out and you write a business letter on your office stationery. For a memory link, associate the *e* in *letter* with the *e* in *stationery*. Students frequently confuse *your* and *you're: your* shows possession, and *you're* is a contraction for *you are.* To differentiate confusing words, create associations and memorize them.

Exercise 2.11 **Confusing Words**

Study the following easily confused words, and then circle the one that is correct in each sentence.

accept: receive
except: all but

1. When children reach adolescence, they begin to (**accept, except**) the values of their peers.

to: a preposition
too: additionally
two: the number

2. Entrapment is used as an excuse from criminal liability in (**to, too, two**) many undercover drug cases.

thorough: careful
threw: tossed
through: by means of

3. A (**thorough, threw, through**) investigation can help reveal whether the murder was premeditated.

consul: foreign representative

council: elected officials

counsel: a lawyer apponited to give advice on legal matters; also a verb: give advice

4. The court will appoint (**consul, council, counsel**) for an armed robbery defendant who has no money to pay for a lawyer.

site: place

cite: quote

sight: vision

5. Attorneys need to (**site, cite, sight**) references from previous trials to support their interpretation of the law.

Recognizing Acronyms

An *acronym* is an abbreviation that is pronounced as a word. Acronyms can thus be considered invented words that are often thoughtfully contrived to simplify a lengthy name and gain quick recognition for an organization or agency. For example, *UNICEF* is the abbreviation for the United Nations International Children's Emergency Fund. The arrangement of consonants and vowels formed by the first letter of each word in the title creates an invented term that we can easily pronounce and quickly recognize. When names are created for new organizations, clever organizers thoughtfully consider the choice and sequence of words in order to engineer a catchy acronym. In some cases, acronyms have become so ingrained in our language that the abbreviations have become accepted as words with lowercase letters. An example of this is the word *radar,* which is a combination of the initial letters of the phrase *radio detecting and ranging.*

Exercise 2.12

Acronyms

The following letters are abbreviations. Write an *A* beside those that are pronounced as words and thus are considered acronyms.

________ 1. CNN
________ 2. NAFTA
________ 3. MP3
________ 4. NASA
________ 5. IRS
________ 6. CD
________ 7. UNESCO
________ 8. OSHA
________ 9. MCI
________ 10. NASDAQ

Recognizing Transitional Words

Transitional words are connecting words that signal the direction of the writer's thought. They are single words or short phrases that lead the reader to anticipate a continuation or a change in thought. For example, the phrase *in addition* signals a continuation, whereas *but* or *however* signals a change.

Reader's Tip

Signals for Transition

* **For addition:** in addition furthermore moreover
* **For examples:** for example for instance to illustrate such as
* **For time:** first secondly finally last afterward
* **For comparison:** similarly likewise in the same manner
* **For contrast:** however but nevertheless whereas on the contrary conversely in contrast
* **For cause and effect:** thus consequently therefore as a result

Exercise 2.13

Transitions

Read to understand the direction of the author's thought and then choose a signal word from the boxed lists to complete the following sentences.

furthermore	similarly	consequently	however	for example

1. The Internet is a valuable research tool; ____________, it can be frustrating.
2. Ragweed causes allergies; ____________, mildew and dust mites also stimulate allergic reactions.
3. The chemist walked to class yesterday in the rain and ____________ has a cold today.

4. Papers are due at the beginning of the period, and __________, they should be put on my desk when you first enter the classroom.
5. Runners train for many different events. __________, the Boston Marathon attracts thousands of athletes.

Summary Points

- **What's the best way to remember new words?**

  To remember new words, associate words in phrases, in families, and in images. Use concept cards to record a new word's definition with a phrase and an image that suggest the meaning.

- **What are context clues?**

  The context clues in a sentence or paragraph can help unlock the meaning of unknown words. These can be definitions, details, examples, and comparisons or contrasts.

- **Why learn prefixes, roots, and suffixes?**

  A knowledge of prefixes, roots, and suffixes can reveal smaller and more familiar word parts in unknown words.

- **What will you find in a dictionary?**

  A collegiate dictionary contains definitions, word origins, pronunciations, and spellings.

- **What is a glossary?**

  A glossary defines words that are unique to a subject-matter area.

- **What is a thesaurus?**

  A thesaurus is a reference book that contains synonyms for frequently used words to add variety to writing.

- **What are analogies?**

  Analogies are comparisons that fall into different categories of relationships.

- **What are acronyms?**

  Acronyms are abbreviations that are pronounced as words.

- **How are transitional words used?**

  Transitional words are used to connect words that signal the writer's thought.

Search the Net

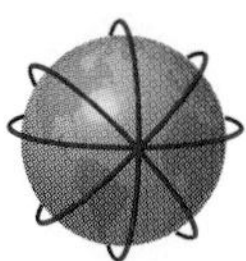

- Search for information on solving analogies. Select three sample analogies from your findings and explain the relationships between the words. Start your own search or begin with the following:

  Puzz.com

  http://www.puzz.com/analogies.html

- Locate information on etymology, the study of the origin of words. List ten words, and give a brief description of the origin of each word. Start your own search, or begin with the following:

  Wordorigins.org

  http://www.wordorigins.org/home.htm

READER'S JOURNAL

Name ______________________ Date __________

CHAPTER 2

Answer the following questions to reflect on your own learning and progress. Use the perforations to tear the assignment out for your instructor.

1. Name and evaluate the quality of the dictionary that you use.

2. What has been your experience with using a dictionary on the computer?

3. How does a thesaurus differ from a dictionary?

4. In the past, which techniques have you used effectively to remember new words? Which ones did not work?

5. Which techniques are you using to remember the new words that you encounter in this book?

6. Name a difficult word that you enjoy using that many of your friends might not understand.

7. Explain how you would teach someone the meaning of the word you named above.

8. Why are the index cards suggested for remembering words called *concept cards?*

3

Reading and Study Strategies

- What is a study strategy?
- What are the three stages of reading?
- What is previewing?
- Why should you activate your schema?
- What is metacognition?
- Why recall or self-test what you have read?

The Lesson #2 *(detail) by Sharon Wilson. Pastel, 19 × 25". Private Collection. © 1991 Sharon Wilson Gallery.*

What Is a Study System?

In 1946, after years of working with college students at Ohio State University, Francis P. Robinson developed a textbook-study system designed to help students efficiently read and learn from textbooks and effectively recall relevant information for subsequent exams. The system was called SQ3R, with the letters standing for the following five steps: survey, question, read, recite, and review.

Numerous variations have been developed since SQ3R was introduced. One researcher, Norman Stahl, analyzed sixty-five textbook study systems and concluded that there are more similarities than differences among the systems.[1] The commonalities in the systems include a previewing stage, a reading stage, and a final self-testing stage. In the *previewing* stage students ask questions, activate past knowledge, and establish a purpose for reading. During the *reading* stage, students answer questions and continually integrate old and new knowledge. The *self-testing* stage of reading involves review to improve recall,

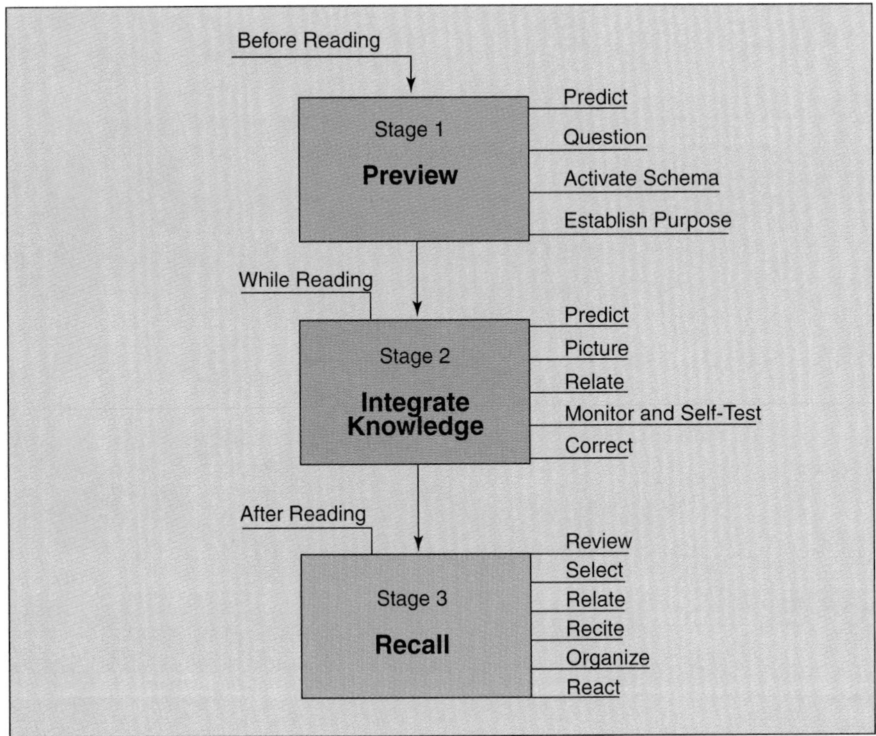

[1]N. A. Stahl, "Historical Analysis of Textbook Study Systems" (Ph.D. diss., University of Pittsburgh, 1983).

evaluation to accept or reject ideas, and integration to blend new information with existing knowledge networks. Strategies used in these stages are depicted in the chart shown on page 80 and are discussed in this chapter.

Why Use a Study System?

When a professor ends a class by saying "Read the assigned pages for your next class meeting," everyone knows that the real message is, "*Actively read, study, and remember* the assigned pages." Reading a textbook means "reading to learn." Rather than being a single task, it is a project that needs an organized approach. Unlike an adventure novel, each chapter—even each page—of a textbook contains new and complex ideas. To be a successful academic reader, you should systematically engage in predicting, summarizing, self-testing, and establishing relationships to prior knowledge. In other words, you need a study system to help you succeed.

Stage 1: Previewing

Previewing is a method of personally connecting with the material before you start to read. When you preview, you look over the material, predict what the material is probably about, ask yourself what you already know about the topic, decide what you will probably know after you read, and make a plan for reading. Does this process sound similar to the concentration technique of sparking an interest before reading? The difference is that with previewing, your questions are related more directly to your purpose for reading. Even though it may take a few extra minutes in the beginning, your increased involvement will mean increased comprehension.

To preview, look over the material, think, and ask questions. The focus is, "What do I already know, what do I need to know, and how do I go about finding it out?"

Signposts for Answering Preview Questions

An often repeated rule for public speaking says, "Tell them what you are going to tell them, tell them, and then tell them what you told them." This same organizational pattern frequently applies to textbook material. Typically, a chapter begins with a brief overview of the topic. The ideas are then developed in paragraphs or sections. Concluding statements at the end summarize the important points the author wants the reader to remember. Although this pattern does not apply in every case, it can serve as a guide in determining what to read when previewing textbook material.

Previewing can be a hit-or-miss activity since there may or may not be an introductory or concluding statement. Because of differences in writing styles, no one set of rules will work for all materials. Consider the following signposts when previewing.

Asking Questions Before Reading

* **What is the topic of the material?** What does the title suggest? What do the subheadings, italics, and summaries suggest?
* **What do I already know?** What do I already know about this topic or a related topic? Is this new topic a small part of a larger idea or issue that I have thought about before?
* **What is my purpose for reading?** What will I need to know when I finish?
* **How is the material organized?** What is the general outline or framework of the material? Is the author listing reasons, explaining a process, or comparing a trend?
* **What will be my plan of attack?** What parts of the textbook seem most important? Do I need to read everything with equal care? Can I skim some parts? Can I skip some sections completely?

Title. Titles are designed to attract attention and reflect the contents of the material. The title of an article, a chapter, or a book is the first and most obvious clue to its content. Think about the title and turn it into a question. If the article is entitled "Acupuncture," a major concern in your reading would probably be to find out "What is acupuncture?" Learn the "five-*W* technique" that journalists often use in the first paragraphs of their articles when they ask *who, what, when, where,* and *why*.

Introductory Material. To get an overview of an entire book, refer to the table of contents and preface. Sophisticated students use the table of contents as a study guide, turning the chapter headings into possible exam items. Many textbooks open each chapter with an outline and preview questions. Italicized inserts, decorative symbols, and color type are also used to overview and highlight contents. In textbook chapters and articles, the first paragraph frequently introduces the topic to be covered and gives the reader a sense of perspective.

Subheadings. Subheadings are titles for sections within chapters. The subheadings, usually appearing in **boldface print** or *italics*, outline the main points of the author's message and thus give the reader an overview of the organization and the content. Turn these subheadings into questions that need to be answered as you read.

Italics, Boldface Print, and Numbers. Italics and boldface print are used to highlight words that merit special attention and emphasis. These are usually new words or key words that students should be prepared to define and remember. For example, a discussion of sterilization in a biology text might emphasize the words *vasectomy* and *tubal ligation* in italics or boldface print. Numbers can also be used to signal a list of important details. In another book on the same subject, the two forms of sterilization might be emphasized with enumeration: (1) vasectomy and (2) tubal ligation.

Concluding Summary. Many textbooks include a summary at the end of each chapter to highlight the important points within the material. The summary can serve not only as a review to follow reading but also as an introduction for overviewing the chapter.

Exercise 3.1

Previewing This Textbook for the Big Picture

To get an overview of the scope of this textbook and its sequence of topics, look over the table of contents and preface. Think about how the different chapter topics fit into the goals of college reading. Glance at the chapters to get a sense of the overall organization, and then answer the following questions.

1. Who is the author? Is the author an instructor? ______________________

   ____

2. What seems to be the purpose of the numbered reading selections?

   ____

3. List six different college disciplines that are represented in the numbered reading selections. ______________________

   ____

4. What seems to be the purpose of the "Contemporary Focus" selections?

   ____

5. Does the text have any study aids such as an index, a glossary, or summaries?

   ____

6. Which reading selection do you think will be the most interesting?

   ____

Exercise 3.2

Previewing This Chapter

To get an overview of this chapter, look first at the table of contents at the beginning of the book and then read the list of questions at the beginning of the chapter. Read the chapter summary points. Use your previewing to answer the following questions.

1. What is a study system? ______________________________

2. What is a schema? ______________________________

3. What is metacognition? ______________________________

4. What is the purpose of a recall diagram? ______________________________

5. Which reading selection do you think will be most interesting? ______________________________

6. What are the five thinking strategies used by good readers? ______________________________

Use your answers to these questions to help establish a purpose for reading the chapter. Why is this chapter important, and what do you hope to gain from reading it?

Preview to Activate Schemata

Despite what you may sometimes think, you are not an empty bucket into which the professor is pouring information. You are a learner who already knows a lot, and you are actively selecting, connecting, and eliminating information.

What do you bring to the printed page? As a reader, you have a responsibility to think and interact before, during, and after reading. Your previewing of material helps you predict the topic. Then, as a further part of the prereading stage, you need to activate your schema for what you perceive the topic to be.

A **schema** (plural, *schemata*) is like a computer chip in your brain that holds all you know on a subject. Each time you learn something new, you pull out the computer chip on that subject, add the new information, and return the chip to storage. The depth of the schema or the amount of information on the chip varies according to previous experience. For example, a scientist would have a more detailed computer chip for DNA than would a freshman biology student.

All college students have a schema for Shakespeare. Suppose your previewing of a ten-page essay led you to predict that the discussion focused on the strength of the main characters in five of Shakespeare's plays. Next you would ask, "What existing knowledge do I have on the subject?" or "What is on my computer chip labeled 'Shakespeare'?" Most students would immediately think of *Macbeth* and *Hamlet*, both the characters and the plays. Others who have studied Shakespeare more might recall *King Lear*, the comedies, and a model of the Globe Theatre. The richness of your background determines the amount you can activate. In general, the more you are able to activate, the more meaningful your reading will be.

Stage 2: Integrating Knowledge While Reading

Is it easier to understand a passage if you already know something about the topic? You already know that the answer is *yes.* Read the following paragraphs for a demonstration.

Passage A: Water Balance

Water may be the single most important nutrient for athletic performance. The body may be able to survive weeks or even months without certain vitamins and minerals, but without water, performance may be compromised in as little as 30 minutes. Our bodies are approximately 60% water, and our muscles are approximately 70%. For an athlete exercising vigorously, water's main function is to remove the heat (calories) generated by exercise. The body's metabolic rate may increase 20 to 25 times during intense exercise. The body gets rid of this heat by picking it up in the circulation and transporting it to the skin, where it is lost through evaporation.

S. Fike et al., "Fluid and Electrolyte Requirements of Exercise," *Sports Nutrition,* ed. by Dan Benardot

Passage B: Echinoderms

Echinoderms have protective skeletal elements embedded in their body walls. They also have an unusual feature called a water vascular system, which is used as a kind of hydraulic pump to extend the soft, pouchlike *tube feet,* with their terminal suckers. They are sluggish creatures with poorly developed nervous systems. However, they are tenacious foragers. Some species feed on shellfish, such as oysters. They wrap around their prey and pull relentlessly until the shells open just a bit. Then they evert their stomachs, squeezing them between the shells, and digest the flesh of the oysters on the spot.

Robert Wallace, *Biology: The Science of Life*

Even if you are a biology major, the first passage is probably easier to read than the second. People tend to be interested in the health of the human body. Thus, most people have greater prior knowledge of the water balance needs of the human body than those of echinoderms. This prior knowledge makes reading more interesting, easier to visualize, and therefore easier to understand. Linking the old with the new provides a schema on which to hang the new ideas.

Before starting to read and while reading, good readers ask, "What do I already know about this topic?" and "How does this new information relate to my previous knowledge?" Although textbook topics may at times seem totally unfamiliar, seldom are all of the ideas completely new. Usually there is a link, an old bit of knowledge that you can associate with the new ideas. For example, although you may not be familiar with the echinoderms described in Passage B, you probably know what an oyster looks like and can visualize the tenacity needed to open its shell.

On the other hand, your view of Passage A or B might have been different if you had known before reading that starfish are echinoderms. You might have found the description of mealtime downright exciting. Reread the second passage with this knowledge and visualize the gruesome drama.

Later in this chapter you will read another passage on echinoderms. Be ready to pull out your already developed "echinoderm knowledge network."

Expanding Knowledge

Most experts agree that the single best predictor of your reading comprehension is what you already know. In other words, the rich get richer. The good news about this conclusion is that once you have struggled and learned about a subject, the next time you encounter the subject, learning about it will be easier. Does this help to explain why some experts say that the freshman year is the hardest? Frequently, students who barely make C's in introductory courses end up making A's and B's during their junior and senior years. Their intellectual energies during their junior and senior years can go into assimilating and arranging new information into previously established frameworks rather than striving to build schemata. Be comforted to know that during that initial struggle with new subjects, you are building schemata that you will later reuse. Tell yourself, "The smart get smarter, and I'm getting smart!"

Integrating Ideas: How Do Good Readers Think?

Understanding and remembering complex material requires as much thinking as reading. Both consciously and subconsciously, the good reader is predicting, visualizing, and drawing comparisons in order to assimilate new knowledge. The suggestions in the box shown on page 87, which were devised by a reading researcher, represents the kind of thinking strategies good readers use.[2]

The first three thinking strategies used by good readers are perhaps the easiest to understand and the quickest to develop. Young readers quickly learn to predict actions and outcomes as the excitement of an adventure escalates. Vivid descriptions and engaging illustrations nurture the imagination to create exciting mental images triggering past experiences. When the ideas get more complicated, however, the last two thinking strategies become essential elements in the pursuit of meaning. College textbooks are tough and require constant use of the monitoring strategy and frequent use of the correction strategy.

These last two strategies involve a higher level of thinking than just picturing an oyster. They reflect a deeper understanding of the process of getting meaning and require a reader who both knows and controls. This ability to know and control is called *metacognition*.

[2]B. Davey, "Think Aloud—Modeling for Cognitive Processes of Reading Comprehension," *Journal of Reading* 27 (October 1983): 44–47.

Using Thinking Strategies While Reading

* **Make predictions.** (Develop hypotheses.)

  "From the title, I predict that this section will give another example of a critical time for rats to learn a behavior."

  "In this next part, I think we'll find out why the ancient Greeks used mnemonic devices."

  "I think this is a description of an acupuncture treatment."

* **Describe the picture you're forming in your head from the information.** (Develop images during reading.)

  "I have a picture of this scene in my mind. My pet is lying on the table with acupuncture needles sticking out of its fur."

* **Share an analogy.** (Link prior knowledge with new information in text.) We call this the *"like-a" step.*

  "This is like my remembering, 'In 1492 Columbus sailed the ocean blue.'"

* **Verbalize a confusing point.** (Monitor your ongoing comprehension.)

  "This is confusing."

  "This just doesn't make sense. How can redwoods and cypress trees both be part of the same family?"

  "This is different from what I had expected."

* **Correct gaps in comprehension.** (Use fix-up strategies.)

  "I'd better reread."

  "Maybe I'll read ahead to see if it gets clearer."

  "I'd better change my picture of the story."

  "This is a new word to me—I'd better check the context to figure it out."

Metacognition

When you look at the following words, what is your reaction?

feeet   thankz   supplyyied

Your reaction is probably, "The words don't look right. They are misspelled." The reason for your realizing the errors so quickly is that you have a global understanding of the manner in which letters can and cannot occur in the English language. You instantly recognize the errors, and immediately scan your knowledge of words and the rules of ordering letters. Through your efficient recognition and correction, you have used information that goes beyond knowing about each of the three individual words. You have demonstrated a metacognitive awareness and understanding of spelling in the English language.[3]

The term **metacognition** is a coined word. *Cognition* refers to knowledge or skills that you possess. The Greek prefix *meta-* suggests an abstract level of understanding as if viewed from the outside. Thus, metacognition not only means having the knowledge but also refers to your own awareness and understanding of the thinking processes involved and your ability to regulate and direct these processes. If you know how to read, you are operating on a cognitive level. To operate on a metacognitive level, you must know the processes involved in reading and be able to regulate them.

Let's take a real-life example. If you are reading a chemistry assignment and failing to understand it, you must first recognize that you are not comprehending. Next you must identify what and why you don't understand. Remember, you will be able to do this because you understand the skills involved in the reading process. Finally, you try to figure out how to eliminate your confusion. You attempt a correction strategy. If it does not work, you try another and remain confident that you will succeed. The point is to understand how to get meaning, to know when you don't have it, and to know what to do about getting it. One researcher calls this "knowing about knowing."[4]

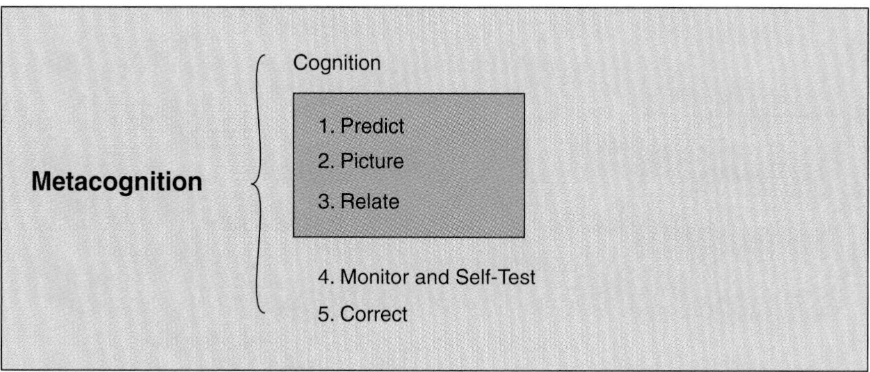

The Strategies of Metacognition

Comparing reading to a similar activity, do you know when you are really studying? Do you know the difference between really studying and simply going through the motions of studying? Sometimes you can study intensely for an hour and accomplish a phenomenal amount. At other times you can put in twice the time with books and notes but learn practically nothing. Do you know the difference and do you know what to do about it? Some students do not.

---

[3]The author is grateful to Professor Jane Thielemann, University of Houston (Downtown), for inspiring this paragraph.

[4]A. L. Brown, "The Development of Memory: Knowing, Knowing About Knowing, and Knowing How to Know," in H. W. Reese, ed., *Advances in Child Development and Behavior*, vol. 10 (New York: Academic Press, 1975), pp. 104–46.

Poor readers see their failure to comprehend as a lack of ability and feel that nothing can be done about it. Successful readers see failure only as a need to reanalyze the task. They know they will eventually correct their problems and succeed.

Reader's Tip

Developing a Metacognitive Sense for Reading

With instruction and practice, you can improve your reading performance.

* **Know about reading.** Are you aware of the many strategies you use to comprehend? These include knowledge about words, main ideas, supporting details, and implied ideas. Also, think about the organization of the text and where meaning can be found.
* **Know how to monitor.** Monitor as an ongoing process throughout your reading. Use predicting and questioning to corroborate or discard ideas. Continually clarify and self-test to reinforce learning and pinpoint gaps in comprehension.
* **Know how to correct confusion.** Reread to reprocess a complex idea. Unravel a confusing writing style on a sentence level. Read ahead for ideas that unfold slowly. Consult a dictionary or other sources to fill in background knowledge you lack.

EXAMPLE Use both your cognitive and metacognitive knowledge to answer the following test item. Interact with the material, monitor, and predict the ending phrase before reading the options. The highlighted handwriting models the thinking of an active reader.

Picture the comparison → "oil spill"; *pollutes and kills* → oil disaster

What is euphemistically called an "oil spill" can very well become an oil disaster for marine life. This is particularly true when refined or semirefined products are being transported. *wants to make more money* As the tankers get bigger, so do the accidents, yet we continue to *key word*

a. fight for clean water

b. search for more oil

c. use profits for cleanup

d. build larger vessels *shows a parallel idea*

Robert Wallace, Biology: The Science of Life

The passage below illustrates the use of these thinking strategies with longer textbook material. Modeled thoughts of the reader are highlighted in handwriting. Keep in mind that each reader reacts differently to material, depending on background and individual differences. This example merely represents one reader's attempt to integrate knowledge.

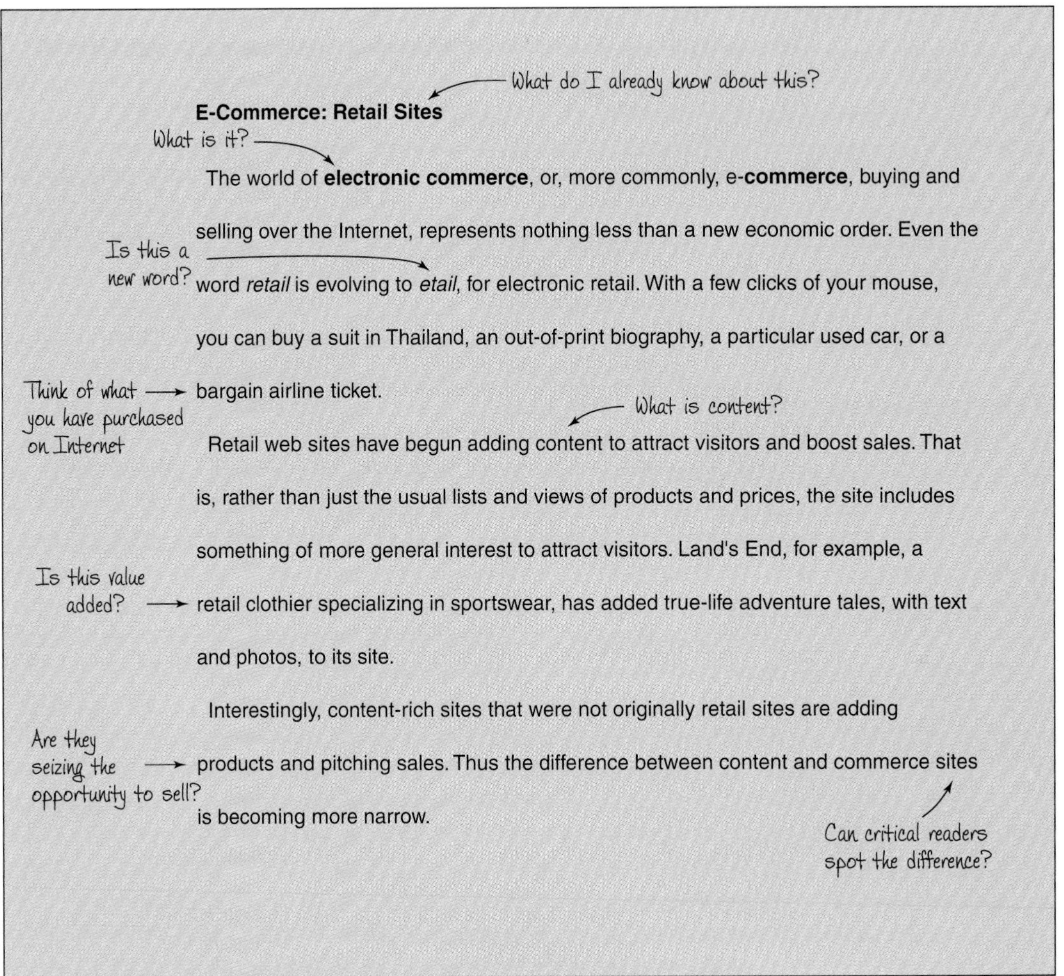

What do I already know about this?
E-Commerce: Retail Sites
What is it?
The world of **electronic commerce**, or, more commonly, e-**commerce**, buying and selling over the Internet, represents nothing less than a new economic order. Even the word *retail* is evolving to *etail*, for electronic retail. With a few clicks of your mouse, you can buy a suit in Thailand, an out-of-print biography, a particular used car, or a bargain airline ticket.
Is this a new word?
Think of what you have purchased on Internet
What is content?
Retail web sites have begun adding content to attract visitors and boost sales. That is, rather than just the usual lists and views of products and prices, the site includes something of more general interest to attract visitors. Land's End, for example, a retail clothier specializing in sportswear, has added true-life adventure tales, with text and photos, to its site.
Is this value added?
Interestingly, content-rich sites that were not originally retail sites are adding products and pitching sales. Thus the difference between content and commerce sites is becoming more narrow.
Are they seizing the opportunity to sell?
Can critical readers spot the difference?

H. L. Capron, Computers

EXPLANATION The examples may be confusing to read because many of the thoughts that are highlighted normally occur on the subconscious level rather than the conscious level. Stopping to consciously analyze these reactions seems artificial and disruptive. It is important, however, to be aware that you are incorporating these thinking strategies into your reading. The following exercise is designed to heighten your awareness of this interaction.

Exercise 3.3

Integrating Knowledge While Reading

For the following passage, demonstrate with written notes the way you use the five thinking strategies as you read. The passage is double-spaced so that you can insert your thoughts and reactions between the lines. Make a conscious effort to experience all of the following strategies as you read:

1. Predict (develop hypotheses).
2. Picture (develop images during reading).
3. Relate (link prior knowledge with new ideas).
4. Clarify points (monitor your ongoing comprehension).
5. Correct gaps in comprehension (use correction strategies).

Sea Stars

Let's take a look at one class of echinoderms—the sea stars. Sea stars (starfish) are well known for their voracious appetite when it comes to gourmet foods, such as oysters and clams. Obviously, they are the sworn enemy of oystermen. But these same oystermen may have inadvertently helped the spread of the sea stars. At one time, when they caught a starfish, they chopped it apart and vengefully kicked the pieces overboard. But they were unfamiliar with the regenerative powers of the starfish. The central disk merely grows new arms, and a single arm can form a new animal.

Stars are slow-moving predators, so their prey, obviously, are even slower-moving or immobile. Their ability to open an oyster shell is a testimony to their persistence. When a sea star finds an oyster or clam, the prey clamps its shell together tightly, a tactic that discourages most would-be predators, but not the starfish. It bends its body over the oyster and attaches its tube feet to the shell, and then begins to pull. Tiring is no problem since it uses tube feet in relays. Finally, the oyster can no longer hold itself shut, and it opens gradually—only a tiny bit, but it is enough. The star then protrudes its stomach out through its mouth. The soft stomach slips into the slightly opened shell, surrounds the oyster, and digests it in its own shell.

Robert Wallace, *Biology: The Science of Life*

At first glance, you probably recognized *echinoderm* as an old friend and activated your newly acquired schema from a previous page. The description of the starfish lends itself to a vivid visualization. Were some of your predictions corroborated as you read the passage? Did you find yourself monitoring to reconcile new facts with old ideas? Did you need to use a correction strategy? Has your computer chip been expanded?

Stage 3: Recalling for Self-Testing

Recall does not have to be a formal process. It involves briefly telling yourself what you have learned, remembering, relating it to what you already know, and forming an opinion and reaction. Actually, all of this also occurs while reading, but an additional stop at the conclusion of an assignment helps you fill in any gaps and assimilate the many parts into an organized and meaningful whole. Improve your comprehension by taking those few extra minutes to digest what you have read; then, have a short conversation with yourself or a friend about the new material.

Recall also involves arranging new information into old schemata and creating new schemata. Not only are you recalling what you just read, but you are also recalling old knowledge and seeking to make connections. While "sorting through" ideas, you are accepting and rejecting information based on your opinions, making decisions about storage, rearranging old networks, and creating new ones. You are updating your computer chip. Good readers take the time to make these connections.

Recall by Writing

Good readers also benefit from taking the time to write about what they have read. Writing is a powerful learning tool that helps students translate and discover their own thinking. Experts define writing as a "mode of learning," which means that writing is a process that helps students blend, reconcile, and gain personal ownership of new knowledge. When you write about a subject, you not only discover how much you know and don't know, but you begin to make meaningful personal connections.

Writing requires an active commitment that goes beyond oral recall and class discussion. When you write, you have to actively wrestle with ideas. A humorous adage about the power of writing says, "How do I know what I think until I see what I say?" Writing can be hard work, but it helps you clarify and crystallize what you have learned. Answering multiple-choice questions after reading requires one type of mental processing, but writing about the reading requires another type of processing. Writing is another valuable resource in the learning process. Use its power to take your recall to a higher level.

How to Recall

To recall, simply take a few minutes after reading to recap what you have learned. This can be done in your head or on paper. To visualize the main points graphically, make a recall diagram. On a straight line across the top, briefly state the topic, or what the selection seems to be mainly about. Indented underneath the topic, state the supporting details that seem to be most significant. Next, make a connection. What do you already know that seems to relate to this information? Your answer will be unique because you are connecting the material to your own knowledge networks. Draw a dotted line, your thought line, and recall a related idea, issue, or concern. Finally, react to the material. Formulate an opinion about the author and the message.

Reader's Tip

Recalling After Reading

* **Pinpoint the topic.** Sift through the generalities and the nonessentials to get focused on the subject. Use the title and the subheading to help you recognize and narrow down the topic.
* **Select the most important points.** Poor readers want to remember everything, thinking facts have equal importance. Good readers pull out the important issues and identify significant supporting information.
* **Relate the information.** Facts are difficult to learn in isolation. Many first-year college students have difficulty with history courses because they have limited schemata. Events appear to be isolated happenings rather than results of previous occurrences. Network your new knowledge to enhance memory.
* **React.** Evaluate and form opinions about the material and the author. Decide what you wish to accept and what you will reject. Blend old and new knowledge, and write about what you have read.

EXAMPLE

Autopsies

Today, many dead people receive some form of autopsy or postmortem examination. At least two main reasons for this are (1) the desire of the family to know the exact cause of death, and (2) the fact that increased medical knowledge results. Because of the important moral and legal restrictions on human experimentation, much of our knowledge of pathology comes from autopsies. This fact prompts many people to donate their bodies to medical schools and/or donate certain organs for possible transplantation.

John Cunningham, *Human Biology*, 2nd ed.

EXPLANATION Remember that the recall diagram is a temporary and artificial format. The diagram below graphically demonstrates a process that you will learn to do in your head. Practice using the diagram will help you learn to organize and visualize your reading.

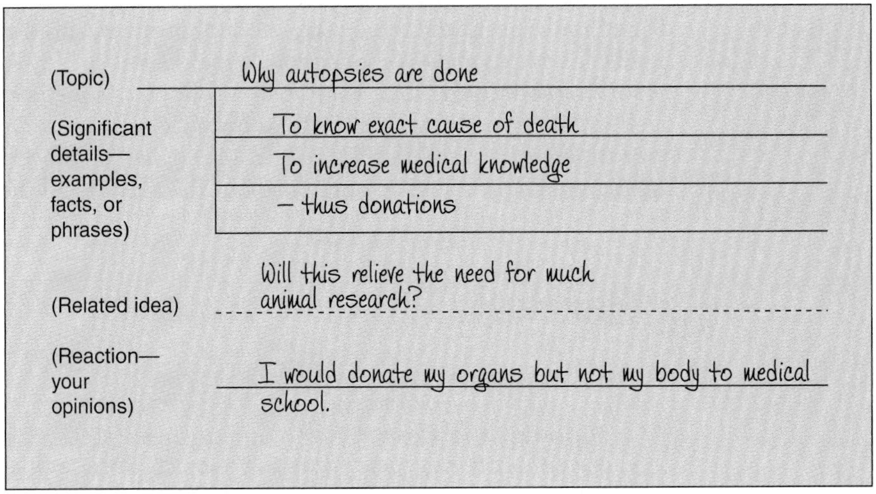

(Topic)	Why autopsies are done
(Significant details—examples, facts, or phrases)	To know exact cause of death To increase medical knowledge – thus donations
(Related idea)	Will this relieve the need for much animal research?
(Reaction—your opinions)	I would donate my organs but not my body to medical school.

Exercise 3.4 Recall Diagrams

After reading each of the following passages, stop to recall what the passage contained. Use the recall diagrams to record what the passage seems to be mainly about, list significant supporting details, identify a related idea, issue, or concern to which you feel the information is connected, and react.

Passage A: The Depression and Its Victims

The depression affected the families of the jobless in many ways. It caused a dramatic drop in the birthrate, from 27.7 per thousand population in 1920 to 18.4 per thousand in the early 1930s, the lowest in American history. Sometimes it strengthened family ties. Some unemployed men spent more time with their children and helped their wives with cooking and housework. Others, however, became impatient when their children demanded attention, refused to help around the house, sulked, or took to drink. The influence of wives in families struck by unemployment tended to increase, and in this respect women suffered less psychologically from the depression. They were usually too busy trying to make ends meet to become apathetic.

Children often caused strains in families. Parental authority declined when there was less money available to supply children's needs. Some youngsters became angry when their allowance was cut or when told they could not have something they particularly wanted. Some adolescents found part-time jobs to help out. Others refused to go to school.

John Garraty and Mark Carnes, *The American Nation*, 10th ed., p. 743

(Topic) ______

(Significant details) ______

(Related idea) ------

(Reaction) ______

Passage B: Kangaroos

Kangaroos and Australia are synonymous for most people, and the abundance of the large kangaroos has gone up since the British colonized Australia. The increase in kangaroo populations has occurred in spite of intensive shooting programs, since kangaroos are considered pests by ranchers and are harvested for meat and hides. The reason seems to be that ranchers have improved the habitat for the large kangaroos in three ways. First, in making water available for their sheep and cattle, the ranchers have also made it available for the kangaroos, removing the impact of water shortage for kangaroos in arid environments. Second, ranchers have cleared timber and produced grasslands for livestock. Kangaroos feed on grass, and so their food supply has been increased as well as the water supply. Third, ranchers have removed a major predator, the dingo. The dingo is a doglike predator, the largest carnivore in Australia. Because dingoes eat sheep, ranchers have built some 9,660 kilometers of fence in southern and eastern Australia to prevent dingoes from moving into sheep country. Intensive poisoning and shooting of dingoes in sheep country, coupled with the dingo fence that prevents recolonization, has produced a classic experiment in predator control.

Charles Krebs, *The Message of Ecology*

(Topic) ______

(Significant details) ______

(Related idea) ------

(Reaction) ______

Summary Points

- **What is a study strategy?**

  All study systems include a previewing stage to ask questions and establish a purpose for reading, a reading stage to answer questions and integrate knowledge, and a final stage of self-testing and reviewing to improve recall.

- **What are the three stages of reading?**

  Reading is an active rather than a passive process. Good readers preview before reading, integrate knowledge while reading, and recall after reading.

- **What is previewing?**

  Previewing is a way to assess your needs before you start to read by deciding what the material is about, what needs to be done, and how to go about doing it.

- **Why should you activate your schema?**

  If you brainstorm to make a connection with your reading topic before you begin to read, the information will be more meaningful and memorable.

- **What is metacognition?**

  Good readers control and direct their thinking strategies as they read. They know about knowing.

- **Why recall or self-test what you have read?**

  Recalling what you have read immediately after reading forces you to select the most important points, to relate the supporting details, to integrate new information into existing networks of knowledge, and to react.

CONTEMPORARY FOCUS

In college and in business, listening can make the difference between success and failure. Recognize the pitfalls of poor listening and study the stages for success.

LISTENING SKILL SAVES TIME AND INCREASES EFFECTIVENESS

Michael Kemp

The American Salesman, Burlington, September 2000

The process of listening begins with the need to devote a certain amount of focused time to someone else. One of the best ways to learn about listening is to see examples of poor listening skills. Take a look around your office. Chances are you'll see examples of associates who fit the following categories:

- The Chatterbox, who can't bear to listen to anyone for more than a few seconds before chiming in with their own thoughts.
- The Star Trekker, who has the perpetually glazed over look of someone whose body is there but whose mind has been beamed to another place.
- The Appeaser, who shakes their head in agreement but hasn't heard a word said.
- The Wanderer, whose eyes are all over the room—to their wristwatch, their hands, out the window, to the nonringing telephone etc.—and gives every indication they would like the moment to end.
- The Nervous Nellie, who can't abide any pauses or silences and has every intention of keeping each meeting to the two minutes they've apparently allotted.
- The Baffler, who pretends to listen but then baffles everyone with the unrelated comments they make.

When you listen effectively, you learn. A clear understanding leads to better decisions. Over time you will discern the individual patterns and styles of the people with whom you meet.

Collaborative Activity

Collaborate on responses to the following questions:

- What speech have you heard lately that you enjoyed listening to?
- When do you tune people out rather than listen?
- How much time do you spend each day listening?

Skill Development—Stage 1: Preview

Preview the next selection to predict the purpose and organization as well as your learning plan.

The author will probably describe the stages of effective listening.

Agree ☐ Disagree ☐

After reading this selection, I will need to know

____

Activate Schema

Why are people so influenced by appearances?

How can you help ensure that people pay attention to you?

Learning Strategy

Recall the five stages of listening.

Word Knowledge

What do you know about these words?

perspective	self-sufficient	makeshift	bewildered	litany
gab	bombarded	notion	intonation	cryptic

Your instructor may give a true-false vocabulary review before or after reading.

Stage 2: Integrate Knowledge While Reading

Since each reader interacts with material in a unique manner, it is artificial to require certain thinking strategies to be used in certain places. In order to heighten awareness, however, several questions and comments have been inserted within this selection. Briefly respond in the margin to the inserted comments or questions. In addition, make a note in the margin of at least one other instance when you used each of the following strategies:

Predict Picture Relate Monitor Correct

The Listening Process

From Joseph DeVito, *The Elements of Public Speaking*, 7th ed.

In the popular mind, listening is often thought to be the same as hearing; it's just something that takes place when you're in hearing range of speech. Actually, listening and hearing are not the same. Listening is a lot more complex than hearing.

When do you hear but not listen?

The Five Stages of Listening

The process of listening can be described as a series of five stages or steps: receiving, understanding, remembering, evaluating, and responding. This process is represented in the figure shown here.

How does the figure show interaction?

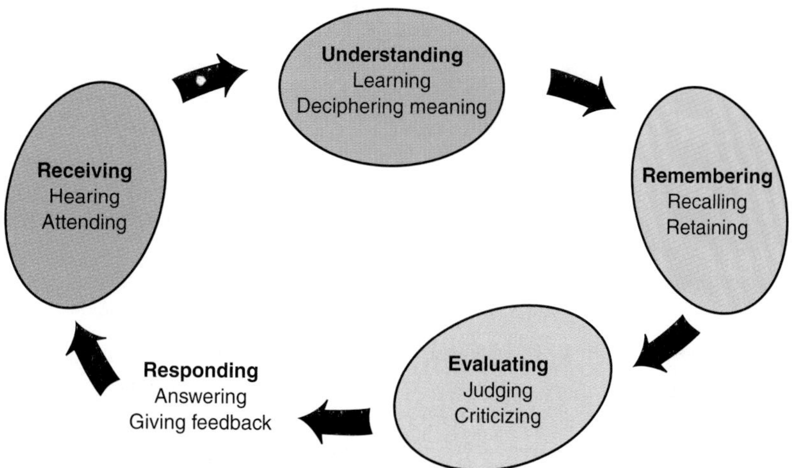

A Five-Stage Model of the Listening Process.
This five-stage model draws on a variety of previous models that listening researchers have developed (for example, Barker and Gaut 1996; Steil, Barker, and Watson 1983; Brownell 1987; and Alessandra 1986).
Source: Joseph A. DeVito, The Elements of Public Speaking, *7th ed. (New York: Longman, 2000), p. 61.*

Receiving. Unlike listening, hearing begins and ends with this first stage of receiving. Hearing is something that just happens when you get within earshot of some auditory stimuli. Listening is quite different; it begins (but does not end) with receiving the messages the speaker sends. The messages are both verbal and nonverbal; they consist of words as well as gestures, facial expressions, variations in volume and rate, and much more.

Understanding. Understanding is the stage at which you learn what the speaker means. This understanding includes both the thoughts that are expressed as well as the emotional tone that accompanies these thoughts—for example, the urgency or the joy or sorrow expressed in the message.

Remembering. What you remember is actually not what was said, but what you think (or remember) was said. Memory for speech isn't reproductive; you don't simply reproduce in your memory what the speaker said. Rather, memory is reconstructive; you actually reconstruct the messages you hear into a system that seems to make sense to you.

What factors affect your reconstructive memory?

Evaluating. At this stage your own biases and prejudices become especially influential; they influence what you single out for evaluation and what you'll just let pass, what you judge good and what you judge bad.

Responding. Responding occurs in two phases: (1) nonverbal (and occasionally verbal) responses you make while the speaker is talking and (2) responses you make after the speaker has stopped talking.

Here is a speech that provides an interesting perspective on the importance of listening, in this case to the medical profession.

What kinds of nonverbal responses do you want from listeners?

Mending the Body by Lending an Ear: The Healing Power of Listening

Address by Carol Koehler, Ph.D., Assistant Professor of Communication and Medicine. Delivered to the International Listening Association Business Conference, at the Ritz-Carlton Hotel, Kansas City, Missouri, March 19, 1998

How did this introduction gain your attention? How did it establish a speaker-audience-topic connection? How did it orient the audience?

I would like to start this morning by telling you two different stories. Each story has the same two characters and happens in the same location. Both stories occur within a twenty-four hour period.

Over the Christmas holidays my husband and I were invited to a formal black tie wedding. This was to be an elegant event so we put on our best evening clothes. Adding to that, I wore my mother's diamond jewelry and this fabulous mink coat that I inherited. Just before we left the house I telephoned my 86-year-old mother-in-law for her daily check up. When she answered, her voice sounded a little strange so my husband and I decided to stop at her apartment to make sure she was all right before we went to the wedding.

Why are the marginal notes inserted for the speech?

When we arrived she seemed slightly disoriented (she was 86 years old but wonderfully healthy, sharp-witted and self-sufficient). We called her physician to ask his advice and he said to bring her to the local Emergency Room and have her checked out. We did that. This was a Saturday night so the Emergency Room was pretty active. When we arrived, I in my mink and my husband in his tux, we looked noticeably different from the general population in the waiting room. While my husband filled out forms, the doctors took my mother-in-law into a makeshift curtained room. When I noticed that the staff had removed both her glasses and her hearing aid, I realized she would experience some anxiety, so at that point I decided to stay with her to keep her from being frightened. As I went into the room, a young doctor said, "Mam, you can't go in there." Without missing a beat I said, "Don't be ridiculous." With that I went and found a chair in the waiting room, brought it into the examination room and sat down. I remember thinking the staff looked a little bewildered but no one challenged me at any time. When my mother-in-law's hands felt a little cool, I asked for a heated blanket and one was brought immediately. So it went for the entire evening, we missed

Were the two stories effective in making the speaker's point that listening is broader than hearing and that people often listen not only with their ears but with their eyes?

In this paragraph the speaker cites the *Journal of the American Medical Association*, the *Wall Street Journal*, and the *New England Journal of Medicine*. Was this sufficient to convince you that listening is an important skill for the health care professional? Would these citations have been more effective if the speaker had given the dates? The authors of the articles?

the wedding but finally got my mother-in-law in a permanent room about 2 a.m.

The next morning, I went to the hospital about 10 o'clock in the morning, dressed in tennis shoes, a sweat suit and no makeup. As I arrived at my mother-in-law's room, an unfamiliar doctor was just entering. I introduced myself and asked him to speak up so my mother-in-law would be aware of why he was there and what he was doing. I told him that she tends to be frightened by the unexpected and without her glasses or hearing aid, she was already frightened enough. This thirty-something male doctor proceeded to examine my mother-in-law without raising his voice so that she could hear, and without acknowledging me or my request in any way. Actually he never really looked at either one of us.

In both those scenarios, I was listened to, not by ears alone, but by eyes, by gender, and age judgments, and by social status assessments. That started me thinking . . .

What was she thinking?

Did the speaker effectively make the point that listening is unwisely neglected in education? If not, what additional evidence and argument would you have liked to hear?

Why did a recent article in the *Journal of the American Medical Association* indicate high dissatisfaction in traditional doctor-patient appointments? Why is it the *Wall Street Journal* claims that perception of physician concern and not physician expertise is the deciding factor in the rising number of malpractice suits? Why did the *New England Journal of Medicine* report that the care and attention quotient is causing "alternative" medical practices to grow by leaps and bounds? Given this litany of events, what does it really mean to listen? And why, in the name of science, don't we produce better listeners in the medical profession?

Notice that the speaker involves the audience with very specific questions, calling for single word answers. In a short speech, you really don't want to invite the audience to discourse at length on the issues you're discussing. If you were a member of the audience, would you have appreciated this opportunity to contribute to the speech? Were there other opportunities to directly involve the audience that also might have been effective?

The reasons are so obvious that they are sometimes overlooked. First, listening is mistakenly equated with hearing and since most of us can hear, no academic priority is given to this subject in either college or med school (this by the way flies in the face of those who measure daily time usage). Time experts say we spend 9% of our day writing, 16% reading, 30% speaking and 45% listening—just the opposite of our academic pursuits. Second, we perceive power in speech. We put a value on those who have the gift of gab. How often have you heard the compliment, "He/she can talk to anyone"? Additionally, we equate speaking with controlling both the conversation and the situation. The third and last reason we don't listen is that we are in an era of information overload. We are bombarded with the relevant and the irrelevant and it is easy to confuse them. Often it's all just so much noise.

How can we address this depressing situation? Don Callahan, a physician and teacher, argues that primacy in health care needs to be given to the notion of care over cure. Caring as well as curing humanizes our doctor patient relationships.

Let's talk about what that might mean for health care. What comes to mind when someone is caring? (The audience responded with the words "warm," "giving," "interested," "genuine" and "sincere.") Now, what comes to mind when you think of the opposite of care? (The audience volunteered "cold," "uninterested," "egotistical," "busy," "distracted" and selfish.")

What might a caring doctor be like? If we take the word CARE and break it down, we find the qualities that are reflective of a therapeutic communicator, in other words, someone who listens not with the ears alone.

What has been your experience with caring doctors?

The speaker organized her speech around the acronym CARE. How effective do you think this organizational strategy was?

C stands for concentrate. Physicians should hear with their eyes and ears. They should avoid the verbal and visual barriers that prevent real listening. It may be as simple as eye contact (some young doctors have told me they have a difficult time with looking people in the eye, and my advice is, when you are uncomfortable, focus on the patient's mouth and as the comfort level increases, move to the eyes). In the placement of office furniture, try and keep the desk from being a barrier between you and the patient. Offer an alternative chair for consultations—one to the side of your desk and one in front of the desk. Let the patient have some control and power to decide their own comfort level.

How would you evaluate the supporting materials used in the discussion of CARE? Did the examples help you understand the points the speaker was making? Were the recommendations for more effective listening clear and meaningful?

A stands for acknowledge. Show them that you are listening by using facial expressions, giving vocal prompts and listening between the lines for intent as well as content. Listen for their vocal intonation when responding to things like prescribed medication. If you hear some hesitation in their voice, say to them, I hear you agreeing but I'm getting the sound of some reservation in your voice. Can you tell me why? And then acknowledge their response. Trust them and they will trust you.

R stands for response. Clarify issues by asking "I'm not sure what you mean." Encourage continuing statements by saying "and then what" or "tell me more." The recurrent headache may mask other problems. Provide periodic recaps to focus information. Learn to take cryptic notes and then return your attention to the patient (note taking is sometimes used as an avoidance tactic and patients sense this). Use body language by leaning toward the patient. Effective listening requires attention, patience, and the ability to resist the urge to control the conversation.

If the speaker wanted to use a presentation aid, what type would you have suggested for this speech?

E stands for exercise emotional control. This means if your "hot buttons" are pushed by people who whine, and in walks someone who does that very thing, you are likely to fake interest in the patient. With your mind elsewhere, you will never really "hear" that person. Emotional blocks are based on previous experiences. They are sometimes activated by words, by tone of voice, by style of clothes or hair, or by ethnicity. It is not possible for us to be free of those emotional reactions, but the first step in controlling them is to recognize when you are losing control. One of the most useful techniques to combat emotional responses is to take a long deep breath when confronted with the urge to interrupt. Deep breathing redirects your response and as a bonus, it is impossible to talk when you are deep breathing. Who of us would not choose the attentive caring physician?

How did the conclusion summarize the speech? Did it contain a motivation? How did the speaker obtain closure?

Did the speaker convince you that health care professionals should devote more attention to listening?

As it nears time for me to take that deep breath, I would just like to reiterate that listening is a learned skill and learning to listen with CARE has valuable benefits for health care professionals and patients. As a wise man named

J. Isham once said, "Listening is an attitude of the heart, a genuine desire to be with another which both attracts and heals."

Thank you very much.

Stage 3: Recall

Stop to self-test, relate, and react. Use the subheadings in the recall diagram shown here to guide your thinking. For each subheading, jot down a key idea that you feel is important to remember.

Your instructor may choose to give you a true-false comprehension review.

(Topic) ______________________________

(Significant details) ______________________________

____

____

____

____

(Related idea) ------------------------------

(Reaction) ______________________________

Thinking About "The Listening Process"

Not only does Carol Koehler's speech give an interesting perspective on listening, it also serves as a model for teaching the elements of an effective speech. Using the marginal queries as a guideline, describe the strengths of Koehler's speech.

Response Suggestion: Either directly or by inference, each query addresses an important element in an effective speech. Pinpoint each element and evaluate her strengths.

Contemporary Link

Use the five stages of listening to analyze your own listening pitfalls. In what routine situations do you tend to fall into any of the six categories of poor listening (from the Chatterbox to the Baffler)? List each and explain why.

Comprehension Questions

After reading the selection, answer the following questions with *a*, *b*, *c*, or *d*. In order to help you analyze your strengths and weaknesses, the question types are indicated.

Main Idea ______ 1. The best statement of the main idea is as follows:
- a. In the medical profession listening is the most important aspect of the patient/physician relationship.
- b. Listening is a valuable success skill that involves much more than just hearing.
- c. Bias and prejudice influence listening and responding.
- d. The ability to make a public speech begins with the ability to be an effective listener.

Inference ______ 2. In the five stages of listening, overcoming your concern for the environment by agreeing with a speaker's argument for a gas pipeline through Alaska would most likely be categorized by the author as
- a. receiving.
- b. understanding.
- c. remembering.
- d. evaluating.

Inference ______ 3. In retelling the two hospital stories Carol Koehler implies that
- a. the medical professionals reacted to her differently based on her appearance.
- b. medical doctors are not biased by age or signs of social status.
- c. medical professionals discriminate against people with signs of elevated social status.
- d. diamonds and mink coats do not influence medical care.

Detail ______ 4. According to the passage, the study indicating that "we spend 9% of our day writing, 16% reading, 30% speaking and 45% listening" was conducted on
- a. college students.
- b. medical students.
- c. practicing medical professionals.
- d. a population that is not clearly defined by the author.

Inference ______ 5. The primary purpose of the comments inserted in the margins of Carol Koehler's speech is to question
- a. the elements of making a good speech.
- b. the five stages of listening.
- c. the meaning of her speech.
- d. the audience participation.

Detail ________ 6. Carol Koehler is a
a. medical student.
b. medical doctor.
c. patient.
d. college professor.

Inference ________ 7. The reader can conclude that Carol Koehler most likely chose the acronym CARE to organize her action points because
a. it was coined by the inventors of the five stages of listening.
b. it appeals to a doctor's mission and was relate to *cure* by Dan Callahan.
c. it was adopted by the American Medical Association to humanize doctors.
d. it has taken on a legal meaning in malpractice suits against doctors.

Inference ________ 8. In discussing her "C stands for concentrate," Koehler focuses primarily on
a. verbal aspects of receiving.
b. mental processing.
c. emotional aspects of listening.
d. physical suggestions.

Inference ________ 9. By including "E stands for emotional control," Koehler suggests that
a. doctors never let emotions interfere with patient treatment.
b. one patient is the same as another with doctors.
c. doctors can react negatively to patients.
d. most doctors fear emotional reactions.

Inference ________ 10. By using the phrase, "This thirty-something male doctor," the author indicates
a. respect.
b. admiration.
c. loyalty.
d. annoyance.

Answer the following with *T* (true) or *F* (false).

Detail ________ 11. The author defines hearing as receiving sound rather than receiving meaning.

Inference ________ 12. The author suggests that malpractice suits are linked to poor listening skills.

Detail ________ 13. Koehler indicates that a patient usually feels more connected when the doctor takes extensive notes during a visit.

Detail ________ 14. The author indicates that in the remembering stage of listening, you mentally rearrange rather than duplicate the message.

Detail ________ 15. Koehler indicates that speaking is typically valued more highly than listening.

Vocabulary

According to the way the italicized word was used in the selection, select *a*, *b*, *c*, or *d* for the word or phase that gives the best definition. The number in parentheses indicates the line of the passage in which the word is located.

________ 1. "an interesting *perspective*" (29)
a. summary
b. point of view
c. essay
d. variation

________ 2. "sharp-witted and *self-sufficient*" (42)
a. interesting
b. independent
c. intelligent
d. strong

________ 3. "*makeshift* curtained room" (48)
a. modern
b. shoddy
c. private
d. quickly assembled

________ 4. "looked a little *bewildered*" (55)
a. confused
b. angry
c. afraid
d. dissatisfied

________ 5. "*litany* of events" (79)
a. list resembling a responsive prayer
b. historical description
c. publication
d. comparison

________ 6. "gift of *gab*" (88)
a. happiness
b. conversation
c. friendliness
d. leadership

________ 7. "*bombarded* with the relevant" (92)
a. attracted
b. attacked
c. fascinated
d. stimulated

________ 8. "*notion* of care over cure" (95)
a. replacement
b. strategy
c. idea
d. question

________ 9. "vocal *intonation*" (117)
a. lapses
b. questions
c. rise and fall in tone
d. pauses

________ 10. "take *cryptic* notes" (125)
a. lengthy
b. brief
c. meaningful
d. complete

Search the Net

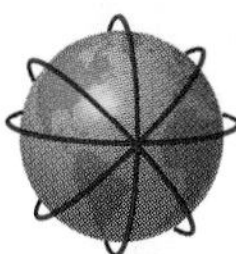

- You can join a "Toastmasters" club to learn and practice listening and speaking skills. Search the Internet for a local Toastmasters club. When does the club meet? What can one gain from participating in a Toastmasters club? What tips does the club give for effective public speaking?

  Toastmasters International: http://www.toastmasters.org/

- Listening is a skill that is critical to success in most career fields, especially in counseling. Search the Internet for three resources, such as seminars, classes, or reading materials, that a counselor could use for improving listening skills. Explain the benefits of each of the resources.

  The International Listening Association: http://www.listen.org/

  The Biz Hotline:
  http://www.bizhotline.com/html/focused listening skills.html

Concept Prep

for Communications and Language

What is communications?

Communications is one of the fastest growing departments in many colleges. It includes speech, journalism, film, and video. The courses are usually interactive and stress group and team performance by learning leadership and responsible group membership skills.

What words are associated with communications?

- A popular word associated with public speaking and leadership is **charisma**. The word refers to a magnetically charming personality and an extraordinary power to inspire loyalty and enthusiasm in others. Leaders such as John F. Kennedy and Martin Luther King, Jr., are described as charismatic.
- **Ethics** is another word associated with leadership, team performance, and business. Ethical decision making and behavior are aimed at distinguishing between right and wrong and acting in a manner that is morally correct and virtuous.
- When speaking formally, use fresh and concise language. Avoid using **clichés** such as "Don't let the cat out of the bag" and "Let's get down to brass tacks." These hackneyed, overused expressions create images that were probably humorous when first used but are now considered tiresome. If interpreted **literally,** exactly word for word, the phrases do not make sense. The words are intentionally designed to take on a new descriptive or **figurative** meaning. In the previous phrases, the "cat in the bag" is a secret, and the "brass tacks" are the "real issues." Such phrases are also called **idioms,** and they are especially confusing to people who speak English as a second language.
- Use appropriate **diction** for your audience. Diction refers to your choice of words. It can also refer to the quality of your pronunciation. Use clear and effective words and enunciate them correctly.
- If you don't want snickers in the audience, avoid **double entendres**—expressions that have a double meaning. The second meaning is usually a mischievous and sexual interpretation of an innocent expression, such as "The athletes were hanging around in the locker room."

American civil rights activist Dr. Martin Luther King, Jr., addresses a large crowd gathered at the Lincoln Memorial for the March on Washington.
Hulton Archive/Getty Images

- More snickers may come if you make a **malapropism,** a humorous confusion of two words that sound alike. Saying "a blue tarpon was spread over the building under repair" will have your audience envisioning a huge blue fish covering the structure rather than a large plastic tarp.
- Give credit when you use the words or ideas of another person. To steal the thoughts of others as your own is **plagiarism.** Acknowledging credit to others does not detract from your work but enhances your status as a researcher.

- If you are duplicating published materials for distribution to a group, obtain **copyright** permission so that you are not acting illegally. A copyright is a legal protection granted to an author or publishing company to prevent others from pirating a body of work. In order to obtain reprint permission, you will probably need to pay a fee.
- When receiving constructive criticism, don't be a **prima donna.** The word is derived from Latin and refers to the "first lady" in an opera. The connotation, however, is that the person is overly sensitive and difficult to work with. If you become a prima donna, you may suddenly discover that you are a **persona non grata,** a person who is no longer acceptable or in favor.
- Strive for excellence and perhaps you will graduate with honors or **cum laude.** Colleges differ on the grade-point averages required for different designations of distinction and high honor. At some institutions, a cumulative grade-point average of 3.500–3.699 is required for **cum laude,** a 3.700–3.899 for **magna cum laude,** and a 3.900–4.000 for **summa cum laude.** Some students, however, are satisfied to graduate with a "Thank the Lordy."

REVIEW QUESTIONS

Study the material and answer the following questions.

1. What areas are usually included in a communications department? ______________________________
2. What is ethical behavior? ______________________________
3. What is a cliché? ______________________________
4. What is good diction? ______________________________
5. What is a double entendre? ______________________________
6. What is a malapropism? ______________________________
7. What is plagiarism? ______________________________
8. What is a prima donna? ______________________________
9. What is a persona non grata? ______________________________
10. What is summa cum laude? ______________________________

Your instructor may choose to give a true-false review of these communications and language concepts.

Selection 2 **SOCIOLOGY**

CONTEMPORARY FOCUS

Customs and culture vary from country to country. What may seem acceptable to us may be offensive to others.

MAKE THE RIGHT GESTURE ON A TRIP TO ASIA

Jane E. Lasky

The Secured Lender, New York, November/December 2000

I have learned a lot about proper Asian etiquette, having lived in the region for three years in the early 1990s. Here are some rules that should help you understand how to mind your P's and Q's through certain gestures in an array of Asian countries.

- **China:** Don't be surprised if you are applauded when entering a room. This is a form of greeting that should be reciprocated. During your visit to China, remember to keep your hands to yourself. It is not a good idea to touch, hug or slap a Chinese colleague on the back when you first meet, as most men and women from this country don't relish being touched by a stranger. In friendship, people of the same sex often hold hands. Don't point with your index finger but with your open hand.
- **India:** The left hand is typically used to wash up after using the toilet. While dining at an Indian table, even if you are left-handed, you should always use your right hand to accept and pass food. Likewise, when you hand money to an Indian. To express remorse or honesty, simply grasp your ear in earnest a la Carol Burnett. Avoid giving a side-to-side wave which often means "hello" in the West. In India this can be interpreted as "go away" or "no." In public, don't whistle a tune no matter how happy you are. Doing so is frowned upon.
- **Indonesia:** Before entering into any conversation, even one that takes place on the street, remove your hat and sunglasses. If an Indonesian colleague pats you on the shoulder, it is a sign of approval. In Indonesia, the left hand is considered unclean. Do not give anything with your left hand. Do not eat with it, do not shake hands with it and do not point with it. If you are invited to an Indonesian home, remove your shoes before entering any carpeted area of the house.
- **Malaysia:** Be sure not to litter. This crime tends to carry harsh penalties in Malaysia where even an apple core or a cigarette butt can cause much trouble. If you're going to give a gift during your stay, hand it over with your right hand. Using your left hand will be considered impolite.

Collaborative Activity

Collaborate on responses to the following questions:

- Do you believe it is wrong to touch or hug people whom you don't know well? Why or why not?
- How do business hours vary in Latin America and the United States?
- What would an Asian executive need to know about doing business in the United States?

Skill Development—Stage 1: Preview

Preview the next selection to predict the purpose, organization, and your learning plan.

The phrase "unity in diversity" is a paradox. What does it mean?

After reading this selection, I will need to know____________________

____

____

____

Activate Schema

Is it wrong for primitive tribal people to wear no clothes?

Does social status exist in primitive cultures?

Could you eat insects if doing so meant survival?

Learning Strategy

Define and use examples to explain cultural universals, adaptation, relativity, ethnocentrism, norms, and values.

Word Knowledge

What do you know about these words?

curb	naiveté	adornments	articulate	bizarre
smirk	abstained	postpartum	agile	consign

Your instructor may give a true-false vocabulary review before or after reading.

Stage 2: Integrate Knowledge While Reading

Since each reader interacts with material in a unique manner, it is artificial to require that certain thinking strategies be used. In order to heighten awareness, however, several questions have been inserted within this selection. Briefly respond in the margin to the inserted questions. In addition, make a note in the margin of at least one other instance when you used each of the following strategies:

Predict   Picture   Relate   Monitor   Correct

Unity in Diversity

From Donald Light, Jr., and Suzanne Keller, *Sociology*[5]

Does this title make sense or are these words opposites?

What is more basic, more "natural" than love between a man and woman? Eskimo men offer their wives to guests and friends as a gesture of hospitality; both husband and wife feel extremely offended if the guest declines. The Banaro of New Guinea believe it would be disastrous for a woman to conceive her first child by her husband and not by one of her father's close friends, as is their custom.

> The real father is a close friend of the bride's father. . . . Nevertheless the first-born child inherits the name and possessions of the husband. An American would deem such a custom immoral, but the Banaro tribesmen would be equally shocked to discover that the first-born child of an American couple is the offspring of the husband.

The Yanomamö of Northern Brazil, whom anthropologist Napoleon A. Chagnon named "the fierce people," encourage what we would consider extreme disrespect. Small boys are applauded for striking their mothers and fathers in the face. Yanomamö parents would laugh at our efforts to curb aggression in children, much as they laughed at Chagnon's naïveté when he first came to live with them.

What would your parents do if you slapped either of them in the face?

In a traditional Indian wedding ceremony the bride and groom pray at the altar.
Fabian Falco/Stock, Boston, Inc.

[5] Light, Donald Jr. and Suzanne Keller. "Unity and Diversity" from *Sociology*, 4th Edition. Copyright © 1986 by McGraw-Hill, Inc. Reproduced with permission of The McGraw-Hill Companies.

The variations among cultures are startling, yet all peoples have customs and beliefs about marriage, the bearing and raising of children, sex, and hospitality—to name just a few of the universals anthropologists have discovered in their cross-cultural explorations. But the *details* of cultures do indeed vary: in this country, not so many years ago, when a girl was serious about a boy and he about her, she wore his fraternity pin over her heart; in the Fiji Islands, girls put hibiscus flowers behind their ears when they are in love. The specific gestures are different but the impulse to symbolize feelings, to dress courtship in ceremonies, is the same. How do we explain this unity in diversity?

Cultural Universals

Cultural universals are all of the behavior patterns and institutions that have been found in all known cultures. Anthropologist George Peter Murdock identified over sixty cultural universals, including a system of social status, marriage, body adornments, dancing, myths and legends, cooking, incest taboos, inheritance rules, puberty customs, and religious rituals.

The universals of culture may derive from the fact that all societies must perform the same essential functions if they are to survive—including organization, motivation, communication, protection, the socialization of new members, and the replacement of those who die. In meeting these prerequisites for group life, people inevitably design similar—though not identical—patterns for living. As Clyde Kluckhohn wrote, "All cultures constitute somewhat distinct answers to essentially the same questions posed by human biology and by the generalities of the human situation."

The way in which a people articulates cultural universals depends in large part on their physical and social environment—that is, on the climate in which they live, the materials they have at hand, and the peoples with whom they establish contact. For example, the wheel has long been considered one of humankind's greatest inventions, and anthropologists were baffled for a long time by the fact that the great civilizations of South America never discovered it. Then researchers uncovered a number of toys with wheels. Apparently the Aztecs and their neighbors did know about wheels; they simply didn't find them useful in their mountainous environment.

Describe your mental picture.

Adaptation, Relativity, and Ethnocentrism

Taken out of context, almost any custom will seem bizarre, perhaps cruel, or just plain ridiculous. To understand why the Yanomamö encourage aggressive behavior in their sons, for example, you have to try to see things through their eyes. The Yanomamö live in a state of chronic warfare; they spend much of their time planning for and defending against raids with neighboring tribes. If Yanomamö parents did *not* encourage aggression in a boy, he would be ill equipped for life in their society. Socializing boys to be aggressive is *adaptive* for the Yanomamö because it enhances their capacity for survival. "In general, culture is . . . adaptive because it often provides people with a means of adjusting to the physiological needs of their own bodies, to their physical-geographical environment and to their social environments as well."

In many tropical societies, there are strong taboos against a mother having sexual intercourse with a man until her child is at least two years old. As a Hausa woman explains,

> A mother should not go to her husband while she has a child such is sucking . . . if she only sleeps with her husband and does not become pregnant, it will not hurt her child, it will not spoil her milk. But if another child enters in, her milk will make the first one ill. (Smith, in Whiting 1969, p. 518)

Undoubtedly, people would smirk at a woman who nursed a two-year-old child in our society and abstained from having sex with her husband. Why do Hausa women behave in a way that seems so overprotective and overindulgent to us? In tropical climates protein is scarce. If a mother were to nurse more than one child at a time, or if she were to wean a child before it reached the age of two, the youngster would be prone to *kwashiorkor*, an often fatal disease resulting from protein deficiency. Thus, long postpartum sex taboos are adaptive. In a tropical environment a postpartum sex taboo and a long period of breast-feeding solve a serious problem.

No custom is good or bad, right or wrong in itself; each one must be examined in light of the culture as a whole and evaluated in terms of how it works in the context of the entire culture. Anthropologists and sociologists call this *cultural relativity*. Although this way of thinking about culture may seem self-evident today, it is a lesson that anthropologists and the missionaries who often preceded them to remote areas learned the hard way, by observing the effects their best intentions had on peoples whose way of life was quite different from their own. In an article on the pitfalls of trying to "uplift" peoples whose ways seem backward and inefficient, Don Adams quotes an old Oriental story:

> Once upon a time there was a great flood, and involved in this flood were two creatures, a monkey and a fish. The monkey, being agile and experienced, was lucky enough to scramble up a tree and escape the raging waters. As he looked down from his safe perch, he saw the poor fish struggling against the swift current. With the very best intentions, he reached down and lifted the fish from the water. The result was inevitable (1960, p. 22).

What is the difference between adaptation and relativity?

Ethnocentrism is the tendency to see one's own way of life, including behaviors, beliefs, values, and norms as the only right way of living. Robin Fox points out that "any human group is ever ready to consign another recognizably different human group to the other side of the boundary. It is not enough to possess culture to be fully human, you have to possess *our* culture."

Values and Norms

The Tangu, who live in a remote part of New Guinea, play a game called *taketak*, which in many ways resembles bowling. The game is played with a top that has been fashioned from a dried fruit and with two groups of coconut stakes that are driven into the ground (more or less like bowling pins). The players divide into two teams. Members of the first team take turns throwing the top into the batch of stakes; every stake the top hits is removed. Then the second team steps to the line and tosses the top into their batch of stakes. The object of the game, surprisingly, is not to knock over as many stakes as possible. Rather, the game continues until both teams have removed the *same* number of stakes. Winning is completely irrelevant.

What will be covered in this next part?

In a sense games are practice for "real life"; they reflect the values of the culture in which they are played. *Values* are the criteria people use in assessing their daily lives, arranging their priorities, measuring their pleasures and pains, choosing between alternative courses of action. The Tangu value equivalence: the idea of one individual or group winning and another losing bothers them, for they believe winning generates ill-will. In fact, when Europeans brought soccer to the Tangu, they altered the rules so that the object of the game was for two teams to score the same number of goals. Sometimes their soccer games went on for days! American games, in contrast, are highly competitive; there are *always* winners and losers. Many rule books include provisions for overtime and "sudden death" to prevent ties, which leave Americans dissatisfied. World Series, Superbowls, championships in basketball and hockey, Olympic Gold Medals are front-page news in this country. In the words of the late football coach Vince Lombardi, "Winning isn't everything, it's the only thing."

Norms, the rules that guide behavior in everyday situations, are derived from values, but norms and values can conflict. You may recall a news item that appeared in American newspapers in December 1972, describing the discovery of survivors of a plane crash 12,000 feet in the Andes. The crash had occurred on October 13; sixteen of the passengers (a rugby team and their supporters) managed to survive for sixty-nine days in near-zero temperatures. The story made headlines because, to stay alive, the survivors had eaten parts of their dead companions. Officials, speaking for the group, stressed how valiantly the survivors had tried to save the lives of the injured people and how they had held religious services regularly. The survivors' explanations are quite interesting, for they reveal how important it is to people to justify their actions, to resolve conflicts in norms and values (here, the positive value of survival vs. the taboo against cannibalism). Some of the survivors compared their action to a heart transplant, using parts of a dead person's body to save another person's life. Others equated their act with the sacrament of communion. In the words of one religious survivor, "If we would have died, it would have been suicide, which is condemned by the Roman Catholic faith."

Stage 3: Recall

Stop to self-test, relate, and react. Use the subheadings in the recall diagram shown here to guide your thinking. For each subheading, jot down a key idea that you feel is important to remember.

Your instructor may choose to give you a true-false comprehension review.

(Topic) ____________________

(Significant details) ____________________

____

____

____

____

(Related idea) ____________________

(Reaction) ____________________

Thinking About "Unity in Diversity"

Define the following terms and describe two examples for each that are not mentioned in the selection:

cultural universals adaptation relativity ethnocentrism
norms values

Response Suggestion: Define the cultural concepts in your own words and relate examples from today's society.

Contemporary Link

From a cultural relativity perspective, discuss using the left hand in different cultures. Why do you think the United States has no such left-hand taboo?

Comprehension Questions

After reading the selection, answer the following questions with *a, b, c,* or *d.*

Main Idea

_____ 1. The best statement of the main idea of this selection is
- a. the variety of practices and customs in society show few threads of cultural unity.
- b. the unusual variations in societies gain acceptability because of the cultural universals in all known societies.
- c. a variety of cultural universals provides adaptive choices for specific societies.
- d. cultural universals are found in all known societies even though the details of the cultures may vary widely.

Inference

_____ 2. The author believes that the primary cultural universal addressed in the Eskimo custom of offering wives to guests is
- a. bearing and raising of children.
- b. social status.
- c. hospitality.
- d. incest taboos.

Detail

_____ 3. The custom of striking practiced by the Yanomamö serves the adaptive function of
- a. developing fierce warriors.
- b. binding parent and child closer together.
- c. developing physical respect for parents.
- d. encouraging early independence from parental care.

Detail

_____ 4. *Cultural universals* might be defined as
- a. each culture in the universe.
- b. similar basic living patterns.
- c. the ability for cultures to live together in harmony.
- d. the differences among cultures.

Inference

_____ 5. The author implies that cultural universals exist because of
- a. a social desire to be more alike.
- b. the differences in cultural behavior patterns.
- c. the competition among societies.
- d. the needs of survival in group life.

Inference

_____ 6. The author suggests that the wheel was not a part of the ancient Aztec civilization because the Aztecs
- a. did not find wheels useful in their mountainous environment.
- b. were not intelligent enough to invent wheels.
- c. were baffled by inventions.
- d. did not have the materials for development.

Inference _________ 7. The underlying reason for the postpartum sexual taboo of the Hausa is
a. sexual.
b. nutritional.
c. moral.
d. religious.

Inference _________ 8. The term *cultural relativity* explains why a custom can be considered
a. right or wrong regardless of culture.
b. right or wrong according to the number of people practicing it.
c. right in one culture and wrong in another.
d. wrong if in conflict with cultural universals.

Inference _________ 9. The author relates Don Adams's oriental story to show that missionaries working in other cultures
a. should be sent back home.
b. can do more harm than good.
c. purposefully harm the culture to seek selfish ends.
d. usually do not have a genuine concern for the people.

Inference _________ 10. The tendency of ethnocentrism would lead most Americans to view the Eskimo practice of wife sharing as
a. right.
b. wrong.
c. right for Eskimos but wrong for most Americans.
d. a custom about which an outsider should have no opinion.

Answer the following questions with *T* (true) or *F* (false).

Inference _________ 11. An American's acceptance of the Banaro tribal custom of fathering the firstborn is an example of an understanding by cultural relativity.

Inference _________ 12. The author feels that the need to symbolize feelings in courtship is a cultural universal.

Inference _________ 13. The author feels that culture is not affected by climate.

Detail _________ 14. The author states that all societies must have a form of organization if they are to survive.

Inference _________ 15. The author implies that the rugby team that crashed in the Andes could have survived without eating human flesh.

Vocabulary

According to the way the italicized word was used in the selection, select *a*, *b*, *c*, or *d* for the word or phrase that gives the best definition. The number in parentheses indicates the line of the passage in which the word is located.

_______ 1. "efforts to *curb* aggression" (15)
- a. stabilize
- b. release
- c. promote
- d. restrain

_______ 2. "at Chagnon's *naïveté*" (16)
- a. lack of knowledge
- b. gentle manner
- c. jolly nature
- d. clumsiness

_______ 3. "body *adornments*" (31)
- a. ailments
- b. treatments
- c. scars
- d. decorations

_______ 4. "*articulates* cultural universals" (41)
- a. remembers
- b. designs
- c. expresses clearly
- d. substitutes

_______ 5. "will seem *bizarre*" (50)
- a. phony
- b. unjust
- c. grotesque
- d. unnecessary

_______ 6. "*smirk* at a woman" (68)
- a. refuse to tolerate
- b. smile conceitedly
- c. lash out
- d. acknowledge approvingly

_______ 7. "*abstained* from having sex" (69)
- a. matured
- b. regained
- c. refrained
- d. reluctantly returned

_______ 8. "long *postpartum* sex taboos" (74)
- a. after childbirth
- b. awaited
- c. subcultural
- d. complicated

_______ 9. "being *agile* and experienced" (quote, 88)
- a. eager
- b. nimble
- c. young
- d. knowledgeable

_______ 10. "ready to *consign*" (96)
- a. assign
- b. remove
- c. reorganize
- d. overlook

Search the Net

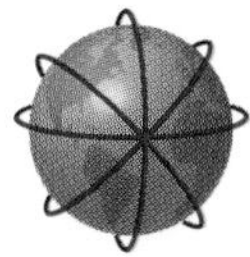

- Cultural etiquette is increasingly important as the workplace becomes more diverse and companies compete in the global economy. Your company has asked you to increase its business in Latin America. Before you can begin, search for information on Latin American business and cultural etiquette and highlight sensitive differences. Summarize your research in a memo to the company president. Plan your own search or begin by trying the following:

The International Business Etiquette Internet Sourcebook: http://atn-riae.agr.ca/public/htmldocs/e2729.htm

Doing Business in Latin America: http://www.omnilingua.com/resource/business/doingbusinesslatinamerica.htm

- Weddings are cultural events that are filled with unique rituals. Choose an ethnic group, and research wedding customs and rituals that are unique to that particular group. Explain the significance of three rituals.

  Chinese wedding customs: http://24.1.238.207/jelly/wedcus.html

  Scottish wedding customs: http://weddingcircle.com/ethnic/scot/

Concept Prep

for Anthropology

Although the "Unity in Diversity" selection is from a sociology textbook, the passage deals with concepts in anthropology. Thus, this section will also explore anthropology.

What is anthropology?

Anthropology is the study of humankind. It focuses on the origins and development of humans and their diverse cultures. By seeking to understand, respect, and applaud human diversity, anthropology might be considered the first multicultural course on college campuses. Special areas that you can study in anthropology include:

- **Physical anthropology:** How did humans evolve? What does genetic and fossil evidence reveal about our place in the animal kingdom?
- **Cultural anthropology:** What was the purpose of primitive customs and behaviors and what do they reveal about contemporary social problems?
- **Archaeology:** What can we reconstruct about extinct societies and their cultures from artifacts such as ancient bones, pieces of pottery, and excavated ruins?

Husband and wife Louis and Mary Leakey study fossilized skull fragments which may belong to the "missing link" between ape and man.
Bettmann/CORBIS

Who are famous anthropologists?

- In search of our human origins, **Louis and Mary Leakey** sifted through the dirt of **Olduvai Gorge** in Tanzania, East Africa, for over twenty-five years. Finally, in 1959 they unearthed a humanlike upper jaw with teeth and a skull. This discovery of a 1.75 million year old hominid revealed that the first humans originated in Africa.
- Cultural anthropology was popularized by **Margaret Mead** with the publication of her book, *Coming of Age in Samoa*, in 1928. Mead observed children moving into adolescence and described the transition as happy. She argued that the stress of adolescence is cultural, but others later disagreed. Mead also studied male and female roles in different societies and argued that gender roles are cultural rather than inborn.

Who were our early ancestors?

- **Lucy,** one of the greatest archaeological finds, is the nickname for the most complete human skeleton of early ancestors ever found. Lucy is over three million years old and was found in Ethiopia.
- The **Cro-Magnons** were the earliest form of modern humans, who developed about 35,000 years ago. Their cave paintings in Europe are the first known human art.
- The earliest societies were **hunting and gathering societies.** People roamed widely to hunt wild animals and fish, and to gather fruits and nuts. Usually this **nomadic** wandering was seasonal and calculated to create the best opportunities for available food. Not until 10,000 years ago did humans begin to domesticate plants and animals and thus remain in one area.

REVIEW QUESTIONS

Study the material and answer the following questions.

1. Digging in New Mexico for prehistoric artifacts suggests what area of anthropology? ______________
2. Living with tribal people in the Amazon to study their ways suggests what area of anthropology? ______________
3. Analyzing DNA to link Asian and African people suggests what area of anthropology? ______________
4. What did Mary and Louis Leakey discover? ______________
5. Why was the Leakey discovery especially significant? ______________
6. What did Margaret Mead investigate in Samoa? ______________
7. Why was Mead's work especially significant? ______________
8. Why is Lucy significant? ______________
9. What was the artistic contribution of Cro-Magnons? ______________
10. What phenomenon usually ends hunting and gathering societies? ______________

Your instructor may choose to give a true-false review of these anthropology concepts.

READER'S JOURNAL

Name ______________________________ Date ____________

CHAPTER 3

Answer the following questions to reflect on your own learning and progress. Use the perforations to tear the assignment out for your instructor.

1. What do you enjoy reading on a regular basis? Why? ____________

   ____

2. How do you preview a book or magazine before purchasing it? ________

   ____

3. What do you plan to do to "train" yourself to use the recall stage?

   ____

4. Which of the five thinking strategies do you tend to use the most while reading? Explain. ______________________________

   ____

5. What seems to be the main cause of confusion in your comprehension?

   ____

6. Compare your thinking when you are really studying and when you are just holding the book. ______________________________

   ____

7. Reflect on the longer selections and review the forty-five multiple-choice items. How many did you answer correctly? ______________

   What types of questions are you missing the most? ____________

8. Identify the page and item numbers and explain the reasons for two of your comprehension errors in this chapter. ______________

   ____

9. Which selection did you enjoy the most? Why? ____________

   ____

   ____

4

Main Idea

- What is a topic?
- What is a main idea?
- What are supporting details?
- What is a summary?

Kabuki Theater *by Utagawa Toyokuni (1795–1825). Color woodblock print, 38.5 × 26.0 cm. Musée des Arts Asiatiques-Guimet, Paris, France. Photo: Arnaudet. Copyright Réunion des Musées Nationaux/Art Resource, NY.*

What Is a Main Idea?

The **main idea** of a passage is the central message that the author is trying to convey about the material. It is a sentence that condenses thoughts and details into a general, all-inclusive statement of the author's message.

Comprehending the main idea is crucial to your comprehension of text, and many experts believe that it is the most important reading skill. In fact, if all reading comprehension techniques were combined and reduced to one essential question, that question might be, "What is the main idea the author is trying to get across to the reader?" Whether you read a single paragraph, a chapter, or an entire book, your most important single task is to understand the main idea of what you read.

Labels for Main Idea

Reading specialists use various terms when referring to the main idea. In classroom discussions, all of the following words are sometimes used to help students understand the meaning of *main idea:*

main point

central focus

gist

controlling idea

central thought

thesis

The last word on the list, *thesis,* is a familiar word in English composition classes. Students usually have had practice in stating a thesis sentence for English essays, but they have not had as much practice in stating the main idea of a reading selection. Recognizing the similarity between a thesis and a main idea statement will help to clarify the concept.

Importance of Prior Knowledge in Main Idea

Research has been done investigating the processes readers use to construct main ideas. One researcher, Peter Afflerbach,[1] asked graduate students and uni-

[1]P. Afflerbach, "How Are Main Idea Statements Constructed? Watch the Experts!," *Journal of Reading* 30 (1987): 512–518; and "The Influence of Prior Knowledge on Expert Readers' Main Idea Construction Strategies," *Reading Research Quarterly* 25 (1990): 31–46.

versity professors to "think aloud" as they read passages on both familiar and unfamiliar topics. These expert readers spoke their thoughts to the researcher before, during, and after reading. From these investigations, Afflerbach concluded that expert readers use different strategies for familiar and unfamiliar materials.

This research showed that *already knowing something about the topic is the key* to easy reading. When readers are familiar with the subject, constructing the main idea is effortless and, in many cases, automatic. These readers quickly assimilate the unfolding text into already well-developed knowledge networks. They seem to organize text into chunks for comprehension and later retrieval. These "informed" readers do not have to struggle with an information overload.

By contrast, expert readers with little prior knowledge of the subject are absorbed in trying to make meaning out of unfamiliar words and confusing sentences. Because they are struggling to recognize ideas, few mental resources remain for constructing a main idea. These "uninformed" experts were reluctant to guess at a main idea and to predict a topic. Instead, they preferred to read all the information before trying to make sense of it. Constructing the main idea was a difficult and deliberate task for these expert readers.

Main Idea Strategies

The following strategies for getting the main idea were reported by Afflerbach's expert readers. Can you see the differences in the thinking processes of the informed and uninformed experts?

"Informed" Expert Readers

Strategy 1: The informed expert readers skimmed the passage before reading and took a guess at the main idea. Then they read for corroboration.

Strategy 2: The informed experts automatically paused while reading to summarize or reduce information. They frequently stopped at natural breaks in the material to let ideas fall into place.

"Uninformed" Expert Readers

Strategy 1: Expert readers who did not know about the subject were unwilling to take a guess at the main idea. Instead they read the material, decided on a topic, and then looked back to pull together a main idea statement.

Strategy 2: The uninformed experts read the material and they reviewed it to find key terms and concepts. They tried to bring the key terms and concepts together into a main idea statement.

Strategy 3: The uninformed experts read the material and then proposed a main idea statement. They double-checked the passage to clarify or revise the main idea statement.

What differences do you see in these approaches? Since introductory college textbooks address many topics that are new and unfamiliar, freshmen readers will frequently need to use the strategies of uninformed expert readers to comprehend the main ideas of their college texts. Until prior knowledge is built for the different college courses, main idea construction for course textbooks is likely to be a *conscious effort* rather than an automatic phenomenon.

What Is a Topic?

The **topic** of a passage is like a title. It is a word, name, or phrase that labels the subject but does not reveal the specific contents of the passage. The topic is a general rather than specific term and forms an umbrella under which the specific ideas or details in the passage can be grouped. For example, what general term would pull together and unify the following items?

Items: carrots
lettuce
onions
potatoes

Topic? ________________

Exercise 4.1 Identifying Topics

Each of the following lists includes four specific items or ideas that could relate to a single topic. At the end of each list, write a general topic that could form an umbrella under which the specific ideas can be grouped.

1. shirt	2. psychology	3. democracy	4. Bermuda	5. coffee
pants	history	autocracy	Cuba	tea
jacket	sociology	oligarchy	Haiti	cola
sweater	political science	monarchy	Tahiti	chocolate
________	________	________	________	________

How Do Topics and Main Ideas Differ?

Topics are general categories, like titles, but they are not main ideas. In the previous list, caffeine is a general term or topic that unifies the items, *coffee, tea, cola,* and *chocolate.* If those items were used as details in a paragraph, the main idea could not be expressed by simply saying "caffeine." The word *caffeine* would answer the question, "What was the passage about?" but not the second question, "What is the author's main idea?"

A writer could actually devise several very different paragraphs about caffeine using the same four details as support. If you were assigned to write a paragraph about caffeine, using the four items as details, what would be the main idea or thesis of your paragraph?

Topic: Caffeine

Main idea or thesis: ____

Read the following examples of different main ideas that could be developed in a paragraph about caffeine.

1. Consumption of caffeine is not good for your health. (Details would enumerate health hazards associated with each item.)
2. Americans annually consume astonishing amounts of caffeine. (Details would describe amounts of each consumed annually.)
3. Caffeine can wake up an otherwise sluggish mind. (Details would explain the popular use of each item as a stimulant.)
4. Reduce caffeine consumption with the decaffeinated version of popular caffeine-containing beverages. (Details would promote the decaffeinated version of each item.)

EXAMPLE Below are examples of a topic, main idea, and supporting detail.

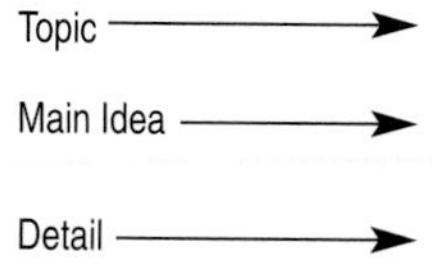

Early Cognitive Development

Cognitive psychologists sometimes study young children to observe the very beginnings of cognitive activity. For example, when children first begin to utter words and sentences, they overgeneralize what they know and make language more consistent than it actually is.

Christopher Peterson, *Introduction to Psychology*

EXPLANATION The topic pulls our attention to a general area, and the main idea provides the focus. The detail offers elaboration and support.

Exercise 4.2 Differentiating Topic, Main Idea, and Supporting Details

This exercise is designed to check your ability to differentiate statements of the main idea from topic and specific supporting details. Compare the items within each group and indicate whether each one is a statement of the main idea *(MI)*, a topic *(T)*, or a specific supporting detail *(SD)*.

Group 1

_______ a. For poor farm families, life on the plains meant a sod house or a dugout carved out of the hillside for protection from the winds.

_______ b. One door and usually no more than a single window provided light and air.

_______ c. Sod houses on the plains

James W. Davidson et al., *Nation of Nations*

Group 2

______ a. She was the daughter of English poet Lord Byron and of a mother who was a gifted mathematician.

______ b. Babbage and the Programming Countess

______ c. Ada, the Countess of Lovelace, helped develop the instructions for doing computer programming computations on Babbage's analytical engine.

______ d. In addition, she published a series of notes that eventually led others to accomplish what Babbage himself had been unable to do.

H. L. Capron, *Computers*, 5th ed. (adapted)

Group 3

______ a. As a group, for instance, Generation Xers try harder to work around employees' childcare needs by creating flexible schedules, and many encourage workers to bring their children—and even their pets—to the workplace for visits.

______ b. Generation X entrepreneurs differ

______ c. Generation Xers are choosing to run their companies differently from how their parents might have done.

______ d. Their goal is to recognize and reward people for the contributions they make rather than for their titles in the corporate hierarchy.

From Ronald Ebert and Ricky Griffin, *Business Essentials*, 2nd ed. (adapted)

Group 4

______ a. Mexican American Political Gains

______ b. During the 1960s four Mexican Americans—Senator Joseph Montoya of New Mexico and representatives Eligio de la Garza and Henry B. Gonzales of Texas and Edward R. Roybal of California—were elected to Congress.

______ c. In 1974 two Chicanos were elected governors—Jerry Apodaca in New Mexico and Raul Castro in Arizona—becoming the first Mexican-American governors since early in this century.

______ d. Since 1960 Mexican Americans have made important political gains.

James Kirby Martin et al., *America and Its Peoples*, 4th ed., vol. 2, pp. 898–99

Questioning for the Main Idea

To determine the main idea of a paragraph, an article, or a book, follow the three basic steps listed in the box on page 131. The order of the questions may vary depending on your prior knowledge of the material. If the material is familiar, main idea construction may be automatic and thus a selection of significant supporting details would follow. If the material is unfamiliar, as frequently occurs in textbook reading, identifying the details through key terms and concepts would come first and from them you would form a main idea statement.

Reader's Tip

Finding the Main Idea

* **Establish the topic.** Who or what is this about? What general word or phrase names the subject? The topic should be broad enough to include all the ideas, yet restrictive enough to focus on the direction of the details. For example, identifying the topic of an article as "politics," "federal politics," or "corruption in federal politics" might all be correct, but the last may be the most descriptive of the actual contents.
* **Identify the key supporting terms.** What are the major supporting details? Look at the details that seem to be significant to see if they point in a particular direction. What aspect of the subject do they address? What seems to be the common message? Details such as kickbacks to senators, overspending on congressional junkets, and lying to the voters could support the idea of "corruption in federal politics."
* **Focus on the message of the topic.** What is the main idea the author is trying to convey about the topic?

  This statement should be

  A complete sentence

  Broad enough to include the important details

  Focused enough to describe the author's slant

The author's main idea about corruption in federal politics might be that voters need to ask for an investigation of seemingly corrupt practices by federal politicians.

Read the following example, and answer the questions for determining the main idea.

EXAMPLE

New high-speed machines also brought danger to the workplace. If a worker succumbed to boredom, fatigue, or simple miscalculation, disaster could strike. Each year of the late nineteenth century some 35,000 wage earners were killed by industrial accidents. In Pittsburgh iron and steel mills alone, in one year 195 men died from hot metal explosions, asphyxiation, and falls, some into pits of molten metal. Men and women working in textile mills were poisoned by the thick dust and fibers in the air; similar toxic atmospheres injured those working in anything from twine-making plants to embroidery factories. Railways, with their heavy equipment and unaccustomed speed, were especially dangerous. In Philadelphia over half the railroad workers who died between 1886 and 1890 were killed by accidents. For injury or death, workers and their families could expect no payment from employers, since the idea of worker's compensation was unknown.

James W. Davidson et al., *Nation of Nations*

1. Who or what is this about? ______________________________

2. What are the major details? ______________________________

3. What is the main idea the author is trying to convey about the topic?

____

EXPLANATION The passage is about injuries from machines. The major details are 35,000 killed, 195 died from explosions, etc., poisoned by dust, and half of rail workers killed. The main idea is that new high-speed machines brought danger to the workplace.

What Do Details Do?

Look at the details in the picture on page 133 to decide what message the photographer is trying to communicate. Determine the topic of the picture, propose a main idea using your prior knowledge, and then list some of the significant details that support this point.

What is the topic? ______________________________

____

What are the significant supporting details? ______________________________

____

What is the point the photograph is trying to convey about the topic?

____

The topic of the picture is baseball. The details show a player, whose name is Jones, making a giant leap into the stands to catch the ball, but the ball is too high and too well hit. The fans are concentrating on the ball while moving back to avoid being hit. One fan, however, reaches with his mitt to catch the ball. This prepared fan also holds a target sign in his lap, indicating the place to hit a homerun ball. To make the photograph even more visually interesting, Jones's body is centered in the middle of the letters POW, as if he were stepping on the letter O. The main idea of the picture is the fielder has failed to

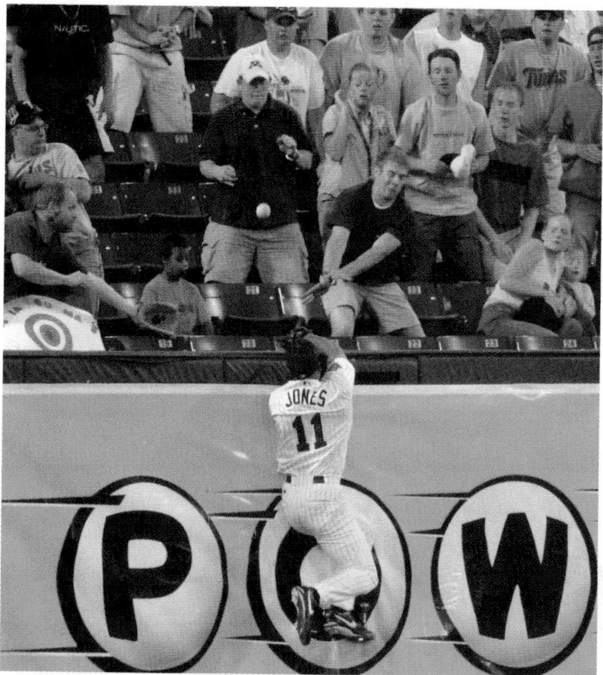

AP/Wide World Photos

catch a homerun hit. For baseball fans who want the exact details that are not disclosed in the picture, left fielder Jacque Jones (11) of the Minnesota Twins missed the homerun hit by Chicago White Sox's Ray Durham in the first inning in Minneapolis, Tuesday, June 26, 2001.

Details support, develop, and explain a main idea. Specific details can include reasons, incidents, facts, examples, steps, and definitions. The task of a reader is to recognize the major supporting details and to pull them together into a main idea. Being able to pick out major details implies that the reader has some degree of prior knowledge on the subject and has probably already begun to form some notion of the main idea.

Textbooks are packed full of details, but fortunately all details are not of equal importance. Major details tend to support, explain, and describe main ideas, whereas minor details tend to support, explain, and describe the major details. Ask the following questions to determine which details are major in importance and which are not:

1. Which details logically develop the main idea?
2. Which details help you understand the main idea?
3. Which details make you think the main idea you have chosen is correct?

Noticing key words that form transitional links from one idea to another can sometimes help the reader distinguish between major and minor details.

Reader's Tip

Signals for Significance

* **Key words for major details:**
  one first another furthermore also finally
* **Key words for minor details:**
  for example to be specific that is this means

Stated and Unstated Main Ideas

Like paragraphs, pictures also suggest main ideas. Artists compose and select to communicate a message. Look at the picture shown here and then answer the questions that follow.

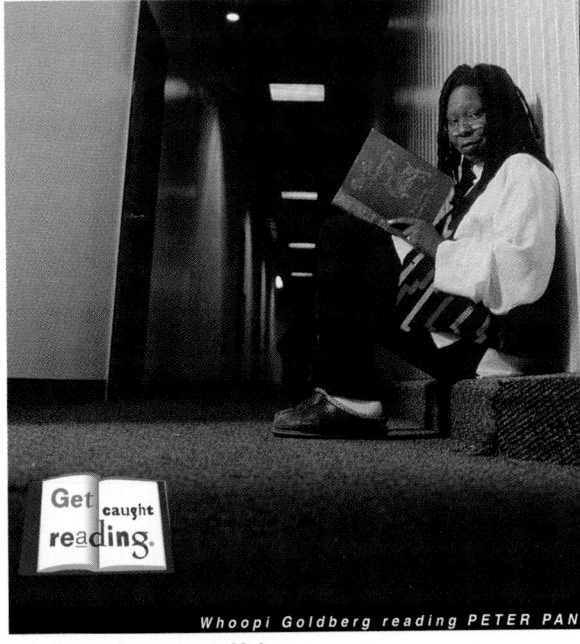

Get caught reading.
Whoopi Goldberg reading PETER PAN.

Association of American Publishers

What is the general topic of the picture? ______________________

What details seem important? ______________________

What is the main idea the artist is trying to convey about the topic?

____

The topic of the picture is reading. The details show the actress Whoopi Goldberg sitting in an empty corridor on an improvised seat reading a book. The book title, *Peter Pan*, is written on the book as well as at the bottom of the page. We can assume that she is reading *Peter Pan* for pleasure, since it is fanciful and seldom required reading. We can also assume she has escaped to a quiet place for a few minutes of pleasurable reading. She is having fun and wants to be alone, but the camera has caught her. The main idea, "Get caught reading," is written at the bottom of the picture. The message is that we should copy this noted comedian and escape to enjoy a good book.

Now look at the picture below, which does not include a slogan or directly stated appeal. Again, answer the questions that follow.

AP/Wide World Photos

What is the general topic of the picture? ______________________________

What details seem important? ______________________________

What is the main idea the artist is trying to convey about the topic?

____

The topic of the picture is a disaster. The building has collapsed and rescue workers with hard hats are moving rocks and looking for survivors and victims. Emergency personnel carry an orange body bag with the remains of a victim. The American flag at the top of the rubble indicates that this is in the United States. A fireman in uniform stands under the flag as smoke still rises from still-simmering fires in the rubble. The disaster is recent, and the site is dangerous. The main idea of this picture is that emergency rescue workers are trying to sort through this enormous disaster for possible pockets of life, as well as for victims. From the details and your prior knowledge, you will recognize that this is the World Trade Center disaster that occurred on September 11, 2001, when two hijacked airliners crashed into the towers in New York and destroyed both buildings.

As in the pictures, an author's main point can either be directly stated in the material or it can be unstated. When the main idea is stated in a sentence, the statement is called a **topic sentence** or **thesis statement.** Such a general statement is helpful to the reader because it provides an overview of the material. It does not, however, always express the author's opinion of the subject. For that reason, although helpful in overviewing, the topic sentence may not always form a complete statement of the author's main point.

Frequency of Stated Main Idea. Research shows that students find passages easier to comprehend when the main idea is directly stated within the passage. How often do stated main ideas appear in college textbooks? Should the reader expect to find that most paragraphs have stated main ideas?

For psychology texts, the answer seems to be about half and half. In a recent study,[2] stated main ideas appeared in *only 58 percent* of the sampled paragraphs in introductory psychology textbooks. In one of the books, the main idea was directly stated in 81 percent of the sampled paragraphs, and the researchers noted that the text was particularly easy to read.

Given these findings, we should recognize the importance of being skilled in locating and, especially, in constructing main ideas. In pulling ideas together to construct a main idea, you will be looking at the big picture and not be bound to the text in search of any single suggestive sentence.

Examples of Stated Main Idea

EXAMPLE

Managers can regain control over their time in several ways. One is by meeting whenever possible in someone else's office, so that they can leave as soon as their business is finished. Another is to start meetings on time without waiting for late-comers. The idea is to let late-comers adjust their schedules rather than everyone else adjusting theirs. A third is to set aside a block of time to work on an important project without interruption. This may require ignoring the telephone, being protected by an aggressive secretary, or hiding out. Whatever it takes is worth it.

Joseph Reitz and Linda Jewell, *Managing*

1. Who or what is this about? ______
2. What are the major details? ______
3. What is the main idea the author is trying to convey about the topic?

______

EXPLANATION The passage is about managers controlling their time. The major details are *meet in another office, start meetings on time,* and *block out time to work*. The main idea, stated in the first sentence, is that managers can do things to control their time.

[2] B. Smith and N. Chase, "The Frequency and Placement of Main Idea Topic Sentences in College Psychology Textbooks." *Journal of College Reading and Learning* 24 (1991): 46–54.

Location of Stated Main Ideas. Should college readers wish for all passages in all textbooks to begin with stated main ideas? Indeed, research indicates that when the main idea is stated at the beginning of the passage, the text tends to be comprehended more easily. In their research, however, Smith and Chase found only 33 percent of the stated main ideas to be positioned as the first sentence of the paragraph.

Main idea statements can be positioned at the beginning, in the middle, or at the end of a paragraph. Both the beginning and concluding sentences of a passage can be combined for a main idea statement. The following examples and diagrams demonstrate the different possible positions for stated main ideas within paragraphs.

1. **An introductory statement of the main idea is given at the beginning of the paragraph.**

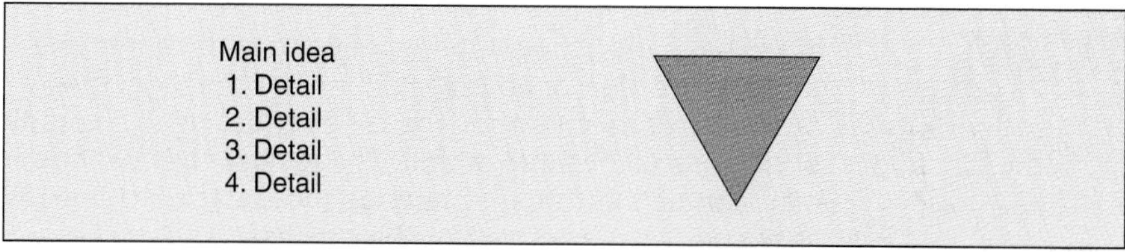

EXAMPLE

Under hypnosis, people may recall things that they are unable to remember spontaneously. Some police departments employ hypnotists to probe for information that crime victims do not realize they have. In 1976, twenty-six young children were kidnapped from a school bus near Chowchilla, California. The driver of the bus caught a quick glimpse of the license plate of the van in which he and the children were driven away. However, he remembered only the first two digits. Under hypnosis, he recalled the other numbers and the van was traced to its owners.

David Dempsey and Philip Zimbardo, *Psychology and You*

2. **A concluding statement of the main idea appears at the end of the paragraph.**

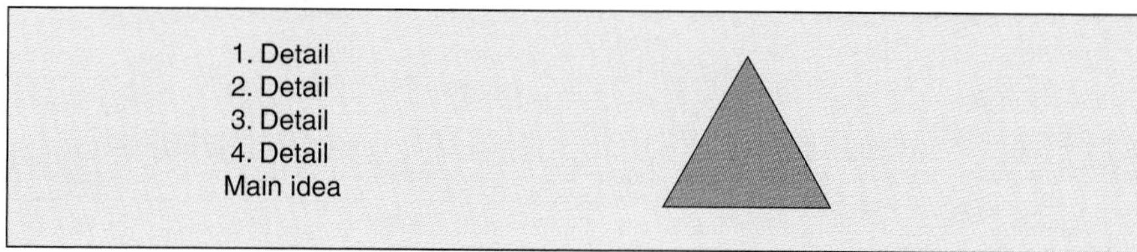

EXAMPLE

Research is not a once-and-for-all-times job. Even sophisticated companies often waste the value of their research. One of the most common errors is not providing a basis for comparisons. A company may research its market, find a need for a new advertising campaign, conduct the campaign, and then neglect to research the results. Another may simply feel the need for a new campaign, conduct it, and research the results. Neither is getting the full benefit of the research. When you fail to research either the results or your position *prior* to the campaign, you cannot know the effects of the campaign. *For good evaluation you must have both before and after data.*

Edward Fox and Edward Wheatley, *Modern Marketing*

3. Details are placed at the beginning to arouse interest, followed by a statement of the main idea in the middle of the paragraph.

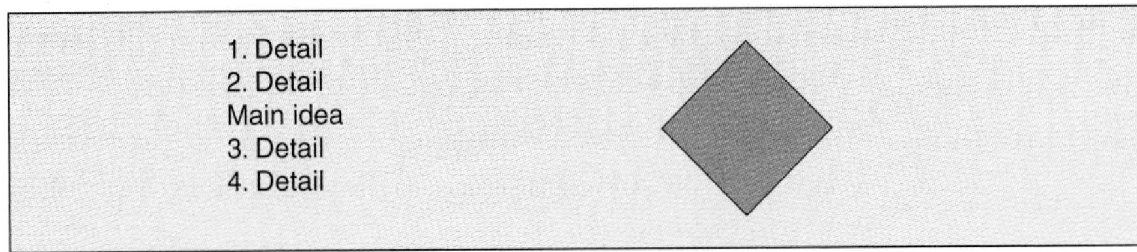

EXAMPLE

What happens when foreign materials do enter the body by breaking through the skin or epithelial linings of the digestive, circulatory, or respiratory systems and after the clotting process is complete? The next line of defense comes into action. Phagocytic cells (wandering and stationary) may engulf the foreign material and destroy it. But there is another and very complicated aspect of the process. *This is the production of specific antibody molecules. Antibodies may circulate in the blood as mentioned or they may be bound to cells;* less is known about these cell-bound antibodies. Antibodies inactivate or destroy the activity of antigens by combining with them. The reaction is a manifestation of the immune response, and the discipline primarily devoted to its study is immunology. Generally immunity is considered to be peculiar to the vertebrates, but recent evidence suggests that a form of immunity occurs in invertebrate animals also.

Willis H. Johnson et al., *Essentials of Biology*

4. Both the introductory and concluding sentences state the main idea.

EXAMPLE

A speech of tribute is designed to create in those who hear it a sense of appreciation for the traits or accomplishments of the person or group to whom tribute is paid. If you cause your audience to realize the essential worth or importance of the person or group, you will have succeeded. But you may go further than this. You may, by honoring a person, arouse deeper devotion to the cause he or she represents. Did this person give distinguished service to community or country? Then strive to enhance the audience's sense of patriotism and service. Was this individual a friend to young people? Then try to arouse the conviction that working to provide opportunities for the young deserves the audience's support. Create a desire in your listeners to emulate the person or persons honored. *Make them want to develop the same virtues, to demonstrate a like devotion.*

Douglas Ehninger et al., *Principles of Speech Communication*

Unfortunately, readers cannot always rely on a stated main idea being provided. For example, fiction writers rarely, if ever, use stated main ideas. The following is an example of a paragraph with an unstated main idea.

5. Details combine to make a point but the main idea is not directly stated.

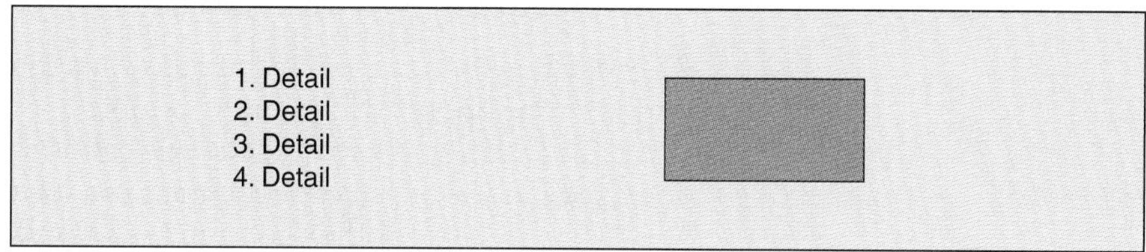

EXAMPLE

This creature's career could produce but one result, and it speedily followed. Boy after boy managed to get on the river. The minister's son became an engineer. The doctor's sons became "mud clerks"; the wholesale liquor dealer's son became a bar-keeper on a boat; four sons of the chief merchant, and two sons of the county judge, became pilots. Pilot was the grandest position of all. The pilot, even in those days of trivial wages, had a princely salary—from a hundred and fifty to two hundred and fifty dollars a month, and no board to pay. Two months of his wages would pay a preacher's salary for a year. Now some of us were left disconsolate. We could not get on the river—at least our parents would not let us.

Mark Twain, *Life on the Mississippi*

EXPLANATION Main idea: Young boys in the area have a strong desire to leave home and get a job on the prestigious Mississippi River.

Exercise 4.3

Identifying Stated Main Ideas

Read the following passages and apply the three-question system. Select the letter of the author's topic, identify major and minor details, and underline the main idea. For each passage in this exercise, the answer to the third question will be stated somewhere within the paragraph.

Passage A

The term vegetarian means different things to different people. Strict vegetarians, or *vegans,* avoid all foods of animal origins, including dairy products and eggs. Far more common are *lacto-vegetarians,* who eat dairy products but avoid flesh foods. Their diets can be low in cholesterol, but only if they consume skim milk and other low- or nonfat products. **Ovo-vegetarians** add eggs to their diet, while *lact-ovo-vegetarians* eat both dairy products and eggs. *Pesco-vegetarians* eat fish, dairy products, and eggs. Some people in the semivegetarian category prefer to call themselves "non-red meat eaters."

Rebecca J. Donatelle, *Health: The Basics,* 4th ed.

_________ 1. The topic of the passage is
   a. Vegetarians Without Dairy Products
   b. Becoming a Vegetarian
   c. Different Vegetarian Categories
   d. Health Issues for Vegetarians

2. Indicate whether each of the following details is major or minor in support of the author's topic.
   _________ a. Pesco-vegetarians eat fish.
   _________ b. Lacto-vegetarians can have low cholesterol if they consume skim milk.
   _________ c. Ovo-vegetarians add eggs to their diet.

3. Underline the sentence that best states the main idea of this passage.

Passage B

Building and equipping the pyramids focused and transformed Egypt's material and human resources. Artisans had to be trained, engineering and transportation problems solved, quarrying and stone-working techniques perfected, and laborers recruited. In the Old Kingdom, whose population has been estimated at perhaps 1.5 million, more than 70,000 workers at a time were employed in building the great temple-tombs. No smaller work force could have built such a massive structure as the Great Pyramid of Khufu.

Mark Kishlansky et al., *Civilization in the West,* 4th ed.

_________ 1. The topic of the passage is
   a. Training Laborers for the Pyramids
   b. Resources Needed for Building Pyramids
   c. Pyramid Building Problems
   d. The Pyramids

2. Indicate whether each of the following details is major or minor in support of the author's topic.
   _________ a. The Old Kingdom had an estimated population of 1.5 million.
   _________ b. More than 70,000 workers at a time were employed in building the great temple-tombs.
   _________ c. Artisans had to be trained.

3. Underline the sentence that best states the main idea of this passage.

Passage C

If you're upset or tired, you're at risk for an emotion-charged confrontation. If you ambush someone with an angry attack, don't expect her or him to be in a productive frame of mind. Instead, give yourself time to cool off before you try to resolve a conflict. In the case of the group project, you could call a meeting for later in the week. By that time, you could gain control of your feelings and think things through. Of course, sometimes issues need to be discussed on the spot; you may not have the luxury to wait. But whenever it's practical, make sure your conflict partner is ready to receive you and your message. Select a mutually acceptable time and place to discuss a conflict.

Steven A. Beebe, Susan J. Beebe, and Diana K. Ivy, *Communication* (adapted)

A______ 1. The topic of the passage is
   a. Planning for Conflict Resolution
   b. Confrontation
   c. Being Productive
   d. Solving Problems

2. Indicate whether each of the following details is major or minor in support of the author's topic.
   ______ a. Give yourself time to cool off before you try to resolve a conflict.
   ______ b. If you are upset, you are at risk for a confrontation.
   ______ c. Call a meeting a week later for a group project.

3. Underline the sentence that best states the main idea of this passage.

Passage D

In a Utah case, the defendant fell asleep in his car on the shoulder of the highway. Police stopped, smelled alcohol on his breath, and arrested him for driving while intoxicated. His conviction was reversed by the Utah Supreme Court, because the defendant was not in physical control of the vehicle at the time as required by the law. In freeing the defendant, the Supreme Court judged that the legal definition of sufficiency was not established in this case because the act observed by the police was not *sufficient* to confirm the existence of a guilty mind. In other words, the case against him failed because he was not violating the law at the time of the arrest and because it was also possible that he could have driven while sober, then pulled over, drank, and fell asleep.

Jay S. Albanese, *Criminal Justice, Brief Edition* (adapted)

D______ 1. The topic of the passage is
   a. Driving Drunk
   b. The Utah Supreme Court
   c. Sleeping Behind the Wheel
   d. Establishing Sufficiency for Drunken Driving

2. Indicate whether each of the following details is major or minor in support of the author's topic.
   ______ a. Police arrested the defendant for driving while intoxicated.
   ______ b. The defendant was not violating a law at the time of the arrest.
   ______ c. The case was tried in Utah.
3. Underline the sentence that best states the main idea of this passage.

Exercise 4.4

Writing Stated Main Ideas

Read the following passages and use the three-question system to determine the author's main idea. For each passage in this exercise, the answer to the third question will be stated somewhere within the paragraph.

Passage A

Time is especially linked to status considerations, and the importance of being on time varies with the status of the individual you are visiting. If the person is extremely important, you had better be there on time or even early just in case he or she is able to see you before schedule. As the person's status decreases, so does the importance of being on time. Junior executives, for example, must be on time for conferences with senior executives, but it is even more important to be on time for the company president or the CEO. Senior executives, however, may be late for conferences with their juniors but not for conferences with the president. Within any hierarchy, similar unwritten rules are followed with respect to time. This is not to imply that these "rules" are just or fair; they simply exist.

Joseph DeVito, *Interpersonal Communication*, 6th ed.

1. Who or what is this about? ______

2. What are the major details? ______

______

______

3. What is the main idea the author is trying to convey about the topic?

______

______

Underline the main idea.

Passage B

Courting behavior in birds is also believed to be instinctive. In one experiment Daniel Lehrman of Rutgers University found that when a male blond ring dove was isolated from females, it soon began to bow and coo to a stuffed model of a female—a model that it had previously ignored. When the model was replaced by a rolled-up cloth, he began to court the cloth; and when this was removed the sex-crazed dove directed his attention to a corner of the cage, where it could at least focus its gaze. It seems that the threshold for release of the behavior pattern became increasingly lower as time went by without the sight of a live female dove. It is almost as though some specific "energy" for performing courting behavior were building up within the male ring dove.

Robert Wallace, *Biology: The World of Life*

1. Who or what is this about? ______________________________
2. What are the major details? ______________________________

____

____

3. What is the main idea the author is trying to convey about the topic?

____

Underline the main idea.

Passage C

To retrieve a fact from a library of stored information, you need a way to gain access to it. In recognition tests, retrieval cues (such as photographs) provide reminders of information (classmates' names) we could not otherwise recall. Retrieval cues also guide us where to look. If you want to know what the pyramid on the back of a dollar bill signifies, you might look in *Collier's Encyclopedia* under "dollar," "currency," or "money." But your efforts would be futile. To get the information you want, you would have to look under "Great Seal of the United States." Like information stored in encyclopedias, memories are inaccessible unless we have cues for retrieving them. The more and better learned the retrieval cues, the more accessible the memory.

David G. Myers. *Psychology*

1. Who or what is this about? ______________________________
2. What are the major details? ______________________________

____

3. What is the main idea the author is trying to convey about the topic?

____

____

Underline the main idea.

Passage D

Most of the Plains Indians believed that land could be utilized, but never owned. The idea of owning land was as absurd as owning the air people breathed. To some, the sacredness of the land made farming against their religion. Chief Somohalla of the Wanapaun explained why his people refused to farm. "You ask me to plow the ground! Shall I take a knife and tear my mother's bosom? . . . You ask me to cut grass and make hay and sell it, and be rich like white men! But how dare I cut off my mother's hair?"

James Kirby Martin et al., *America and Its Peoples*, 4th ed.

1. Who or what is this about? ____________________________________

____

2. What are the major details? ____________________________________

____

3. What is the main idea the author is trying to convey about the topic?

____

Underline the main idea.

Passage E

A crab lives at the bottom of its ocean of water and looks upward at jellyfish drifting above it. Similarly, we live at the bottom of our ocean of air and look upward at balloons drifting above us. A balloon is suspended in air and a jellyfish is suspended in water for the same reason: each is buoyed upward by a displaced weight of fluid equal to its own weight. In one case the displaced fluid is air, and in the other case it is water. In water, immersed objects are buoyed upward because the pressure acting up against the bottom of the object exceeds the pressure acting down against the top. Likewise, air pressure acting up against an object immersed in air is greater than the pressure above pushing down. The buoyancy in both cases is numerically equal to the weight of fluid displaced. **Archimedes' principle** holds for air just as it does for water: An object surrounded by air is buoyed up by a force equal to the weight of the air displaced.

Paul Hewitt, *Conceptual Physics*, 8th ed.

1. Who or what is this about? ____________________________________
2. What are the major details? ____________________________________

____

3. What is the main idea the author is trying to convey about the topic?

____

Underline the main idea.

Examples of Unstated Main Idea

EXAMPLE

Michael Harner proposes an ecological interpretation of Aztec sacrifice and cannibalism. He holds that human sacrifice was a response to certain diet deficiencies in the population. In the Aztec environment, wild game was getting scarce, and the population was growing. Although the maize-beans combination of food that was the basis of the diet was usually adequate, these crops were subject to seasonal failure. Famine was frequent in the absence of edible domesticated animals. To meet essential protein requirements, cannibalism was the only solution. Although only the upper classes were allowed to consume human flesh, a commoner who distinguished himself in a war could also have the privilege of giving a cannibalistic feast. Thus, although it was the upper strata who benefited most from ritual cannibalism, members of the commoner class could also benefit. Furthermore, as Harner explains, the social mobility and cannibalistic privileges available to the commoners through warfare provided a strong motivation for the "aggressive war machine" that was such a prominent feature of the Aztec state.

Serena Nanda, *Cultural Anthropology*, 4th ed.

1. Who or what is this about? ______________________
2. What are the major details? ______________________
3. What is the main idea the author is trying to convey about the topic?

____

EXPLANATION The passage is about Aztec sacrifice and cannibalism. The major details are: *diet deficiencies occurred, animals were not available,* and *members of the upper class and commoners who were war heroes could eat human flesh.* The main idea is that *Aztec sacrifice and cannibalism met protein needs of the diet and motivated warriors to achieve.*

Exercise 4.5

Identifying Unstated Main Ideas

Read the following passages and apply the three-question system. Select the letter of the author's topic, identify major and minor details, and choose the letter of the sentence that best states the main idea.

Passage A

Until recently, the U.S. census, which is taken every ten years, offered only the following categories: Caucasian, Negro, Indian, and Oriental. After years of complaints from the public the list was expanded. In the year of 2000 census, everyone had to declare that they were or were not "Spanish/Hispanic/Latino." They had to mark "one or more races" that they "considered themselves to be." Finally, if these didn't do it, you could check a box called "Some Other Race" and then write whatever you wanted. For example, Tiger Woods, one of the top golfers of all time, calls himself Cablinasian. Woods invented this term as a boy to try to explain to himself just who he was—a combination of Caucasian, Black, Indian, and Asian. Woods wants to embrace both sides of his family.

James M. Henslin, *Sociology*, 5th ed. (adapted)

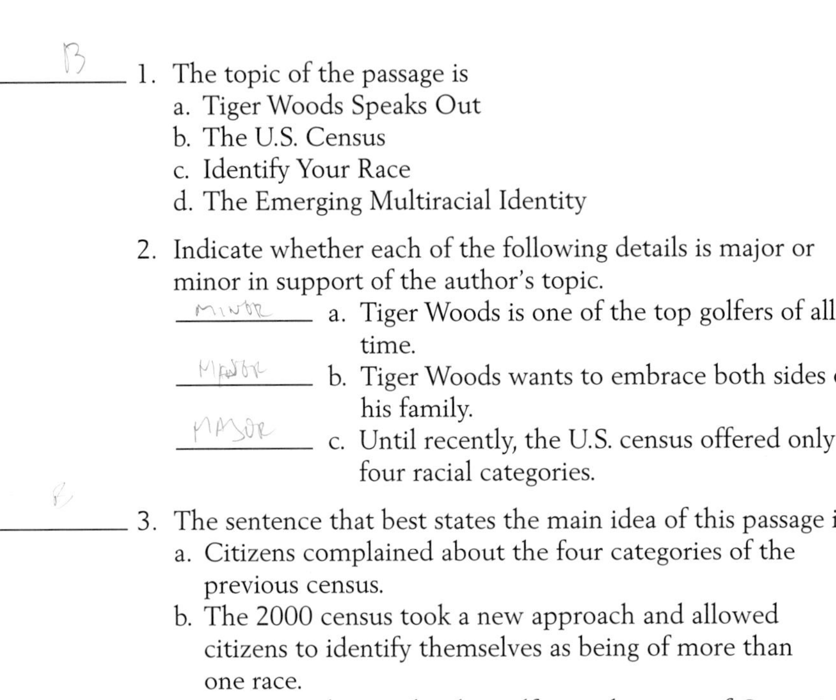

_______ 1. The topic of the passage is
   a. Tiger Woods Speaks Out
   b. The U.S. Census
   c. Identify Your Race
   d. The Emerging Multiracial Identity

2. Indicate whether each of the following details is major or minor in support of the author's topic.
   _______ a. Tiger Woods is one of the top golfers of all time.
   _______ b. Tiger Woods wants to embrace both sides of his family.
   _______ c. Until recently, the U.S. census offered only four racial categories.

_______ 3. The sentence that best states the main idea of this passage is
   a. Citizens complained about the four categories of the previous census.
   b. The 2000 census took a new approach and allowed citizens to identify themselves as being of more than one race.
   c. Tiger Woods considers himself a combination of Caucasian, Black, Indian, and Asian.
   d. Information from the 2000 census will be more useful than data gathered from the previous census.

Passage B

The rate of incarceration in prison increased from 27 per 100,000 women in 1985 to 57 per 100,000 in 1998. Men still outnumber women in the inmate population by a factor of about 14 to 1, but the gap is narrowing—from 17 to 1 a decade ago. Women constituted only 4 percent of the total prison and jail population in the United States in 1980 but more than 6 percent in 1998.

Jay S. Albanese, *Criminal Justice*

_______ 1. The topic of the passage is
   a. Men Versus Women in Jail
   b. Incarceration in America
   c. The Increasing Number of Women in Jail
   d. Overcrowded Prisons

2. Indicate whether each of the following details is major or minor in support of the author's topic.
   ________ a. The rate of incarceration of women in prison in 1985 was 27 per 100,000.
   ________ b. The rate of incarceration of women in prison in 1998 was 57 per 100,000.
   ________ c. A decade ago men outnumbered women 17 to 1.

__C__ 3. Which sentence best states the main idea of this passage?
   a. Men continue to outnumber women in the prison and jail population.
   b. The rate of incarceration is increasing for both men and women.
   c. In the last decade the rate of women incarcerated has doubled.
   d. The role of women in society has changed in the last decade.

Passage C

Each year in the United States approximately 50,000 miscarriages are attributed to smoking during pregnancy. On average, babies born to mothers who smoke weigh less than those born to nonsmokers, and low birth weight is correlated with many developmental problems. Pregnant women who stop smoking in the first three or four months of their pregnancies give birth to higher-birth-weight babies than do women who smoke throughout their pregnancies. Infant mortality rates are also higher among babies born to smokers.

Rebecca J. Donatelle, *Health: The Basics*, 4th ed.

________ 1. The topic of the passage is
   a. Infant Mortality
   b. Smoking
   c. Smoking and Pregnancy
   d. Smoking and Miscarriages

2. Indicate whether each of the following details is major or minor in support of the author's topic.
   ________ a. Low birth weight is correlated with many developmental problems.
   ________ b. Infant mortality rates are also higher among babies born to smokers.
   ________ c. Babies born to mothers who smoke weigh less than those born to nonsmokers.

__________ 3. Which sentence best states the main idea of this passage?
a. Smoking during pregnancy increases the chance of miscarriages, low-weight babies, and infant mortality.
b. Smoking during pregnancy causes many miscarriages.
c. Ceasing smoking during pregnancy can increase infant birth weight.
d. Smoking is a major contributor to infant mortality.

Passage D

The young reporter with the slow Missouri drawl stamped the cold of the high Nevada desert out of his feet as he entered the offices of the Virginia City *Territorial Enterprise*. It was early in 1863. The newspaper's editor, Joseph T. Goodman, looked puzzled at seeing his Carson City correspondent in the home office, but Samuel Clemens came right to the point: "Joe, I want to sign my articles. I want to be identified to a wider audience." The editor, already impressed with his colleague of six months, readily agreed. Then came the question of a pen name, since few aspiring writers of the time used their legal names. Clemens had something in mind: "I want to sign them 'Mark Twain,'" he declared. "It is an old river term, a leadsman's call, signifying two fathoms—twelve feet. It has a richness about it; it was always a pleasant sound for a pilot to hear on a dark night; it meant safe water."

Roderick Nash and Gregory Graves, *From These Beginnings*, 6th ed., vol. 2.

__________ 1. The topic of the passage is
a. Becoming a Reporter
b. How Mark Twain Got His Name
c. Safe Water on the River
d. Working for the Virginia City *Territorial Enterprise*

2. Indicate whether each of the following details is major or minor in support of the author's topic.
__________ a. Clemens had worked for the newspaper for six months.
__________ b. The newspaper's editor was Joseph T. Goodman.
__________ c. Clemens wanted to sign his articles in order to be known to a wider audience.

__________ 3. Which sentence best states the main idea of this passage?
a. Samuel Clemens worked as a young reporter for the Virginia City *Territorial Enterprise.*
b. The newspaper's editor, Joseph T. Goodman, was impressed with the young reporter, Samuel Clemens.
c. "Mark Twain" is a river term that means two fathoms—twelve feet.
d. The young reporter, Samuel Clemens, decided to take the pen name "Mark Twain."

Exercise 4.6

Writing Unstated Main Ideas

Read the following passages and use the three-question system to determine the author's main idea. Pull the ideas together to state the main ideas in your own words.

Passage A

According to the U.S. Department of the Census, the demographic shift in the population will be "profound" in the next 50 years. By 2050, Hispanics will make up 24.5 percent of the population, up from 10.2 percent in 1996. The annual growth rate of the Hispanic population is expected to be 2 percent through the year 2030. To put this growth in perspective, consider the fact that even at the height of the baby boom explosion in the late 1940s and early 1950s, the country's annual population increase never reached 2 percent. Demographers, it seems, are alerting us to the enormous importance of such change. Says Gregory Spencer, Director of the Census Bureau's Population Projections Branch, "The world is not going to be the same in thirty years as it is now."

Ronald Ebert and Ricky Griffin, *Business Essentials*, 2nd ed.

1. Who or what is this about? HISPANIC POPULATION GROWTH
2. What are the major details? ______________________________

____

3. What is the main idea the author is trying to convey about the topic?
GROWING POPULATION OF HISPANICS

____

Passage B

Prior to the time of Jan Baptiste van Helmont, a Belgian physician of the 17th century, it was commonly accepted that plants derived their matter from materials in the soil. (Probably, many people who haven't studied photosynthesis would go along with this today.) We aren't sure why, but van Helmont decided to test the idea. He carefully stripped a young willow sapling of all surrounding soil, weighed it, and planted it in a tub of soil that had also been carefully weighed. After five years of diligent watering (with rain water), van Helmont removed the greatly enlarged willow and again stripped away the soil and weighed it. The young tree had gained 164 pounds. Upon weighing the soil, van Helmont was amazed to learn that it had lost only 2 ounces.

Robert Wallace et al., *Biology: The Science of Life*, 3rd ed.

1. Who or what is this about? ______________________________
2. What are the major details? ______________________________

____

3. What is the main idea the author is trying to convey about the topic?

____

____

Passage C

The Aswan High Dam, built in Egypt with Russian support, was supposed to provide hydroelectric power and to increase Egypt's food supply by controlling the unpredictable Nile River. The project meant that great art treasures were flooded as submerged land was drained for cultivation. However, only one-tenth of an acre of land was made available for each person added to Egypt's population during the period of construction. One result of the dam was that the Nile no longer flooded the delta farmlands annually. These annual floods served to restore the farmland fertility with deposited silt. This no longer the case, the quality of the farmland decreased. The dam also cut off the nutrients that had been washed to the Mediterranean Sea as a result of the annual floodings. Because of this, or the change in the salinity of the sea that the dam produced, the sardine catch dropped from 18,000 tons per year to 500 tons per year. The stable lake created by the dam allowed aquatic snails to flourish. The snails serve as an intermediate host to a blood fluke that bores into humans causing the dreaded disease, schistosomiasis. The construction of the dam had important political implications at the time.

Robert Wallace, *Biology: The World of Life*

1. Who or what is this about? ______________________________

2. What are the major details? ______________________________

____

____

3. What is the main idea the author is trying to convey about the topic?

____

____

Passage D

If using sunscreen, apply it at least 30–45 minutes before exposure, then reapply it periodically, especially after you swim or sweat. It is especially important to protect children. One or more severe sunburns with blisters in childhood or adolescence can double the risk of the skin cancer melanoma later in life. Additional protection can be provided by a wide-brimmed hat to protect your head and face, and opaque clothing to cover those body areas you wish to protect. Any fabric or material you can see through, including some beach umbrellas, does not give full protection. You should stay out of the sun between 10 A.M. and 2 P.M. when the rays are strongest.

Curtis O. Byer and Louis W. Shainberg, *Living Well: Health in Your Hands,* 2nd ed.

1. Who or what is this about? ______________________________

2. What are the major details? ______________________________

____

____

3. What is the main idea the author is trying to convey about the topic?

____

____

Passage E

In 1979 when University of Minnesota psychologist Thomas Bouchard read a newspaper account of the reuniting of 39-year-old twins who had been separated from infancy, he seized the opportunity and flew them to Minneapolis for extensive tests. Bouchard was looking for differences. What "the Jim twins," Jim Lewis and Jim Springer, presented were amazing similarities. Both had married women named Linda, divorced, and married women named Betty. One had a son James Alan, the other a son James Allan. Both had dogs named Toy, chainsmoked Salems, served as sheriff's deputies, drove Chevrolets, chewed their fingernails to the nub, enjoyed stock car racing, had basement workshops, and had built circular white benches around trees in their yards. They also had similar medical histories: Both gained 10 pounds at about the same time and then lost it; both suffered what they mistakenly believed were heart attacks, and both began having late-afternoon headaches at age 18.

Identical twins Oskar Stohr and Jack Yufe presented equally striking similarities. One was raised by his grandmother in Germany as a Catholic and a Nazi, while the other was raised by his father in the Caribbean as a Jew. Nevertheless, they share traits and habits galore. They like spicy foods and sweet liqueurs, have a habit of falling asleep in front of the television, flush the toilet before using it, store rubber bands on their wrists, and dip buttered toast in their coffee. Stohr is domineering toward women and yells at his wife, as did Yufe before he was separated.

David G. Myers, *Psychology*

1. Who or what is this about? ______________________________

2. What are the major details? ______________________________

____

____

3. What is the main idea the author is trying to convey about the topic?

____

____

Interpreting Longer Selections

Understanding the main idea of longer selections requires a little more thinking than finding the main idea of a single paragraph. Since longer selections such as articles or chapters involve more material, the challenge of tying the ideas together can be confusing and complicated. Each paragraph of a longer selection usually represents a new aspect of a supporting detail. In addition, several major ideas may contribute to developing the overall main idea. The reader, therefore, must fit the many pieces together under one central theme.

For longer selections, the reader needs to add an extra step between the two questions, "What is the topic?" and "What is the main idea the author is trying to convey?" The step involves organizing the material into manageable subunits and then relating those to the whole. Two additional questions to ask are, "Under what subsections can these ideas be grouped?" and "How do these subsections contribute to the whole?"

Use the suggestions in the box below to determine the main idea of longer selections. The techniques are similar to those used in previewing and skimming, two skills that also focus on the overall central theme.

Reader's Tip

Getting the Main Idea of Longer Selections

* **Think about the significance of the title.** What does the title suggest about the topic?
* **Read the first paragraph or two for a statement of the topic or thesis.** What does the selection seem to be about?
* **Read the subheadings and, if necessary, glance at the first sentences of some of the paragraphs.** Based on these clues, what does the article seem to be about?
* **Look for clues that indicate how the material is organized.** Is the purpose to define a term, to prove an opinion or explain a concept, to describe a situation, or to persuade the reader toward a particular point of view?

  Is the material organized into a list of examples, a time order or sequence, a comparison or contrast, or a cause-and-effect relationship?
* **As you read, organize the paragraphs into subsections.** Give each subsection a title. These become your significant supporting details.
* **Determine how the overall organization and subsections relate to the whole.** Answer the question, "What is the main idea the author is trying to convey in this selection?"

Summary Writing: A Main Idea Skill

A **summary** is a series of brief, concise statements in your own words of the main idea and the significant supporting details. The first sentence should state the main idea or thesis, and subsequent sentences should incorporate the significant details. Minor details and material irrelevant to the learner's purpose should be omitted. The summary should be in paragraph form and should always be shorter than the material being summarized.

Why Summarize?

Summaries can be used for textbook study and are particularly useful in anticipating answers for essay exam questions. For writing research papers, summarizing is an essential skill. Using your own words to put the essence of an article into concise sentences requires a thorough understanding of the material. As one researcher noted, "Since so much summarizing is necessary for writing papers, students should have the skill before starting work on research papers. How much plagiarism is the result of inadequate summarizing skills?"[3]

Writing a research paper may mean that you will have to read as many as thirty articles and four books over a period of a month or two. After each reading, you want to take enough notes so you can write your paper without returning to the library for another look at the original reference. Since you will be using so many different references, the notetaking should be done carefully. The complete sentences of a summary are more explicit than underscored text or the highlighted topic-phrase format of an outline. Your summary should demonstrate a synthesis of the information.

EXAMPLE Read the following excerpt on political authority as if you were researching for a term paper and writing a summary on a note card. Mark key terms that you would include in your summary. Before reading the example provided, anticipate what you would include in your own summary.

Types of Authority

Where is the source of the state's authority? Weber described three possible sources of the right to command, which produce what he called traditional authority, charismatic authority, and legal authority.

Traditional Authority

In many societies, people have obeyed those in power because, in essence, "that is the way it has always been." Thus, kings, queens, feudal lords, and tribal chiefs did not need written rules in order to govern. Their authority was based on tradition, on long-standing customs, and it was handed down from parent to child, maintaining traditional authority from one generation to the next. Often, traditional authority has been

[3]K. Taylor, "Can College Students Summarize?" *Journal of Reading* 26 (March 1983): 540–44.

Reader's Tip

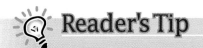

How to Summarize

* **Keep in mind the purpose of your summary.** Your projected needs will determine which details are important and how many should be included.
* **Decide on the main idea the author is trying to convey.** Make this main idea the first sentence in your summary.
* **Decide on the major ideas and details that support the author's point.** Mark the key terms and phrases. Include in your summary the major ideas and as many of the significant supporting details as your purpose demands.
* **Do not include irrelevant or repeated information in your summary.**
* **Use appropriate transitional words and phrases to show relationships between points.**
* **Use paragraph form.**
* **Do not add your personal opinion as part of the summary.**

justified by religious tradition. For example, medieval European kings were said to rule by divine right, and Japanese emperors were considered the embodiment of heaven.

Charismatic Authority

People may also submit to authority, not because of tradition, but because of the extraordinary attraction of an individual. Napoleon, Gandhi, Mao Tse-tung, and Ayatollah Khomeini all illustrate authority that derives its legitimacy from *charisma*—an exceptional personal quality popularly attributed to certain individuals. Their followers perceive charismatic leaders as persons of destiny endowed with remarkable vision, the power of a savior, or God's grace. Charismatic authority is inherently unstable. It cannot be transferred to another person.

Legal Authority

The political systems of industrial states are based largely on a third type of authority: legal authority, which Weber also called *rational authority.* These systems derive legitimacy from a set of explicit rules and procedures that spell out the ruler's rights and duties. Typically, the rules and procedures are put in writing. The people grant their obedience to "the law." It specifies procedures by which certain individuals hold offices of power, such as governor or president or prime minister. But the authority is vested in those offices, not in the individuals who temporarily hold the offices. Thus, a political system based on legal authority is often called a "government of laws, not of men." Individuals come and go, as American presidents have come and gone, but the office, "the presidency," remains. If individual officeholders overstep their authority, they may be forced out of office and replaced.

Alex Thio, *Sociology*, 3rd ed.

1. To begin your summary, what is the main point? ______________________

____

2. What are the major areas of support? ______________________

____

3. Should you include an example for each area? ______________________

____

EXPLANATION Begin your summary with the main point, which is that Weber describes the three sources of authority as traditional, charismatic, and legal. Then define each of the three sources but do not include examples.

Read the summary below and notice how closely it fits your own ideas.

Political Authority

Weber describes the three command sources as traditional, charismatic, and legal authority. Traditional authority is not written but based on long-standing custom such as the power of queens or tribal chiefs. Charismatic authority is based on the charm and vision of a leader such as Gandhi. Legal authority, such as that of American presidents, comes from written laws and is vested in the office rather than the person.

Exercise 4.7 Summarizing

Read the following passages and mark the key terms and phrases. Begin your summary with a statement of the main point and add the appropriate supporting details. Use your markings to help you write the summary. Be brief but include the essential elements.

Passage A: Prosecutors

The task of prosecutors is to represent the community in bringing charges against an accused person. The job of the prosecutor is constrained by political factors, caseloads, and relationships with other actors in the adjudication process.

First, most prosecutors are elected (although some are appointed by the governor), so it is in their interests to make "popular" prosecution decisions—and in some cases these may run counter to the ideals of justice. For example, prosecution "to the full extent of the law" of a college student caught possessing a small amount of marijuana may be unwarranted, but failure to prosecute may be used by political opponents as evidence that the prosecutor is "soft on crime."

A second constraint is caseload pressures, which often force prosecutors to make decisions based on expediency rather than justice. A prosecutor in a jurisdiction where many serious crimes occur may have to choose which to prosecute to the full extent of the law and which ones to plea-bargain.

Third, prosecutors must maintain good relationships with the other participants in the adjudication process: police, judges, juries, defense attorneys, victims, and witnesses. Cases typically are brought to prosecutors by the police, and police officers usually serve as witnesses.

Jay S. Albanese, *Criminal Justice*

Use your marked text to write a summary.

Passage B: Suicide Among College Students

Compared to nonstudents of the same age, the suicide rate among college students is somewhat higher. Why is this so? For one thing, among the younger college students who commit suicide (ages 18–22), a common thread is the inability to separate themselves from their family and to solve problems on their own. College presents many of these younger students with the challenge of having to be independent in many ways while remaining dependent on family in other ways, such as financially and emotionally.

Several other characteristics of the college experience may relate to suicide. A great emphasis is put on attaining high grades and the significance of grades may be blown out of proportion. A student may come to perceive grades as a measurement of his or her total worth as a person, rather than just one of many ways a person can be evaluated. If a student is unable to achieve expected grades, there may be a total loss of self-esteem and loss of hope for any success in life.

In the college setting, where self-esteem can be tenuous, the end of a relationship can also be devastating. A student who has recently lost a close friend or lover can become so deeply depressed that suicide becomes an attractive alternative. The problem can be compounded when depression interferes with coursework and grades slip.

Curtis O. Byer and Louis W. Shainberg, *Living Well: Health in Your Hands*, 2nd ed.

Use your marked text to write a summary.

Passage C: Alcohol Advertising and College Students

The alcohol industry knows a receptive market when it sees it. Each year, college students spend a reported $5.5 billion ($446 per student) on alcohol, consuming some 4 billion cans' worth of alcohol and accounting for 10 percent of total beer sales. For brewers, student drinking spells not just current sales, but future profits as well, because most people develop loyalty to a specific beer between the ages of 18 and 24. To secure this lucrative market, brewers and other alcohol producers spend millions of dollars each year promoting their products to college students. One conservative estimate places annual expenditures for college marketing between $15 million and $20 million. According to one survey, alcohol advertising of local specials in many college newspapers has increased by more than half over the past decade, stymieing college and community efforts to reduce binge drinking.

Rebecca J. Donatelle, *Health: The Basics*, 4th ed.

Use your marked text to write a summary.

Summary Points

- **What is a topic?**

  The topic of a passage is the general term that forms an umbrella for the specific ideas presented.

- **What is a main idea?**

  The main idea is the point the author is trying to convey about the topic. In some passages the main idea is stated in a sentence, and in others it is unstated.

- **What are significant details?**

  Details support, develop, and explain the main idea. Some details are of major significance and others are only of minor significance in supporting the main idea.

- **What is a summary?**

  Summaries condense material and include the main ideas and major details.

Selection 1 PSYCHOLOGY

CONTEMPORARY FOCUS

Humans owe a debt to animals whose lives are manipulated and sacrificed for the sake of knowledge. Is there a line that marks the point when animal research is acceptable and when it is unethical?

BRAIN RESEARCH ON MONKEYS

Gail Schontzler

From *Bozeman Daily Chronicle* (MT), December 3, 2000

Tall and bearded, Charlie Gray looks like a rugged outdoorsman, not like what you might expect of a research scientist, and not like a man afraid to be photographed.

Gray, 42, is doing research at Montana State University, trying to unlock the mysteries of the brain. He is excited about his work, and proud that his knowledge has already helped provide a cure for patients suffering the uncontrollable tremors of Parkinson's disease.

"I'm incredibly fascinated by the brain," Gray said. "It's an incredibly mysterious and fascinating thing to learn about. It's probably the greatest mystery there is. Everything we are is what goes on inside our head."

Yet Gray advances scientific knowledge by drilling holes in the skulls of rhesus monkeys and cats and poking electrodes into their brains. When the research is completed after one to five years, the animals must be euthanized. It's a use of animals that could incense animal-rights activists. That is why he refuses to be photographed.

Collaborative Activity

Collaborate on responses to the following questions:

- What are the positive and negative arguments for a university conducting research on animals?
- How do animal-rights activists apply pressure for animal protection?
- Why are students invited to participate in research projects in psychology and education?

Skill Development—Stage 1: Preview

Preview the next selection to predict the purpose and your learning plan.

The author's main purpose is to describe the infant-mother relationship.
Agree ☐ Disagree ☐

After reading this selection, I will need to know the meaning of contact comfort. Agree ☐ Disagree ☐

Activate Schema

Do parents who were abused as children later abuse their own children?

As a child, what did you use as a "security blanket"?

Learning Strategy

Explain the psychological needs of an infant monkey and the effect that deprivation of those needs can have on the whole pattern of psychological development.

Word Knowledge

What do you know about these words?

surrogate	functional	anatomy	tentatively	novel
desensitized	ingenious	deprived	persisted	deficient

Your instructor may give a true-false vocabulary review before or after reading.

Stage 2: Integrate Knowledge While Reading

Predict Picture Relate Monitor Correct

MONKEY LOVE

From James V. McConnell, *Understanding Human Behavior*

The scientist who has conducted the best long-term laboratory experiments on love is surely Harry Harlow, a psychologist at the University of Wisconsin. Professor Harlow did not set out to study love—it happened by accident. Like many other psychologists, he was at first primarily interested in how organisms learn. Rather than working with rats, Harlow chose to work with monkeys.

Since he needed a place to house and raise the monkeys, he built the Primate Laboratory at Wisconsin. Then he began to study the effects of brain lesions on monkey learning. But he soon found that young animals reacted somewhat differently to brain damage than did older monkeys, so he and his wife Margaret devised a breeding program and tried various ways of raising monkeys in the laboratory. They rapidly discovered that monkey infants raised by their mothers often caught diseases from their parents, so the Harlows began taking the infants away from their mothers at birth and tried raising them by hand. The baby monkeys had been given cheesecloth diapers to serve as baby blankets. Almost from the start, it became obvious to the Harlows that their little animals developed such strong attachments to the blankets that, in the Harlows' own terms, it was often hard to tell where the diaper ended and the baby began. Not only this, but if the Harlows removed the "security" blanket in order to clean it, the infant monkey often became greatly disturbed—just as if its own mother had deserted it.

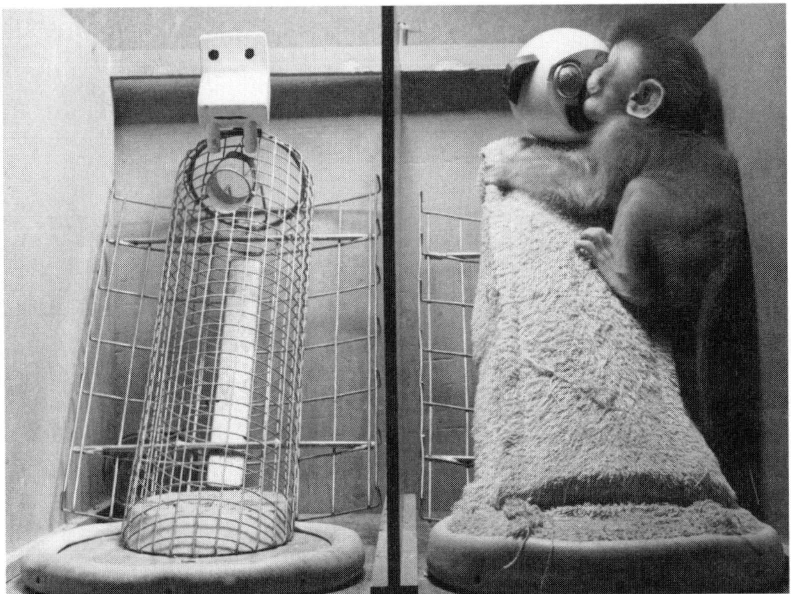

Although the baby monkey receives milk from Harlow's wire mother, it spends most of its time with the terry-cloth version and clings to the terry-cloth mother when frightened.
Harlow Primate Library, University of Wisconsin

The Surrogate Mother

What the baby monkeys obviously needed was an artificial or *surrogate* mother—something they could cling to as tightly as they typically clung to their own mother's chest. The Harlows sketched out many different designs, but none really appealed to them. Then, in 1957, while enjoying a champagne flight high over the city of Detroit, Harry Harlow glanced out of the airplane window and "saw" an image of an artificial monkey mother. It was a hollow wire cylinder, wrapped with a terry-cloth bath towel, with a silly wooden head at the top. The tiny monkey could cling to this "model mother" as closely as to its real mother's body hair. This surrogate mother could be provided with a functional breast simply by placing a milk bottle so that the nipple stuck through the cloth at an appropriate place on the surrogate's anatomy. The cloth mother could be heated or cooled; it could be rocked mechanically or made to stand still; and, most important, it could be removed at will.

While still sipping his champagne, Harlow mentally outlined much of the research that kept him, his wife, and their associates occupied for many years to come. And without realizing it, Harlow had shifted from studying monkey learning to monkey love.

Infant-Mother Love

The chimpanzee or monkey infant is much more developed at birth than the human infant, and apes develop or mature much faster than we do. Almost from the moment it is born, the monkey infant can move around and hold tightly to its mother. During the first few days of its life the infant will approach and cling to almost any large, warm, and soft object in its environment, particularly if that object also gives it milk. After a week or so, however, the monkey infant begins to avoid newcomers and focuses its attentions on "mother"—real or surrogate.

During the first two weeks of its life warmth is perhaps the most important psychological thing that a monkey mother has to give to its baby. The Harlows discovered this fact by offering infant monkeys a choice of two types of mother-substitutes—one wrapped in terry cloth and one that was made of bare wire. If the two artificial mothers were both the same temperature, the little monkeys always preferred the cloth mother. However, if the wire model was heated, while the cloth model was cool, for the first two weeks after birth the baby primates picked the warm wire mother-substitutes as their favorites. Thereafter they switched and spent most of their time on the more comfortable cloth mother.

Why is cloth preferable to bare wire? Something that the Harlows called *contact comfort* seems to be the answer, and a most powerful influence it is. Infant monkeys (and chimps too) spend much of their time rubbing against their mothers' skins, putting themselves in as close contact with the parent as they can. Whenever the young animal is frightened, disturbed, or annoyed, it typically rushes to its mother and rubs itself against her body. Wire doesn't "rub" as well as does soft cloth. Prolonged "contact comfort" with a surrogate cloth mother appears to instill confidence in baby monkeys and is much more rewarding to them than is either warmth or milk. Infant monkeys also prefer a "rocking" surrogate to one that is stationary.

According to the Harlows, the basic quality of an infant's love for its mother is *trust*. If the infant is put into an unfamiliar playroom without its mother, the infant ignores the toys no matter how interesting they might be. It *screeches* in terror and curls up into a furry little ball. If its cloth mother is now introduced into the playroom, the infant rushes to the surrogate and clings to it for dear life. After a few minutes of contact comfort, it apparently begins to feel more secure. It then climbs down from the mother-substitute and begins tentatively to explore the toys, but often rushes back for a deep embrace as if to reassure itself that its mother is still there and that all is well. Bit by bit its fears of the novel environment are "desensitized" and it spends more and more time playing with the toys and less and less time clinging to its "mother."

Good Mothers and Bad

The Harlows found that, once a baby monkey has come to accept its mother (real or surrogate), the mother can do almost no wrong. In one of their studies, the Harlows tried to create "monster mothers" whose behavior would be so abnormal that the infants would desert the mothers. Their purpose was to determine whether maternal rejection might cause abnormal behavior patterns in the infant monkeys similar to those responses found in human babies whose mothers ignore or punish their children severely. The problem was—how can you get a terry-cloth mother to reject or punish its baby? Their solutions were ingenious—but most of them failed in their main purpose. Four types of "monster mothers" were tried, but none of them was apparently "evil" enough to impart fear or loathing to the infant monkeys. One such "monster" occasionally blasted its babies with compressed air; a second shook so violently that the baby often fell off; a third contained a catapult that frequently flung the infant away from it. The most evil-appearing of all had a set of metal spikes buried beneath the terry cloth; from time to time the spikes would poke through the cloth making it impossible for the infant to cling to the surrogate.

The baby monkeys brought up on the "monster mothers" did show a brief period of emotional disturbance when the "wicked" temperament of the surrogates first showed up. The infants would cry for a time when displaced from their mothers, but as soon as the surrogates returned to normal, the infant would return to the surrogate and continue clinging, as if all were forgiven. As the Harlows tell the story, the only prolonged distress created by the experiment seemed to be that felt by the experimenters!

There was, however, one type of surrogate that uniformly "turned off" the infant monkeys. S. J. Suomi, working with the Harlows, built a terry-cloth mother with ice water in its veins. Newborn monkeys would attach themselves to this "cool momma" for a brief period of time, but then retreated to a corner of the cage and rejected her forever.

From their many brilliant studies, the Harlows conclude that the love of an infant for its mother is *primarily a response to certain stimuli the mother offers.* Warmth is the most important stimulus for the first two weeks of the monkey's life, then contact comfort becomes paramount. Contact comfort is determined by the softness and "rub-ability" of the surface of the mother's body—terry cloth is better than are satin and silk, but all such materials are more effective in creating love and trust than bare metal is. Food and mild "shaking" or "rocking" are important too, but less so than warmth and contact comfort. These needs—and the rather primitive responses the infant makes in order to obtain their satisfaction—are programmed into the monkey's genetic blueprint. The growing infant's requirement for social and intellectual stimulation becomes critical only later in a monkey's life. And yet, if the baby primate is deprived of contact with other young of its own species, its whole pattern of development can be profoundly disturbed.

Mother-Infant Love

The Harlows were eventually able to find ways of getting female isolates pregnant, usually by confining them in a small cage for long periods of time with a patient and highly experienced normal male. At times, however, the Harlows were forced to help matters along by strapping the female to a piece of apparatus. When these isolated females gave birth to their first monkey baby, they turned out to be the "monster mothers" the Harlows had tried to create with mechanical surrogates. Having had no contact with other animals as they grew up, they simply did not know what to do with the furry little strangers that suddenly appeared on the scene. These motherless mothers at first totally ignored their children, although if the infant persisted, the mothers occasionally gave in and provided the baby with some of the contact and comfort it demanded.

Surprisingly enough, once these mothers learned how to handle a baby, they did reasonably well. Then, when they were again impregnated and gave birth to a second infant, they took care of this next baby fairly adequately.

Maternal affection was totally lacking in a few of the motherless monkeys, however. To them the newborn monkey was little more than an object to be abused the way a human child might abuse a doll or a toy train. These motherless mothers stepped on their babies, crushed the infant's face into the floor of the cage, and once or twice chewed off their baby's feet and fingers before they could be stopped. The most terrible mother of all popped her infant's head into her mouth and crunched it like a potato chip.

We tend to think of most mothers—no matter what their species—as having some kind of almost divine "maternal instinct" that makes them love their children and take care of them no matter what the cost or circumstance. While it is true that most females have built into their genetic blueprint the tendency to be interested in (and to care for) their offspring, this inborn tendency is always expressed in a given environment. The "maternal instinct" is strongly influenced by the mother's past experiences. Humans seem to have weaker instincts of all kinds than do other animals—since our behavior patterns are more affected by learning than by our genes, we have greater flexibility in what we do and become. But we pay a sometimes severe price for this freedom from genetic control.

Normal monkey and chimpanzee mothers seldom appear to inflict real physical harm on their children; human mothers and fathers often do. Serapio R. Zalba, writing in a journal called *Trans-action*, estimated in 1971 that in the United States alone, perhaps 250,000 children suffer physical abuse by their parents each year. Of these "battered babies," almost 40,000 may be very badly injured. The number of young boys and girls killed by their parents annually is not known, but Zalba suggests that the figure may run into the thousands. Parents have locked their children in tiny cages, raised them in dark closets, burned them, boiled them, slashed them with knives, shot them, and broken almost every bone in their bodies. How can we reconcile these facts with the much-discussed maternal and paternal "instincts"?

The research by the Harlows on the "motherless mothers" perhaps gives us a clue. Mother monkeys who were themselves socially deprived or isolated when young seemed singularly lacking in affection for their infants. Zalba states that most of the abusive human parents that were studied turned out to have been abused and neglected *themselves* as children. Like the isolated monkeys who seemed unable to control their aggressive impulses when put in contact with normal animals, the abusive parents seem to be greatly deficient in what psychologists call "impulse control." Most of these parents also were described as being socially isolated, as having troubles adjusting to marriage, often deeply in debt, and as being unable to build up warm and loving relationships with other people—including their own children. Since they did not learn how to love from their own parents, these mothers and fathers simply did not acquire the social skills necessary for bringing up their own infants in a healthy fashion.

Stage 3: Recall

Stop to self-test, relate, and react.

Your instructor may choose to give you a true-false comprehension review.

Thinking About "Monkey Love"

Explain and give examples of findings from Harlow's experiment that you believe are applicable to human infants.

Response Suggestion: Describe the experimental finding and use examples to relate it to the psychological needs of human infants.

Contemporary Link

Why might some people feel that Harlow's animal research is less acceptable than Gray's research on the brain? Give specific examples to support your statement.

Skill Development: Summarizing

Using this selection as a source, summarize on index cards the information that you might want to include in a research paper entitled "Animal Rights: Do Scientists Go Too Far?"

Skill Development: Main Idea

Answer the following with *T* (true) or *F* (false).

_________ 1. The main point of the first four paragraphs is that Harlow's shift to studying monkey love occurred by accident.

_________ 2. In the second section titled "Infant-Mother Love," the main point is that an infant monkey needs the "contact comfort" of the mother to give it a feeling of security while interacting with the environment.

_________ 3. In the beginning of the section titled "Good Mothers and Bad," the main point is that baby monkeys will reject monster mothers.

_________ 4. In the beginning of the section titled "Mother-Infant Love," the main point is that the maternal instinct is not influenced by the mother's past experiences.

Comprehension Questions

After reading the selection, answer the following questions with *a, b, c,* or *d.* In order to help you analyze your strengths and weaknesses, the question types are indicated.

Main Idea

1. Who or what is the topic? ______________________________

____

What is the main idea the author is trying to convey about the topic?

____

____

Inference

_______ 2. When Harry Harlow originally started his experiments with monkeys, his purpose was to study
   a. love.
   b. breeding.
   c. learning.
   d. disease.

Inference

_______ 3. The reason that the author mentions Harry Harlow's revelations on the airplane is to show
   a. that he had extrasensory perception.
   b. that he liked to travel.
   c. that he was always thinking of his work.
   d. in what an unexpected way brilliant work often starts.

Detail

_______ 4. In his experiments Harlow used all of the following in designing his surrogate mothers except
   a. a terry-cloth bath towel.
   b. real body hair.
   c. a rocking movement.
   d. temperature controls.

Detail

_______ 5. Harlow manipulated his experiments to show the early significance of warmth by
   a. heating wire.
   b. changing from satin to terry cloth.
   c. equalizing temperature.
   d. creating "monster mothers."

Inference

_______ 6. Harlow feels that for contact comfort the cloth mother was preferable to the wire mother for all of the following reasons except
   a. the cloth mother instilled confidence.
   b. the wire mother didn't "rub" as well.
   c. the wire mother was stationary.
   d. with the cloth mother, the infant felt a greater sense of security when upset.

Detail ________ 7. Harlow's studies show that when abused by its mother, the infant will
a. leave the mother.
b. seek a new mother.
c. return to the mother.
d. fight with the mother.

Detail ________ 8. For an infant to love its mother, Harlow's studies show that in the first two weeks the most important element is
a. milk.
b. warmth.
c. contact comfort.
d. love expressed by the mother.

Inference ________ 9. In Harlow's studies with motherless monkeys, he showed that the techniques of mothering are
a. instinctive.
b. learned.
c. inborn.
d. natural.

Inference ________ 10. The Harlows feel that child abuse is caused by all of the following problems except
a. parents who were abused as children.
b. socially isolated parents.
c. parents who cannot control their impulses.
d. parents who are instinctively evil.

Answer the following with *T* (true) or *F* (false).

Inference ________ 11. The author feels that love in infant monkeys has a great deal of similarity to love in human children.

Inference ________ 12. The author implies that isolated monkeys have difficulty engaging in normal peer relationships.

Detail ________ 13. After learning how to handle the first baby, many motherless mothers became better parents with the second infant.

Inference ________ 14. Zalba's studies support many of the findings of the Harlow studies.

Detail ________ 15. Harlow had initially planned to perform drug experiments on the monkeys.

Vocabulary

According to the way the italicized word was used in the selection, indicate *a*, *b*, *c*, or *d* for the word or phrase that gives the best definition. The number in parentheses indictes the line nmber of the passage in which the word is located.

_______ 1. "the *surrogate* mother" (20–21)
a. mean
b. thoughtless
c. loving
d. substitute

_______ 2. "a *functional* breast" (29)
a. mechanical
b. operational
c. wholesome
d. imitation

_______ 3. "on the surrogate's *anatomy*" (30)
a. body
b. head
c. offspring
d. personality

_______ 4. "begins *tentatively* to explore" (71–72)
a. rapidly
b. hesitantly
c. aggressively
d. readily

_______ 5. "fears of the *novel* environment" (74)
a. hostile
b. literary
c. dangerous
d. new

_______ 6. "fears . . . are *desensitized*" (74)
a. made less sensitive
b. made more sensitive
c. electrified
d. communicated

_______ 7. "solutions were *ingenious*" (83–84)
a. incorrect
b. noble
c. clever
d. honest

_______ 8. "*deprived* of contact" (116)
a. encouraged
b. denied
c. assured
d. ordered into

_______ 9. "if the infant *persisted*" (127)
a. stopped
b. continued
c. fought
d. relaxed

_______ 10. "to be greatly *deficient*" (167)
a. lacking
b. supplied
c. overwhelmed
d. secretive

Search the Net

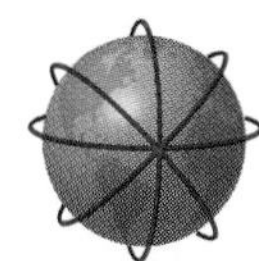

- Conduct a search on the signs of child abuse. List five indicators that a child may be suffering from abuse or neglect. List three agencies that can be contacted to report suspected abuse. Plan your own search or begin by trying the following:

  National Foundation for Abused and Neglected Children:
  http://www.gangfreekids.com/index.html

- Conduct a search on the causes of delinquency among children and teenagers. List the different types of abuse and neglect that can cause delinquency. List steps that can be taken to prevent delinquency. Plan your own search or begin by trying the following:

  Coordinating Council on Juvenile Justice and Delinquency:
  http://ojjdp.ncjrs.org/council/index.html

Concept Prep for Psychology

What is classical conditioning?

Classical conditioning is the learning that takes place when a subject is taught, or conditioned, to make a new response to a neutral stimulus. This is illustrated by the research of **Ivan Pavlov,** a Russian scientist in the late nineteenth century. Pavlov was studying the basic processes of digestion, focusing on salivation in dogs. Since salivation is a **reflex,** it is an unlearned, automatic response in dogs. When food is presented, dogs will automatically salivate. As his research progressed, Pavlov noticed that the dogs would salivate at the sight of the assistant who delivered the food. At this point, Pavlov decided to investigate learning.

Pavlov reasoned that no learning was involved in the dog's automatic salivation (the **unconditioned response**) when presented with food (the **unconditioned stimulus**). He wondered, however, if he could teach the dogs to salivate at the sound of a bell. To investigate this, Pavlov decided to pair the sound of a bell with the presentation of the food, sound first and food second. The bell alone was a **neutral stimulus** that had never before caused salivation. After a number of **trials** (presenting sound and food together), the dogs became conditioned to associate the sound of the bell with the food. The dogs soon would salivate at the sound, even when the food was withheld. Learning had taken place; Pavlov had taught the dogs to react to a neutral stimulus. Once learning or conditioning had taken place, the sound became a **conditioned stimulus** and the salivation became a **conditioned response.** To take this experiment a step further, if the sound is consistently presented without food, the salivation response will gradually weaken until the dogs completely stop salivating at the sound of the bell **(extinction).** Pavlov's work on animals and learning laid the groundwork for the American behaviorists of the twentieth century.

Two pigeons seek food in a box developed by psychologist B. F. Skinner as part of his operant conditioning research.
Bettmann/CORBIS

What is behaviorism?

At the beginning of the twentieth century, many American psychologists disagreed with Freud's psychoanalytical approach (see page 46). They wanted to measure behavior in the laboratory and explain personality in terms of learning theories and observable behaviors. **B. F. Skinner** was a leader in this new movement. He borrowed from Pavlov's work and conducted research on operant conditioning.

Skinner posed questions such as, What are your beliefs about rewards and punishments? Do consequences affect your behaviors? Are you a reflection of your positive and negative experiences? Skinner believed that consequences shape behavior and that your personality is merely a reflection of your many learned behaviors.

Skinner demonstrated **operant conditioning** (behaviors used to operate something) by putting a rat inside a small box that came to be known as a **"Skinner box."** The rat explored the box until eventually it found that by pressing a lever, it could make food appear. The rat enjoyed the food and dramatically increased the lever-pressings. The food was a **positive reinforcer** for the lever-pressing. In other words, the food reinforced the behavior and increased it. To stop the lever-pressing behavior **(extinction),** the rat was given a shock each time the lever was touched. The shock is a **negative reinforcer.** Rewards are positive reinforcers, and punishments are negative reinforcers.

Behavior modification, a type of **behavior therapy,** uses the principles of classical and operant conditioning to increase desired behaviors and decrease problem behaviors. You can use these principles to train a pet, stop a smoking habit, or overcome a fear of flying. Does the desire to make a good grade (reward) affect your studying behavior? Skinner would say, "Yes."

REVIEW QUESTIONS

Study the material and answer the following questions.

1. Who was Ivan Pavlov? __________

2. What is a reflex? __________

3. What is a neutral stimulus? __________

4. Why is the response to the food called unconditioned? __________

5. What is a conditioned stimulus? __________

6. What is extinction? __________

7. How did B. F. Skinner differ from Freud? __________

8. How does operant conditioning differ from classical conditioning? __________

9. What is the role of a positive reinforcer? __________

10. In behavior modification, what makes you want to change behaviors? __________

Your instructor may choose to give a true-false review of these psychology concepts.

Selection 2 ART HISTORY

CONTEMPORARY FOCUS

What drives the price of a painting to astronomical levels? Is it the potential for pleasure in viewing the work or the potential for profit?

A BLUE PERIOD FOR ART BUYERS

Thane Peterson

Londoner Michael G. Wilson, a producer of James Bond movies, is a renowned photo collector. But these days, when he peruses the offerings of dealers, he's often shocked to find classic works by such artists as Man Ray or Gustave Le Gray priced at $500,000 or more. "I used to say a good photo cost the price of a used car," Wilson says. "Then it was a new car, and then a condo. Now, it's measured in houses."

Prices for top modern works are astonishing. *Woman with Crossed Arms*, an ultra-rare canvas from Picasso's Blue Period, went for $55 million at Christie's International, an all-time record for the artist. An Alberto Giacometti sculpture, *Grande Femme Debout*, fetched $14.3 million.

Serious collectors never stop buying. But with prices so high, many are taking precautions. The first rule—always—is don't buy art solely as an investment. Rather, buy works you enjoy living with. And don't be afraid to wait if you don't find exactly what you want.

Collaborative Activity

Collaborate on responses to the following questions:

- What makes a photograph worth a half million dollars?
- Is the greatest profit on art made by the artists or the art dealers?
- How does the phrase "art is subjective" apply to a $55 million Picasso?

Skill Development—Stage 1: Preview

Preview the next selection to predict the purpose and your learning plan.

What is the purpose of writing about art?

What painting is analyzed in the passage?

Activate Schema

What style are Picasso's most famous paintings?

Who is your favorite artist?

Learning Strategy

Understand the questions that you ask when writing about art and see how the example illustrates a way of answering.

Word Knowledge

What do you know about these words?

eluding	bourgeois	enhance	prominence	wisps
wedded	stubble	ponderously	sensate	untainted

Your instructor may give a true-false vocabulary review before or after reading.

Stage 2: Integrate Knowledge While Reading

Predict Picture Relate Monitor Correct

Why Write About Art?

From Sylvan Barnet, *A Short Guide to Writing About Art,* 5th ed.

We write about art in order to clarify and to account for our responses to works that interest or excite or frustrate us. In putting words on paper we have to take a second and a third look at what is in front of us and at what is within us. Picasso said, "To know what you want to draw, you have to begin drawing"; similarly, writing is a way of finding what you want to write, a way of learning. The last word is never said about complex thoughts and feelings—and works of art, as well as our responses to them, embody complex thoughts and feelings. But when we write about art we hope to make at least a little progress in the difficult but rewarding job of talking about our responses. As Arthur C. Danto says in the introduction to *Embodied Meanings* (1994), a collection of essays about art:

> Until one tries to write about it, the work of art remains a sort of aesthetic blur. . . . After seeing the work, write about it. You cannot be satisfied for very long in simply putting down what you felt. You have to go further. (p. 14)

When we write, we learn; we also hope to interest our reader by communicating our responses to material that for one reason or another is worth talking about.

The Function of Critical Writing

In everyday language the most common meaning of criticism is "finding fault," and to be critical is to be censorious. But a critic can see excellences as well as faults. Because we turn to criticism with the hope that the critic has seen something we have missed, the most valuable criticism is not that which shakes its finger at fault but that which calls attention to interesting matters going on in the work of art.

Getting Ideas: Asking Questions to Get Answers

The painter Ad Reinhardt once said that "Looking is not as simple as it looks." What are some of the basic things to look for in trying to acquire an understanding of the languages of art; that is, in trying to understand what a work of art expresses?

Basic Questions

One can begin a discussion of the complex business of expression in the arts almost anywhere, but let's begin with some questions that can be asked of almost any work of art—whether a painting or a drawing or a sculpture or even a building.

- **What is my first response to the work?** Later you may modify or even reject this response, but begin by trying to study it. Jot down your responses—even your free associations. Do you find the work puzzling, boring, pretty, ugly, offensive, sexy, or what? The act of jotting down a response may help you to deepen the response, or to move beyond it to a different response.
- **When and where was the work made?** Does it reveal the qualities that your textbook attributes to the culture? (Don't assume that it does; works of art have a way of eluding easy generalization.)
- **Where would the work originally have been seen?** Perhaps in a church or a palace, or a bourgeois home, or (if the work is an African mask) worn by a costumed dancer, but surely not in a museum (unless it is a contemporary work) or in a textbook. For Picasso, "The picture-hook is the ruination of a painting. . . . As soon as a painting is bought and hung on a wall, it takes on quite a different significance, and the painting is done for." If the work is now part of an exhibition in a museum, how does the museum's presentation of the work affect your response?
- **What purpose did the work serve?** To stimulate devotion? To impress the viewer with the owner's power? To enhance family pride? To teach? To delight? Does the work present a likeness, or express a feeling, or illustrate a mystery?
- **In what condition has the work survived?** Is it exactly as it left the artist's hands, or has it been damaged, repaired, or in some way altered? What evidence of change can be seen?
- **What is the title?** Does it help to illuminate the work? Sometimes it is useful to ask yourself, "What would I call the work?" Picasso called one of his early self-portraits *Yo Picasso* (i.e., "I, Picasso"), rather than, say, *Portrait of the Artist*, and indeed his title goes well with the depicted self-confidence.

A Sample Essay

The following essay on Jean-François Millet's *The Gleaners,* written by Robert Herbert, was originally a note in the catalog issued in conjunction with the art exposition at the Canadian World's Fair, Expo 67.

In this brief essay, in fact, Herbert skillfully sets forth material that might have made half a dozen essays: Millet's life, the background of Millet's thought, Millet's political and social views, the composition of *The Gleaners,* Millet's depiction of peasants, Millet's connection with later painters. But the aim is always to make us see. In *The Gleaners* Millet tried to show us certain things, and now Robert Herbert tries to show us—tries to make us see—what Millet was doing and how he did it.

"Millet's *The Gleaners*"

by Robert Herbert

The Gleaners, *by Jean-François Millet, 1857. Oil on canvas, 83.6 × 111 cm. Musée d'Orsay, Paris, France. Photo: Jean Schormans/Réunion des Musées Nationaux/Art Resource, NY.*

Jean-François Millet, born of well-to-do Norman peasants, began his artistic training in Cherbourg. In 1837 he moved to Paris where he lived until 1849, except for a few extended visits to Normandy. With the sounds of the Revolution of 1848 still rumbling, he moved to Barbizon on the edge of the Forest of Fontainebleau, already noted as a resort of landscape painters, and there he spent the rest of his life. One of the major painters of what came to be called the Barbizon School, Millet began to celebrate the labors of the peasant, granting him a heroic dignity which expressed the aspirations of 1848. Millet's identification with the new social ideals was a result not of overtly radical views, but of his instinctive humanitarianism and his rediscovery in the actual peasant life of the eternal rural world of the Bible and of Virgil, his favorite reading since youth. By elevating to a new prominence the life of the common people, the revolutionary era released the stimulus which enabled him to continue this essential pursuit of his art and of his life.

The Gleaners, exhibited in the Salon of 1857, presents the very poorest of the peasants who are fated to bend their backs to gather with clubbed fingers the wisps of overlooked grain. That they seem so entirely wedded to the soil results from the perfect harmony of Millet's fatalistic view of man with the images which he created by a careful disposition of lines, colors, and shapes. The three women are alone in the bronzed stubble of the foreground, far removed from the bustling activity of the harvesters in the distance, the riches of whose labors have left behind a few gleanings. Millet has weighted his figures ponderously downward, the busy harvest scene is literally above them, and the high horizon line which the taller woman's cap just touches emphasizes their earth-bound role, suggesting that the sky is a barrier which presses down upon them, and not a source of release.

The humility of primeval labor is shown, too, in the creation of primitive archetypes rather than of individuals. Introspection such as that seen in Velazquez's *Water Carrier of Seville*, in which the three men are distinct individuals, is denied by suppressing the gleaners' features, and where the precise, fingered gestures of La Tour's *Saint Jerome* bring his intellectual work toward his sensate mind, Millet gives his women clublike hands which reach away from their bent bodies toward the earth.

It was, paradoxically, the urban-industrial revolution in the nineteenth century which prompted a return to images of the preindustrial, ageless labors of man. For all their differences, both Degas and Van Gogh were to share these concerns later, and even Gauguin was to find in the fishermen of the South Seas that humble being, untainted by the modern city, who is given such memorable form in Millet's *Gleaners*.

Stage 3: Recall

Stop to self-test, relate, and react.

Your instructor may choose to give you a true-false comprehension review.

Thinking About "Why Write About Art?"

What does the author mean in referring to Millet's "instinctive humanitarianism" and the paradox of the urban-industrial revolution in the nineteenth century prompting a return to images of the labors of man?

Response Suggestion: Define instinctive humanitarianism, paradox, and urban-industrial revolution. Relate the meanings to Millet's historical times and to his painting.

Contemporary Link

In order to write about art and clarify your understanding, the author suggests six basic questions to guide your thinking. Expand on this concept from a purchaser's point of view. List six additional questions that you think a collector should ask before paying $15 million for a work of art.

Skill Development: Main Idea

Answer the following with *T* (true) or *F* (false).

_________ 1. The main idea of the first paragraph is that writing about art helps us understand art.

_________ 2. The main idea of the paragraph beginning with "In everyday language" is that art does not deserve criticism.

_________ 3. The main idea of the last paragraph is that Millet was a greater painter than Degas or Van Gogh.

Comprehension Questions

After reading the selection, answer the following questions with *a*, *b*, *c*, or *d*. In order to help you analyze your strengths and weaknesses, the question types are indicated.

Main Idea _________ 1. The best statement of the main idea is
a. the act of writing to explore and answer basic questions about art helps us clarify our responses and learn.
b. in *The Gleaners*, Millet depicts poor peasants who are harvesting grain.
c. Picasso believed that you have to experience in order to appreciate.
d. the purpose of writing about art is to learn and to find flaws.

Inference _________ 2. The author believes that the ultimate goal of criticism is to
a. find fault.
b. be censorious.
c. contrast and thus highlight excellences.
d. uncover new aspects of interest.

Inference _________ 3. The author uses Ad Reinhardt's quotation, "Looking is not as simple as it looks," to suggest that
a. most people are ignorant of good art.
b. guidelines for examining art are needed.
c. what you see does not control what you feel.
d. Reinhardt did not understand art.

Detail ________ 4. The author believes that our initial responses to art
a. are never valid.
b. may change with study.
c. only reveal our own biases.
d. demonstrate our own ignorance.

Inference ________ 5. In Picasso's statement about the "picture-hook," he implies that taking a painting from its origins and hanging it on a wall
a. gives more people an opportunity to view it.
b. enhances the painting.
c. allows for a greater appreciation of the painting.
d. changes the painting for the worse.

Inference ________ 6. The author suggests that Millet moved to Barbizon because
a. he wanted to attend college there and become a landscape painter.
b. he wanted to work with the peasants and learn their ways.
c. it was an artistic colony that was somewhat sheltered from the conflicts of war.
d. it was located in Normandy where the artist was born.

Inference ________ 7. Herbert suggests that the women in Millet's *The Gleaners* are
a. searching for leftovers for personal use.
b. harvesting grain for the wealthy landowner.
c. working with the harvesters.
d. stealing something they should not be taking.

Inference ________ 8. According to Herbert, Millet depicts the three women as
a. independently in charge of their own destinies.
b. sinners being punished.
c. tied to the earth.
d. reaching toward heaven.

Detail ________ 9. According to Herbert, Millet's portrayal of peasants
a. was similar to La Tour's *Saint Jerome*.
b. gave them heroic dignity.
c. ridiculed primeval labor.
d. was a result of his radical politics.

Detail ________ 10. According to the passage, an artist who created primitive archetypes similar to Millet's three women was
a. Picasso.
b. Velazquez.
c. La Tour.
d. Gauguin.

Answer the following with *T* (true) or *F* (false).

Inference _________ 11. The author suggests that the one who benefits most from writing about art is the writer.

Detail _________ 12. Herbert's essay was originally written as an explanation for attendees at the Canadian World's Fair.

Detail _________ 13. Herbert suggests that the three women in Millet's painting are portrayed in a similar manner to the three men in Velazquez's *Water Carrier of Seville*.

Detail _________ 14. Millet was born into a very poor family.

Detail _________ 15. According to Herbert, the hands of Millet's gleaners are slim and agile.

Vocabulary

According to the way the italicized word was used in the selection, select *a*, *b*, *c*, or *d* for the word or phrase that gives the best definition. The number in parentheses indicates the line number of the passage in which the word is located.

_________ 1. "*eluding* easy generalizations" (30, item 2)
a. generating
b. skillfully avoiding
c. capturing
d. copying

_________ 2. "*bourgeois* home" (30, item 3)
a. peasant
b. middle class
c. modern
d. decorated

_________ 3. "*enhance* family pride" (30, item 4)
a. mimic
b. increase
c. validate
d. insure

_________ 4. "new *prominence*" (53–54)
a. era
b. importance
c. art form
d. style of interpretation

_________ 5. "*wisps* of overlooked grain" (59)
a. small fragments
b. bundles
c. handfuls
d. buckets

_________ 6. "*wedded* to the soil" (59–60)
a. indebted
b. contrasted
c. removed
d. joined

_________ 7. "bronzed *stubble*" (62)
a. oil painting
b. rough growth
c. dim light
d. smooth grass

_________ 8. "*ponderously* downward" (65)
a. heavily
b. curved
c. carelessly
d. needlessly

_______ 9. "his *sensate* mind" (75)
a. logical
b. relating to the senses
c. narrow
d. curious

_______ 10. "*untainted* by the modern city" (81)
a. uncontaminated
b. uncontrolled
c. unimpressed
d. unmatched

Search the Net

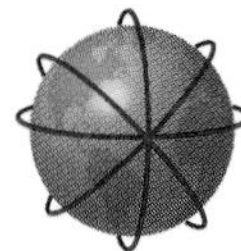

- Search for and print a picture of a piece of art by an artist of your choice, such as Paul Cezanne, Georgia O'Keeffe, or Diego Rivera. Describe your first response to the work, where and when the work was created, where the work may have originally been seen, and the purpose that the work originally had. Begin your own search, or start with one of the following:

  Constable.net: http://www.constable.net/index.html

  Art Without Artifice—The Truth About Famous Paintings: http://painting.netfirms.com/

  Internet Art Museum: http://library.thinkquest.org/29313/

- Search for and print two different pictures of pieces of artwork that illustrate different styles of painting. Compare and contrast your first response to each work, where each work may have originally been seen, and the original purpose of each piece. Begin your own search, or start with one of the following:

  Museum Suite: http://www.museum.suite.dk/

  National Museum of Women in the Arts Permanent Collection Tour: http://dir.yahoo.com/Arts/Art_History/Collections/

  El Museo del Barrio: http://www.elmuseo.org/

Concept Prep

for Art

When we say "the arts," what do we mean?

The **arts** and the **fine arts** refer to creative works in painting, sculpture, literature, architecture, drama, music, opera, dance, and film. A work that is exceptionally well crafted is said to aspire to the level of fine art.

Museums, a word derived from Greek to mean places presided over by the Muses, display fine arts in paintings and sculpture. Some of the greatest museums in the world are the **Louvre** in Paris, the **Prado** in Madrid, and the **Metropolitan Museum of Art** in New York. Art tells us about people and their culture as illustrated in the earliest primitive cave drawings depicting animals and hunters or in the elaborately decorated tombs in the Egyptian pyramids built for the ascension of pharaohs into heaven.

Who are considered some of the greatest artists?

- One of the most extraordinary artists was **Leonardo da Vinci** (1452–1519). He was considered a **Renaissance man** because of his genius, insatiable curiosity, and wide interests in art, engineering, anatomy, and aeronautics. He painted the **Mona Lisa,** the world's most famous painting. This woman with the mysterious smile whose eyes seem to follow you is displayed in the Louvre behind several layers of bulletproof glass.
- **Michelangelo** (1475–1564) was a sculptor, painter, architect, and poet. Before he was thirty years old, he created the famous marble statue of **David,** which portrays the biblical king in his youth. Michelangelo was commissioned by the Pope to paint the ceiling of the **Sistine Chapel** in the Vatican in Rome. For four years, the artist worked on his back in the chapel to complete the biblical story, **The Creation of Adam,** which contains more than 400 individual figures.
- The founder and leading artist of the **Impressionists** was **Claude Monet** (1840–1926). Critics said the feathery brushstrokes and play of light in his works conveyed the "impression" of a particular moment. Monet advocated getting out of the studio and painting outdoors facing the subject. He painted many scenes of the gardens and water lily ponds surrounding his home in **Giverny** near Paris.

This self portrait of Vincent van Gogh was painted in 1887, three years before he died.
Self Portrait, 1887 by Vincent van Gogh, Musée d'Orsay, Paris, France. Copyright Réunion des Musées Nationaux/Art Resource, NY.

- **Van Gogh** (1853–1890) borrowed from the Impressionists but achieved another dimension in the swirling brushstrokes of his work to convey his unique vision. His sunflower paintings and **Starry Night** are among his most famous works, now popularized in mass reproductions, but in his lifetime Van Gogh sold only one painting. He suffered from depression and spent his last years in a mental institution. In an argument with another artist, he cut off his own ear, which he later sent to a prostitute.

- **Pablo Picasso** (1881–1973) is one of the most influential of all modern artists. Because traditional skills in painting were so easy for him, he looked for new modes of expression. He was the originator of Cubism, an abstract style of painting that displays several perspectives of an object simultaneously. One of his most acclaimed paintings is **Guernica,** a haunting visual protest against the savagery of war.

REVIEW QUESTIONS

Study the material and answer the following questions.

1. What do works included in "the arts" have in common? ________________

2. Where is the Louvre? ________________

3. What is a Renaissance Man? ________________

4. What is unusually engaging about Mona Lisa's face? ________________

5. What story is painted on the ceiling of the Sistine Chapel? ________________

6. How did the Impressionists get the name? ________________

7. What scenes did Monet paint at Giverny? ________________

8. Which painter advocated painting outdoors? ________________

9. How did Van Gogh disfigure himself? ________________

10. Why did Picasso turn to Cubism? ________________

Your instructor may choose to give a true-false review of these art concepts.

Selection 3 SOCIOLOGY

CONTEMPORARY FOCUS

The world is becoming increasingly urban as people leave rural areas and seek economic opportunity in cities. The new immigrants congregate in shantytowns, overcrowded settlements that lack basic city services. How can individuals and governments solve these squatter problems?

LETTER FROM BRAZIL

Robert Neuwirth

The Nation, New York, July 10, 2000

Many Brazilians will tell you that the favelas are slums or shantytowns, but that is simply the dictionary definition. The favelas may once have been urban wastelands, but over the past two decades favelados have transformed their junkyard colonies into desirable neighborhoods, achieving something most illegal settlers can only dream of: permanence. Their new brand of self help urban development could become a model for the rest of the world. Here are its two simple steps: Let the poor build, then work with them to stabilize their self built communities.

Other countries have huge squatter populations, of course, but Brazil is one of the few places where squatters have transformed their domains into thriving neighborhoods. Here are some of the reasons why the favelados have succeeded where most other squatters have not.

The favelados defy many stereotypes. They aren't anarchists or punks or people raging against the system; most favelados are simply trying to create a better life for themselves and their kids.

The squatters are shrewd and strategic. Early on, they recognized that one of the legacies of authoritarian rule was that there was a huge amount of fallow land under government control. So they tended to invade these parcels.

The favelados also understand the need for coordinated action. Since a single person has a hard time erecting a house, the favelas became natural collectives. The residents united in *mutiroes*—cooperative building associations—and erected their communities collectively.

The squatters realized they had to work inside the system. Some favelas cut deals with local politicians—promising support if the officials helped them get city services like running water, sanitation or access to mass transit.

The favelados have also been aided in their quest by a marvelous quirk of Brazilian law and by responsive governments. In contrast to the United States, where property rights are king, Brazil's Constitution explicitly protects squatters.

Collaborative Activity

Collaborate on responses to the following questions:

- Why didn't Brazilian cities outlaw the favelas?
- How has the human spirit and cooperation changed the favelas?
- What happens to new immigrants who go to the favelas?

Skill Development—Stage 1: Preview

Preview the next selection to predict its purpose, organization, and your learning plan.

The author probably describes the problems of city slums.
Agree ☐ Disagree ☐

After reading this selection, I will need to know the ten major cities in the world. Agree ☐ Disagree ☐

Activate Schema

Why do so many people flock to Mexico City?

Why do so many people prefer city life to farm life?

Learning Strategy

Seek to understand the reasons for urbanization and the problems.

Word Knowledge

What do you know about these words?

pursuits	endeavors	transcends	serene	pastoral
spigot	distort	deteriorating	dismal	enclaves

Your instructor may give a true-false vocabulary review before or after reading.

Stage 2: Integrate Knowledge While Reading

Predict Picture Relate Monitor Correct

Urbanization

From James M. Henslin, *Sociology,* 5th ed.

The key to the origin of cities is the development of more efficient agriculture (Lenski and Lenski 1987). Only when farming produces a surplus can some people stop being food producers and gather in cities to spend time in other pursuits. A **city,** in fact, can be defined as a place in which a large number of people are permanently based and do not produce their own food. The invention of the plow between five and six thousand years ago created widespread agricultural surpluses, stimulating the development of towns and cities (Curwin and Hart 1961).

Slum houses on the hillside in Mexico are built with brick walls and wooden boards.
Jonathan Nourok/PhotoEdit

The Industrial Revolution and the Size of Cities

Most early cities were tiny by comparison with those of today, merely a collection of a few thousand people in agricultural centers or on major trade routes. The most notable exceptions are two cities that reached 1 million for a brief period of time before they declined—Changan in China about A.D. 800 and Bagdad in Persia about A.D. 900 (Chandler and Fox 1974). Even Athens at the peak of its power in the fifth century B.C. had less than 200,000 inhabitants. Rome, at its peak, may have had a million or more (Flanagan 1990).

Even 200 years ago, the only city in the world that had a population of more than a million was Peking (now Beijing), China (Chandler and Fox 1974). Then in just 100 years, by 1900, the number of such cities jumped to sixteen. The reason was the Industrial Revolution, which drew people to cities by providing work. The Industrial Revolution also stimulated rapid transportation and communication, and allowed people, resources, and products to be moved efficiently—all essential factors (called infrastructure) on which large cities depend. Today about 300 cities have a million or more people (Frisbie and Kasarda 1988).

City Life

Cities are intended to be solutions to problems. They are the result of human endeavors that seek to improve life collectively, to develop a way of life that transcends the limitations of farm and village. Cities hold out the hope of jobs, education, and other advantages. The perception of opportunity underlies mass migration to cities throughout the world.

City Slums in the Least Industrialized Nations

Images of the Least Industrialized Nations that portray serene pastoral scenes distort today's reality. In these nations, poor rural people have flocked to the cities in such numbers that these nations now contain most of the world's largest cities. Each year the cities of the Least Industrialized Nations grow by 62 million people (Annez 1998). That's more than all the Italians who live in Italy, the equivalent of adding twice the population of Canada every year. In the Most Industrialized Nations, industrialization usually preceded urbanization, but here *urbanization is preceding industrialization*.

The settlement patterns are also different. When rural migrants and immigrants move to U.S. cities, they usually settle in deteriorating houses near the city's center. The wealthy reside in suburbs and luxurious city enclaves. Migrants to cities of the Least Industrialized Nations, in contrast, establish illegal squatter settlements outside the city. There they build shacks from scrap board, cardboard, and bits of corrugated metal. Even flattened tin cans are used for building material. The squatters enjoy no city facilities—roads, public transportation, water, sewers, or garbage pickup. After thousands of squatters have settled an area, the city acknowledges their right to live there and adds bus service and minimal water lines. Hundreds of people use a single spigot. About 5 *million* of Mexico City's residents live in such conditions, with hundreds of thousands more pouring in each year.

This story is repeated throughout South America, Africa, India, and the rest of the so-called underdeveloped world. Why this vast rush to live in the city under such miserable conditions? The explanation lies in the many "push" factors that arise from the breakdown of traditional rural life. With the importation of modern medicine, a safer water supply, and better transportation and distribution of food, the death rate has dropped, and the rural populations are multiplying. There is not enough land for everyone, and rural life can no longer support so many people. "Pull" factors also draw people to the cities—the hope of jobs, education, better housing, and even a more stimulating life.

At the bottom of a ravine near Mexico City is a dismal bunch of shacks. Some of the families living in them have 14 children.

"We used to live up there," Senora Gonzalez gestured toward the mountain, "in those caves. Our only hope was one day to have a place to live. And now we do." She smiled with pride at the jerry-built shacks . . . each one had a collection of flowers planted in tin cans. "One day, we hope to extend the water pipes and drainage—perhaps even pave . . ."

And what was the name of her community? Senora Gonzalez beamed. "Esperanza!" (McDowell 1984:172)

Esperanza is the Spanish word for hope. This is what lies behind the rush to these cities—the hope of a better life. And this is why the rush won't slow down. In 1930, only one Latin American city had more than a million people—now fifty do! The world's cities are growing by one million people each week (Brockerhoff 1996).

Will the Least Industrialized Nations adjust to this vast, unwanted migration? They have no choice. Authorities in Brazil, Guatemala, Venezuela, and other countries have sent in the police and the army to evict the settlers. It doesn't work. It just leads to violence, and the settlers keep streaming in. The adjustment will be painful. The infrastructure (roads, water, sewers, electricity, and so on) must be built, but these poor countries don't have the resources to build them. As the desperate flock to the cities, the problems will worsen.

Stage 3: Recall

Stop to self-test, relate, and react.

Your instructor may choose to give you a true-false comprehension review.

Thinking About "Urbanization"

What is the relationship of cities to farming?

Response Suggestion: Describe historically how one must come before the other and how one supports the other.

Contemporary Link

How can other cities solve urban slum problems by using the success of the favelas? Explain the conditions that are necessary for the favela model to work.

Skill Development: Main Idea

Answer the following with *T* (true) or *F* (false).

_________ 1. The main idea of the selection is stated in the first sentence of the second paragraph.

_________ 2. The topic of the third paragraph is the Industrial Revolution in China.

_________ 3. The main topic for the entire selection is the failure of the farms to support the people.

_________ 4. The need for cities to have adequate infrastructure to serve new rural migrants is a major detail in support of the main idea of this selection.

Comprehension Questions

After reading the selection, answer the following questions with *a*, *b*, *c*, or *d*. In order to help you analyze your strengths and weaknesses, the question types are indicated.

Main Idea ________ 1. Which is the best statement of the main idea?
a. City slums in the Least Industrialized Nations lack sewage and sanitation.
b. Without efficient agriculture and industrialization to support the development of cities, city slums are now emerging in underdeveloped countries.
c. A surplus of farm produce is the key factor in the development of the many cities that now have over a million people.
d. Cities offer solutions to problems and attract mass migrations of people looking for opportunities.

Detail ________ 2. In 1900, how many cities had over a million people?
a. 2
b. 4
c. 16
d. 300

Detail ________ 3. Infrastructure includes all of the following except
a. roads.
b. migrants.
c. water.
d. electricity.

Inference ________ 4. By using the word *perception* in the phrase, "The perception of opportunity underlies mass migration," the author suggests that
a. the opportunity is not always a reality for migrants.
b. migrants usually get what they expect.
c. migrants have developed clear goals for their migrations.
d. mass migrations are usually caused by famine in underdeveloped countries.

Detail ________ 5. The pattern of migrants to the cities in the Least Industrialized Nations is
a. to move to the inner city.
b. to move to the luxurious city enclaves.
c. to settle in deteriorating housing near the city's center.
d. to settle outside the city.

Inference ________ 6. The author suggests that all of the following nations are included in the Least Industrialized Nations except
a. Canada.
b. Mexico.
c. India.
d. Brazil.

Detail ________ 7. The author attributes the breakdown of traditional rural life and the move to city slums to all of the following except
a. reduced death rate.
b. the urban infrastructure readily available to the new squatters.
c. safer water supply.
d. better transportation.

Inference ________ 8. The primary reason the author includes the story of Senora Gonzalez is to
a. argue for better transportation for the squatters.
b. explain why violence is prevalent in squatter communities.
c. show that most squatters will leave the community and find jobs.
d. dramatize the hope, pride, and determination of the squatters.

Inference ________ 9. In the statement, "urbanization is preceding industrialization," the author means that
a. the people are needed for the jobs in the cities.
b. the people are coming before the jobs.
c. the people come to the cities and do not want to work.
d. the people who are coming are not trained to fill the jobs.

Inference ________ 10. The reader can conclude that
a. cities encourage migrants to locate in squatter communities.
b. cities can regulate the flow of migrants into the squatter communities.
c. cities have little control over the establishment of squatter communities.
d. cities first provide the land, water, and electricity and then the squatter communities are built.

Answer the following with *T* (true) or *F* (false).

Detail ________ 11. The author attributes the development of cities to the creation of the plow.

Detail ________ 12. The author defines a "pull" factor as a positive motivation to migrate to a city.

Detail ________ 13. According to the passage, every year each of the major cities in the Least Industrialized Nations grows by 62 million people.

Detail ________ 14. According to the passage, the first city in history to reach a million in population was Athens.

Detail ________ 15. Senora Gonzalez lives in a shack in a ravine near Mexico City.

Vocabulary

According to the way the italicized word was used in the selection, select *a, b, c,* or *d* for the word or phrase that gives the best definition. The number in parentheses indicates the line of the passage in which the word is located.

_______ 1. "in other *pursuits*" (3–4)
a. communities
b. occupations
c. locations
d. environments

_______ 2. "human *endeavors*" (26–27)
a. efforts
b. mysteries
c. misfortunes
d. miseries

_______ 3. "*transcends* the limitations" (28)
a. combines
b. changes
c. rises above
d. compares

_______ 4. "portray *serene* pastoral scenes" (31)
a. peaceful
b. unsanitary
c. lonely
d. shameful

_______ 5. "portray serene *pastoral* scenes" (31)
a. religious
b. mountainous
c. small town
d. country

_______ 6. "*distort* today's reality" (32)
a. confirm
b. describe
c. compliment
d. twist

_______ 7. "*deteriorating* houses" (40)
a. antique
b. remodeled
c. falling apart
d. vacant

_______ 8. "luxurious city *enclaves*" (41)
a. exclusive enclosed areas
b. houses
c. country clubs
d. apartment buildings

_______ 9. "use a single *spigot*" (48)
a. water hose
b. sink
c. faucet
d. shower

_______ 10. "*dismal* bunch of shacks" (60)
a. newly erected
b. dreadful
c. dangerous
d. illegal

Search the Net

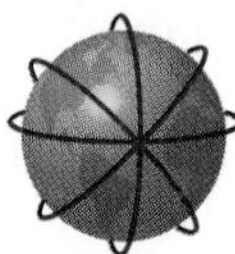

- List the names and locations of three different shantytowns. Briefly describe the living conditions, the population, and some of the factors that led to the creation of each shantytown. Start your own search, or begin with one of the following:

Gypsy Journal: http://www.gypsyjournal.com/Chapter.asp?ChapterID=346

Scriptnet2000: http://www.scriptnet2000.org.uk/ghana/ghcities.html

Caritas.org: http://www.caritas.org.au/what_we_do/where_la1.htm

- While industrialization draws people to urban areas, cities are not always prepared to serve the needs of a growing population. Discuss five of the problems that arise as a result of overpopulation. Provide Web site addresses for each source of your information. Start your own search, or begin with one of the following:

  Facing the Future; People and the Planet: http://www.facingthefuture.org/

  Negative Population Growth: http://www.npg.org/

  Population Action: http://www.populationaction.org/

Concept Prep for Sociology

What is sociology?

While psychology focuses on the individual, **sociology** focuses on explaining group behaviors and society. **Sociologists** use logic and the scientific method to observe and explain interpersonal interaction, group membership, and social institutions. Students majoring in sociology may concentrate on family and community services, social justice, cultural issues, urban issues, or gerontology (the study of issues of aging).

What is a counterculture movement?

In the late 1950s the **Beat Generation** began to question the accepted American values. These **beatniks** scorned materialism, traditional family life, religion, and politics. They embraced radical politics and exotic music, art, and literature. Their slang included words like *chick, Big Apple,* and *square,* and their appeal on college campuses scattered the seeds for change in the next decade.

By the 1960s, young people were beginning to see themselves as a social force for change. Many protested and demonstrated for civil rights, women's rights, gay and lesbian rights, and abortion. They declared a **generation gap** between themselves and the decision makers, feeling that no one over thirty years of age could be trusted. These young people rejected the traditional dreams of success and values of conservative Middle America. They rebelled against the expected path to success and chose an alternative lifestyle. They became **hippies** or **flower children,** wearing unconventional clothing, using drugs, and practicing free love and communal living. By the late 1960s they were protesting U.S. military involvement in Vietnam. To celebrate their new culture or **counterculture,** 400,000 young people gathered near **Woodstock**, a small town in New York state, for a rock music festival in 1969. They listened to music, took drugs, and made love.

Counterculture groups join the Fourth of July celebration in 1968 in El Rito, N.M.
Lisa Law/The Image Works

What is feminism?

Feminism is a political movement for women's rights, asserting that women and men should have equal legal, economic, social, and political rights. In 1963 **Betty Friedan's** book, ***The Feminine Mystique,*** launched this new movement that was to redefine female roles in American society. Basing her information on interviews and questionnaires, Friedan wrote about the sense of discontent, frustration, and exhaustion felt by educated American women. She criticized educators and the mass media for thinking women could only be mothers and housewives. **Gloria Steinem,** founder of *Ms.* magazine, was also a leader in the women's liberation movement.

What is an environmentalist?

An **environmentalist** is a person dedicated to protecting our natural resources from destruction and pollution. **Rachel Carson,** a marine biologist, popularized a mass movement for environmental protection in 1962 with the publication of her book, ***Silent Spring.*** In the book, she described how DDT and other pesticides contaminated the food chain, killed birds and fish, and caused human illnesses.

REVIEW QUESTIONS

Study the material and answer the following questions.

1. What is sociology? ______________________

2. Who were the beatniks? ______________________

3. What is a counterculture? ______________________

4. Who were the hippies? ______________________

5. What was the significance of Woodstock? ______________________

6. What is feminism? ______________________

7. What was the point of *The Feminine Mystique?* ______________________

8. Who is Gloria Steinem? ______________________

9. What was the significance of *Silent Spring?* ______________________

10. What is DDT? ______________________

Your instructor may choose to give a true-false review of these sociology concepts.

READER'S JOURNAL

Name ______________________________ Date ______________

CHAPTER 4

Answer the following questions to reflect on your own learning and progress. Use the perforations to tear the assignment out for your instructor.

1. When trying to determine the author's point, why is it important to determine the topic first? ______________________________
2. Why is prior knowledge important in stating the main idea? __________
3. Why should the main idea be stated in a complete sentence? __________
4. When you write a term paper, where do you usually state the main idea? Why? ______________________________
5. For what purpose have you written a summary as part of your school work? What was difficult about writing it? ______________________________
6. Reflect on the multiple-choice items in the longer selections. How were your errors similar to or different from your errors in the last chapter? ______________________________
7. Compare your concentration on the psychology, art history, and sociology selections. Which did you feel most focused on and why? __________
8. How many of the thirty vocabulary items did you answer correctly? ______________________________

5

Patterns of Organization

- How do transitional words signal organizational patterns?
- What organizational patterns are used in textbooks?

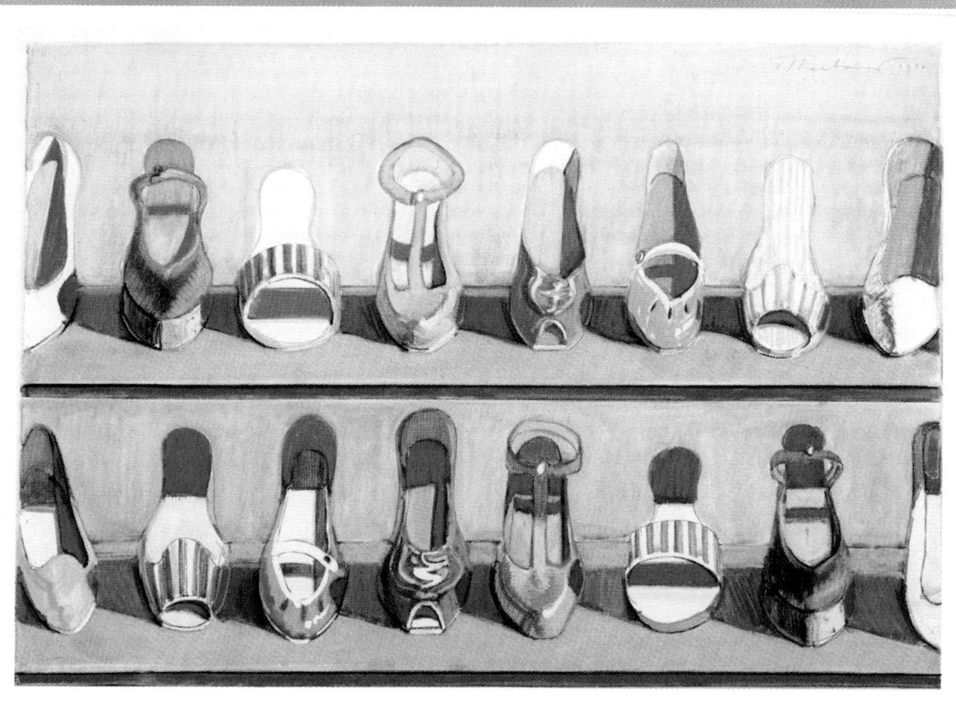

Shoes (Shoe Rows) *by Wayne Thiebaud, 1980. Watercolor and pastel on etching, 17 7/8 × 26 1/2" (sight) (45.4 × 67.3 cm). Photo courtesy of Allan Stone Gallery, NYC. © Wayne Thiebaud/Licensed by VAGA, New York, NY.*

Textbook Organization

Why is it important to identify organizational patterns in textbooks and other readings? Basically, such patterns are important because they serve as the blueprints that you can use while reading as well as writing. They signal how facts and ideas will be presented. The number of details in a textbook can be overwhelming. Identifying a section's or chapter's pattern of organization can help you master the complexities of the material. If you know the pattern of organization, you can predict the format of upcoming information.

Although key transitional words can signal a particular pattern, the most important clue to the pattern is the main idea itself. This idea usually dictates the organizational pattern. Your aim as a reader is to identify the main idea, be alert to the signal words, anticipate the overall pattern of organization, and place the major supporting details into the outline or pattern employed by the author.

What Do Transitional Words Do?

Small words can carry a big load. Single words can signal levels of importance, connections, and the direction of thoughts. For example, if a friend begins a sentence with "I owe you $100," would you prefer that the next word be *and* or *but*? The word *and* signals addition and would give you high hopes for the return of your money. However, the word *but* signals a change of thought which, in this case, would be in a negative direction. If the next word were *first*, you would anticipate a sequence of events before repayment. If it were *consequently*, you would hope the positive result would be your $100.

Such words are **transitional words,** or signal words, that connect parts of sentences or whole sentences and lead you to anticipate a continuation or a change in thought. Transitions show the relationships of ideas within sentences, between sentences, and between paragraphs. Writers use transitions to keep their readers' comprehension on track and to guide them through the logic of the message. To avoid repetition, authors choose from a variety of signal words to indicate the transition of thought. These signal words or transitions can be categorized as follows.

Words That Signal Addition

in addition   moreover   furthermore   and   also   another

EXAMPLE

José was given a raise after six months at his job. In addition, he became eligible for health insurance benefits.

After causing a disturbance in the movie theater, Brian and his friends were asked to leave. Furthermore, they were barred from attending that theater ever again.

Words That Signal Examples or Illustrations

for example for instance to illustrate such as including

EXAMPLE

Traffic seems to be getting heavier. For instance, last year it took only twenty minutes to get to school, and now it takes thirty.

Some experts believe that a fetus in the womb can be affected by sounds such as classical music or the mother's voice.

Words That Signal Time or Sequence

first	second	finally	last	afterwards	after	during
while	before	then	previously	until	now	next

EXAMPLE

Apply sunscreen while walking on the beach and before swimming in the surf. Afterward, reapply the sunscreen even if it is waterproof.

To build a good financial foundation, first pay yourself in the form of savings, and then pay your bills.

Words That Signal Comparison

similarly	likewise	in the same manner	like
as	just as	as well	

EXAMPLE

If you treat someone with kindness, they will probably treat you in kind. Likewise, if you treat someone with disrespect, you will probably be disrespected.

Portland is a port city in Oregon; similarly, it is a seaport in Maine.

Words That Signal Contrast

however	but	nevertheless	whereas
on the contrary	conversely	yet	in contrast
even though	on the other hand	although	instead

EXAMPLE

Using a knife to cut a bagel can be dangerous to the fingers. On the other hand, using a bagel holder keeps fingers safe from the falling blade.

Today many families eat dinner separately and on the run, whereas in the past the family dinner hour was a time for bonding and an opportunity to instill values or share dreams.

Words That Signal Cause and Effect

thus	consequently	therefore	as a result	because
accordingly	since	so	because of	

EXAMPLE

Because of his work to end apartheid in South Africa, Nelson Mandela spent twenty-seven years in prison. Upon his release, Mandela treated his oppressors with respect and worked to unite the country. Consequently, he shared a Nobel Peace Prize with then-president de Klerk.

There has been a severe shortage of rainfall this year. Therefore, we have instituted an outdoor watering ban.

Reader's Tip

Signal Words for Transition

* **Addition:** in addition furthermore moreover
* **Examples:** for example for instance to illustrate such as
* **Time:** first secondly finally last afterward
* **Comparison:** similarly likewise in the same manner
* **Contrast:** however but nevertheless whereas on the contrary conversely in contrast
* **Cause and Effect:** thus consequently therefore as a result

Exercise 5.1

Signal Words

Choose a signal word from the boxed lists to complete the sentences that follow.

however	for example	in addition	consequently	in the meantime

1. New roller coasters are providing extreme thrill rides for their aficionados. ________________, the Hypersonic Coaster has a face-first drop that speeds from zero to eighty miles per hour in less than two seconds.
2. The United States has an ever-increasing demand for oil. ________________, we are researching alternative sources of energy, such as solar energy, in order to reduce our dependence on oil.

3. _______________ to alternative energy research, we may begin drilling for oil on a small portion of our public lands to lessen our dependence on foreign sources of oil.

4. Drilling on public lands, _______________, is not popular with environmentalists who believe the drilling cannot be done without spoiling the land.

5. _______________, we can strive to be more fuel-efficient to help reduce our demand for energy.

therefore	on the contrary	for instance	in the same manner	furthermore

6. One way to be more fuel efficient is in our choice of cars to drive. _______________, some hybrid cars that run on both gas and electricity are currently available. _______________, these cars get up to 68 miles per gallon.

7. The ancient Chinese practice of acupuncture is based on a belief that chi, a life force, flows along meridians throughout the body. _______________, Feng Shui practitioners believe that the same chi flows throughout the earth, and that by harnessing the chi of our surroundings we can improve the flow of energy in our bodies.

8. Coretta Scott King felt strongly that her husband's legacy should be celebrated nationally. _______________, she worked successfully with others to have Martin Luther King, Jr.'s birthday recognized as a federal holiday beginning in 1983.

9. The U.S. Postal Service works to raise social awareness of important issues. _______________, the USPS has issued commemorative stamps including Diabetes Awareness, Breast Cancer Awareness, and Hospice Care.

10. The popular Harry Potter books are not only for children. _______________, many adults enjoy reading about Harry's magical adventures at Hogwarts.

furthermore	for example	nevertheless	finally	in contrast

11. African-American music in twentieth-century America evolved from ragtime, to jazz, to rhythm and blues, to soul, and, _______________, to rap.

12. Gloria Estefan and the Miami Sound Machine's recording of "Conga" was on Billboard's Pop, Latin, Soul, and Dance Charts at the same time. _______________, it was the only song in history to have this distinction.

13. Mardi Gras as celebrated in New Orleans is similar to Carnaval as celebrated throughout Latin America. Carnaval lasts for five days; _______________, Mardi Gras lasts only one day.

14. Internet car sales, rather than hurting auto dealerships, have actually helped them. _______________, most customers research the Net, but still visit a dealer to actually buy an automobile. A well-informed consumer who is ready to purchase makes the salesperson's job easier.

15. The concert tickets were outrageously priced. ________________, this was a once-in-a-lifetime opportunity and other luxuries would have to be sacrificed to compensate for the expense.

moreover	but	simultaneously	as a result	similarly

16. Is chocolate a food or a drug? Chocolate contains antioxidants and minerals like many foods, ________________ it also contains a neurotransmitter naturally found in the brain that, like many drugs, makes us feel good.

17. The 2000 U.S. Census shows a dramatic increase in the Hispanic population in the South. This influx was due to a recession in California occurring ________________ with a robust economy in the South during the 1990s.

18. Vicente Fox, the president of Mexico, has vowed to improve his country's economy with foreign investment and jobs programs. ________________, he has pledged to work toward an open border between Mexico and the United States, where workers would be able to cross the border freely.

19. Musicians protested the swapping of their songs on the Napster Internet Web site without royalties being paid. ________________, journalists have protested their past works being electronically reproduced without royalty payments.

20. Maria was exercising for two hours every day and following a very low-calorie diet that proved to be too stressful on her body. ________________, she ended up in extremely poor health and feeling fatigued all the time.

Patterns of Organization in Textbooks

As transitional words signal connections and relationships of ideas within and among sentences, they also help signal the overall organizational pattern of the message. This **pattern of organization** is the presentation plan, format, or structure for the message. When you write, you have a pattern for organizing your thoughts that enables you to present your ideas with logic. That organizational pattern is probably dictated by the main idea of your message. Before beginning to write, you must ask, "If this is what I want to say, what is the best way to organize my message?"

Suppose you were writing an orientation article describing support services available at your own college. You could summarize the resources in a **simple listing** pattern, or you could discuss them in the **sequence** or **time order** in which a freshman is likely to need them. Within your article, you might use a **description** or **definition** pattern to identify a relatively unknown service on campus, with **examples** of how it has helped others. You might also choose to **compare and contrast** a special service with that at another college. Thus, one long article might have an overall **simple listing** pattern of organization yet contain individual paragraphs that follow other patterns.

The following are examples of the patterns of organization found in textbooks. Some are used much more frequently than others, and some are more frequent in particular disciplines. For example, history textbooks often use the time order and the cause and effect patterns. Management textbooks frequently use the simple listing pattern, and psychology textbooks make heavy use of the definition and example pattern.

Notice the outline that accompanies each pattern of organization. After reading each example paragraph, enter the key points into the blank outline display to show that you understand the pattern.

Simple Listing

With a **simple listing,** items are randomly listed in a series of supporting facts or details. These supporting elements are of equal value, and the order in which they are presented is of no importance. Changing the order of the items does not change the meaning of the paragraph.

Signal words, often used as transitional words to link ideas in a paragraph with a pattern of simple listing, include *in addition, also, another, several, for example, a number of.*

EXAMPLE

Work-related Stress

Work-related stress has increased significantly in the last few years. People are spending more hours at work and bringing more work home with them. Job security has decreased in almost every industry. Pay, for many, has failed to keep up with the cost of living. Women are subject to exceptionally high stress levels as they try to live up to all of the expectations placed upon them. Finally, many people feel that they are trapped in jobs they hate, but can't escape.

Curtis O. Byer and Louis W. Shainberg, *Living Well: Health in Your Hands*, 2nd ed.

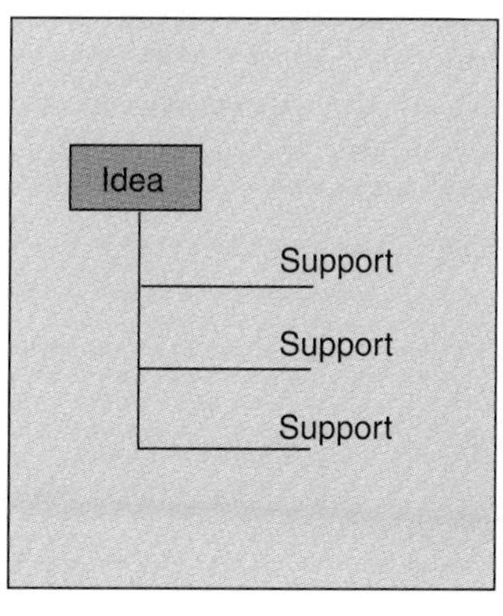

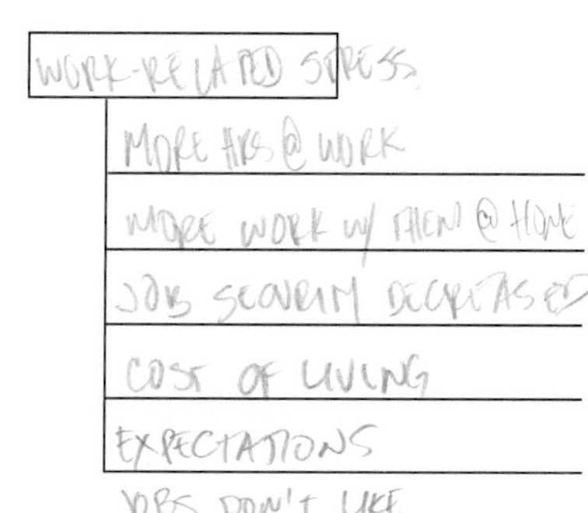

Definition

Frequently in a textbook, an entire paragraph is devoted to defining a complex term or idea. With **definition,** the concept is defined initially and then expanded with examples and restatements. In a textbook, a defined term is usually signaled by *italicized* or **boldfaced** type.

EXAMPLE

Ultrasound

Ultrasound is a relatively new technique that uses sound waves to produce an image that enables a physician to detect structural abnormalities. Useful pictures can be obtained as early as 7 weeks into pregnancy. Ultrasound is frequently used in conjunction with other techniques such as amniocentesis and fetoscopy.

John Dacey and John Travers, *Human Development*, 2nd ed.

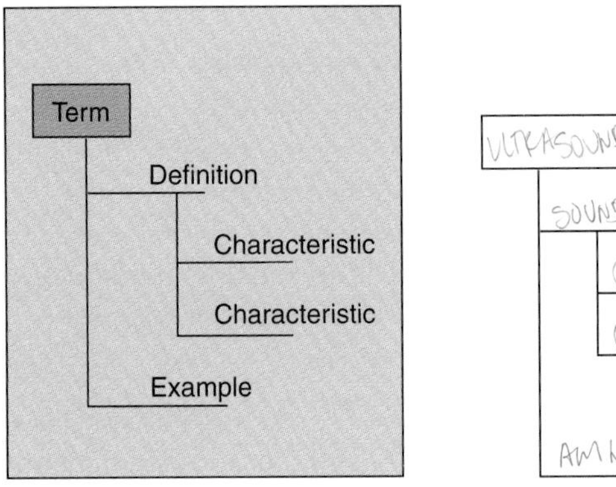

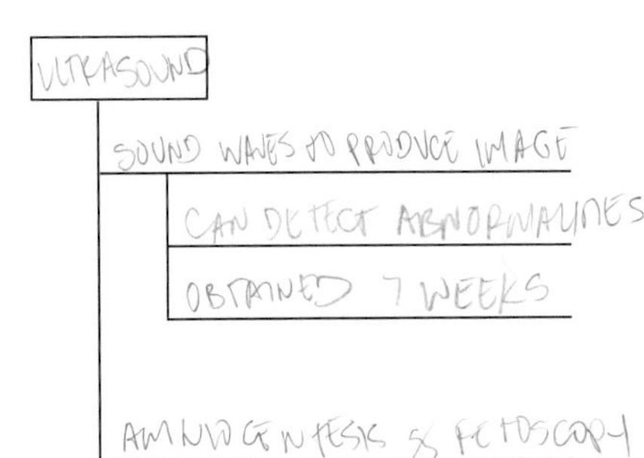

Description

Description is like listing; the characteristics that make up a description are no more than a definition or a simple list of details.

EXAMPLE

Caribbean

Caribbean America today is a land crowded with so many people that, as a region (encompassing the Greater and Lesser Antilles), it is the most densely populated part of the Americas. It is also a place of grinding poverty and, in all too many localities, unrelenting misery with little chance for escape.

H. J. De Blij and Peter O. Muller, *Geography: Realms, Regions, and Concepts*, 7th ed.

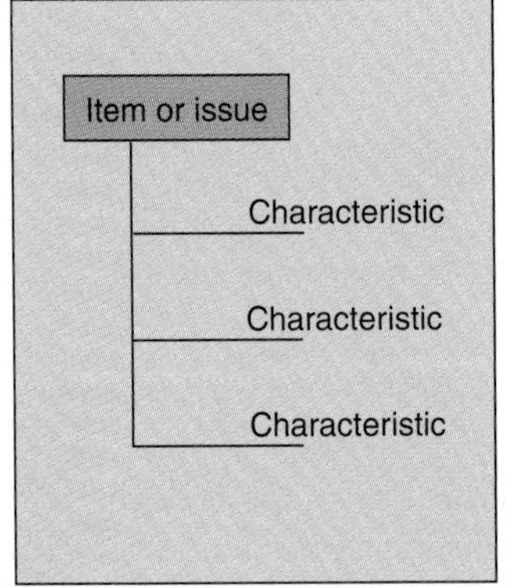

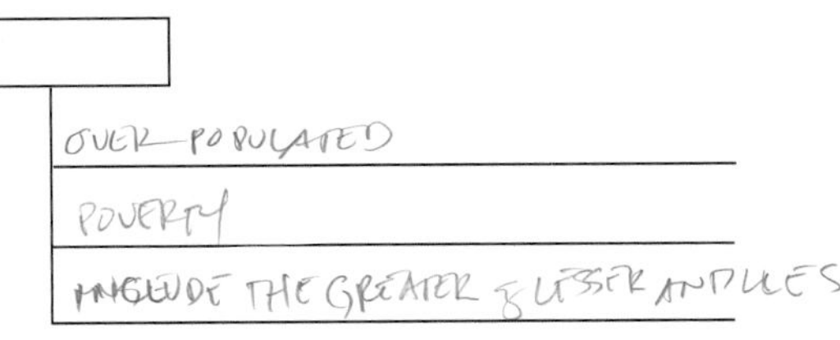

Time Order or Sequence

Items are listed in the order in which they occurred or in a specifically planned order in which they must develop. In this case, the **time order** is important, and changing it would change the meaning. Narrative writing, which tells a story, is an example of writing in which time order is important.

Signal words that are often used for time order, sequence, or narration include *first, second, third, after, before, when, until, at last, next, later.* Actual time periods, such as days or years, also signal sequence and time.

EXAMPLE

Mormon Movement

The idea of the Mormon church began when a young Joseph Smith, Jr., went into the New York woods in 1820 and was told by spirits that the true church of God would be reestablished. In 1823 another revelation led him to find buried golden plates and translate the *Book of Mormon.* Smith attracted thousands of followers and in the 1830s moved from Ohio to Missouri to Illinois to seek religious freedom for his group. In 1844 Smith was shot by an angry mob. After his death, a new leader, Brigham Young, led the Mormons to the Great Salt Lake.

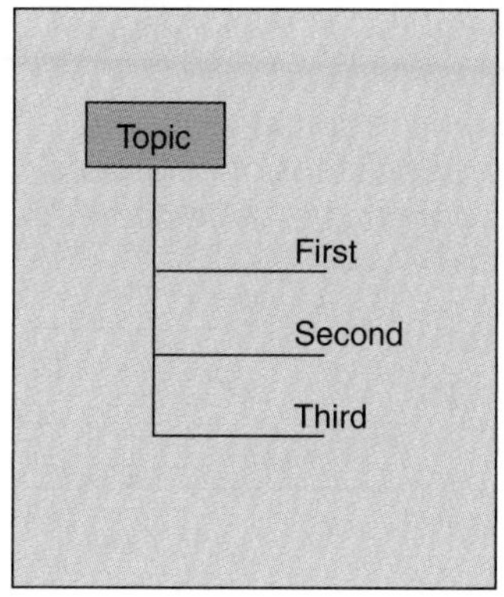

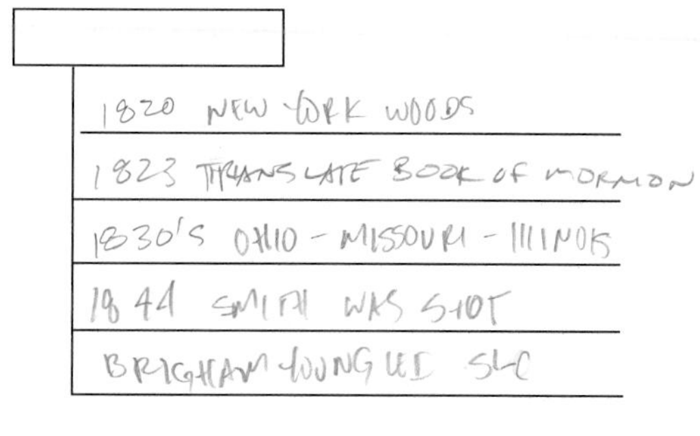

1820 NEW YORK WOODS
1823 TRANSLATE BOOK OF MORMON
1830'S OHIO - MISSOURI - ILLINOIS
1844 SMITH WAS SHOT
BRIGHAM YOUNG LED SLC

Contrast

With **contrast,** items are presented according to differences between or among them. Signal words that are often used for contrast include *different, in contrast, on the other hand, but, however, bigger than.*

EXAMPLE

Oranges

An orange grown in Florida usually has a thin and tightly fitting skin, and it is also heavy with juice. Californians say that if you want to eat a Florida orange you have to get into a bathtub first. On the other hand, California oranges are light in weight and have thick skins that break easily and come off in hunks.

John McPhee, *Oranges*

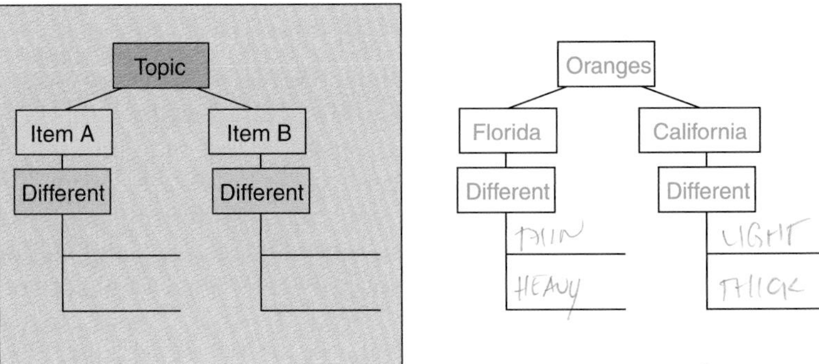

Comparison

With **comparison,** items are presented according to similarities between or among them. Signal words that are often used for comparison include *similar, in the same way, parallels.*

EXAMPLE

Jazz Greats

Jazz greats Louis Armstrong and Billie Holiday overcame similar obstacles in their struggling early years. Both were raised in the slums by working mothers, and both learned the discipline needed for success through hard work. As a teen, Armstrong hauled coal from 7 a.m. to 5 p.m. for 75 cents a day and then practiced on his trumpet after work. Similarly, after school Holiday scrubbed the white stone steps of neighbors' houses to earn an average of 90 cents a day, and then she came home to practice her singing.

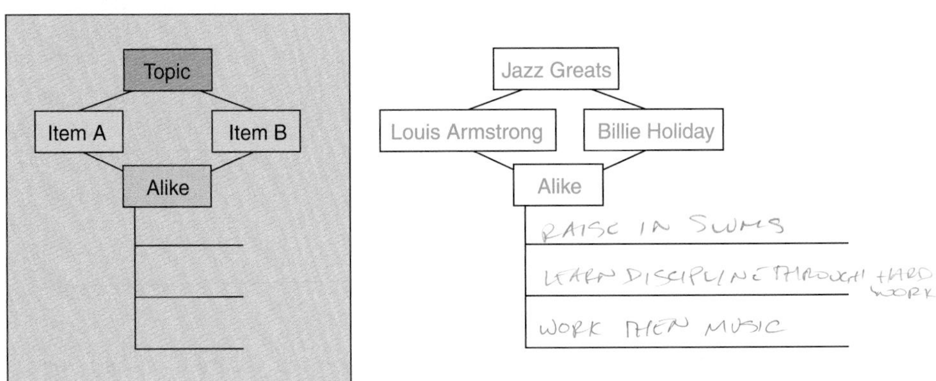

Comparison and Contrast

Some passages combine both comparisons and contrasts together into a single paragraph. This combination is called a **comparison-contrast pattern** and is demonstrated in the following examples.

EXAMPLE

Hispanic Americans

The primary groups in the rising new minority are Mexican Americans and Cuban Americans. Mexican Americans are heavily concentrated in the Southwest, whereas Cuban Americans are concentrated in Florida, particularly in the Miami area. Together the groups are called Hispanic Americans or Latinos. Although their histories are different, they share several similarities. They both speak the Spanish language and most of them, at least 85 percent, are Roman Catholic.

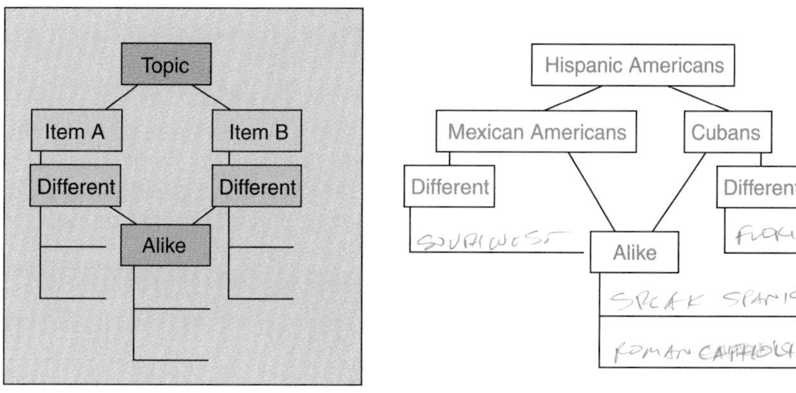

Cause and Effect

With **cause and effect,** an element is shown as producing another element. One is the *cause* or the "happening" that stimulated the particular result or *effect*. A paragraph may describe one cause or many causes, as well as one or many results. Signal words that are often used for cause and effect include *for this reason, consequently, on that account, hence, because.*

EXAMPLE

Winter Camp at Valley Forge

General George Washington's Continental army set up camp on the frozen grounds of Valley Forge in December of 1777 and experienced dire consequences. The winter was particularly cold that year and the soldiers lacked straw and blankets. Many froze in their beds. Food was scarce and soldiers died of malnutrition. Because of the misery and disease in the camp, many soldiers deserted the army and went home.

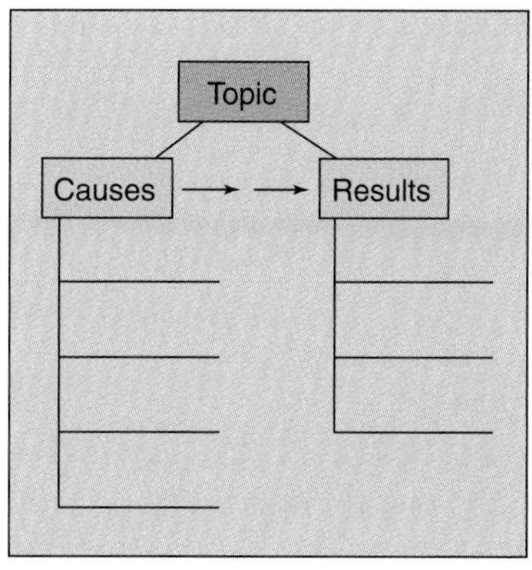

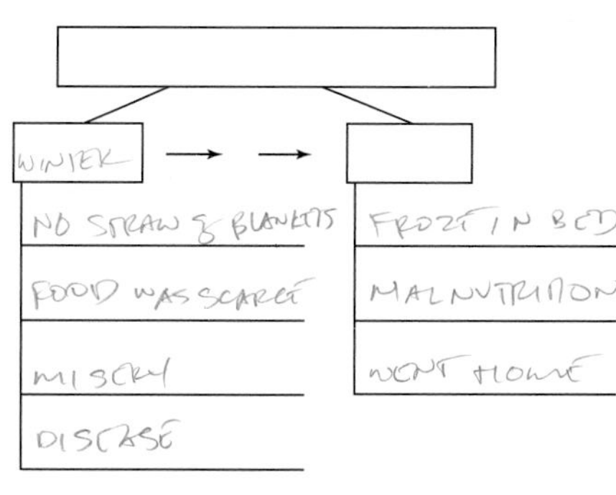

Classification

In order to simplify a complex topic, authors frequently begin introductory paragraphs by stating that the information that follows is divided into a certain number of groups or categories. The divisions are then named and the parts are explained. Signal words often used for classification include *two divisions, three groups, four elements, five classes, six levels, seven categories,* and so on.

EXAMPLE

Predation

Predation, the interaction in which one species kills and eats another, involves two groups. The predator, or consumer, must be alert and skillful to locate and capture the prey. The consumable group, or prey, constantly must adapt its behavior to defend against being eaten.

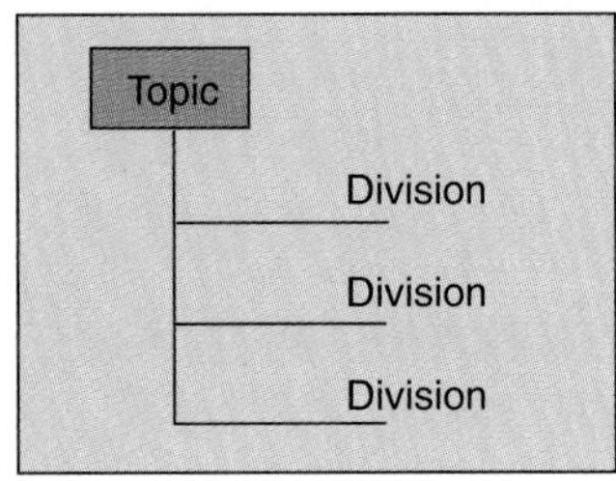

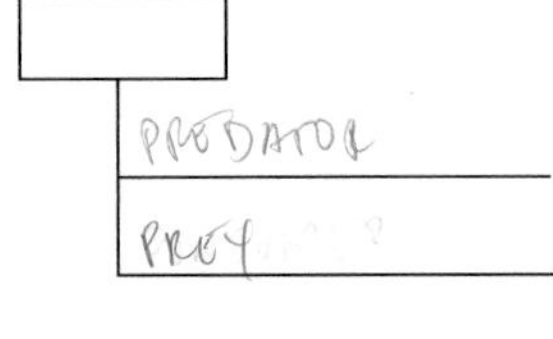

Addition

The addition pattern is used to provide more information to something that has already been explained. Signal words are *furthermore, again, also, further, moreover, besides, likewise.*

EXAMPLE

Entrepreneur Quincy Jones

Not only is Quincy Jones the talented producer who helped drive Michael Jackson's "Beat It" to a No. 1 hit and "Thriller" to the best-selling album of all time, he is also the founder of VIBE magazine and the co-owner of SPIN magazine. Furthermore, Jones, who has been awarded 26 Grammys and a Grammy Legend, is Chairman and CEO of the Quincy Jones Media Group.

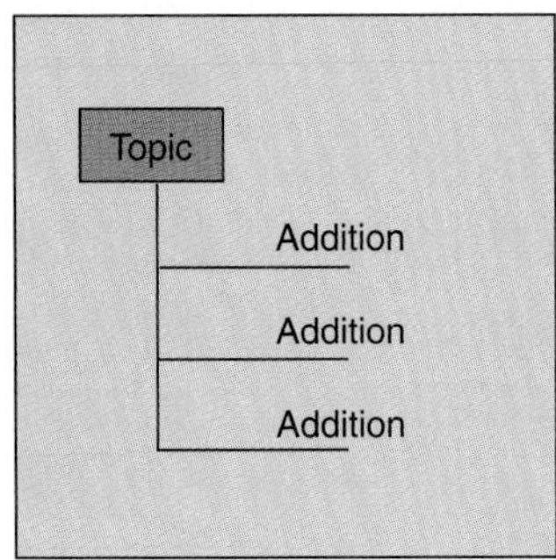

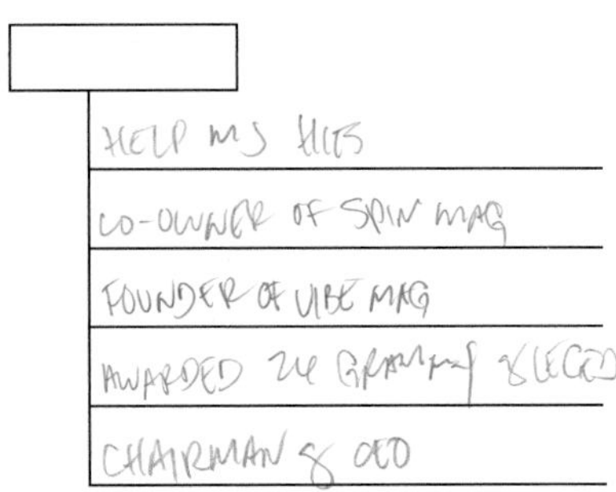

HELP MJ HITS
CO-OWNER OF SPIN MAG
FOUNDER OF VIBE MAG
CHAIRMAN & CEO

Summary

A summary usually comes at the end of an article or chapter and condenses the main idea or thesis into a short and simple concluding statement with a few major supporting details. Signal words are *in conclusion, briefly, to sum up, in short, in a nutshell.*

EXAMPLE

Remember the Alamo

In conclusion, the 1836 phrase "Remember the Alamo," became an unfair threat to Mexican Texans. Many Mexican Texans had lived within the borders of Texas for generations and fought and died for Texas independence. They were not defenders of Santa Anna and did not deserve the ethnic prejudice the phrase stimulated.

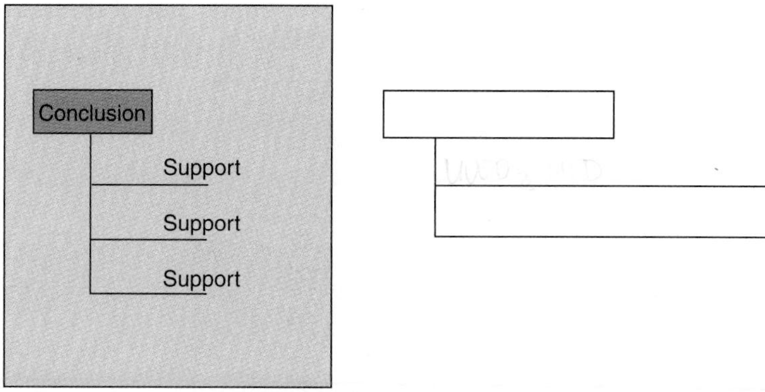

Location or Spatial Order

Location or spatial order identifies the whereabouts of a place or object. Signal words are *north, east, south, west, next to, near, below, above, close by, within, without, adjacent to, beside, around, to the right or left side, opposite.*

EXAMPLE

Egypt

The Republic of Egypt is located in the northeastern corner of Africa. The northern border of Egypt is the Mediterranean Sea. Libya is the country to the west and the Sudan lies to the south. Across the Suez Canal and to the east lies Israel.

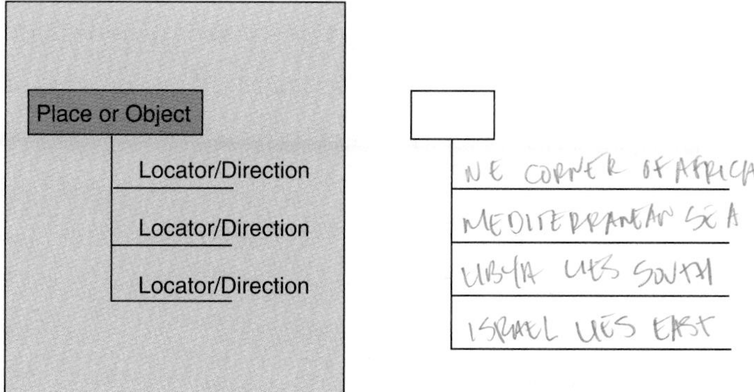

Generalization and Example

In the generalization and example pattern, a general statement or conclusion is supported with specific examples. Signal words include *to restate that, that is, for example, to illustrate, for instance.*

EXAMPLE

Smoking

To restate it in simple terms, smoking kills. The American Cancer Society estimates that tobacco smoking is the cause of 30 percent of all deaths from cancer. Lung cancer is the leading cause of death from cancer in the United States, with 85 to 90 percent of these cases being from smoking. Save your life by not smoking.

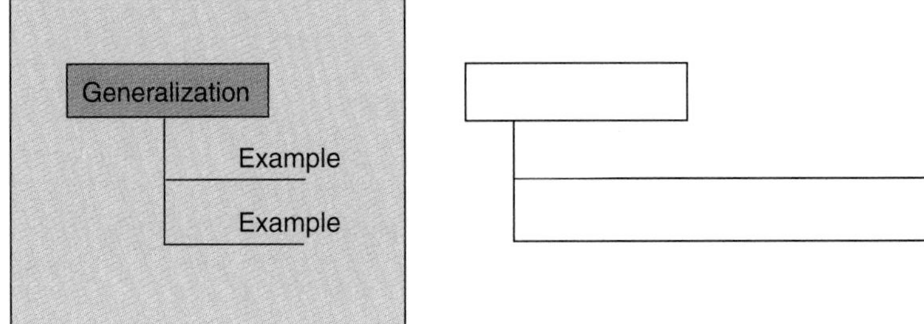

Reader's Tip

Patterns of Organization and Signal Words

* **Addition:** furthermore • again • also • further • moreover • besides • likewise
  (providing more information)
* **Cause and Effect:** because • for this reason • consequently • hence • as a result • thus • due to • therefore
  (showing one element as producing or causing a result or effect)
* **Classification:** groups • categories • elements • classes • parts
  (dividing items into groups or categories)
* **Comparison:** in a similar way • similar • parallels • likewise • in a like manner
  (listing similarities among items)
* **Contrast:** on the other hand • bigger than • but • however • conversely • on the contrary • although • nevertheless
  (listing differences among items)

(continued)

- **Definition:** can be defined • means • for example • like
(initially defining a concept and expanding with examples and restatements)
- **Description:** is • as • like • could be described
(listing characteristics or details)
- **Generalization and Example:** to restate • that is • for example • to illustrate • for instance
(explaining with examples to illustrate)
- **Location or Spatial Order:** next to • near • below • above • close by • within • without • adjacent to • beside • around • to the right or left side • opposite
(identifying the whereabouts of objects)
- **Simple Listing:** also • another • several • for example
(randomly listing items in a series)
- **Summary:** in conclusion • briefly • to sum up • in short • in a nutshell
(condensing major points)
- **Time Order, Sequence, or Narration:** first • second • finally • after • before • next • later • now • at last • until • thereupon • while • during
(listing events in order of occurrence)

Exercise 5.2

Identifying Paragraph Patterns

Each of the following items presents the first two sentences of a paragraph stating the main idea and a major supporting detail. Select the letter that indicates the pattern of organization that you would predict for each.

_________ 1. Often called the "kissing disease," mononucleosis is caused by the Epstein-Barr virus. The symptoms include sore throat, fever, headache, nausea, chills, and weakness.
a. summary
b. classification
c. definition
d. comparison/contrast

_________ 2. There are several preventive measures that you can take to avoid back pain. Try not to sleep on your stomach, and buy a good chair for doing your work.
a. description
b. simple listing
c. time order
d. classification

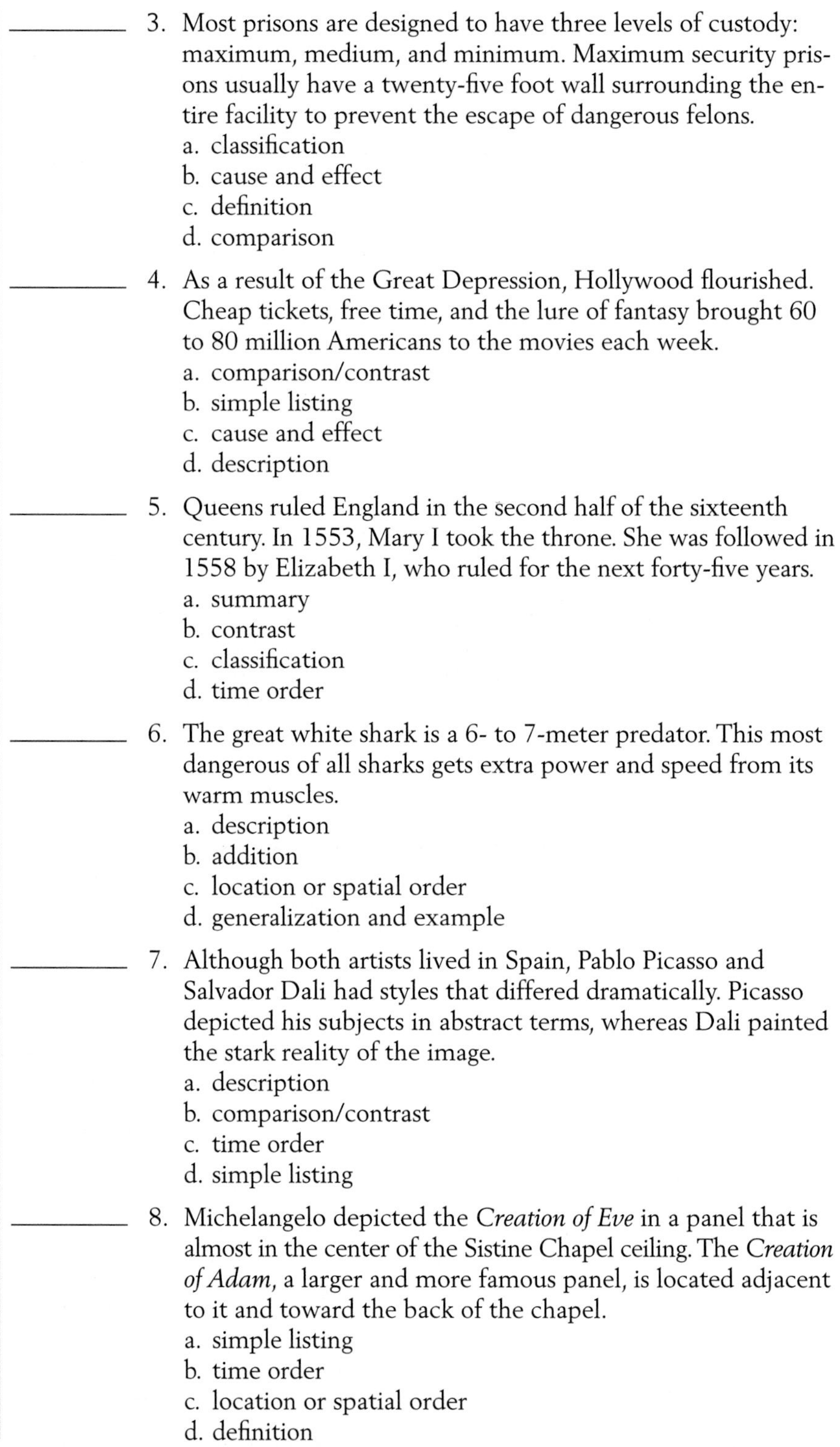

_____ 3. Most prisons are designed to have three levels of custody: maximum, medium, and minimum. Maximum security prisons usually have a twenty-five foot wall surrounding the entire facility to prevent the escape of dangerous felons.
   a. classification
   b. cause and effect
   c. definition
   d. comparison

_____ 4. As a result of the Great Depression, Hollywood flourished. Cheap tickets, free time, and the lure of fantasy brought 60 to 80 million Americans to the movies each week.
   a. comparison/contrast
   b. simple listing
   c. cause and effect
   d. description

_____ 5. Queens ruled England in the second half of the sixteenth century. In 1553, Mary I took the throne. She was followed in 1558 by Elizabeth I, who ruled for the next forty-five years.
   a. summary
   b. contrast
   c. classification
   d. time order

_____ 6. The great white shark is a 6- to 7-meter predator. This most dangerous of all sharks gets extra power and speed from its warm muscles.
   a. description
   b. addition
   c. location or spatial order
   d. generalization and example

_____ 7. Although both artists lived in Spain, Pablo Picasso and Salvador Dali had styles that differed dramatically. Picasso depicted his subjects in abstract terms, whereas Dali painted the stark reality of the image.
   a. description
   b. comparison/contrast
   c. time order
   d. simple listing

_____ 8. Michelangelo depicted the *Creation of Eve* in a panel that is almost in the center of the Sistine Chapel ceiling. The *Creation of Adam,* a larger and more famous panel, is located adjacent to it and toward the back of the chapel.
   a. simple listing
   b. time order
   c. location or spatial order
   d. definition

_______ 9. In short, the Internet can be a source of dangerous misinformation. Anyone can develop a Website and fill it with distortions of the truth and inflammatory accusations.
a. classification
b. summary
c. definition
d. time order

_______ 10. In case of a sprained ankle, you should first apply ice to constrict the blood vessels to stop internal bleeding. Next, elevate your foot above the level of your heart to further control bleeding by making the blood run downhill.
a. summary
b. classification
c. generalization and example
d. sequence

Exercise 5.3

Patterns of Organization and Main Idea

Read the following passages and use the three-question system you learned in Chapter 4 to determine the author's main idea. In addition, indicate the dominant pattern of organization used by the author. Select from the following list:

simple listing	definition	description
time order	comparison-contrast	cause and effect

Passage A

Let us follow the story of how rabbits were introduced into Australia. European rabbits reached Australia with the first European settlers in 1788 and repeated introductions followed. By the early 1800s rabbits were being kept in every large settlement and had been liberated many times. All the early rabbit introductions either died out or remained localized. No one knows why.

On Christmas Day, 1859, the brig H.M.S. *Lightning* arrived at Melbourne with about a dozen wild European rabbits bound for an estate in western Victoria. Within three years rabbits had started to spread, after a bush fire destroyed the fences enclosing one colony. From a slow spread at first the colonization picked up speed during the 1870s, and by 1900 the European rabbit had spread 1,000 miles to the north and west, changing the entire economy of nature in southeastern Australia.

Charles Krebs, *The Message of Ecology*

1. Who or what is this about? _______________

2. What are the major details? _______________

____

____

____

3. What is the overall pattern of organization? ______________________

4. What is the main idea the author is trying to convey about the topic?

____

____

Passage B

Sloppy people can't bear to part with anything. They give loving attention to every detail. When sloppy people say they're going to tackle the surface of a desk, they really mean it. Not a paper will go unturned; not a rubber band will go unboxed.

Neat people are bums and clods at heart. They have cavalier attitudes toward possessions, including family heirlooms. Everything is just another dust-catcher to them. If anything collects dust, it's got to go and that's that.

Suzanne Britt, *Neat People vs. Sloppy People*

1. Who or what is this about? ______________________

2. What are the major details? ______________________

____

____

3. What is the overall pattern of organization? ______________________

4. What is the main idea the author is trying to convey about the topic?

____

Passage C

The disadvantage faced by children who attempt morning schoolwork on an empty stomach appears to be at least partly due to hypoglycemia. The average child up to the age of ten or so needs to eat every four to six hours to maintain a blood glucose concentration high enough to support the activity of the brain and nervous system. A child's brain is as big as an adult's, and the brain is the body's chief glucose consumer. A child's liver is considerably smaller, and the liver is the organ responsible for storing glucose (as glycogen) and for releasing it into the blood as needed. The liver can't store more than about four hours' worth of glycogen; hence the need to eat fairly often. Teachers aware of the late-morning slump in their classrooms wisely request that a midmorning snack be provided; it improves classroom performance all the way to lunch time. But for the child who hasn't had breakfast, the morning may be lost altogether.

Eva May Nunnelley Hamilton et al., *Nutrition*, 5th ed.

1. Who or what is this about? ______________________

2. What are the major details? ______________________

____

____

3. What is the overall pattern of organization? ____________________

4. What is the main idea the author is trying to convey about the topic?

____

____

Passage D

The media do influence public opinion to some degree. Their power comes largely from their role as gatekeepers—determining what information will be passed on to large numbers of people. There are at least five ways in which the media affect opinion. First, they *authenticate* information, making it more credible to the audience. A news item reported in the mass media often seems more believable than one passed by word of mouth. Second, the media *validate* private opinions, preferences, and values. If a famous commentator offers a view similar to our own, we are likely to feel more confident of our own opinion. Third, the media *legitimize* unconventional viewpoints. The wildest idea may eventually sound reasonable, or at least worth considering, if we read it repeatedly on the editorial pages of newspapers or hear it on the evening news. Fourth, the mass media *concretize* free-floating anxieties and ill-defined preferences. By supplying such labels as "population explosion," "the crime wave," and "the great racial divide," the media in effect create a world of objects against which feelings can be specifically expressed. Fifth, the mass media help *establish a hierarchy* of importance and prestige among persons, objects, and opinions. If the national media never interview the senators from your state, the public is not likely to consider them important, even if they are very influential among their colleagues in the Senate.

Alex Thio, *Sociology*, 3rd ed.

1. Who or what is this about? ____________________

2. What are the major details? ____________________

____

____

3. What is the overall pattern of organization? ____________________

4. What is the main idea the author is trying to convey about the topic?

____

Passage E

Intellectual property is created through a person's creative activities. Books, articles, songs, paintings, screenplays, and computer software are all intellectual property. The U.S. Constitution grants protection to intellectual property by means of copyrights, trademarks, and patents. Copyrights and patents apply to tangible expressions of an idea—not to the ideas themselves. Thus, you could not copyright the idea of cloning dinosaurs from fossil DNA. Michael Crichton could copyright his novel

Jurassic Park, which is a tangible result of that idea, and sell the film rights to producer-director Steven Spielberg.

Ronald Ebert and Ricky Griffin, *Business Essentials*, 2nd ed.

1. Who or what is this about? __________
2. What are the major details? __________
3. What is the overall pattern of organization? __________
4. What is the main idea the author is trying to convey about the topic? __________

Summary Points

- **What are transitional words?**

  Transitions or signal words connect parts of sentences and lead you to anticipate a continuation or a change in thoughts. They guide you through the logic of the message by showing the relationships of ideas within sentences, between sentences, and between paragraphs.

- **What is an organizational pattern?**

  An organizational pattern is the presentation plan, format, or structure for the message. It is a pattern for organizing your thoughts that enables you to present your ideas with logic. These patterns for presenting details and developing details can vary.

Selection 1 ECONOMICS

CONTEMPORARY FOCUS

Human rights violations occur throughout the world. How can those of us who enjoy freedom work to liberate those around the world who are less fortunate?

IN SUDAN, CHILDHOODS OF SLAVERY

Dale Gavlak

Christian Science Monitor, August, 22, 2000

In a halfway house run by a Dinka tribal chief, 14-year-old Shama Amal waits for the day when he will see his mother again.

If that day ever comes, it would put an end to an ordeal that began nine years ago, when the Dinka boy, then 5, was kidnapped by an Arab cattleman and made a slave. Shama escaped after his master put burning coal in his palm—punishment for letting livestock stray.

In this impoverished African nation, some 14,000 southern Sudanese children and women have been abducted in recent years, according to government figures.

Officials in the capital, Khartoum, say the kidnappings are simply part of intertribal conflicts. But critics insist that the abducted, whom they call "slaves," number far greater and that their enslavement is part of a government-sponsored program of forced Islamization—an accusation Sudanese officials dismiss as false propaganda.

The attackers take livestock, belongings, and harvests—and need carriers to transport the goods. Consequently, captive women and children become part of the Baggara's workforce. They fetch water and firewood, herd livestock, and do heavy manual labor.

Collaborative Activity

Collaborate on responses to the following questions:

- Are there ways in which the government can control the kidnappings and enslavement?
- What aspects of this slavery problem are religious in nature?
- How might paying for the release of slaves stop the problem?

Stage 1: Preview

After reading this selection, I will know what slave redemption has to do with economics. Agree ☐ Disagree ☐

Activate Schema

Where is the Sudan, and what countries are adjacent to it?

Learning Strategy

Explain the reasons why the slave redemption has not worked as envisioned.

Word Knowledge

What do you know about these words?

adherents	alleviate	suppressed	inception	unilateral
vicious circle	maritime	vein	incentive	enticing

Your instructor may give a true-false vocabulary review before or after reading.

Stage 2: Integrate Knowledge While Reading

Predict Picture Relate Monitor Correct

SLAVE REDEMPTION IN SUDAN

From Roger LeRoy Miller, Daniel K. Benjamin, and Douglass C. North, *The Economics of Public Issues*, 12th ed.

Sudan is Africa's largest nation. Located immediately south of Egypt, it encompasses nearly one million square miles and is home to 35 million people. It is also home to poverty, disease, civil war—and the emergence of modern-day slavery. The slave trade, in turn, has given rise to a new humanitarian movement, whose adherents seek to alleviate Sudan's misery by buying freedom for its slaves. Well-intentioned though they are, these humanitarian efforts may be making things worse.

Slavery is a centuries-old practice in Sudan, one that colonial British rulers finally managed to halt during World War I. The Sudanese gained independence in 1956 but, despite ensuing periods of civil war, the slave trade initially remained a piece of history. This changed in 1989, when the National Islamic Front (NIF) took control of the government. The NIF quickly began arming the Muslim Baggara tribe in the northern part of the country to fight against the rebellious Christian tribes of the south. The Baggara previously had made a regular practice of enslaving members of the southern Dinka tribe, and once armed by the NIF the Baggara resumed the slave raids the British had suppressed. This activity was further aided by the government, which supplied horses to the Baggara and permitted slave markets to open in the cities controlled by the NIF. Perhaps as many as 20,000 Dinkas, mostly women and children, were enslaved and taken north, selling for as little as $15 each. The

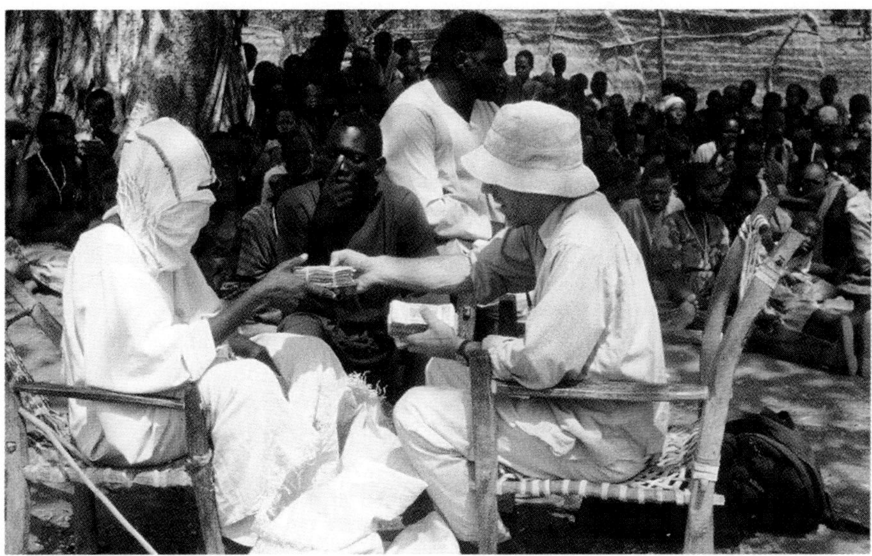

In a slave trade in the Sudan, John Eibner hands over money to a slave retriever in Sudan in order to buy freedom for the slaves.
Getty Images

slaves were branded with the names of their owners and put to work as cooks, maids, field hands, and concubines.

Within a few years, word of the revived slave trade began filtering out of Sudan. In response, a variety of humanitarian groups from other nations began buying slaves in large batches and setting them free. The process is called "slave redemption," and its purpose—one hopes—is to reduce the number of people who are enslaved.

Raising money for slave redemption has become big business, spreading rapidly among public schools and evangelical churches. A middle school in Oregon, for example, raised $2500 to be used for slave redemption. Even more impressive was an elementary school class in Colorado. After the children's efforts caught the media's eye, the class raised more than $50,000 for slave redemption.

The largest of the humanitarian groups involved in slave redemption is Christian Solidarity International (CSI). This group says it has freed almost 8000 slaves since 1995, most at prices of about $50 each. In 1999 alone, for example, CSI purchased the freedom of nearly 3000 slaves. Several other groups also purchased the freedom of several hundred slaves that year, sometimes at prices of up to $100 each.

Per capita income in Sudan is about $500 per year, which makes slave prices of $50 to $100 apiece quite attractive to the Baggara slave raiders. This is particularly true when the redeemers are buying in the south, where the targeted Dinkas live, and prices in the north, the traditional market for slaves, are as low as $15 apiece. In fact, says one individual who used to be active in slave redemption, "We've made slave redemption more profitable than narcotics." What are the consequences of such profitability?

There have been two sets of responses. First, on the demand side, the higher prices for slaves make it more costly for owners in the north to hold slaves. So rather than own slaves, some of them have offered their slaves to the redeemers. This, of course, is exactly the effect the slave redemption movement has desired. But there is also a supply response: When the market value of slaves rises due to an increase in demand (the demand of the slave redeemers), we expect an increase in the quantity supplied. That is, we expect the raiders who produce slaves by capturing them to engage in more of that activity. This is exactly what has happened in Sudan.

Slave redemption began in earnest in 1995 and, according to local authorities, the number of slave raids has grown each year since. Moreover, the size of a typical raiding party has grown from roughly 400 attackers to more than 2500. Why the growth? Slaves used to be traded in relatively small batches, but the redeemers prefer to buy in large lots—1000 or more at a time. Collecting and assembling the number of slaves required to satisfy the redemption buyers thus requires considerably more manpower. Hence, the slave trade is gradually being transformed from a cottage industry into a large-scale business enterprise. Overall, it is estimated that the number of slaves captured in raids each year has risen steadily since the inception of slave redemption. Initially, it is likely that the impact of slave redemption was chiefly on the demand side: that is, the first slaves redeemed were almost surely "freed from slavery" in the sense that we would normally use the terminology. But once the stock of slave holdings in the north had adjusted downward in response to the newly elevated equilibrium price, there was only one place for the slave traders to get the slaves demanded by the redemption buyers. This was from the raiders who were now taking slaves for one purpose only—sale to the redeemers. Thus, once the stock of slaves in the north is adjusted to its lower equilibrium level, *all* of the slaves subsequently "freed" by the redeemers are in fact individuals who never would have been enslaved had the redeemers not first made a market for them. In addition, because large numbers of new slaves now spend some time in captivity awaiting redemption, it is even possible that the total number of people in slavery at any point in time is actually *higher* because of the well-intentioned efforts of the slave redeemers.

As unpleasant as such reasoning is, it agrees with the opinions of people who observe the slave trade firsthand. As a local humanitarian worker says, "Giving money to the slave traders only encourages the trade. It is wrong and must stop. Where does the money go? It goes to the raiders to buy more guns, raid more villages . . . It is a vicious circle." In a similar vein, the chief of one village that has been targeted by the slave raiders says, "Redemption is not the solution. It means you are encouraging the raiders."

In addition to encouraging the capture of new slaves, redemption also reduces any incentive for owners to set free their less productive slaves. Prior to 1995, about 10 percent of all slaves, chiefly older women and young children, were allowed to escape or even told to go home, because the costs of feeding, clothing, and housing them exceeded their value to their owners. Now slaves who have been freed on their own are instead held in captivity until a trader can be found to haul them south for sale to the redeemers.

The final effect of redemption has been to create a trade in fictitious slaves—individuals who are paid to pose as slaves for the purposes of redemption, and who are then given a cut of the redemption price after they are "freed." Although redemption groups obviously try to avoid participating in such deals, observers familiar with the trade consider them a regular part of the redemption business.

Is there another way to combat slavery in Sudan? On the demand side, the U.S. government has long refused to negotiate with terrorists or pay ransom to kidnappers, simply because it believes that such tactics encourage terrorism and kidnapping. It recognizes that paying a ransom increases the profits of kidnapping, thus enticing more individuals into the trade.

On the supply side, the British were originally successful in ending the slave trade in Sudan and elsewhere in their empire by dispatching soldiers to kill or disarm slave raiders, and by sending warships to close off maritime slave-trading routes. Sudan, of course, is an independent sovereign nation today; both the United Nations and the British electorate would likely oppose unilateral military action by the British government against Sudanese slave raiders. Yet even the people who used to be subject to British colonial rule have mixed feelings. When asked to compare the colonial British policies to the redeemers' policies of today, a schoolmaster in the affected area remarked, "If the colonial government were standing for election, I would vote for them." So too might the victims of the slave trade in Sudan.

Stage 3: Recall

Stop to self-test, relate, and react. Your instructor may choose to give you a true-false comprehension review.

Thinking About "Slave Redemption in Sudan"

What are the demand and supply sides of the slavery redemption program? Describe the intended and the actual results of each.

Response Suggestion: Define both sides and list the intended and actual results of each.

Contemporary Link

Given the existing problems with slave redemption, what other solutions would you suggest to end the slavery in the Sudan?

Skill Development: Organizational Patterns

Fill in the organizational diagram on page 218 to reflect the cause and effect pattern of the selection.

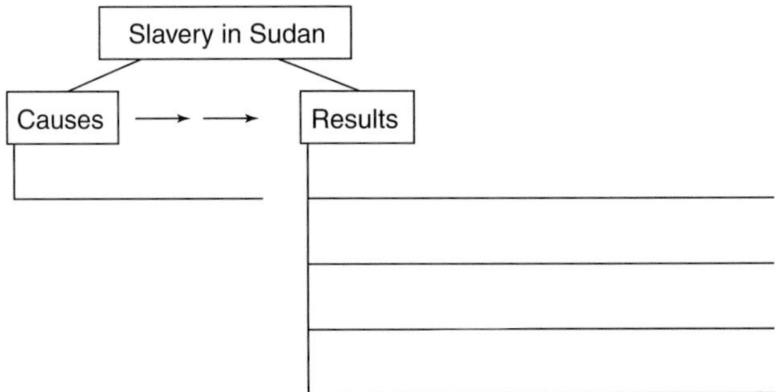

Comprehension Questions

After reading the selection, answer the following questions with *a, b, c,* or *d*. In order to help you analyze your strengths and weaknesses, the question types are indicated.

Main Idea _______ 1. Which is the best statement of the main idea?
a. Humanitarian efforts in the Sudan have captured world wide attention.
b. The government and the humanitarians have united to free slaves from the Sudan.
c. The slave redemption program in the Sudan has increased rather than decreased the number of slaves captured.
d. The new government has brought independence to most of the people of the Sudan.

Detail _______ 2. The slave trade in the Sudan reemerged in 1989 because
a. the British never got rid of the slave trade.
b. the Muslim government failed in its attempt to stop the slave trade.
c. the NIF lost in a civil war against the Muslim Baggara tribe.
d. The Muslim government allowed and even encouraged the enslavement of members of rebellious Christian tribes.

Detail _______ 3. Slave redemption is a process of
a. capturing slaves.
b. selling victims into slavery.
c. buying the freedom of slaves.
d. the government allowing slavery.

Detail _______ 4. The resumption of the slave trade in 1989 was aided by all of the following except
a. the NIF.
b. the Baggara tribe.
c. Muslims in the Sudan.
d. Christian tribes.

Inference _________ 5. From an economic perspective, the author implies that humanitarian efforts would have worked to reduce slavery if
a. the demand were met and the supply was not increased.
b. both supply and demand increased.
c. only the supply increased.
d. supply grew greater than demand.

Inference _________ 6. The author implies that a "cottage industry" is
a. a small business.
b. a large-scale business enterprise.
c. a corporation.
d. a government program.

Detail _________ 7. The desire of redeemers to purchase slaves in large lots created all of the following except
a. a dramatic increase in the number of attackers.
b. fictitious slaves.
c. the voluntary release of slaves whose costs for owners exceeded their value.
d. a greater effort to increase supply.

Detail _________ 8. A fictitious slave is a
a. recaptured slave who is sold twice.
b. person who is paid to pretend to be a slave.
c. person who, by false accounting, is sold but the person does not physically exist.
d. kidnapped slave.

Detail _________ 9. The British ended slavery in the Sudan by
a. paying ransoms.
b. kidnapping slave raiders.
c. attacking slave raiders.
d. voting in elections.

Inference _________ 10. The reader can conclude that
a. the Sudanese government will join with the United Nations to use force against the slave raiders.
b. the humanitarian groups are beginning to support military force rather than redemption as a means of ridding the Sudan of slavery.
c. the success of the humanitarian group in raising money for slave redemption has also led to the failure in ridding the Sudan of slavery.
d. the United Nations and the British will use force to cut the maritime slave-trade routes.

Answer the following with *T* (true) or *F* (false).

Detail _________ 11. Prior to World War II, the Baggara tribe conducted slave raids against the Dinka tribe.

Inference _________ 12. The primary purpose of initially reviving the slave trade was to profit from slave redemption.

Detail _________ 13. As soon as the Sudanese gained independence in 1956, the slave trade resumed.

Inference _________ 14. The author feels that organizations such as Christian Solidarity International have intensified the slave problem.

Inference _________ 15. In the final quotation, the author suggests that some people in the Sudan feel that the British were better rulers than the Sudanese.

Vocabulary

According to the way the italicized word was used in the selection, select *a*, *b*, *c*, or *d* for the word or phrase that gives the best definition. The number in parentheses indicates the line of the passage in which the word is located.

_________ 1. "*adherents* seek" (5)
a. followers
b. founders
c. opponents
d. demonstrators

_________ 2. "*alleviate* Sudan's misery" (5)
a. assault
b. relieve
c. confront
d. recognize

_________ 3. "British had *suppressed*" (16–17)
a. stopped
b. started
c. disliked
d. disowned

_________ 4. "*inception* of slave redemption" (65)
a. violation
b. reduction
c. justification
d. beginning

_________ 5. "It is a *vicious circle*" (84)
a. unethical act
b. crime against humanity
c. solution creates problem
d. religious challenge

_________ 6. "In a similar *vein*" (84)
a. line of thought
b. community
c. strategy
d. phase

_________ 7. "*incentive* for owners" (88)
a. allowance
b. reluctance
c. financial motivation
d. power

_________ 8. "*enticing* more individuals" (103)
a. surrendering
b. attracting
c. surrounding
d. demanding

_________ 9. "*maritime* slave-trading routes" (106–107)
a. popular
b. sea
c. successful
d. temporary

_________ 10. "*unilateral* military action" (109)
a. one-sided
b. two-sided
c. immediate
d. united

Search the Net

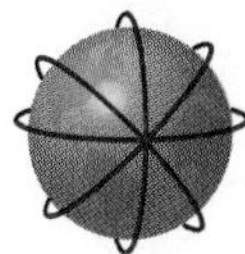

What happens to children in the Sudan who are kidnapped and enslaved? How are young women treated compared to young men? Begin your own search, or start with one of the following:

The London Free Press Online: http://www.lfpress.com/sudan/

Oneworld.net: http://www.oneworld.org/

The country of Sudan is plagued not only by slavery, but also by war and hunger. What other countries have efforts under way to help Sudan? Describe their efforts to improve conditions in Sudan. Begin your own search, or start with one of the following:

World Food Programme: http://www.wfp.org/index.htm

Oxfam Community Aid Abroad: http://www.caa.org.au/world/africa/sudan/

Concept Prep for Economics

What is economics?

Economics involves analyzing different aspects of the demands of the marketplace and the supply or scarcity of available products and services. Economists study inflation, minimum wages, unemployment, taxation, and the many factors that affect our economic well-being. One such factor is the stock market.

What is a stock?

A **stock** is a share of the ownership in a company. Corporations sell shares in order to raise money, and a large company may have millions of shareholders. If a private company desires to go public (sell stock) and meets the qualifications of the stock exchange, the price of a share of stock is set for the **initial public offering (IPO)**. The company then sells shares to get money for reinvestment or for the owners to get some of their investment money out. The shares are traded on one of the exchanges of the stock market.

Usually shares are purchased in lots of 100, but you can buy any amount you wish. You pay a fee to a licensed **broker** for completing the purchase. Many investors buy with online discount brokers and pay a fee of approximately $30 for each purchase and each sale. No longer do you get certificates for your stocks, but instead the documentation for your purchase is held by the brokerage firm in **"Street Name"** (in the broker's name).

Traders buy and sell stocks on the floor of the New York Stock Exchange in lower Manhattan.
Chris Hondros/Getty Images

The price of a stock should reflect the value of the company, including its **earnings** (profits) and **assets** (holdings that have a monetary value). All too often, however, the price of a stock represents what people are willing to pay for it. Thus a stock can be overvalued because of wild expectations, as happened with Internet stocks, or a stock can be undervalued because of temporary problems with earnings or sales.

Financial rewards from stocks come in two ways. The first is through annual **dividends,** which are shares of the profits based on the number of stocks owned. The second and greatest reward, however, will come if the company flourishes and your shares appreciate. After a few years, you might triple your money and sell 100 shares of a $25 stock for $75 each and make a nice profit. On the other hand, there are no guarantees with stocks. The price of the stocks may decline and you may lose money. You will hope for a **bull market,** a rising trend in stock prices, rather than a **bear market,** which is a declining price trend.

What are stock exchanges?

Stock exchanges are organizations that are formed to sell the stocks of their members.

- The **New York Stock Exchange (NYSE),** with its trading floor located on **Wall Street** in New York City, is the oldest exchange. Known as the **"Big Board,"** it is also the largest exchange and sells many of the **blue chip stocks** issued by large established companies such as Coca-Cola and General Electric. These blue chips are well known, widely held by investors, and unlikely to go bankrupt. The name comes from poker, where the blue chips have the highest value.

- The **American Stock Exchange (AMEX)** is also located in New York. Its minimum requirements for membership are less stringent. As firms grow, they often transfer from the AMEX to the NYSE.
- The **National Association of Securities Dealers Automated Quotation (NASDAQ)** system has no trading floor but is an electronic network for trading stocks. Many high-tech and dot-com stocks, such as Microsoft, Oracle, and Cisco, are traded on the NASDAQ.

What are stock indexes?

- The **Dow-Jones Industrial Average** (the **Dow**) is an index or sum of the market prices for thirty of the largest industrial firms listed on the NYSE. If the many blue chips indexed by the Dow are increasing in value, the Dow is up.
- The **Standard & Poor's Composite Index (the S & P)** gives a broader view of the strength of the market. It is a sum of the market prices for 500 stocks, which includes 400 industrial, 40 utilities, 40 financial institutions, and 20 transportation companies.

REVIEW QUESTIONS

Study the material and answer the following questions.

1. Why would a company go public and sell stock? ______________________
2. What is an IPO? ______________________
3. What is the discount broker's commission on a stock purchase? ______________________
4. Who keeps the stock if it is in "Street Name"? ______________________
5. Is the greater potential for gain in a stock dividend or in stock appreciation? ______________________
6. If you are forced to sell, is it usually better to sell a stock in a bear or a bull market? ______________________
7. What are blue chip companies? ______________________
8. Which stock exchange is the oldest and most established? ______________________
9. Which stock exchange is on an electronic network with no trading floor? ______________________
10. Which of the indexes mentioned summarizes more stocks? ______________________

Your instructor may choose to give a true-false review of these economics concepts.

Selection 2 HISTORY

CONTEMPORARY FOCUS

Condoleezza Rice is President George W. Bush's national security advisor. She is the first African-American woman to hold that position. How does she exemplify the characteristics of a modern female leader?

BUSH'S SECRET WEAPON

Steve Kettmann

Salon Politics 2000, March 20, 2000

In a recent phone interview, Rice recalled her rise to political renown. She was born in Birmingham, Ala., in 1954, and since both parents were teachers, education was a major theme of her youth. So was faith. Her father, John Rice, was an ordained Presbyterian minister, as well as dean of Stillman College in Tuscaloosa, and later vice chancellor of the University of Denver. He was also a Republican who influenced the political thinking of his daughter, who calls herself an "all-over-the-map Republican." Rice considers herself "very conservative" on foreign policy but "almost shockingly libertarian" or "moderate" on some issues.

A gifted student who skipped two grades, Rice enrolled at the University of Denver when she was 15, and graduated when she was 19. She gave up on a career as a pianist midway through, and eventually wound up falling under the spell of Josef Korbel, a former Czech diplomat best known for being the father of Madeleine Albright. Rice sometimes dined at the Korbel home, along with the future secretary of state—but emerged with views much more in line with Korbel's than Albright's.

Rice mixes confidence and a light touch, as she made clear in a recent interview. Recalling the time she met Russia's acting president, Vladimir Putin, at a reception (when Putin was working for the mayor of St. Petersburg), Rice insisted he would not remember her. Right. No doubt he meets smart, charming, Russian-speaking Americans with names like Condoleezza all the time. (The name, by the way, came from her mother, like Rice a pianist, who made a variation on the musical direction *con dolcezza*, or "with sweetness.")

Her mentor at Stanford, Coit Blacker, said Rice possesses "a kind of intellectual agility mixed with velvet-glove forcefulness."

Collaborative Activity

Collaborate on responses to the following questions:

- What is the job of the chief foreign policy advisor?
- Who is Madeleine Albright?
- What other president did Condoleezza Rice work for and what was her job?

Stage 1: Preview

The pattern of organization in the first part of the following selection is

____

After reading this selection, I will know Sojourner Truth's feelings on the weakness of women. Agree ☐ Disagree ☐

Activate Schema

Why did the Civil War throw women into many leadership roles?

Learning Strategy

Explain the contributions of individuals and groups toward changing the image of women.

Word Knowledge

What do you know about these words?

restrictive	detriment	defiant	communal	hecklers
pursue	hygiene	incessant	convalescent	naive

Your instructor may give a true-false vocabulary review before or after reading.

Stage 2: Integrate Knowledge While Reading

Predict Picture Relate Monitor Correct

WOMEN IN HISTORY

From Leonard Pitt, *We Americans*

Three Radical Women

Amelia Bloomer (1818–1894) published the first newspaper issued expressly for women. She called it *The Lily*. Her fame, however, rests chiefly in dress reform. For six or eight years she wore an outfit composed of a knee-length skirt over full pants gathered at the ankle, which were soon known everywhere as "bloomers." Wherever she went, this style created great excitement and brought her enormous audiences—including hecklers. She was trying to make the serious point that women's fashions, often designed by men to suit their own tastes, were too restrictive, often to the detriment of the health of those who wore them. Still, some of her contemporaries thought she did the feminist movement as much harm as good.

Very few feminists hoped to destroy marriage as such. Most of them had husbands and lived conventional, if hectic, lives. And many of the husbands supported their cause. Yet the feminists did challenge certain marital customs. When Lucy Stone married Henry Blackwell, she insisted on being called "Mrs. Stone," a defiant gesture that brought her a lifetime of ridicule. Both she and her husband signed a marriage contract, vowing "to recognize the wife as an independent, rational being." They agreed to break any law which brought the husband "an injurious and unnatural superiority." But few of the radical feminists indulged in "free love" or joined communal marriage experiments. The movement was intended mainly to help women gain control over their own property and earnings and gain better legal guardianship over their children. Voting also interested them, but women's suffrage did not become a central issue until later in the century.

Many black women were part of the movement, including the legendary Sojourner Truth (1797–1883). Born a slave in New York and forced to marry a man approved by her owner, Sojourner Truth was freed when the state abolished slavery. After participating in religious revivals, she became an active abolitionist and feminist. In 1851 she saved the day at a women's rights convention in Ohio, silencing hecklers and replying to a man who had belittled the weakness of women:

> The man over there says women need to be helped into carriages and lifted over ditches, and to have the best place everywhere. Nobody ever helps me into carriages or over puddles, or gives me the best place—and ain't I a woman? . . . Look at my arm! I have ploughed and planted and gathered into barns, and no man could head me—and ain't I a woman? I could work as much and eat as much as a man—when I could get it—and bear the lash as well! And ain't I a woman? I have borne thirteen children, and seen most of 'em sold into slavery, and when I cried out my mother's grief, none but Jesus heard me—and ain't I a woman?

Changing the Image and the Reality

The accomplishments of a few women who dared pursue professional careers had somewhat altered the image of the submissive and brainless child-woman. Maria Mitchell of Nantucket, whose father was an astronomer, discovered a comet at the age of twenty-eight. She became the first woman professor of astronomy in the U.S. (at Vassar in 1865). Mitchell was also the first woman elected to the American Academy of Arts and Sciences and a founder of the Association for the Advancement of Women. Elizabeth Blackwell applied to twenty-nine medical schools before she was accepted. She attended all classes, even anatomy class, despite the sneers of some male students. As a physician, she went on to make important contributions in sanitation and hygiene.

By about 1860 women had effected notable improvements in their status. Organized feminists had eliminated some of the worst legal disadvantages in fifteen states. The Civil War altered the role—and the image—of women even more drastically than the feminist movement did. As men went off to fight,

Former slave Isabella Van Wagener became the abolitionist Sojourner Truth.
Hulton Archive/Getty Images

women flocked into government clerical jobs. And they were accepted in teaching jobs as never before. Tens of thousands of women ran farms and businesses while the men were gone. Anna Howard Shaw, whose mother ran a pioneer farm, recalled:

> It was an incessant struggle to keep our land, to pay our taxes, and to live. Calico was selling at fifty cents a yard. Coffee was one dollar a pound. There were no men left to grind our corn, to get in our crops, or to care for our livestock; and all around us we saw our struggle reflected in the lives of our neighbors.

Women took part in crucial relief efforts. The Sanitary Commission, the Union's volunteer nursing program and a forerunner of the Red Cross, owed much of its success to women. They raised millions of dollars for medicine, bandages, food, hospitals, relief camps, and convalescent homes.

North and South, black and white, many women served as nurses, some as spies and even as soldiers. Dorothea Dix, already famous as a reformer of prisons and insane asylums, became head of the Union army nurse corps. Clara Barton and "Mother" Bickerdyke saved thousands of lives by working close behind the front lines at Antietam, Chancellorsville, and Fredericksburg. Harriet Tubman led a party up the Combahee River to rescue 756 slaves. Late in life she was recognized for her heroic act by being granted a government pension of twenty dollars per month.

Southern white women suffered more from the disruptions of the Civil War than did their northern sisters. The proportion of men who went to war or were killed in battle was greater in the South. This made many women self-sufficient during the war. Still, there was hardly a whisper of feminism in the South.

The Civil War also brought women into the political limelight. Anna Dickson skyrocketed to fame as a Republican speaker, climaxing her career with an address to the House of Representatives on abolition. Stanton and Anthony formed the National Woman's Loyal League to press for a constitutional amendment banning slavery. With Anthony's genius for organization, the League in one year collected 400,000 signatures in favor of the Thirteenth Amendment.

Once abolition was finally assured in 1865, most feminists felt certain that suffrage would follow quickly. They believed that women had earned the vote by their patriotic wartime efforts. Besides, it appeared certain that black men would soon be allowed to vote. And once black men had the ballot in hand, how could anyone justify keeping it from white women—or black women? Any feminist who had predicted in 1865 that women would have to wait another fifty-five years for suffrage would have been called politically naive.

Stage 3: Recall

Stop to self-test, relate, and react. Your instructor may choose to give you a true-false comprehension review.

Thinking About "Women in History"

How did the actions of many early women "somewhat alter the image of the submissive and brainless child-woman"? List the women and discuss how each changed stereotypical thinking.

Contemporary Link

How does Condoleezza Rice continue to change the image and the reality for women? What characteristics do you admire about her? How would you compare her to the three radical women in the selection?

Skill Development: Organizational Patterns

Fill in the organizational diagram on page 229 to reflect the simple listing pattern of the first part of the selection.

Women & Accomplishments

Comprehension Questions

After reading the selection, answer the following questions with *a*, *b*, *c*, or *d*.

Main Idea

_______ 1. What is the best statement of the main point of this selection?
- a. Women made impressive gains because of their work during the Civil War.
- b. Many women made early contributions toward changing the stereotypical image of the female role.
- c. Bloomer, Stone, and Truth changed a radical image into a reality.
- d. Women were slow to get the right to vote despite their efforts.

Detail

_______ 2. In originating "bloomers," Amelia Bloomer's greatest concern was
- a. fashion.
- b. principle.
- c. expense.
- d. good taste.

Inference

_______ 3. The major purpose of Sojourner Truth's quoted speech was to
- a. prove that women are stronger than men.
- b. reprimand men for social courtesy.
- c. dramatize the strengths of women.
- d. praise childbearing as a womanly virtue.

Detail

_______ 4. Lucy Stone's major motive in retaining the name "Mrs. Stone" after marriage was to
- a. condone "free love" without marriage.
- b. de-emphasize the responsibilities of marriage.
- c. purchase property in her own name.
- d. be recognized as an independent person equal to her husband.

Detail

_______ 5. The article explicitly states that women worked during the Civil War in all of the following except
a. farms and businesses.
b. the military.
c. government clerical jobs.
d. the Red Cross.

Inference

_______ 6. The author implies that the eventual assumption of responsible roles by large numbers of women was primarily due to
a. the feminist movement.
b. the determination and accomplishments of female professionals.
c. a desire to give women a chance.
d. economic necessity.

Inference

_______ 7. The author believes that the Civil War showed southern women to be
a. as capable but less vocal than northern women.
b. more capable than their northern sisters.
c. capable workers and eager feminists.
d. less able to assume responsible roles than northern women.

Inference

_______ 8. The author's main purpose in mentioning the accomplishments of Maria Mitchell is to point out that
a. she discovered a comet.
b. her professional achievements in astronomy were exceptional and thus somewhat improved the image of women.
c. she was the first woman professor of astronomy in the United States.
d. she was a founder of the Association for the Advancement of Women.

Detail

_______ 9. The article states or implies that all of the following women worked to abolish slavery except
a. Anna Howard Shaw.
b. Harriet Tubman.
c. Anna Dickson.
d. Stanton and Anthony.

Inference

_______ 10. In the author's opinion, the long wait by women after the Civil War for suffrage
a. was predictable in 1865.
b. would not have been expected in 1865.
c. was due to the vote of black men.
d. was justified.

Answer the following with *T* (true) or *F* (false).

Detail ________ 11. Women were granted the right to vote in 1920.

Detail ________ 12. Sojourner Truth had been a southern slave.

Inference ________ 13. The author implies that feminist leaders were more concerned with their own right to vote than with the abolition of slavery.

Detail ________ 14. From the very beginning, the right to vote was the focal point of the women's movement.

Detail ________ 15. Sojourner Truth had thirteen children.

Vocabulary

According to the way the italicized word was used in the selection, indicate *a*, *b*, *c*, or *d* for the word or phrase that gives the best definition. The number in parentheses indicates the line of the passage in which the word is located.

________ 1. "were too *restrictive*" (8)
a. showy
b. expensive
c. complicated
d. confining

________ 2. "to the *detriment of*" (8)
a. harm
b. anger
c. apology
d. objection

________ 3. "a *defiant* gesture" (15)
a. unlucky
b. resistive
c. admirable
d. ignorant

________ 4. "*communal* marriage experiments" (19)
a. permanent
b. living together in groups
c. illegal
d. uncommon

________ 5. "silencing *hecklers*" (29)
a. soldiers
b. rioters
c. disciples
d. verbal harassers

________ 6. "*pursue* professional careers" (40)
a. strive for
b. abandon
c. acknowledge
d. indicate

________ 7. "sanitation and *hygiene*" (49)
a. garbage disposal
b. biology
c. health care
d. mental disorders

________ 8. "an *incessant* struggle" (line 1 of quote, p. 227)
a. earlier
b. final
c. novel
d. unceasing

________ 9. "*convalescent* homes" (66)
a. sanitary
b. government
c. reclaimed
d. recuperating

________ 10. "called politically *naive*" (92–93)
a. unsophisticated
b. well informed
c. dishonest
d. unfortunate

Search the Net

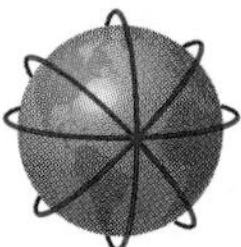

- How did the roles and responsibilities of women change during World War II? What kinds of jobs were opened up to women during this time? How did women contribute to war efforts both at home and abroad? Begin your own search, or start with one of the following:

  Women and World War II:
  http://www.stg.brown.edu/projects/WWII_Women/WomenInWWII.html

  Women Pilots of World War II: http://www.womenofcourage.com/

  Women Come to the Front; Journalists, Photographers, and Broadcasters During World War II: http://www.loc.gov/exhibits/wcf/wcf0001.html

- What role did women play in the Civil Rights Movement? Identify three women who made significant contributions to the movement, and explain the importance of their work. Begin your own search, or start with one of the following:

  Student Nonviolent Coordinating Committee:
  http://www.stanford.edu/~ccarson/articles/black_women_3.htm

  The Role of Women in the Civil Rights Movement:
  http://www.clas.ufl.edu/users/brundage/website/roleofwomen.htm

  Representation of Women in the 1960s Civil Rights Movement:
  http://nimbus.ocis.temple.edu/~rkarras/winters2.htm

Concept Prep for History

What events led up to World War II?

After Germany was defeated in World War I, supposedly the "war to end all wars," the **Allies** (United States, Britain, France, and Russia) expected Germany to pay for the war they helped start. The Allies also changed the world map by taking away much of the German empire. The German people were stunned at their defeat, angry over the demands of the victors, and eventually unable to meet their debt payments. **Adolf Hitler,** a skillful and charismatic leader, seized this opportunity and tapped into the country's anger. He promised to restore national pride, and consequently many Germans were drawn to him. He became the leader of the **Nazi** party, created the **swastika** as its symbol, and eventually became dictator of Germany.

Hitler strengthened the military, forged an alliance with Japan and Italy, and attacked and conquered much of continental Europe. When Britain, under the leadership of Prime Minister **Winston Churchill,** refused to bargain with Hitler, he ordered the **Luftwaffe,** the German air force, to destroy Britain from the air. The air raids, known as the **blitz,** failed in their purpose when the Royal Air Force (RAF) won the Battle of Britain. Hitler then attacked Russia.

Prime Minister Sir Winston Churchill, President Franklin Roosevelt, and Soviet leader Joseph Stalin pose for pictures at the Yalta Conference in 1945.
Hulton Archive/Getty Images

What was the U.S. role in the war?

The United States, under **Franklin D. Roosevelt,** remained neutral. **Isolationists** opposed foreign involvement. That changed, however, on December 7, 1941, at 7:02 A.M., when the Japanese bombed **Pearl Harbor,** an American naval base in Hawaii. America declared war on that day. **General Douglas MacArthur** was put in charge of all army troops in the Pacific, and **General Dwight D. Eisenhower** led the Allied soldiers in Europe.

What was D-Day?

Allied forces planned the liberation of Europe, and on June 6, 1944—on what came to be known as **D-Day**—thousands of brave soldiers secretly left England and stormed the beaches of Normandy, France. After two weeks of desperate fighting, the troops moved inland and liberated Paris by August. The Allied armies drove toward **Berlin,** the capital of Germany, and by April 30, Hitler committed suicide to avoid capture. The Germans surrendered one week later, and the European part of the war was over. Hitler, with his anti-Semitic hatred, had killed over six million innocent Jews. Many were taken by trains to concentration camps for extermination in gas chambers. This horrible carnage was called the **Holocaust.**

How did the war with Japan end?

The American forces in the Pacific were moving from island to island against fierce Japanese resistance. Victories were won with great loss of life. Harry Truman had become president and was told of the **Manhattan Project,** a top-secret plan to develop an atomic bomb. On August 6, 1945, the **Enola Gay** flew over **Hiroshima, Japan,** and dropped an atomic bomb that obliterated the city. Three days later a second bomb was dropped over **Nagasaki.** Within a few days the Japanese asked for peace, and a month later they officially surrendered to General MacArthur aboard the battleship **U.S.S. Missouri** in Tokyo Bay. World War II had come to an end.

REVIEW QUESTIONS

Study the material and answer the following questions.

1. How did the end of World War I affect the beginning of World War II? ________________

2. Why were the Germans drawn to Hitler's message? ________________

3. Who were Germany's allies in World War II? ________________

4. Why did the Luftwaffe strike England? ________________

5. Who were the isolationists? ________________

6. What prompted the United States to enter the war? ________________

7. What was the Holocaust? ________________

8. What was D-Day? ________________

9. What ended the war in Europe? ________________

10. What ended the war in Japan? ________________

Your instructor may choose to give a true-false review of these history concepts.

Selection 3 BUSINESS

CONTEMPORARY FOCUS

As a part of your college experience, do you plan to spend a semester studying abroad? With businesses becoming more international and global communication becoming easier through the Internet, how could studying abroad give you a career advantage?

GLOBAL EXPERIENCE THROUGH STUDY ABROAD

Jackie Elowsky

American Society of Agricultural Engineers, August 2000

When Michigan State University senior April Pasutti decided to study abroad for a month last summer, she had to choose a country. "Koala bears are my favorite animal," she says, which led her to an adventure in the land Down Under.

Each student successfully completing the program earned six credits toward their academic goals. But Pasutti says she got much more from the program than just a grade. "I'm more aware of cultural beliefs," she says. "A global experience makes you feel more well rounded. More understanding."

Pasutti graduated in May 2000 with a bachelor's degree in biosystems engineering and is now bulk storage coordinator for the Michigan Department of Agriculture in Lansing, Mich. She believes her overseas studies will help her career. But it also allowed her to fulfill a dream.

University of Illinois junior Mathew Rund also picked Australia. "It made me a lot more open to other things," Rund, 24, says of his experience. "The biggest thing I got out of it was to see that everything in the world doesn't revolve around us." He believes his travels have prepared him for the challenges posed by his new job.

University of Idaho agricultural engineering student Tina Carpenter, 22, spent a semester in Lulea, Sweden, last fall, about a 90-minute drive from the Arctic Circle. She completed four engineering courses at the Lulea University of Technology where she met students from around the world.

Between studies, Carpenter found time to travel to England, Denmark, Germany and the Arctic Circle. She met potential employers and ate plenty of Swedish meatballs. "I think I would have had a good time anywhere," she says. "But I wouldn't trade this trip for anything."

Collaborative Activity

Collaborate on responses to the following questions:

- How is the value of studying abroad affected if you don't need to learn a foreign language?
- Where would you wish to study abroad and why?
- How has the Internet affected global thinking?

Stage 1: Preview

After reading this selection, I will know what Robert Goizueta did for Coca-Cola. Agree ☐ Disagree ☐

Activate Schema

Why does a company like Coca-Cola want to be a sponsor of the Olympics?

Learning Strategy

Explain how Coca-Cola became a global company.

Word Knowledge

What do you know about these words?

formidable	immensely	inconsequential	aspiring	protégé
slated	stagnation	enhancing	tapered	deriving

Your instructor may give a true-false vocabulary review before or after reading.

Stage 2: Integrate Knowledge While Reading

Predict Picture Relate Monitor Correct

Expanding into the International Marketplace

From Samuel Certo, *Modern Management*, 8th ed.

Most U.S. companies see great opportunities in the international marketplace today. Although the U.S. population is growing steadily but slowly, the population in many other countries is exploding. For example, it has been estimated that in 1990, China, India, and Indonesia together had more than 2 billion people, or 40 percent of the world's population. Obviously, such countries offer a strong profit potential for aggressive businesspeople throughout the world.

This potential does not come without serious risk, however. Managers who attempt to manage in a global context face formidable challenges. Some of these challenges are the cultural differences among workers from different countries, different technology levels from country to country, and laws and political systems that can vary immensely from one nation to the next.

The trend toward increased international management, or globalization, is now widely recognized. The primary question for most firms is not *whether* to globalize, but *how* and *how fast* to do so and how to measure global progress over time.

Transnational organizations, also called global organizations, take the entire world as their business arena. Doing business wherever it makes sense is primary; national borders are considered inconsequential. The transnational organization transcends any single home country, with ownership, control, and management being from many different countries.

Case Study: A Global Success Story

Robert Goizueta, Coca-Cola's president and CEO since 1981, believed that "soft drinks are very much a local product. I'd love for the Chinese to arrive in New York" he explains, "and say, 'My goodness, they have Coca-Cola here, too,'" The hand-picked protégé of longtime Coca-Cola chairman Robert Woodruff, Goizueta recognized when he became CEO that changes had to be made in the company's way of doing business around the world to overcome the 1970s stagnation in Coca-Cola's growth. In the past, he says, "You'd plant your flag in a new country every time you needed to grow. We ran out of countries, so I had to do something different." In fact, Goizueta was recognized by *Fortune* magazine for his success in enhancing shareholder value—a crucial investment value that showed a significant loss in the 10-year period before he took over.

Atlanta-based Coca-Cola boasts one of the best-recognized logos in the world. Whether he or she speaks Japanese, Hebrew, or Russian, the world traveler knows the product inside the familiar tapered bottle or distinctively labeled can and trusts its consistently high quality. Even five years ago, however,

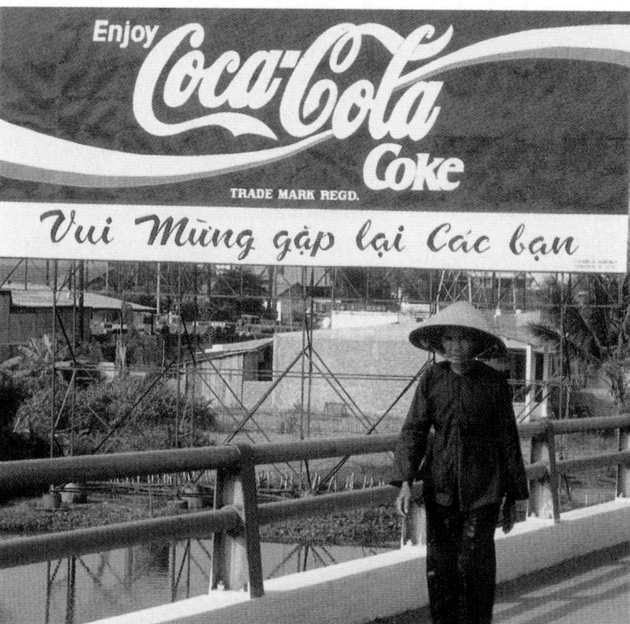

American products are advertised in Asia. The cola competition is evident in Ho Chi Minh City.
Radhika Chlasani/ Getty Images

Goizueta believed that Coca-Cola's marketing was flawed. Too much marketing money, he felt, was being devoted to advertising and too little to brand strategy and packaging. So Coca-Cola hired hundreds of new marketers to take a more "holistic" approach to the international market. At the same time, however, Goizueta cautioned a worldwide gathering of Coca-Cola's quality assurance staff about the dangers of change for its own sake. "It's extremely important," he reminded them, "that you show some sensitivity to your past in order to show the proper respect for the future."

Coca-Cola's push into the international market began during World War II, when company president Robert Woodruff announced, "We will see that every man in uniform gets a bottle of Coca-Cola for 5 cents wherever he is and whatever it costs." General Dwight D. Eisenhower, a Coca-Cola fancier, agreed. Thus, as competing soft-drink companies watched helplessly, Coca-Cola established bottling plants near every battlefront. By the end of the war, the company had 64 international bottling plants, most of them built at the expense of the U.S. taxpayer.

During the Cold War, however, the company faced severe criticism in certain countries as a symbol of American imperialism. For example, efforts were made to drive Coke from the shelves of French stores. "The moral landscape of France," declared the respected French newspaper *Le Monde*, "is at stake." In the end, of course, the company won this and other fights on foreign soil. Coca-Cola was once boycotted by Arabic countries because it had a franchised bottler in Israel, but over time, the company's persistence—and consumer demand—broke down this barrier.

Coca-Cola currently does business in 195 countries, deriving close to 70 percent of its total revenues and 80 percent of its operating profits from outside the United States. In 1994, Coke had revenues exceeding $15 billion and had more than doubled sales from the decade before. Today, the international market remains the key to Coca-Cola's future. With domestic per capita consumption leveling, the global market offers enormous potential.

Goizueta recognizes that Coca-Cola's present success comes from operating in different geographic locations. First, Coke pushed aggressively into foreign markets when the domestic market matured. Indeed facing just 2 to 4 percent annual growth domestically, Coca-Cola had to concentrate on the world market. Coke managers reason that when sales drop in troubled economies like those of Mexico or Argentina, growth in new markets like India or China can create a hedge.

Today, Coca-Cola's International Business Sector is divided into four operating groups: the Greater Europe Group, the Latin America Group, the Middle and Far East Group, and the Africa Group. Moreover, Coca-Cola is putting major resources into continued international growth. The company has, for instance, targeted Eastern Europe and China for future expansion and has spent liberally to support business in these sizable markets. In addition, Coca-Cola plans a $250 million expansion in Russia. Bottlers in Venezuela anticipate a $200 million expansion, and in Brazil, $2 billion is slated to be spent in the next five years to add vending machines and coolers. Not forgetting the home market, Coca-Cola will also continue to add vending machines and coolers in

U.S. gas stations, convenience stores, and grocery stores to help catch up with archrival Pepsi Cola in these areas.

Finally, since 1928, Coca-Cola has supported Olympic Games and athletes—this is the longest continuous support provided by a corporation. Through international and national sponsorship programs, Coca-Cola helps finance teams and aspiring athletes in 195 countries.

The key to Coca-Cola's future success is management's commitment to create value for shareholders. One of its major assets in this effort is the company's "strong global leadership in the beverage industry in particular and in the business world in general."

Stage 3: Recall

Stop to self-test, relate, and react. Your instructor may choose to give you a true-false comprehension review.

Thinking About "Expanding into the International Marketplace"

What does Goizueta mean when he says that "soft drinks are very much a local product"? What steps do you think will be necessary for Goizueta's vision to become a reality?

Response Suggestion: Define the meaning of "local" product, and list strategies that you think would convince people to accept Coca-Cola as local.

Contemporary Link

Students have studied abroad for many years in order to learn a foreign language and enjoy personal growth. Now those purposes seem to be expanding into business goals. Why do you think that shift has occurred? What do you think are the career advantages for you in studying abroad?.

Skill Development: Organizational Patterns

Answer the following with *T* (true) or *F* (false).

_________ 1. The pattern of organization in the fourth paragraph is <u>definition</u>.

_________ 2. The story of Goizueta and Coca-Cola serves as an example for a successful global organization.

_________ 3. Although patterns may vary within the selection, the overall organization of the selection is definition and example.

Comprehension Questions

After reading the selection, answer the following questions with *a, b, c,* or *d*. In order to help you analyze your strengths and weaknesses, the question types are indicated.

Main Idea ________ 1. Which is the best statement of the main idea?
a. Managers face overwhelming difficulties in expanding into international markets.
b. Transnational organizations face cultural differences from different countries as they take the entire world as a business market.
c. Robert Goizueta had the vision to successfully move Coca-Cola from a regional to a global company.
d. As illustrated by Coca-Cola, strategically expanding into international markets offers a strong profit potential for U.S. companies.

Inference ________ 2. The primary driving motive behind globalization is
a. multiculturalism.
b. the exploding potential for new customers.
c. the prestige of being an international company.
d. the availability of new technology to meet international needs.

Inference ________ 3. Goizueta has stated his hope that Chinese arriving in New York would say, "My goodness, they have Coca-Cola here too." The statement suggests that
a. Coca-Cola has expanded into a country with one of the largest world populations.
b. marketers had been effective in convincing the Chinese to enjoy an American product.
c. American trademarks can be identified worldwide.
d. the company has succeeded in making Coca-Cola into a local Chinese product.

Inference ________ 4. The expansion strategy of the past, "You plant your flag in a new country," suggests that the company
a. remained American on foreign soil.
b. sought to create a local product to reflect each foreign country.
c. integrated ownership and management with the foreign hosts.
d. purchased land for factories and stores in each foreign country.

Inference _________ 5. By reminding marketers of the need to "show some sensitivity to your past in order to show the proper respect for the future," Goizueta wants them to
a. make drastic changes for future success.
b. build on past successes.
c. learn form their own mistakes.
d. map out a plan that will last, not just for a year, but for a millennium.

Detail _________ 6. Coca-Cola's original entry into foreign markets was all of the following except
a. paid for by the U.S. taxpayer.
b. begun during World War II.
c. spearheaded by Goizueta.
d. designed to get Coca-Colas to soldiers on foreign soil.

Detail _________ 7. According to the author, the percentage of Coca-Cola's total revenues that come from the United States is
a. 30%.
b. 70%.
c. 80%.
d. 95%.

Inference _________ 8. The reader can conclude that the phrase "domestic markets matured" means
a. the customers in the United States have grown older.
b. growth was leveling off with only a small percent of new U.S. customers.
c. young people drink more Coca-Cola than older adults.
d. the U.S. population rate has declined.

Inference _________ 9. The reader can conclude that
a. Pepsi has more vending machines in U.S. stores than Coca-Cola.
b. Pepsi and Coca-Cola work together to open new markets.
c. Pepsi opened foreign markets at the U.S. taxpayer's expense.
d. Pepsi does business in more countries than Coca-Cola.

Inference _________ 10. All of the following can be concluded from this selection except that
a. shareholders want more than 2 to 4% annual growth in a company.
b. advertising at the Olympic Games is part of Coca-Cola's global strategy.
c. Coca-Cola is opposed to doing business in countries that are not democracies.
d. the Coca-Cola company has already globalized and built a transnational organization.

Answer the following with *T* (true) or *F* (false).

Detail ________ 11. The author indicates that most firms are still in the phase of deciding whether or not to globalize.

Detail ________ 12. The author indicates that Goizueta increased the value of the company for shareholders.

Inference ________ 13. The reader can conclude that American imperialism can be considered a threat by other countries.

Inference ________ 14. The reader can conclude that Coca-Cola finances Olympic athletes in every country in which it does business.

Detail ________ 15. China, India, and Indonesia have over 60 percent of the world's population.

Vocabulary

According to the way the italicized word was used in the selection, select *a, b, c,* or *d* for the word or phase that gives the best definition. The number in parentheses indicates the line of the passage in which the word is located.

________ 1. "face *formidable* challenges" (8)
a. unlimited
b. intimidating
c. surprising
d. hidden

________ 2. "can vary *immensely*" (11)
a. enormously
b. irregularly
c. unexpectedly
d. differently

________ 3. "are considered *inconsequential*" (18)
a. complicated
b. undefined
c. invisible
d. unimportant

________ 4. "hand-picked *protégé*" (24)
a. partner
b. boss
c. relative
d. protected trainee

________ 5. "*stagnation* in Coca-Cola's growth" (27)
a. inflation
b. acceleration
c. slowdown
d. orientation

________ 6. "*enhancing* shareholder value" (30)
a. advertising
b. increasing
c. marketing
d. maintaining

________ 7. "familiar *tapered* bottle" (35)
a. gradually diminishing
b. decorated
c. glass
d. tall

________ 8. "*deriving* close to 70 percent" (61–62)
a. inheriting
b. selling
c. spending
d. obtaining

_________ 9. "*slated* to be spent" (81)
a. designated
b. announced
c. divided
d. wished

_________ 10. "*aspiring* athletes" (88)
a. new
b. young
c. handicapped
d. hopeful

Search the Net

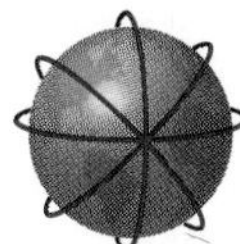

- How is Coca-Cola marketed differently across the world? Compare how it is marketed in three different countries. Print examples of how the product looks different for different market segments. Begin your own search, or start with one of the following:

  Coca-Cola Bottles of the World: http://www.pl8s.com/coke.htm

  Coca-Cola.com: http://www.coca-cola.com/gateway.html

- What is the North American Free Trade Agreement? How has this agreement affected job growth and trade? List three benefits of this agreement. Begin your own search, or start with one of the following:

  Association of American Chambers of Commerce in Latin America: http://www.aaccla.org/issues/western/NAfreetrade.htm

  Global Trade Watch: NAFTA: http://www.citizen.org/pctrade/nafta/naftapg.html

  Notes on NAFTA: The Masters of Mankind: http://www.cs.unb.ca/~alopez-o/politics/chomnafta.html

Concept Prep
for Business

What is a CD?

A **CD (certificate of deposit)** is a loan to a bank for a fixed interest rate and for a designated period of time. The CD may be for one month or up to five years, and the interest rate increases with the extent of the time period. Banks then lend out the money at a higher rate for people to buy cars or houses. With a CD, the return of your **principal** (original money) is guaranteed. You do not have to worry about losing your money.

What is a bond?

A **bond** is a loan to a government or a corporation. For example, many cities sell **municipal bonds** to finance infrastructure improvements or schools. You lend the city money and the taxpayers pay you interest. The interest rate on bonds is usually higher than CDs, but the risk is greater. You have a promise that you will be paid back at **maturity** (a specified time period), and you hope the city will be able to fulfill this promise. If you buy a **U.S. Treasury Bill** or a **savings bond,** you are lending money to the U.S. government, which uses the money to pay down the national debt. Because U.S. Treasury bills are backed by the U.S. government, they are safer investments than municipal bonds.

What is a mutual fund?

A **mutual fund** is a company that pools the investment money of many individuals and purchases a **portfolio** (array of holdings) of stocks, bonds, and other securities. Each investor then shares accordingly in the profits or losses. Investors also pay a fee for professionals to manage the portfolio, which includes bookkeeping, researching, buying, and selling. All fees for management come out of profits before they are shared.

An advantage of mutual funds is that they offer instant **diversification.** With a $1,000 purchase, you can have a part ownership in many different stocks and bonds. Also, if you do not have the expertise to research individual stocks, you can rely on the judgment of the professional money managers. Different mutual funds specialize in different areas such as large companies, small companies, or even IPOs. You would want to find one that matches your investment interests and also has a positive track record of growth.

What is a capital gain?

A capital gain is a profit on the sale of a property or a security. A **short-term capital gain** is a profit made on a property or security owned for less than one year. This profit is taxed as ordinary income and may be as high as 40 percent for people in upper tax brackets. A **long-term capital gain,** on the other hand, is a profit on a property or security owned for over a year. On this, investors are taxed at a maximum of 20%.

REVIEW QUESTIONS

Study the material and answer the following questions.

1. Are CD rates better for a month or a year? ____________________

2. What does the bank do with your CD money? ____________________

3. What is your principal? ____________________

4. What is a municipal bond? ____________________

5. What are the advantages of a mutual fund? ____________________

6. Is tax greater on a short- or long-term capital gain? ____________________

7. How long must you hold a property before selling to achieve a long-term capital gain? ____________________

8. What is a portfolio? ____________________

9. For the safest choice, should you pick bonds, CDs, or a mutual fund? ____________________

10. What does diversification mean? ____________________

Your instructor may choose to give a true-false review of these business concepts.

READER'S JOURNAL

Name ______________________________ Date ____________

CHAPTER 5

Answer the following questions to reflect on your own learning and progress. Use the perforations to tear the assignment out for your instructor.

1. How do transitions direct logic? ______________________________

   ____
2. What pattern of organization do you use most frequently in your papers?

   ____
3. Why is cause and effect a frequently used pattern in history? __________

   ____
4. Why is definition and example a frequently used pattern in psychology?

   ____
5. Why does a cause and effect pattern fit economics? ______________

   ____
6. Why do many speakers use a simple listing pattern? ______________

   ____
7. Which patterns of organization do you find most difficult to recognize? Why? ______________________________

   ____
8. What effect do you think e-mail has had on international business? Explain. ______________________________

   ____

6

Organizing Textbook Information

- What is study reading?
- What is annotating?
- What is the Cornell Method of notetaking?
- What is outlining?
- What is mapping?

Proposition #5, *1966 by Allan D'Archangelo. Acrylic on canvas, 72 × 72" (183 × 183 cm). Photo courtesy of JPMorgan Chase Art Collection. © Estate of Allan D'Arcangelo/Licensed by VAGA, New York, NY.*

The Demands of College Study

Your first assignment in most college courses will be to read Chapter 1 of the appointed textbook, at which time you will immediately discover that a textbook chapter contains an amazing amount of information. Your instructor will continue to make similar assignments designating the remaining chapters in rapid succession. Your task is to select the information that needs to be remembered, try to learn it, and organize it for future study for a midterm or final exam that is weeks or months away.

In an extensive study, three college professors investigated the question, "What are the demands on students in introductory college history courses?"[1] They observed classes for a ten-week period and analyzed the actual reading demands, finding that students were asked to read an average of 825 pages in each class over the ten-week period. The average length of weekly assignments was more than 80 pages, but the amount varied both with the professor and the topic. In one class, students had to read 287 pages in only ten days.

The college history professors expected students to be able to see relationships between parts and wholes, to place people and events into a historical context, and to retain facts. Professors spent 85 percent of the class time lecturing and 6 percent of the time testing. In short, the demands were high and students were expected to work independently to organize textbook material efficiently and effectively to prepare for that crucial 6 percent of test-taking time.

Building Knowledge Networks

The old notion of studying and learning is that studying is an information-gathering activity. Knowledge is the "product" and the student acquires "it" by transferring information from the text to memory. With this view, good learners locate important information, review it, and then transfer the information into long-term memory. The problem with this model is that review does not always guarantee recall, and rehearsal is not always enough to ensure that information is encoded into long-term memory.

More recent theories of studying and learning reflect the thinking of cognitive psychologists and focus on schemata, prior knowledge, and the learner's own goals. To understand and remember, the learner hooks new information to

[1]J. G. Carson, N. D. Chase, S. U. Gibson, and M. F. Hargrove. "Literacy Demands of the Undergraduate Curriculum." *Reading, Research, and Instruction* 31 (1992): 25–30.

already existing schemata, or networks of knowledge. As the reader's personal knowledge expands, new networks are created. The learner, not the professor, decides how much effort should be expended and adjusts studying according to the answers to questions such as "How much do I need to know?" "Will the test be multiple-choice or essay?" and "Do I want to remember this forever?" The learner makes judgments and selects the material to be remembered and integrated into knowledge networks.

Methods of Organizing Textbook Information

This chapter will discuss four methods of organizing textbook information for future study: (1) annotating, (2) notetaking, (3) outlining, and (4) mapping. In a review of more than 500 research studies on organizing textbook information, two college developmental reading professors concluded that "no one study strategy is appropriate for all students in all study situations."[2] They encourage students to develop a repertoire of skills. They feel that students need to know, for example, that underlining takes less time than notetaking, but notetaking or outlining produces better test results.

Your selection of a study strategy for organizing textbook material will vary according to the announced testing demands, the nature of the material, the amount of time you have to devote to study, and your preference for a particular strategy. Being familiar with all four strategies affords a repertoire of choices.

The following comments on organizing textbook and lecture materials come from college freshmen taking an introductory course in American history. These history students were all enrolled in a Learning Strategies for History course that focused on how to be a successful student. Their comments probably address some of your experiences in trying to rapidly organize large amounts of textbook material.

From a student who made an A in history:

Organization of my class notes is very important. The notes can be very easy to refer to if they are organized. This enables me to go back and fill in information and it also helps me to understand the cycle of events that is taking place. I generally try to outline my notes by creating sections. Sections help me to understand the main idea or add a description of a singular activity. I usually go back and number the sections to make them easy for reference.

Taking notes can be very difficult sometimes. In class, if my mind strays just a few times, I can easily lose track of where my notes were going. Then again, when I am reading my textbook, I may read without even realizing what I just read. The difference in class and the textbook is that I can go back and reread the text.

[2]D. Caverly and V. Orlando, *Textbook Strategies in Teaching Reading and Study Strategies at the College Level* (Newark, NJ: International Reading Association, 1991), pp. 86–165.

It is very easy to overdo the notes that I take from the text. Originally, I tended to take too much information from the book, but now, as I read more, I can better grasp the main idea. Underlining also makes a big difference. When I underline, I can go back and reread the book.

From a student who made a B in history:

Taking notes is no longer something that you can just do and expect to have good and complete notes. I have learned that taking notes is a process of learning within itself.

From a student who made a C in history:

In starting college, I have made a few changes in how I take notes. For instance, I am leaving a lot more space in taking notes. I find that they are easier to read when they are spread out. I have also been using a highlighter and marking topics and definitions and people's names. I make checks near notes that will definitely be on a test so I can go over them.

When I am reading, I have begun to do a lot of underlining in the book, which I would never do before because my school would not take back books if they were marked. I have also started to note important parts with a little star and confusing parts with a question mark.

From a student who made an A in history:

I think that the best way to do it is to completely read the assignment and then go back over it to clear up any confusion. I would also recommend going over your lecture notes before starting your reading assignment, which is something I didn't do this past week. I also try to key in on words like "two significant changes" or "major factors." Sometimes you may go three or four pages without seeing anything like that. My question is, "What do you do then?" I think that you should write down the point or points that were repeated the most or stressed the most.

All of these students were successful in history, although the final grades vary. Each student's reflection offers sincere and sound advice. However you organize material—by annotating, notetaking, outlining, or mapping—seek to make meaning by making connections.

Annotating

Which of the following would seem to indicate the most effective use of the textbook as a learning tool?

1. A text without a single mark—not even the owner's name has spoiled the sacred pages
2. A text ablaze with color—almost every line is adorned with a red, blue, yellow, and/or green colored marker
3. A text with a scattered variety of markings—highlighting, underlines, numbers, and stars are interspersed with circles, arrows, and short, written notes

Naturally, option three is the best. The rationale for the first is probably for a better book resale value, but usually used books resell for the same price whether they are marked or unmarked. The reason for the second is probably procrastination in decision making. Students who highlight everything rely on coming back later to figure out what is *really* important. Although selective highlighting in a light color such as yellow is a helpful strategy, highlighting everything is inefficient. The variety of markings in the third strategy enables you to pinpoint ideas for later study.

Why Annotate?

The textbook is a learning tool and should be used as such; it should not be preserved as a treasure. A college professor requires a particular text because it contains information vital to your understanding of the course material. The text places a vast body of knowledge in your hands, much more material than the professor could possibly give in class. It is your job to cull through this information, to make some sense out of it, and to select the important points that need to be remembered.

Annotating is a method of highlighting main ideas, major supporting details, and key terms. The word *annotate* means to add marks. By using a system of symbols and notation and not just colored markers, you mark the text after the first reading so that a complete rereading will not be necessary. The markings indicate pertinent points to review for an exam. If you are running short on time, highlighting with a colored marker is better than not making any marks at all.

Marking in the textbook itself is frequently faster than summarizing, outlining, or notetaking. In addition, since your choices and reactions are all in one place, you can view them at a glance for later study rather than referring to separate notebooks. Your textbook has become a workbook.

Students who annotate, however, will probably want to make a list of key terms and ideas on their own paper in order to have a reduced form of the information for review and self-testing.

When to Annotate

Annotations are best done after a unit of thought has been presented and the information can be viewed as a whole. This may mean marking after a single paragraph or after three pages; marking varies with the material. When you are first reading, every sentence seems of major importance as each new idea unfolds, and the tendency is to annotate too much. Overmarking serves no useful purpose and wastes both reading and review time. If you wait until a complete thought has been developed, the major points will emerge from a background of lesser details. You will then have all the facts, and you can decide what you want to remember. At the end of the course your textbook should have that worn but well-organized look.

Reader's Tip

How to Annotate

Develop a system of notations. Use circles, stars, numbers, and whatever else helps you put the material visually into perspective. *Anything that makes sense to you is a correct notation.* Here is an example of one student's marking system:

Main idea	( )
Supporting material	______
Major trend or possible essay exam question	*
Important smaller point to know for multiple-choice item	✓
Word that you must be able to define	(oval)
Section of material to reread for review	{ }
Numbering of important details under a major issue	(1), (2), (3)
Didn't understand and must seek advice	?
Notes in the margin	Ex., Def., Topic
Questions in the margin	Why signif.?
Indicating relationships	~
Related issue or idea	← R

EXAMPLE

The passage shown below is taken from a biology textbook. Notice how the notations have been used to highlight main ideas and significant supporting details. This same passage will be used throughout this chapter to demonstrate each of the four methods of organizing textbook material.

Circulatory Systems

When we examine the systems by which blood reaches all the cells of an animal, we find two general types, known as open and closed circulatory systems.

Def. I

Open Circulatory Systems

The essential feature of the **open circulatory system** is that the [1] blood moves through a body cavity—such as the abdominal cavity—and bathes the cells directly. The open circulatory system is particularly [2] characteristic of insects and other arthropods, although it is also found in some other organisms. Ex.

In most insects the blood does not take a major part in oxygen transport. 3 Oxygen enters the animal's body through a separate network of branching tubes that open to the atmosphere on the outside of the animal. (This type of respiratory system will be discussed in more detail in the next chapter.) 4 Blood in an open circulatory system moves somewhat more slowly than in the average closed system. The slower system is adequate for insects because it does not have to supply the cells with oxygen.

Def. II

Closed Circulatory Systems

In a **closed circulatory system**, the blood flows through a well-defined system of 1 vessels with many branches. In the majority of closed systems the blood is responsible for oxygen transport. To supply all the body cells with sufficient oxygen, the blood must 2 move quickly through the blood vessels. A closed circulatory system must therefore have an efficient 3 pumping mechanism, or heart, to set the blood in motion and keep it moving briskly through the body.

Ex. 4 All vertebrates possess closed circulatory systems. Simple closed systems are also found in some invertebrates, including annelid worms. A good example of such a simple closed circulatory system can be seen in the 5 earthworm.

Ex. R ⟶ regeneration?

Exercise 6.1 Annotating

Using a variety of notations, annotate the following passage as if you were preparing for a quiz on the material. Remember, do not underscore as you read, but wait until you finish a paragraph or a section and then mark the important points.

Stress Management

Each of us has our own optimum stress level, which is influenced by heredity and other factors. Some people thrive at stress levels that would quickly lead others to the state of exhaustion. How can we tell if we are stressed beyond our optimum level? Sometimes it is obvious; but, more often we fail to associate the symptoms we experience with their cause.

Different people respond to stress differently. For example, one person might gorge him- or herself with food while another might lose his or her appetite. One person might have trouble falling asleep at night while another person might sleep most of the time.

General Guidelines for Stress Management

Adopt a new way of looking at life. Stress management begins with adopting the philosophy that you, as an individual, are basically responsible for your own emotional and physical well-being. You can no longer allow other people to determine whether or not you are happy. You have little control over the behavior of anyone but yourself, and your emotional well-being is too important to trust to anyone but yourself. Your goal should be to develop such positive emotional wellness that nobody can ruin your day.

A positive outlook on life. This is absolutely essential to successful stress management. Your perception of events, not the events themselves, is what causes stress. Almost any life situation can be perceived as either stressful or nonstressful, depending on your interpretation. A negative view of life guarantees a high stress level. People who habitually view life negatively can recondition themselves to be more positive. One way is by applying a thought-stopping technique: Whenever you catch yourself thinking negatively, force yourself to think about the positive aspects of your situation. Eventually you will just automatically begin to see life more positively.

A regular exercise program. Exercise is an excellent tension reliever. In addition to the physical benefits, exercise is also good for the mind. Participating in at least three aerobic exercise sessions a week for at least 20 minutes each can greatly reduce stress. Daily stretching exercises provide relaxation and improve flexibility and posture. Participate in leisure activities that keep you physically active.

Be reasonably organized. Disorganization, sloppiness, chaos, and procrastination may seem very relaxed, but they are stressful. Set short-term, intermediate-term, and long-term goals for yourself. Every morning list the things you want and need to accomplish that day.

Learn to say no. Some people accept too many responsibilities. If you spread yourself too thin, not only will you be highly stressed, but important things will be done poorly or not at all. Know your limits and be assertive. If you don't have time to do something or simply don't want to do it, don't. Practice saying no effectively. Try, "I'm flattered that you've asked me, but given my commitments at this time, I won't be able to. . . ."

Learn to enjoy the process. Our culture is extremely goal oriented. Many of the things we do are directed toward achieving a goal, with no thought or expectation of enjoying the process. You may go to college for a degree, but you should enjoy the process of obtaining that degree. You may go to work for a paycheck, but you should enjoy your work. Happiness can seldom be achieved when pursued as a goal. It is usually a byproduct of other activities. In whatever you do, focus on and enjoy the activity itself, rather than on how well you perform the activity or what the activity will bring you.

Don't be a perfectionist. Perfectionists set impossible goals for themselves, because perfection is unattainable. Learn to tolerate and forgive both yourself and others. Intolerance of your own imperfections leads to stress and low self-esteem. Intolerance of others leads to anger, blame, and poor relationships, all of which increase stress.

Look for the humor in life. Humor can be an effective part of stress management. Humor results in both psychological and physical changes. Its psychological effects include relief from anxiety, stress, and tension, an escape from reality, and a means of tolerating difficult life situations. Physically, laughter increases muscle activity, breathing rate, heart rate, and release of brain chemicals such as catecholamines and endorphins.

Practice altruism. **Altruism** is unselfishness, placing the well-being of others ahead of one's own. Altruism is one of the best roads to happiness, emotional health, and stress management. As soon as you start feeling concern for the needs of others, you immediately feel less stressed over the frustration of your own needs. Invariably, the most selfish people are the most highly stressed as they focus their attention on the complete fulfillment of their own needs, which can never happen.

Let go of the past. Everyone can list things in the past that he or she might have done differently. Other than learning through experience and trying not to make the same mistakes again, there is nothing to be gained by worrying about what you did or didn't do in the past. To focus on the past is nonproductive, stressful, and robs the present of its joy and vitality.

Eat a proper diet. How you eat affects your emotions and your ability to cope. When your diet is good you feel better and deal better with difficult situations. Try eating more carefully for two weeks and feel the difference it makes.

There is no unique stress-reduction diet, despite many claims to the contrary. The same diet that helps prevent heart disease, cancer, obesity, and diabetes (low in sugar, salt, fat, and total calories; adequate in vitamins, minerals, and protein) will also reduce stress.

Get adequate sleep. Sleep is essential for successfully managing stress and maintaining your health. People have varying sleep requirements, but most people function best with seven to eight hours of sleep per day. Some people simply don't allot enough time to sleep, while others find that stress makes it difficult for them to sleep.

Avoid alcohol and other drugs. The use of alcohol and other drugs in an effort to reduce stress levels actually contributes to stress in several ways. In the first place, it does *not* reduce the stress from a regularly occurring stressor such as an unpleasant job or relationship problems. Further, as alcohol and other drugs wear off, the rebound effect makes the user feel very uncomfortable and more stressed than before.

Don't overlook the possibility that excess caffeine intake is contributing to your stress. Caffeine is a powerful stimulant that, by itself, produces many of the physiological manifestations of stress. Plus, its effect of increased "nervous" energy contributes to more stressful, rushed behavior patterns. Remember that not only coffee and tea, but chocolate and many soft drinks contain caffeine.

Checkpoint

1. Why might two people in the same situation experience very different stress levels?
2. What is meant by "learn to enjoy the process"?
3. In what ways can being other-centered help reduce stress?

Curtis O. Boyer and Louis W. Shainberg, *Living Well*

Review your annotations. Have you sufficiently highlighted the main idea and the significant supporting details?

Notetaking

Many students prefer **notetaking,** or jotting down on their own paper brief sentence summaries of important textbook information. Margin space to the left of the summaries can be used to identify topics. Thus, topics of importance and explanations are side-by-side on notepaper for later study. In order to reduce notes for review, key terms can be further highlighted with a yellow marker to trigger thoughts for self-testing.

Why Take Textbook Notes?

Students who prefer this method say that working with a pencil and paper while reading keeps them involved with the material and thus improves concentration. Notetaking takes longer than annotating, but sometimes a student who has already annotated the text may feel the need, based on later testing

Reader's Tip

How to Take Notes

One of the most popular systems of notetaking is called the Cornell Method. The steps are as follows:

1. Draw a line down your paper two and one-half inches from the left side to create a two-and-one-half-inch margin for noting key words and a six-inch area on the right for sentence summaries.
2. After you have finished reading a section, tell yourself what you have read and jot down sentence summaries in the six-inch area on the right side of your paper. Use your own words and make sure you have included the main ideas and significant supporting details. Be brief, but use complete sentences.
3. Review your summary sentences and underline key words. Write these key words in the column on the left side of your paper. These words can be used to stimulate your memory of the material for later study.

demands, time, and the complexity of the material, to organize the information further into notes.

Although the following notetaking system recommends sentence summaries, writing short phrases can sometimes be more efficient and still adequately communicate the message for later study.

The Cornell Method can be used for taking notes on classroom lectures. The chart shown on the following page, developed by Norman Stahl and James King, both explains the procedure and gives a visual display of the results. The example below applies the Cornell Method of notetaking to the biology passage on the circulatory system that you have already read (see pages 252–253).

	Circulatory System
Two types Open and closed	There are two types, the open and the closed, by which blood reaches the cells of an animal.
Open Bathes cells Oxygen from outside	In the open system, found mostly in insects and other arthropods, blood moves through the body and bathes the cells directly. The blood moves slower than in the closed system, and oxygen is supplied from the outside air through tubes.
Closed Blood vessels Blood carries oxygen Heart pumps	In the closed system, blood flows through a system of vessels, oxygen is carried by the blood so it must move quickly, and the heart serves as a pumping mechanism. All vertebrates, as well as earthworms, have closed systems.

Taking Class Notes: The Cornell Method	
← $2^1/_2$ INCHES → *REDUCE IDEAS TO CONCISE JOTTINGS AND SUMMARIES AS CUES FOR RECITING.*	*← 6 INCHES →* *RECORD THE LECTURE AS FULLY AND AS MEANINGFULLY AS POSSIBLE.*
Cornell Method	This sheet demonstrates the Cornell Method of taking classroom notes. It is recommended by experts from the Learning Center at Cornell University.
Line drawn down paper	You should draw a line down your notepage about $2^1/_2$ inches from the left side. On the right side of the line simply record your classroom notes as you usually do. Be sure that you write legibly.
After the lecture	After the lecture you should read the notes, fill in materials that you missed, make your writing legible, and underline any important materials. Ask another classmate for help if you missed something during the lecture.
Use the recall column for key phrases	The recall column on the left will help you when you study for your tests. Jot down any important words or key phrases in the recall column. This activity forces you to rethink and summarize your notes. The key words should stick in your mind.
Five Rs	The Five Rs will help you take better notes based on the Cornell Method.
Record	1. Record any information given during the lecture which you believe will be important.
Reduce	2. When you reduce your information you are summarizing and listing key words/phrases in the recall column.
Recite	3. Cover the notes you took for your class. Test yourself on the words in the recall section. This is what we mean by recite.
Reflect	4. You should reflect on the information you received during the lecture. Determine how your ideas fit in with the information.
Review	5. If you review your notes you will remember a great deal more when you take your midterm.
Binder & paper	Remember it is a good idea to keep your notes in a standard-sized binder. Also you should use only full-sized binder paper. You will be able to add mimeographed materials easily to your binder.
Hints	Abbreviations and symbols should be used when possible. Abbrev. & sym. give you time when used automatically.

Exercise 6.2 **Notetaking**

In college courses, you will usually take notes on lengthy chapters or entire books. For practice with notetaking here, use the passage, "Stress Management," which you have already annotated (pages 253–256). Prepare a two-columned sheet and take notes using the Cornell Method.

Outlining

Outlining enables you to organize and highlight major points and subordinates items of lesser importance. In a glance the indentations, Roman numerals, numbers, and letters quickly show how one idea relates to another and how all aspects relate to the whole. The layout of the outline is simply a graphic display of main ideas and significant supporting details.

The example below is the picture-perfect version of the basic outline form. In practice your "working outline" would probably not be as detailed or as regular as this.

Use the tools of the outline format, *especially the indentations and numbers,* to devise your own system for organizing information.

Title

I. First main idea
  A. Supporting idea
    1. Detail
    2. Detail
    3. Detail
      a. Minor detail
      b. Minor detail
  B. Supporting idea
    1. Detail
    2. Detail
  C. Supporting idea
II. Second main idea
  A. Supporting idea
  B. Supporting idea

Why Outline?

Students who outline usually drop the preciseness of picture-perfect outlines, but make good use of the numbers, letters, indentations, and mixture of topics and phrases from the system to take notes and show levels of importance. A quick look to the far left of an outline indicates the topic with subordinate ideas indented underneath. The letters, numbers, and indentations form a visual display of the significance of the parts that make up the whole. Good outliners use plenty of paper so the levels of importance are evident at a glance.

Another use of the outline is to organize notes from class lectures. During class, most professors try to add to the material in the textbook and put it into perspective for students. Since the notes taken in class represent a large percentage of the material you need to know in order to pass the course, they are extremely important. While listening to a class lecture, you must almost instantly receive, synthesize, and select material and, at the same time, record something on paper for future reference. The difficulty of the task demands order and decision making. Do not be so eager to copy down every detail that you miss the big picture. One of the most efficient methods of taking lecture notes is to use a modified outline form, a version with the addition of stars, circles, and underlines to emphasize further the levels of importance.

How to Outline

Professors say that they can walk around a classroom and look at the notes students have taken from the text or from a lecture and tell how well each has understood the lesson. The errors most frequently observed fall into the following categories:

1. Poor organization
2. Failure to show importance
3. Writing too much
4. Writing too little

Reader's Tip

Avoiding Pitfalls in Outlining

The most important thing to remember when outlining is to ask yourself, *"What is my purpose?"* You don't need to include everything and you don't need a picture-perfect version for study notes. Include only what you believe you will need to remember later, and use a numbering system and indentations to show how one item relates to another. There are several other important guidelines to remember:

* **Get a general overview before you start.** How many main topics do there seem to be?
* **Use phrases rather than sentences.** Can you state it in a few short words?
* **Put it in your own words.** If you cannot paraphrase it, do you really understand it?
* **Be selective.** Are you highlighting or completely rewriting?
* **After outlining, indicate key terms with a yellow marker.** Highlighting makes them highly visible for later review and self-testing.

EXAMPLE Notice how numbers, letters, and indentations are used in the following outline to show levels of importance.

Circulatory System

I. Open circulatory system
   A. Blood moves through the body and bathes cells directly
   B. Examples—insects and other arthropods
   C. Oxygen supplied from outside air through tubes
   D. Slower blood movement since not supplying cells with oxygen
II. Closed circulatory system
   A. Blood flows through system of vessels
   B. Oxygen carried by blood so it must move quickly
   C. Heart serves as pumping mechanism
   D. Example—all vertebrates
   E. Example—earthworms

Exercise 6.3 Outlining

Outline the key ideas in the following selection as if you were planning to use your notes to study for a quiz. You may want to annotate before you outline.

Reacting to Stress with Defense Mechanisms

Stress may occasionally promote positive outcomes. Motivated to overcome stress and the situations that produce it, we may learn new and adaptive responses. It is also clear, however, that stress involves a very unpleasant emotional component. **Anxiety** is a general feeling of tension or apprehension that often accompanies a perceived threat to one's well-being. It is this unpleasant emotional component that often prompts us to learn new responses to rid ourselves of stress.

There are a number of techniques, essentially self-deception, that we may employ to keep from feeling the unpleasantness associated with stress. These techniques, or tricks we play on ourselves, are not adaptive in the sense of helping us to get rid of anxiety by getting rid of the source of stress. Rather, they are mechanisms that we can and do use to defend ourselves against the *feelings* of stress. They are called **defense mechanisms.** Freud believed defense mechanisms to be the work of the unconscious mind. He claimed that they are ploys that our unconscious mind uses to protect us (our *self* or *ego*) from stress and anxiety. Many psychologists take issue with Freud's interpretation of defense mechanisms and consider defense mechanisms in more general terms than did Freud, but few will deny that defense mechanisms exist. It *is* true that they are generally ineffective if consciously or purposively employed. The list of defense mechanisms is a long one. Here, we'll review some of the more common defense mechanisms, providing an example of each, to give you an idea of how they might serve as a reaction to stress.

Repression. The notion of **repression** came up earlier in our discussion of memory. In a way, it is the most basic of all the defense mechanisms. It is sometimes referred to as *motivated forgetting,* which gives us a good idea of what is involved. Repression is a matter of conveniently forgetting about some stressful, anxiety-producing event, conflict, or frustration. Paul had a teacher in high school he did not get along with at all. After spending an entire semester trying his best to do whatever was asked, Paul failed the course. The following summer, while walking with his girlfriend, Paul encountered this teacher. When he tried to introduce his girlfriend, Paul could not remember his teacher's name. He had repressed it. As a long-term reaction to stress, repressing the names of people we don't like or that we associate with unpleasant, stressful experiences is certainly not a very adaptive reaction. But at least it can protect us from dwelling on such unpleasantness.

Denial. **Denial** is a very basic mechanism of defense against stress. In denial, a person simply refuses to acknowledge the realities of a stressful situation. When a physician first tells a patient that he or she has a terminal illness, a common reaction is denial; the patient refuses to believe that there is anything seriously wrong.

Other less stressful events than serious illness sometimes evoke denial. Many smokers are intelligent individuals who are well aware of the data and the statistics that can readily convince them that they are slowly (or rapidly) killing themselves by continuing to smoke. But they deny the evidence. Somehow they are able to convince themselves that they aren't going to die from smoking; that's something that happens to other people, and besides, they *could* stop whenever they wanted.

Rationalization. **Rationalization** amounts to making excuses for our behaviors when facing the real reasons for our behaviors would be stressful. The real reason Kevin failed his psychology midterm is that he didn't study for it and has missed a number of classes. Kevin hates to admit, even to himself, that he could have been so stupid as to flunk that exam because of his own actions. As a result, he rationalizes: "It wasn't really *my* fault. I had a lousy instructor. We used a rotten text. The tests were grossly unfair. I've been fighting the darn flu all semester. And Marjorie had that big party the night before the exam." Now Susan, on the other hand, really did want to go to Marjorie's party, but she decided that she wouldn't go unless somebody asked her. As it happens, no one did. In short order, Susan rationalized that she "didn't want to go to that dumb party anyway"; she needed to "stay home and study."

Compensation. We might best think of **compensation** in the context of personal frustration. This defense mechanism is a matter of overemphasizing some positive trait or ability to counterbalance a shortcoming in some other trait or ability. If some particular goal-directed behavior becomes blocked, a person may compensate by putting extra effort and attention into some other aspect of behavior. For example, Karen, a seventh grader, wants to be popular. She's a reasonably bright and pleasant teenager, but isn't—in the judgment of her classmates—very pretty. Karen *may* compensate for her lack of good looks by studying very hard to be a good student, or by memorizing jokes and funny stories, or by becoming a good musician. Compensation is not just an attempt to be a well-rounded individual. It is a matter of expending *extra* energy and resources in one direction to offset shortcomings in other directions.

Fantasy. **Fantasy** is one of the more common defense mechanisms used by college students. It is often quite useful. Particularly after a hard day when stress levels are high, isn't it pleasant to sit in a comfortable chair, kick off your shoes, lie back, close your eyes, and daydream, perhaps about graduation day, picturing yourself walking across the stage to pick up your diploma—with honors?

When things are not going well for us, we may retreat into a world of fantasy where everything always goes well. Remember that to engage from time to time in fantasizing is a normal and acceptable response to stress. You should not get worried if you fantasize occasionally. On the other hand, you should realize that there are some potential dangers here. You need to be able to keep separate those activities that are real and those that occur in your fantasies. And you should realize that fantasy in itself will not solve whatever problem is causing you stress. Fantasizing about academic successes may help you feel better for a while, but it is not likely to make you a better student.

Projection. **Projection** is a matter of seeing in others those very traits and motives that cause us stress when we see them in ourselves. Under pressure to do well on an exam, Mark may want to cheat, but his conscience won't let him. Because of projection, he may think he sees cheating going on all around him.

Projection is a mechanism that is often used in conjunction with hostility and aggression. When people begin to feel uncomfortable about their own levels of hostility, they often project their aggressiveness onto others, coming to believe that others are "out to do me harm," and "I'm only defending myself."

Regression. To employ **regression** is to return to earlier, even childish, levels of behavior that were once productive or reinforced. Curiously enough, we often find regression in children. Imagine a four-year-old who until very recently was an only child. Now Mommy has returned from the hospital with a new baby sister. The four-year-old is no longer "the center of the universe," as her new little sister now gets parental attention. The four-year-old reverts to earlier behaviors and starts wetting the bed, screaming for a bottle of her own, and crawling on all fours in an attempt to get attention. She is regressing.

Many defense mechanisms can be seen on the golf course, including regression. After Doug knocks three golf balls into the lake, he throws a temper tantrum, stamps his feet, and tosses his three-iron in the lake. His childish regressive behavior won't help his score, but it may act as a release from the tension of his stress at the moment.

Displacement. The defense mechanism of **displacement** is usually discussed in the context of aggression. Your goal-directed behavior becomes blocked or thwarted. You are frustrated, under stress, and somewhat aggressive. You cannot vent your aggression directly at the source of the frustration, so you displace it to a safer outlet. Dorothy expects to get promoted at work, but someone else gets the new job she wanted. Her goal-directed behavior has been frustrated. She's upset and angry at her boss, but feels (perhaps correctly) that blowing her top at her boss will do more harm than good. She's still frustrated, so she displaces her hostility toward her husband, children, and/or the family cat.

Displacement doesn't have to involve hostility and aggression. A young couple discovers that having children is not going to be as easy as they thought. They want children badly, but there's an infertility problem that is causing considerable stress. Their motivation for love, sharing, and caring may be displaced toward a pet, nephews and nieces, or some neighborhood children—at least until their own goals can be realized with children of their own.

The list of defense mechanisms provided above is not an exhaustive one. These are among the most common, and this list gives you an idea of what defense mechanisms are like.

Josh Gerow, *Psychology: An Introduction*, 2nd ed.

Exercise 6.4 **Outlining**

For additional practice, outline the previous passage on "Stress Management" beginning on page 253. Use your annotations and notes to help.

Mapping

Mapping is a visual system of condensing material to show relationships and importance. A map is a diagram of the major points, with their significant subpoints, that support a topic. The purpose of mapping as an organizing strategy is to improve memory by grouping material in a highly visual way.

Why Map?

Proponents of popular learning style theories would say that mapping offers a visual organization that appeals to learners with a preference for spatial representation, as opposed to the linear mode offered by outlining and notetaking. A map provides a quick reference to overviewing an article or a chapter and can be used to reduce notes for later study.

Maps are not restricted to any one pattern, but can be formed in a variety of creative shapes, as the diagrams on the next page illustrate.

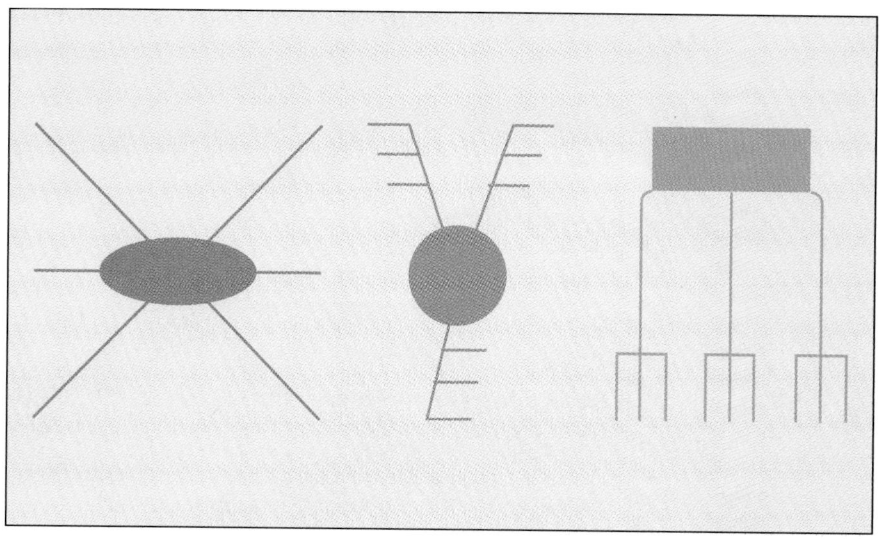

The following map highlights the biology passage on the circulatory system (see pages 252–253). Notice how the visual display emphasizes the groups of ideas supporting the topic.

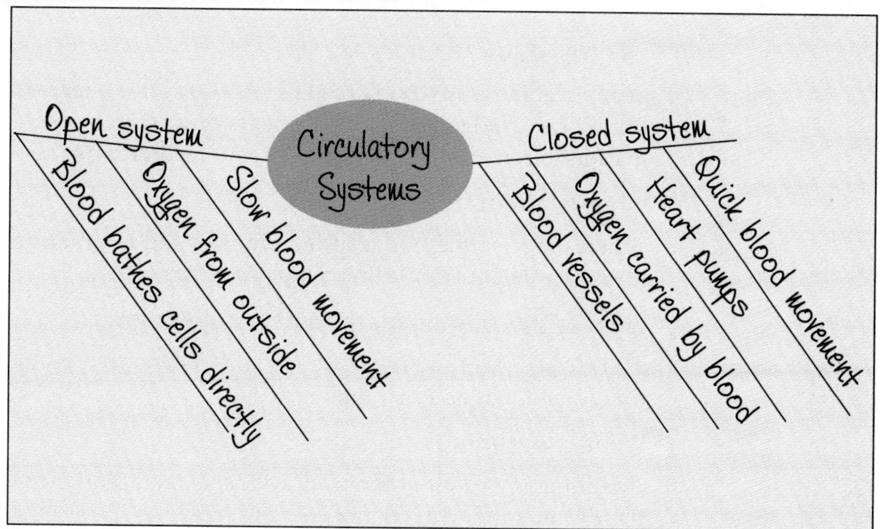

Exercise 6.5 Mapping

Refer to Exercise 6.3 and design a map for the passage entitled "Reacting to Stress with Defense Mechanisms," which you previously outlined. Use your outline to help you in making the map. Experiment with several different shapes for your map patterns on notebook or unlined paper. For additional practice, design a map for the passage in Exercise 6.1 (p. 253).

Reader's Tip

How to Map

Use the following steps for mapping:

* **Draw a circle or a box** in the middle of a page and in it write the subject or topic of the material.
* **Determine the main ideas** that support the subject and write them on lines radiating from the central circle or box.
* **Determine the significant details** and write them on lines attached to each main idea. The number of details you include will depend on the material and your purpose.

Summary Points

- What is study reading?

  Study reading is textbook reading. It is reading to learn and involves establishing knowledge networks. Students must select which textbook information to remember and organize it to facilitate further study.

- What is annotating?

  Annotating is a method of using symbols and notations to highlight main ideas, significant supporting details, and key terms.

- What is the Cornell Method of notetaking?

  The Cornell Method is a system of notetaking that includes writing summary sentences and marginal notes.

- What is outlining?

  Outlining is a method that follows a specified sequence of main ideas and significant supporting details.

- What is mapping?

  Mapping is a visual system of condensing material to show relationships and importance.

Selection 1 BIOLOGY

CONTEMPORARY FOCUS

The miracle of life becomes a double miracle with the advent of a new medical discovery. How can a fetus save the life of another person?

BLOOD THERAPY

Sarah Avery

The News & Observer (Raleigh, N.C.), February 11, 2001, pp. 1A, 15A

For Clay, the prospect of doing regular 9-year-old boy stuff is tantalizing. But he has leukemia, and six months ago, he had a cord blood transplant at Duke University Medical Center. His doctor, Joanne Kurtzberg, has six more months to go before she can pronounce him cured.

For more than two decades, Kurtzberg has sought ways to give ordinary lives to children who suffer from blood-based cancers and other life-threatening diseases. Short of a magic bullet, she swears by cord blood, which is collected from the placenta and umbilical cords after full-term births and can be used in transplants when bone marrow can't. Kurtzberg has pioneered the use of cord blood.

The success of the cord blood transplantation depends in large part on the availability of the blood itself, which, until a decade ago, was considered medical waste. The more people who know the uses of cord blood, the more who might donate.

At 5 feet 1 inch tall, Kurtzberg presents an unimposing presence to her young transplant patients. She's never seen in a white lab coat during her clinical rounds—it scares children—and instead wears overalls or cargo pants with ample pockets to carry a mobile office. She conveys an essence of Earth Mother, which is compounded by her curly, gray-flecked hair parted just off center.

Her patients love her. Her patients' parents love her more.

Collaborative Activity

Collaborate on responses to the following questions:

- What special traits enhance a doctor's ability to work with children?
- If you donated your child's umbilical cord blood, would you want to know the person who received it?
- If you had cancer and were not near a major research hospital, what would you do to find out about new treatments?

Stage 1: Preview

Preview the next selection to predict its purpose and organization as well as your learning plan.

This selection is divided into how many sections? ________________

After reading this selection, I will need to know ________________

____

Activate Schema

What hour of which day of the week were you born?

How much did you weigh?

Learning Strategy

Describe fetal growth in each trimester.

Stage 2: Integrate Knowledge While Reading

Predict Picture Relate Monitor Correct

Skill Development: Outlining

Outline or map the key ideas in each section as if you were planning to use your notes to study for a quiz.

PREGNANCY AND BIRTH

From Robert Wallace, *Biology: The World of Life*, 5th ed.

Descriptions in bus-station novels notwithstanding, fertilization occurs with the mother-to-be totally unaware of the event. If there are sperm cells thrashing around in the genital tract at any time within forty-eight hours before ovulation to about twelve hours after, the odds are very good that pregnancy will occur. As soon as the egg is touched by the head of a sperm, it undergoes violent pulsating movements which unite the twenty-three chromosomes of the sperm with its own genetic complement. From this single cell, about $\frac{1}{175}$ of an inch in diameter, a baby weighing several pounds and composed of trillions of cells will be delivered about 266 days later.

For convenience, we will divide the 266 days, or nine months, into three periods of three months each. We can consider these *trimesters* separately, since each is characterized by different sorts of events.

The First Trimester

In the first trimester the embryo begins the delicate structural differentiations that will lead to its final form. It is therefore particularly susceptible during this period to any number of factors that might influence its development. In fact the embryo often fails to survive this stage.

The first cell divisions result in cells that all look about alike and have roughly the same potentials. In other words, at this stage the cells are, theoretically anyway, interchangeable. Seventy-two hours after fertilization the embryo will consist of sixteen such cells. (So, how many divisions will have taken place?) Each cell will divide before it reaches the size of the cell that has produced it; hence the cells will become progressively smaller with each division. By the end of the first month the embryo will have reached a length of only ⅛ inch, but it will consist of millions of cells.

In the second month the features of the embryo become more recognizable. Bone begins to form throughout the body, primarily in the jaw and shoulder areas. The head and brain are developing at a much faster rate than the rest of the body, so that at this point the ears appear and open, lidless eyes stare blankly into the amniotic fluid. The circulatory system is developing and blood is pumped through the umbilical cord out to the chorion, where it receives life-sustaining nutrients and deposits the poisons it has removed from the developing embryo. The nitrogenous wastes and carbon dioxide filter into the mother's bloodstream, where they will be circulated to her own kidneys and lungs for removal. At about day 46 the primordial reproductive organs begin to form, either as testes or ovaries, and it is now, for the first time, that the sex of the embryo becomes apparent. Near the end of the second month fingers and toes begin to appear on the flattened paddles which have formed from the limb buds. By this time the embryo is about two inches long and is more or less human in appearance; it is now called a *fetus.* Growth and differentiation continue during the third month, but now the fetus begins to move.

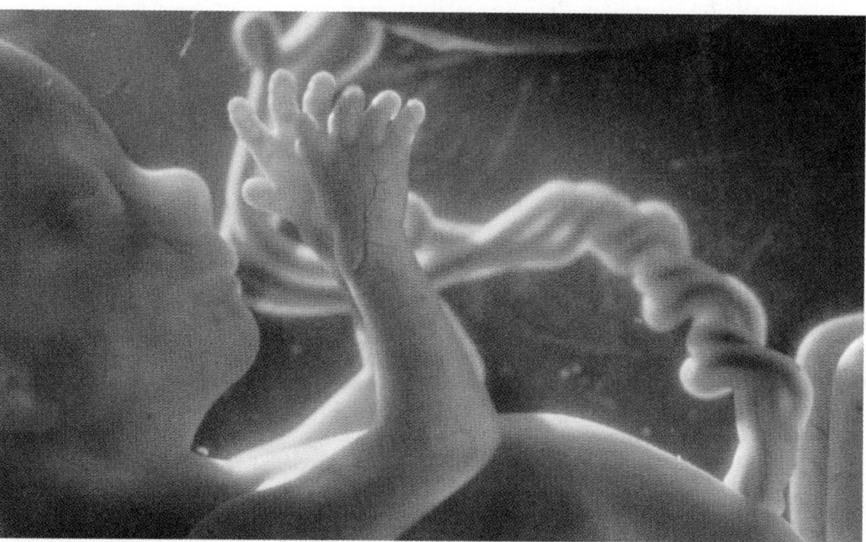

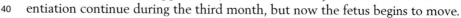

A four-month-old fetus grows inside the mother's womb.
Gui Goz/Petit Format, Science Source/Photo Researchers

It breathes the amniotic fluid in and out of bulblike lungs and swallowing motions become distinct. At this point individual differences can be distinguished in the behavior of fetuses. The clearest differences are in their facial expressions. Some frown a lot; others smile or grimace. It would be interesting to correlate this early behavior with the personality traits that develop after birth.

The Second Trimester

In the second trimester the fetus grows rapidly, and by the end of the sixth month it may be about a foot long, although it will weigh only about a pound and a half. Whereas the predominant growth of the fetus during the first trimester was in the head and brain areas, during the second trimester the body grows at a much faster relative rate than the brain and begins to catch up in size with the head.

The fetus is by this time behaving more vigorously. It is able to move freely within its sea of amniotic fluid and the delighted mother can feel it kicking and thrashing about. Interestingly, the fetus must sleep now, so there are periods when it is inactive. It is capable of reacting to more types of stimuli as time passes. For example, by the fifth month the eyes are sensitive to light, although there is still no sensitivity to sound. Other organs seem to be complete, but remain nonfunctional. For example, the lungs are developed, but they cannot exchange oxygen. The digestive organs are present, but they cannot digest food. Even the skin is not prepared to cope with the temperature changes in the outside world. In fact, at the end of the fifth month the skin is covered by a protective cheesy paste consisting of wax and sweatlike secretions mixed with loosened skin cells *(vernix caseosa)*. The fetus is still incapable in nearly all instances of surviving alone.

By the sixth month the fetus is kicking and turning so constantly that the mother often must time her own sleep periods to coincide with her baby's. The distracting effect has been described as similar to being continually tapped on the shoulder, but not exactly. The fetus moves with such vigor that its movements are not only felt from the inside, but can be seen clearly from the outside. To add to the mother's distraction, the fetus may even have periods of hiccups. By this stage it is so large and demanding that it places a tremendous drain on the mother's reserves.

At the end of the second trimester the fetus has the unmistakable appearance of a human baby (or a very old person, since its skin is loose and wrinkled at this stage). In the event of a premature birth around the end of this trimester, the fetus may be able to survive.

The Third Trimester

During the third trimester the fetus grows until it is no longer floating free in its amniotic pool. It now fills the abdominal area of the mother. The fetus is crowded so tightly into the greatly enlarged uterus that its movement is restricted. In these last three months the mother's abdomen becomes greatly distended and heavy, and her posture and gait may be noticeably altered in response to the shift in her center of gravity. The mass of tissue and amniotic fluid that accompanies the fetus ordinarily weighs almost twice as much as the fetus itself. Toward the end of this period, milk begins to form in the mother's mammary glands, which in the previous trimester have undergone a sudden surge of growth.

At this time, the mother is at a great disadvantage in several ways in terms of her physical well-being. About 85 percent of the calcium she eats goes to the fetal skeleton, and about the same percentage of her iron intake goes to the fetal blood cells. Of the protein she eats, much of the nitrogen goes to the brain and other nerve tissues of the fetus.

Some interesting questions arise here. If a woman is unable to afford expensive protein-rich foods during the third trimester, what is the probability of a lowered IQ in her offspring? On the average the poorer people in this country show lower IQ scores. Are they poor because their IQ's are low, or are IQ's low because they are poor? Is there a self-perpetuating nature about either of these alternatives?

In the third trimester, the fetus is large. It requires increasingly greater amounts of food, and each day it produces more poisonous wastes for the mother's body to carry away. Her heart must work harder to provide food and oxygen for two bodies. She must breathe, now, for two individuals. Her blood pressure and heart rate rise. The fetus and the tissues maintaining it form a large mass that crowds the internal organs of the mother. In fact, the crowding of the fetus against the mother's diaphragm may make breathing difficult for her in these months. Several weeks before delivery, however, the fetus will change its position, dropping lower in the pelvis (called *"lightening"*) and thus relieve the pressure against the mother's lungs.

There are important changes occurring in the fetus in these last three months, and some of these are not very well understood. The effects of these changes, however, are reflected in the survival rate of babies delivered by Caesarian section (an incision through the mother's side). In the seventh month, only 10 percent survive; in the eighth month, 70 percent; and in the ninth, 95 percent survive.

Interestingly, there is another change in the relationship of the fetus and mother at this time. Whereas measles and certain other infectious diseases would have affected the embryo during the first trimester of pregnancy, at this stage the mother's antibodies confer an immunity to the fetus, a protection that may last through the first few weeks of infancy.

At some point about 255 to 265 days from the time of conception the life-sustaining placenta begins to break down. Certain parts shrink, the tissue structure begins changing, and the capillaries begin to disintegrate. The result is a less hospitable environment for the fetus, and premature births at this time are not unusual. At about this time the fetus slows its growth, and drops into position with its head toward the bottom of the uterus. Meanwhile, the internal organs undergo the final changes that will enable the newborn to survive in an entirely different kind of world. Its home has been warm, rather constant in its qualities, protected, and confining. It is not likely to encounter anything quite so secure again.

Birth

The signal that there will soon be a new member of the earth's most dominant species is the onset of *labor,* a series of uterine contractions that usually begin at about half-hour intervals and gradually increase in frequency. Meanwhile, the sphincter muscle around the cervix dilates, and as the periodic contractions become stronger, the baby's head pushes through the extended cervical canal to the opening of the vagina. The infant is finally about to emerge into its new environment, one that, in time, may give it the chance to propel its own genes into the gene pool of the species.

Once the baby's head emerges, the pattern of uterine contractions changes. The contractions become milder and more frequent. After the head gradually emerges through the vaginal opening, the smaller shoulders and the body appear. Then with a rush the baby slips into a new world. As soon as the baby has emerged, the umbilicus by which it is attached to the placenta is tied off and cut. The placenta is expelled by further contractions as the *afterbirth.* The mother recovers surprisingly rapidly. In other species, which deliver their young unaided, the mother immediately chews through the umbilicus and eats the afterbirth so that it will not advertise to predators the presence of a helpless newborn. Fortunately, the behavior never became popular in our own species.

The cutting of the umbilicus stops the only source of oxygen the infant has known. There is a resulting rapid buildup of carbon dioxide in the blood, which affects a breathing center in the brain. An impulse is fired to the diaphragm, and the baby gasps its first breath. Its exhaling cry signals that it is breathing on its own.

In American hospitals the newborn is then given the first series of the many tests it will encounter during its lifetime. This one is called the *Apgar test series,* in which muscle tone, breathing, reflexes, and heart rate are evaluated. The obstetrician then checks for skin lesions and evidence of hernias. If the infant is a boy, it is checked to see whether the testes have properly descended into the scrotum. A footprint is then recorded as a means of identification, since the new individual, despite the protestations of proud parents, does not yet have many other distinctive features that would be apparent to the casual observer. And there have been more than a few cases of accidental baby-switching.

Stage 3: Recall

Stop to self-test, relate, and react.

Your instructor may choose to give you a true-false comprehension review.

Thinking About "Pregnancy and Birth"

Why it is important for pregnant women to get regular medical checkups, to avoid smoking, and to avoid consuming alcohol? Use information from the text to discuss your reasoning.

Contemporary Link

Should a company, parents, and/or a newborn baby make a profit from the sale of umbilical cord blood? If you were a new parent, what would you think are the ethical issues surrounding the donation or sale of this cord blood?

Comprehension Questions

Mark each statement with *T* (true) or *F* (false).

_________ 1. Newborns are footprinted as a means of identification.

_________ 2. The fetus is most susceptible to measles during the last trimester.

_________ 3. During fertilization, the mother can feel the sperm and the egg touch.

_________ 4. During the first trimester, changes in the facial expression of the fetus occur.

_________ 5. During the second trimester, the fetus can have the hiccups.

_________ 6. During the third trimester, the fetus floats freely with room to move in the uterus.

_________ 7. The author implies that the mother's body works the hardest during the third trimester.

_________ 8. The baby is forced to breathe when the cervix dilates.

_________ 9. Sperm can live for several hours in the genital tract.

_________ 10. During the third trimester, the mother's antibodies confer immunity to the fetus.

Search the Net

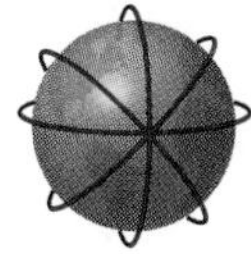

- Many difficulties can occur for expectant mothers during their pregnancies. Conduct a search to investigate pregnancy complications. Describe two complications, including the symptoms, the health risks they pose, and treatment options. Plan your own search or begin by trying the following:

  Preeclampsia: http://familydoctor.org/handouts/064.html

  Ectopic pregnancy:
  http://www.rxmed.com/illnesses/ectopic_pregnancy.html

- During each month of a pregnancy, distinct developments take place in the fetus. Describe one significant development that happens during each month of a healthy pregnancy. Plan your own search or begin by trying the following:

  Just the Facts; Your First Nine Months: http://www.justthefacts.org/continue.asp

  Kinderstart.com: http://www.kinderstart.com/pregnancyandbirth/

Concept Prep

for Life Science

How are living things organized?

The **life sciences,** sometimes called biology, encompass the study and classification of the millions of living things on earth, from the tiniest microorganisms to the largest ecosystems. Biologists organize life into a hierarchy of structural levels with each level building on the level below it. The basic unit of life is the **cell,** which has reproductive powers and contains **genes,** the units of inheritance, which are made of DNA.

A recent system of classification divides all organisms into two major groups: **prokaryotes** and **eukaryotes.** Prokaryotes, which are bacteria and blue-green algae, have very simple cells with no distinct subcellular structures. Comprising all other forms of life, eukaryotes are more complex cells with structures called **organelles** and a **nucleus** containing DNA.

Eukaryotes are divided into four groups: (1) **protists,** which have only one single cell; (2) **animals,** which are multicellular and obtain energy by eating other organisms; (3) **fungi,** which are multicellular and obtain energy by absorbing food directly through their cell membranes; and (4) **plants,** which are multicellular and use light energy to make food. The five major groups of living things (prokaryotes, protists, animals, fungi, and plants) are referred to as the **five kingdoms** of living things.

The five kingdoms continue to be subdivided into **phyla** (plural for **phylum**) for animals and **divisions** for plants and plantlike protists. These groups are then further divided into classes, orders, families, genera, and finally into single **species,** particular groups of organisms with shared characteristics that can mate and produce fertile offspring. The scientists who study animals are **zoologists,** and those who study plants are **botanists.**

After an expedition to the Galapagos Islands, British scientist Charles Darwin founded the principles of evolutionary theory.
Bettmann/CORBIS

What is natural selection?

One of the great contributions to biology was made by the British naturalist **Charles Darwin** (1809–1882). As a young man in 1831, Darwin set sail on ***HMS Beagle*** to help chart the South American coastline. He observed nature, kept records, and collected specimens. By the mid 1800s, Charles Darwin presented a logical argument for evolution in his book, ***On the Origin of Species.*** He used his observations on the coast and the **Galapagos Islands** to explain **natural selection,** a process in which organisms adapt to their environment with varying degrees of success. Those that are best adapted are the ones that survive, reproduce, and pass their characteristics to the next generation. Over time natural selection thus works as a natural editing process that favors traits best suited to the environment.

What is genetic engineering?

Another important contribution to the life sciences was made by **Gregor Mendel** (1822–1884), an Austrian monk born in what is today the Czech Republic. Mendel discovered the basic **laws of genetics** by experimenting with the size, seed appearance, and flower color of pea plants. He was the first person to experiment and reason that genetic traits are inherited as separate particles from each parent. Today those separate particles are known as genes. Genes are made of **DNA,** the molecule that carries genetic information in all living things, and are studied by **geneticists.** DNA can be manipulated by **genetic engineering** to produce modified organisms, such as disease-resistant crops, by inserting or deleting genes. Through **cloning,** scientists now have the capability to reproduce identical organisms.

The most recent controversy in genetics involves **stem cell research,** the extraction of stem cells from the inner core of a newly fertilized human embryo for medical experimentation. Scientists say they can trigger these stem cells to grow tissues to treat spinal cord injuries and diseases such as heart failure, Alzheimer's, Parkinson's, diabetes, and cancer.

REVIEW QUESTIONS

Study the material and answer the following questions.

1. What is the basic unit of life? ______________________

2. How do prokaryotes differ from eukaryotes? ______________________

3. Are plants and animals eukaryotes or prokaryotes? ______________________

4. In the classification system, how does a phylum relate to a species? ______________________

5. What was the contribution of Charles Darwin? ______________________

6. Why do the characteristics of a species change over time through natural selection? ______________________

7. What area of life science did Mendel research? ______________________

8. What is DNA? ______________________

9. What is genetic engineering? ______________________

10. What is a clone? ______________________

Your instructor may choose to give a true-false review of these life science concepts.

Selection 2 ALLIED HEALTH

CONTEMPORARY FOCUS

Are the foods that taste the best always the worst for you? How can your knowledge of nutrition improve your performance and reduce stress?

FOOD AND STRESS

Martin Zucker

From *Better Nutrition*, May 2000

Can some foods trigger or increase stress? Yes. These foods are called "pseudostressors" or "sympathomimetics," because they imitate stimulation of the sympathetic nervous system.

- *Refined sugar and carbohydrates.* Foods which have refined sugar and refined carbohydrates—such as white flour, rice and high-fructose corn syrup—are stressors, and a body under stress has an even harder time processing these carbs. In addition, taking in a lot of sugar in a short period of time (or missing meals and then consuming sugar) can result in hypoglycemia, which is marked by headache, dizziness, anxiety, trembling and irritability. A sugar-caused stress response and accompanying cortisol production raise blood glucose levels which, in turn, burdens the pancreas. This heightened blood-sugar level leads to insulin resistance and can bring on fatigue, depression and emotional instability.
- *Fats.* Consuming the wrong kinds of fat can cause "stress damage" to your body. The consumption of too much fat prevents your body from properly using carbohydrates, initiating the cascade of problems mentioned above.
- *Processed foods.* Processed foods, such as junk foods and fast foods, contain synthetic additives—preservatives, emulsifiers, thickeners, stabilizers and flavor-enhancers. Some of these, including Tartrazine and Sodium Yellow, are thought to cause stress-related responses. These colorants are believed to excite the central nervous system, and have been implicated in stress-related conditions, such as childhood hypersensitivity, attention deficit disorder and certain allergies.

Collaborative Activity

Collaborate on responses to the following questions:

- What food do you regularly eat that can cause stress?
- What healthy food options do you regularly incorporate into your diet?
- What effects does sugar have on the body?

Stage 1: Preview

Preview the next selection to predict the purpose and organization as well as your learning plan.

After reading this selection, I would like to know ____________________

____

Activate Schema

What causes stress for you?

What is your typical response to stress?

Learning Strategy

Explain the scientific impact of nutrition, exercise, and stress on the body.

Word Knowledge

What do you know about these words?

attribute	crankiness	optimal	judiciously	mimic
aroused	prone	precursor	salient	euphoria

Your instructor may give a true-false vocabulary review before or after reading.

Stage 2: Integrate Knowledge While Reading

Predict Picture Relate Monitor Correct

Skill Development: Notetaking

Use an informal outline to take notes for later study.

NUTRITION, HEALTH, AND STRESS

From Barbara Brehm, *Stress Management*

Nutrition and Stress: Running on Empty

Good nutrition and eating habits contribute significantly to good health and stress resistance. They are especially important during high-stress times, but these may be the times when we are least likely to eat well! The cupboard is bare, we have no time to plan a shopping list and no money to go shopping, so we skip meals or grab whatever fast food is closest at hand. Sometimes we depend on a dining hall whose schedule doesn't match our own, or whose ideas of good nutrition and fine cuisine are limited to meat, potatoes, and overcooked vegetables with lots of butter. Dessert is usually the high point of every meal.

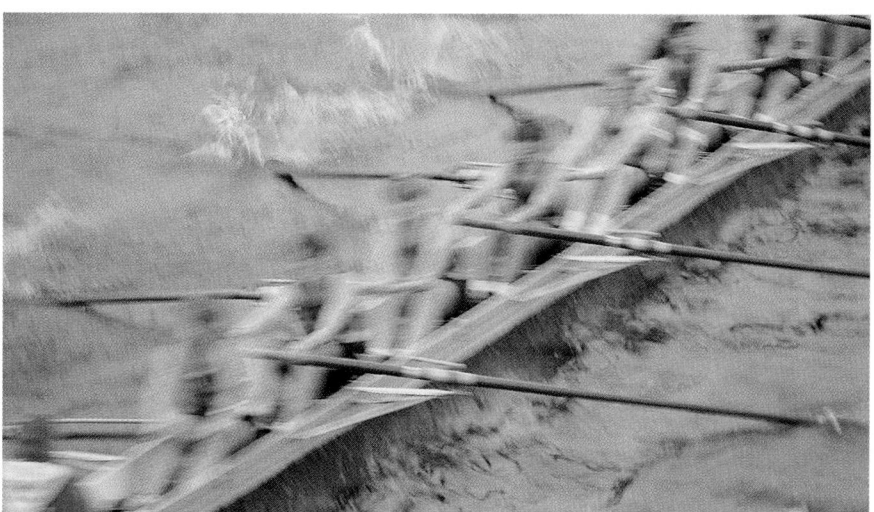

A woman's crew team races on the Charles River in Cambridge, Massachusetts.
James Lemass/Getty Images

Food and Energy: The Role of Blood Sugar

Everyone has experienced the fatigue and irritability that can result from being hungry. While many of the body's systems can make energy from fat, the central nervous system, including the brain, relies primarily on blood sugar, or glucose, for fuel. When blood sugar falls, these symptoms of fatigue result. Parents and people who work with children have observed the hungry-cranky connection on many occasions. As adults, we tend to attribute our moods to external events and ignore our internal physiology, but hunger can cause crankiness in us just the same.

After you consume a meal, your blood glucose level rises as sugar enters the bloodstream from the digestive tract. A rising blood sugar level signals the pancreas to release **insulin.** Insulin is a hormone that allows sugar to enter the cells and be used for energy. As the glucose gradually leaves the bloodstream, blood glucose levels begin to decrease.

Some people have more trouble regulating blood sugar than others and are prone to **hypoglycemia,** or low blood sugar, especially if they forget to eat or when they participate in physical activity. Symptoms of hypoglycemia include hunger, shakiness, nervousness, dizziness, nausea, and disorientation.

The following are recommendations for keeping your blood sugar at a healthful level without peaks and dips.

Eat Regularly

Your body likes a regular schedule. Skipping meals means guaranteed hypoglycemia in people prone to this condition. Set up times for meals and snacks that are convenient for your schedule and stick to this routine as much as possible. This may mean planning ahead and carrying snacks with you if you are at work or out running errands. Many people, including those with hypoglycemia, find that eating five or six small meals or snacks each day helps them feel more energetic than three large meals.

Include Protein Foods at Every Meal

Carbohydrate foods eaten without foods containing much protein are digested and enter the bloodstream quickly and are thus likely to challenge blood sugar regulatory processes in people prone to hypoglycemia. Protein slows digestion and allows blood sugar to rise more gradually. Protein servings may be small: a slice or two of meat or cheese; a half-cup of cottage cheese, yogurt, or tuna salad; small servings of fish or shellfish; a dish made with lentils or other legumes; or soy products like tofu.

Avoid Sugar Overload

When you eat a large amount of carbohydrates, blood sugar rises quickly. A high blood sugar level calls forth a high insulin response, which in some people causes a sort of rebound effect: glucose enters the cells, and the blood sugar level drops quickly, causing hypoglycemia. While you may feel energized for a short period of time after too much sugar, you may eventually begin to feel tired, irritable, and hungry.

Drink Plenty of Fluids

Many people fail to maintain optimal levels of hydration. The next time you feel tired, try drinking a glass of water. Dehydration causes fatigue and irritability. Thirst is not an adequate indicator of dehydration; you become dehydrated before you get thirsty. Nutritionists advise drinking at least four cups of fluid each day, more with physical activity or hot weather. Caffeinated and alcoholic beverages don't count. Not only do they increase your stress but they also dehydrate you and thus increase your fluid needs. Your urine will be pale if you are adequately hydrated; dark-colored urine is a sign of dehydration.

Limit Caffeine

Caffeine is a **sympathomimetic** substance, which means its effects mimic those of the sympathetic nervous system and thus cause the fight-or-flight response. If you add caffeine to an already aroused sympathetic nervous system, the results can be stressful and produce high levels of anxiety, irritability, headache, and stress-related illness. Most caffeine drinks, including coffee, tea, and cola soft drinks, can also cause stomachaches and nausea, which often get worse under stress.

One or two caffeinated beverages consumed judiciously at appropriate times during the day appear to do no harm for most people. Indeed, a little caffeine can increase alertness. The problem with caffeine is that people are likely to overindulge in it when they are stressed. When summoning the energy necessary to get through the day feels like trying to squeeze water from a rock, they reach for a shot of caffeine. Caffeine cannot substitute for a good night's sleep, however. When you are truly fatigued, caffeine does not help you concentrate; it simply leaves you wired, too jittery to sleep, and too tired to do anything productive.

Eating in Response to Stress: Feeding the Hungry Heart

Few people look on eating and food only in terms of hunger and nutrition. Every culture in the world has evolved rituals around food and eating. Feasting and fasting carry layers of religious, cultural, and emotional overtones. As children, we learn to associate food with security, comfort, love, reward, punishment, anger, restraint. It's no wonder that we eat for many reasons other than hunger: because we're lonely, angry, sad, happy, nervous, or depressed. Unlike alcohol, which we can give up if we are prone to a drinking problem, we must learn to live with food. If eating is the only way we take the time to nurture ourselves, we eat more than we are really hungry for. In extreme cases, an inability to control eating can develop into an eating disorder known as **compulsive overeating,** that often gets worse under stress.

Food and Mood: The Role of Neurotransmitters

Most people feel relaxed and lazy after a big feast. For this reason many cultures have incorporated a siesta after the large midday meal, and professors who teach a class right after lunch or dinner rarely turn out the lights for a slide show. Why do we feel tired? Certainly our blood sugar should be adequate after eating all that food. Changes in brain biochemistry may be the reason. The food we eat supplies the precursor molecules for manufacturing neurotransmitters that influence our emotions and mood. Some researchers believe that by selecting the right kinds of food we can encourage states of relaxation or alertness.

Big meals, especially those with a lot of fat, take a long time to digest, and with a full stomach we feel like relaxing rather than working. On the other hand, smaller meals low in fat take less time and energy to digest and leave us feeling more energetic and alert.

Meals that are composed primarily of carbohydrates encourage production of the neurotransmitter *serotonin,* which makes us feel drowsy and relaxed. High-carbohydrate meals are a prescription for relaxation and may be the reason some people overeat: it makes them feel good. A small, high-carbohydrate snack before bedtime can encourage sleep. Many people find that eating carbohydrates helps them feel less stressed and more relaxed. Some people find that a meal or snack with carbohydrate but little protein, especially in the middle of the day, leaves them feeling tired.

Meals that include a small serving of protein foods, with or without carbohydrates, encourage alertness by favoring production of neurotransmitters such as *dopamine* and *norepinephrine.* A small lunch that includes protein foods is best for students who need to stay alert for a 1:00 class.

Physical Activity and Stress Resistance

Participation in regular physical activity is one of the most effective ways to increase your stress resistance. Countless studies comparing people with high and low levels of stress resistance have found exercise to be one of the most salient discriminators between these two groups. An important note is that the amount and intensity of exercise required to produce stress management benefits need not be overwhelming. While many athletes enjoy extended periods of intense activity, other people find stress relief with a brisk walk, an hour of gardening, or a game of volleyball on the beach.

Exercise High: Endorphins, Hormones, and Neurotransmitters

In addition to canceling the negative effects of stress, exercise may induce some positive biochemical changes. Many exercisers report feelings of euphoria and states of consciousness similar to those described by people using drugs such as heroin. Such accounts have led to use of the term *runner's high*, since these descriptions first came primarily from long-distance runners. These reports have intrigued both exercise scientists and the lay public and have suggested the possibility that certain types of exercise, particularly vigorous exercise of long duration, may cause biochemical changes that mimic drug-induced euphoria.

As scientists have come to understand something of brain biochemistry, some interesting hypotheses have emerged. The most publicized of these has focused on a group of chemical messengers found in the central nervous system (brain and spinal cord) called opioids, since they are similar in structure and function to the drugs that come from the poppy flower: opium, morphine, and heroin. **Beta-endorphins** belong to this group. They not only inhibit pain but also seem to have other roles in the brain as well, such as aiding in memory and learning and registering emotions. It is difficult for scientists to measure opioid concentrations in the central nervous system of humans, but animal research has suggested that endogenous (produced by the body) opioid concentrations increase with level of exercise: more exercise, more opioids.

Rhythmic Exercise: Relaxed Brain Waves

Rhythmic exercises such as walking, running, rowing, and swimming increase **alpha-wave** activity in the brain. The electrical activity of the brain can be monitored in the laboratory using an instrument called an **electroencephalograph (EEG).** Alpha waves are associated with a calm mental state, such as that produced by meditation or chanting. The rhythmic breathing that occurs during some forms of exercise also contributes to an increase in alpha-wave activity. Rhythmic activity performed to music may be stress relieving in other ways as well.

Stage 3: Recall

Stop to self-test, relate, and react.

Your instructor may choose to give you a true-false comprehension review.

Thinking About "Nutrition, Health, and Stress"

Explain how you can use the health and nutritional information in this selection to energize and stimulate your mental performance during exam week. Explain the purpose for each part of your plan and give specific examples.

Contemporary Link

The "Freshman 15" refers not to an athletic team but to the 15 pounds that students often gain during the first year of college. How do you plan to use this information about nutrition and cafeteria/fast food choices to avoid this weight gain?

Comprehension Questions

After reading the selection, answer the following questions with *a, b, c,* or *d.*

Main Idea ________ 1. Which is the best statement of the main idea of this selection?
   a. A balanced diet is the most effective way to decrease stress.
   b. Regular exercise and good eating habits contribute to stress reduction and both physical and emotional well being.
   c. Stress negatively affects mental and physical performance.
   d. Avoiding sugar overload and including protein at every meal help regulate blood sugar.

Detail ________ 2. The pancreas is signaled to release insulin when
   a. protein is consumed.
   b. blood glucose levels rise.
   c. physical activity increases.
   d. blood sugar levels decrease.

Inference ________ 3. By using the term "fine cuisine," the author suggests that
   a. "fine" meals include meat, potatoes, and vegetables.
   b. dessert is an important part of "fine dining."
   c. dining halls do not always serve good, nutritional meals.
   d. vegetables should be cooked without fats.

Detail ________ 4. People who experience symptoms of hypoglycemia should do all of the following except
   a. eat three large meals per day and vary the times.
   b. combine proteins with carbohydrates.
   c. limit sugar intake.
   d. eat several small meals or snacks per day.

Inference ________ 5. The implied similarity between drinking and eating problems is that
a. many people who abuse alcohol are also prone to eating problems.
b. compulsive eating is treated more easily than compulsive drinking.
c. drinking alcohol and eating food sometimes are misguided responses to stress.
d. the consumption of both food and alcohol releases endorphins, which reduce stress.

Detail ________ 6. The production of norepinephrine is stimulated by eating
a. proteins.
b. fats.
c. carbohydrates.
d. caffeine.

Detail ________ 7. The beta-endorphins believed to be released by exercise have all of the following benefits except
a. inducing feelings of euphoria.
b. inhibiting pain.
c. regulating blood sugar.
d. aiding memory.

Inference ________ 8. The activity most likely to increase alpha-wave activity in the brain would be
a. playing a game of chess.
b. jogging.
c. lifting weights.
d. playing baseball.

Inference ________ 9. For a midnight snack before bed, the author would most likely recommend
a. a bagel.
b. cappuccino.
c. peanuts.
d. a chicken leg.

Detail ________ 10. The author's attitude toward the use of caffeine by most people is that
a. caffeine can be used to decrease fear because it arouses the fight-or-flight response.
b. light amounts of caffeine appear harmless and can increase alertness.
c. caffeine should be avoided because it causes stomachaches, nausea, headaches, and irritability.
d. when a person is truly fatigued, caffeine can increase concentration.

Answer the following with *T* (true) or *F* (false).

Detail ________ 11. Glucose provides the primary fuel for the brain.

Detail ________ 12. Thirst is an adequate indicator of the body's optimal hydration level.

Inference ________ 13. The term *hungry heart* implies a need that food cannot satisfy.

Detail ________ 14. A glass of cola can be counted toward the number of cups of fluid the body needs each day.

Inference ________ 15. The author suggests that serotonin is more important for effective studying than dopamine and norepinephrine.

Vocabulary

According to the way the italicized word was used in the selection, select *a, b, c,* or *d* for the word or phrase that gives the best definition. The number in parentheses indicates the line of the passage in which the word is located.

________ 1. "to *attribute* our moods" (15)
a. to dissociate
b. to credit
c. to explain
d. to reject

________ 2. "can cause *crankiness*" (16–17)
a. rage
b. irritability
c. drowsiness
d. fatigue

________ 3. "*optimal* levels" (49)
a. medium
b. low
c. satisfactory
d. regulatory

________ 4. "its effects *mimic*" (57)
a. distort
b. imitate
c. confuse
d. falsify

________ 5. "an already *aroused*" (59)
a. excited
b. not stimulated
c. settled
d. relaxed

________ 6. "beverages consumed *judiciously*" (64)
a. recklessly
b. hastily
c. cautiously
d. carelessly

________ 7. "we are *prone*" (78)
a. damaged by
b. inclined
c. addicted
d. connected

________ 8. "the *precursor* molecules" (88)
a. necessary
b. final
c. active
d. forerunner

_________ 9. "*salient* discriminators" (110)
a. noticeable
b. instructive
c. irrelevant
d. damaging

_________ 10. "drug-induced *euphoria*" (122–123)
a. insanity
b. disorientation
c. exhilaration
d. serenity

Search the Net

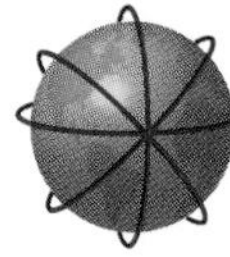

- The body needs certain nutrients to help it cope with stress. List five of these nutrients. Which foods contain these nutrients? Plan your own search or begin by trying one of the following:

  Wholehealthmd.com: http://www.wholehealthmd.com

  Homearts: http://homearts.com/

- Foods can serve as remedies for specific ailments. Search for foods that help the body fight the following: acne, cold sores, high blood pressure, and insomnia. Plan your own search or begin by trying one of the following:

  Wholehealthmd.com: http://www.wholehealthmd.com/hk/remedies/0,1458,,00.html

  Foods that Heal: http://www.picoftheweb.com/healing/foods_healing/

Concept Prep

for Health

What is blood pressure?

Blood pressure is the measure of the pressure exerted by the blood as it flows through the arteries. Blood moves in waves and is thus measured in two phases. The **systolic pressure** is the pressure at the height of the blood wave when the left ventricle of the heart contracts to push the blood through the body. The **diastolic pressure** is the pressure when the ventricles are at rest and filling with blood. The figures are expressed as the systolic "over" the diastolic pressure. The average blood pressure of a healthy adult is **120 over 80.**

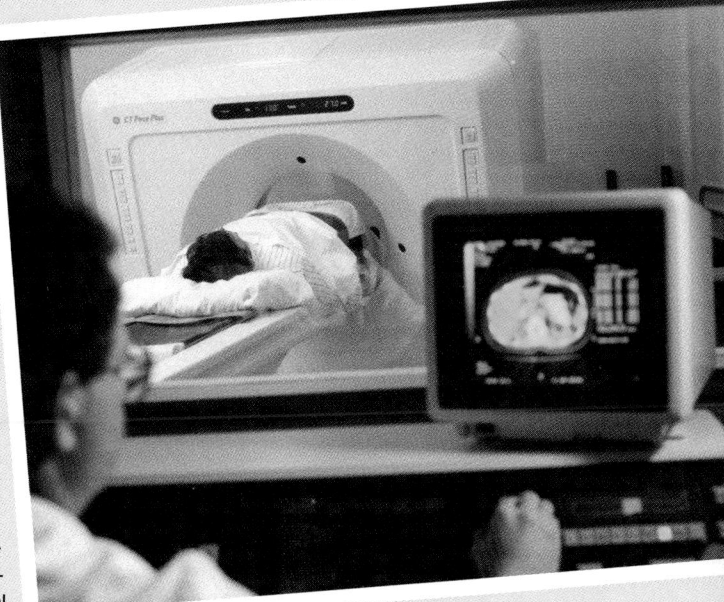

The technician uses the computer to administer an MRI.
Ed Eckstein/CORBIS

What can happen to arteries as we age?

Cholesterol—a white soapy substance that is found in the body and in foods such as animal fats—can accumulate on the inner walls of arteries—blood vessels that carry blood away from the heart—and narrow the channels through which blood flows. Nutritionists recommend eating **unsaturated fats** such as vegetable or olive oils as opposed to **saturated fats** (animal fats), which are solid at room temperature.

Another condition that lessens the flow of blood through the arteries is hardening of the arteries or **arteriosclerosis**. A surgical technique called an **angioplasty** is used to clear the arteries. A catheter with a small balloon is inserted into the arteries around the heart to compress fatty deposits and restore the flow of blood.

What are some frequently discussed medical procedures?

- A **CAT scan** (computerized axial tomography) is a painless, noninvasive procedure that uses radiation to show a three-dimensional image of the body. The diagnostic procedure is used to detect tumors and other conditions. It shows differences in the density of soft tissue with high-density substances appearing white and low-density substances appearing dark.
- An **MRI** (magnetic resonance imaging) uses magnetic fields and radio waves to detect hidden tumors and other conditions by mapping the vibration of atoms. The MRI is painless and does not use radiation.
- **Chemotherapy** is a treatment for cancer in which chemicals are given to destroy cancer cells. Currently more than fifty anticancer drugs are available for use. Temporary hair loss is a common side effect of chemotherapy.
- **Radiation** is another treatment for destroying malignant cancer cells. Unfortunately, it also destroys some healthy cells.
- A **mammogram** is an X-ray of the breast to detect tumors that are too small to be detected by other means.
- A **Pap test** is a procedure in which cells are taken from the cervical region and tested for cancer.

- **PSA** (prostate-specific antigen) levels in the blood are used to detect prostate cancer in men. A prostatic ultrasound can also be used.
- A **sonogram** or **ultrasound** test uses high-frequency sound waves to detect abnormalities. It is a noninvasive procedure that can be used to view the size, position, and sex of a fetus.
- **Amniocentesis** is a procedure for detecting abnormalities in the fetus. Fluid is drawn from the liquid surrounding the fetus by a needle through the mother's stomach. The fluid contains cells of the fetus that can be analyzed.

REVIEW QUESTIONS

Study the material and answer the following questions.

1. What is the difference between systolic and diastolic pressure? ______________________________
____
____

2. Which type of pressure should be higher? ______________________________
____

3. How does cholesterol harm the body? ______________________________
____

4. How can you distinguish saturated fats? ______________________________
____

5. What does an angioplasty do? ______________________________
____

6. What medical procedure uses drugs to cure cancer? ______________________________
____

7. What procedure uses magnetic fields and radio waves to detect tumors and other conditions without radiation? ______________________________
____

8. What test can indicate prostate cancer? ______________________________
____

9. What procedure extracts fetal cells for diagnosis? ______________________________
____

10. What type of X-ray is used to detect breast cancer? ______________________________
____

Your instructor may choose to give a true-false review of these health concepts.

READER'S JOURNAL

Name ______________________________ Date ______________

CHAPTER 6

Answer the following questions to reflect on your own learning and progress. Use the perforations to tear the assignment out for your instructor.

1. Why would you tend to learn more from notetaking than from annotating? ______________________________

____

2. Why is it important to indent outlined notes? ______________________________

____

3. Do you prefer the Cornell System of notetaking or outlining? Why?

____

____

4. When taking notes from a text, why do many students tend to write too much? ______________________________

____

5. When you take lecture notes, do you tend to write too much or too little? Why? ______________________________

____

6. Why is it more difficult to take notes on the selection on pregnancy than on the one about nutrition, health, and stress? ______________________________

____

7. Why do experts recommend that you review class lecture notes within twenty-four hours after taking them? ______________________________

____

8. How do the written critical thinking response questions enrich your understanding of the selection? ______________________________

____

7

Inference

- What is an inference?
- What is the connotation of a word?
- What is figurative language?
- Why is prior knowledge needed for implied meaning?
- How does a reader draw conclusions?

Man in Brick Maze *by Roger Leyonmark. Pen, ink, and airbrush. © Roger Leyonmark/The Stock Illustration Source*

What Is an Inference?

The first and most basic level of reading is the *literal level*—that is, the level that presents the facts. In reacting to a literal comprehension question, you can actually point to the words on the page that answer the question. Reading, however, progresses beyond this initial stage. A second and more sophisticated level of reading deals with motives, feelings, and judgments; this is the *inferential level.* At this level you no longer can point to the answer in the text but instead must form the answer from suggestions within the selection. In a manner of speaking, you must read between the lines for the implied meaning.

With inference, rather than directly stating a fact, authors often subtly suggest and thus manipulate the reader. Suggestion can be a more effective method of getting the message across than a direct statement. Suggestion requires greater writing skill, and it is also usually more artistic, creative, and entertaining. The responsible reader searches beyond the printed word for insights into what was left unsaid.

For example, in cigarette advertisements the public is enticed through suggestion, not facts, into spending millions of dollars on a product that is known to be unhealthful. Depending on the brand, smoking offers the refreshment of a mountain stream or the sophisticated elegance of the rich and famous. Never in the ads is smoking directly praised or pleasure promised; instead, the positive aspects are *implied.* A lawsuit for false advertising is avoided because nothing tangible has been put into print. The emotionalism of a full-page advertisement is so overwhelming that the consumer hardly notices the warning peeking from the bottom of the page—"Warning: The Surgeon General Has Determined That Cigarette Smoking Is Dangerous to Your Health."

Reprinted with special permission of King Features Syndicate.

Exercise 7.1 **Implied Meaning in Advertisements**

Look through magazines and newspapers to locate advertisements for cigarettes, alcoholic beverages, and fragrances. What characteristics do all three types of advertisements have in common? Select one advertisement for each product and answer the following questions about each.

1. What is directly stated about the product?
2. What does the advertisement say about the product?
3. Who seems to be the potential customer for the product?

Authors and advertisers have not invented a new comprehension skill; they are merely capitalizing on an already highly developed skill of daily life. When asked by a student in her class, "How do you like the new president of the college?" the professor might answer, "I think he wears nice suits and is always on time," rather than say, "I don't like the new president." A lack of approval has been suggested by an absence of information, and the professor has avoided making a direct negative statement. In everyday life, we make inferences about people by examining what people say, what they do, and what others say about them. The intuition of everyday life applied to the printed word is the inferential level of reading.

Connotation of Words

Notice the power of suggested meaning in responding to the following questions:

1. If you read an author's description of classmates, which student would you assume is smartest?
   a. A student annotating items on a computer printout
   b. A student with earphones listening to a CD
   c. A student talking with classmates about *The Sopranos*
2. Which would you find described in a vintage small town of the 1960s?
   a. Movies
   b. Cinema
   c. Picture shows
3. Who probably earns the most money?
   a. A businessperson in a dark suit, white shirt, and tie
   b. A businessperson in slacks and a sport shirt
   c. A businessperson in a pale blue uniform

Can you prove your answers? It's not the same as proving when the Declaration of Independence was signed, yet you still have a feeling for how each question should be answered. Even though a right or wrong answer is difficult to explain in this type of question, certain answers can still be defended as most accurate—they are *a*, *c*, and *a*. The answers are based on feelings, attitudes, and knowledge commonly shared by members of society.

A seemingly innocent tool, word choice is the first key to implied meaning. For example, if a person is skinny, he is unattractive, but if he is slender or slim he must be attractive. All three words might refer to the same underweight person, but *skinny* communicates a negative feeling while *slender* or *slim* communicates a positive one. This feeling or emotionalism surrounding a word is called **connotation. Denotation** is the specific meaning of a word, but the connotative meaning goes beyond this to reflect certain attitudes and prejudices of society. Even though it may not seem premeditated, writers select words, just as advertisers select symbols and models, to manipulate the reader's opinions.

Exercise 7.2 Recognizing Connotation in Familiar Words

In each of the following word pairs, write the letter of the word that connotes the more positive feeling:

________	1. (a) guest	(b) boarder
________	2. (a) surplus	(b) waste
________	3. (a) conceited	(b) proud
________	4. (a) buzzard	(b) robin
________	5. (a) heavyset	(b) obese
________	6. (a) explain	(b) brag
________	7. (a) house	(b) mansion
________	8. (a) song	(b) serenade
________	9. (a) calculating	(b) clever
________	10. (a) neglected	(b) deteriorated
________	11. (a) colleague	(b) accomplice
________	12. (a) ambition	(b) greed
________	13. (a) kitten	(b) cat
________	14. (a) courageous	(b) audacious
________	15. (a) contrived	(b) designed
________	16. (a) flower	(b) orchid
________	17. (a) distinctive	(b) peculiar
________	18. (a) baby	(b) kid
________	19. (a) persuasion	(b) propaganda
________	20. (a) gold	(b) tin
________	21. (a) slump	(b) decline
________	22. (a) lie	(b) misrepresentation
________	23. (a) janitor	(b) custodian
________	24. (a) offering	(b) collection
________	25. (a) soldiers	(b) mercenaries

Exercise 7.3 Connotation in Textbooks

For each of the underlined words in the following sentences, indicate the meaning of the word and reasons why the connotation is positive or negative. Note the following example:

While the unions fought mainly for better wages and hours, they also championed various social reforms.

Leonard Pitt, *We Americans*

championed: ______________________________

____

1. The ad was part of the oil companies' program to sell their image rather than their product to the public. In the ad they boasted that they were reseeding all the disrupted areas with a newly developed grass that grows five times faster than the grass that normally occurs there.

Robert Wallace, *Biology: The World of Life*

boasted: ______________________________

2. At noon, a group of prominent bankers met. To stop the hemorrhaging of stock prices, the bankers' pool agreed to buy stocks well above the market.

James Kirby Martin et al., *America and Its People*

hemorrhaging: ______________________________

____

3. Tinbergen, like Lorenz and von Frisch, entered retirement by continuing to work. Tinbergen was a hyperactive child who, at school, was allowed to periodically dance on his desk to let off steam. So in "retirement" he entered a new arena, stimulating the use of ethological methods in autism.

Robert Wallace, *Biology: The World of Life*

"retirement": ______________________________

4. The nation's capital is crawling with lawyers, lobbyists, registered foreign agents, public relations consultants, and others—more than 14,000 individuals representing nearly 12,000 organizations at last count—all seeking to influence Congress.

Robert Lineberry et al., *Government in America, Brief Version,* 2nd ed.

crawling: ______________________________

5. Not since Wilson had tried to ram the League of Nations through the Senate had any president put more on the line.

Leonard Pitt, *We Americans*

ram: ______________________________

Figurative Language

Figurative language requires readers to make inferences about comparisons that are not literally true and sometimes not logically related. What does it mean to say, "She worked like a dog"? To most readers it means that she worked hard, but since few dogs work, the comparison is not literally true or particularly logical. **Figurative language** is, in a sense, another language because it is a different way of using "regular" words so that they take on new meaning. For example, "It was raining buckets" and "raining cats and dogs" are lively, figurative ways of describing a heavy rain. New speakers of English, however, who comprehend on a literal level, might look up in the sky for the descending pails or animals. The two expressions create an exaggerated, humorous effect, but on the literal level, they do not make sense.

Idioms

When first used, "works like a dog" and "raining cats and dogs" were probably very clever. Now the phrases have lost their freshness, but still convey meaning for those who are "in the know." Such phrases are called **idioms,** or expressions that do not make literal sense but have taken on a new generally accepted meaning over many years of use.

EXAMPLE

She tried to *keep a stiff upper lip* during the ordeal.

His eyes were *bigger than his stomach.*

EXPLANATION The first means to maintain control and the second means to ask for more food than you are able to eat.

Exercise 7.4 **Understanding Idioms**

What do the following idioms mean?

1. to lay an egg ______________________________
2. a bone to pick ______________________________
3. born with a silver spoon in her mouth ______________________________

   ____
4. chip on his shoulder ______________________________
5. burn the midnight oil ______________________________

Similes

A **simile** is a comparison of two unlike things using the words *like* or *as.*

EXAMPLE

The spring flower pushed up its bloom *like a lighthouse* beckoning on a gloomy night.

And every soul, it passed me by,
Like the whizz of my crossbow!

Samuel Taylor Coleridge, *The Rime of the Ancient Mariner*

Metaphors

A **metaphor** is a direct comparison of two unlike things (without using *like* or *as*).

EXAMPLE

The corporate accountant is a computer from nine to five.

Miss Rosie was a wet brown bag of a woman who used to be the best looking gal in Georgia.

Lucille Clifton, *Good Times*

Personification

Personification is the process of attributing human characteristics to nonhuman things.

EXAMPLE

The *birds speak* from the forest.

Time marches on.

Verbal Irony

Verbal irony is the use of words to express a meaning that is the opposite of what is literally said.[1] If the intent is to hurt, the irony is called **sarcasm.**

EXAMPLE

"What a great looking corporate outfit!" [said to someone wearing torn jeans]

"There is nothing like a sunny day for a picnic." [said to pouring rain]

Exercise 7.5

Figurative Language in Textbooks

The figurative expressions in the following sentences are underlined. Identify the figurative type, define each expression, and suggest, if possible, the reason for its use. Follow this example:

[1]In situational irony, events occur contrary to what is expected, as if in a cruel twist of fate. For example, Juliet awakens and finds that Romeo has killed himself because he thought she was dead.

As a trained nurse working in the immigrant slums of New York, she knew that table-top abortions were common among poor women, and she had seen some of the tragic results.

Leonard Pitt, *We Americans*

It is a metaphor, which may now be an idiom, and means illegal. The connotation suggests the reality of where the operations probably occurred.

1. The War of 1812 was Tecumseh's final test. Although his alliance was incomplete, he recognized that the war was his last chance to prevail against the "Long Knives," as the Americans were called. He cast his lot with the British, who at one point gave him command over a red coat army.

   Leonard Pitt, *We Americans*

   cast his lot: ______

   red coat army: ______

2. She asked for another whiskey and, fingers trembling, lit a cigarette. She was a stone rolling downhill.

   Pedro Juan Soto, *God in Harlem*

   She was a stone rolling downhill. ______

3. Americans "discovered" the Spanish Southwest in the 1820s. Yankee settlers Moses and Stephen Austin took a party of settlers into Texas in 1821.

   Leonard Pitt, *We Americans*

   "discovered": ______

   ______

4. I can still see myself, like a wild bird set free of a cage, running from one berry bush to another, filling my little play bucket, my heart beating with delight at the sight of beautiful mariposa lilies.

   Maya Angelou, "Sister Monroe"

   like a wild bird set free of a cage: ______

5. The Moving Finger writes; and, having writ,
   Moves on; nor all your Piety nor Wit
   Shall lure it back to cancel half a Line,
   Nor all your Tears wash out a Word of it.

   Edward FitzGerald, trans., *The Rubáiyát of Omar Khayyám*

Moving Finger: ______

your Piety nor Wit: ______

to cancel half a Line: ______

Tears wash out a Word of it: ______

Inferences from Facts

Inferences can be suggested simply by juxtaposing facts. For example, an author selected the following facts from issues of *Time* magazine and presented them side-by-side in order to suggest an inference. No direct connection is stated, so the reader must thoughtfully reflect on the suggested message. This pause for thought adds power to the message.

EXAMPLE

343,000 Amount by which the population of all European Union countries combined grew last year.

343,000 Amount by which India's population grew in the first week of 2001.

Inference: ______

EXPLANATION The inference is that India's population is increasing at an alarming rate that is 52 times greater than the rate in the European Union.

Exercise 7.6 **Inferring from Facts**

$59,500 Usual amount Colin Powell received per speaking engagement after retiring from military service in 1993.

10 Number of speeches, on average, Powell gave per month in 2000.

1. Inference: ______

______

______

$662 Maximum fine a 16-year-old "mafiaboy" could pay for hacking into computers at Yahoo, eBay, and Dell, among others.

$1.7 billion Estimated amount of damage he caused.

2. Inference: ______

______

61,000 Items, worth a total of nearly $70 million, found missing from the Immigration and Naturalization Service during an audit.

539 Weapons listed in the report as missing, including six guns later linked to crimes.

3. Inference: ____

____

____

89 Percentage of nightly network-news stories reported by whites in 2000.

76 Percentage of nightly network-news stories reported by men in 2000.

4. Inference: ____

____

38 Average age at which Americans surveyed believe they reach their peak physical attractiveness.

22 Average age of *Vogue* cover models in 2000.

5. Inference: ____

____

Implied Meaning

Reading would be rather dull if the author stated every idea, never giving you a chance to figure things out for yourself. For example, in a mystery novel you carefully weigh each word, each action, each conversation, each description, and each fact in an effort to identify the villain and solve the crime before it is revealed at the end. Although textbook material may not have the Sherlock Holmes spirit of high adventure, authors use the same techniques to imply meaning.

Note the inferences in the following example:

EXAMPLE

Johnson in Action

Lyndon Johnson suffered from the inevitable comparison with his young and stylish predecessor. LBJ was acutely aware of his own lack of polish; he sought to surround himself with Kennedy advisers and insiders, hoping that their learning and sophistication would rub off on him. Johnson's assets were very real—an intimate knowledge of Congress, an incredible energy and determination to succeed, and a fierce ego. When a young marine officer tried to direct him to the proper helicopter, saying, "This one is yours," Johnson replied, "Son, they are all my helicopters."

LBJ's height and intensity gave him a powerful presence; he dominated any room he entered, and he delighted in using his physical power of persuasion. One Texas politician explained why he had given in to Johnson: "Lyndon got me by the lapels and put his face on top of mine and he talked and talked and talked. I figured it was either getting drowned or joining."

Robert A. Divine et al., *America Past and Present*

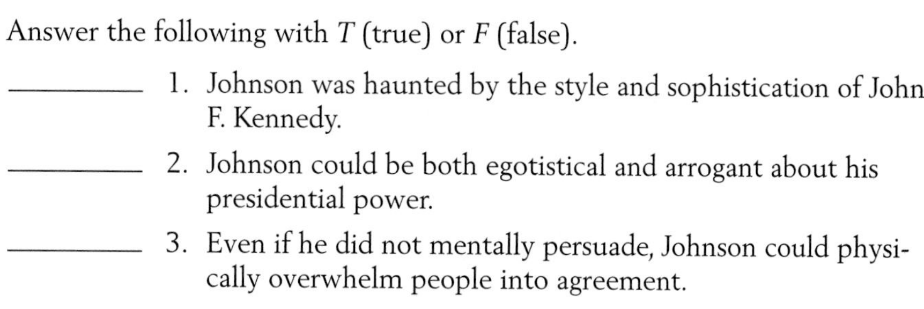

Answer the following with *T* (true) or *F* (false).

________ 1. Johnson was haunted by the style and sophistication of John F. Kennedy.

________ 2. Johnson could be both egotistical and arrogant about his presidential power.

________ 3. Even if he did not mentally persuade, Johnson could physically overwhelm people into agreement.

EXPLANATION The answer to question 1 is *True.* He "suffered from the inevitable comparison" and he went so far as to retain the Kennedy advisers. Question 2 is *True.* The anecdote about the helicopters proves that. Question 3 is *True.* His delight in "using his physical powers of persuasion" and the anecdote about the Texas politician support that.

In the following exercises, you can see how authors use suggestions. From the clues given, you can deduce the facts.

Exercise 7.7 Inference from Description

Looking back on the Revolutionary War, one cannot say enough about Washington's leadership. While his military skills proved less than brilliant and he and his generals lost many battles, George Washington was the single most important figure of the colonial war effort. His original appointment was partly political, for the rebellion that had started in Massachusetts needed a commander from the South to give geographic balance to the cause. The choice fell to Washington, a wealthy and respectable Virginia planter with military experience dating back to the French and Indian War. He had been denied a commission in the English army and had never forgiven the English for the insult. During the war he shared the physical suffering of his men, rarely wavered on important questions, and always used his officers to good advantage. His correspondence with Congress to ask for sorely needed supplies was tireless and forceful. He recruited several new armies in a row, as short-term enlistments gave out.

Leonard Pitt, *We Americans*

Answer the following with *T* (true) or *F* (false).

________ 1. The author regards George Washington as the most brilliant military genius in American history.

_________ 2. A prime factor in Washington's becoming president of the United States was a need for geographic balance.

_________ 3. Washington resented the British for a past injustice.

_________ 4. The Revolutionary War started as a rebellion in the Northeast.

_________ 5. The author believes that Washington's leadership was courageous and persistent even though not infallible.

Exercise 7.8 Inference from Action

When he came to the surface he was conscious of little but the noisy water. Afterward he saw his companions in the sea. The oiler was ahead in the race. He was swimming strongly and rapidly. Off to the correspondent's left, the cook's great white and corked back bulged out of the water, and in the rear the captain was hanging with his one good hand to the keel of the overturned dinghy.

There is a certain immovable quality to a shore, and the correspondent wondered at it amid the confusion of the sea.

Stephen Crane, *The Open Boat*

Answer the following with *a, b, c,* or *d*. Draw a map indicating the shore and the positions of the four people in the water to help you visualize the scene.

_________ 1. The reason that the people are in the water is because of
a. a swimming race.
b. an airplane crash.
c. a capsized boat.
d. a group decision.

_________ 2. In relation to his companions, the correspondent is
a. closest to the shore.
b. the second or third closest to the shore.
c. farthest from the shore.
d. in a position that is impossible to determine.

_________ 3. The member of the group that had probably suffered a previous injury is the
a. oiler.
b. correspondent.
c. cook.
d. captain.

_________ 4. The member of the group that the author seems to stereotype negatively as least physically fit is the
a. oiler.
b. correspondent.
c. cook.
d. captain.

_____ 5. The story is being told through the eyes of the
a. oiler.
b. correspondent.
c. cook.
d. captain.

Exercise 7.9 Inference from Factual Material

Except for some minor internal disturbances in the nineteenth century, Switzerland has been at peace inside stable boundaries since 1815. The basic factors underlying this long period of peace seem to have been (1) Switzerland's position as a buffer between larger powers, (2) the comparative defensibility of much of the country's terrain, (3) the relatively small value of Swiss economic production to an aggressive state, (4) the country's value as an intermediary between belligerents in wartime, and (5) Switzerland's own policy of strict and heavily armed neutrality. The difficulties which a great power might encounter in attempting to conquer Switzerland have often been popularly exaggerated since the Swiss Plateau, the heart of the country, lies open to Germany and France, and even the Alps have frequently been traversed by strong military forces in past times. On the other hand, resistance in the mountains might well be hard to thoroughly extinguish. In World War II Switzerland was able to hold a club over the head of Germany by mining the tunnels through which Swiss rail lines avoid the crests of Alpine passes. Destruction of these tunnels would have been very costly to Germany, as well as to its military partner, Italy.

Jesse H. Wheeler et al., *Regional Geography of the World*

Answer the following with *T* (true) or *F* (false).

_____ 1. The author implies that Switzerland is rich with raw materials for economic production.

_____ 2. The most important economic area of Switzerland is protected from its neighbors by the Alps.

_____ 3. In World War II Germany did not invade Switzerland primarily because of the fear of the strong Swiss army.

_____ 4. The maintenance of a neutral Swiss position in World War II was due in part to a kind of international blackmail.

_____ 5. The Swiss have avoided international war on their soil for almost two hundred years.

Prior Knowledge and Implied Meaning

Have you ever considered what makes a joke funny? Why is it no longer funny when you have to explain the meaning of a joke to someone who didn't understand it? The answer is that jokes are funny because of implied connections. The meaning that you may have to reluctantly explain is the inference or **implied meaning.** If the listener does not share the background knowledge to which the joke refers, your hilarious comic attempt will fall flat because the listener cannot understand the implied meaning. Listeners cannot connect with something they don't know, so you must choose the right joke for the right audience.

College reading may not be filled with comedy, but **prior knowledge** is expected and specifics are frequently implied rather than directly spelled out. For example, if a sentence began, "Previously wealthy investors were leaping from buildings in the financial district," you would know that the author was referring to the Stock Market Crash of 1929 on Wall Street in New York City. The details fall into an already existing schema. Although the specifics are not directly stated, you have used prior knowledge and have "added up" the details that are meaningful to you to infer time and place.

Exercise 7.10 Inferring Time and Place

Read the following passages and indicate *a, b,* or *c* for the suggested time or place. Use your prior knowledge of "anchor" dates in history to logically think about the possible responses. Underline the clues that helped you arrive at your answer.

Passage A

As women strove to maintain a semblance of home on the trail, they often experienced a profound sense of loss. The Sabbath, which had been ladies' day back home and an emblem of women's moral authority, was often spent working or traveling, especially once the going got rough. "Oh dear me I did not think we would have abused the sabbath in such a manner," wrote one guilt-stricken female emigrant. Women also felt the lack of close companions, to whom they could turn for comfort. One woman, whose husband separated their wagon from the train after a dispute, sadly watched the other wagons pull away: "I felt that indeed I had left all my friends to journey over the dreaded plains without one female acquaintance even for a companion—of course I wept and grieved about it but to no purpose."

James Davidson et al., *Nation of Nations*

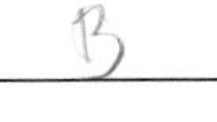

1. The time when this takes place is probably in the
   a. 1710s.
   b. 1840s.
   c. 1920s.

_______ 2. The section of the United States is most likely the
   a. west.
   b. south.
   c. north.

3. Underline the clues to your answers.

Passage B

There was an average of fifty storms a year. Cities kept their street lights on for twenty-four hours a day. Dust covered everything from food to bedspreads and piled up in dunes in city streets and barnyards. Thousands died of "dust pneumonia." One woman remembered what it was like at night: "A trip for water to rinse the grit from our lips, and then back to bed with washclothes over our noses, we try to lie still, because every turn stirs the dust on the blankets."

By the end of the decade three and a half million people had abandoned their farms and joined a massive migration to find a better life. Not all were forced out by the dust storms; some fell victim to large-scale agriculture, and many tenant farmers and hired hands were expendable during the depression. In most cases they not only lost their jobs, but they also were evicted from their houses.

Gary B. Nash et al., *The American People*

_________ 4. The time is probably in the
a. 1690s.
b. 1770s.
c. 1930s.

_________ 5. The place is most likely
a. New England.
b. the Great Plains.
c. the Deep South.

6. Underline the clues to your answers.

Passage C

On November 28 the first tea ship, the *Dartmouth,* docked. The local customs collectors fled to Fort Castle William, and the local committee of correspondence, headed by Samuel Adams and his associates, put guards on the *Dartmouth* and two other tea ships entering the port within the next few days. Repeatedly the popular rights faction insisted that the three tea ships be sent back to England. But Governor Hutchinson refused. Instead, he called upon Royal Naval vessels in the vicinity to block off the port's entrance.

James Martin et al., *America and Its People*

_________ 7. The time is probably in the
a. 1770s.
b. 1850s.
c. 1920s.

_________ 8. The place is probably
a. Washington, D.C.
b. Boston.
c. New Orleans.

9. Underline the clues to your answers.

Expanding Prior Knowledge

Your response on these passages depends on your previous knowledge of history and your general knowledge. If you did not understand many of the inferences, you might ask, "How can I expand my prior knowledge?" The answer is not an easy formula or a quick fix. The answer is part of the reason that you are in college; it is a combination of broadening your horizons, reading more widely, and being an active participant in your own life. Expanding prior knowledge is a slow and steady daily process.

Drawing Conclusions

To arrive at a conclusion, you must make a logical deduction from both stated and unstated ideas. Using the hints as well as the facts, you rely on prior knowledge and experience to interpret motives, actions, and outcomes. You draw conclusions on the basis of perceived evidence, but because perceptions differ, conclusions can vary from reader to reader. Generally, however, authors attempt to direct readers to preconceived conclusions. Read the following example and look for a basis for the stated conclusion.

EXAMPLE

Underground Conductor

Harriet Tubman was on a northbound train when she overheard her name spoken by a white passenger. He was reading aloud an ad which accused her of stealing $50,000 worth of property in slaves, and which offered a $5000 reward for her capture. She lowered her head so that the sunbonnet she was wearing hid her face. At the next station she slipped off the train and boarded another that was headed south, reasoning that no one would pay attention to a black woman traveling in that direction. She deserted the second train near her hometown in Maryland and bought two chickens as part of her disguise. With her back hunched over in imitation of an old woman, she drove the chickens down the dusty road, calling angrily and chasing them with her stick whenever she sensed danger. In this manner Harriet Tubman was passed by her former owner who did not even notice her. The reward continued to mount until it reached $40,000.

Leonard Pitt, *We Americans*

Conclusion: Harriet Tubman was a clever woman who became a severe irritant to white slave owners.

What is the basis for this conclusion?

____

____

EXPLANATION Her disguise and subsequent escape from the train station provide evidence for her intelligence. The escalating amount of the reward, finally $40,000, proves the severity of the sentiment against her.

Exercise 7.11

Drawing Conclusions

Read the following passages. For the first two passages indicate evidence for the conclusions that have been drawn. For the latter passages, write your own conclusion as well as indicate evidence.

Passage A

Coolidge was a stern-faced, tight-lipped New Englander. Coolidge had no desire to be a strong president in the tradition of a Teddy Roosevelt or a Woodrow Wilson. A firm believer in the wisdom of inactivity, Coolidge slept ten hours a night, napped every afternoon, and seldom worked more than four hours a day.

James Kirby Martin et al., *America and Its People*

Conclusion: Calvin Coolidge was a quiet and lazy president.

What is the basis for this conclusion?

____

____

Passage B

Pesticides are biologically rather interesting substances. They have no known counterpart in the natural world, and most of them didn't even exist thirty years ago. Today, however, a metabolic product of DDT, called DDE, may be the most common and widely distributed man-made chemical on earth. It has been found in the tissues of living things from the polar regions to the remotest parts of the oceans, forests, and mountains. Although the permissible level of DDT in cow's milk, set by the U.S. Food and Drug Administration, is 0.05 parts per million, it often occurs in human milk in concentrations as high as 5 parts per million and in human fat at levels of more than 12 parts per million.

Robert Wallace, *Biology: The World of Life*

Conclusion: DDT accumulates in the environment far beyond the areas where it was directly applied.

What is the basis for this conclusion?

____

____

Passage C

Writing is untidy and disconcerting. No successful ad company would want to market it. It's not fast, it's not predictable, it's not sweet. First we fantasize about that hushed moment when we'll be wonderfully alone with all our familiar, comforting writing implements at hand. I visualize a sunny room and my cup of tea. We savor the moment when, bulging with inspiration and wisdom, we at last lift our pen or start our computer and begin a new work. And work it is, though we forget that aspect in the amnesia necessary to bring us back to the blank page.

Pat Moro, "Universities" in *Nepantla*

Conclusion: ____

____

What is the basis for this conclusion? ____

____

Passage D

As social psychologist Sharon Brehm explains, "To meet people is not necessarily to love them, but to love them we must first meet them." In your classes, you are more likely to form relationships with classmates sitting on either side of you than with someone seated at the opposite end of the room. This is partly because physical **proximity** increases communication opportunities. We are more likely to talk, and therefore to feel attracted, to neighbors who live right next door than those who live down the block.

Steven Beebe et al., *Communications*

Conclusion: ____

____

What is the basis for this conclusion? ____

____

Reader's Tip

Making Inferences

- ✱ Consider attitude in the choice of words.
- ✱ Unravel actions.
- ✱ Interpret motives.
- ✱ Use suggested meaning and facts to make assumptions.
- ✱ Draw on prior knowledge to make connections.
- ✱ Base conclusions on stated ideas and unstated assumptions.

Exercise 7.12

Building a Story with Inferences

The following story unfolds as the reader uses the clues to predict and make inferences. To make sense out of the story, the reader is never told—but must figure out—who the main character is, what he is doing, and why he is doing it. Like a mystery, the story is fun to read because you are actively involved. Review the strategies for making inferences and then use your inferential skills to figure it out.

Caged

Emphatically, Mr. Purcell did not believe in ghosts. Nevertheless, the man who bought the two doves, and his strange act immediately thereafter, left him with a distinct sense of the eerie.

Purcell was a small, fussy man; red cheeks and a tight, melon stomach. He owned a pet shop. He sold cats and dogs and monkeys; he dealt in fish food and bird seed, and prescribed remedies for ailing canaries. He considered himself something of a professional man.

There was a bell over the door that jangled whenever a customer entered. This morning, however, for the first time Mr. Purcell could recall, it failed to ring. Simply he glanced up, and there was the stranger, standing just inside the door, as if he had materialized out of thin air.

The storekeeper slid off his stool. From the first instant he knew instinctively, unreasonably, that the man hated him; but out of habit he rubbed his hands briskly together, smiled and nodded.

"Good morning," he beamed. "What can I do for you?"

The man's shiny shoes squeaked forward. His suit was cheap, ill-fitting, but obviously new. A gray pallor deadened his pinched features. He had a shuttling glance and close-cropped hair. He stared closely at Purcell and said, "I want something in a cage."

"Something in a cage?" Mr. Purcell was a bit confused. "You mean—some kind of pet?"

"I mean what I said!" snapped the man. "Something alive that's in a cage."

"I see," hastened the storekeeper, not at all certain that he did. "Now let me think. A white rat, perhaps."

"No!" said the man. "Not rats. Something with wings. Something that flies."

"A bird!" exclaimed Mr. Purcell.

"A bird's all right." The customer pointed suddenly to a suspended cage which contained two snowy birds. "Doves? How much for those?"

"Five-fifty. And a very reasonable price."

"Five-fifty?" The sallow man was obviously crestfallen. He hesitantly produced a five-dollar bill. "I'd like to have those birds. But this is all I got. Just five dollars."

Mentally, Mr. Purcell made a quick calculation, which told him that at a fifty-cent reduction he could still reap a tidy profit. He smiled magnanimously. "My dear man, if you want them that badly, you can certainly have them for five dollars."

"I'll take them." He laid his five dollars on the counter. Mr. Purcell teetered on tiptoe, unhooked the cage, and handed it to his customer.

The man cocked his head to one side, listening to the constant chittering, the rushing scurry of the shop. "That noise?" he blurted. "Doesn't it get you? I mean all this caged stuff. Drives you crazy, doesn't it?"

Purcell drew back. Either the man was insane, or drunk.

"Listen." The staring eyes came closer. "How long d'you think it took me to make that five dollars?"

The merchant wanted to order him out of the shop. But he heard himself dutifully asking, "Why—why, how long *did* it take you?"

The other laughed. "Ten years! At hard labor. Ten years to earn five dollars. Fifty cents a year."

It was best, Purcell decided, to humor him. "My, my! Ten years—"

"They give you five dollars," laughed the man, "and a cheap suit, and tell you not to get caught again."

Mr. Purcell mopped his sweating brow. "Now, about the care and feeding of—"

"Bah!" The sallow man swung around, and stalked abruptly from the store.

Purcell sighed with sudden relief. He waddled to the window and stared out. Just outside, his peculiar customer had halted. He was holding the cage shoulder-high, staring at his purchase. Then, opening the cage, he reached inside and drew out one of the doves. He tossed it into the air. He drew out the second and tossed it after the first. They rose like wind-blown balls of fluff and were lost in the smoky grey of the wintry city. For an instant the liberator's silent and lifted gaze watched after them. Then he dropped the cage. A futile, suddenly forlorn figure, he shoved both hands deep in his trouser pockets, hunched down his head and shuffled away. . . .

The merchant's brow was puckered with perplexity. "Now why," Mr. Purcell muttered, "did he do that?" He felt vaguely insulted.

Lloyd Eric Reeve, *Household Magazine*

1. Where had the man been? ______________________________

2. How do you know for sure? Underline the clues. ______________________________

____

3. When did you figure it out? Circle the clincher. ______________________________

____

4. Why does he want to set the birds free? ______________________________

____

5. Why should the shopkeeper feel insulted? ______________________________

____

6. After freeing the birds, why is the stranger "a futile, suddenly forlorn figure," rather than happy and excited? ______________________________

____

Summary Points

- **What is an inference?**

  The inferential level of reading deals with motives, feelings, and judgments. The reader must read between the lines and look for the implied meaning in words and actions.

- **What is the connotation of a word?**

  The feeling or emotionalism surrounding a word is its connotation. The connotation reflects certain attitudes and prejudices of society that can be positive or negative. The author's choice of words can manipulate the reader.

- **What is figurative language?**

  Figurative language creates images to suggest attitudes. It is a different way of using "regular" words so that the words take on a new meaning. A simile is a comparison of two unlike things using the words *like* or *as,* whereas a metaphor is a directly stated comparison. Personification attributes human characteristics to nonhuman things. Verbal irony expresses a meaning the opposite of what is literally said.

- **Why is prior knowledge needed for implied meaning?**

  The reader must have background knowledge in a subject in order to understand the suggested or implied meaning.

- **How does a reader draw conclusions?**

  The reader makes a logical deduction from hints, facts, and prior knowledge.

Selection 1 SHORT STORY

CONTEMPORARY FOCUS

Short stories are carefully crafted works of literary art in which every word and idea counts. The short story by Somerset Maugham included here is considered a masterpiece of the genre. How has the author used the rules of short story telling to make a lasting impact on the reader?

A SHORT COURSE IN SHORT-SHORT FICTION

Geoff Fuller and Pamelyn Casto

Writer's Digest, February, 2001

Call them short-shorts, call them flash fiction, call them sudden fiction, it's harder than it looks to keep stories to 2,000 words or less. But the impact these stories can have makes them worth the effort. Unfortunately, simple elegance is seldom simple to achieve.

A short-short must remain simple, from conception through execution. Not simplistic, but simple. The key is to find a good port of entry by determining the point of the story in advance. Think of the point literally. Imagine that in any story you'd like to tell there's a tiny point, a small jewel of hidden reality to polish into a brilliant fictional truth. Hold your focus on that small dot, that potent speck that can explode into truth and realization. Around that point, your story will germinate and come alive.

While many short-shorts rely on a sudden shock at the end—the victim turns out to be the aggressor, the man turns out to be a woman—the most enduring manage not merely to surprise us, but also to transcend their few words. They compound meaning by linking the surface story to layers that exist above, behind and beneath them.

The writer needs to make sure that every element links to the kernel of truth the story contains. Unlike in longer fiction, everything in a short-short has to link to that central point. All the elements, all the actions that characters take, must be absolutely clear so that readers can focus on the point of the story. Writers must spend the time and the words to link to every element of the story: links among the elements and links to the reader's understanding.

Collaborative Activity

Collaborate on responses to the following questions:

- What is your favorite short story? Why do you like it so much?
- What short stories have you read by Somerset Maugham? Why have they endured as masterpieces?
- What are the elements of a short story?

Stage 1: Preview

Preview the next selection to predict its purpose and organization.

The author's purpose is to ______________________________

Activate Schema

What is a fable?

Word Knowledge

What do you know about these words?

industry	larder	perversity	prudence	unscrupulous
qualm	vindictive	scoundrel	rogue	trifle

Your instructor may give a true-false vocabulary review before or after reading.

Stage 2: Integrate Knowledge While Reading

Predict Picture Relate Monitor Correct

THE ANT AND THE GRASSHOPPER

By Somerset Maugham, 1924, from *75 Short Masterpieces from the World's Literature,* ed. Roger Goodman

When I was a very small boy I was made to learn by heart certain of the fables of La Fontaine, and the moral of each was carefully explained to me. Among those learned was The Ant and the Grasshopper, which is devised to bring home to the young the useful lesson that in an imperfect world industry is rewarded and giddiness punished. In this admirable fable (I apologize for telling something which everyone is politely, but inexactly, supposed to know) the ant spends a laborious summer gathering its winter store, while the grasshopper sits on a blade of grass singing to the sun. Winter comes and the ant is comfortably provided for, but the grasshopper has an empty larder: he goes to the ant and begs for a little food. Then the ant gives him her classic answer:

"What were you doing in the summer time?"

"Saving your presence, I sang. I sang all day, all night."

"You sang. Why, then go and dance."

I do not ascribe it to perversity on my part, but rather to the consequence of childhood, which is deficient in moral sense, that I could never quite reconcile myself to the lesson. My sympathies were with the grasshopper and for some time I never saw an ant without putting my foot on it. In this summary (and as I have discovered since, entirely human) fashion I sought to express my disapproval of prudence and common sense.

I could not help thinking of this fable when the other day I saw George Ramsay lunching by himself in a restaurant. I never saw anyone wear an expression of such deep gloom. He was staring into space. He looked as though

Illustration for "The Ant and the Grasshopper" by Milo Winter from The AESOP for CHILDREN with pictures by MILO WINTER *(1919).*

the burden of the whole world sat upon his shoulders. I was sorry for him: I suspected at once that his unfortunate brother had been causing trouble again. I went up to him and held out my hand.

"How are you?" I asked

"I'm not in hilarious spirits," he answered.

"Is it Tom again?"

He sighed.

"Yes, it's Tom again."

"Why don't you chuck him? You've done everything in the world for him. You must know by now that he's quite hopeless."

I suppose every family has a black sheep. Tom had been a sore trial to his for twenty years. He had begun life decently enough: he went into business, married and had two children. The Ramsays were perfectly respectable people and there was every reason to suppose that Tom Ramsay would have a useful and honorable career. But one day, without warning, he announced that he didn't like work and that he wasn't suited for marriage. He wanted to enjoy himself. He would listen to no expostulations. He left his wife and his office. He had a little money and he spent two happy years in various capitals of Europe. Rumors of his doings reached his relations from time to time and they were profoundly shocked. He certainly had a very good time. They shook their heads and asked what would happen when his money was spent. They soon found out: he borrowed. He was charming and unscrupulous. I have never met anyone to whom it was more difficult to refuse a loan. He made a steady income from his friends and he made friends easily. But he always said that the money you spent on necessities was boring; the money that was amusing to spend was the money you spent on luxuries. For this he depended on his brother George. He did not waste his charm on him. George was respectable. Once or twice he fell to Tom's promises of amendment and gave him considerable sums in order that he might make a fresh start. On these Tom bought a motorcar and some very nice jewelry. But when circumstances forced George to realize that his brother would never settle down and he washed his hands of him, Tom, with a qualm, began to blackmail him. It was not very nice for a respectable lawyer to find his brother shaking cocktails behind the bar of his favorite restaurant or to see him waiting on the box-seat of a taxi outside his club. Tom said that to serve in a bar or to drive a taxi was a perfectly decent occupation, but if George could oblige him with a couple of hundred pounds he didn't mind for the honor of the family giving it up. George paid.

Once Tom nearly went to prison. George was terribly upset. He went into the whole discreditable affair. Really Tom had gone too far. He had been wild, thoughtless and selfish, but he had never before done anything dishonest, by which George meant illegal; and if he were prosecuted he would assuredly be convicted. But you cannot allow your only brother to go to jail. The man Tom had cheated, a man called Cronshaw, was vindictive. He was determined to take the matter into court; he said Tom was a scoundrel and should be punished. It cost George an infinite deal of trouble and five hundred pounds to settle the affair. I have never seen him in such a rage as when he heard that Tom and Cronshaw had gone off together to Monte Carlo the moment they cashed the check. They spent a happy month there.

For twenty years Tom raced and gambled, philandered with the prettiest girls, danced, ate in the most expensive restaurants, and dressed beautifully. He always looked as if he had just stepped out of a bandbox. Though he was forty-six you would never have taken him for more than thirty-five. He was a most amusing companion and though you knew he was perfectly worthless you could not but enjoy his society. He had high spirits, an unfailing gaiety and incredible charm. I never grudged the contributions he regularly levied on me for the necessities of his existence. I never lent him fifty pounds without feeling that I was in his debt. Tom Ramsay knew everyone and everyone knew Tom Ramsay. You could not approve of him, but you could not help liking him. Poor George, only a year older than his scapegrace brother, looked sixty. He had never taken more than a fortnight's holiday in the year for a quarter of a century. He was in his office every morning at nine-thirty and never left it till six. He was honest, industrious and worthy. He had a good wife, to whom he had never been unfaithful even in thought, and four daughters to whom he was the best of fathers. He made a point of saving a third of his income and his plan was to retire at fifty-five to a little house in the country where he proposed to cultivate his garden and play golf. His life was blameless. He was glad that he was growing old because Tom was growing old too. He rubbed his hands and said:

"It was all very well when Tom was young and good-looking, but he's only a year younger than I am. In four years he'll be fifty. He won't find life too easy then. I shall have thirty thousand pounds by the time I'm fifty. For twenty-five years I've said that Tom would end in the gutter. And we shall see how he likes that. We shall see if it really pays best to work or be idle."

Poor George! I sympathized with him. I wondered now as I sat down beside him what infamous thing Tom had done. George was evidently very much upset.

"Do you know what's happened now?" he asked me.

I was prepared for the worst. I wondered if Tom had got into the hands of the police at last. George could hardly bring himself to speak.

"You're not going to deny that all my life I've been hard working, decent, respectable and straightforward. After a life of industry and thrift I can look forward to retiring on a small income in gilt-edged securities. I've always done my duty in that state of life in which it has pleased Providence to place me."

"True."

"And you can't deny that Tom has been an idle, worthless dissolute and dishonorable rogue. If there were any justice he'd be in the workhouse."

"True."

George grew red in the face.

"A few weeks ago he became engaged to a woman old enough to be his mother. And now she's died and left him everything she had. Half a million pounds, a yacht, a house in London and a house in the country."

George Ramsay beat his clenched fist on the table.

I could not help it. I burst into a shout of laughter as I looked at George's wrathful face. I rolled in my chair, I very nearly fell on the floor. George never forgave me. But Tom often asks me to excellent dinners in his charming house in Mayfair, and if he occasionally borrows a trifle from me, that is merely from force of habit. It is never more than a sovereign.

Stage 3: Recall

Stop to self-test, relate, and react.

Your instructor may choose to give you a true-false comprehension review.

Thinking About "The Ant and the Grasshopper"

What does the fable add to the story? Could the story be told without it? Explain why you think the fable is masterful or unnecessary.

Response Suggestion: Discuss the contribution of the fable to the point of the story, the layers of meaning, and the suspense of the story.

Contemporary Link

Reflect on the craftsmanship of the author. Why do you think this story is considered a masterpiece? Give specific examples.

Skill Development: Implied Meaning

According to the implied meaning in the selection, answer the following with *T* (true) or *F* (false).

_________ 1. The author suggests that Tom planned to bring his wife and children to Mayfair.

_________ 2. The author suggests that he enjoyed being with George more than Tom

_________ 3. The author suggests that George attended parties at Mayfair.

_________ 4. The author laughed at the end because injustice prevailed.

_________ 5. The reader can conclude that George wanted to prevent Tom from going to prison because a jail sentence would reflect negatively on the family name.

Comprehension Questions

After reading the selection, answer the following questions with *a, b, c,* or *d.* In order to help you analyze your strengths and weaknesses, the question types are indicated.

Main Idea _________ 1. Which is the best statement of the main idea of this selection?
a. The story of George and Tom prove the fable of the ant and the grasshopper.
b. The case of George and Tom shows that it is not always true that industry is rewarded and giddiness is punished.
c. A fable about insects can teach a useful lesson about life.
d. The success of the two brothers was predicted by the fable of the ant and the grasshopper.

Inference _________ 2. In the fable of the ant and the grasshopper, the ant
a. has sympathy for the grasshopper.
b. shares her food with the grasshopper.
c. does not give the grasshopper food.
d. tells the grasshopper how to find food.

Inference _________ 3. By saying, "You sang. Why, then go and dance," the ant is being
a. heartless.
b. helpful.
c. sincere.
d. kind.

Inference _________ 4. In recalling the fable of the ant and the grasshopper, the author's feeling about the moral of the story suggests
a. acceptance.
b. rebellion.
c. gratitude.
d. reconciliation.

Detail _________ 5. On the day that the author saw George Ramsay lunching by himself in a restaurant, George was upset about
a. Tom's wanting to borrow more money.
b. the Monte Carlo trip.
c. Tom's blackmail.
d. Tom's success.

Detail _________ 6. The review of Tom's background reveals that
a. he had no children.
b. he had been married before.
c. he had never been in a business.
d. he was twenty years younger than his brother.

Inference _________ 7. In blackmailing George, Tom was crafty enough to take advantage of George's
a. appreciation of an honest day's work.
b. willingness for his brother to suffer the consequences of his behavior.
c. belief that his brother would change his ways.
d. concern about appearance and the judgment of others.

Inference _________ 8. From the results of the Monte Carlo incident, the reader can conclude that
a. Tom and Cronshaw were partners in a scheme to get George's money.
b. Tom was in prison because of Cronshaw.
c. Cronshaw took Tom to court because of a cheating incident.
d. George paid the money to have Tom released from jail.

Inference _________ 9. From past experiences, the reader can conclude that Tom's engagement occurred because
a. Tom was in love.
b. Tom finally wanted to settle down.
c. Tom was planning to marry for money.
d. Tom wanted to have a family.

Inference _________ 10. George is distressed primarily because
a. a lifetime of hard work paid off for him.
b. idleness ultimately was victorious.
c. crime does not pay.
d. he lost money on Tom.

Answer the following with *T* (true) or *F* (false).

Detail _______ 11. Tom blackmailed George by threatening to tell family secrets.

Infrerence _______ 12. Tom was a dishonorable man who took advantage of his brother.

Detail _______ 13. La Fontaine wrote *The Ant and the Grasshopper.*

Detail _______ 14. The author expressed his resentment by stepping on ants.

Detail _______ 15. George was sixty and his brother was forty-six.

Vocabulary

According to the way the italicized word was used in the selection, select *a, b, c,* or *d* for the word or phase that gives the best definition. The number in parentheses indicates the line of the passage in which the word is located.

_______ 1. "*industry* is rewarded" (4–5)
a. manufacturing
b. business
c. generosity
d. hard work

_______ 2. "empty *larder*" (9)
a. house
b. supply of food
c. plate
d. hand

_______ 3. "ascribe it to *perversity*" (15)
a. ignorance
b. corruption
c. imagination
d. humor

_______ 4. "disapproval of *prudence*" (20)
a. politeness
b. honesty
c. carefulness
d. disobedience

_______ 5. "charming and *unscrupulous*" (45)
a. handsome
b. humorous
c. entertaining
d. dishonest

_______ 6. "with a *qualm*" (55)
a. grin
b. moral hesitation
c. laugh
d. strong determination

_______ 7. "Cronshaw was *vindictive*" (67)
a. revengeful
b. nervous
c. poor
d. cowardly

_______ 8. "Tom was a *scoundrel*" (68)
a. murderer
b. beggar
c. fighter
d. villain

_______ 9. "dishonorable *rogue*" (111–112)
a. worthless person
b. relative
c. brother
d. victim

_______ 10. "borrows a *trifle*" (122)
a. dollar
b. favor
c. small amount
d. nickel

Search the Net

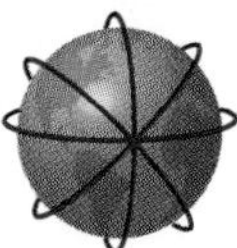

- Search the Internet for biographical information about Somerset Maugham. Describe where he lived and the lifestyle he maintained. What were some of the influences upon his writing? In what ways is the character "Tom" similar to Maugham himself?

  Somerset Maugham; World Traveler, Famed Storyteller:
  http://www.caxtonclub.org/reading/smaugham.html

  The W. Somerset Maugham Center:
  http://members.home.net/winluc/maugham/

- Somerset Maugham was a prolific writer. Search the Net for information on his plays, novels, and short stories. Select one of his works from each of these genres, and briefly describe the setting and plot. What similarities do you see in his works?

  Spartacus Educational:
  http://www.spartacus.schoolnet.co.uk/Jmaugham.htm

  William Somerset Maugham (1874–1965):
  http://www.kirjasto.sci.fi/maugham.htm

Concept Prep

for Philosophy and Literature

The ancient Greeks laid the foundations for Western traditions in science, philosophy, literature, and the arts. They set the standards for proportion and beauty in art and architecture, and we continue to ponder their questions about the good life, the duties of a citizen, and the nature of the universe.

In Raphael's painting School of Athens, *Plato and Aristotle converse.*

School of Athens (detail) by Raphael. Vatican. Erich Lessing/Art Resource NY.

Who were the most notable Greek philosophers?

- One of the most notable philosophers was **Socrates,** the teacher of Plato. Socrates sought an understanding of the world while other teachers of the time taught students how to get along in the world. Socrates proclaimed himself to be the wisest of all the thinkers because he knew how little he knew. He used a method of teaching that explored a subject from all sides with questions and answers, as opposed to the lecture method. This is today known as the **Socratic method.** Socrates took no pay for his teachings. As an old man, he was condemned to death by the citizens of Athens who claimed he denied the gods and corrupted the youth. More likely, however, Socrates was a natural target for enemies and was made the scapegoat for the city's military defeat. As ordered, Socrates drank poison hemlock and died. He left behind no written works, but his pupil Plato later immortalized his lively discussions in his own works.
- **Plato** is often considered the most important figure in Western philosophy. Without him, the thoughts of Socrates and previous philosophers might not be recorded. Plato used a dialogue format to explore many subjects such as ethics and politics. He founded a school in Athens called the Academy and became the teacher of Aristotle.
- **Aristotle** was a disciple of Plato and then broke away to develop his own philosophy and school, called the Lyceum. He wrote on virtually every subject and laid the foundation for analytical reasoning and logic. He was the tutor of Alexander the Great. In the political unrest following Alexander's death, Aristotle remembered the fate of Socrates and fled Athens to escape prosecution.

What are the literary genres?

Over hundreds of years, certain stories, essays, and poems have remained timeless in their appeal and relevance to human life. These works are considered **literature,** the art form of language. As you read a piece of literature, you are allowed inside the minds of characters, and you feel what they feel. You learn about life as the characters live it or as the poet entices you to feel it. After reading, you are enriched, as well as entertained. As defined in most college courses, literature includes four categories, or **genres:** poetry, drama, fiction, and essays

Poetry

Poetry has its roots in the pleasure of rhythm, repetition, and sound. Before the written word, rhythm and repetition were used to help people organize and recall episodes in history. Poetry was danced, chanted, and performed with the whole body in tribal cultures as a way of keeping cultural truths alive. In the **Odyssey,** an ancient Greek epic by **Homer** that recounts the adventures of Odysseus during his return from the war in Troy to his home on a Greek island, the rhyme format made the epic easier to remember. Thus the poem became a vehicle for preserving the lore of the sea, warfare, and Greek mythology.

Poetry appeals to the senses, offering strong visual images and suggestive symbolism to enhance the pleasure. **Lyric** poems are brief and emotional, **narrative** poems tell a story with plot and characters, **dramatic** poems use dialogue to express emotional conflict, and **epic** poems tell a long narrative with a central hero of historical significance.

Drama

The origins of **drama** lie in religious ceremonies in ancient Greece, when masters of Greek drama competed for prizes by means of their plays. Without movies and television, the ancient Greeks created plays for religious instruction and for entertainment. These dramatic performances eventually evolved into comedy, tragedy, and romantic tragedy.

Plays are narratives and thus contain all of the literary elements of short stories and novels. As in works of fiction, the main character in a play is sometimes called a **protagonist,** from the Greek word for "first actor." The character who is trying to move against or harm the main character is called the **antagonist** (from the prefix *anti*).

Plays are written to be performed rather than read. The actors interpret for the audience, and a single play can seem vastly different depending on which production company performs it. After hundreds of years, the plays of **William Shakespeare** are still relevant to the human condition; they entertained audiences in England in the late 1500s, on the American frontier in the mid 1800s, and both on stages and in movie theaters in the 2000s.

Fiction

Fiction creates an illusion of reality to share an experience and communicate universal truths about the human condition. Since each work of fiction is deliberate, each element has a meaning that is subject to interpretation on many different levels. Short stories and novels are written to entertain by engaging you in the life of another human being.

- A **short story** is a brief work of fiction ranging from 500 to 15,000 words. It is a narrative with a beginning, middle, and end that tells about a sequence of events. The **plot** of the story involves **characters** in one or more **conflicts.** As the conflict intensifies, the **suspense** rises to a **climax,** or turning point, which is followed by the **denouement,** or unraveling. Then the action falls for a **resolution.** Because the short story is brief and carefully crafted, some literary experts recommend reading a short story three times: first to enjoy the plot, second to recognize the elements, and third to appreciate how the elements work together to support the theme. Setting, point of view, tone, and symbolism all contribute to this appreciation.
- The **novel** is an extended fictional work that has all of the elements of a short story. Because of its length, a novel usually has more characters and more conflicts than a short story.

The Essay

An **essay** is a short work of nonfiction that discusses a specific topic. Much of your own college writing will follow an essay format. The **title** of an essay suggests the contents, the **thesis** is usually stated in the **introduction,** the **body** provides evidence to prove the thesis, and the **conclusion** summarizes in a manner to provoke further thought.

REVIEW QUESTIONS

1. What is the Socratic method of teaching? ______________________

2. What was the underlying reason Socrates was forced to drink poison? ______________________

3. Why was Plato particularly important to the teaching of Socrates? ______________________

4. What acronym could you devise to remind you of the chronological order of the three famous philosophers? __________

5. What was a significant contribution of Aristotle? __________

6. What is a literary genre? __________

7. What was the original purpose of drama? __________

8. What was the purpose of the *Odyssey?* __________

9. Which genre is most frequently written by the majority of college students? __________

10. What is the typical relationship between the protagonist and the antagonist? __________

Your instructor may choose to give a true-false review of these philosophy and literature concepts.

Selection 2 ESSAY

CONTEMPORARY FOCUS

In addition to approving new drugs, the Food and Drug Administration alerts the American public to foods that are potential health hazards. Do we get so much negative information from the FDA that we can't enjoy a simple meal, or does the FDA need more power to enforce food safety?

DANGEROUS FOODS: THE SHOCKING TRUTH THAT PUTS YOUR FAMILY AT RISK

Barry Yeoman

Redbook, August, 2000

Like most of us, Nancy Donley assumed the government was protecting the food she served her family. And then her son died from eating a tainted hamburger at a family backyard cookout—and a crusader was born.

At the time Alex died, his mother discovered, meat was being inspected using a turn-of-the-century system nicknamed "poke and sniff," where inspectors touched and smelled the carcasses and looked for lesions that might indicate a diseased animal. Says Donley, "Even Alex, at the age of 6, knew that you needed to use a microscope to see bacteria."

Thanks in part to Donley's lobbying efforts, the nation's meat and poultry inspection system has undergone a major overhaul. Yet it's still far too easy for contaminated meat to make its way from farms to slaughterhouses to our dinner tables, argues Donley. "The public thinks that every single carcass is getting tested for both E. coli and salmonella, and this is just not the case," she says.

Another reason for the continued outbreaks is that the government lacks the power to recall meat when it's found to be contaminated. The Department of Agriculture can pressure companies to do voluntary recalls, but sometimes days will pass while a business negotiates how much meat to pull off the shelves. Notes the Agriculture Department's Margaret Glavin, "If we have dangerous food out there, even hours are important."

What's more, the department has trouble cracking down on repeat offenders because it's not authorized to levy fines. "The Secretary of Agriculture can issue civil penalties for the abuse of a circus elephant," says Senator Tom Harkin, a Democrat from Iowa, "but not for the shipment of adulterated meat."

Collaborative Activity

Collaborate on responses to the following questions:

- How does hamburger get contaminated with E. coli?
- What precautions should you take in handling food in the kitchen to guard against the spread of dangerous bacteria?
- What kills bacteria in contaminated meat and poultry?

Stage 1: Preview

The title suggests that the author is being humorous.
Agree ☐ Disagree ☐

Activate Schema

Why is it recommended that you do not eat eggs every day for breakfast?

How can caffeine be dangerous to your health?

Stage 2: Integrate Knowledge While Reading

Predict Picture Relate Monitor Correct

BREAKFAST AT THE FDA CAFE

by John R. Alden, from *Motives for Writing*, 3rd ed., edited by Robert Keith Miller

"I'll have two eggs over easy, home fries, a blueberry muffin, decaf coffee and the fresh-squeezed orange juice," I told my waiter.

"Very good, sir," he said, and hurried away.

I had just unfolded my paper as he came back with the coffee.

"Here you are," he said. "But before you can have this, our corporate legal department insists that we warn you that recent studies indicate that consumption of three or more cups of coffee a day may increase your risk of stroke and bladder cancer. This is decaffeinated, so I don't need to say that caffeine is addictive and can cause temporary but significant increases in your blood pressure and heartbeat. However, FDA regulations do require me to notify you that the decaffeination process may leave minute traces of carcinogenic solvents in the coffee beans." He poured.

I had nearly finished the front page when he returned with my breakfast.

"Your eggs," he said as he put my plate in front of me, "are fried in a polyunsaturated oil high in fat and calories. Eggs that are only lightly cooked may contain salmonella, an organism causing food poisoning, and the National Society for the Alleviation of Allergies warns that many Americans exhibit a mild allergic response to the ova of domestic fowl. Egg yolks contain large quantities of cholesterol, and the American Association of Cardiological Surgeons recommends that people over 40, particularly those who smoke or are more than 10 pounds overweight, limit their consumption to four eggs per week."

I sucked in my stomach.

"Potatoes," he continued, "are a member of the nightshade family, and any greenish patches on their skin may contain traces of an alkaloid poison called solanine. The Physician's Reference Manual says solanine can cause

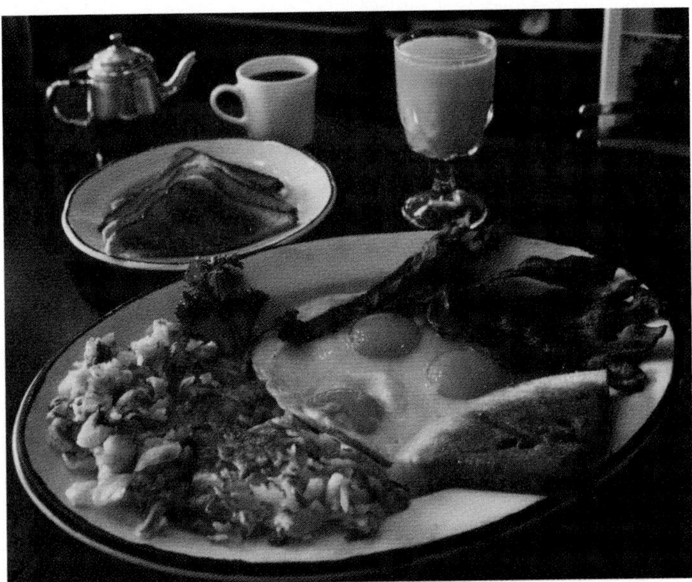

The hearty American breakfast appeals and surprises.
Chad Slattery/Getty Images

vomiting, diarrhea, and acute nausea. However, your potatoes have been carefully peeled, and our supplier has agreed to assume any liability that may arise from their consumption.

"The blueberry muffin contains enriched flour, cane sugar, eggs, butter, blueberries and low-sodium baking powder. The Institute of Alimentary Studies warns that a diet high in processed flour may add to your risk of stomach and intestinal cancer. The Center for Dietary Purity warns that processed wheat flour may be contaminated with up to two tenths of a part per billion of fungicides and rodenticides. It has been bleached and brominated and in cool wet years might also contain minute traces of ergot. Ingested in sufficient quantities, ergot can cause hallucinations and convulsions, arterial spasms, and induce abortions in pregnant women.

"Citizens Against Empty Calories, an independent research organization funded in part by the American Beet Sugar Producers Association, warns that cane sugar is high in calories, low in nutritional value, and one of the principal dietary factors associated with dental cavities.

"Butter, like eggs, is high in cholesterol, a material that studies have identified as playing a potentially significant role in the development of arteriosclerosis and heart disease, particularly in genetically susceptible individuals. If any of your close relatives ever had a heart attack, the Department of Health and Human Services warns that your personal physician might advise you to limit your intake of butter, cream and other dairy products.

"Our blueberries are from Maine. They have not been fertilized or treated with pesticides. However, the U.S. Geological Survey has reported that many Maine blueberry barrens are located on granite, and granitic rock frequently contains measurable amounts of radioactive uranium, radium and radon gas.

"Finally, the baking powder used in these muffins contains sodium aluminum sulfate. Aluminum, some researchers suggest, may be a contributing factor in the development of Alzheimer's disease. The National Institute of Mental Health has not stated a position on this, but it has asked us to inform our customers that it will be funding a seven-year, $47 million study examining the association between aluminum consumption and senility syndromes."

He picked up a pitcher. "I have to inform you that our 'fresh-squeezed' orange juice was actually prepared before 6 this morning. It is now 8:30. The FDA and the Justice Department recently sued a restaurant in Georgia (*U.S.* v. *Mom's Home-baked Cafe*) for describing three-hour-old juice as 'fresh-squeezed.' Until that case is decided, our legal advisers have required us to get a waiver from any customer ordering a similar product."

I signed the form he handed me, and he stapled a copy to my bill. But as I reached for the glass, he stopped me.

"Excuse me, please. Our salt and pepper shakers are clearly labeled, but corporate policy requires that I repeat the warnings to you verbally. On the salt it says, 'If consumed in large quantities, sodium chloride can be highly toxic, and habitual ingestion of this compound has been shown to cause life-threatening hypertension.' The other shaker says: 'Pepper. Use with extreme caution! The Center for Communicable Disease warns that sneezing associated with careless use of this powder may contribute to the transmission of rhinoviral and influenza-type diseases.' Finally, the Department of Consumer Safety has determined that the tines of your fork are sharp, and new regulations require me to caution customers to use that utensil with extreme care."

He turned, and with a cheery "Enjoy your breakfast, sir," headed off to the next table. I picked at my meal but couldn't finish it. The food had gotten cold, and somehow I had lost my appetite.

Stage 3: Recall

Stop to self-test, relate, and react.

Your instructor may choose to give you a true-false comprehension review.

Thinking About "Breakfast at the FDA Cafe"

What would the FDA say about what you usually have for breakfast? Write a scenario similar to the author's in which you describe your typical breakfast along with the possible FDA warnings. Use exaggeration to add humor.

Contemporary Link

The author of the Contemporary Link and the author of the selection address two different functions of the FDA. What are these functions and how do the authors' attitudes differ?

Skill Development: Implied Meaning

Answer the following questions according to the implied meaning in the selection.

1. What do you think prompted the author to write this essay?

2. How does the author use exaggeration to achieve humor? Give examples.

3. How does repetition add to the humor of the essay? Give examples.

4. What inference can you make when you hear that the beet sugar company is funding the cane sugar study? ______

5. Why is the last warning about the fork humorous? ______

6. Why do food producers and eating establishments print warnings about products? ______

Comprehension Questions

After reading the selection, answer the following with *T* (true) or *F* (false).

Inference _________ 1. The author's purpose is to make fun of the abundance of FDA warnings about the foods we eat.

Inference _________ 2. The FDA cafe is a creation of the author's imagination and does not actually exist.

Detail _________ 3. The waiter says that decaffeinated coffee increases blood pressure and heart beat.

Inference _________ 4. The reader can be certain that there is a National Society for the Alleviation of Allergies.

Inference _________ 5. The author's discussion of the potato serves to add unappetizing details that are not relevant to the author's potato.

Inference _________ 6. In discussing flour, the reader can be certain that there is an Institute of Alimentary Studies and a Center for Dietary Purity.

Detail _________ 7. The author implies that all flour contains ergot.

Inference _________ 8. The author includes the time limit on the 'fresh-squeezed' orange juice to show how reasonable FDA regulations can be.

Inference _________ 9. *U.S.* v. *Mom's Home-baked Cafe* is a fictional rather than an actual case.

Inference _________ 10. The reader can be certain of the existence of a seven-year, $47 million study that will research aluminum consumption and senility syndromes.

Search the Net

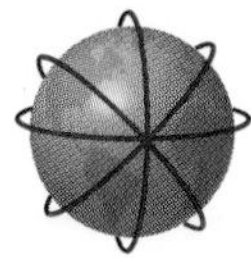

- Search the Internet for information on foods that are considered to be dangerous or foods that have recently been recalled. Identify at least three of these foods and briefly describe why they are considered to be dangerous.

  Journal of Longevity: http://www.journaloflongevity.com/JOLWeb/Archives/11November2000/prostatehealth.html

  SafetyAgent.com: http://www.safetyagent.com/SearchResults.asp

  FDA Enforcement Report: http://www.fda.gov/opacom/Enforce.html

- With proper care and handling of food products, the ever-present threat of food poisoning can be diminished. Search the Internet for the primary cause of food poisoning. Describe several bacteria that cause food poisoning. What steps can you take to prevent food poisoning?

  Bacterial food poisoning: http://aggie-horticulture.tamu.edu/extension/poison.html

  Digestive disorders: http://www.digestivedisorders.org.uk/leaflets/foodpoi.html

Selection 3 NARRATIVE NONFICTION

CONTEMPORARY FOCUS

Colin Powell has served his country most of his adult life. He rose from a soldier in the army to four-star general. He was National Security Advisor and then Chairman of the Joint Chiefs of Staff under President George Bush, and now he serves as Secretary of State under President George W. Bush. What attributes have led Colin Powell to his success?

LEADING PEOPLE

Oren Harari (including words from Colin Powell's *My American Journey*)

Executive Excellence, Provo, June 2000

When General Colin Powell made the transformation from a human being to phenomenon, I paid little attention, as I have little interest in celebrities. But then I found myself on the same speaking platform with General Powell. I was impressed with him. Powell was witty, erudite, insightful, articulate, and self-deprecating. So I decided to buy his book, *My American Journey*. In it, I found many gems of wisdom.

- Being responsible sometimes means pissing people off. Leaders are responsible for the welfare of the group, meaning some people will get angry at your actions and decisions. It's inevitable if you're honorable. Trying to get everyone to like you is a sign of mediocrity. Ironically, by not making difficult choices, by trying not to get anyone mad, and by treating everyone equally "nicely," you'll anger your most creative and productive people.
- The day people stop bringing you their problems is the day you stop leading them. They have either lost confidence that you can help them or concluded that you do not care. Real leaders make themselves accessible and available. They show concern for the efforts and challenges faced by others—even as they demand high standards.
- Never neglect details. When everyone's mind is dulled or distracted, the leader must be doubly vigilant. All the great ideas and visions in the world are worthless if they can't be implemented rapidly and efficiently. Good leaders delegate and empower others liberally, but they pay attention to details, every day.
- Have fun in your command. Don't always run at a breakneck pace. Take leave when you've earned it. Spend time with your families. Surround yourself with people who take their work seriously, but not themselves, those who work hard and play hard.

Collaborative Activity

Collaborate on responses to the following questions:

- Why would Powell say that trying to get everyone to like you is a sign of mediocrity?
- According to Powell, why should leaders welcome personnel with problems?
- What was Desert Storm?

Stage 1: Preview

The author's main purpose is to explain the military.

Agree ☐ Disagree ☐

After reading this selection, I will need to explain how Colin Powell managed Desert Storm.

Agree ☐ Disagree ☐

Activate Schema

Who is the senior George Bush?

Who is Ronald Reagan?

Word Knowledge

What do you know about these words?

pronto	coercion	brandishing	contorted	stockade
mulling	culminated	sector	eminence	demotion

Your instructor may give a true-false vocabulary review before or after reading.

Stage 2: Integrate Knowledge While Reading

Predict Picture Relate Monitor Correct

COLIN POWELL

From Colin Powell, *My American Journey*

Colin Powell is the embodiment of the American dream. He was born in Harlem to immigrant parents from Jamaica. He knew the rough life of the streets. He overcame a barely average start at school. Then he joined the Army. The rest is history—Vietnam, the Pentagon, Panama, Desert Storm. Each of the following excerpts, taken from Colin Powell's autobiography entitled My American Journey, *shows a different part of Powell's personality.*

Korea, 1953

"Colin Powell, you got to come down to C Company pronto." The caller this Saturday afternoon was the company commander, a promising young officer

Secretary of State Colin Powell discusses the diplomatic aspects of the Sept. 11, 2001, terrorist attacks on the World Trade Center.
AP/Wide World Photos

who had not yet found that fine balance in handling his men between coercion and persuasion.

I hurried from my hooch to discover a small crowd at an intersection near C Company's rec room. The men parted to let me through. At the center stood a soldier, either drunk or doped up, brandishing a pool cue. His eyes were afire and his face contorted. "Somebody's gonna die first!"

"I called the MPs, Colonel," the lieutenant informed me. "They're on the way."

I nodded and started toward the assailant, maintaining a distance of one pool cue. "What are you gonna do, son?" I said. "Hit me?"

"Somebody's gonna die," he repeated.

I spoke gently. "Son, put the cue down."

"No, sir."

"Do you know who I am?"

"Yes, sir, Colonel Powell."

"I want you to put the cue down before you hurt somebody. I want you to put it down before somebody hurts you." I came closer. "You see, if you don't do what I tell you, all these men are going to whip the hell out of you. Then, when they're done, you're going to the stockade for a year. What sense does that make? So put the cue down, and we'll have a nice talk."

His arm dropped, the pool cue dropped. And he started to cry. "Nobody understands. Nobody cares." Suddenly the homicidal maniac had become a confused, hurt kid.

We put him on restriction for a couple of weeks. Soon afterward, I passed him on the post and he threw me a snappy salute. "Colonel, how you doin', sir." He grinned to some of his pals. "That's Bro P, Brother Powell, he's all right." And Bro P became my nickname, at least among the black troops, for the rest of the tour. (p. 182)

Washington, D.C., 1988

Mike Powell and Jane Knott were married on October 1. I kidded my son about postponing his honeymoon so that he could accept a speaking invitation. Strange priorities for a red-blooded American youth, I said. The speech, however, meant a great deal to Mike. Frank Carlucci had asked him to speak at a ceremony honoring handicapped employees at the Department of Defense, where Mike was now working. Alma and I went to the Pentagon auditorium with our new daughter-in-law and Kick and Eleanor Knott, her parents. We had no idea what Mike intended to say. We watched him, supported by his cane, make his way slowly to the rostrum.

He began to speak in a clear, firm voice. He likened the struggle of the handicapped to combat. He described his feelings in the hospital as the painkillers were reduced and the stream of visitors, cards, and flowers began to dwindle. He spoke of the day when two rehabilitation therapists told him, bluntly, that the easy part, being sick, was over, and the hard part, making his broken body work again, was about to begin. The next morning, he said, "I looked in the mirror. My hair was a mess, dried out by medication. I had lost a great deal of weight. My face was colorless and unshaven. I stood supported by my crutches with a catheter coming out of my stomach. I stood trembling, and I began to cry, uncontrollably. I was at the lowest point of my entire life. This was real, and I was losing." Mike went on to describe how he went from rock bottom that day to fight back to his present renewal of hope, the war that every handicapped person has to fight, and little different from the struggle of a soldier wounded in battle. "The power of human will is amazing," he concluded. "It lifted me from a bed; it stood me up from a wheelchair; it handed me a cane; and it has allowed me to walk through life again."

Tears were streaming down my face. I glance at Alma and Jane, who smiled. We did not have to exchange a word. The pride was in our eyes. (p. 373)

Washington, D.C., 1988

On November 9, after the presidential election, the White House staff held a simple ceremony in the Rose Garden to welcome the victorious George Bush back from the campaign trail. Afterwards, I was returning to my West Wing office, and since we were next-door neighbors, the Vice President and I walked together. "Well Mr. Vice Pres—excuse me, Mr. Pres- Mr President-elect. What should it be now?" I asked. Bush laughed and said he did not know.

When we got to his office, he said, "Come on in. Let's chat for a bit. I need an update on what's been happening." I gave him a quick survey of the international scene. When I finished, he said, "You're one of the few people in the White House I want to consider for the new team. I have some options I hope you'll think about. Jim Baker would like you as deputy secretary of state"—which confirmed where Baker was going. "Or you can have the CIA. Or you can stay on as National Security Advisor for a while, until you decide what you want to do."

"I'm flattered," I said, "but I'm certainly not owed anything."

"No, no," Bush said, "we want you. Take some time. Think it over."

That night I stopped by Carl Vuono's house at Fort Myer. Carl's brilliant career had culminated in his rise to the top as the four-star Army Chief of Staff. He led me to his upstairs study at Quarters 1, where I told him about my conversation with the President-elect. I added that the Army certainly did not owe me anything either and, with the NSC job coming to an end, this might be the time for me to retire. I had thirty years in, and I was getting interesting offers from the private sector. One retired military gray eminence had recently stopped by to tell me he was leaving the board of a major corporation and thought I would make a good replacement. When he told me the five-figure salary I would get just for sitting on a board, I was staggered. "Carl," I said, "I've been away for a while, but what I really want is to stay in the Army, if there's a job for me."

Carl is a no-nonsense guy and came right to the point. Forget this business about being away too long, he said. My standing with the Army college of cardinals was still good. He wanted me back, and the Army wants me back. In fact, he said, he had a job for me, commander in chief of Forces Command, FORSCOM, responsible for all Army field forces based in the United States, almost one million troops, including National and Reserve units.

When I got home, I did what I usually do when faced with a personal decision: I drew up a balance sheet. I put "Stay" on the left side and "Go" on the right side, since staying in the Army or going out were my only intentions. I did not want to go to the State Department as number two. It would be a demotion. And I did not want to be the nation's chief spook at the CIA. That was not me. And there was no point lingering at the NSC, since I knew Bush had his own man in mind, the able Brent Scowcroft. I wound up with nineteen reasons on the "Stay" side and only a few on the "Go" side, which came down to "new career, make some money." After mulling the matter over for a couple of days, I went in and told Vice President Bush that I wanted to return to the Army, a decision which he accepted graciously. Immediately afterward, at our regular morning briefing, I told President Reagan what I had decided. "FORSCOM is four stars, isn't it?" he asked. Yes, I answered, the Army's highest rank. "Good, good," he said.

Stage 3: Recall

Stop to self-test, relate, and react.

Your instructor may choose to give you a true-false comprehension review.

Thinking About "Colin Powell"

After Desert Storm, Colin Powell retired from the military, wrote a book, served on corporate boards, and toured the country for paid speaking engagements. During these few years, he accumulated wealth stated to be over $20 million. Now Colin Powell is back in the service of his country as Secretary of

State and earning a government salary. From what you have learned about Powell, why do you think he would choose a position at the State Department when he could continue earning big money in the private sector?

Response Suggestion: Support your reasons with what you have learned from the text.

Contemporary Link

By reflecting on both his words and his actions, list and explain the characteristics that you think make Colin Powell an effective manager of people and events.

Skill Development: Implied Meaning

According to the implied meaning in the selection, answer the following with *T* (true) or *F* (false).

_________ 1. In retelling the story of Mike Powell's speech, Colin Powell shows himself as a proud father.

_________ 2. The author suggests that Mike Powell's speech to the Department of Defense was scheduled almost immediately after his wedding to Jane Knott.

_________ 3. The author suggests that Bush should not have been elected president.

_________ 4. The reader can conclude that the young soldier with the pool cue was African American.

_________ 5. The reader can conclude that Powell's love of the army was greater than his love of money.

Comprehension Questions

After reading the selection, answer the following questions with *a*, *b*, *c*, or *d*. In order to help you analyze your strengths and weaknesses, the question types are indicated.

Main Idea _________ 1. The main point of this selection is

a. to recall the most important experiences in Colin Powell's life.
b. to describe how Colin Powell became a general.
c. to show Colin Powell's determination to get to the top.
d. to reveal Colin Powell's character through his experiences.

Inference ________ 2. In the pool cue incident with the young soldier in Korea, Colin Powell demonstrates all of the following except
a. his ability to persuade.
b. his primary concern for adherence to army rules and regulations.
c. his desire to take care of his soldiers in a humane manner.
d. his courage in confronting difficult problems.

Inference ________ 3. The later response of the young soldier in the pool cue incident showed that the soldier
a. respected Colonel Powell for his help.
b. resented Colonel Powell's intervention.
c. felt he was mistreated by Colonel Powell.
d. wished that Colonel Powell had let the lieutenant handle the situation.

Inference ________ 4. The reader can conclude that Mike Powell was asked to speak at the Department of Defense ceremony primarily because
a. he was the son of Colin Powell.
b. he was a friend of Frank Carlucci.
c. he was a handicapped employee who had overcome adversity.
d. he was a brave soldier who had been injured.

Detail ________ 5. In his speech, Mike Powell attributes his ability to walk again to
a. the power of the human spirit.
b. his father's military leadership.
c. the visitors, cards, and flowers he received.
d. the support of his family.

Inference ________ 6. Powell's hesitation over what to call George Bush was because Bush
a. had not yet been elected president.
b. was resigning from his position as vice president.
c. would be serving as both president and vice president.
d. was both vice president and the newly elected next president.

Inference ________ 7. Colin Powell's ultimate response to the job offers made by George Bush was
a. "Yes."
b. "No."
c. "Maybe."
d. "Yes, but."

Inference

_________ 8. Colin Powell went to see Carl Vuono because
a. Vuono was George Bush's friend.
b. Vuono could assess his career possibilities and offer him a job in the army.
c. Vuono was his mentor, best friend, and chief advisor.
d. Vuono worked for the State Department.

Inference

_________ 9. Colin Powell's use of a balance sheet in decision making primarily demonstrates his
a. drive for success.
b. courage.
c. logic.
d. fear.

Inference

_________ 10. The reader can conclude that on November 9, 1988,
a. Reagan was president, Bush was vice president, and Powell was deputy secretary of state.
b. Reagan was president, Bush was vice president, and Powell was national security advisor.
c. Reagan was president, Bush was vice president, and Vuono was head of FORSCOM.
d. Bush was president and Powell was national security advisor.

Answer the following with *T* (true) or *F* (false).

Inference

_________ 11. Colin Powell suggests that the young lieutenant was not capable of handling the young soldier with the pool cue and should have been discharged from the army.

Inference

_________ 12. The author suggests that he accepted the nickname "Bro P" as a sign of respect and affection.

Detail

_________ 13. Colin Powell and Vice President Bush had offices next door to each other in the West Wing of the White House.

Inference

_________ 14. The reader can conclude that the desire to finally make some money led to Colin Powell's decision to accept the FORSCOM job.

Inference

_________ 15. The reader can conclude that Bush named Jim Baker as his Secretary of State.

Vocabulary

According to the way the italicized word was used in the selection, select *a*, *b*, *c*, or *d* for the word or phase that gives the best definition. The number in parentheses indicates the line of the passage in which the word is located.

_________ 1. "to C Company *pronto*" (1)
a. cautiously
b. immediately
c. carefully
d. alone

_________ 2. "between *coercion* and persuasion" (3–4)
a. force
b. conversation
c. friendliness
d. necessity

_________ 3. "*brandishing* a pool cue" (7)
a. lifting
b. tapping
c. waving
d. gripping

_________ 4. "his face *contorted*" (8)
a. emotionless
b. twisted
c. lifeless
d. eager

_________ 5. "going to the *stockade*" (20)
a. solitary confinement
b. island facility
c. mental institution
d. prison enclosure

_________ 6. "career had *culminated*" (73)
a. been stopped short
b. accumulated
c. reached its highest point
d. been recognized

_________ 7. "private *sector*" (78)
a. economic subdivision of society
b. governmental department
c. individual leaders
d. secret organizations

_________ 8. "military gray *eminence*" (78)
a. general
b. retired person
c. consultant
d. person of prominence

_________ 9. "would be a *demotion*" (93)
a. step down
b. tense situation
c. job without meaning
d. embarrassing situation

_________ 10. "*mulling* the matter over" (98)
a. writing
b. talking
c. pondering
d. acting

Search the Net

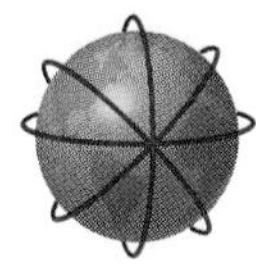

- What position did Colin Powell hold during the Persian Gulf War? How did he shape the U.S. government's plans for removing Iraqi forces from Kuwait? How would the war have been different if Colin Powell's strategy had not been implemented?

  Washingtonpost.com: http://www.washingtonpost.com/wp-srv/inatl/longterm/fogofwar/wargoals.htm

  The Gulf War: http://www.pbs.org/wgbh/pages/frontline/gulf/index.html

- Find information about America's Promise, the organization that Colin Powell founded. When and why was this organization founded? What is its mission? What are the five promises? Where can you volunteer in your local area to be involved in this organization?

  America's Promise: http://www.americaspromise.org/

Concept Prep for Political Science

What is the U.S. Constitution?

The **Constitution** is a document that defines the structure of our government and the roles, powers, and responsibilities of public officials. It was signed in Philadelphia in 1787. Prior to the Constitution, the **Declaration of Independence** in 1776 declared our independence from England. The **Articles of Confederation** were written to govern the resulting new union of states that joined to fight for freedom and forge a new democracy. The articles created a loose union and left most of the authority with the individual states. After the Revolution, as economic conflicts arose and more central control was needed, the Constitution was written to give more power to the federal government, replacing the Articles of Confederation. Our country is still governed by this same Constitution of 1787, which also guarantees our civil liberties and civil rights, including freedom of expression, due process, and equal protection.

A Republican delegate supports the ticket as balloons fall at the National Convention in Philadelpha in 2000.
Chris Hondros/Getty Images

What are the three branches of government?

The Constitution divides the federal government into the executive, legislative, and judicial branches.

- The **executive branch** consists of the president, whose powers include approving or vetoing (refusing to sign) laws passed by Congress, and the **president's cabinet,** an advisory group of thirteen government department heads appointed by the president. For example, as Secretary of State, Colin Powell is a member of President George Bush's presidential cabinet.
- The **legislative branch** of the government consists of the two houses of Congress: the Senate and the House of Representatives. The **Senate** with 100 members (two from each state) and the **House of Representatives** with 435 members (apportioned to each state according to population) pass federal laws and serve on committees that investigate problems and oversee the executive branch.
- The **judicial branch** consists of a system of federal courts, the highest of which is the **Supreme Court.** It consists of a chief justice and eight associate justices who are appointed by sitting presidents. The Supreme Court resolves conflicts among states and ensures uniformity in the interpretation of national laws.

Each of the three branches has checks and balances over the other branches so that errors can be addressed and power is shared.

What are political parties?

- Our president, senators, and representatives are nominated for office by a political party, an organization formed to support and elect candidates who uphold the views and beliefs of the group. Over the years, political parties have changed and some have disappeared. Today the two major parties are the Republicans and the Democrats. The **Republican Party,** also called the GOP for "Grand Old Party," began in 1854. Its symbol is the elephant, and Abraham Lincoln was the first Republican president. The party tends to be against expanding the size and responsibilities of the federal government and to support private enterprise. The party image is **conservative,** an ideology or set of beliefs that prefers the existing order and opposes change.
- The **Democratic Party** was organized by Thomas Jefferson in the late eighteenth century, and its first elected president was Andrew Jackson. The party tends to support the expansion of federal programs and a tax system with a greater burden on the rich and corporations. Its symbol is the donkey. The party image is **liberal,** an ideology that supports the strong role of government in economic and social issues.

Prior to elections, both parties pay organizations such as **Gallup** to conduct **polls,** questioning voters about the most important issues and sampling public opinion on voting preferences.

What are capitalism, communism, and socialism?

- **Capitalism** is an economic system based on a free market for goods and services. Production centers such as factories seek profits and are owned by individuals as well as corporations and their stockholders, not the government. The United States has a capitalist economy, although it is not purely capitalistic since government does impose regulations on business.
- **Communism** is almost the opposite of capitalism. It is an economic, political, and social system in which there is no individual ownership. The government controls businesses, and goods and property are owned in common by all citizens. Goods are available to all people as they are needed. The communist system was envisioned by Karl Marx and is associated with the former Soviet Union and China.
- **Socialism** is an economic system advocating government or collective ownership of the goods, rather than private ownership. In Karl Marx's theory, it is the transition between capitalism and communism in which people are paid according to work done. Communists are socialists, but not all socialists are communists.

REVIEW QUESTIONS

1. Why were the Articles of Confederation replaced? ____________________
2. How does the Declaration of Independence differ from the Constitution? ____________________
3. Which branch of the government has the fewest principal members? ____________________
4. In which branch of the government do members of the Cabinet serve? ____________________
5. Which branch of the government has the most elected members? ____________________
6. In which house of Congress does each state have equal representation? ____________________
7. How do Republican and Democratic views on federal government expansion differ? ____________________
8. Would a push to reduce corporate taxes most likely be a liberal or conservative cause? ____________________
9. Would a dynamic business owner prefer capitalism or socialism? ____________________
10. In theory, under which system—capitalism or communism—does a worker share equally in goods regardless of the work he or she does? ____________________

Your instructor may choose to give a true-false review of these computer science concepts.

READER'S JOURNAL

Name ______________________ Date __________

CHAPTER 7

Answer the following questions to learn about your own learning and reflect on your progress. Use the perforations to tear the assignment out for your instructor.

1. Why is it interesting to read material with many inferences? ____________

2. Describe the inference of a "clean" joke that you know. ____________

3. Why would literature tend to contain more inferences than a biology text? ____________

4. "Reading between the lines" is an idiom. What does it mean? ____________

5. What clues do you use to guess a person's age by his or her voice on the telephone? ____________

6. What clues do you use to draw conclusions when you overhear conversations in public places? ____________

7. On what do you base your assumptions when you first meet a person? ____________

8. Do you prefer to read fiction or nonfiction? Why? ____________

9. Why are there no subheadings in works of fiction? ____________

8

Point of View

- Is a textbook influenced by the author's point of view?
- What is the author's point of view?
- What is the reader's point of view?
- What is the difference between a fact and an opinion?
- What is the author's purpose?
- What is the author's tone?

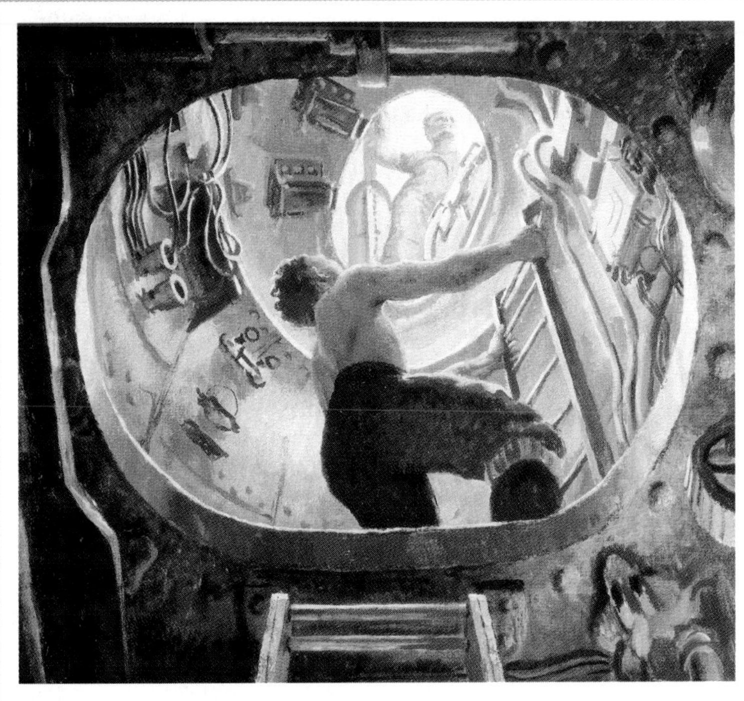

On Board an S-Class Submarine: Up the Conning Tower *(detail) by Stephen Bone, 1944. Oil on canvas,* $30\frac{1}{2} \times 25\frac{1}{2}$" *(77.5 × 65 cm).* © *National Maritime Museum, London. Neg. No. BHC1553.*

Is a Textbook Influenced by the Author's Point of View?

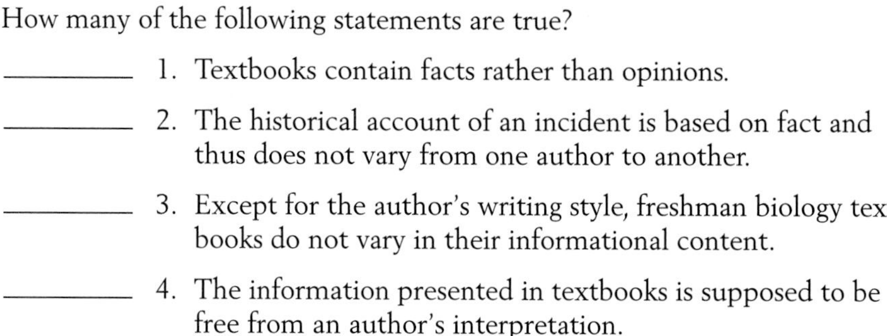

How many of the following statements are true?

_________ 1. Textbooks contain facts rather than opinions.

_________ 2. The historical account of an incident is based on fact and thus does not vary from one author to another.

_________ 3. Except for the author's writing style, freshman biology textbooks do not vary in their informational content.

_________ 4. The information presented in textbooks is supposed to be free from an author's interpretation.

Unfortunately, too many students tend to answer "true" to all of the above. Paying big money for a thick history book with lots of facts and an authoritative title does not mean, contrary to student belief, that the text is a cleansed chronicle of the nation's past. No purity rule applies to textbook writing. In the case of history, the author portrays the past from a uniquely personal perspective. The name of the first president of the United States does not vary from one book to another, but, depending on the point of view of the author, the emphasis on the importance of Washington's administration might vary.

In short, *everything you read is affected by the author's point of view, purpose, tone, and presentation of facts and opinions.*

What Is the Author's Point of View?

Authors of factual material, like authors of fiction, have opinions and theories that influence their presentation of the subject matter. For example, would a British professor's account of American history during the Revolutionary period be the same as a version written by a U.S.-born scholar from Philadelphia? Because of national loyalties and different biases in their own educational histories, the two scholars might look at the events from two different angles—the first as a colonial uprising on a distant continent and the second as a struggle for personal freedom and survival. Each of the two authors would write from a different **point of view** and express particular opinions because they have different ways of looking at the subject.

Recognizing the author's point of view is part of understanding what you read. Sophisticated readers seek to identify the beliefs of the author in order to "know where he or she is coming from." When the point of view is not directly stated, the author's choice of words and information provides clues for the reader.

NON SEQUITUR © 1992 Wiley Miller. Distributed by UNIVERSAL PRESS SYNDICATE. Reprinted with permission. All rights reserved.

The terms *point of view* and *bias* are very similar and are sometimes used interchangeably. When facts are slanted, though not necessarily distorted, toward the author's personal beliefs, the written material is said to reflect the author's bias. Thus, a **bias** is simply an opinion or position on a subject. As commonly used, however, *bias* has a negative connotation suggesting narrow-mindedness and prejudice, whereas *point of view* suggests thoughtfulness and openness. Perhaps you would like to refer to your own opinion as point of view and to those of others, particularly if they disagree with you, as biases!

EXAMPLE Read the following passage and use the choice of information and words to identify the author's point of view on whaling.

> Our own species is providing us with clear examples of how density-dependent regulation can fail. The great whales have been hunted to the brink of oblivion over the past few decades as modern whaling methods have reduced personal risk while increasing profits. Although there is nothing that whales provide that can't be obtained elsewhere, the demand for whale products (and their price) hasn't diminished, especially in Japan. Thus, instead of the human predators relaxing their pressure and allowing the whale population to recover, whaling fleets continue to exert their depressing effect on populations of the great mammals. . . . Then, as whales decrease in number, the price of whale products goes up, and the hunt becomes still more avid. If humans actually starved when they couldn't catch whales (which might once have been the case among the Eskimos), both populations might eventually stabilize (or cycle). But the current decline in whale numbers has had no effect on the growth of the human population.
>
> Robert Wallace et al., *Biology: Science of Life*, 6th ed.

What is the author's point of view? Underline clues that suggest your answer.

____

EXPLANATION The author is against commercial whaling because the whale population is severely declining. Whaling is for profit and seemingly unlimited greed and not for products that cannot be obtained elsewhere.

Exercise 8.1 Comparing Authors' Points of View

Read the following two descriptions of Mary Stuart, Queen of Scotland, from two different history books. Although both include positive and negative comments, the second author obviously finds the subject more engaging and has chosen to include more positive details.

Passage A

Mary Stuart returned to Scotland in 1561 after her husband's death. She was a far more charming and romantic figure than her cousin Elizabeth, but she was no stateswoman. A convinced Catholic, she soon ran head-on into the granitelike opposition of Knox and the Kirk. In 1567 she was forced to abdicate, and in the following year she fled from Scotland and sought protection in England from Elizabeth. No visitor could have been more unwelcome.

Joseph R. Strayer et al., *The Mainstream of Civilization,* 4th ed.

Passage B

Mary Stuart was an altogether remarkable young woman, about whom it is almost impossible to remain objectively impartial. Even when one discounts the flattery that crept into descriptions of her, one is inclined to accept the contemporary evidence that Mary was extraordinarily beautiful, though tall for a girl—perhaps over six feet. In addition to beauty, she had almost every other attractive attribute in high degree: courage, wit, resourcefulness, loyalty, and responsiveness, in short everything needful for worldly greatness save discretion in her relations with men and a willingness to compromise, if need be, on matters of religion. She was a thoroughgoing Roman Catholic, a good lover, and a magnificent hater.

Shepard B. Clough et al., *A History of the Western World*

1. How are the two descriptions alike? ______________________________

____

2. How do the two descriptions differ? ______________________________

____

3. Which do you like better, and why? ______________________________

____

4. What clues signal that the author of the second description is more biased than the first? ______________________________

____

5. What is the suggested meaning in the following phrases:

   a. "no stateswoman" ______

   b. "A convinced Catholic" ______

   c. "granitelike opposition" ______

   d. "more unwelcome" ______

   e. "save discretion in her relations with men" ______

   f. "thoroughgoing Roman Catholic" ______

   g. "magnificent hater" ______

   ______

What Is the Reader's Point of View?

To recognize a point of view, a reader must know enough about the subject to realize that there is another opinion beyond the one being expressed. Thus, prior knowledge and a slightly suspicious nature open the mind to countless other views and alternative arguments.

On the other hand, prior knowledge can also lead to a closed mind and rigid thinking. Existing opinions affect how much readers accept or reject what they read. If their beliefs are particularly strong, sometimes they refuse to hear what is said or they hear something that is not said. Research has shown that readers will actually "tune out" new material that is drastically different from their own views. For example, if you were reading that the AIDS virus should not be a concern for most middle-class Americans, would you be "tuned in" or "tuned out"?

EXAMPLE Read the following passage on smoking first from the point of view of a nonsmoker and second from the point of view of a smoker, and then answer the questions.

> Smoke can permanently paralyze the tiny cilia that sweep the breathing passages clean and can cause the lining of the respiratory tract to thicken irregularly. The body's attempt to rid itself of the smoking toxins may produce a deep, hacking cough in the person next to you at the lunch counter. Console yourself with the knowledge that these hackers are only trying to rid their bodies of nicotines, "tars," formaldehyde, hydrogen sulfide, resins, and who knows what. Just enjoy your meal.
>
> Robert Wallace, Biology: *The World of Life*

1. Is the author a smoker? Underline the clues suggesting your answer.

   ______

2. What is your view on smoking? ______

   ______

3. Reading this passage in the guise of a nonsmoker, what message is conveyed to you? ______________________________

____

4. Assuming the role of a smoker, what message is conveyed to you?

____

5. What is the main point the author is trying to convey? ______________________________

____

EXPLANATION Although it is possible that both the smoker and nonsmoker would get exactly the same message, it is more likely that the nonsmoker would be disgusted by the health risks, whereas the smoker would claim exaggeration and discrimination. The main point is that smoking causes permanent physical damage. The attitude suggests that the author is probably not a smoker.

Exercise 8.2 Identifying Points of View

Read the following passages and answer the questions about point of view.

Passage A: Columbus

On August 3, 1492, Columbus and some ninety mariners set sail from Palos, Spain, in the *Niña, Pinta,* and *Santa Maria.* Based on faulty calculations, the Admiral estimated Asia to be no more than 4500 miles to the west (the actual distance is closer to 12,000 miles). Some 3000 miles out, his crew became fearful and wanted to return home. But he convinced them to keep sailing west. Just two days later, on October 12, they landed on a small island in the Bahamas, which Columbus named San Salvador (holy savior).

A fearless explorer, Columbus turned out to be an ineffective administrator and a poor geographer. He ended up in debtor's prison, and to his dying day in 1506 he never admitted to locating a world unknown to Europeans. Geographers overlooked his contribution and named the Western continents after another mariner, Amerigo Vespucci, a merchant from Florence who participated in a Portuguese expedition to South America in 1501. In a widely reprinted letter, Vespucci claimed that a new world had been found, and it was his name that caught on.

James Kirby Martin et al., *America and Its People*

1. Which paragraph sounds more like the Columbus you learned about in elementary school? ______________________________

2. What is the author's position on Columbus? Underline clues for your answer.

____

3. What is your view of Columbus? What has influenced your view?

____

____

4. What is the main point the author is trying to convey? _______________

____

Passage B: Mexican Cession

The tragedy of the Mexican cession is that most Anglo-Americans have not accepted the fact that the United States committed an act of violence against the Mexican people when it took Mexico's northwestern territory. Violence was not limited to the taking of the land; Mexico's territory was invaded, her people murdered, her land raped, and her possessions plundered. Memory of this destruction generated a distrust and dislike that is still vivid in the minds of many Mexicans, for the violence of the United States left deep scars. And for Chicanos—Mexicans remaining within the boundaries of the new United States territories—aggression was even more insidious, for the outcome of the Texas and Mexican-American wars made them a conquered people. Anglo-Americans were the conquerors, and they evinced all the arrogance of military victors.

In material terms, in exchange for 12,000 lives and more than $100,000,000 the United States acquired a colony two and a half times as large as France, containing rich farm lands and natural resources such as gold, silver, zinc, copper, oil, and uranium which would make possible its unprecedented industrial boom. It acquired ports on the Pacific which generated further economic expansion across that ocean. Mexico was left with its shrunken resources to face the continued advances of the expanding capitalist force on its border.

Rodolfo Acuña, *Occupied America: A History of Chicanos*

1. What is the author's point of view? Underline clues. _______________

____

____

2. How does this author's view differ from what you would expect in most American history texts? _______________

____

3. What is your point of view on the subject? _______________

____

4. What is the main point the author is trying to convey? _______________

____

____

Passage C: Surviving in Vietnam

Vietnam ranks after World War II as America's second most expensive war. Between 1950 and 1975, the United States spent $123 billion on combat in Southeast Asia. More importantly, Vietnam ranks—after our Civil War and World Wars I and II—as the nation's fourth deadliest war, with 57,661 Americans killed in action.

Yet, when the last U.S. helicopter left Saigon, Americans suffered what historian George Herring terms "collective amnesia." Everyone, even those who had fought in 'Nam, seemed to want to forget Southeast Asia. It took nearly ten years for the government to erect a national monument to honor those who died in Vietnam.

Few who served in Vietnam survived unscathed, whether psychologically or physically. One of the 303,600 Americans wounded during the long war was 101st Airborne platoon leader James Bombard, first shot and then blown up by a mortar round during the bitter Tet fighting at Hue in February 1968. He describes his traumatic experience as

> feeling the bullet rip into your flesh, the shrapnel tear the flesh from your bones and the blood run down your leg. . . . To put your hand on your chest and to come away with your hand red with your own blood, and to feel it running out of your eyes and out of your mouth, and seeing it spurt out of your guts, realizing you were dying. . . . I was ripped open from the top of my head to the tip of my toes. I had forty-five holes in me.

Somehow Bombard survived Vietnam.

Withdrawing U.S. forces from Vietnam ended only the combat. Returning veterans fought government disclaimers concerning the toxicity of the defoliant Agent Orange. VA hospitals across the nation still contain thousands of para- and quadriplegic Vietnam veterans, as well as the maimed from earlier wars. Throughout America the "walking wounded" find themselves still embroiled in the psychological aftermath of Vietnam.

James Divine et al., *America: Past and Present*

1. What is the author's own view of the war? Underline clues for your answer. ______________________________

____

2. What is your own position on the Vietnam War? ______________________________

____

3. What is the purpose of Bombard's quotation? ______________________________

____

4. How do you feel about war after reading this passage? ______________________________

____

5. What is the main point the author is trying to convey? ______________________________

____

What Is a Fact and What Is an Opinion?

For both the reader and the writer, a point of view is a position or belief that logically evolves over time with knowledge and experience and is usually based on both facts and opinions. For example, what is your position on city curfews for youth, on helping the homeless, on abortion? Are your views on these issues supported solely by facts? Do you recognize the difference between the facts and the opinions used in your thinking?

Both facts and opinions are used persuasively to support positions. You have to determine which is which and then judge the issue accordingly. A fact is a statement based on actual evidence or personal observation. It can be checked objectively with empirical data and proved to be either true or false. By contrast, an opinion is a statement of personal feeling or a judgment. It reflects a belief or an interpretation rather than an accumulation of evidence, and it cannot be proved true or false. Adding the quoted opinion of a well-known authority to a few bits of evidence does not improve the data, yet this is an effective persuasive technique. Even though you may believe an opinion is valid, it is still an opinion.

EXAMPLE

Fact: Freud developed a theory of personality.
Fact: Freud believed that the personality is divided into three parts.

Opinion: Freud constructed the most complete theory of personality development.
Opinion: The personality is divided into three parts: the id, the ego, and the superego.

Reader's Tip

Questioning to Uncover Bias

* What is your opinion on the subject?
* What is the author's opinion on the subject?
* What are the author's credentials for writing on the subject?
* What does the author have to gain?
* Does the author use facts or opinions as support?
* Are the facts selected and slanted to reflect the author's bias?

Authors mix facts and opinions, sometimes in the same sentence, in order to win you over to a particular point of view. Persuasive tricks include factually quoting sources who then voice opinions or hedging a statement with "It is a fact that" and attaching a disguised opinion. Recognize that both facts and opinions are valuable but be able to distinguish between the two.

Exercise 8.3

Fact or Opinion

Read each of the following and indicate *F* for fact and O for opinion.

_________ 1. Electronic mail, generally called e-mail, is one of the most useful Internet features for business.

Courtland Bovee and John Thill, *Business Communication Today*

_________ 2. A survey of 600 university students found that 34 percent had pirated software and 16 percent had gained illegal access to a computer system

Jay Albanese, *Criminal Justice*

_________ 3. Company sources attribute Coors' success to product quality, boasting that it "is the most expensively brewed beer in the world."

Louis Boone and David L. Kurtz, *Contemporary Business*

_________ 4. If you wish to "break the hunger habit" in order to gain better control over your own food intake, you might be wise to do so slowly—by putting yourself on a very irregular eating schedule.

James V. McConnell, *Understanding Human Behavior*

_________ 5. The first step in running for the nomination is to build a personal organization, because the party organization is supposed to stay neutral until the nomination is decided.

James M. Burns et al., *Government by the People*

_________ 6. It is true that American politics often rewards with power those who have proved that they can direct the large institutions of commerce and business, of banking, and of law, education, and philanthropy.

Kenneth Prewitt and Sidney Verba, *An Introduction to American Government*

_________ 7. Precipitation is not uniform, and neither is the distribution of population.

Robert J. Foster, *Physical Geology*

_________ 8. Massively built, with eyes so piercing they seemed like the headlights of an onrushing train, J. P. Morgan was the most powerful figure in American finance.

Robert Divine et al., *America Past and Present*

_________ 9. At least 10 percent of the world's available food is destroyed by pests, waste, and spoilage somewhere between the marketplace and the stomach of the consumer.

Robert Wallace, *Biology: The World of Life*

_________ 10. Women, young girls, and even mere children were tortured by driving needles under their nails, roasting their feet in the fire, or crushing their legs under heavy weights until the marrow spurted from their bones, in order to force them to confess to filthy orgies with demons.

Edward M. Burns, *Western Civilization*

Exercise 8.4

Fact and Opinion in Textbooks

The following passage from a history text describes Franklin D. Roosevelt. Notice the mixture of facts and opinions in developing a view of Roosevelt. Mark the items that follow as fact (*F*) or opinion (O).

> Franklin D. Roosevelt won the Democratic nomination in June 1932. At first glance he did not look like someone who could relate to suffering people; he had spent his entire life in the lap of luxury.
>
> Handsome and outgoing, Roosevelt had a bright political future. Then disaster struck. In 1921, he developed polio. The disease left him paralyzed from the waist down and confined to a wheelchair for the rest of his life. Instead of retiring, however, Roosevelt threw himself into a rehabilitation program and labored diligently to return to the public life. "If you had spent two years in bed trying to wiggle your toe," he later observed, "after that anything would seem easy."
>
> Few intellectuals had a high opinion of him. Walter Lippmann described Roosevelt as "a pleasant man who, without any important qualifications for the office, would very much like to be President."
>
> The people saw Roosevelt differently. During the campaign, he calmed their fears and gave them hope. Even a member of Hoover's administration had to admit: "The people seem to be lifting eager faces to Franklin Roosevelt, having the impression that he is talking intimately to them." Charismatic and utterly charming, Roosevelt radiated confidence. He even managed to turn his lack of a blueprint into an asset. Instead of offering plans, he advocated the experimental method. "It is common sense to take a method and try it," he declared, "if it fails, admit it frankly and try another."
>
> James Kirby Martin et al., *America and Its People*

________ 1. Roosevelt won the Democratic nomination in June 1932.

________ 2. He was handsome and outgoing.

________ 3. He developed polio in 1921.

________ 4. Few intellectuals thought highly of him.

________ 5. Roosevelt radiated confidence.

What Is the Author's Purpose?

Be aware that a textbook author can shift from an objective and factual explanation of a topic to a subjective and opinionated treatment of the facts. Recognizing the author's purpose does not mean that you won't buy the product; it just means that you are a more cautious, well-informed consumer.

An author always has a purpose in mind when putting words on paper. The reader of a textbook expects that the author's purpose will be to inform or explain objectively—and in general this is true. At times, however, texts can slip from factual explanation to opinionated treatment of the facts, or persuasion. The sophisticated reader recognizes this shift in purpose and thus is more critical in evaluating the content. For example, a persuasive paragraph for or against more air quality control regulations should alert you to be more skeptical and less accepting than a paragraph explaining how air quality control works.

The author can have a single purpose or a combination of the following:

to inform	to argue	to entertain
to explain	to persuade	to narrate
to describe	to condemn	to shock
to enlighten	to ridicule	to investigate

Read the following passage to determine the author's purpose.

EXAMPLE

love, *n.* A temporary insanity curable by marriage or by removal of the patient from the influences under which he incurred the disorder. This disease, like caries and many other ailments, is prevalent only among civilized races living under artificial conditions; barbarous nations breathing pure air and eating simple food enjoy immunity from its ravages. It is sometimes fatal, but more frequently to the physician than to the patient.

Ambrose Bierce, *The Devil's Dictionary*

EXPLANATION The author defines love in a humorous and exaggerated manner for the purpose of entertaining the reader.

Exercise 8.5 Determining the Author's Purpose

Read the following passage and answer the questions about the author's purpose.

Isabella Katz and the Holocaust: A Living Testimony

No statistics can adequately render the enormity of the Holocaust, and its human meaning can perhaps only be understood through the experience of a single human being who was cast into the nightmare of the Final Solution. Isabella Katz was the eldest of six children—Isabella, brother Philip, and sisters Rachel, Chicha, Cipi, and baby Potyo—from a family of Hungarian Jews. She lived in the ghetto of Kisvarda, a provincial town of 20,000 people, where hers was a typical Jewish family of the region—middle-class, attached to Orthodox traditions, and imbued with a love of learning.

In 1938 and 1939 Hitler pressured Hungary's regent, Miklós Horthy, into adopting anti-Jewish laws. By 1941 Hungary had become a German ally, and deportations and massacres were added to the restrictions. Isabella's father left for the United States, where he hoped to obtain entry papers for his family, but after Pearl Harbor, Hungary was at war with America and the family was trapped. In the spring of 1944, when Hitler occupied Hungary, the horror of the Final Solution struck Isabella. On March 19 Adolf Eichmann, as SS officer in charge of deportation, ordered the roundup of Jews in Hungary, who numbered some 650,000. On May 28, Isabella's nineteenth birthday, the Jews in Kisvarda were told to prepare for transportation to Auschwitz on the following morning. Isabella recalled:

> And now an SS man is here, spick-and-span, with a dog, a silver pistol, and a whip. And he is all of sixteen years old. On his list appears the name of every Jew in the ghetto. . . . "Teresa Kata," he calls—my mother. She steps forward. . . . Now the SS man moves toward my mother. He raises his whip and, for no apparent reason at all, lashes out at her.

En route to Auschwitz, crammed into hot, airless boxcars, Isabella's mother told her children to "stay alive":

> Out there, when it's all over, a world's waiting for you to give it all I gave you. Despite what you see here. . . . believe me, there is humanity out there, there is dignity. . . . And when this is all over, you must add to it, because sometimes it is a little short, a little skimpy.

Isabella and her family were among more than 437,000 Jews sent to Auschwitz from Hungary.

When they arrived at Auschwitz, the SS and camp guards divided the prisoners into groups, often separating family members. Amid the screams and confusion, Isabella remembered:

> We had just spotted the back of my mother's head when Mengele, the notorious Dr. Josef Mengele, points to my sister and me and says, "Die Zwei" [those two]. This trim, very good-looking German, with a flick of his thumb and a whistle, is selecting who is to live and who is to die.

Isabella's mother and her baby sister perished within a few days.

> The day we arrived in Auschwitz, there were so many people to be burned that the four crematoriums couldn't handle the task. So the Germans built big open fires to throw the children in. Alive? I do not know. I saw the flames. I heard the shrieks.

Isabella was to endure the hell of Auschwitz for nine months.

The inmates were stripped, the hair on their heads and bodies was shaved, and they were herded into crude, overcrowded barracks. As if starvation, forced labor, and disease were not enough, they were subjected to unspeakable torture, humiliation, and terror, a mass of living skeletons for whom the difference between life and death could be measured only in an occasional flicker of spirit that determined to resist against impossible odds. Isabella put it this way:

> Have you ever weighed 120 pounds and gone down to 40? Something like that—not quite alive, yet not quite dead. Can anyone, can even I, picture it? . . . Our eyes sank deeper. Our skin rotted. Our bones screamed out of our bodies. Indeed, there was barely a body to house the mind, yet the mind was still working, sending out the messages "Live! Live!"

In November, just as Isabella and her family were lined up outside a crematorium, they were suddenly moved to Birnbäumel, in eastern Germany—

the Russians were getting nearer and the Nazis were closing down their death camps and moving the human evidence of their barbarism out of reach of the enemy. In January, as the Russians and the frigid weather closed in, the prisoners were forced to march through the snows deeper into Germany, heading toward the camp at Bergen-Belsen. Those who could not endure the trial fell by the side, shot or frozen to death. On January 23, while stumbling through a blizzard with the sound of Russian guns in the distance, Isabella, Rachel, and Chicha made a successful dash from the death march and hid in an abandoned house. Two days later Russian soldiers found them. Philip had been sent to a labor camp, and Cipi made it to Bergen-Belsen, where she died.

Isabella later married and had two children of her own, making a new life in America. Yet the images of the Holocaust remain forever in her memory. "Now I am older," she says, "and I don't remember all the pain. . . . That is not happiness, only relief, and relief is blessed. . . . And children someday will plant flowers in Auschwitz, where the sun couldn't crack through the smoke of burning flesh."

Richard L. Greaves et al., *Civilizations of the World*

1. What is the author's purpose for including this story in a history textbook?

____

2. What does the author mean by "its human meaning can perhaps only be understood through the experience of a single human being"? _______________

____

____

3. Why does the author include Isabella's quote? _______________

____

4. Why does the author include Isabella's quote about the SS man?

____

____

5. What is Isabella's purpose in relating her story? _______________

____

6. Is the passage predominantly developed through facts or opinions? Give an example of each. _______________

____

7. How does the passage influence your thinking about the Holocaust?

____

____

What Is the Author's Tone?

The tone of an author's writing is similar to the tone of a speaker's voice. For listeners, it is fairly easy to tell the difference between an angry tone and a romantic tone by noticing the speaker's voice. Distinguishing among humor, sarcasm, and irony, however, may be more difficult. **Humorous** remarks are designed to be comical and amusing, while **sarcastic** remarks are designed to cut or give pain. As stated in the discussion of figurative language in Chapter 7, **ironic** remarks express something other than the literal meaning and are designed to show the incongruity between the actual and the expected. Making such precise distinctions requires more than just listening to sounds; it requires a careful evaluation of what is said. Because the sound of the voice is not heard in reading, clues to the tone must come from the writer's presentation of the message. Your job is to look for clues to answer the question "What is the author's attitude toward the topic?"

Try being the author yourself. Let's say that your friend is already a half-hour late for a meeting. You can wait no longer but you can leave a note. On your own paper, write your friend three different notes—one in a sympathetic tone, one in an angry tone, and one in a sarcastic tone. Notice in doing this how your tone reflects your purpose. Which note would you really leave and to which friend?

Reader's Tip

Recognizing an Author's Tone

The following list of words with explanations can describe an author's tone or attitude:

* **Absurd, farcical, ridiculous:** laughable or a joke
* **Apathetic, detached:** not caring
* **Ambivalent:** having contradictory attitudes or feelings
* **Angry, bitter, hateful:** feeling bad and upset about the topic
* **Arrogant, condescending:** acting conceited or above others
* **Awestruck, wondering:** filled with wonder
* **Cheerful, joyous, happy:** feeling good about the topic
* **Compassionate, sympathetic:** feeling sorrow at the distress of others
* **Complex:** intricate, complicated, and entangled with confusing parts

(continued)

Reader's Tip, *continued*

* **Congratulatory, celebratory:** honoring an achievement or festive occasion
* **Cruel, malicious:** mean-spirited
* **Cynical:** expecting the worst from people
* **Depressed, melancholy:** sad, dejected, or having low spirits
* **Disapproving:** judging unfavorably
* **Distressed:** suffering strain, misery, or agony
* **Evasive, abstruse:** avoiding or confusing the issue
* **Formal:** using an official style
* **Frustrated:** blocked from a goal
* **Gentle:** kind or of a high social class, genteel
* **Ghoulish, grim:** robbing graves or feeding on corpses; stern and forbidding
* **Hard:** unfeeling, strict, and unrelenting
* **Humorous, jovial, comic, playful, amused:** being funny
* **Incredulous:** unbelieving
* **Indignant:** outraged
* **Intense, impassioned:** extremely involved, zealous, or agitated
* **Ironic:** the opposite of what is expected; a twist at the end
* **Irreverent:** lacking respect for authority
* **Mocking, scornful, caustic, condemning:** ridiculing the topic
* **Objective, factual, straightforward, critical:** using facts without emotions
* **Obsequious:** fawning for attention
* **Optimistic:** looking on the bright side
* **Outspoken:** speaking one's mind on issues
* **Pathetic:** moving one to compassion or pity
* **Pessimistic:** looking on the negative side
* **Prayerful:** religiously thankful

(continued)

Reader's Tip, *continued*

* **Reticent:** shy and not speaking out
* **Reverent:** showing respect
* **Righteous:** morally correct
* **Romantic, intimate, loving:** expressing love or affection
* **Sarcastic:** saying one thing and meaning another
* **Satiric:** using irony, wit, and sarcasm to discredit or ridicule
* **Sensational:** overdramatized or overhyped
* **Sentimental, nostalgic:** remembering the good old days
* **Serious, sincere, earnest, solemn:** being honest and concerned
* **Straightforward:** forthright
* **Subjective, opinionated:** expressing opinions and feelings
* **Tragic:** regrettable or deplorable mistake
* **Uneasy:** restless or uncertain
* **Vindictive:** seeking revenge

EXAMPLE Identify the tone of the following passage.

> As a father of two pre-teen boys, I have in the last year or so become a huge fan of the word "duh." This is a word much maligned by educators, linguistic brahmins and purists, but they are all quite wrong.
>
> Duh has elegance. Duh has shades of meaning, even sophistication. Duh and its perfectly paired linguistic partner, "yeah, right," are the ideal terms to usher in the millennium and the information age, and to highlight the differences from the stolid old 20th century.
>
> From Kirk Johnson. "Today's Kids Are, Like, Killing the English Language," *The New York Times*, August 9, 1998. Copyright © 1998 by The New York Times Co. Reprinted by permission.

The author's tone is ______________________________.

a. nostalgic.
b. humorous.
c. angry.

EXPLANATION The author's tone is humorous. The author is poking fun at the way teens communicate or fail to communicate. Along with the word or nonword "duh," the author uses complex terms such as "linguistic brahmins" and "linguistic partner." For an additional clue to the author's tone and intent, read the title of the selection from which this excerpt is taken.

Exercise 8.6

Identifying Tone in Sentences

Mark the letter that identifies the tone for each of the following examples:

_________ 1. Must I recycle everything? I don't want any more gifts of brown, "earth friendly" stationery. I want to exercise my right to burn my newspapers and throw my soda can in the trash.
a. objective b. nostalgic c. angry

_________ 2. Health experts and environmentalists now look to birth control to save us from a growing world population that already exceeds 5.5 billion. Yet, as recently as 1914, the distribution of birth control information was illegal. In that year, Margaret Higgins Sanger, founder of The Woman Rebel, was arrested and indicted for sending birth control information through the mail.
a. optimistic b. ironic c. sentimental

_________ 3. The Golden Age or heyday of Hollywood was in the 1930s. Americans, economically crippled by the Great Depression, went to movies for fantasy escapes into worlds created by entertainers such as Clark Gable, Greta Garbo, and the Marx Brothers.
a. objective b. nostalgic c. bitter

_________ 4. Doublespeak hides the truth, evades the issues, and misleads. No one gets fired these days. They disappear due to downsizing, workforce adjustments, and headcount reductions. After eliminating 8,000 jobs, an automobile company called it "a volume-related production schedule adjustment." Perhaps the families of the workers called it an "involuntary lifestyle reduction."
a. sensational b. impassioned c. bitter

_________ 5. In his early thirties, Beethoven's gradual hearing loss became total. This prevented him from playing the piano properly but not from continuing to write music. His three most complex and acclaimed symphonies were written when he was stone deaf. He never heard them played.
a. ironic b. sarcastic c. opinionated

Exercise 8.7

Identifying the Author's Tone in Paragraphs

Read the following passages to determine the author's tone and attitude toward the subject.

Passage A: Water Pollution

In many locales the water is not safe to drink, as evidenced by the recent outbreaks of infectious hepatitis in the United States. Infectious hepatitis is believed to be caused by a virus carried in human waste, usually through a water supply that is contaminated by sewage. There is some disturbing evidence that this virus may be resistant to chlorine, especially in the presence of high levels of organic material. Despite our national pride in indoor plumbing and walk-in bathrooms, sewage treatment for many communities in the United States is grossly inadequate, and waste that has been only partially treated is discharged into waterways. Recently the news services carried a story announcing that the New Orleans water supply may be dangerous to drink. However, we have been assured that there is no cause for alarm—a committee has been appointed to study the problem!

Robert Wallace, *Biology: The World of Life*

1. What is the author's tone? ____

   ____

2. Circle the words and phrases that suggest this tone.
3. What is the author's point of view? ____

   ____

4. What is your own point of view on the subject? ____

   ____

5. What is the main point the author is trying to convey? ____

   ____

Passage B: The Redwoods

It is impossible to live in the redwood region without being profoundly affected by the massive destruction of this once-magnificent ecosystem. Miles and miles of clearcuts cover our bleeding hillsides. Ancient forests are being strip-logged to pay off corporate junk bonds. Log trucks fill our roads, heading to the sawmills with loads ranging from 1,000-year-old redwoods, one tree trunk filling an entire logging truck, to six-inch-diameter baby trees that are chipped for pulp.

Judi Bari, "The Feminization of Earth First!"

1. What is the author's tone? ____
2. Circle the words and phrases that suggest this tone.
3. What is the author's point of view? ____
4. What is your own point of view on the subject? ____

   ____

5. What is the main point the author is trying to convey? ____

   ____

Passage C: Why Women Smile

After smiling brilliantly for nearly four decades, I now find myself trying to quit. Or, at the very least, seeking to lower the wattage a bit.

Smiles are not the small and innocuous things they appear to be: Too many of us smile in lieu of showing what's really on our minds. Despite all the work we American women have done to get and maintain full legal control of our bodies, not to mention our destinies, we still don't seem to be fully in charge of a couple of small muscle groups in our faces.

Our smiles have their roots in the greetings of monkeys, who pull their lips up and back to show their fear of attack, as well as their reluctance to vie for a position of dominance. And like the opossum caught in the light by a clattering garbage can, we, too, flash toothy grimaces when we make major mistakes. By declaring ourselves nonthreatening, our smiles provide an extremely versatile means of protection.

Amy Cunningham, "Why Women Smile"

1. What is the author's tone? ______________________________
2. Circle the words and phrases that suggest this tone.
3. What is the author's point of view? ______________________________

____
4. What is your own point of view on the subject? ______________________
5. What is the main point the author is trying to convey? __________________

____

Passage D: The Comma

The commas are the most useful and usable of all the stops. It is highly important to put them in place as you go along. If you try to come back after doing a paragraph and stick them in the various spots that tempt you will discover that they tend to swarm like minnows into all sorts of crevices whose existence you hadn't realized and before you know it the whole long sentence becomes immobilized and lashed up squirming in commas. Better to use them sparingly, and with affection, precisely when the need for each one arises, nicely, by itself.

Lewis Thomas, *The Medusa and the Snail.*

1. What is the author's tone? ______________________________
2. Circle the words and phrases that suggest this tone.
3. What is the author's point of view? ______________________________
4. What is your own point of view on the subject? ______________________
5. What is the main point the author is trying to convey?

____

Editorial Cartoons

Editorial cartoons vividly illustrate how an author or an artist can effectively communicate point of view without making a direct verbal statement. Through their drawings, cartoonists have great freedom to be extremely harsh and judgmental. For example, they take positions on local and national news events and frequently depict politicians as crooks, thieves, or even murderers. Because the accusations are implied rather than directly stated, the cartoonist communicates a point of view but is still safe from libel charges.

EXAMPLE Study the cartoon below to determine what the cartoonist believes and is saying about the subject. Use the following steps to help you analyze the implied meaning and point of view.

Reprinted with permission of the St. Louis Post-Dispatch, 2001.

1. Glance at the cartoon for an overview and read the book and box titles.
2. Answer the question, "What is this about?" to determine the general topic.

____

3. Study the details for symbolism. Who is Harry Potter? What is the boy's expression? What do the machines mean, and why are they so big? What is in the boxes beside the machines? Why is the scene depicted behind the boy's chair?

____

____

____

____

____

4. With all the information in mind, explain the main point that the cartoonist is trying to get across. _______________

____

5. What is the tone of the cartoon? _______________

____

6. What is the cartoonist's purpose? _______________

____

7. What is the cartoonist's point of view or position on the subject? What is your point of view? _______________

____

EXPLANATION Harry Potter is the main character in a series of bestselling novels that children are eagerly reading and enjoying. The books are so engaging that children are ignoring the lure of television, computers, and video games to escape into the fanciful adventures of Harry Potter. The cartoonist is gleefully proclaiming the triumph of the old-fashioned book over modern technology. The scene behind the boy's chair represents the window of the child's imagination as it soars with the bird to new heights. The tone, like the boy's expression, is happy, gleeful, and optimistic. The purpose is to praise the fictional character that has allowed children to return to the simple pleasures of combining a story with their own imagination. The cartoonist likes books and feels that children should read.

Exercise 8.8

Interpreting an Editorial Cartoon

Use the same steps to analyze the message and answer the questions about the cartoon shown on page 365.

1. What is the general topic of this cartoon? _______________

____

WASHINGTON ZOO
"REMIND ME WHY THEY'RE CONSIDERED THE MORE EVOLVED SPECIES"

Mike Thompson/Detroit Free Press

2. What do the people and objects represent? ______________________
____
____
____

3. What is the main point the cartoonist is trying to convey? ______________________
____
____

4. What is the cartoonist's purpose? ______________________
____
____

5. What is the tone of the cartoon? ______________________
____

6. What is the cartoonist's point of view? ______________________
____

7. What is your point of view on the subject? ______________________
____

Cartoons are fun but challenging, because they require prior knowledge for interpretation. For current news cartoons, you have to be familiar with the latest happenings in order to make connections and understand the message.

Look on the editorial page of your newspaper to enjoy world events from a cartoonist's point of view.

As stated in the beginning of the chapter, even in college textbooks the author's attitudes and biases slip through. It is your responsibility as a reader to be alert for signs of manipulation and to be ready to question interpretations and conclusions. Sophisticated readers are aware and draw their own conclusions based on their own interpretation of the facts.

Summary Points

- **Is a textbook influenced by the author's point of view?**

  Authors have opinions, theories, and prejudices that influence their presentation of material. When facts are slanted, though not necessarily distorted, the material is biased toward the author's beliefs.

- **What is the author's point of view?**

  A bias is a prejudice, a mental leaning, or an inclination. The bias, in a sense, creates the point of view, the particular angle from which the author views the material.

- **What is the reader's point of view?**

  The reader's point of view is prejudice or bias with which the reader views the subject. Readers should not let their viewpoints impede their understanding of the author's opinions and ideas.

- **What is the difference between a fact and an opinion?**

  A fact is a statement that can be proved to be either true or false; an opinion is a statement of feeling or a judgment. Both facts and opinions are used persuasively to support positions.

- **What is the author's purpose?**

  The author's purpose is usually informational, argumentative, or entertaining. An author always has a purpose in mind, and a sophisticated reader should recognize that purpose in order to be a well-informed consumer.

- **What is the author's tone?**

  The tone of an author's writing is similar to the tone of a speaker's voice. The reader's job is to look for clues to determine the author's attitude about the subject.

Selection 1 ESSAY

CONTEMPORARY FOCUS

With people living longer than ever, care for elderly parents in America requires increasingly more time and money. How does elder care vary in different cultures? We can learn about this issue and gain an appreciation for humanity from other cultures.

50 NOT SO NIFTY FOR BABY BOOMERS

Sandra Block

USA TODAY, September 20, 2000, p.1B

Every 7 seconds, a baby boomer turns 50. Listen closely, and you can hear their screams.

Forced to juggle conflicting demands from children and parents, boomers in their 50s must also get serious about saving for their own retirement, cope with the demands of blended families and negotiate a rapidly changing workforce. How they manage those challenges will have far-reaching effects on everything from new car sales to Medicare.

The problems of the so-called Sandwich Generation—middle-aged adults with some responsibility for children and aging parents—aren't new. But the sandwich is getting bigger every day. About 64 million boomers will turn 50 in the next 14 years.

Jann Selle, 50, of Kansas City, Kan., helps care for her 73-year-old mother, who has emphysema, and her late husband's mother, who lives in an assisted care facility. Both live nearby. Selle also has a 16-year-old son at home.

She says she sometimes returns home from running errands for her recently widowed mother-in-law too drained to spend time with her son. "One of the most devastating things about being in the Sandwich Generation is having to choose between taking care of your parent and your child," she says.

The rise in longevity will continue to squeeze the health care system and family members. The number of Americans over 65 requiring long-term care will top 9 million by 2005, AARP estimates. Some will end up in nursing homes, but most of the care will be provided by family and friends.

Collaborative Activity

Collaborate on responses to the following questions:

- Who are the baby boomers?
- What prompted the name *Sandwich Generation* and what problems does it imply?
- What are the responsibilities of the primary caregiver for an elderly parent?

Stage 1: Preview

Preview the next selection to predict its purpose and organization, as well as your learning plan.

The author will probably discuss ________________________________.

Activate Schema

Why was the Vietnam War fought?

Why did many Vietnamese flee their country?

Stage 2: Integrate Knowledge While Reading

Predict Picture Relate Monitor Correct

ELDERLY PARENTS: A CULTURAL DUTY

From Ta Thuc Phu, *Orlando Sentinel*, May 2, 1998, p. A-19

A Vietnamese saying goes: "The father's creative work is as great as the Thai Son mountain; the mother's love is as large as the river flowing out to sea. Respect and love your parents from the bottom of your hearts. Achieve your duty of filial piety as a proper standard of well-behaved children."

I am pleased to answer the question, "How do you deal with your parents as they get older?" I want to relate some characteristics of the Vietnamese culture.

Living together with elderly parents under the same roof is one of our national traditions. In fact, I am honored to have my 92-year-old mother-in-law living with me and my wife.

The family is the basic institution with which to perpetuate society and provide protection to individuals. Generally speaking, the family structure in Southeastern Asia is more complex than the American family structure.

In Vietnamese society, the father is the head of the family. However, the father shares with his wife and children collective responsibilities—legally, morally and spiritually—and these responsibilities continue, even after children are grown up and married. Always, the mother has the same status as the father. In addition, she is the embodiment of love and the spirit of self-denial and sacrifice.

Vietnamese parents consider the parent-child relationship their most important responsibility, and they train their children for a lifetime. In effect, the family is the small school where children learn to follow rules of behavior and speaking. The cornerstone of the children's behavior in the family is filial

Vietnamese family honor: Ta Thuc Phu, M.D., poses with his 92-year-old mother-in-law, Duong Thi Tri, and his wife, Hoang Thi Hanh.
© Angela Peterson/The Orlando Sentinel

piety. Filial piety consists of loving, respecting and obeying one's parents. As a result, the obligation to obey parents does not end with the coming of age or marriage. Filial piety means solicitude and support of one's parents, chiefly in their old age. Vietnamese elders never live by themselves or in nursing homes. Instead, they live with one of their children, usually the eldest son. This is a family custom practiced in all Vietnamese homes.

We do not want to live far apart from our parents, regardless of whether they are young or old, healthy or infirm, because we want to take care of them at any time until their deaths. That is our concept of gratitude to our parents for their hard work and sacrifice throughout the years.

I recall that, when I was growing up, my mother was severely crippled. When we walked together, she held on to my arm for balance. It was difficult to coordinate our steps. My wife and I took turns holding my mother when she cried, and we helped her to walk two hours a day to exercise her body.

By living with our aging parents under the same roof, we also have many occasions to demonstrate our respect for them in the solemn days of the lunar year, such as New Year's Day (Tet), and to celebrate their anniversaries. Our children would present New Year's wishes and symbols of good luck, such as bright red ribbons, to their grandparents to represent prosperity and longevity.

Most important in the Vietnamese value system is undoubtedly our belief that children ought to be grateful to parents for the debt of birth, rearing and education. Children are taught to think of parents first, even at their own expense, to make sacrifices for their parents' sake, to love and care for them in their old age. Unfortunately, that practice is denied now by the communist regime in Vietnam. Children have been taught to spy on their parents and report to the Communist Party any subversive talk or irregular behavior.

Above all, since April 30, 1975, after the collapse of Saigon with the communist takeover of South Vietnam and the tragic exodus of more than 2 million refugees to all parts of the world in search of freedom and a better future, Vietnamese families still practice the custom of living with the parents under the same roof. Deep feelings for families and ties to elders are still strong. These feelings and ties will endure despite these times of change. Even when our parents have been gone many years, we still think of them as living with us.

Stage 3: Recall

Stop to self-test, relate, and react.

Your instructor may choose to give you a true-false comprehension review.

Thinking About "Elderly Parents: A Cultural Duty"

Describe your family tradition and your philosophical view on the care of elderly parents. Also, describe your plan for the care of your own parents.

Contemporary Link

Why do you feel that American baby boomers are stressed with caring for elderly parents while the author is honored to have his elderly mother-in-law under the same roof? What contributes to the difference in attitude?

Skill Development: Exploring Point of View

Form a collaborative group to discuss the following questions:

- What is your view on nursing homes?
- What do you feel is the government's responsibility in the care of the elderly?
- If financial assistance is needed, who should pay for the care of the elderly?
- Is the question of elder care only about money?

Comprehension Questions

After reading the selection, answer the following with *T* (true) or *F* (false).

Inference ________ 1. The author's primary purpose is to argue that Americans should have elderly parents living with them under the same roof.

Inference ________ 2. The author's tone is objective.

Inference	_______	3. The author feels both honored and happy to have an elderly parent living in his home.
Inference	_______	4. The author implies that the Communists in Vietnam are undermining the traditional parent-child relationship.
Detail	_______	5. According to the author, there are no nursing homes in Vietnam.
Inference	_______	6. The author's statement that a mother "is the embodiment of love and the spirit of self-denial and sacrifice" is a statement of fact.
Detail	_______	7. The author suggests that in Vietnamese culture, the mother is the actual head of the family.
Inference	_______	8. The author suggests that Vietnamese refugees in America have begun to abandon the custom of living with parents under the same roof.
Inference	_______	9. The author probably supported the Communist takeover of South Vietnam.
Inference	_______	10. The author implies that family comes before business in the Vietnamese culture.

Vocabulary

1. Define *filial* ____________________
2. Define *piety* ____________________
3. In your own words, define *filial piety* as used in the passage. ____________________

____

Search the Net

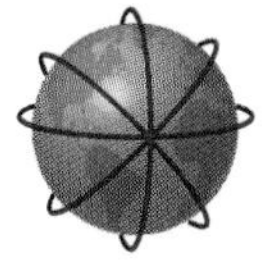

The Internet can be a valuable resource for the elderly. Prepare a resource guide for an elderly friend or grandparent that includes Websites or links, or both, with useful information on retirement, healthcare, and homecare. Select at least four sites, and describe the information given in each. Plan your search or begin by trying the following:

http://www.caregiving.com

http://www.nahc.org

http://www.senior.com/

http://katesdrm.home.mindspring.com/

http://www.aahsa.org/

Selection 2 BUSINESS

CONTEMPORARY FOCUS

Economic cooperation in the European marketplace and the Internet have been working to make English a global language. Yet, the United States is becoming more accepting of different languages and more culturally diverse than ever before. Should companies in the United States enforce English-only standards on the job or should they encourage employees to speak many languages?

THE TRIUMPH OF ENGLISH

Justin Fox

Fortune, New York, September 18, 2000

To compete globally, more and more European businesses are making English their official language. Even the French—quelle horreur!—are adopting it as their lingua franca.

Didier Benchimol lives in Paris. He grew up in Paris. He went to college in Paris. He runs a company founded in Paris and based in Paris. But from the moment he gets to work in the morning till he goes home at night, he speaks nothing but English.

He speaks it well, with lots of American business jargon and only the charming residue of a French accent. But that's not good enough for him. He's been working with a speech coach to conquer that blandest and least identifiable brand of American English: Californian.

The 39-year-old Benchimol, CEO of an e-commerce software company called mediation, is admittedly an extreme case. But he's not the only French executive speaking a lot of English these days. Turn on CNBC or CNN.

English's lead as the world's most spoken language is only going to widen. More important than the numbers is where English is found. It's spoken all over the world; it's the global language of commerce and of science; it's disseminated constantly and instantaneously by radio, TV, and the Internet. No language has ever had this kind of reach, and never has there been so much communication between the different corners of the globe.

Collaborative Activity

Collaborate on responses to the following questions:

- If you owned an Internet company, why would speaking English become increasingly more important?
- Why does the author imply that the French consider speaking English a last resort?
- What is the Euro, and what does it mean for trading within Europe?

Stage 1: Preview

Preview the next selection to predict its purpose and organization, as well as your learning plan.

This selection seems to be about ________________________________.

Activate Schema

If you worked in Spain, would you speak Spanish or English to an American coworker during work breaks?

Stage 2: Integrate Knowledge While Reading

Predict Picture Relate Monitor Correct

SHOULD COMPANIES STRESS ENGLISH ONLY ON THE JOB?

From Courtland L. Bovee and John V. Thill, *Business Communication Today*

When Frances Arreola read the memo announcing that employees should speak only English on the job, she was outraged. Arreola, a lens inspector for Signet Amoralite, a lens-manufacturing firm in southern California, remembers having been punished and humiliated by elementary school teachers for speaking in her native Spanish but feels that the English-only rules stressed in some corporate cultures constitute discrimination.

More than half of Signet Amoralite's 900 employees are Asian, Filipino, or Hispanic. The company defends its English-only rule on the grounds that "speaking in another language that friends and associates cannot fully understand can lead to misunderstandings, is impolite, and can even be unsafe." The company claims that the English-only requirement is not written policy, just a guideline, and that violating it carries no punishment. Nevertheless, this policy—and ones like it at hundreds of companies throughout the United States—is incorporated into the company's culture, and it is considered by critics to violate federal laws against discrimination on the basis of national origin. According to Equal Employment Opportunity Commission rules, employers can establish language restrictions only when such restrictions are required by valid business necessities.

A similar situation occurred at the Allied Insurance Agency in Amarillo, Texas. Two clerks at the agency, Rosa Gonzales and Ester Hernandez, were

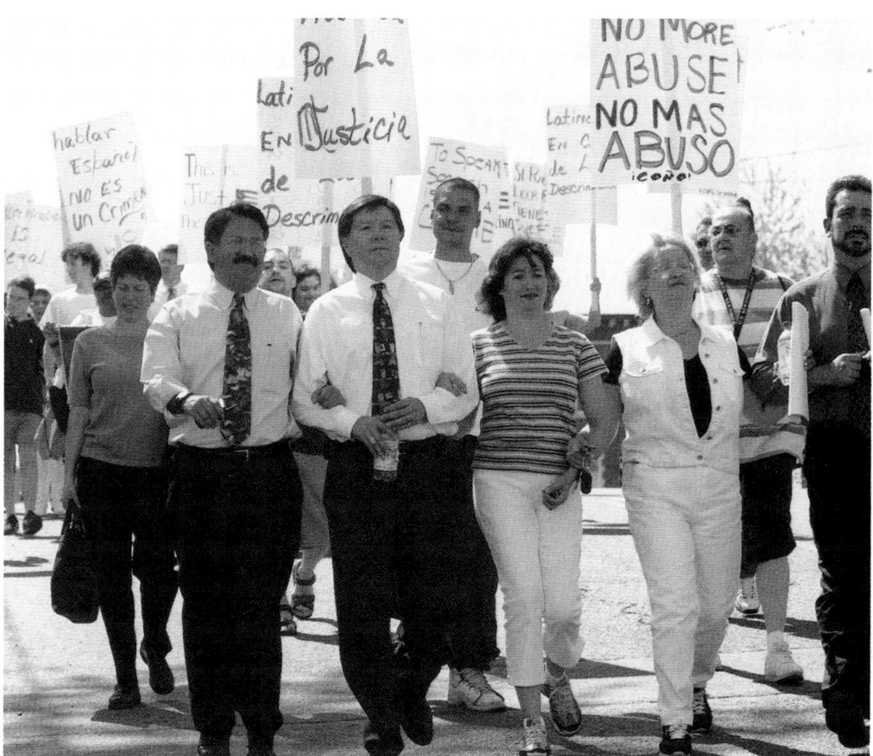

Workers parade to protest English-only restrictions. *AP/Wide World Photos*

hired partially because both are fluent in Spanish and were therefore able to communicate with Spanish-speaking customers. However, the agency's owners became irritated when the two women chatted with each other in Spanish during the workday. Both women were subsequently let go after they refused to sign a pledge that would make Allied "an English-speaking office except when we have customers who can't speak our language." Since then, the agency has been boycotted by two Hispanic groups and has been threatened with lawsuits.

Managers are caught in the middle. On the one side are employees who are disturbed by coworkers' speaking to each other in a language they don't understand, an act they consider to be rude. According to Allied Insurance's owners, the women's chatting in Spanish was "almost like they were whispering behind our backs." On the other side are employees who feel they have a right to speak in a more familiar language as long as it doesn't affect their work. "I'm not doing it to offend anybody. It just feels comfortable," says Gonzales. What is a manager to do?

The best solution, according to experts, is to offer culture sensitivity training that will eliminate misconceptions on both sides and create a more open corporate culture. Native English speakers often assume that nonnative speakers are highly motivated to learn English because they believe it will improve their chances for advancing in the work world. "They tend to speak English as often as they can," says Michael Adams, who helps run culture sensitivity programs for employees at the University of California at San Francisco. "When they speak another language, it's done in order to help a fellow employee understand something."

Colleagues may empathize if they step into the nonnative speaker's shoes. They can be asked to imagine traveling overseas and encountering someone from their home country. What language would they converse in? Would that be rude, or would it simply be more comfortable?

Stage 3: Recall

Stop to self-test, relate, and react.

Your instructor may choose to give you a true-false comprehension review.

Thinking About "Should Companies Stress English Only on the Job?"

Based on what you have read, if you owned a manufacturing company that made semiconductors, what language rules would you impose? Depending on your policy, what would be your method of enforcement?

Contemporary Link

How do English-only rules in American companies discriminate against immigrants? How does not demanding English on the job in the United States also discriminate against immigrants? If you owned a company, what language rules would you impose?

Skill Development: Exploring Point of View

1. From a manager's point of view, what are the conflicts in enforcing an English-only work environment? ________________________________

____

____

2. From the point of view of fellow employees who speak only English, what are the conflicts with employees who speak other languages on the job?

____

____

3. From the point of view of non–native-speaking employees, what are the conflicts with an employer who enforces an English-only policy?

____

____

4. Describe what you believe to be the point of view of the author on the English-only business controversy. _______________________

____

5. What do you believe are the ethical differences between a company that clearly states an English-only policy before hiring and a company that hires and then states an English-only policy? _______________

____

6. If you were working in Spain, what would your feelings be about speaking English on the job to a coworker? _______________________

____

Comprehension Questions

After reading the selection, answer the following with *T* (true) or *F* (false).

Detail ________ 1. Arreola received a memo, rather than a punishment from Signet Amoralite, for speaking Spanish on the job.

Inference ________ 2. Arreola probably went to elementary school in the United States.

Detail ________ 3. According to the passage, Arreola has filed a discrimination lawsuit against Signet Amoralite.

Inference ________ 4. The author suggests that the employer documented that Arreola's Spanish contributed to errors on the job.

Inference ________ 5. The author suggests that Arreola was hired because she was fluent in Spanish.

Inference ________ 6. The reader can conclude that Signet Amoralite could argue with the Equal Employment Opportunity Commission rules on the safety issue.

Inference ________ 7. The author suggests that Gonzales and Hernandez were told of the English-only policy at Allied prior to being hired.

Inference ________ 8. The reader can conclude that local Hispanic groups disagreed with the firing of Gonzales and Hernandez.

Detail ________ 9. The author suggests that most nonnative speakers do not want to learn to speak English.

Inference ________ 10. The author suggests that employees at Allied felt that Gonzales and Hernandez were using Spanish for clarification as suggested by the quote from Michael Adams.

Search the Net

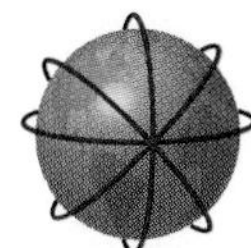

- There are thousands of languages spoken throughout the world. Many of these languages are in danger of becoming extinct. Search the Internet for three languages that are in danger of disappearing. Where are these languages spoken? Why are they disappearing? What is being done to preserve them?

  Foundation for Endangered Languages: http://www.ogmios.org/

  The International Clearing House for Endangered Languages: http://www.tooyoo.l.u-tokyo.ac.jp/ichel.html

- You are the new mayor of a major city, a city that has a large population of immigrants from many countries, including Mexico, Russia, China, Poland, Ghana, and Vietnam. You must take a position in the citywide debate on whether to use several languages or to make English the official language for all government departments, including the police and fire departments. Search the Internet for information about this debate, and use the resources you find to help you make your decision. Briefly describe your decision and refer to the resources that influenced your thinking.

  American Civil Liberties Union: http://www.aclu.org/library/pbp6.html

  English Language Advocates: http://www.elausa.org/

Selection 3 ESSAY

CONTEMPORARY FOCUS

How do you assess the truthfulness of what you read in print? Do you give more credibility to some newspapers than to others? Can you rely on our libel laws to protect you from printed untruths?

RAMSEYS SUE EX-COP

Owen S. Good

Rocky Mountain News (CO), March 30, 2001

A libel and slander lawsuit filed Thursday by John and Patsy Ramsey says they are victims of an embittered ex-cop bent on "vigilante justice" in the form of a tell-all book. The suit accuses former Boulder police detective Steve Thomas of securing a six-figure book contract with the promise he would say Patsy Ramsey killed her 6-year-old daughter, Jon-Benet, on Dec. 26, 1996, and that John Ramsey covered up the crime.

Thomas did not return two messages left for him Thursday at his residence.

The Ramseys are seeking $65 million from Thomas, publisher St. Martin's Press, and several other defendants, including unnamed Boulder police officials who the Ramseys allege supplied Thomas with material for his work.

To prove libel, a plaintiff must show the statements are false or made with a reckless disregard for the truth. If the plaintiffs are public figures, as John and Patsy Ramsey are, they must prove the statements were made with actual malice.

Thomas' work is especially damaging because of his position in the case, Wood said. When supermarket tabloids or talk show hosts accuse the Ramseys, "I don't think the public puts a lot of stock in it," he said. "But it's another thing when a guy claiming to be the lead investigator on the case makes the accusation."

He said that when a grand jury declined to indict either parent in 1999, Thomas pursued "his version of vigilante justice. He knows they will never be charged, so he'll just write a book convicting them of the crime by bootstrapping his credibility as a former detective," Wood said.

Collaborative Activity

Collaborate on responses to the following questions:

- What is the motivation of the detective and of the Ramseys in this case?
- Does not being charged with a crime mean that someone is innocent of the crime?
- What does the phrase "vigilante justice" mean?

Stage 1: Preview

Preview the next selection to predict its purpose and organization as well as your learning plan.

This passage probably defines issues concerning negligence and liability. Agree ☐ Disagree ☐

Activate Schema

How can tabloids print untrue stories and not get sued?

Stage 2: Integrate Knowledge While Reading

Predict Picture Relate Monitor Correct

Tracking the Werewolf

From Daniel McDonald, "Skeptical Inquirer," in *Language of Argument*, 9th ed. by Daniel McDonald and Larry W. Burton

As a longtime student of the tabloids, I'm used to seeing reports of vampires in Venezuela, space aliens in Borneo, and Elvis in Kalamazoo. So it was a rich surprise one day earlier this year when I picked up the *Weekly World News* (dated February 2, 1993) and discovered there was a werewolf downtown, right here in Mobile, Alabama, prowling the State Docks.

The report was written by Tim Skelly, identified as a "Special correspondent in Mobile, Ala." A small photo of Skelly appeared with the article.

The story was titled "Werewolf Battles Cops in Alabama," and the main facts were given in the opening paragraphs:

Bettmann/CORBIS

> MOBILE, Ala.—A howling, snarling werewolf escaped from a foreign freighter, savagely bit seven cops and turned a police cruiser over before he was captured in a darkened alley near the docks.
>
> Heavily armed police are now guarding the wolf-man around the clock at an undisclosed location in Mobile County until he can be placed back aboard the ship he escaped from.

Much of this information came from "a police spokesman," who was quoted at length.

The most impressive evidence was photographic. There were four pictures:

- A profile of the creature's head, which took up most of one page of the two-page story. (He looks like Lon Chaney, Jr., in the Wolfman movies.) At the top of the picture is an identification number: "Mobile P.D. #702419-92."
- A photo of Laura Schindler, a 58-year-old housewife, who stood five feet from the werewolf when he jumped off the ship. She is quoted as saying, "I never saw anything so frightening." Schindler had come to the State

Docks to pick up her husband, a merchant seaman.

- A picture of an overturned car, with four wheels pointing in the air and with a spare tire stored under the trunk.
- A photo of a man with his entire head bandaged. Only his mouth is showing, there are little slit spaces for his eyes. By the picture is a caption, "Ripped to Shreds."

The article fascinated me, and I was in a good position to check it out. Tom Jennings, who serves as Public Information officer for the Mobile Police Department, is a former student of mine. So I phoned him to get the official version. Tom said, "We've had a lot of calls about that crazy story."

Then he gave me the facts.

- The police department couldn't find any "police spokesman" who told the story to the *Weekly World News*.
- They couldn't identify a foreign freighter that had lost a deckhand.
- The "undisclosed location in Mobile County" where the wolfman was being held remained undisclosed. Nobody in the department knew anything about it.
- The police had had no success in locating Laura Schindler. They could find no reference to her merchant-seaman husband.
- The identification number on the werewolf photo is not a sequence used by the Mobile Police Department.
- The police department has had no reports of an overturned vehicle, nor does it have a police cruiser that carries a spare tire under the car.
- There had been no injury reports relating to such an incident, certainly no report of a police officer "ripped to shreds."

Jennings was emphatic on the last two points. He said: "Around here, if an officer gets cut on the hand, there's a lot of paperwork that has to be filled out. If police property is destroyed, it's just the same. There are liability areas." He repeated that there were no reports relating to a werewolf incident. The article, he said, was a "total fabrication."

Jennings suggested I call Nancy Wilstach, a reporter for the *Birmingham News*. He said she had more information about the story.

Indeed she did. Wilstach had interviewed Eddie Clontz, editor of the *Weekly World News*. She found him pleasant and cooperative. He told her they got the werewolf reports from Tim Skelly and that he considers Skelly a reliable source. He said, "Usually his stuff is right on the money."

According to Clontz, tabloids call these articles "harmless." They know that a werewolf story (or a vampire or space-alien story) won't offend anybody and won't bring a lawsuit. So the Weekly World News didn't try to verify the Mobile incident. They just got the report and published it. Clontz said, "We put it out there and let our readers decide."

He added, "Maybe it didn't happen."

Wilstach asked Clontz how she could get in touch with Tim Skelly. He told her it might be difficult, that Skelly is now doing research in Caracas, Venezuela. Clontz said, "He's covering our vampire beat."

Stage 3: Recall

Stop to self-test, relate, and react.

Your instructor may choose to give you a true-false comprehension review.

Thinking About "Tracking the Werewolf"

With an accepted credibility problem, why do you think people buy tabloids? Why would someone read a story about a wolfman? Describe the customers for these publications.

Contemporary Link

To prove guilt in a libel suit, what would distinguish the Steve Thomas book from the wolfman story? How are the purposes for writing each similar or different?

Skill Development: Exploring Point of View

Form a collaborative group to discuss the following questions:

- What is your point of view, opinion, or bias on tabloids? Why?
- What is the author's point of view on tabloids?
- From Clontz's point of view, tabloid articles on a werewolf, vampire, or space-alien are "harmless." What is your point of view on this issue? Are the articles harmless or harmful? Explain your thinking.
- From the reader's point of view, how do the photos affect the validity of the story?

Comprehension Questions

After reading the selection, answer the following with *T* (true) or *F* (false).

Inference ________ 1. The author's primary purpose is to show that the tabloid knowingly published an untrue story.

Inference ________ 2. The tone of the inserted tabloid excerpt is humorous.

Inference ________ 3. The reader can conclude that the vampire and alien stories in tabloids are untrue.

Inference ________ 4. The author implies that he has researched the validity of several tabloid stories.

Inference ________ 5. The reader can conclude that Mobile is a seacoast town.

Inference ________ 6. The tabloid statement that the werewolf "bit seven cops and turned a police cruiser over" is a statement of fact, be it true or false.

Detail ________ 7. The photo provides evidence that the overturned car was not a Mobile police car.

Inference ________ 8. The reader can conclude that Laura Schindler does not exist.

Inference ________ 9. The author implies that the *Birmingham News* is a more reliable newspaper than the *Weekly World News*.

Inference ________ 10. The reader can conclude from the facts presented by the author that Tim Skelly is an actual reporter for the *Weekly World News.*

Search the Net

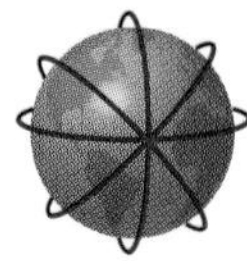

- Find a tabloid magazine article that has questionable validity. Summarize the article as well as the author's purpose and point of view. Is the story presented as fact? How do you think the author and the publishing company have protected themselves from a lawsuit?

  Star Magazine: http://www.starmagazine.com/

  National Enquirer: http://www.nationalenquirer.com/

- Compare two articles about the same subject from two different tabloid magazines. How do the stories differ? How do the sources of information differ?

  The Globe: http://globeonthenet.com/

  Duncan Expose: http://www.dxpnet.com/news/

READER'S JOURNAL

Name ______________________________ Date ______________

CHAPTER 8

Answer the following questions to learn about your own learning and reflect on your progress. Use the perforations to tear the assignment out for your instructor.

1. How can your point of view cloud your understanding of material you read?

____

____

2. Select a current and controversial news issue and describe your position.

____

____

3. When you read for pleasure, what type of material do you enjoy? What tends to be the author's main purpose in that material? ______________

____

____

4. Define the following tones and give an example:

Sarcastic ______________________________

____

Skeptical ______________________________

____

Cynical ______________________________

____

5. How is multiculturalism connected to point of view? ______________

____

____

6. How can education give us greater appreciation for different cultural views?

____

____

9

Critical Thinking

- What is critical thinking?
- What are the characteristics of critical thinkers?
- What are the barriers to critical thinking?
- Why do critical thinkers have power?
- How do critical thinkers analyze an argument?
- What is the difference between inductive and deductive reasoners?
- What does creative thinking add to critical thinking?

Trial by Jury *by Thomas Hart Benton, 1964. Oil on canvas, 30 × 40" (76.2 × 101.6 cm). The Nelson-Atkins Museum of Art, Kansas City, Missouri. Bequest of the artist. F75-21/11. © T. H. Benton and R. P. Benton Testamentary Trusts/Licensed by VAGA, New York, NY.*

What Is Critical Thinking?

Do you accept the thinking of others or do you think for yourself? Do you examine and judge? Can you identify important questions and systematically search for answers? Can you justify what you believe? If so, you are thinking critically. For example, if each of the following questions represents a textbook portrayal of Christopher Columbus, which would you tend to accept most readily and why?

Was he a courageous hero?

Was he a despot who enslaved the Indians?

Was he a hapless explorer who failed to find India or gold?

Rather than answer immediately, most students would say, "I need more information. I want to consider the arguments, weigh the facts, and draw my own conclusions."

Thinking critically means deliberating in a purposeful, organized manner in order to assess the value of information, both old and new. Critical thinkers search, compare, analyze, clarify, evaluate, and conclude. Critical thinkers do not start from scratch; they build on previous knowledge or schemata to forge new relationships. They recognize both sides of an issue and evaluate the reasons and evidence in support of each.

Some professors speak of critical thinking as if it were a special discipline rather than an application of many known skills. Frank Smith, an educator who has written eleven books on thinking, says that thinking critically refers simply to the manner in which thinking is done.[1] It is merely an approach to thinking, in the same sense that thinking impulsively or thinking seriously are approaches, and the approach can be practiced and learned.

Applying Skills to Meet College Goals

Many colleges cite the ability to think critically as one of the essential academic outcome goals for students graduating after four years of college work. An educated person is expected to think systematically, to evaluate, and to draw conclusions based on logic. At your college, an emphasis on critical thinking probably crosses the curriculum, and thus becomes a part of every college course. When an instructor returns a paper to you and comments, "Good logic" or "Not enough support," the comments are referring to critical

[1]Frank Smith, *To Think* (New York: Teachers' College Press, 1990).

thinking. The same is true if you make a class presentation and are told either that your thesis is very convincing or that you are missing vital support.

Critical thinking is thus not a new skill; it is the systematic application of many well-learned skills. These include identifying details, inferences, and point of view. In this chapter we will also discuss a few new techniques for evaluating the support for an argument or thesis.

Critical thinking instruction has its own specialized vocabulary, often using seemingly complex terms for simple ideas. As you work through this chapter, you will become familiar with the critical thinking application of the following terminology:

analogy	argument	assertion	believability	conclusion	consistency
deduction	fallacy	induction	premise	relevance	reliability

Reader's Tip

How to Think Critically

* **Be willing to plan.** Think first and write later. Don't be impulsive. Develop a habit of planning.
* **Be flexible.** Be open to new ideas. Consider new solutions for old problems.
* **Be persistent.** Continue to work even when you are tired and discouraged. Good thinking is hard work.
* **Be willing to self-correct.** Don't be defensive about errors. Figure out what went wrong and learn from your mistakes.

Barriers to Critical Thinking

Some people will not allow themselves to think critically. They are mired in their own belief system and do not want to change or be challenged. They are gullible and thus easily persuaded by a slick presentation or an illogical argument. In their book *Invitation to Critical Thinking*, Joel Rudinow and Vincent E. Barry identified the following barriers to critical thinking:[2]

1. *Frame of reference:* Each of us has an existing belief system that influences the way we deal with incoming information. We interpret new experiences according to what we already believe. We are culturally conditioned to resist change and feel that our own way is best. We refuse to look at the merits of something our belief system rejects, such as the advantages of legalizing drugs, for example.

[2]J. Rudinow and V. E. Barry, *Invitation to Critical Thinking* (New York: Harcourt Brace, 1994), pp. 11–19.

2. *Wishful thinking:* We talk ourselves into believing things that we know are not true because we want them to be true. We irrationally deceive ourselves and engage in self-denial. For example, we might refuse to believe well-founded claims of moral corruption leveled at our favorite politician or relative.
3. *Hasty moral judgments:* We tend to evaluate someone or something as good or bad, right or wrong, and remain fixed in this thinking. Such judgments are often prejudiced, intolerant, emotional, and self-righteous. An example of such a barrier to thinking critically would be the statement, "Abortion should never be legal."
4. *Reliance on authority:* An authority such as a clergy member, a doctor, or a teacher is an expert source of information. We give authorities and institutions such as church or government the power to think for us and thus block our own ability to question and reason.
5. *Labels:* Labels ignore individual differences and lump people and things into categories. Labels oversimplify, distort the truth, and usually incite anger and rejection. To say, "People who love America and people who do not," forces others to take sides as a knee-jerk reaction.

Exercise 9.1

Identify Types of Barriers

Read the numbered statements below and identify with *a, b, c,* or *d* the type of barrier the statement best represents:

a. Wishful thinking
b. Frame of reference or hasty moral judgments
c. Reliance on authority
d. Labels

EXAMPLE The new drug will not be helpful because the FDA has not yet approved it.

EXPLANATION The answer is *c,* reliance on authority, which in this case is a government agency. A critical thinker might argue that the FDA is slow to test and respond to new drugs, and that many drugs are used safely and successfully in other countries before the FDA grants approval for Americans.

________ 1. Our country is divided into two groups of people: those who work and those who don't work.

________ 2. In some countries people eat horse meat and dog meat, but it is wrong to do so because these animals are friends of humans.

________ 3. My daughter has never taken drugs because she could not do such a horrible thing.

________ 4. I am not buying bottled water because Dr. Juan Garcia of the Duke Medical School reported that some bottled waters are unsafe.

Power of Critical Thinking

Critical thinkers are willing to hold their own opinions up to scrutiny and to consider over and over again, "Is this position worth holding?" They drive to the heart of issues and assess reasons for opposing views. They solve problems and gain knowledge. They do not feel the need to persuade or to argue for right or wrong, but they are not afraid of questions. As a result of logical thinking and the ability to justify their own positions, critical thinkers gain confidence.

Courtroom Analogy

Jurors use critical thinking in deciding court cases. The judge defines the issue and clever lawyers argue "conflicting versions of the truth" before the jury. Each presents reasons and selected evidence to support the case of the client. Needless to say, in the summation to the jury, each attorney interprets the truth in the client's best interest. The jury is left to weigh the validity of the evidence, to reflect on what might be missing, and to decide between two logical arguments. Through the critical thinking process, the jurors systematically answer the following questions:

1. What is the issue?
2. What are the arguments?
3. What is the evidence?
4. What is the verdict?

College students can adapt the jury's critical thinking approach to textbook reading. The same four questions are as relevant in weighing information about Christopher Columbus, genetic engineering, or manic depression as they are to making life-or-death courtroom decisions.

"Your Honor, the jury finds the defendant weakly developed as a central character, overshadowed by the principal witnesses, unconvincingly portrayed as a victim of society, and guilty as charged."

Recognizing an Argument

We often make statements that are not arguments. Assertions such as "I like milk" or "We had a huge overnight snowfall, and my car is covered" are not meant to trigger extensive thought, provoke questions, and lead to analysis. These are nonargumentative statements that are intended to inform or explain. An argument, on the other hand, is an assertion or set of assertions that supports a conclusion and is intended to persuade.

The basic difference between an argument and a nonargumentative statement is the intent or purpose. Nonargumentative statements do not question truth but simply offer information to explain and thereby help us understand. For example, the statement, "The grass is wet because it rained last night" is an explanation, not an argument. To say, however, "You should water the grass tonight because rain is not predicted for several days" constitutes an argument. In the latter case, the conclusion of watering the grass is based on a "fact," the forecast, and the intent is to persuade by appealing to reason. To identify arguments we must use inferential skills and recognize the underlying purpose or intent of the author.

Exercise 9.2

Identify the Argument

Practice recognizing arguments by identifying each of the following statements with *A* for argument or *N* for a nonargumentative statement of information.

EXAMPLE

The foods in salad bars sometimes contain preservatives to keep them looking fresh and appealing.

EXPLANATION This is not an argument. It is not intended to move you to action. It is a statement of fact similar to "It sometimes snows at night."

________ 1. Food preservatives can cause cancer, and you should thus avoid eating food that contains them.

________ 2. According to a famed Nobel laureate, you should take vitamin C regularly in order to prevent colds.

________ 3. Tropical fish have a variety of different colors.

________ 4. Parrots talk because people have taught them how to speak and to understand.

Steps in Critical Thinking

Analyzing an argument through critical thinking and evaluation combines the use of most of the skills that have been taught in this text. The amount of analysis depends on the complexity of the argument. Some arguments are simple, while others are lengthy and complicated. The following is a four-step procedure that can be used as a format to guide your critical thinking:

1. Identify the issue.
2. Identify the support for the argument.
3. Evaluate the support.
4. Evaluate the argument.

Step 1: Identify the Issue

In the courtroom, the judge instructs the jury on the issue and the lawyers provide the arguments. In reading, however, the issues may not be as obvious or clearly defined. The reader must cut through the verbiage to recognize underlying issues as well as to identify support.

Good readers are "tuned in" to look for issues that have opposing points of view. Writers strive to convince readers but are under no obligation to explain, or even to admit persuasion. Knowledgeable readers, however, sense possible biases; they look for the hidden agendas. Good readers constantly ask, "How am I being manipulated or persuaded?" to detect an argument and then ask, "What is the debatable question or central issue in this argument?"

In a college course on critical thinking or logic, the parts of an argument that you would be asked to identify would probably be called the *conclusion* and the *premises*. The conclusion is an assertion or position statement. It is what the author is trying to convince you to believe or to do. For example, in the statement "You should water the grass because rain is not in the forecast," the conclusion is "You should water the grass." The premise, or support, is "because rain is not in the forecast." In the terminology of this textbook, the conclusion also could be viewed as a statement of the main point.

To identify the issue or conclusion in persuasive writing, use your main-idea reading skills. First ask yourself, "What is the passage primarily about?" to determine the topic. Then ask, "What is the main point the author is trying to convey about the topic?" Your answer will be a statement of the issue that is being argued, which could also be called the main point, the thesis, or the conclusion.

Begin by reading the material all the way through. Do not allow your own beliefs to cloud your thinking. Set aside your own urge to agree or disagree, but be alert to the bias of the author. Be aware of the barriers to critical thinking that include limited frame of reference, wishful thinking, hasty moral judgments, reliance on authority, and labeling. Be sensitive to emotional language and the connotation of words. Cut through the rhetoric and get to the heart of the matter.

EXAMPLE Read the following passage and identify the issue that is being argued.

> The technology for television has far exceeded the programming. Viewers are recipients of crystal clear junk. Network programming appeals to the masses for ratings and advertising money and offers little creative or stimulating entertainment.

EXPLANATION Several debatable issues about television are suggested by this passage. They include the abundance of technological advancement, the power of ratings, and the importance of advertising money. The central issue, however, concerns the quality of network programming. Although it is not directly stated, the argument or central issue is "Network television programming is not any good."

Recognizing Analogies as a Familiar Pattern in Issues. George Polya, a pioneer in mathematical problem solving, said we cannot imagine or solve a problem that is totally new and absolutely unlike any problem we have ever known.[3] We seek connections and look for similarities to previous experiences. Such comparisons are called **analogies.**

Analogies are most easily made on a personal level. We think about how the issue has affected or could affect us or someone we know. For example, if high school principals were seeking your input on the issue of declining mathematics scores, you would first relate the problem to your own experience. How did you score in math? Why do you think you did or did not do well? What about your friends? From your memory of high school, what would you identify as the key reasons for the declining scores? The problem now has a personal meaning and is linked to prior knowledge.

Linking new knowledge with personal and expanded comparisons applies past experience to new situations. Two researchers tested the importance of analogies by asking students to read technical passages with and without analogies to familiar topics.[4] The students who read the material containing the analogies scored higher on tests of comprehension and recall than students who did not have the benefit of the familiar comparisons.

Referring back to the previous example on television programming, what analogies could you draw from your own personal experience? What television programs do you consider junk? Are they all junk? What network programs do you feel are high-quality entertainment?

Identifying the Issue Through Signal Words. The central issue may be stated as the thesis or main point at the beginning of an argument, it may be embedded within the passage, or it may be stated at the end as a conclusion. The following key words are sometimes used to signal the central issue being argued:

as a result	finally	in summary	therefore
consequently	for these reasons	it follows that	thus

EXAMPLE What is the central issue that is being argued in the following passage?

> A year in a United States prison costs more than a year at Harvard; however, almost no one is rehabilitated. Prisoners meet and share information with other hardened criminals to refine their skills. It seems reasonable, therefore, to conclude that prisons in the U.S. are societal failures.

[3]George Polya, *How to Solve It*, 2nd ed. (Princeton, NJ: Princeton University Press, 1957).

[4]C. C. Hansen and D. F. Halpern, "Using Analogies to Improve Comprehension and Recall of Scientific Passages." Paper presented at the annual meeting of Psychonomic Society, Seattle, 1987.

EXPLANATION The central issue in this argument is directly stated in the last sentence. Note the inclusion of the signal word *therefore.*

Exercise 9.3

Identify the Issue

Read the following sentence groups and underline or state in a sentence the central issue that is being argued in each.

1. Weekly television comedies frequently show parents in an unflattering light. The parents are usually bettered by the kids, who are portrayed as smarter. The kids win laughs with rude and sarcastic comments directed at the parents.
2. The price of oil, gas, and electricity continues to rise for heating and cooling homes. This rise could lead to renewed interest in solar heating. If the price of installing solar heating panels declined, the result could be that more people would use solar energy as a source for home heating and cooling.
3. Shoplifting raises the price of what we purchase by more than 2 percent. Medicare fraud costs the average taxpayer several hundred dollars each year. The cost of exaggerated insurance claims is passed along to all policy holders in increased premiums. For these reasons it follows that when we cheat corporations, we cheat ourselves and our friends.
4. The director of a film has chosen whether the film will be done in color or in black and white. Colorizers should not be allowed to add color to an original black and white movie. Perhaps the director wanted no one to view the work in color.
5. As soon as East Coast voting booths are closed, the network reporters begin reporting private polling results and predicting a presidential front-runner. Yet, many West Coast voters have not cast their ballots. Reporting polling results before all national votes are cast allows the media too much influence on election results.

Step 2: Identify Support for the Argument

In a college logic course, after identifying the central issue of an argument, you would be asked to identify and number the premises. In the example presented earlier about watering the grass, only one premise, "because rain is not in the forecast," was offered. Other premises such as "the grass will die without water" and "water is plentiful right now" would have added further evidence in support of the conclusion. In reality, the identification of premises is simply the identification of significant supporting details for the main point.

Identifying Supporting Reasons Through Signal Words. Supporting reasons may be directly stated or may be signaled. The key words that signal support for an argument are in some cases the same as those that signal significant supporting details. They include the following:

because	if	assuming that
since	first . . . second . . . finally	given that

EXAMPLE In the previous passage about U.S. prisons, signal words can be used to introduce supporting details:

> One can conclude that prisons in the United States are failures. First, almost no one is rehabilitated. Second, prisoners meet and share information with other hardened criminals to refine their skills. Taxpayers should also consider that a year in prison costs more than a year at Harvard.

EXPLANATION The argument is the same with or without the signal words. In a longer passage the signal words usually make it easier to identify the significant supporting details or reasons.

Exercise 9.4 Identify Support for the Argument

Read the following sentence groups and identify the central issue that is being argued and the supporting reasons. Place the letter *I* before phrases containing the central issue and the letter *S* before those containing supporting reasons.

1. The shad or any fish that runs upstream is an excellent choice for sea ranching. Such fish use their own energies to swim and grow in open waters and then swim back to be harvested.
2. Major game reserves in Africa such as the Ngorongoro Crater are in protected areas, but many lie adjacent to large tracts of land with no conservation status. Animals who migrate off the reserves compete with humans for food and are endangered. Thus, clear boundaries between areas for animals and people would minimize friction.
3. In some states, laws prohibit the sale of obscene material to minors. In these states musicians who sell CDs with obscene lyrics should be prosecuted. Such lyrics brutalize women and should be considered audio pornography.
4. A visit to a doctor's office is a lesson in humility for the patient. First, you see the receptionist who tells you to fill out forms and wait your turn. Next, the nurse takes your blood pressure and extracts blood while you look at the diplomas on the wall. Finally, you are led into a bare room to strip down and wait still longer for the doctor to appear for a few expensive minutes of consultation.
5. In most companies, college graduates get higher-paying jobs than those who do not attend college. As the years go by in a company, promotions and their accompanying raises tend to go primarily to the college graduates. Thus, it can be concluded that a college degree is worth money.

Identifying Types of Supporting Reasons. As support for arguments, readers would probably prefer the simplicity of a smoking gun with fingerprints on it, but such conclusive evidence is usually hard to find. Evidence comes in many different forms, and may be tainted with opinion. The box below contains some categories of "evidence" typically used as supporting reasons in an argument. Each type, however, has its pitfalls and should be immediately tested with an evaluative question.

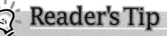

Reader's Tip

Categories of Support for Arguments

* **Facts:** objective truths
  Ask: How were the facts gathered? Are they true?
* **Examples:** anecdotes to demonstrate the truth
  Ask: Are the examples true and relevant?
* **Analogies:** comparisons to similar cases
  Ask: Are the analogies accurate and relevant?
* **Authority:** words from a recognized expert
  Ask: What are the credentials and biases of the expert?
* **Causal relationship:** saying one thing caused another
  Ask: Is it an actual cause or merely an association?
* **Common knowledge claim:** assertion of wide acceptance
  Ask: Is it relevant? Does everyone really believe it?
* **Statistics:** numerical data
  Ask: Do the numbers accurately describe the population?
* **Personal experiences:** personal anecdotes
  Ask: Is the experience applicable to other situations?

Step 3: Evaluate the Support

As a reader, you will decide to accept or reject the author's conclusion based on the strength and acceptability of the reasons and evidence. Strong arguments are logically supported by well-crafted reasons and evidence, but clever arguments can be supported by the crafty use of reason and evidence.

In evaluating the support for an argument, teachers of logic warn students to beware of fallacies. A **fallacy** is an inference that appears to be reasonable at first glance, but closer inspection proves it to be unrelated, unreliable, or illogical. For example, to say that something is right because everybody is doing it is not a convincing reason for accepting an idea. Such "reasoning," however, can be compelling and is so frequently used that it is labeled a *bandwagon fallacy.*

Logicians have categorized, labeled, and defined over 200 types of fallacies or tricks of persuasion. The emphasis for the critical thinker should not be on memorizing a long list of fallacy types but rather on understanding how such irrelevant reasoning techniques can manipulate logical thinking. Fallacies are tools employed in constructing a weak argument that critical thinkers should spot. In a court of law, the opposing attorney would shout "Irrelevant, Your Honor!" to alert the jury to the introduction of fallacious evidence.

Evaluate the support for an argument according to three areas of reasoning: (1) relevance, (2) believability, and (3) consistency. The following list of fallacies common to each area can sensitize you to the "tools" of constructing a weak argument.

1. ***Relevance fallacies: Is the support related to the conclusion?***
   - ***Ad hominem:*** an attack on the person rather than the issue, the hope being that the idea will be opposed if the person is opposed
     Example: Do not listen to Mr. Hite's views on education because he is a banker.
   - **Bandwagon:** the idea that everybody is doing it and you will be left out if you do not quickly join the crowd
     Example: Everybody around the world is drinking Coke so you should too.
   - **Misleading analogy:** a comparison of two things suggesting that they are similar when they are in fact distinctly different
     Example: College students are just like elementary school students; they need to be taught self-discipline.
   - **Straw person:** a setup in which a distorted or exaggerated form of the opponent's argument is introduced and knocked down as if to represent a totally weak opposition
     Example: When a teenaged daughter is told she cannot go out on the weeknight before a test, she replies with "That's unreasonable to say that I can never go out on a weeknight."
   - **Testimonials:** opinions of agreement from respected celebrities who are not actually experts
     Example: A famous actor endorses a headache pill.
   - **Transfer:** an association with a positively or negatively regarded person or thing in order to lend the same association to the argument (also guilt or virtue by association)
     Example: A local politician quotes President Lincoln in a speech as if Lincoln would have agreed with and voted for the candidate.
2. ***Believability fallacies: Is the support believable or highly suspicious?***
   - **Incomplete facts** or **card stacking:** omission of factual details in order to misrepresent reality
     Example: Buy stock in this particular restaurant chain because it is under new management and people eat out a lot.
   - **Misinterpreted statistics:** numerical data misapplied to unrelated populations that they were never intended to represent
     Example: Over 20 percent of people exercise daily and thus do not need fitness training.

- **Overgeneralizations:** examples and anecdotes asserted to apply to all cases rather than a select few
  Example: High school students do little work during their senior year and thus are overwhelmed at college.
- **Questionable authority:** testimonial suggesting authority from people who are not experts
  Example: Dr. Lee, a university sociology professor, testified that the DNA reports were 100 percent accurate.

3. ***Consistency fallacies: Does the support hold together or does it fall apart and contradict itself?***
   - **Appeals to emotions:** highly charged language used for emotional manipulation
     Example: Give money to our organization to help the children who are starving orphans in desperate need of medical attention.
   - **Appeals to pity:** pleas to support the underdog, the person or issue that needs your help
     Example: Please give me an A for the course because I need it to get into law school.
   - **Begging the question** or **circular reasoning:** support for the conclusion that is merely a restatement of it
     Example: Drugs should not be legalized because it should be against the law to take illegal drugs.
   - **Oversimplification:** reduction of an issue to two simple choices, without consideration of other alternatives or "gray areas" in between
     Example: The choices are very simple in supporting our foreign-policy decision to send troops. You are either for America or against it.

Signe Wilkerson/Cartoonists & Writers Syndicate

- **Slippery slope:** objecting to something because it will lead to greater evil and disastrous consequences
  Example: Support for assisting the suicide of a terminally ill patient will lead to the ultimate disposal of the marginally sick and elderly.

Exercise 9.5 Identify the Fallacy

Identify the type of fallacy in each of the following statements by indicating *a*, *b*, or *c*.

_________ 1. Hollywood movie stars and rock musicians are not experts on the environment and should not be dictating our environmental policy.
a. testimonial
b. *ad hominem*
c. bandwagon

_________ 2. Michael Jordan says, "I always wear this brand of athletic shoes. They are the best."
a. *ad hominem*
b. misleading analogy
c. testimonial

_________ 3. The fight for equal rights is designed to force men out of jobs and encourage women to leave their young children alone at home.
a. bandwagon
b. questionable authority
c. straw person

_________ 4. People should give blood because it is important to give blood.
a. begging the question
b. appeal to pity
c. appeal to emotions

_________ 5. Prayer in the schools is like cereal for breakfast. They both get the morning off to a good start.
a. circular reasoning
b. appeal to emotions
c. misleading analogy

_________ 6. The advocate for rezoning of the property concluded by saying, "George Washington was also concerned about land and freedom."
a. transfer
b. *ad hominem*
c. straw person

_______ 7. The explanation for the distribution of grades is simple. College students either study or they do not study.
a. misinterpreted statistics
b. oversimplification
c. appeal to pity

_______ 8. Your written agreement with my position will enable me to keep my job.
a. misinterpreted statistics
b. appeal to pity
c. card stacking

_______ 9. Everyone in the neighborhood has worked on the new park design and agreed to it. Now we need your signature of support.
a. bandwagon
b. appeal to emotions
c. begging the question

_______ 10. Democrats go to Washington to spend money with no regard for the hardworking taxpayer.
a. circular reasoning
b. bandwagon
c. overgeneralization

_______ 11. The suicide rate is highest over the Christmas holidays, which means that Thanksgiving is a safe and happy holiday.
a. misinterpreted statistics
b. card stacking
c. questionable authority

_______ 12. The workers' fingers were swollen and infected, insects walked on their exposed skin, and their red eyes begged for mercy and relief. We all must join their effort.
a. oversimplification
b. appeal to emotions
c. overgeneralization

_______ 13. Our minister, Dr. Johnson, assured the family that our cousin's cancer was a slow-growing one so that a brief delay in treatment would not be detrimental.
a. transfer
b. straw person
c. questionable authority

_______ 14. Crime in this city has been successfully addressed by increasing the number of police officers, seeking neighborhood support against drug dealers, and keeping teenagers off the streets at night. The city is to be commended.
a. misleading analogy
b. incomplete facts
c. misinterpreted statistics

_________ 15. A biology professor cannot possibly advise the swim coach on the placement of swimmers in the different races.
a. *ad hominem*
b. testimonial
c. transfer

Determining What Support Is Missing. Arguments are written to persuade, and thus include the proponent's version of the convincing reasons. Writers do not usually supply the reader with any more than one or two weak points that could be made by the other side. In analyzing an argument, ask yourself, "What is left out?" Be an advocate for the opposing point of view and guess at the evidence that would be presented. Decide if evidence was consciously omitted because of its adverse effect on the conclusion. For example, a businessperson arguing for an increased monthly service fee might neglect to mention how much of the cost is administrative overhead and profit.

Step 4: Evaluate the Argument

Important decisions are rarely quick or easy. A span of incubation time is often needed for deliberating among alternatives. Allow yourself time to go over arguments, weighing the support, and looking at the issues from different perspectives. Good critical thinkers are persistent in seeking solutions.

Diane Halpern expresses the difficulty of decision making by saying, "There is never just one war fought. Each side has its own version, and rarely do they agree."[5] The reader must consider all factors carefully in seeking the truth. Halpern uses a picture of a table and compares the legs of the table to four different degrees of support.

1. Unrelated reasons give no support.
2. A few weak reasons do not adequately support.
3. Many weak reasons can support.
4. Strong related reasons provide support.

Remember, in critical thinking there is no "I'm right, and you are wrong." There are, however, strong and weak arguments. Strong relevant, believable, and consistent reasons build a good argument.

Exercise 9.6

Evaluate Your Own Decision Making

Now that you are familiar with the critical thinking process, analyze your own thinking in making an important recent decision of where to attend college. No college is perfect; many factors must be considered. The issue or conclusion is that you have decided to attend the college where you are now enrolled. List relevant reasons and/or evidence that supported your decision. Evaluate the strength of your reasoning. Are any of your reasons fallacies?

[5]Diane Halpern, *Thought and Knowledge*, 2nd ed. (Hillsdale, NJ: Lawrence Erlbaum, 1989), p. 191.

1. ____
2. ____
3. ____
4. ____
5. ____

How would you evaluate your own critical thinking in making a choice of colleges? Perhaps you relied heavily on information from others. Were those sources credible?

Inductive and Deductive Reasoning

In choosing a college, did you follow an inductive or deductive reasoning process? Did you collect extensive information on several colleges and then weigh the advantages and disadvantages of each? **Inductive reasoners** start by gathering data, and then, after considering all available material, they formulate a conclusion. Textbooks written in this manner give details first and lead you into the main idea or conclusion. They strive to put the parts into a logical whole and thus reason "up" from particular details to a broad generalization.

Deductive reasoners, on the other hand, follow the opposite pattern. They start with the conclusion of a previous experience and apply it to a new situation. Perhaps your college choice is a family tradition; your parents are alumni, and you have always expected to attend. Although your thinking may have begun with this premise for your choice, you may have since discovered many reasons why the college is right for you. When writers use a deductive pattern, they first give a general statement and then enumerate the reasons.

Despite this formal distinction between inductive and deductive reasoning, in real life we switch back and forth as we think. Our everyday observations lead to conclusions that we then reuse and modify to form new conclusions.

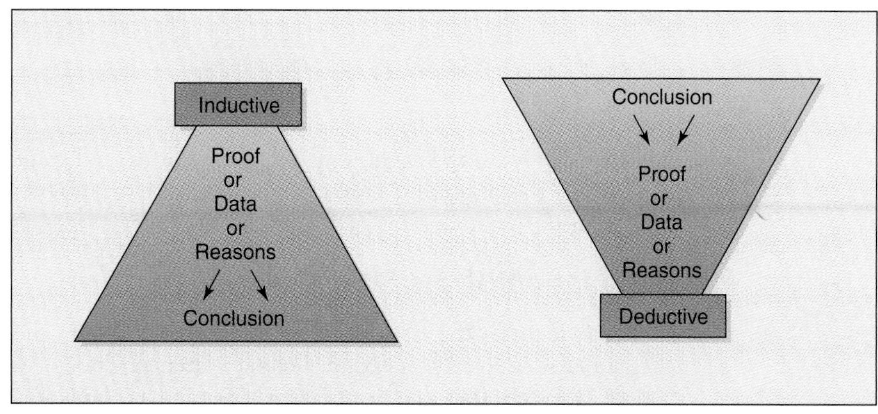

Applying the Four-Step Format for Critical Thinking: An Example

The following is an example of how the four-step format can be used to evaluate an argument. Read the argument, analyze according to the directions for each step, and then read the explanation of how the critical thinking process was applied.

The Argument: Extraterrestrial Life

Surely life exists elsewhere in the universe. After all, most space scientists today admit the possibility that life has evolved on other planets. Besides, other planets in our solar system are strikingly like Earth. They revolve around the sun, they borrow light from the sun, and several are known to revolve on their axes, and to be subject to the same laws of gravitation as Earth. What's more, aren't those who make light of extraterrestrial life soft-headed fundamentalists clinging to the foolish notion that life is unique to their planet?

Joel Rudinow and Vincent Barry, *Invitation to Critical Thinking*, 3rd ed.

- *Step 1:* Identify the issue. What is the topic of this argument and what is the main point the writer is trying to convey? Although many ideas may be included, what is the central concern that is being discussed and supported? Underline the central issue if it is directly stated or write it above the passage if it is implied.
- *Step 2:* Identify the support for the argument. What are the significant supporting details that support the central issue that is being argued? Put brackets at the beginning and end of each assertion of support and number the assertions separately and consecutively. Do not number background information or examples that merely illustrate a point.
- *Step 3:* Evaluate the support. Examine each supporting assertion separately for relevance, believability, and consistency. Can you identify any as fallacies that are intended to sell a weak argument? Also list the type of supporting information that you feel is missing.

  1. ______________________________
  2. ______________________________
  3. ______________________________

  What is missing? ______________________________

- *Step 4:* Evaluate the argument. What is your overall evaluation of the argument? Is the argument convincing? Does the argument provide good reasons and/or evidence for believing the thesis?

Explanation of the Steps

- *Step 1:* Identify the issue. The central issue, assertion, thesis, main point, or conclusion is directly stated in the first sentence. Good critical thinkers would note, however, that "life" is not clearly defined as plant, animal, or human.

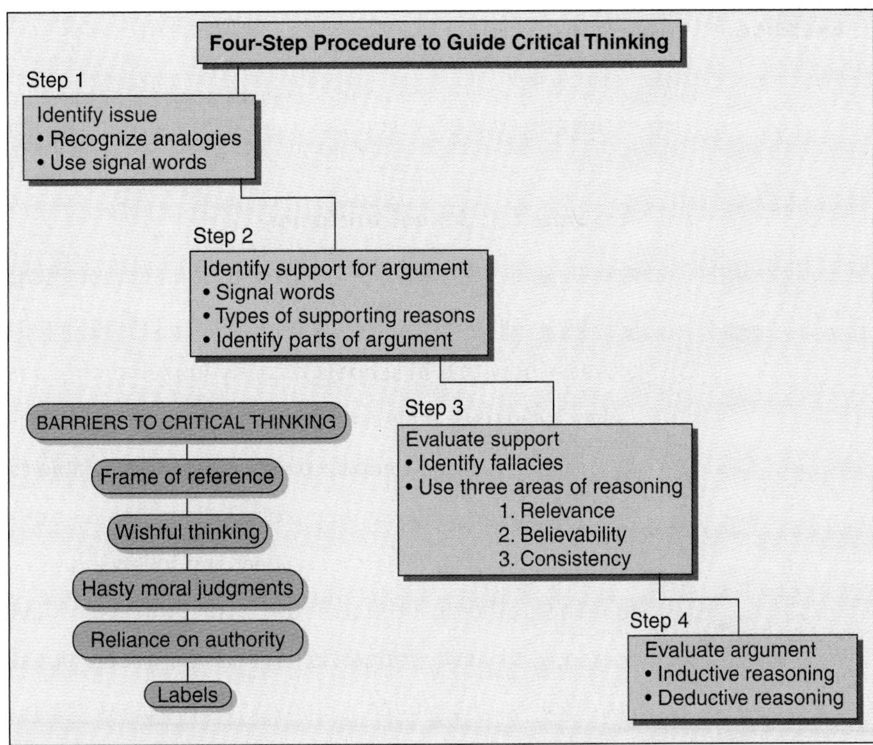

Helen R. Carr, San Antonio College.

- *Step 2:* Identify the support for the argument. This argument contains the three main premises or significant supporting details, which can be numbered as follows:

  1. Space scientists admit the possibility that life has evolved from other planets.
  2. Other planets in our solar system are strikingly like Earth.
  3. Those who make light of extraterrestrial life are soft-headed fundamentalists clinging to the foolish notion that life is unique to this planet.

- *Step 3:* Evaluate the support. The first supporting detail is a vague appeal to authority that does not reveal who "most space scientists" are. Do the scientists work for NASA? The second statement is also vague and presented as a misleading comparison. Other planets may be round, but they have different temperatures and different atmospheres. The third statement is an oversimplified, personal attack on those who may not agree with the argument. Scientific support for this argument seems to be missing.

- *Step 4:* Evaluate the argument. This is not a good argument. There may be good reasons to believe that life exists on other planets, but this argument fails to provide them. The possibility of extraterrestrial life might be argued through statistics from astronomy and a specific definition of "life."

Exercise 9.7

Apply the Steps

Read the following three arguments and apply the four-step format for evaluation. Identify the issue and the support, then evaluate the support and the argument.

Argument 1: School Uniforms

A review of the evidence shows that a mandatory school uniform policy can be a solution to many high school learning and behavior problems. Studies show that in schools recently implementing a mandatory uniform policy, academic achievement has gone up and discipline problems have decreased. With the uniform policy, students are able to spend more time on their studies because they are not distracted by clothing choices. In addition, students who learn to respect and follow a dress code will also learn to respect other institutional rules. The principal of Taylor High School reported, "Our newly found success can be traced directly back to our uniform policy. The students enjoy and appreciate the opportunity to wear our school uniform." In light of this evidence, one can only conclude that denying our students the opportunity for uniforms is denying them academic success.

Joel Rudinow and Vincent E. Barry, *Invitation to Critical Thinking*, 3rd ed.

- *Step 1:* Identify the issue. State or underline the main point or issue the author is arguing.
- *Step 2:* Identify the support for the argument. Put brackets at the beginning and end of each major assertion of support and letter the assertions.
- *Step 3:* Evaluate the support. Examine each supporting assertion for relevance, believability, and consistency. Identify and label any fallacies. List missing support.

____

____

____

____

- *Step 4:* Evaluate the argument. What is your overall evaluation and why?

____

____

Argument 2: Invasion of Privacy

When you call 911 in an emergency, some police departments have a way of telling your telephone number and address without your saying a word. The chief value of this, say the police, is that if the caller is unable to communicate for any reason, the dispatcher knows where to send help. But don't be duped by such paternalistic explanations. This technology is a despicable invasion of privacy, for callers may be unaware of the insidious device. Even if they are, some persons who wish anonymity may be reluctant to call for emergency help. Remember that the names of complainants and witnesses are recorded in many communities' criminal justice systems. A fairer and more effective system seemingly would include an auxiliary number for callers who wish anonymity.

Joel Rudinow and Vincent E. Barry, *Invitation to Critical Thinking,* 3rd ed.

- *Step 1:* Identify the issue. State or underline the main point or issue the author is arguing.
- *Step 2:* Identify the support for the argument. Put brackets at the beginning and end of each major assertion of support and letter the assertions.
- *Step 3:* Evaluate the support. Examine each supporting assertion for relevance, believability, and consistency. Identify and label any fallacies. List missing support.

____

____

____

- *Step 4:* Evaluate the argument. What is your overall evaluation and why?

____

____

Argument 3: Ban Boxing

As a practicing physician, I am convinced that boxing should be banned.

First, boxing is a very visible example that violence is accepted behavior in our society—outside the ring as well as inside. This sends the wrong message to America's youth, and at a time when so many kinds of violence are on the rise, it is a message we should stop.

Second, boxing is the only sport where the sole object is to injure the opponent. Think about what a knockout really is. It is a cerebral concussion that knocks the victim senseless! Boxing, then, is morally offensive because its intent is to inflict brain injuries on another person. And it is medically indefensible because these injuries so often lead to irreversible medical consequences, such as subdural hematoma, nonfatal acute intracranial hemorrhages, "punch drunk syndrome," progressive neurological disorder and serious eye conditions.

Third, medical science can't take someone who has suffered repeated blows to the head and restore that person to normal function. Many physicians, with new methods of brain scanning, have seen an otherwise young and healthy individual sustain serious and permanently disabling injuries due to boxing, sometimes in just one fight. This causes many physicians to conclude that our society should ban boxing. And sadly—slowly but surely—as many of our nationally known veteran boxers can no longer hide the long-term effects of brain injury, the public is beginning to understand what only doctors and family members previously knew.

What about the argument that injuries occur in other sports? Quite simply, in those sports, injuring the opponent is not the accepted method of scoring or winning. And in those sports, there is an attempt to wear protective equipment that will minimize injury. But scientific evidence shows there is no really effective way to prevent boxing injuries that may have a lifetime effect—even from one fight.

And finally, to those who say boxing "gives poor kids an opportunity to get out of the ghetto," I have a better suggestion. Let's take each young person with that precious, undamaged brain and combine some education with that same commitment to excellence he has for boxing. I guarantee that youngster better success over a lifetime—and perhaps a longer and healthier life, too.

Boxing is morally and medically offensive. So as a physician, I believe boxing should be banned.

From Robert E. McAfee, *USA Today*, in *The Language of Argument*, 9th ed., by Daniel McDonald and Larry W. Burton

- *Step 1:* Identify the issue. State or underline the main point or issue the author is arguing.

____

- *Step 2:* Identify the support for the argument. Put brackets at the beginning and end of each major assertion of support and letter the assertions.
- *Step 3:* Evaluate the support. Examine each supporting assertion for relevance, believability, and consistency. Identify and label any fallacies. List missing support.

____

____

____

- *Step 4:* Evaluate the argument. What is your overall evaluation and why?

____

____

Creative and Critical Thinking

A chapter on critical thinking would not be complete without an appeal for creative thinking. You may ask, "Are critical thinking and creative thinking different?" Creative thinking refers to the ability to generate many possible solutions to a problem, whereas critical thinking refers to the examination of those solutions for the selection of the best of all possibilities. Both ways of thinking are essential for good problem solving.

Diane Halpern uses the following story to illustrate creative thinking:[6]

> Many years ago when a person who owed money could be thrown into jail, a merchant in London had the misfortune to owe a huge sum to a money-lender. The money-lender, who was old and ugly, fancied the merchant's beautiful teenage daughter. He proposed a bargain. He said he would cancel the merchant's debt if he could have the girl instead.
>
> Both the merchant and his daughter were horrified at the proposal. So the cunning money-lender proposed that they let Providence decide the matter. He told them that he would put a black pebble and a white pebble into an empty money-bag and then the girl would have to pick out one of the pebbles. If she chose the black pebble she would become his wife and her father's debt would be canceled. If she chose the white pebble she would stay with her father and the debt would still be canceled. But if she refused to pick out a pebble her father would be thrown into jail and she would starve.
>
> Reluctantly the merchant agreed. They were standing on a pebble-strewn path in the merchant's garden as they talked and the money-lender

[6]Halpern, *Thought and Knowledge*, p. 408.

> stooped down to pick up two pebbles. As he picked up the pebbles the girl, sharp-eyed with fright, noticed that he picked up two black pebbles and put them into the money-bag. He then asked the girl to pick out the pebble that was to decide her fate and that of her father.

If you were the girl, what would you do? Think creatively, and, without evaluating your thoughts, list at least five possible solutions. Next think critically to evaluate and then circle your final choice.

1. ______________________________
2. ______________________________
3. ______________________________
4. ______________________________
5. ______________________________

In discussing the possible solutions to the problem, Halpern talks about two kinds of creative thinking, vertical thinking and lateral thinking. **Vertical thinking** is a straightforward and logical way of thinking that would typically result in a solution like, "Call his hand and expose the money-lender as a crook." The disadvantage of this solution is that the merchant is still in debt so the original problem has still not been solved. **Lateral thinking,** on the other hand, is a way of thinking *around* a problem or even redefining the problem. DeBono suggests that a lateral thinker might redefine the problem from "What happens when I get the black pebble?"[7] to "How can I avoid the black pebble?" Using this new definition of the problem and other seemingly irrelevant information, DeBono's lateral thinker came up with a winning solution. When the girl reaches into the bag, she should fumble and drop one of the stones on the "pebble-strewn path." The color of the pebble she dropped could then be determined by looking at the one left in the bag. Since the remaining pebble is black, the dropped one that is now mingled in the path must have been white. Any other admission would expose the money-lender as a crook. Probably the heroine thought of many alternatives, but thanks to her ability ultimately to generate a novel solution and evaluate its effectiveness, the daughter and the merchant lived happily free of debt.

DeBono defines vertical thinking as "digging the same hole deeper" and lateral thinking as "digging the hole somewhere else."[8] For example, after many years of researching a cure for smallpox, Dr. Edward Jenner stopped focusing on patients who were sick with the disease and instead began studying groups of people who never seemed to get the smallpox. Shortly thereafter, using this different perspective, Dr. Jenner discovered the clues that led him to the smallpox vaccine.

---

[7]E. DeBono, *New Think: The Use of Lateral Thinking in the Generation of New Ideas* (New York: Basic Books, 1968), p. 195.

[8]E. DeBono, "Information Processing and New Ideas—Lateral and Vertical Thinking," in S. J. Parnes, R. B. Noller, and A. M. Biondi, eds., *Guide to Creative Action: Revised Edition of Creative Behavior Guidebook* (New York: Scribner's, 1977).

Creative and critical thinking enable us to see new relationships. We blend knowledge and see new similarities and differences, a new sequence of events, or a new solution for an old problem. We create new knowledge by using old learning differently.

Summary Points

- **What is critical thinking?**

  Thinking critically means deliberating in a purposeful, organized manner in order to assess the value of information, both old and new.

- **What are the characteristics of critical thinkers?**

  Critical thinkers are flexible, persistent, and willing to plan and self-correct.

- **What are the barriers to critical thinking?**

  Some people do not allow themselves to think critically because of their frame of reference or because of wishful thinking, hasty moral judgments, reliance on authority, and labeling.

- **Why do critical thinkers have power?**

  Critical thinkers have power because they accept scrutiny and are willing to question and reconsider their opinions.

- **How do critical thinkers analyze an argument?**

  Critical thinkers can use a four-step plan for analyzing an argument: (1) identify the issue; (2) identify the support for the argument; (3) evaluate the support; and (4) evaluate the argument.

- **What is the difference between inductive and deductive reasoners?**

  Inductive reasoners start by gathering data; deductive reasoners start with the conclusion and apply it to a new situation.

- **What does creative thinking add to critical thinking?**

  Creative thinking involves both vertical and lateral thinking.

Selection 1 ESSAY

CONTEMPORARY FOCUS

Does personal appearance affect the way people are treated? Do attractive people have more advantages than their unattractive counterparts? If so, is this a form of discrimination that can be measured and proven?

WHY LOOKS MATTER

Pam Adams

Journal Star (Peoria, IL), June 27, 1999

Mirror, mirror on the wall,
Who's the fairest of them all?

Now come two economists with one explanation for why that evil queen was so obsessed with beauty.

"It pays to be good looking," says Dan Hamermesh, an economist at the University of Texas at Austin and coauthor of several studies provocatively titled "Beauty and the Labor Market," "Beauty and Business Success" and "Business Success and Businesses' Beauty Capital."

Handsome men and pretty women earn more money in the labor market, according to Hamermesh's research. The beauty standard affects men's earnings more than women's; occupation makes little difference—the standard is as true for auto mechanics and lawyers as it is for waiters and car salesmen.

Hamermesh and coauthor Jeff Biddle of Michigan State University tracked the salaries and career paths of 2,500 law school graduates for 15 years. They had four raters judge each graduate's photograph. Though none of them knew the others' ratings, they all agreed on each graduate's attractiveness.

"And as it turned out, the good-looking lawyers got more money, even working in the same kinds of jobs," Hamermesh says of the study, published in the *Journal of Labor Economics* in 1998.

"Interestingly, the difference in earnings between the good-looking lawyers and the ugly lawyers grew over time."

Collaborative Activity

Collaborate on responses to the following questions:

- In what situations have you discriminated according to looks?
- Considering the manner in which lawyers get and do business, what occupational factors might contribute to good-looking lawyers making more money than ugly lawyers?
- If we willingly engage in discrimination according to looks, is this an issue worth worrying about? Why or why not?

Stage 1: Preview

The author seems to be against beauty. Agree ☐ Disagree ☐

Activate Schema

Why are most politicians good looking?

Stage 2: Integrate Knowledge While Reading

Predict Picture Relate Monitor Correct

The Importance of Being Beautiful

From Sidney Katz, in *Motives for Writing*, 3rd ed., Robert Miller, ed.

Unlike many people, I was neither shocked nor surprised when the national Israeli TV network fired a competent female broadcaster because she was not beautiful. I received the news with aplomb because I had just finished extensive research into "person perception," an esoteric branch of psychology that examines the many ways in which physical attractiveness—or lack of it—affects all aspects of your life.

Unless you're a 10—or close to it—most of you will respond to my findings with at least some feelings of frustration or perhaps disbelief. In a nutshell, you can't overestimate the importance of being beautiful. If you're beautiful, without effort you attract hordes of friends and lovers. You are given higher school grades than your smarter—but less appealing—classmates. You compete successfully for jobs against men or women who are better qualified but less alluring. Promotions and pay raises come your way more easily. You are able to go into a bank or store and cash a check with far less hassle than a plain Jane or John. And these are only a few of the many advantages enjoyed by those with a ravishing face and body.

"We were surprised to find that beauty had such powerful effects," confessed Karen Dion, a University of Toronto social psychologist who does person perception research. "Our findings also go against the cultural grain. People like to think that success depends on talent, intelligence, and hard work." But the scientific evidence is undeniable.

In large part, the beautiful person can attribute his or her idyllic life to a puzzling phenomenon that social scientists have dubbed the "halo effect." It defies human reason, but if you resemble Jane Fonda or Paul Newman it's assumed that you're more generous, trustworthy, sociable, modest, sensitive, interesting, and sexually responsive than the rest of us. Conversely, if you're somewhat physically unattractive, because of the "horns effect" you're stigmatized as being mean, sneaky, dishonest, antisocial, and a poor sport to boot.

The existence of the halo/horns effect has been established by several studies. One, by Dion, looked at perceptions of misbehavior in children. Dion provided 243 female university students with identical detailed accounts of the misbehavior of a seven-year-old school child. She described how the youngster had pelted a sleeping dog with sharp stones until its leg bled. As the animal

Multiethnic models present international fashions on the runway for Fashion Week in Florida.
Jeff Greenberg/PhotoEdit

limped away, yelping in pain, the child continued the barrage of stones. The 243 women were asked to assess the seriousness of the child's offense and to give their impression of the child's normal behavior. Clipped to half of the reports were photos of seven-year-old boys or girls who had been rated "high" in physical attractiveness; the other half contained photos of youngsters of "low" attractiveness. "We found," said Dion, "that the opinions of the adults were markedly influenced by the appearance of the children."

One evaluator described the stone thrower, who in her report happened to be an angelic-looking little girl, in these glowing terms: "She appears to be a perfectly charming little girl, well mannered and basically unselfish. She plays well with everyone, but, like everyone else, a bad day may occur . . . Her cruelty need not be taken too seriously." For the same offense, a homely girl evoked this comment from another evaluator: "I think this child would be quite bratty and would be a problem to teachers. She'd probably try to pick a fight with other children . . . She would be a brat at home. All in all, she would be a real problem." The tendency throughout the 243 adult responses was to judge beautiful children as ordinarily well behaved and unlikely to engage in wanton cruelty in the future; the unbeautiful were viewed as being chronically antisocial, untrustworthy, and likely to commit similar transgressions again.

The same standards apply in judging adults. The beautiful are assumed innocent. John Jurens, a colorful private investigator, was once consulted by a small Toronto firm which employed 40 people. Ten thousand dollars' worth of merchandise had disappeared, and it was definitely an inside job. After an intensive investigation, which included the use of a lie detector, Jurens was certain he had caught the thief. She was 24 years old and gorgeous—a lithe princess with high cheekbones, green eyes and shining, long black hair. The employer dismissed Juren's proof with the comment, "You've made a mistake. It just can't be her." Jurens commented sadly, "A lot of people refuse to believe that beautiful can be bad."

David Humphrey, a prominent Ontario criminal lawyer, observed, "If a beautiful woman is on trial, you practically have to show the judge and jury a movie of her committing the crime in order to get a conviction." The halo and horns effect often plays an important role in sentencing by courts. After spending 17 days observing cases heard in an Ontario traffic court, Joan Finegan, a graduate psychology student at the University of Western Ontario, concluded that pleasant and neat-looking defendants were fined an average of $6.31 less than those who were "messy."

Careers

If you're a good-looking male over six feet tall, don't worry about succeeding at your career.

A study of university graduates by the *Wall Street Journal* revealed that well-proportioned wage earners who were six-foot-two or taller earned 12 percent more than men under six feet. "For some reason," explained Ronald Burke, a York University psychologist and industrial consultant, "tall men are assumed to be dynamic, decisive, and powerful. In other words, born leaders." A Toronto consultant for Drake Personnel, one of the largest employment agencies in Canada, recalled trying to find a sales manager for an industrial firm. He sent four highly qualified candidates, only to have them all turned down. "The fifth guy I sent over was different," said the consultant. "He stood six-foot-four. He was promptly hired."

The well-favored woman also has a distinct edge when it comes to getting a job she's after. "We send out three prospects to be interviewed, and it's almost always the most glamorous one that's hired," said Edith Geddes of the Personnel Centre, a Toronto agency that specializes in female placements. "We sometimes feel bad because the best qualified person is not chosen." Dr. Pam Ennis, a consultant to several large corporations, observed. "Look at the photos announcing promotions in the *Globe and Mail* business section. It's no accident that so many of the women happen to be attractive and sexy-looking." Ennis, an elegant woman herself, attributes at least part of her career success to good looks. Her photograph appears on the brochures she mails out to companies soliciting new clients. "About eight out of 10 company presidents give me an appointment," she said. "I'm sure that many of them are curious to see me in person. Beauty makes it easier to establish rapport."

Old Age

An elderly person's attractiveness influences the way in which he or she is treated in nursing homes and hospitals. Doctors and nurses give better care to the beautiful ones.

Lena Nordholm, an Australian behavioral scientist, presented 289 doctors, nurses, social workers, speech therapists, and physiotherapists with photos of eight attractive and unattractive men and women. They were asked to speculate about what kind of patients they would be. The good-lookers were judged to be more cooperative, better motivated, and more likely to improve than their less attractive counterparts. Pam Ennis, the consultant, commented, "Because the doctor feels that beautiful patients are more likely to respond to his treatment, he'll give them more time and attention."

We like to think we have moved beyond the era when the most desirable woman was the beauty queen, but we haven't. Every day we make assumptions about the personality of the bank teller, the delivery man, or the waitress by their looks. The way in which we attribute good and bad characteristics still has very little to do with fact. People seldom look beyond a pleasing façade, a superficial attractiveness. But the professors of person perception are not discouraged by this. They want to educate us. Perhaps by arming us with the knowledge and awareness of why we discriminate against the unattractive, we'll learn how to prevent this unwitting bigotry. Just maybe, we can change human nature.

Stage 3: Recall

Stop to self-test, relate, and react.

Skill Development: Critical Thinking

Apply the four-step format for evaluating the argument. Use the perforations to tear out and hand this page to your instructor.

- *Step 1:* Identify the issue. State the main point or issue the author is arguing.

  ____

- *Step 2:* Identify the support for the argument. List and letter each major assertion of support.

  ____

  ____

  ____

  ____

  ____

  ____

  ____

  ____

  ____

  ____

- *Step 3:* Evaluate the support. Comment on weaknesses in relevance, believability, and consistency for the assertions listed above. Label the fallacies.

  ____

  ____

  ____

  ____

  What support do you feel is missing? ______________________

  ____

- *Step 4:* Evaluate the argument. What is your overall evaluation and why?

  ____

  ____

  What is your opinion on the issue? ______________________

  ____

Thinking About "The Importance of Being Beautiful"

How do you plan to use the ideas from this selection to your benefit and apply the author's documented awareness of discrimination according to looks? Discuss this from two points of view: the way you manage yourself and the way you manage others.

Contemporary Link

Both authors of the selections presented here seek to prove their arguments by quantifying or measuring unequal treatment according to looks. Review their research studies, and then devise a research study of your own to prove the argument that attractive students are given better grades than their smarter but less attractive counterparts. Design your study to account for different levels of ability.

Comprehension Questions

Answer the following questions about the selection.

1. Why do we like to believe that success depends on talent, intelligence, and hard work? ______________________

2. How does the study of the misbehaving seven-year-old prove the existence of the halo/horns effect? ______________________

   ____

   ____

3. What does the phrase, "you're a 10" mean? ______________________________

4. What evidence shows that the beautiful are treated differently in legal matters? ______________________________

5. Why do you think tall men are assumed to be born leaders?

6. What does the author mean by "Beauty makes it easier to establish rapport"?

7. For the elderly, why can looks be a life-and-death matter?

Search the Net

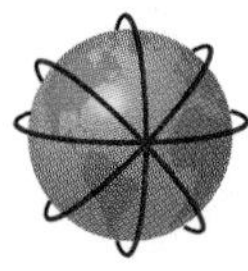

- Art illustrates how concepts of beauty have changed over hundreds of years. Search the Internet for examples of artistic depictions of beauty in previous centuries and choose two time periods to compare and contrast.

  The Mayan beauty ideal: http://www.beautyworlds.com/mayans.htm

  History of women through art: http://www.wic.org/artwork/idex_art.htm

- Are there cultural variations in today's perceptions and definitions of beauty? Locate the Websites of two fashion magazines that target different cultural groups. Compare and contrast how beauty is portrayed for the group by each magazine, using specific examples such as hairstyles, body types, and clothing.

  Essence: http://www.essence.com/

  Cosmopolitan: http://www.cosmomag.com/

  Latina Magazine: http://www.latina.com/

Selection 2 EDITORIAL ESSAY

CONTEMPORARY FOCUS

Thomas Sowell, a noted American scholar, writes newspaper columns, has taught at Cornell University, UCLA, and Stanford, and has written more than thirty books on economics, ethnicity, and education. In one of his columns, he has written that students are taught to express their opinions on topics and issues even before the ideas are fully explored and developed. How does his life as revealed in his new book, *A Personal Odyssey,* reflect his beliefs? Does Sowell have the credentials to express opinions about teaching?

PRACTICING WHAT HE PREACHES

James W. Michaels

Forbes, October 2, 2000

The Oxford dictionary defines *odyssey* as "a series of adventurous journeys marked by many changes of fortune." Tom's odyssey was all of that. It began 70 years ago in Charleston, S.C., in a little frame house that lacked electricity and indoor plumbing. Tom was raised by a barely literate great-aunt, his father having died before he was born and his mother too poor to support a fifth child on a domestic's earnings.

By the time the journey concludes at the Hoover Institution in Palo Alto, Calif., he is Dr. Thomas Sowell, public figure, newspaper columnist and author of such splendid books as *A Conflict of Visions*. The voyage from the Jim Crow South to intellectual eminence involved bloody noses, a home for wayward boys, a near court-martial, unemployment, a busted marriage, brushes with southern racists and abuse from white liberals and black politicians.

Of his critics, including many self-anointed black leaders, Sowell says: "I lived through experiences they can only theorize about." A chapter in one of his books is entitled "The Economics of Discrimination." But he never forgot a warning given him by a beloved professor of English at Howard University when Sowell was leaving the all-black institution for Harvard: If you flunk out, the prof told him, "Don't come back here and tell me you didn't make it because white folks were mean."

With his somewhat spotty early education, Sowell did nearly flunk out of Harvard. He had two Fs and two Ds in his first semester. Instead of feeling sorry for himself, Sowell hit the books hard. He graduated *magna cum laude*.

Collaborative Activity

Collaborate on responses to the following questions:

- What does the author mean by "Jim Crow South"?
- Why is it unusual that Sowell would have conflicts with a combination of white racists, white liberals, and black politicians?
- What does it mean to graduate *magna cum laude?*

Stage 1: Preview

The author seems to be giving his opinion. Agree ☐ Disagree ☐

Activate Schema

Have you ever written a letter to an author?

Stage 2: Integrate Knowledge While Reading

Predict Picture Relate Monitor Correct

STUDENTS LED TO BELIEVE OPINIONS MORE IMPORTANT THAN KNOWLEDGE

Thomas Sowell, *Arizona Republic*, August 18, 1998. By permission of Thomas Sowell and Creators Syndicate, Inc.

Reaching the public also means that the public reaches you. My mail ranges from fan mail to hate mail. But there is a special kind of letter that bothers me more than the most idiotic obscenities.

That is the letter from some teenager (or younger) who is writing because his school has led him to believe that he ought to have opinions on some **issue** or other—and ought to express those opinions to strangers he has read about and expect those strangers to take up their time discussing his opinions.

A single word in a recent letter from a 15-year-old boy epitomized what is so wrong with such premature presumption. He said that American military leaders "over-estimated" the casualties that would have resulted from an invasion of Japan in World War II, so that we were unjustified in dropping the atomic bomb instead.

This particular issue is not the point. The point is that people expect to have their opinions taken seriously just because these are their opinions.

Here is someone with no military training or experience, much less achievements, blithely second-guessing General Douglas MacArthur, who served in the military more than twice as long as this kid has been in the world. Here is someone in the safety and comfort of a classroom issuing pronouncements about assessments made by someone who fought on the battlefields of two world wars and left a record of stunning victories with low casualties that have caused him to be ranked among the great military minds in history.

If this were just one kid who has gotten too big for his britches, then it would only be a small part of the passing parade of human foibles. But schoolchildren all across the country are being encouraged or assigned to engage in letter-writing campaigns, taking up the time of people ranging from journalists

Thomas Sowell is a senior fellow at Stanford University's Hoover Institution.
James D. Wilson/Getty Images

to congressmen and presidents. Worse, these pupils are led to believe that having opinions is more important than knowing what you are talking about.

Few things are more dangerous than articulate superficiality. Glib demagogues have been the curse of the twentieth century and tens of millions of human beings have paid with their lives for the heady visions and clever talk of political egotists. Yet the danger is not that a particular child will follow in the footsteps of Lenin, Hitler, or Mao. The danger is that great numbers of people will never know what it is to know, as distinguished from sounding off. They will be sitting ducks for the demagogues of their times.

If our so-called educators cannot be bothered to teach our children knowledge and logic, they can at least refrain from undermining the importance of knowledge and logic by leading students to believe that how you feel and express yourself are what matter.

It takes considerable knowledge just to realize the extent of your own ignorance. Back in 1982, when I began an international study of peoples and cultures, I planned to write a chapter on India. It was only after reading books about India, visiting India twice and talking with Indian scholars, officials, businessmen, and journalists that I realized what a monumental job it would be to write about this vast and complex society.

Although my study took 15 years and resulted in three books, there was no chapter on India. I realized that I didn't know enough to write one.

Assigning students to write letters and papers on vast topics is training them in irresponsibility. It is putting the cart before the horse. There will never be a shortage of ignorant audacity. What is always scarce is thorough knowledge and carefully reasoned analysis, systematically checked against factual evidence.

Our education-is-fun approach is setting up the next generation to be patsies for any political manipulator who knows how to take advantage of their weaknesses. Educators who are constantly chirping about how this or that is "exciting" ignore the reality that education is not about how you feel at the moment but how well the young are being prepared for future responsibilities.

Classroom letter-writing assignments are not just silliness. They are a dangerous betrayal of the young and an abdication of adult responsibility by self-indulgent teachers.

Stage 3: Recall

Stop to self-test, relate, and react.

Skill Development: Critical Thinking

Apply the four-step format for evaluating the argument. Use the perforations to tear out and hand the page to your instructor.

- *Step 1:* Identify the issue. State the main point or issue the author is arguing.

____

____

- *Step 2:* Identify the support for the argument. List and letter each major assertion of support.

____

____

____

____

____

____

- *Step 3:* Evaluate the support. Comment on weaknesses in relevance, believability, and consistency for the assertions listed above. Label the fallacies.

____

____

____

____

What support do you feel is missing?

____

____

- *Step 4:* Evaluate the argument. What is your overall evaluation and why?

  ____

  ____

  What is your opinion?

  ____

  ____

  ____

Thinking About "Students Led to Believe Opinions More Important Than Knowledge"

Why does Sowell believe that it is particularly dangerous to be both articulate and superficial?

Contemporary Link

From what you can gather about Sowell in both selections, give specific examples of how Sowell practices what he preaches. Why do you think his work has stirred controversy?

Comprehension Questions

Answer the following questions about the selection.

1. What prompted the writing of this editorial? ______________________________

   ____

2. What does the author mean by "They will be sitting ducks for the demagogues of their times"? ______________________________

   ____

3. Why does the author feel letter-writing assignments are "a dangerous betrayal of the young"? ______________________________

   ____

4. Would you describe the author's views as liberal or conservative? Explain.

   ____

   ____

5. Define the following phrases as used by the author:

   idiotic obscenities ____________________

   epitomized what is so wrong ____________________

   blithely second-guessing ____________________

   human foibles ____________________

   articulate superficiality ____________________

   glib demagogues ____________________

   ignorant audacity ____________________

Search the Net

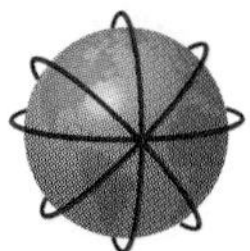

Thomas Sowell is a syndicated columnist whose editorials appear in many newspapers around the country. Conduct a search to find out more about his work.

- List the title and briefly describe the contents of one of his books.
- Locate and read another of his editorials. Briefly summarize his message.

Selection 3 EDITORIAL ESSAY

CONTEMPORARY FOCUS

The market for human eggs is largely unregulated and the subject of a variety of ethical issues that stir controversy. Should women be paid for egg donations, and, if so, how much? How much choice should consumers, the infertile couples, have in the purchase of eggs? Since more eggs are fertilized than are usually needed, what happens to the leftover eggs? Should they be used in stem cell research to seek cures for spinal injuries and diseases? The list of questions, like the technological possibilities, seems endless.

THE ETHICS OF EGGS

Brenda D. Smith

An advertisement in an Ivy League college newspaper requested the eggs of a tall, athletic coed with high SAT scores for a payment of $50,000. Is this an easy way to make money or does it entail the stress, work, and worry that is normally associated with earning a large sum of money?

To participate in the process, women who "donate" eggs must make frequent visits to doctors at designated fertility clinics. These women receive daily hormone injections, experience bloated ovaries, and endure several minor surgeries to extract the eggs. Aside from these physical challenges, the donor never knows if she became a biological mother with one or several children or if her eggs still exist for future use.

The ownership of the eggs resides exclusively with the couples who purchased them from the donors. In the in vitro fertilization process, eggs are fertilized outside a woman's body and after three to five days are either used or stored. Some of the stored eggs are later used by the infertile couple for additional fertility attempts or to create more children. Some eggs are donated to other infertile couples, some are discarded, and some are stored indefinitely. At present, thousands of embryos are stored at 200 degrees below zero in fertility centers at a cost to a couple of $100 a year. Many couples are reluctant to destroy these eggs.

Collaborative Activity

Collaborate on responses to the following questions:

- What is the ethical difference in randomly receiving an egg and selecting an egg for IQ and attractiveness?
- Would it bother you to know that you had unknown biological offspring?

Stage 1: Preview

The listed opinions of the experts probably differ. Agree ☐ Disagree ☐

Activate Schema

Would you sell your eggs or sperm for reproductive technology?

Stage 2: Integrate Knowledge While Reading

Predict Picture Relate Monitor Correct

MARKETING FERTILITY

From Sheila Cooper and Rosemary Patton, *Writing Logically, Thinking Critically with Readings*

A married woman of 63 gives birth to a daughter fathered by her husband with another woman's egg. A single woman of 51 delivers her first child, a son created from a donor egg and a donor sperm nurtured in her uterus. A small industry has grown up around women who serve as surrogate mothers. Using frozen sperm, doctors help men give life after they have died. In Boston, a man citing "wrongful birth" sued his ex-wife for conceiving a child by implanting a frozen embryo fertilized before their divorce and then demanding child support. Beyond in vitro fertilization, considered almost routine today, a mother can order a custom-tailored embryo, even select a child's sex. Fertilized eggs, frozen and waiting, are now available for "adoption."

TOLES. © "The Buffalo News". Reprinted with permission of UNIVERSAL PRESS SYNDICATE. All rights reserved.

Fertility for Sale

[The following section is from "Life by Design; Fertility for Sale," Editorial Desk, *The New York Times*, March 4, 1998. Copyright © 1998 by The New York Times Co. Reprinted by permission.]

As donor eggs become a valuable commodity, the controversy over the price tag and also the health risks is heating up. Here, experts discuss whether or not women should be able to sell their eggs. As reproductive technology has advanced, the law of supply and demand has inevitably clicked in. Some clinics have had trouble finding women to donate their eggs for implantation in infertile women. That has led to a medical and ethical debate over whether donors should charge for their eggs and, if so, how much. The St. Barnabas Medical Center in Livingston, N.J., recently accelerated that debate by offering $5,000 for donors, double the rate of many clinics. A variety of experts were asked whether women should be permitted to sell their eggs on the open market:

Robert Wright is the author of "The Moral Animal: Evolutionary Psychology and Everyday Life."

Is a woman who gets several thousand dollars for a few eggs being exploited? The claim is not on its face ridiculous; a donor undergoes an unpleasant and risky procedure that is invasive both physically and in a less tangible sense. What is ridiculous is the idea that the woman is more exploited if she gets $5,000 than if she gets $2,000. Yet that is the implicit logic of some who argue for limiting fees lest we degrade women by turning their eggs into commodities.

Critics of high fees say it's all right to compensate donors, just not to entice them. But that distinction faded years ago, when infertile women began paying more than a few dollars for eggs. They found that if they didn't pay real money, they'd get no eggs. This is the market at work: a willing buyer, a willing seller. Is there any reason to get between them?

Cynthia Gorney is the author of "Articles of Faith: A Frontline History of the Abortion Wars."

Galloping technology and the escalating hopes of infertile couples are working together to push us much too far, too fast. There has got to be a point at which society declares to the infertile couple: We are sorry for your situation, but you cannot buy everything you want. We will not let you offer that young woman $10,000 for some of her eggs, just as we will not let you offer her brother $10,000 for one of his kidneys. The potential cost to both of them—and to all the rest of us—is too high.

Lee M. Silver, a biology professor at Princeton, is the author of "Remaking Eden: Cloning and Beyond in a Brave New World."

Why are physicians and bioethicists—who are mostly male—trying to limit monetary compensation to women who donate their eggs? In no other part of the economy do we limit the amount of money that can be paid to people who participate in risky or demeaning activities. Indeed, college students have long been enticed by high fees into participating in risky medical experiments.

But society expects women to be altruistic, not venal. And it insists that women be protected from themselves, on the assumption that they are unable to make rational decisions about their own bodies. And perhaps men feel threatened by the idea that women now also have a way to spread their seed upon the earth.

Elizabeth Bartholet, a professor at Harvard Law School, is the author of "Family Bonds: Adoption and the Politics of Parenting."

The selling of human eggs puts at risk the donors' health and sacrifices their human dignity. It also encourages women to bear children who are not genetically related to them, so that their mates can have genetic offspring. This practice produces children who have lost one genetic parent—in a world that already has an abundance of orphans who need homes.

We need to call a halt to further commercialization of reproduction to give policy makers a chance to consider the ethical issues involved in reproductive technology like egg selling, cloning and sex selection. We should follow the lead of other countries and establish a national commission to resolve these issues rather than leave them to the market.

Lori Arnold is a doctor at the Fertility and I.V.F. Center of Miami.

Most women who donate their eggs at our clinic do so because they want to help provide the gift of life. Many have children of their own: they want to help others experience the joys of motherhood.

The motive is altruistic, but that should not blind anyone to the practical difficulties. Donors are required to undergo treatment with fertility drugs, counseling, screening, ultrasound monitoring, blood work and numerous office visits. It takes weeks. And retrieving the eggs from their ovaries is a surgical procedure.

Also worth factoring in is that the donors are giving a couple the chance to have a family, with a child who has the father's genetic makeup. The donor also gives the recipient a chance to experience pregnancy, delivery and breastfeeding, thereby facilitating mother-baby bonding.

Thus compensation given to an egg donor is well deserved. Of course, there comes a point when a fee becomes self-defeating, since the cost is paid by the recipient—few couples can afford to pay an unlimited amount. But donors deserve something more than a token. Ours receive $1,500 to $2,000: no one should begrudge them that.

Stage 3: Recall

Stop to self-test, relate, and react.

Skill Development: Critical Thinking

In this selection, five different arguments are given in response to the question, "Should women be permitted to sell their eggs on the open market?" For each response, state the argument and list the support. Evaluate the strength of the support and overall argument.

1. Robert Wright

   Argument: ____________________

   Support: ____________________

   ____

   Evaluation: ____________________

2. Cynthia Gorney

   Argument: ____________________

   Support: ____________________

   Evaluation: ____________________

3. Lee M. Silver

   Argument: ____________________

   Support: ____________________

   ____

   ____

   ____

   Evaluation: ____________________

4. Elizabeth Bartholet

   Argument: ____________________

   Support: ____________________

   ____

   Evaluation: ____________________

5. Lori Arnold

   Argument: ____________________

   Support: ____________________

   ____

   ____

   Evaluation: ____________________

6. If your name were added to the selection with a sixth response, what would you argue? State your argument and list support for your position.

Contemporary Link

What do you feel are five important ethical questions concerning in vitro fertilization, the donations of eggs and sperm, and the future of unused eggs? List the five questions and state your opinions in response to each.

Comprehension Questions

Answer the following questions about the selection.

1. Other than egg donors, who else can potentially profit from the new reproductive technology?

2. What does Robert Wright mean by saying that critics agree with compensation but not enticement?

3. In both Silver's and Arnold's responses, the word *altruistic* is used. What does this word mean and how does it relate to the issue?

4. How does Elizabeth Bartholet's response reflect her occupation?

5. Why would you expect Lori Arnold's reply to be positive?

Search the Net

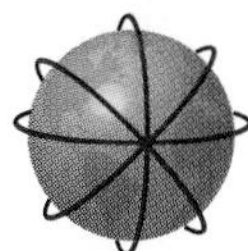

- Infertile couples who would like to have children can turn to many resources—including infertility clinics, egg donation, surrogacy, adoption, and others. Investigate two of these options in order to compare and contrast the costs and benefits of each. Consider financial, ethical, medical, or psychological issues in your discussion.

  Infertility resources: http://www.ihr.com/infertility/

  Fertilitext: http://www.fertilitext.org/

- In vitro fertilization is one method of treating fertility problems. Search the Internet for factors that affect the success rate of this method. Describe the process and discuss the success factors.

  NYU Medical Center: http://www.nyuivf.com/stats/stats.html

  The World Medical Association: http://www.wma.net/e/policy/17-n_e.html

READER'S JOURNAL

Name ______________________ Date __________

CHAPTER 9

Answer the following questions to learn about your own learning and reflect on your progress. Use the perforations to tear the assignment out for your instructor.

1. Before reading this chapter, what was your definition of critical thinking?
____
____

2. How has your definition changed? ______________________
____
____

3. Would you like to be a lawyer or to be on a college debating team? Why or why not?______________________
____
____

4. Recall a recent conversation in which a position was supported with fallacious thinking. What was the fallacy that was most used? __________
____
____

5. How do you think you will use critical thinking when you have graduated from college? Give an example at work and an example in your personal life. ______________________
____
____

6. What fallacies do you use the most when you argue with your parents?
____
____

7. What is your strongest barrier to critical thinking? Explain. __________
____
____

10

Graphic Illustrations

- What do graphics do?
- What is a diagram?
- What does a table do?
- What is most helpful on a typical map?
- What does a pie graph represent?
- How do you read a bar graph?
- What is a line graph?
- What information does a flowchart convey?

Now Cow-Vinox Cake *(detail) by Giovanopoulos. Acrylic on canvas, 63 × 48". © 1986 Paul Giovanopoulos.*

What Graphics Do

If a picture is worth a thousand words, a graphic illustration is worth at least several pages of facts and figures. Graphics express complex interrelationships in simplified form. Instead of plodding through repetitious data, you can glance at a chart, a map, or a graph and immediately see how everything fits together as well as how one part compares with another. Instead of reading several lengthy paragraphs and trying to visualize comparisons, you can study an organized design. The graphic illustration is a logically constructed aid for understanding many small bits of information.

Graphic illustrations are generally used for the following reasons:

1. **To condense.** Pages of repetitious, detailed information can be organized into one explanatory design.
2. **To clarify.** Processes and interrelationships can be more clearly defined through visual representations.
3. **To convince.** Developing trends and gross inequities can be forcefully dramatized.

There are five kinds of graphic illustrations: (1) diagrams, (2) tables, (3) maps, (4) graphs, and (5) flowcharts. All are used in textbooks, and the choice of which is best to use depends on the type of material presented. This chapter contains explanations and exercises for five types of graphic illustrations. Read the explanations, study the illustrations, and respond to the questions as instructed.

Diagrams

A *diagram* is an outline drawing or picture of an object or a process. It shows the labeled parts of a complicated form such as the muscles of the human body, the organizational makeup of a company's management and production teams, or the flow of nutrients in a natural ecological system.

Exercise 10.1

Diagrams

The diagrams shown on page 433 display the major structures of the human ear. Refer to the diagrams to respond to the following items with *T* (true), *F* (false), or *CT* (can't tell).

_________ 1. Sound enters the ear through the auditory canal.
_________ 2. The cochlea can be seen by looking through the auditory canal.
_________ 3. Sound travels through the cochlea to the auditory nerve.

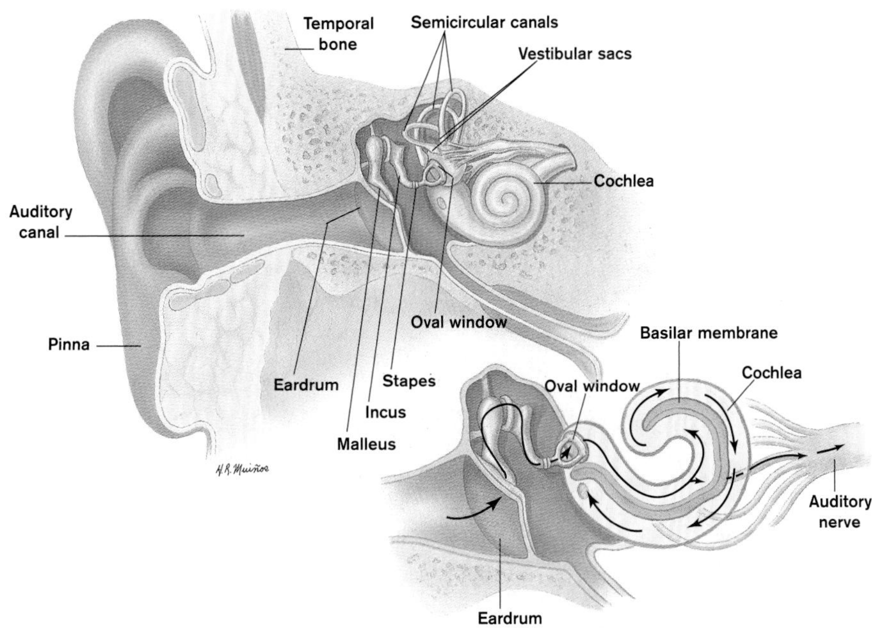

The Major Structures of the Human Ear
Illustration on page 90, Psychology: An Introduction *by Josh R. Gerow. © 1997 Addison-Wesley Educational Publishers Inc.*

________ 4. Most hearing problems result from damage to the eardrum.
________ 5. The nerves in the pinna conduct sound directly to the oval window.
________ 6. The basilar membrane is a part of the cochlea.
________ 7. The malleus, incus, and stapes are positioned to transmit sound from the eardrum to the oval window.
________ 8. According to the diagram, the semicircular canals contain the basilar membrane.
________ 9. If punctured, the eardrum cannot be adequately repaired.
________ 10. The cochlea could be described as snail-like in appearance.

11. The purpose of each diagram is ____________________

____

Tables

A *table* is a listing of facts and figures in columns and rows for quick and easy reference. The information in the columns and rows is usually labeled in two different directions. First read the title for the topic and then read the footnotes to judge the source. Determine what each column represents and how they interact.

Reader's Tip

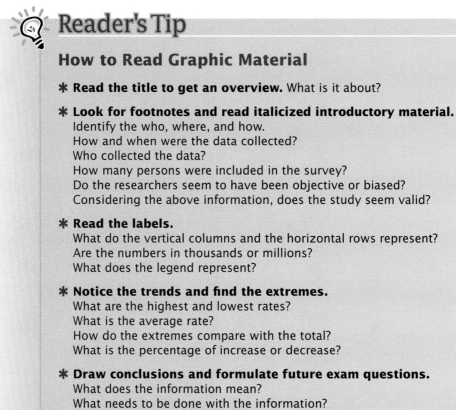

How to Read Graphic Material

* **Read the title to get an overview.** What is it about?
* **Look for footnotes and read italicized introductory material.**
  Identify the who, where, and how.
  How and when were the data collected?
  Who collected the data?
  How many persons were included in the survey?
  Do the researchers seem to have been objective or biased?
  Considering the above information, does the study seem valid?
* **Read the labels.**
  What do the vertical columns and the horizontal rows represent?
  Are the numbers in thousands or millions?
  What does the legend represent?
* **Notice the trends and find the extremes.**
  What are the highest and lowest rates?
  What is the average rate?
  How do the extremes compare with the total?
  What is the percentage of increase or decrease?
* **Draw conclusions and formulate future exam questions.**
  What does the information mean?
  What needs to be done with the information?
  What wasn't included?
  Where do we go from here?

Exercise 10.2

Tables

Refer to the tables shown on page 435 to respond to the following with *T* (true), *F* (false), or *CT* (can't tell). Note the amounts being compared, the average, and the range.

_________ 1. Decaffeinated brewed coffee contains no caffeine.

_________ 2. Imported brands of brewed tea can range higher in caffeine than U.S. brands.

_________ 3. The amount of iced tea measured for caffeine was the same as the amount of brewed tea.

_________ 4. On the average, two ounces of dark chocolate contains more caffeine than two ounces of milk chocolate.

_________ 5. A twelve-ounce serving of Coca-Cola has more caffeine than an equal serving of Pepsi.

_________ 6. On the average, iced tea has more caffeine than an equal amount of Coca-Cola.

Caffeine in Beverages and Foods

Item	Caffeine (mg) Average	Range
Coffee (5-oz. cup)		
Brewed, drip method	115	60–180
Brewed, percolator	80	40–170
Instant	65	30–120
Decaffeinated, brewed	3	2–5
Decaffeinated, instant	2	1–5
Tea (5-oz.cup)		
Brewed, major U.S. brands	40	20–90
Brewed, imported brands	60	25–110
Instant	30	25–50
Iced (12-oz. glass)	70	67–76
Cocoa beverage (5-oz. cup)	4	2–20
Chocolate milk beverage (8-oz. glass)	5	2–7
Milk chocolate (1 oz.)	6	1–15
Dark chocolate, semisweet (1 oz.)	20	5–35
Baker's chocolate (1 oz.)	26	26
Chocolate-flavored syrup (1 oz.)	4	4

Caffeine in Popular Soft Drinks

Brand	Caffeine (mg)*
Sugar-Free Mr. Pibb	58.8
Mountain Dew	54.0
Mello Yello	52.8
Tab	46.8
Coca-Cola	45.6
Diet Coke	45.6
Shasta Cola	44.4
Mr. Pibb	40.8
Dr. Pepper	39.6
Big Red	38.4
Pepsi-Cola	38.4
Diet Pepsi	36.0
Pepsi Light	36.0
RC Cola	36.0
Diet Rite	36.0
Canada Dry Jamaica Cola	30.0
Canada Dry Diet Cola	1.2

*Per 12-oz. serving

Source: From Oakley Ray and Charles Ksir, *Drugs, Society, and Human Behavior.*

_________ 7. In equal amounts, brewed coffee has over twice as much caffeine as a Canada Dry Jamaica Cola.

_________ 8. The caffeine is easier to put in dark drinks and food as opposed to lighter ones.

_________ 9. On the average, instant tea and coffee contain less caffeine than their brewed counterparts.

_________ 10. Mello Yello is light in color and thus most people assume that it does not contain caffeine.

11. The purpose of each table is ______________________________

____

Maps

Traditional *maps,* such as road maps and atlas maps, show the location of cities, waterways, sites, and roads, as well as the differences in the physical terrain of specified areas. A modern use of the map as a visual aid is to highlight special characteristics or population distributions of a particular area. For example, a map of the United States might highlight all states with gun control laws in red and all states without gun control laws in blue.

Begin reading a map by noting the title, source, and date. The legend of a map, which usually appears in a corner box, explains the meanings of symbols and shading.

Exercise 10.3

Maps

Use the legend on the map shown on page 437 to help you respond to the following with *T* (true), *F* (false), or *CT* (can't tell).

_________ 1. In Arizona less than 4 percent of all businesses are owned by foreign corporations.

_________ 2. In Kentucky more than 6 percent of all businesses are owned by foreign corporations.

_________ 3. Georgia has a higher percentage of foreign-owned businesses than Texas.

_________ 4. Georgia has a higher number of foreign-owned businesses than Texas.

_________ 5. Florida has more foreign-owned businesses than Alabama and Mississippi combined.

_________ 6. In all states that border the ocean, at least 4 percent of all businesses are foreign owned.

_________ 7. California and New York have the same percentage of foreign-owned businesses.

_________ 8. Most of the states with a higher than average percentage of foreign-owned businesses are in the east.

_________ 9. Hawaii has the highest number of foreign-owned businesses because it is an island.

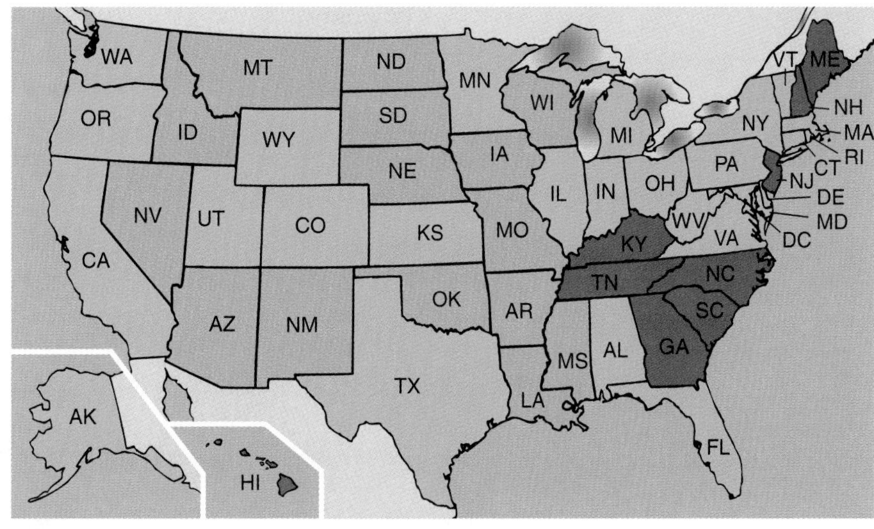

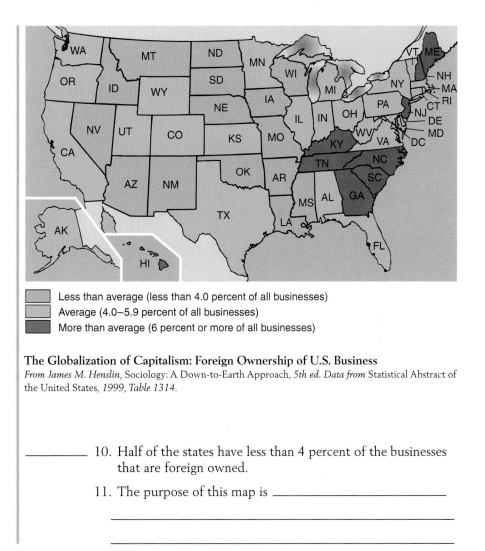

Less than average (less than 4.0 percent of all businesses)
Average (4.0–5.9 percent of all businesses)
More than average (6 percent or more of all businesses)

The Globalization of Capitalism: Foreign Ownership of U.S. Business
From James M. Henslin, Sociology: A Down-to-Earth Approach, *5th ed. Data from* Statistical Abstract of the United States, *1999, Table 1314.*

________ 10. Half of the states have less than 4 percent of the businesses that are foreign owned.

11. The purpose of this map is ____________________

____

____

Exercise 10.4

Geographic Review

Use the map on page 438 to test your knowledge of world geography.

Citizens of the World Show Little Knowledge of Geography

In the spring of 1988, twelve thousand people in ten nations were asked to identify sixteen places on the following world map. The average citizen in the United States could identify barely more than half. Believe it or not, 14 percent of Americans tested could not even find their own country on the map. Despite years of fighting in Vietnam, 68 percent could not locate this Southeast Asian country. Such lack of basic geographic knowledge is quite common throughout the world. Here is the average score for each of the ten countries in which the test was administered.

Country	Average Score
1 Sweden	11.6
2 West Germany	11.2
3 Japan	9.7
4 France	9.3
5 Canada	9.2
6 United States	8.6
7 Britain	8.5
8 Italy	7.6
9 Mexico	7.4
10 Former Soviet Union	7.4

How would you do? To take the test yourself, match the numbers on the map to the places listed.

Robert L. Lineberry et al., *Government in America*

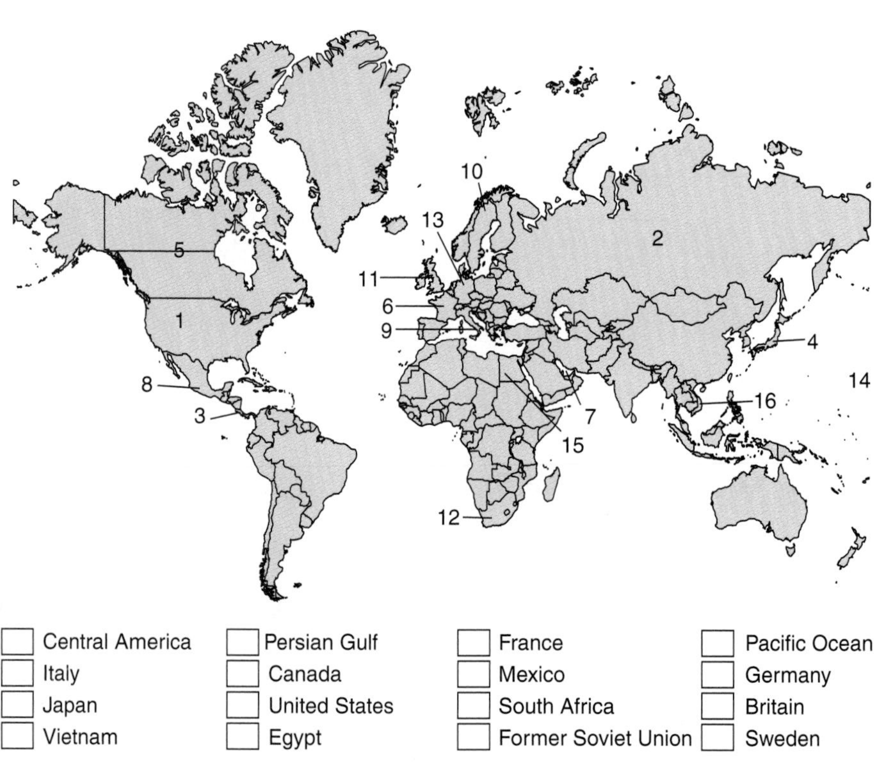

From Warren E. Leary. "Two Superpowers' Citizens Do Badly in Geography." New York Times, *November 9, 1989, A6.*

Pie Graphs

A *pie graph* is a circle that is divided into wedge-shaped slices. The complete pie or circle represents a total, or 100 percent. Each slice is a percent or fraction of that whole. Budgets, such as the annual expenditure of the federal or state governments, are frequently illustrated by pie graphs.

Exercise 10.5

Pie Graphs

Refer to the pie graph below to respond to the following statements with *T* (true), *F* (false), or *CT* (can't tell). To assist you in reading the chart, an *entrepreneur* starts and manages new businesses, and *serendipitously* means discovering something by chance that you were not looking for.

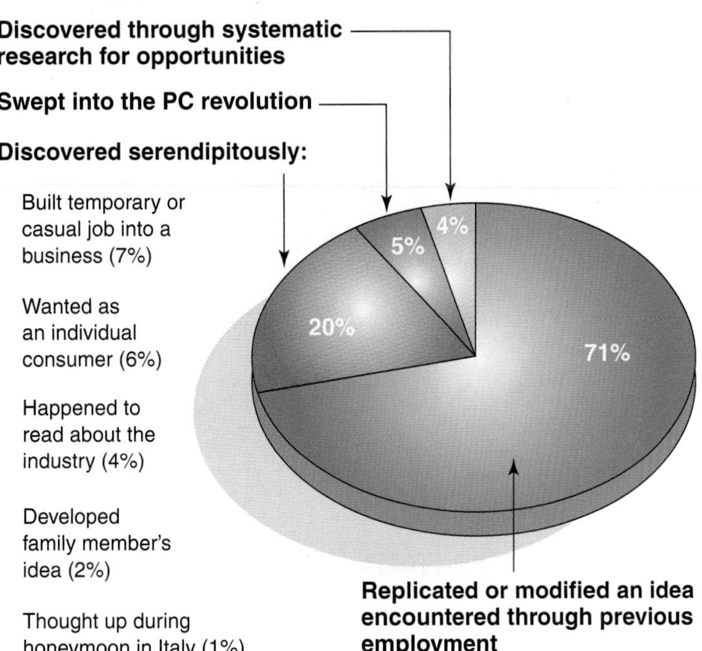

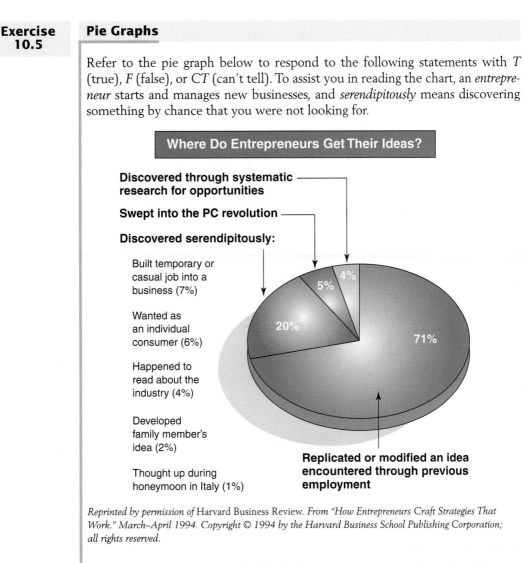

Reprinted by permission of Harvard Business Review. *From "How Entrepreneurs Craft Strategies That Work." March–April 1994. Copyright © 1994 by the Harvard Business School Publishing Corporation; all rights reserved.*

_________ 1. Over two-thirds of the entrepreneurs acted on ideas from previous jobs as opposed to thinking up totally new ideas for business.

_________ 2. The public has a misconception that entrepreneurs discover or invent new products that make them enormously wealthy.

_________ 3. More entrepreneurs got an idea from something they wanted as a customer than got ideas from systematic research for opportunities.

_________ 4. More than a thousand entrepreneurs were questioned for this study.

_________ 5. According to this study, 10 percent of the ideas that were discovered serendipitously were developed from a family member's idea.

6. The purpose of the pie graph is to _________________________

____

____

Bar Graphs

A *bar graph* is a series of horizontal or vertical bars in which the length of each bar represents a particular amount or number of what is being discussed. A series of different items can be quickly compared by noting the different bar lengths.

Exercise 10.6

Bar Graphs

Refer to the bar graph shown here to respond to the following with *T* (true), *F* (false), or *CT* (can't tell).

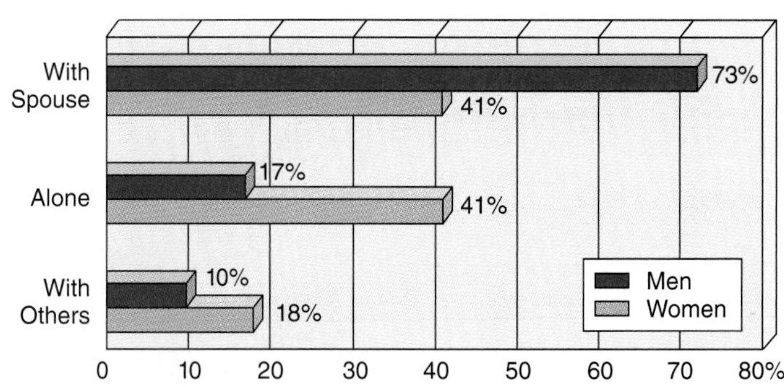

Where Do the Elderly Live?

From James M. Henslin, Sociology: A Down-to-Earth Approach, *5th ed. Data from* Statistical Abstract of the United States, *1999, Table 50.*

_________ 1. The largest percentage of elderly men live with their wives.

_________ 2. According to the graph, the reason that more elderly women than men live alone is that women live ten years longer than men on average.

_________ 3. Elderly men are more likely to live alone than to live with others.

_________ 4. A higher percentage of women live alone than live with a spouse.

_________ 5. In this study the elderly are defined as being over age 70.

6. The purpose of the bar graph is to _________________________

____

Cumulative Bar Graphs

Both *bar graphs* and *line graphs* can be designed to show a cumulative effect in which all the lines or segments add up to the top line or total amount. Rather than having multiple bars or lines, the groups are stacked on top of each other to dramatically show differences. The bar graph below illustrates this cumulative effect.

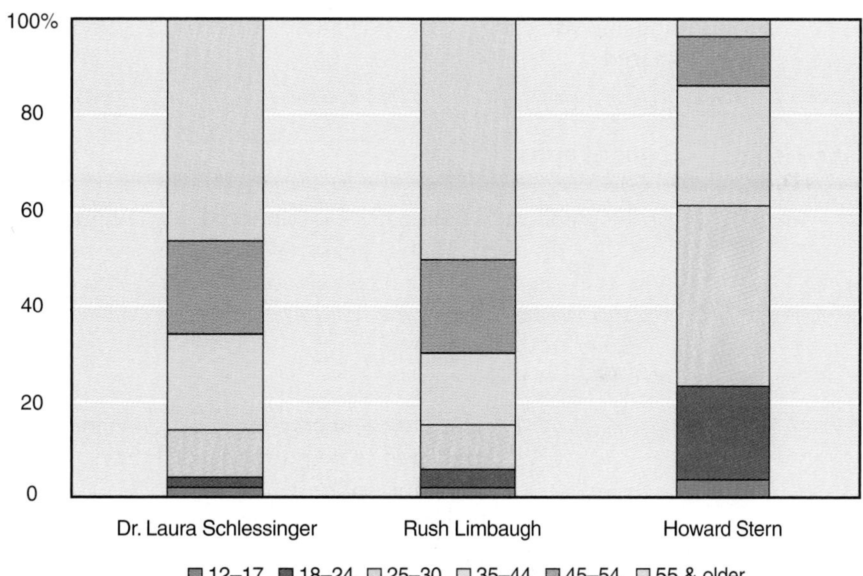

Targeted Talk: Age distribution of listening audience for selected talk radio shows, 1999.
From Courtland L. Bovee and John V. Thill, Business Communication Today, *6th ed.*

Exercise 10.7

Cumulative Bar Graphs

Refer to the bar graph above to respond to the following with *T* (true), *F* (false), or *CT* (can't tell).

_________ 1. Listeners 55 and older comprise over half of Dr. Laura's and Rush Limbaugh's audience.

_________ 2. Of the three talk shows, Howard Stern's attracts the youngest audience.

_________ 3. Stern attracts more 45- to 54-year-olds than Limbaugh or Schlessinger.

_________ 4. Young people do not listen to Dr. Laura because she is sometimes harsh.

_________ 5. Stern attracts more than twice as many 25- to 30-year-olds as Limbaugh or Schlessinger.

6. The purpose of the bar graph is to _________________________

____

Line Graphs

A *line graph* is a continuous curve or frequency distribution in which numbers are plotted in an unbroken line. The horizontal scale measures one aspect of the data and the vertical line measures another aspect. As the data fluctuate, the line will change direction and, with extreme differences, will become very jagged.

Exercise 10.8

Line Graphs

In the graph shown on page 443, notice that the horizontal axis indicates the year and the vertical axis measures income in the thousands of dollars. Also note that the women's percentage of male income has been inserted for each year on the female income line.

Refer to the line graph to respond to the following with *T* (true), *F* (false), or *CT* (can't tell).

_________ 1. The average income for both men and women in 2005 is predicted to be more than 10 times the 1960 average income for each.

_________ 2. In 1990 the average male worker made over $8,000 more than the average female worker.

_________ 3. In 2005 the average male worker is predicted to make over $17,000 more than the average female worker.

_________ 4. Although the dollar gap between the average income for men and women is predicted to be greater in 2005 than in 1990, the percentage difference was greater for 1990.

_________ 5. The gender pay gap is widening because men are graduating from college in higher numbers and have more postgraduate degrees than women.

_________ 6. In 1970 the average woman worker made over $5,000 less than the average male worker.

_________ 7. The highest five-year jump for the average woman worker was from 1985 to 1990.

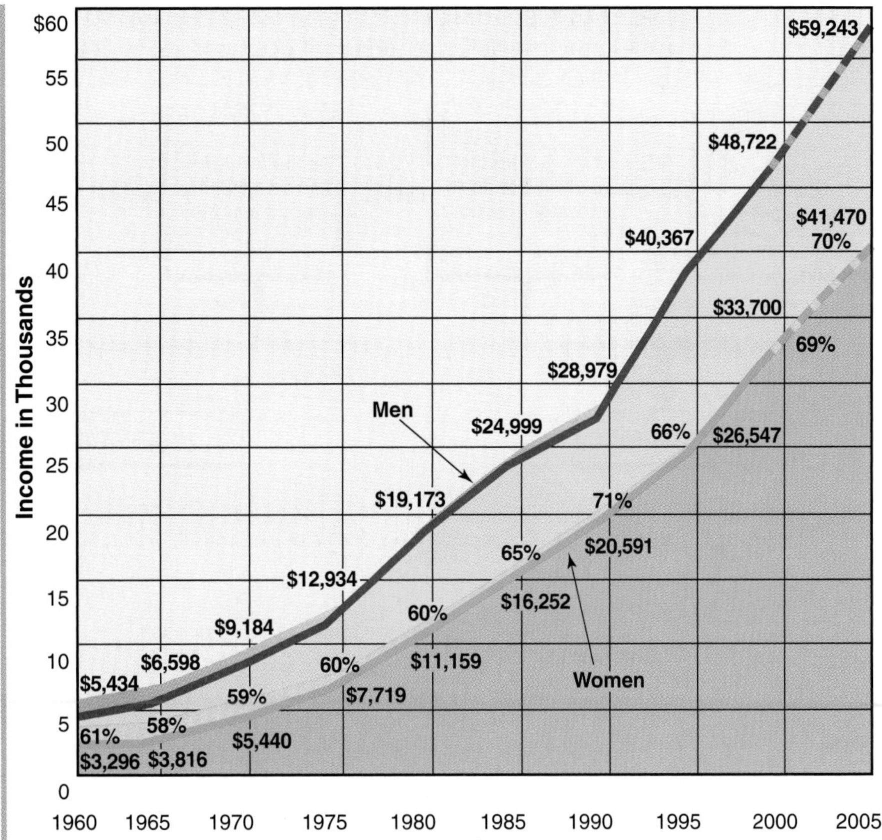

What Percentage of Men's Income Do Women Earn? The Gender Gap over Time
From James M. Henslin, Sociology: A Down-to-Earth Approach, *5th ed. Data from Beeghley, 1989, p. 239;* Statistical Abstract of the United States, *1995, Table 739; 1999, Table 758.*

__________ 8. Three times the number of women were working in the 1990s as were working in the 1960s.

__________ 9. The predicted average income for women in 2005 is about ten years behind the average male income.

__________ 10. In 2005 the average male income is predicted to be 30 percent more than the predicted average female income.

11. The purpose of the line graph is to ____________________

____

____

Flowcharts

Flowcharts provide a diagram of the relationships and sequence of elements. They were first used in computer programming. Key ideas are stated in boxes, along with supporting ideas that are linked by arrows. In the flowchart below, arrows point toward a sequence of decisions about doing business overseas.

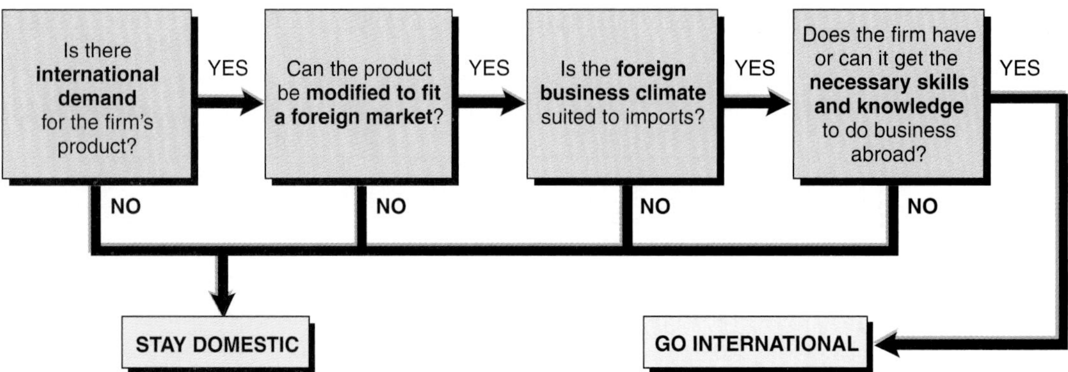

Going International
From Ronald J. Ebert and Ricky W. Griffin, Business Essentials, *2nd ed. Upper Saddle River, N.J., Prentice-Hall, 1998, p. 105.*

Exercise 10.9

Flowcharts

Refer to the flowchart above to respond to the following with *T* (true), *F* (false), or *CT* (can't tell).

_________ 1. According to the flowchart, if there is no international demand for the product, the company should stay domestic.

_________ 2. If a firm can get the necessary skills and knowledge to do business abroad but the foreign climate is not suited to imports, the company should go international.

_________ 3. According to the flowchart, if three out of four questions are answered with "Yes," the company should stay domestic.

_________ 4. Most products are substantially changed to fit the market needs in each foreign country.

_________ 5. Companies can usually make much more money in international markets than they can make in domestic markets.

6. The purpose of the flowchart is _________________________

____

Summary Points

- **What do graphics do?**

Graphic illustrations condense, clarify, and convince. They express complex interrelationships in simplified form.

- **What is a diagram?**

  A diagram is an outline drawing or picture of an object or a process with labeled parts.

- **What does a table do?**

  A table lists facts and figures in columns for quick and easy reference. You must determine what the columns represent and how they interact.

- **What is most helpful on a typical map?**

  The legend on a map of a geographic area explains the symbols and shading used to convey information.

- **What does a pie graph represent?**

  A pie graph depicts a total, or 100 percent, divided into wedge-shaped slices.

- **How do you read a bar graph?**

  You must determine what is represented by the length of a series of horizontal or vertical bars.

- **What is a line graph?**

  A line graph is a frequency distribution. You must identify what is measured by the horizontal and vertical scales in order to read a point on the continuous line.

- **What information does a flowchart convey?**

  A flowchart provides a diagram of the relationship and sequence of events of a group of elements. The key ideas usually appear in boxes and arrows are used to connect the elements.

Selection 1 ALLIED HEALTH

CONTEMPORARY FOCUS

Most colleges offer programs to educate students about drinking, hoping that knowledge about how alcohol is processed by the body will influence student alcohol consumption decisions. Do you think such educational programs can have any impact on ritual drinking? Should colleges offer other options in order to respect the rights of nondrinkers?

SCOUTING A DRY CAMPUS

Daniel McGinn

Newsweek, November 27, 2000

They are stories that make every parent's heart ache. On Nov. 10, University of Michigan sophomore Byung Soo Kim celebrated his 21st birthday by trying to drink 21 shots of whisky. He downed 20, then passed out, turned blue and stopped breathing. As Kim lay dying in a Michigan hospital later that next night, seven college students hopped into a Jeep 500 miles away on the campus of Colgate University. Moments later, the driver, a Colgate student who authorities say was dangerously intoxicated, veered off the road and struck a tree, killing four of the passengers. And by the time Monday classes began, five proud families who'd sent their children away to school were busy planning their funerals.

As tragedies like these fill the evening news, they're increasing the anxiety for parents of college-bound students. While this year's seniors winnow through applications, experts see families beginning to consider campus alcohol abuse as a factor in college selection.

That's a message Cat O'Shaughnessy already understands. As the relative of a recovering alcoholic, she was determined to find a college where she didn't have to drink to fit in. That resolve grew after visiting schools that seemed awash in liquor. "You'd walk down the dorm hallways on Saturday afternoon and people would still be puking," she says. O'Shaughnessy didn't consider schools where fraternities dominated social life. On campus tours she grilled students about the party scene. She liked what she found at George Washington University. "The urban environment in Washington, D.C., made her feel like the campus extended beyond tailgating and Friday-night parties," says Andrew Bryan, a college consultant who helped with her search.

O'Shaughnessy, now a freshman, has sipped a few drinks, but she happily spends most weekend nights at dance clubs or watching DVDs. Reliable school-by-school data on student drinking isn't readily available. The best-known ranking of "party schools," done by *The Princeton Review*, is based on student opinions, and its editor admits it's not scientific. Experts offer other rules of thumb. Schools with large fraternity systems traditionally harbor more excessive drinkers. Some studies also show heavier drinking at rural colleges, which have fewer off-campus entertainment options.

Collaborative Activity

Collaborate on responses to the following questions:

- How does college drinking adversely affect you?
- Why do some college students decide to drink excessively?
- What can realistically be done to limit college drinking?

Stage 1: Preview

The author's main purpose is to condemn alcohol.
Agree □ Disagree □

The different sections describe the cause-and-effect relationship of alcohol on the body. Agree □ Disagree □

After reading this selection, I will need to know how alcohol affects the brain. Agree □ Disagree □

Activate Schema

What is the legal limit on a breathalyzer test for driving a car?

Word Knowledge

What do you know about these words?

counterparts	diffuse	sedating	lethal	toxic
enhanced	prudent	ruefully	abstinence	devastates

Stage 2: Integrate Knowledge While Reading

Predict Picture Relate Monitor Correct

ALCOHOL AND NUTRITION

From Eva May Nunnelley Hamilton et al., *Nutrition*

People naturally congregate to enjoy conversation and companionship, and it is natural, too, to offer beverages to companions. All beverages ease conversation whether or not they contain alcohol. Still, some people choose alcohol over cola, milk, or coffee, and they should know a few things about alcohol's short-term and long-term effects on health. One consideration is energy—alcohol yields energy to the body, and many alcoholic drinks are much more fattening than their nonalcoholic counterparts. Additionally, alcohol has a tremendous impact on the overall well-being of the body.

People consume alcohol in servings they call "a drink." However, the serving that some people consider one drink may not be the same as the standard drink that delivers ½ ounce pure ethanol:

3 to 4 ounces wine
10 ounces wine cooler
12 ounces beer
1 ounce hard liquor (whiskey, gin, brandy, rum, vodka)

The percentage of alcohol in distilled liquor is stated as *proof:* 100-proof liquor is 50 percent alcohol; 90-proof is 45 percent, and so forth. Compared with hard liquor, beer and wine have a relatively low percentage of alcohol.

Alcohol Enters the Body

From the moment an alcoholic beverage is swallowed, the body confers special status on it. Unlike foods, which require digestion, the tiny alcohol molecules are all ready to be absorbed; they can diffuse right through the walls of an empty stomach and reach the brain within a minute. A person can become intoxicated almost immediately when drinking, especially if the person's stomach is empty. When the stomach is full of food, molecules of alcohol have less chance of touching the walls and diffusing through, so alcohol affects the brain a little less immediately. (By the time the stomach contents are emptied into the small intestine, it doesn't matter that food is mixed with the alcohol. The alcohol is absorbed rapidly anyway.)

A practical pointer derives from this information. If a person wants to drink socially and not become intoxicated, the person should eat the snacks provided by the host (avoid the salty ones; they make you thirstier). Carbohydrate snacks are best suited for slowing alcohol absorption. High-fat snacks help too because they slow peristalsis, keeping the alcohol in the stomach longer.

If one drinks slowly enough, the alcohol, after absorption, will be collected into the liver and processed without much affecting other parts of the body. If one drinks more rapidly, however, some of the alcohol bypasses the liver and flows for a while through the rest of the body and the brain.

Alcohol Arrives in the Brain

People use alcohol today as a kind of social anesthetic to help them relax or to relieve anxiety. One drink relieves inhibitions, and this gives people the impression that alcohol is a stimulant. Actually the way it does this is by sedating *inhibitory* nerves, allowing excitatory nerves to take over. This is temporary. Ultimately alcohol acts as a depressant and sedates all the nerve cells. Figure R1 describes alcohol's effects on the brain.

It is lucky that the brain centers respond to elevating blood alcohol in the order described in Figure R1 because a person usually passes out before managing to drink a lethal dose. It is possible, though, for a person to drink fast enough so that the effects of alcohol continue to accelerate after the person has gone to sleep. The occasional death that takes place during a drinking contest is attributed to this effect. The drinker drinks fast enough, before passing out, to receive a lethal dose. Table R1 shows the blood alcohol levels that correspond with progressively greater intoxication and Table R2 shows the brain responses that occur at these blood levels.

Brain cells are particularly sensitive to excessive exposure to alcohol. The brain shrinks, even in people who drink only moderately. The extent of the shrinkage is proportional to the amount drunk. Abstinence, together with

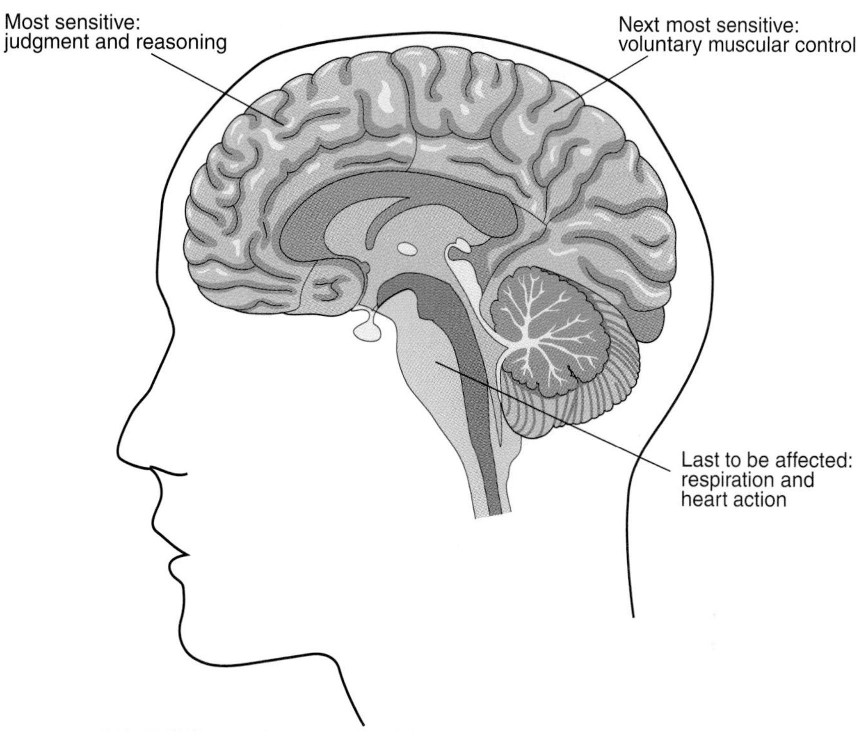

Figure R1. Alcohol's Effects on the Brain

good nutrition, reverses some of the brain damage—possibly all of it if heavy drinking has not continued for more than a few years—but prolonged drinking beyond an individual's capacity to recover can cause severe and irreversible effects on vision, memory, learning ability, and other functions.

Anyone who has had an alcoholic drink knows that alcohol increases urine output. This is because alcohol depresses the brain's production of **antidiuretic hormone.** Loss of body water leads to thirst. The only fluid that will relieve dehydration is water, but if alcohol is the only drink available, the thirsty person may choose another alcoholic beverage and worsen the problem. The smart drinker, then, alternates alcoholic beverages with nonalcoholic choices and when thirsty chooses the latter.

The water loss caused by hormone depression involves loss of more than just water. The water takes with it important minerals, such as magnesium, potassium, calcium, and zinc, depleting the body's reserves. These minerals are vital to the maintenance of fluid balance and to nerve and muscle action and coordination.

Alcohol Arrives in the Liver

The capillaries that surround the digestive tract merge into veins that carry the alcohol-laden blood to the liver. Here the veins branch and rebranch into

Table R1 **Alcohol Doses and Blood Levels**

	Percent Blood Alcohol by Body Weight				
Number of Drinks[a]	**100 lb**	**120 lb**	**150 lb**	**180 lb**	**200 lb**
2	0.08	0.06	0.05	0.04	0.04
4	0.15	0.13	0.10	0.08	0.08
6	0.23	0.19	0.15	0.13	0.11
8	0.30	0.25	0.20	0.17	0.15
12	0.45	0.36	0.30	0.25	0.23
14	0.52	0.42	0.35	0.34	0.27

[a]*Taken within an hour or so.*

Table R2 **Alcohol Blood Levels and Brain Responses**

Blood Level (%)	Brain Response
0.05	Judgment impaired
0.10	Emotional control impaired
0.15	Muscle coordination and reflexes impaired
0.20	Vision impaired
0.30	Drunk, totally out of control
0.35	Stupor
0.50–0.60	Total loss of consciousness, finally death

capillaries that touch every liver cell. The liver cells make nearly all of the body's alcohol-processing machinery, and the routing of blood through the liver allows the cells to go right to work on the alcohol. The liver's location at this point along the circulatory system guarantees that it gets the chance to remove toxic substances before they reach other body organs such as the heart and brain.

The liver makes and maintains two sets of equipment for metabolizing alcohol. One is an enzyme that removes hydrogen from alcohol to break it down; the name almost says what it does—**alcohol dehydrogenase (ADH).**[1]

[1]There are actually two ADH enzymes, each for a specific task in alcohol breakdown. Enzyme 1, alcohol dehydrogenase, converts alcohol to acetaldehyde. Enzyme 2, acetaldehyde dehydrogenase, converts acetaldehyde to a common body compound, acetyl CoA, identical to that derived from carbohydrate and fat during their breakdown.

This handles about 80 percent or more of body alcohol. The other alcohol-metabolizing equipment is a chain of enzymes (known as the **MEOS**) thought to handle about 10 to 20 percent of body alcohol. With high blood alcohol concentrations, the MEOS activity is enhanced, as will be shown later. But let us look at the ADH system first.

The amount of alcohol a person's body can process in a given time is limited by the number of ADH enzymes that reside in the liver.[2] If more molecules of alcohol arrive at the liver cells than the enzymes can handle, the extra alcohol must wait. It enters the general circulation and is carried to all parts of the body, circulating again and again through the liver until enzymes are available to degrade it.

The number of ADH enzymes present is affected by whether or not a person eats. Fasting for as little as a day causes degradation of body proteins, including the ADH enzymes in the liver, and this can reduce the rate of alcohol metabolism by half. Prudent drinkers drink slowly, with food in their stomachs, to allow the alcohol molecules to move to the liver cells gradually enough for the enzymes to handle the load. It takes about an hour and a half to metabolize one drink, depending on a person's body size, on previous drinking experience, on how recently the person has eaten, and on general health at the time. The liver is the only organ that can dispose of significant quantities of alcohol, and its maximum rate of alcohol clearance is fixed. This explains why only time will restore sobriety. Walking will not; muscles cannot metabolize alcohol. Nor will it help to drink a cup of coffee. Caffeine is a stimulant, but it won't speed up the metabolism of alcohol. The police say ruefully that a cup of coffee will only make a sleepy drunk into a wide-awake drunk.

As the ADH enzymes break alcohol down, they produce hydrogen ions (acid), which must be picked up by a compound that contains the B vitamin niacin as part of its structure. Normally this acid is disposed of through a metabolic pathway, but when alcohol is present in the system, this pathway shuts down. The niacin-containing compound remains loaded with hydrogens that it cannot get rid of and so becomes unavailable for a multitude of other vital body processes for which it is required.

The synthesis of fatty acids also accelerates as a result of the liver's exposure to alcohol. Fat accumulation can be seen in the liver after a single night of heavy drinking. **Fatty liver,** the first stage of liver deterioration seen in heavy drinkers, interferes with the distribution of nutrients and oxygen to the liver cells. If the condition lasts long enough, the liver cells die, and fibrous scar tissue invades the area—the second stage of liver deterioration called **fibrosis.** Fibrosis is reversible with good nutrition and abstinence from alcohol, but the next (last) stage—**cirrhosis**—is not. All of this points to the importance of moderation in the use of alcohol.

The presence of alcohol alters amino acid metabolism in the liver cells. Synthesis of some proteins important in the immune system slows down,

[2]Some ADH enzymes reside in the stomach, offering a protective barrier against alcohol entering the blood. Research shows that alcoholics make less stomach ADH, and so do women. Women may absorb about one-third more alcohol than men, even when they are the same size and drink the same amount of alcoholic beverage.

weakening the body's defenses against infection. Synthesis of lipoproteins speeds up, increasing blood triglyceride levels. In addition, excessive alcohol increases the body's acid burden and interferes with normal uric acid metabolism, causing symptoms like those of **gout.**

Liver metabolism clears most of the alcohol from the blood. However, about 10 percent is excreted through the breath and in the urine. This fact is the basis for the breathalyzer test that law enforcement officers administer when they suspect someone of driving under the influence of alcohol.

Alcohol's Long-Term Effects

By far the longest term effects of alcohol are those felt by the child of a woman who drinks during pregnancy. Pregnant women should not drink at all. For nonpregnant adults, however, what are the effects of alcohol over the long term?

A couple of drinks set in motion many destructive processes in the body, but the next day's abstinence reverses them. As long as the doses taken are moderate, time between them is ample, and nutrition is adequate meanwhile, recovery is probably complete.

If the doses of alcohol are heavy and the time between them is short, complete recovery cannot take place, and repeated onslaughts of alcohol gradually take a toll on the body. For example, alcohol is directly toxic to skeletal and cardiac muscle, causing weakness and deterioration in a dose-related manner. Alcoholism makes heart disease more likely probably because alcohol in high doses raises the blood pressure. Cirrhosis can develop after 10 to 20 years from the additive effects of frequent heavy drinking episodes. Alcohol abuse also increases a person's risk of cancer of the mouth, throat, esophagus, rectum, and lungs. Women who drink even moderately may run an increased risk of developing breast cancer. Although some dispute these findings, a reliable source tentatively ranks daily human exposure to ethanol as high in relation to other possible carcinogenic hazards. Other long-term effects of alcohol abuse include:

Ulcers of the stomach and intestines
Psychological depression
Kidney damage, bladder damage, prostate gland damage, pancreas damage
Skin rashes and sores
Impaired immune response
Deterioration in the testicles and adrenal glands, leading to feminization and sexual impotence in men
Central nervous system damage
Malnutrition
Increased risk of violent death

This list is by no means all inclusive. Alcohol has direct toxic effects, independent of the effect of malnutrition, on all body organs.

The more alcohol a person drinks, the less likely that he or she will eat enough food to obtain adequate nutrients. Alcohol is empty calories, like pure

Table R3 **Calories in Alcoholic Beverages and Mixers**

Beverage	**Amount (ounces)**	**Energy (calories)**
Beer	12	150
Light beer	12	100
Gin, rum, vodka, whiskey (86 proof)	1½	105
Dessert wine	3½	140
Table wine	3½	85
Tonic, ginger ale, other sweetened carbonated waters	8	80
Cola, root beer	8	100
Fruit-flavored soda, Tom Collins mix	8	115
Club soda, plain seltzer, diet drinks	8	1

sugar and pure fat; it displaces nutrients. In a sense, each time you drink 150 calories of alcohol, you are spending those calories on a luxury item and getting no nutritional value in return. The more calories you spend this way, the fewer you have left to spend on nutritious foods. Table R3 shows the calorie amounts of typical alcoholic beverages.

Alcohol abuse not only displaces nutrients from the diet but also affects every tissue's metabolism of nutrients. Alcohol causes stomach cells to oversecrete both acid and an agent of the immune system, histamine, that produces inflammation. These changes make the stomach and esophagus linings vulnerable to ulcer formation. Intestinal cells fail to absorb thiamin, folate, and vitamin B_{12}. Liver cells lose efficiency in activating vitamin D and alter their production and excretion of bile. Rod cells in the retina, which normally process vitamin A alcohol (retinol) to the form needed in vision, find themselves processing drinking alcohol instead. The kidneys excrete magnesium, calcium, potassium, and zinc.

Alcohol's intermediate products interfere with metabolism too. They dislodge vitamin B_6 from its protective binding protein so that it is destroyed, causing a vitamin B_6 deficiency and thereby lowered production of red blood cells.

Most dramatic is alcohol's effect on folate. When alcohol is present, it is as though the body were actively trying to expel folate from all its sites of action and storage. The liver, which normally contains enough folate to meet all needs, leaks folate into the blood. As the blood folate concentration rises, the kidneys are deceived into excreting it, as though it were in excess. The intestine normally releases and retrieves folate continuously, but it becomes damaged by folate deficiency and alcohol toxicity; so it fails to retrieve its own folate and misses out on any that may trickle in from food as well. Alcohol also interferes with the action of what little folate is left, and this inhibits the production of new cells, especially the rapidly dividing cells of the intestine and the blood. Alcohol abuse causes a folate deficiency that devastates digestive system function.

Nutrient deficiencies are thus a virtually inevitable consequence of alcohol abuse, not only because alcohol displaces food but also because alcohol directly interferes with the body's use of nutrients, making them ineffective even if they are present. Over a lifetime, excessive drinking, whether or not accompanied by attention to nutrition, brings about deficits of all the nutrients mentioned in this discussion and many more besides.

Alcohol and Drugs

The liver's reaction to alcohol affects its handling of drugs as well as nutrients. In addition to the ADH enzymes, the liver possesses an enzyme system that metabolizes *both* alcohol and drugs—any compounds that have certain chemical features in common. As mentioned earlier, at low blood alcohol concentrations, the MEOS handles about 10 to 20 percent of the alcohol consumed. However, at high blood alcohol concentrations, or if repeatedly exposed to alcohol, the MEOS is enhanced.

As a person's blood alcohol concentration rises, the alcohol competes with—and wins out over—other drugs whose metabolism relies on the MEOS. If a person drinks and uses another drug at the same time, the drug will be metabolized more slowly and so will be much more potent. The MEOS is busy disposing of alcohol, so the drug cannot be handled until later; the dose may build up to where its effects are greatly amplified—sometimes to the point of killing the user.

In contrast, once a heavy drinker stops drinking and alcohol is not present to compete with other drugs, the enhanced MEOS metabolizes those drugs much faster than before. This can make it confusing and tricky to work out the correct dosages of medications. The doctor who prescribes sedatives every four hours, for example, unaware that the person has recently gone from being a heavy drinker to an abstainer, expects the MEOS to dispose of the drug at a certain predicted rate. The MEOS is adapted to metabolizing large quantities of alcohol, however. It therefore metabolizes the drug extra fast. The drug's effects wear off unexpectedly fast, leaving the client undersedated. Imagine the doctor's alarm should a patient wake up on the table during an operation! A skilled anesthesiologist always asks the patient about his drinking pattern before putting him to sleep.

This discussion has touched on some of the ways alcohol affects health and nutrition. Despite some possible benefits of moderate alcohol consumption, the potential for harm is great, especially with excessive alcohol consumption. Consider that over 50 percent of all fatal auto accidents are alcohol related. Translated to human lives, more than 25,000 people die each year in alcohol-related traffic accidents. The best way to avoid the harmful effects of alcohol is, of course, to avoid alcohol altogether. If you do drink, do so with care—for yourself and for others—and in moderation.

Stage 3: Recall

Stop to self-test, relate, and react. Your instructor may choose to give you a true-false comprehension review.

Thinking About "Alcohol and Nutrition"

Use the information in this selection to write a letter to a friend who drinks and drives. In a scientific manner explain to your friend why driving after having a few drinks is dangerous.

Contemporary Link

Use your own knowledge and the information in this selection to explain why binge drinking, such as having twenty shots in one night, can kill you.

Skill Development: Reading Graphics

Refer to the designated graphic and answer the following items with *T* (true) or *F* (false).

_______ 1. According to Figure R1, alcohol first affects muscular control.

_______ 2. According to Table R1, a person who has two drinks and weighs 120 pounds would have 13 percent blood alcohol level.

_______ 3. According to Table R2, a blood alcohol level of 0.35 will cause a stupor.

_______ 4. According to Tables R1 and R2, a person weighing 150 pounds who has eight drinks would have impaired vision.

_______ 5. According to Table R3, vodka has more calories than rum.

Comprehension Questions

After reading the selection, answer the following questions with *a*, *b*, *c*, or *d*.

Main Idea

_______ 1. What is the best statement of the main idea of this selection?

a. Alcohol is involved in over half of the fatal auto accidents each year.
b. Alcohol is processed by the liver.
c. Alcohol is a drug rather than a food.
d. Alcohol is a drug that has a complex and interrelated impact on the body.

Detail _________ 2. When the stomach is full of food, alcohol
a. goes directly to the liver.
b. bypasses the liver for the bloodstream.
c. affects the brain less immediately.
d. rapidly diffuses through the walls of the stomach.

Detail _________ 3. The brain responds to elevated blood alcohol in all of the following ways except
a. loss of consciousness.
b. shrinking.
c. sedating nerve cells.
d. increasing production of antidiuretic hormones.

Detail _________ 4. Most of the body's processing of alcohol is done by the
a. liver.
b. brain.
c. stomach.
d. blood.

Detail _________ 5. Alcohol reaches the liver through
a. direct absorption.
b. veins and capillaries.
c. the intestines.
d. loss of body water.

Detail _________ 6. When enzymes are not available to degrade the total amount of alcohol consumed, this extra alcohol that cannot be immediately processed by the liver
a. waits in the liver for enzymes to become available.
b. circulates to all parts of the body.
c. is metabolized by the MEOS.
d. is sent to the stomach for storage.

Detail _________ 7. All of the following are true about ADH except
a. its production can be accelerated to meet increased demand.
b. it removes hydrogen from the alcohol.
c. the number of ADH enzymes is affected by the presence of food in the stomach.
d. ADH enzymes can reside in the stomach.

Detail _________ 8. The destruction of vitamin B_6 by alcohol results in
a. the excretion of bile.
b. a reduction in the number of red blood cells.
c. the oversecretion of acid and histamine.
d. loss of retinol by the rod cells in the eye.

Detail ________ 9. The negative influence of alcohol on production of new cells is due to
a. folate excretion.
b. ulcer formation.
c. esophagus inflammation.
d. carcinogenic hazards.

Detail ________ 10. If a doctor knows that a patient has recently progressed from being a heavy drinker to an abstainer, the doctor should expect that prescribed drugs will be metabolized
a. at a normal rate.
b. slower than normal.
c. faster than normal.
d. only when the MEOS has returned to normal.

Answer the following with *T* (true) or *F* (false).

Inference ________ 11. The sentence in the first paragraph, "All beverages ease conversation whether or not they contain alcohol," is a statement of fact.

Detail ________ 12. Carbohydrate snacks slow alcohol absorption.

Detail ________ 13. Alcohol can bypass the liver and flow directly to the brain.

Detail ________ 14. High doses of alcohol can raise blood pressure.

Detail ________ 15. Men absorb alcohol faster than women.

Vocabulary

According to the way the italicized word was used in the selection, indicate *a*, *b*, *c*, or *d* for the word or phrase that gives the best definition. The number in the parentheses indicates the line of the passage in which the line is located.

________ 1. "their nonalcoholic *counterparts*" (7)
a. duplicates
b. sugars
c. energy sources
d. stimulants

________ 2. "*diffuse* right through the walls" (17)
a. disappear
b. weaken
c. stick together
d. spread widely

________ 3. "*sedating* inhibitory nerves" (37–38)
a. soothing
b. connecting
c. closing
d. exciting

________ 4. "drink a *lethal* dose" (43)
a. complete
b. large
c. legal
d. deadly

________ 5. "remove *toxic* substances" (74–75)
a. inhibiting
b. foreign
c. poisonous
d. digestive

________ 6. "MEOS activity is *enhanced*" (83)
a. increased
b. condensed
c. redirected
d. consolidated

________ 7. "*Prudent* drinkers" (94)
a. older
b. wise
c. experienced
d. addicted

________ 8. "police say *ruefully*" (103)
a. happily
b. angrily
c. mournfully
d. humorously

________ 9. "next day's *abstinence*" (136)
a. headache
b. sickness
c. repentance
d. giving up drinking

________ 10. "*devastates* digestive system" (185)
a. destroys
b. divides
c. follows
d. loosens

Search the Net

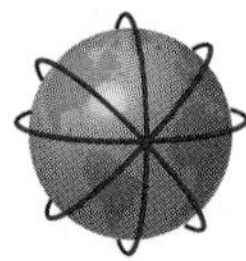

- How do you know if a friend or loved one who drinks alcohol is an alcoholic? Search for information on ten signs or symptoms of alcoholism.

  National Council on Alcohol and Drug Dependence:
  http://www.ncadd.org/

  Oak House Rehabilitation and Recovery Program:
  http://www.oakhouse.com/signs_alc.htm

- There are many different ways of treating alcoholism. Find information on three different treatment programs. Explain how the programs differ.

  Alcoholism/Treatment: http://www.alcoholismtreatment.org/

  National Council on Alcohol and Drug Dependence:
  http://www.ncadd.org/

Concept Prep

for Physical and Earth Sciences

What are the physical sciences?

The **physical sciences** include physics, chemistry, and astronomy. **Physics** is the study of the relationship between energy and matter, and it covers subjects like motion, forces, mass, energy, heat, sound, light, and subatomic particles. The field of physics can be divided into specialty areas such as **mechanics,** which is the study of motion; **thermodynamics,** which is the study of heat; and electricity and magnetism. **Sir Isaac Newton** (1642–1727), a leading physicist, was twenty-three years old when he developed **Newton's laws of motion,** his three important laws that explain the motion of objects. After observing an apple fall to the ground, Newton explained the principle of gravity. Newton was also a mathematician; he invented calculus as a tool for studying science. Another outstanding physicist, **Albert Einstein** (1879–1955), built on Newton's work to develop a **theory of relativity** and a new theory of gravitation. Einstein was born in Germany but opposed Hitler and moved to the United States. He accepted a research position at Princeton University and wrote a famous letter to President Roosevelt describing the scientific possibilities of a **nuclear bomb.** The United States subsequently began a project to develop the atomic bomb.

Chemistry is the study of the composition, structure, and properties of matter, the stuff from which things are made. **Matter** is made up of **atoms,** the smallest units associated with chemical behavior, and **molecules,** larger units composed of groups of atoms. Chemistry students study how matter is put together and interacts. They use the **periodic table,** which places the **elements,** the different types of atoms of which all matter is made, into a meaningful arrangement according to atomic weight. The periodic table has vertical columns that indicate groups or families with similar properties. The horizontal rows are called **periods,** which indicate an opening to the next main energy level.

Astronomy is the study of the universe. Initially astronomy was concerned with the location and movement of celestial objects. Now the emphasis has shifted to an investigation of these objects. **Copernicus** (1473–1543), a Polish scholar, was the first to offer a model of a solar system in which planets revolved around the sun. He was criticized for suggesting that the earth moves rather than stands still. **Galileo** (1564–1642), an Italian scientist, agreed with Copernicus and was the first to use a telescope to examine the planets. Although no one is certain, the most popular theory of how the universe began is the **Big Bang Theory,** which states that the universe began billions of years ago in an explosion at a single point in space and time.

Albert Einstein
AP/Wide World Photos

What are the earth sciences?

Earth sciences cover the formation and functions of our planet from its origins when the solar system was born, to the last **Ice Age,** a period ending less than 20,000 years ago when the earth was covered with glaciers, to the present. **Geologists** trace the history of the earth by examining rocks and studying the changes that occur in the shifting of continents, the erupting of volcanoes, and other processes that cause land surfaces to change. **Plate tectonics** is the currently accepted theory of the structure of the earth. According to this theory, the earth's surface layer is made up of about twenty large plates that fit together like a jigsaw puzzle. These plates, which are many miles thick, move in response to forces within the earth. Thus the continents shift over time, and earthquakes and erupting volcanoes tend to occur at the boundaries between plates. The **San Andreas Fault** in California is on such a boundary.

Specialists in geology also study the earth's climate and water, two important physical concerns in maintaining human life. Heat from the sun and the earth's rotations create winds that affect our weather systems. Both the prevailing winds on the surface and the **jet streams** of rapidly moving air at high altitudes carry the earth's major weather changes. **Meteorologists** study these short-term weather patterns, long-term climate changes, and atmospheric changes. **Hydrologists** study the cycle of the earth's water as it evaporates and then returns as rain or snow.

Ecologists in both the life and physical sciences are concerned about pollution and its short and long-term effects on the planet. Much of our present energy comes from **fossil fuels** such as coal, petroleum, and natural gas. These fuels were formed from fossils or the remains of ancient plants and animals. When the fuels are burned, they release chemicals and carbon dioxide into the atmosphere. These chemicals in the air combine with moisture and fall to the ground as **acid rain** or snow, polluting rivers and forests. The carbon dioxide discharged into the air traps the return or escape of the sun's radiation back into space, and thus warms the earth. Because this process operates much as the glass in a greenhouse traps the sun's heat for flowers, scientists call it the **greenhouse effect** and predict the result will be **global warming,** an increase in the earth's overall temperature.

REVIEW QUESTIONS

Study the material and answer the following questions.

1. What did Newton observe to prompt his theory of gravitation? ______________________________

2. What was Einstein's interest in the atomic bomb? ______________________________

3. What is the periodic table? ______________________________

4. What model did Copernicus offer for the solar system? ______________________________

5. Who was the first astronomer to use the telescope? ______________________________

6. What is the Big Bang Theory? ______________________________

7. What was the last Ice Age? ______________________________

8. What is the theory of plate tectonics? ______________________________

9. How do winds in the jet stream differ from surface winds? ______________________________

____

10. How do fossil fuels contribute to pollution and global warming? ______________________

____

Your instructor may choose to give a true-false review of these science concepts.

READER'S JOURNAL

Name ______________________ Date __________

CHAPTER 10

Answer the following to learn about your own learning and reflect on your progress. Use the perforations to tear the assignment out for your instructor.

1. Which of the graphic illustrations did you find easiest to understand? Why? ______________________
2. When would you use a pie graph rather than a bar graph? ______________________
3. When would you use a flowchart rather than a table? ______________________
4. When would you use a bar graph rather than a line graph? ______________________
5. Why were almost all of the questions on the alcohol selection detail rather than inference questions? ______________________
6. How did the complex, technical nature of the material affect your comprehension? ______________________
7. How did your background in science help you with the selection? ______________________

11

Rate Flexibility

- What is your reading rate?
- How fast should you read?
- How do faster readers maintain a better reading rate?
- What are some techniques for faster reading?
- What happens during regression?
- Why skim?
- What is scanning?

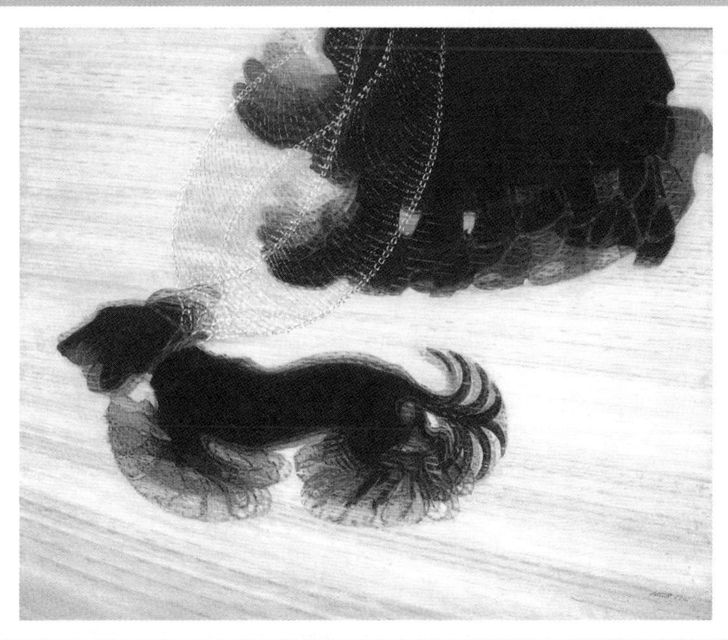

Dynamism of Dog on a Leash *by Giacoma Balla, 1912. Oil on canvas, overall: 35⅜ × 43¼" (89.85 × 109.85 cm). Albright-Knox Art Gallery, Buffalo, New York, bequest of A. Conger Goodyear and gift of George F. Goodyear, 1964. © 2003 Artists Rights Society (ARS), New York/SIAE, Rome.*

Why Is Rate Important?

Professors of college reading are far more concerned with comprehension than with a student's rate of reading. They would say that students should not attempt to "speed read" textbooks, and they would be right.

However, when students are asked what they would like to change about their reading, most will say, "I read too slowly. I would like to improve my reading speed." Whether or not this perception is accurate, rate is definitely a concern of college students. Whether you are reading a magazine or a textbook, reading 150 words per minute takes twice as long as reading 300 words per minute. Understanding the factors that contribute to rate can both quell anxiety and help increase reading efficiency.

What Is Your Reading Rate?

How many words do you read on the average each minute? To find out, read the following selection at your usual reading rate, just as you would have read it before you started thinking about speed. Time your reading of the selection so that you can calculate your rate. Read carefully enough to answer the ten comprehension questions that follow the selection.

Exercise 11.1 **Assessing Rate**

Directions: Time your reading of this selection so that you can compute your words-per-minute rate. To make the calculations easier, try to begin reading on the exact minute, with zero seconds. In other words, begin when the second hand points to twelve. Record your starting and finishing times in minutes and seconds. Then answer the questions that follow. Remember, read the selection at your normal rate.

Starting time: ______ minutes ______ seconds

Sea Lions

"Hey, you guys, hurry up? They're gonna feed the seals!" No visit to the zoo or the circus would be complete without the playful antics of the trained "seal." However, the noisy animal that barks enthusiastically while balancing a ball on its nose is not really a seal at all. In reality, it is a small species of sea lion.

Like all mammals, sea lions are air breathers. Nevertheless, they spend most of their lives in the ocean and are skilled and graceful swimmers. Two species live off the Pacific coast of North America. The California sea lion is the smaller and more southerly. This is the circus "seal." An adult male may measure over seven feet in length and weigh more than 500 pounds. Females are considerably smaller, with a length of six feet and a weight of 200 pounds.

The larger northern, or Steller, sea lion lives off the Alaskan shore in summer and off the California coast in winter. Bulls may weigh over a ton and reach a length of more than eleven feet. Cows weigh some 750 pounds and are about nine feet long. The northern sea lion is generally not as noisy as the California sea lion, but it can bellow loudly when it wants to make its presence known.

At one time, sea lions were hunted almost to extinction for their hides, meat, and oil. Eskimos even stored the valuable oil in pouches made from the sea lion's stomach. Today, sea lions are protected by law, but many fall prey to their natural enemies, the shark and the killer whale. Sea lions are often disliked and sometimes killed by fishermen who accuse them of eating valuable fish and damaging nets. For the most part, the accusations are untrue. The northern sea lion eats mostly "trash fish," which are of little commercial value. The California sea lion prefers squid. Although sea lions do eat salmon, they also eat lampreys, a snakelike parasitic fish that devours salmon in great numbers. By controlling the lamprey population, the sea lion probably saves more salmon than it eats.

Sea lions come ashore in early summer to give birth and to mate. First to arrive are the bulls, which immediately stake out individual territories along the beach. The cows follow and soon give birth to the single pup that each has been carrying since the previous summer. The newborn pup has about a dozen teeth. Its big blue eyes are open from birth and will turn brown after a few weeks.

The pup is born into a tumultuous world of huge, bellowing adults, and it must mature quickly to avoid being trampled by the teeming mob around it. It can move about within an hour, and can be seen scrambling nimbly among its elders within a few days. It doubles its weight in the first month or two. The quick weight gain is largely attributable to the extremely rich milk of the sea lion mother. Low in water and high in protein, the milk is almost 50 percent fat, whereas cow's milk is about 4 percent fat. Zookeepers have found it difficult to provide sea lion pups with adequate nourishment in the absence of the mother. At Marineland of the Pacific, an orphaned pup was successfully raised on a diet of whipping cream, liquefied mackerel muscle, calcium caseinate, and a multivitamin syrup. Not a very delectable-sounding menu, perhaps, but the pup loved it.

Throw a human infant into the ocean and it would drown. So would a sea lion baby. The only mammals that are known to swim from birth are whales and manatees. Although it will spend most of its twenty-year life in the ocean, the sea lion pup is at first terrified of water. The mother must spend about two months teaching it to swim.

Mating is no quiet affair among the sea lions. Almost immediately after the birth of the pups the huge bulls begin to wage bloody battles, trying to keep control of their harems of about a dozen cows. Using their long canine teeth as weapons, they fight with great ferocity for possession of the females. Fighting and mating consume so much of the bulls' time and energy during this period that little time is left for sleeping or eating.

At the end of the summer, the sea lions return to the ocean. The bulls, thin and scarred after a busy breeding season, regain their lost weight with several months of active feeding. As the weather grows colder, the huge northern sea lions begin their southward migration, leaving deserted the northern beaches which in warm weather were covered with their massive dark bodies.

The sea lion has to adapt to a considerable range of climate conditions. Its thick blubber and rapid metabolism are assets in the cold northern waters. But the California sea lion ranges as far south as the Galapagos Islands off the coast of South America. How does it adapt to a hot and dry environment?

The most important thing that the sea lion does to stay cool is to sleep in the daytime and take care of business during the cooler night hours. Sea lions in warm climates spend a great deal of time sleeping on the wet sand. Their bodies are designed in such a way that a large surface of the torso comes in contact with the cool ground when the animal lies down. About 10 percent of body heat can be lost in this way. Furthermore, the animal produces nearly 25 percent less heat while it sleeps than it does when awake and active.

Unfortunately, none of the sea lion's cooling mechanisms are highly effective. Ultimately, the animal relies on immersion in the ocean to keep itself cool.

Victor A. Greulach and Vincent J. Chiappetta, *Biology*

958 Words

Finishing time: ______ minutes ______ seconds

Reading time in seconds ______

Words per minute ______ (see chart on page 467)

Comprehension (% correct) ______ %

Mark each statement with *T* for true or *F* for false.

_________ 1. The author focuses mainly on the sea lion's insatiable appetite for high-protein food.

_________ 2. The larger northern sea lion is the circus "seal."

_________ 3. Sea lions eat lampreys, which eat salmon.

_________ 4. Sea lions both give birth and get pregnant in the summer.

_________ 5. Sea lion milk contains a higher percentage of fat than cow's milk.

_________ 6. Baby sea lions, like whales and manatees, are natural swimmers.

_________ 7. Male sea lions mate with more than one female.

Time (Min.)	Words per Minute	Time (Min.)	Words per Minute
3:00	319	5:10	185
3:10	303	5:20	180
3:20	287	5:30	174
3:30	274	5:40	169
3:40	261	5:50	164
3:50	250	6:00	160
4:00	240	6:10	155
4:10	230	6:20	151
4:20	221	6:30	147
4:30	213	6:40	144
4:40	205	6:50	140
4:50	198	7:00	137
5:00	190		

_________ 8. The cool ground provides the sea lion with a greater release of body heat than the ocean water.

_________ 9. In warm climates sea lions sleep more at night than during the day.

_________ 10. Sea lions are able to stay under water because they have gills.

How Fast Should You Read?

Reading specialists say that the average adult reading speed on relatively easy material is approximately 250 words per minute at 70 percent comprehension. The rate for college students tends to be a little higher, averaging about 300 words per minute on the same type of material with 70 percent comprehension. However, these figures are misleading for a number of reasons.

Anyone who says to you, "My reading rate is 500 words per minute" is not telling the whole story. The question that immediately comes to mind is, "Is that the rate for reading the newspaper or for a physics textbook?" For an efficient reader, no one reading rate serves for all purposes for all materials. Efficient readers demonstrate their flexibility by varying their rate according to their own purpose for reading or according to their prior knowledge of the material being read.

Rate Variations and Prior Knowledge

One reason textbooks usually require slower reading than newspapers is that the sentences are longer, the language is more formal, the vocabulary and ideas are new, and prior knowledge is limited. If you already have a lot of knowledge on a topic, you can usually read about it at a faster rate than if you are exploring a totally new subject. For example, a student who is already involved in the field of advertising will probably be able to work through the advertising chapter in a business textbook at a faster rate than would be likely with a chapter on a less familiar topic, like supply-side economics. The student may need to slow to a crawl at the beginning of the economics chapter in order to understand the new concepts, but as the new ideas become more familiar, the student can perhaps read at a faster rate toward the end of the chapter.

The "difficulty level" of a textbook is primarily measured according to a student's prior knowledge of the subject. Another measure combines the length of the sentences and the number of syllables in the words. The longer sentences and words indicate a more difficult level of reading. Freshman textbooks vary greatly in difficulty from field to field and from book to book. Some are written at levels as high as the sixteenth grade level (senior in college), whereas others may be on the eleventh or twelfth grade level. Even within a single textbook the levels vary from one section or paragraph to another. Unfamiliar technical vocabulary can bring a reader to a complete stop. Complex sentences are more difficult to read than simple, concise statements. Sometimes the difficulty is caused by the complexity of the ideas expressed and sometimes, perhaps unnecessarily, by the formality of the author's writing style.

Before starting on the first word and moving automatically on to the second, third, and fourth at the same pace, take a minute to ask yourself, "Why am I reading this material?" and, based on your answer, vary your speed according to your purpose. Do you want 100 percent, 70 percent, or 50 percent comprehension? In other words, figure out what you want to know when you finish and read accordingly. If you are studying for an examination, you probably need to read slowly and carefully, taking time to monitor your comprehension as you progress. Because 100 percent comprehension is not always your goal, be willing to switch gears and move faster over low-priority material even though you may sacrifice a few details. If you are reading only to get an overview or to verify a particular detail, read as rapidly as possible to achieve your specific purpose.

Techniques for Faster Reading

Concentrate

Fast readers, like fast race car drivers, concentrate on what they are doing; they try to think quickly while they take in the important aspects of the course before them. Although we use our eyes, we actually read with our minds. If our attention is veering off course, we lose some of that cutting-edge quickness necessary for success. Slow readers tend to become bored because ideas are coming too slowly to keep their minds alert. Fast readers are curious to learn, mentally alert, and motivated to achieve.

Distractions that interfere with concentration, as mentioned in Chapter 1, fall into two categories: external and internal. External distractions, the physical happenings around you, are fairly easy to control with a little assertiveness. You can turn the television off or get up and go to another room. You can ask people not to interrupt or choose a place to read where interruptions will be at a minimum. Through prior planning, set yourself up for success and create a physical environment over which you have control.

Internal distractions, the irrelevant ideas that pop into your head while reading, are more difficult to control. As mentioned in Chapter 1, a to-do list will help. Write down your nagging concerns as a reminder for action. Spend less time worrying and more time doing, and you will clear your head for success. Visualize as you read so that you will become wrapped up in the material.

Stop Regressing

During your initial reading of material, have you ever realized halfway down the page that you have no idea what you have read? Your eyes were engaged, but your mind was wandering. Do you ever go back and reread sentences or paragraphs? Were you rereading because the material was difficult to understand, because you were tired and not concentrating, or because you were daydreaming? This type of rereading is called a **regression.**

Regression can be a crutch that allows you to make up for wasted time. If this is a problem for you, analyze when and why you are regressing. If you discern that your regression is due to thinking of something else, start denying yourself the privilege in order to break the habit. Say, "OK, I missed that paragraph because I was thinking of something else, but I'm going to keep going and start paying close attention."

Rereading because you did not understand is a legitimate correction strategy used by good readers who monitor their own comprehension. Rereading because your mind was asleep is a waste of time and a habit of many slow readers.

Daydreaming is a habit caused by lack of involvement with the material. Be demanding on yourself and expect 100 percent attention to the task. Visualize the incoming ideas, and relate the new material to what you already know. Don't just read the words; think the ideas.

Expand Fixations

Your eyes must stop in order to read. These stops, called **fixations,** last a fraction of a second. On the average, 5 to 10 percent of reading time is spent on fixations. Thus, reading more than one word per fixation will reduce your total reading time.

Research on vision shows that the eye is able to see about one-half inch on either side of a fixation point. This means that a reader can see two or possibly three words per fixation. To illustrate, read the following phrase.

in the car

Did you make three fixations, two, or one? Now read the following word.

entertainment

You can read this word automatically with one fixation. As a beginning reader, however, you probably stopped for each syllable for a total of four fixations. If you can read *entertainment,* which has thirteen letters, with one fixation, you can certainly read the eight-letter phrase *in the car* with only one fixation.

Use your peripheral vision on either side of the fixation point to help you read two or three words per fixation. In expanding your fixations, take in phrases or thought units that seem to go together automatically. To illustrate, the following sentence has been grouped into thought units with fixation points.

After lunch,   I studied   in the library   at a table.

By expanding your fixations, the sentence can easily be read with four fixations rather than ten and thus reduce your total reading time.

Monitor Subvocalization

Subvocalization is the little voice in your head that reads for you. Some experts say that subvocalization is necessary for difficult materials, and others say that fast readers are totally visual and do not need to hear the words. Good college readers will probably experience some of both. With easy reading tasks you may find yourself speeding up to the point that you are not hearing every word, particularly the unimportant "filler" phrases. However, with more difficult textbook readings, your inner voice may speak every word. The voice seems to add another sensory dimension to help you comprehend. Because experts say that the inner voice can read up to about 400 words per minute, many college students can make a considerable improvement in speed while still experiencing the inner voice.

Vocalizers, on the other hand, move their lips while reading to pronounce each word. This is an immature habit that should be stopped. Putting a slip of paper or a pencil in your mouth while reading will alert you to lip movement and inspire you to stop.

Preview

Size up your reading assignment before you get started. If it is a chapter, glance through the pages and read the subheadings. Look at the pictures and notice the italicized words and boldface print. Make predictions about what you think the chapter will cover. Activate your schema or prior knowledge on the subject. Pull out your mental computer chip and prepare to bring something to the printed page.

Use Your Pen as a Pacer

The technique of using your pen or fingers as a pacer means pointing under the words in a smooth, flowing motion, moving back and forth from line to line. Although as a child you were probably told never to point to words, it is a very effective technique for improving reading speed. The technique seems to have several benefits. After you overcome the initial distraction, the physical act of pointing tends to improve concentration by drawing your attention directly to the words. The forward motion of your pen tends to keep you from regressing because rereading would interrupt your established rhythm. By pulling your eyes down the page, the pen movement helps set a rapid, steady pace for reading and tends to shift you out of word-by-word reading and move you automatically into phrase reading. Obviously, you cannot read a whole book using your pen as a pacer, but you can start out with this technique. Later, if you feel yourself slowing down, use your pen again to get back on track.

The technique is demonstrated in the following passage. Your pen moves in a *Z* pattern from one side of the column to the other. Because you are trying to read several words at each fixation, your pen does not have to go to the extreme end of either side of the column.

> Rapid reading requires quick thinking
> and intense concentration. The reader
> must be alert and aggressive. Being
> interested in the subject helps improve speed.

As you begin to read faster and become more proficient with the *Z* pattern, you will notice the corners starting to round into an *S*. The *Z* pattern is turning into a more relaxed *S* swirl. When you get to the point of using the *S* swirl, you will be reading for ideas and not be reading every word. You are reading actively and aggressively, with good concentration. Use the *Z* pattern until you find your pen or hand movement has automatically turned into an *S*. The illustration below compares the two.

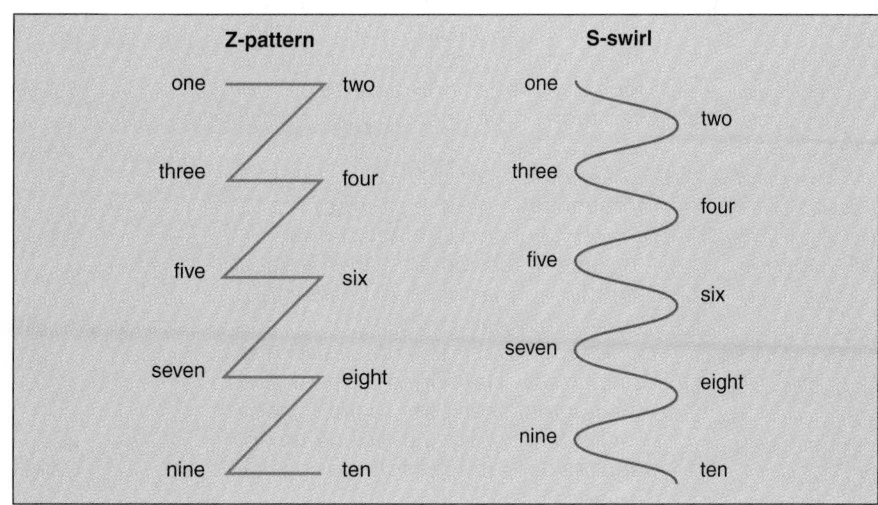

Push and Pace

Be alert and aggressive and try to read faster. Sit up straight and attack the text. Get uncomfortable and force yourself to hurry. Changing old habits is difficult. You will never read faster unless you try to read faster.

Set goals and pace yourself. Count the number of pages in your homework assignments and estimate according to your reading rate how many pages you can read in thirty minutes. Use a paper clip or a sticky note to mark the page you are trying to reach. Push yourself to achieve your goal.

Exercise 11.2 **Pacing**

The following passages are written in columns with approximately six words on each line. Using your pen as a pacer, read each passage, and try to make only two fixations per line. A dashed line has been placed down the middle of the column to help you with the fixations. Record your time for reading each passage and then answer the comprehension questions.

Determine your rate from the rate chart at the end of the passage. Before reading, use the title and any clues in the passage to predict organization: Is it definition or description? ___________

Skunks

Skunks are small, omnivorous
animals found throughout most of
the United States. Striped skunks
are at home in practically every
habitat in every state, living in dens
and often beneath abandoned
buildings. They can be seen
wandering around on cloudy days
and at sunset. They eat a variety of
fruits, berries, insects, earthworms,
other small invertebrates, and some
rodents. They sport many color
variations, from almost black to
almost white.

Spotted skunks are also found
throughout a good portion of the
country, but they are not common
in some of the more northerly states
and the northern part of the East
Coast. They eat a variety of
invertebrates, eggs, and sometimes
small birds. The hognose skunk and
the hooded skunk are found in the
Pacific Southwest and extend down
into Mexico and parts of Central
America.

In a country where millions of dollars are spent every year on human deodorants, it is not to be wondered that the skunk is not favored. Then, too, the animal can carry rabies. Thus removal procedures are the order of the day when skunks invade suburban areas or campgrounds in large numbers. They can be kept away from buildings by repellents—moth balls (paradichlorobenzene) are effective. Screens can prevent them from getting under buildings. Proper fencing will keep them from chicken coops or apiaries (skunks like honeybees). Removal of insects from golf-course grasses is useful.

Despite their bad reputation, skunks do help keep small rodent and insect populations in check.

Stanley Anderson, *Managing Our Wildlife Resources*

245 words

Time _________

Time (Min.)	Words per Minute	Time (Min.)	Words per Minute
0:30	490	1:10	210
0:40	368	1:20	184
0:50	294	1:30	163
1:00	245	1:40	147

Words per minute _________

Mark each statement with *T* for true or *F* for false.

_________ 1. Skunks eat rats and insects.
_________ 2. Skunks are repelled by moth balls.

Exercise 11.3 Pacing

Predict organization: Is the following passage organized in a time order or definition with examples? _________

Cultural Time

Attitudes toward time vary from one culture to another. In one study, for example, the accuracy of clocks was measured in six cultures—Japanese, Indonesian, Italian, English, Taiwanese, and North American (U.S.). The Japanese had the most accurate and Indonesians had the least accurate clocks. A measure of the speed at which people in these six cultures walked, found that the Japanese walked the fastest, the Indonesians the slowest. Another very interesting aspect of cultural time is your "social clock." Your culture and your more specific society maintain a time schedule for the right time to do a variety of important things—for example, the right time to start dating, to finish college, to buy your own home, to have a child. And you no doubt learned about this clock as you were growing up. Based on this social clock you then evaluate your own social and professional development. If you are on time with the rest of your peers —for example, you all started dating at around the same age or you're all finishing college at around the same age —then you will feel well adjusted, competent, and a part of the group. If you are late ("Everyone I graduated with is settled down and well into a career and here I am still waiting tables, waiting for my big break"), you will probably experience feelings of dissatisfaction.

Joseph DeVito, *Messages*

229 words

Time ________

Time (Min.)	Words per Minute	Time (Min.)	Words per Minute
0:30	458	1:10	196
0:40	344	1:20	171
0:50	275	1:30	153
1:00	229	1:40	137

Words per minute __________

Mark each statement with *T* for true or *F* for false.

__________ 1. In the study of cultures, the Indonesians walked the fastest.

__________ 2. According to the author, your position on your social clock is probably connected with your self-satisfaction.

Exercise 11.4 Pacing

Predict organization: Is the following passage organized in an order of definition with examples or a simple listing? ______________________________

The Impact of the Automobile

If we try to pick the single item that has had the greatest impact on social life in the past 100 years, the automobile stands out. Let's look at some of the ways in which it has changed U.S. society.

The decline in the use of streetcars changed the shape of U.S. cities. U.S. cities had been web-shaped, for residences and businesses had located along the streetcar lines. When automobiles freed people from having to live so close to the tracks, they filled in the areas between the "webs."

The automobile had a profound impact on farm life and villages. Before the 1920s, most farmers were isolated from the city. Because using horses for a trip to town was slow and cumbersome, they made such trips infrequently. By the 1920s, however, the popularity and low price of the Model T made the "Saturday trip to town" a standard event. There, farmers would market products, shop, and visit with friends. This changed farm life. Mail-order catalogs stopped being the primary source of shopping, and access to better medical care and education improved. Farmers also began to travel to bigger towns, where they found more variety of goods. As farmers began to use the nearby villages only for immediate needs, these flourishing centers of social and commercial dried up.

James M. Henslin, *Sociology*, 5th ed.

222 words

Time ____________

Time (Min.)	Words per Minute	Time (Min.)	Words per Minute
0:30	444	1:10	190
0:40	333	1:20	167
0:50	266	1:30	148
1:00	222	1:40	133

Words per minute __________

Mark each statement with *T* for true or *F* for false.

_________ 1. The popularity of the automobile led to a decline in the mail order catalog business.

_________ 2. With the rise of the automobile, small villages grew because farmers were able to drive to them quickly.

Exercise 11.5 Pacing

Predict organization: Is it simple listing or description? _______________

Listing and Gender

According to Deborah Tannen (1990) in her best-selling *You Just Don't Understand: Women and Men in Conversation*, women seek to build rapport and establish a closer relationship, and they use listening to achieve these ends. Men, on the other hand, will play up their expertise, emphasize it and use it to dominate the interaction. Women play down their expertise and are more interested in communicating supportiveness. Tannen argues that the goal of a man in conversation is to be accorded respect and so he seeks to show his knowledge and expertise. A woman, on the other hand, seeks to be liked and so she expresses agreement.

Men and women also show that they're listening in different ways. In conversation, a woman is more apt to give many listening cues such as interjecting *yeah, uh-uh,* nodding in agreement, and smiling. A man is more likely to listen quietly, without giving many listening cues as feedback. Tannen argues, however, that men do listen less to women than women listen to men. The reason, says Tannen, is that listening places the person in an inferior position whereas speaking places the person in a superior one.

We can try to apply these gender differences to listening in public speaking. Men may seem to assume a more argumentative posture while listening, as if getting ready to argue. They may also appear to ask questions that are more argumentative or that are designed to puncture holes in your position as a way to play up their expertise. Women are more likely to ask supportive questions and perhaps offer criticism that is more positive than men.

Joseph A. DeVito, *The Elements of Public Speaking*, 7th ed.

272 words

Time ___________

Time (Min.)	Words per Minute	Time (Min.)	Words per Minute
0:30	544	1:10	233
0:40	408	1:20	204
0:50	326	1:30	181
1:00	272	1:40	163

Words per minute ___________

Mark each statement with *T* for true or *F* for false.

_________ 1. According to Tannen, men are more likely to give listening cues than women.

_________ 2. According to Tannen, women listen to argue and men listen to support.

Skimming

Skimming is a technique of selectively reading for the main idea. Because it involves processing material at rates of around 900 words per minute, it is not defined by some experts as reading. Skimming involves skipping words, sentences, paragraphs, and even pages. It is a method of quickly overviewing material to answer the question, "What is this about?"

Skimming and previewing are very similar in that both involve getting an overview. Previewing sets the stage for later careful reading, whereas skimming is a substitute for a complete reading. Skimming is useful for material that you want to know about but don't have the time to read. For example, you might want to skim some supplemental articles that have been placed on reserve in the library because your professor expects you only to understand the main idea of each article and a complete reading would be unnecessary. Or you may want to pick up a book and just "get the idea" but not read it completely. Skimming is a useful tool. The technique is presented in the box on page 478.

Scanning

Because **scanning** is a process of searching for a single bit of information, it is more of a locating skill than a reading skill. A common use of scanning is looking up a number in a telephone book. When scanning for information, you do not need to understand the meaning of the material, but instead you merely need to pinpoint a specific detail. For example, you might find that after reading a chapter on pricing in your marketing textbook, you cannot recall the definition of *price lining*. To locate the information, you would not reread, but scan the chapter to find the key phrase *price lining* and then review the definition. This same scanning technique works well when using a glossary or an index or when doing research on the Internet.

Researchers use a combination of skimming and scanning. If you are working on a research paper on paranoia, you might have a list of thirty books and articles to read. A complete reading of each reference is probably unnecessary. Instead, you can scan to locate the information relevant to your topic and skim to get the main idea.

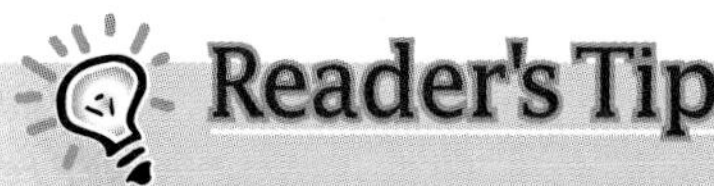

Techniques for Skimming

* Read the title and subheadings as well as words in italics and boldface print to get an idea of what the material is about.
* Try to get an insight into the organization of the material as discussed in Chapter 5 to help you anticipate where the important points will be located. Look for certain organizational patterns and understand their functions:

  Listing: Explains items of equal value.

  Definition and examples: Defines a term and gives examples to help the reader understand the term.

  Time order or sequence: Presents items in chronological order.

  Comparison-contrast: Compares similarities and differences of items.

  Description: Explains characteristics of an item.

  Cause and effect: Shows how one item has produced another.

  Problem-solution: Explains the problem, causes, and effects and also suggests a solution.

  Opinion-proof: Gives an opinion and then supports it with proof.
* If the first paragraph is introductory, read it. If not, skip to a paragraph that seems to introduce the topic.
* Move rapidly, letting your eyes float over the words. Try to grasp the main ideas and the significant supporting details.
* Notice first sentences in paragraphs and read them if they seem to be summary statements.
* Skip words that seem to have little meaning, like *a, an,* and *the.*
* Skip sentences or sections that seem to contain the following:

  Familiar ideas

  Unnecessary details

  Superfluous examples

  Restatements or unneeded summaries

  Material irrelevant to your purpose
* If the last paragraph of a section is a summary, read it if you need to check your understanding.

Reader's Tip

Techniques for Scanning

* Figure out the organization of the material. Get an overview of which section will probably contain the information you are looking for.
* Know specifically what you are looking for. Decide on a key expression that will signal your information, but be ready to switch to a related idea if that doesn't work.
* Repeat the phrase and hold the image in your mind. Concentrate on the image so that you will recognize it when it comes into view.
* Move quickly and aggressively. Remember, you are scanning, not reading.
* Verify through careful reading. After locating your information, read carefully to make sure you have really found it.

Summary Points

- What is your reading rate?

  Your individual reading rate can be calculated if you know your total reading time and the total number of words read during that time.

- How fast should you read?

  The average adult reading speed on relatively easy material is approximately 250 words per minute at 70 percent comprehension.

- How do faster readers maintain a better reading rate?

  Faster readers concentrate, are curious to learn, stay mentally alert, and are motivated to achieve.

- What are some techniques for faster reading?

  Before reading, faster readers make predictions, anticipate organization, and activate schemata. Using the pen as a pacer is an important technique that can improve both concentration and rate.

- What happens during regression?

  With regression, you must go back and reread material because of inattention. Regression thus wastes time.

- **Why skim?**

  Skimming is a technique that allows you to get a quick overview of the material.

- **What is scanning?**

  Scanning is the process of searching for a single bit of information.

Selection 1 ALLIED HEALTH

Skill Development: Skimming

Skim to find the definition of asthma, which is ______________________

____

____

Skill Development: Scanning

Scan to find the likely number of passive smoke lung cancer deaths each year as reported by the 1993 EPA report. ______________ deaths per year

Skill Development: Rate

Now read the selection in order to answer five true-false items. Use your pen as a pacer and time your reading.

Starting time: ______ minutes ______ seconds

Passive Smoking

From Curtis Byer and Louis Shainberg, *Living Well*

The right of nonsmokers to a smoke-free environment has become an emotional issue. The controversy centers around how seriously the nonsmoker is threatened by **passive smoke,** also called "second-hand" or "side-stream" smoke.

Studies have shown that the danger from passive smoking is very real. The smoke rising from a burning cigarette resting in an ashtray or in a smoker's hand is *not* the same as the smoker is inhaling. The smoker is inhaling smoke that has been filtered through the tobacco along the length of the cigarette (and usually by its filter) while the nonsmoker is inhaling smoke that is totally unfiltered. Of course, the smoker also inhales this unfiltered smoke. Unfiltered "side-stream" smoke contains 50 times the amounts of carcinogens, is twice as high in tar and nicotine, has 5 times the carbon monoxide, and has 50 times as much ammonia as smoke inhaled through the cigarette. Although the nonsmoker does not usually inhale side-stream smoke in the concentration that the smoker inhales the **mainstream smoke,** the concentration inhaled still amounts to, for the average person in the United States, the equivalent of smoking one cigarette per day. For people working in very smoky places, such as a bar or office, passive smoking can reach the equivalent of 14 cigarettes per day.

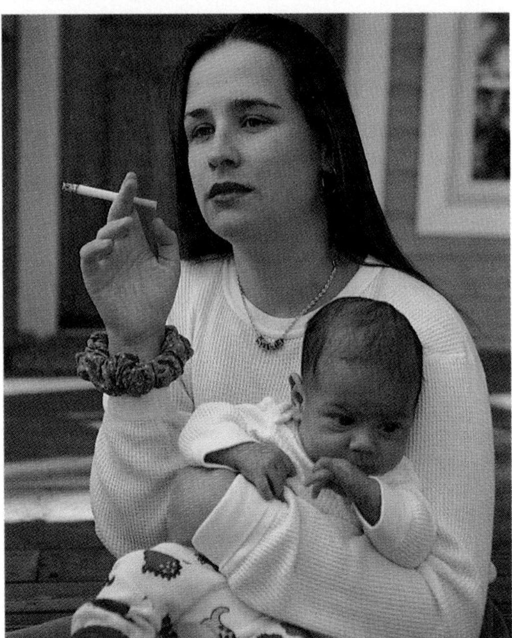

Secondhand smoke can harm a child's health.
David Young-Wolff/PhotoEdit

Cancer Affecting Passive Smokers

In January 1993, a long-awaited Environmental Protection Agency (EPA) report classified passive cigarette smoke as a human carcinogen that causes lung cancer in nonsmokers. According to the report, passive smoking causes somewhere between 700 and 7000 lung cancer deaths a year in the United States. The agency said that the most likely number is about 3000 deaths a year. This report is expected to result in additional limits on smoking in public places and federal regulations on smoking in the workplace. Predictably, the tobacco industry said that the report was based on inadequate scientific data.

Other Effects

Passive tobacco smoke is a major lung irritant. At the very least, breathing second-hand smoke causes discomfort and coughing. Research has demonstrated that children raised in homes of smokers show early signs of conditions known to lead to heart disease in adulthood. For example, they show increased stiffness of the arteries, thickened walls of the heart chambers, and an unfavorable change in the blood's ratio of high-density lipoprotein to low-density lipoprotein.

For people susceptible to **asthma** (attacks of difficult breathing caused by narrowing of the bronchioles), passive smoking can bring on a full-blown asthma attack. This is especially true for children. The incidence of asthma is higher among children who live in homes where someone smokes than among those from homes in which no one smokes. One estimate is that passive smoking may cause up to 100,000 new cases of childhood asthma in the

United States each year. Further, asthmatic children from homes in which someone smokes are likely to be in poorer health than asthmatic children from homes where no one smokes. Infants living in homes with smokers also experience twice as many respiratory infections as other infants.

Societal Issues

Many people do not enjoy the smell of burning tobacco, do not want to have the taste of their dinner spoiled by the smell of smoke, do not want their clothing or hair contaminated with the smell of stale smoke, and consider it very rude to be subjected to these intrusions.

Conversely, many smokers are addicted to nicotine and are thus uncomfortable if required to forgo smoking for extended periods. Many have tried to quit smoking without success. To be denied the right to smoke in public places makes it difficult or impossible for them to enjoy restaurant dining and other activities. As long as there are both smokers and nonsmokers we can expect to see conflicts regarding the rights of each group.

629 words

Finishing time: ______ minutes ______ seconds

Calculate Your Reading Rate

Subtract your starting time from your finishing time and then use the time chart to find your rate in words per minute.

Time (Min.)	Words per Minute	Time (Min.)	Words per Minute	Time (Min.)	Words per Minute
1:00	629	2:10	290	3:20	189
1:10	539	2:20	270	3:30	180
1:20	471	2:30	252	3:40	175
1:30	419	2:40	236	3:50	164
1:40	377	2:50	222	4:00	157
1:50	343	3:00	210	4:10	151
2:00	314	3:10	199	4:20	145

Words per minute ______

Comprehension Questions

Mark each statement with *T* for true or *F* for false.

_________ 1. Side-stream smoke contains 50 times the carcinogens as smoke inhaled through a cigarette.

_________ 2. The smoker inhales passive smoke and the observer inhales mainstream smoke.

_________ 3. A nonsmoker in an environment with smokers can inhale the equivalent of 14 cigarettes per day.

_________ 4. The author suggests that the rate of lung cancer deaths and the incidence of asthma are higher among nonsmokers than among smokers.

_________ 5. The author suggests that government regulations eventually will solve most of the problems between smokers and nonsmokers.

Thinking About "Passive Smoking"

Why are nonsmokers sometimes reluctant to ask others not to smoke? Why should they not be reluctant?

Selection 2 SOCIOLOGY

Skill Development: Skimming

Skim the first paragraph to find the subject that Jaime Escalante teaches, which is ________________.

Skill Development: Scanning

Scan to find Escalante's motto, which is ______________________________

Skill Development: Rate

Now read the selection in order to answer five true-false items. Use your pen as a pacer and time your reading.

Starting time: ______ minutes ______ seconds

THE JAIME ESCALANTE APPROACH TO RESTRUCTURING THE CLASSROOM

From James M. Henslin, *Sociology,* 5th ed.

Called "the best teacher in America," Jaime Escalante taught in an East Los Angeles inner-city school that was plagued with poverty, crime, drugs, gangs, and the usual miserably low student scores. In this desolate environment, he taught calculus. Escalante's students scored so high on national tests that test officials, suspecting cheating, asked his students to retake the test. They did. Again they passed—this time with even higher scores.

Escalante's school ranks fourth in the nation in the number of students who have taken and passed the Advanced Placement SAT Calculus examination. For students to even take the test, they must complete Algebra I, Geometry, Algebra II, Trigonometry or Math Analysis, and Calculus for first-year college and/or Calculus for second-year college.

How did Escalante overcome such odds? His success is *not* due to recruitment of brightest students. Students' poor academic performance did not stand in the way of being admitted to the math program. The *only* requirement was an interest in math. What did Escalante do right, and what can we learn from his approach?

"Success starts with attitude" could be Escalante's motto. He noted that few Latino students were taking math. Most were tracked into craft classes, where they learned to make jewelry and birdhouses. "Our kids are just as talented as anyone else. They just need the opportunity to show it. And for that,

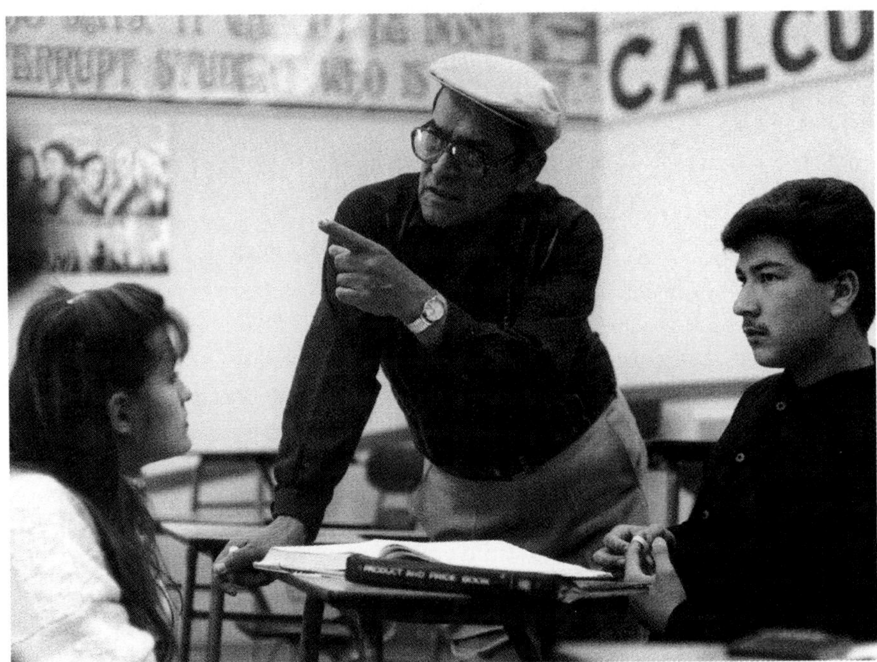

Jaime Escalante, the teacher on whom the movie *Stand and Deliver* is based, teaches math at Garfield High School in California.
AP/Wide World Photos

they must be motivated," he said. "They just don't think about becoming scientists or engineers."

Here are the keys to what Escalante accomplished. First, teaching and learning can't take place unless there is discipline. For that the teachers, not gangs, must control the classroom. Second, the students must believe in themselves. The teacher must inspire students with the idea that they *can* learn (remember teacher expectations). Third, the students must be motivated to perform, in this case to see learning as a way out of the barrio, and as the path to good jobs.

Escalante used a team approach. He had his students think of themselves as a team, with him as the coach and the national exams as a sort of Olympics for which they were preparing. To stimulate team identity, the students wore team jackets, caps, and T-shirts with logos that identified them as part of the team. Before class, his students did "warm-ups" (hand clapping and foot stomping to a rock song).

His team had practice schedules as rigorous as a championship football team. Students had to sign a contract that bound them to participate in the summer program he developed, to complete the daily homework, and to attend Saturday morning and after-school study sessions. To get in his class, even the student's parents had to sign the contract. To make sure his students were mindful of the principle that self-discipline pays off, Escalante covered his room with posters of sports figures in action—Michael Jordan, Babe Ruth, Jackie Joyner-Kersie, and Scottie Pippin.

"How have I been successful with students from such backgrounds?" he asks. "Very simple. I use a time-honored tradition—hard work, lots of it, for teacher and student alike."

Here's how Escalante challenged his students to think of what is possible in life, instead of focusing on obstacles that make achievement seem impossible:

The first day when these kids walk into my room, I have a bunch of names of schools and colleges on the chalkboard. I ask each student to memorize one. The next day I pick one kid and ask, "What school did you pick?" He says USC or UCLA or Stanford, MIT, Colgate, and so on. So I say, "Okay, keep that in mind. I'm going to bring in somebody who'll be talking about the schools."

Escalante then had a college adviser talk to the class. But more than this, he also arranged for foundation money to help the students attend the colleges of their choice.

The sociological point is that the problem was not the ability of the students. Their failure to do well in school was not due to something *within* them. The problem was what we sociologists call *social structure*—the *system*, the way classroom instruction is arranged. When Escalante changed the structure—the system of instruction—both attitudes and performance changed. Escalante makes this very point—that student performance does not depend on the charismatic personality of a single person, but on how we structure the learning setting.

727 Words

Finishing time: ______ minutes ______ seconds

Calculate Your Reading Rate

Subtract your starting time from your finishing time and then use the time chart to find your rate in words per minute.

Time (Min.)	Words per Minute	Time (Min.)	Words per Minute	Time (Min.)	Words per Minute	Time (Min.)	Words per Minute
1:00	727	2:00	363	3:00	242	4:00	182
1:10	623	2:10	336	3:10	230	4:10	174
1:20	545	2:20	312	3:20	218	4:20	168
1:30	485	2:30	291	3:30	208	4:30	162
1:40	436	2:40	273	3:40	198	4:40	156
1:50	397	2:50	257	3:50	190	4:50	150
						5:00	145

Words per minute ______

Comprehension Questions

Mark each statement with *T* for true or *F* for false.

Detail ________ 1. After test officials suspected cheating on national tests, Escalante's students scored higher on their retesting.

Detail ________ 2. Escalante taught in an inner-city school in New York.

Detail ________ 3. Escalante's school ranks first in the nation in the number of students who have taken and passed the Advanced Placement SAT Calculus examination.

Detail ________ 4. Escalante recruited the brightest kids for his calculus class.

Inference ________ 5. The author implies that many of Escalante's students were Latino.

Detail ________ 6. Escalante did not believe in the need for discipline.

Inference ________ 7. The author implies that Escalante believed that intelligence was more important than attitude in student success.

Detail ________ 8. Escalante's students divided into two teams and competed against each other.

Inference ________ 9. The article suggests that both Escalante and his students put in more than the normal school hours to achieve academic success.

Inference ________ 10. The reader can conclude that Escalante used calculus as a means of helping his students achieve lifetime success.

Thinking About "The Jaime Escalante Approach to Restructuring the Classroom"

Excelling in calculus is a difficult academic task, not a brief game. How does Jaime Escalante change the *structure* of the learning setting to achieve success? From a sociological perspective, list and explain at least six ways in which you think the underlying system is changed. Would Escalante's system have been allowed in your high school?

Selection 3 HISTORY

Skill Development: Skimming

Skim the first paragraph to find how the Altair was different than previously available computers, which is ______________________________

____

Skill Development: Scanning

Scan to find Gates's SAT score on the math section, which was __________

Skill Development: Rate

Now read the selection in order to answer ten true-false items. Use your pen as a pacer and time your reading.

Starting time: _____ minutes _____ seconds

AMERICAN LIVES: BILL GATES

From John A. Garraty and Mark C. Carnes, *The American Nation*, 10th ed.

"Project Breakthrough! World's First Minicomputer Kit to Rival Commercial Models." This headline in the January 1975 issue of *Popular Electronics* fired the neurons in Bill Gates's brain. The revolution had begun. Most earlier computers cost hundreds of thousands of dollars, filled room-sized air-conditioned vaults, and were found in university science centers, government agencies and corporate headquarters. But this kit cost only $397. The computer, its name—*Altair*—came from a planet in the TV series *Star Trek*, could fit on a desktop. Gates believed that computers like this would soon be as much a part of life as telephones or automobiles. Armed with the slogan, "A computer on every desktop," he resolved to become the Henry Ford of the computer revolution (and to become, like Ford, immensely rich). He was twenty years old.

Gates recognized the Altair's fatal flaw: it did little more than cause a few lights to blink in complex ways. It lacked internal instructions to convert electrical signals into letters and numbers. He determined to write instructions—the software—to make the personal computer useful. Gates and Paul Allen, a school chum, telephoned Ed Roberts, the president of MITS, manufacturer of the Altair. They told him they had written operating software for the machine. Roberts was skeptical. Scores of programmers had made such claims, he said,

Bill Gates, who would become chairman, CEO, and cofounder of Microsoft Corporation, poses for a photograph in the 1980s.
Doug Wilson/CORBIS

but none had actually done it. He told them to bring their software to the company headquarters in Albuquerque, New Mexico, within two months.

Allen and Gates were euphoric, but not for long: they had not even begun to write a program for the Altair. The challenge of doing so in five weeks would have been unimaginable but for one thing: the electronic core of the Altair was the Intel 8080 computer chip, and for years Allen and Gates had been devising machines and software based on the Intel 8008, whose logic was similar to the 8080.

The boys had met in 1967 at Lakeside, an elite private school, when Gates was in the seventh grade, Allen in the ninth grade. That year, the Lakeside Mothers' Club had bought time on a digital training terminal that connected by phone to a company that leased a mainframe computer. Within weeks of its installation this computer had become Gates's life. He remained in the terminal room after school and late into the evenings, breaking only for coke and pizza. Sometimes he conked out while staring at the screen; his clothes were perpetually wrinkled and spattered with pizza sauce. "He lived and breathed computers," a friend recalled.

Gates learned programming by writing programs and seeing what worked. His first was for playing tic-tac-toe. He also designed a program for students' schedules at Lakeside. He placed "all the good girls in the school" (and very few males of any kind) in his own classes—an early manifestation of his penchant for defeating competitors by conniving to eliminate them.

Gates, who scored 800 on the math SATs (a perfect score), chose a complex strategy to gain admission to the most competitive colleges. In his application to Harvard, he emphasized his political involvement (he had worked one summer as a congressional page); to Yale, he cited his creativity (a starring role in a dramatic production) and character (a former Boy Scout); and to Princeton, "I positioned myself as a computer nerd." Admitted to all three, he went to Harvard. Allen went to work as a programmer for Honeywell. But when they began work on the Altair operating program, Allen moved into Gates's dormitory and Gates skipped most classes. To save time, they built a simulator based on the published specifications and feverishly churned out the operating software.

They completed the program just hours before Allen boarded the plane to Albuquerque. (Allen went because he was older and presumably a more credible "corporate spokesman.") The next morning, Allen fed long rolls of punched yellow paper tape—the software—into an Altair while company executives looked on skeptically. For fifteen minutes the machine chunked along. Misgivings mounted. Then the teletype clacked out the word, "READY." Allen coolly typed: "PRINT 2+2." The teletype spat out: "4." The program worked. Gates and Allen had a deal.

Gates dropped out of Harvard and formed a partnership with Allen. They called their company Microsoft and moved to Albuquerque. They wrote operating programs for personal computers introduced by Apple, Commodore, and Radio Shack. Soon money was pouring into Microsoft. In 1979 they moved Microsoft to Bellevue, near Seattle. Then came the blockbuster.

In 1980, IBM, the nation's foremost manufacturer of mainframe computers, belatedly entered the burgeoning home computer market. IBM approached Gates to write the operating software for its new, state-of-the-art personal computer. IBM intended to keep the computer's specifications secret so that other manufacturers could not copy its design, but Gates shrewdly proposed that IBM make its specifications public. Doing so would allow the IBM personal computer to become the industry standard, giving IBM the edge in developing peripherals—printers, monitors, keyboards, and various applications. IBM agreed. Now Gates's software, called Microsoft-Disk Operating System (MS-DOS), would run every IBM personal computer as well as every IBM clone. In a single stroke, Gates had virtually monopolized the market for PC operating software. By 1991, Gates was the wealthiest man in the world.

880 Words

Finishing time: ______ minutes ______ seconds

Calculate Your Reading Rate

Subtract your starting time from your finishing time and then use the time chart on page 492 to find your rate in words per minute.

Words per minute ______

Time (Min.)	Words per Minute	Time (Min.)	Words per Minute	Time (Min.)	Words per Minute	Time (Min.)	Words per Minute
1:00	880	3:00	293	4:20	203	5:30	160
2:00	440	3:10	278	4:30	196	5:40	155
2:10	406	3:20	264	4:40	189	5:50	151
2:20	377	3:30	251	4:50	182	6:00	147
2:30	352	3:40	240	5:00	176		
2:40	330	3:50	230	5:10	170		
2:50	311	4:10	211	5:20	165		

Thinking About "American Lives: Bill Gates"

How does Bill Gates exemplify the American dream that working smart and working hard can bring enormous financial success?

Comprehension Questions

Mark each statement with *T* for true or *F* for false.

Detail ________ 1. Bill Gates invented Altair.

Detail ________ 2. The Gates and Allen software converted Altair's electrical signals into letters and numbers.

Detail ________ 3. Gates and Allen based the Altair software on software they had written for the Intel 8008 computer chip.

Inference ________ 4. The reader can conclude that without the Lakeside Mothers' Club, Gates might not have had such an early access to computers.

Inference ________ 5. The author suggests that Gates manipulates to defeat competition.

Detail ________ 6. In choosing colleges, Gates preferred Princeton because of its strong computer science courses.

Detail ________ 7. Gates was a college dropout.

Detail ________ 8. To impress Ed Roberts, Allen showed that the computer could add.

Inference ________ 9. The reader can conclude that the Altair deal made more money for Gates and Allen than the IBM contract.

Inference ________ 10. The reader can conclude that if IBM had kept its specifications secret, Bill Gates might not have become the wealthiest man in the world.

READER'S JOURNAL

Name ______________________________ Date ____________

CHAPTER 11

Answer the following to reflect on your own learning and progress. Use the perforations to tear the assignment out for your instructor.

1. How would you describe your concentration on different reading materials? Give at least two examples. ______________________________

____

2. When your mind wanders as you read, what are you usually thinking about? ______________________________

____

3. If your rate of reading is a concern for you, how would you describe the problem? ______________________________

____

4. Did the timed exercises help you read faster? Why or why not? __________

____

5. Will you continue to use your pen as a pacer to speed up your reading? Why or why not? ______________________________

____

6. How much did your reading speed increase as you worked through this chapter? ______________________________

____

7. How did your increased speed affect your comprehension? ____________

____

8. On what type of reading materials will you try to practice and increase your speed? ______________________________

____

12

Test Taking

- Can testwiseness help?
- How should you prepare before a test?
- What should you notice during a test?
- What strategies should you use to read a comprehension passage?
- What are the major question types?
- What hints help with multiple-choice items?
- How do you answer an essay question?

"Blondin Crossing Niagara Falls on a Tightrope" by unidentified artist, ca 1859–1860. Oil on canvas, 46 × 58¾", 1959.107. Collection of The New-York Historical Society.

Can Testwiseness Help?

Receiving a passing grade on a test should not be the result of a trick; your grade should be a genuine assessment of the mastery of a skill or the understanding of a body of information. High scores, therefore, should depend on preparation, both mental and physical—not on schemes involving length of responses or the likelihood of *b* or *c* being the right answer. Research has proven many such gimmicks don't work.[1] Tricks will not get you through college. For a well-constructed examination, the only magic formula is mastery of the skill and an understanding of the material being tested.

Insight into test construction and the testing situation, however, will help you achieve your highest potential. You will perhaps discover answers that you know but didn't think you knew.

The purpose of this chapter is to help you gain points by being aware. You can improve your score by understanding how tests are constructed and what is needed for maximum performance. Study the following and do everything you can both mentally and physically to gain an edge.

Strategies for Mental and Physical Awareness

Before Taking a Test

Get Plenty of Sleep the Night Before. How alert can you be with inadequate sleep? Would you want a physician operating on you who had had only a few hours of sleep the night before? The mental alertness that comes from a good night's sleep could add two, four, or even six points to your score and might mean the difference between passing or failing. Why take a chance by staying up late and gambling at such high stakes?

Arrive Five or Ten Minutes Early and Get Settled. If you run in flustered at the last second, you will spend the first five minutes of the test calming yourself rather than getting immediately to work. Do your nerves a favor and arrive early. Find a seat, get settled with pen or pencil and paper, and relax with a classmate by making small talk.

[1]W. G. Brozo, R. V. Schmelzer, and H. A. Spires, "A Study of Test-Wiseness Clues in College and University Teacher-Made Tests with Implications for Academic Assistance Centers," *College Reading and Learning Assistance*, Technical Report 84-01 (ERIC 1984), ED 240928.

Know What to Expect on the Test. Check beforehand to see if the test will be essay or multiple choice so that you can anticipate the format. Research has shown that studying for both types should stress main ideas, and that it is as difficult to get a good grade on one as it is on another.[2]

Have Confidence in Your Abilities. The best way to achieve self-confidence is to be well prepared. Be optimistic, and approach the test with a positive mental attitude. Lack of preparation breeds anxiety, but positive testing experiences tend to breed confidence. Research shows that students who have frequent quizzes during a course tend to do better on the final exam.[3]

Know How the Test Will Be Scored. If the test has several sections, be very clear on how many points can be earned from each section so that you can set priorities on your time and effort.

Find out if there is a penalty for guessing and, if so, what it is. Because most test scores are based on answering all of the questions, you are usually better off guessing than leaving items unanswered. Research shows that guessing can add points to your score.[4] Know the answers to the following questions and act accordingly:

Are some items worth more points than others?

Will the items omitted count against you?

Is there a penalty for guessing?

Plan Your Attack. At least a week before the test, take an inventory of what needs to be done and make plans to achieve your goals. Preparation can make a difference for both standardized tests and with content area exams. (See the box on page 498.)

During the Test

Concentrate. Tune out both internal and external distractions and focus your attention on the material on the test. Visualize and integrate old and new knowledge as you work. Read with curiosity and an eagerness to learn something new. If you become anxious or distracted, close your eyes and take a few deep breaths to relax and get yourself back on track.

On a teacher-made test, you may have a few thoughts that you want to jot down immediately on the back of the test so that you don't forget them. Do so, and proceed with confidence.

---

[2]P. M. Clark, "Examination Performance and Examination Set," in D. M. Wark, ed., *Fifth Yearbook of the North Central Reading Association* (Minneapolis: Central Reading Association, 1968), pp. 114–22.

[3]M. L. Fitch, A. J. Drucker, and J. A. Norton, "Frequent Testing as a Motivating Factor in Large Lecture Classes," *Journal of Educational Psychology* 42 (1951): 1–20.

[4]R. C. Preston, "Ability of Students to Identify Correct Responses Before Reading," *Journal of Educational Research* 58 (1964): 181–83.

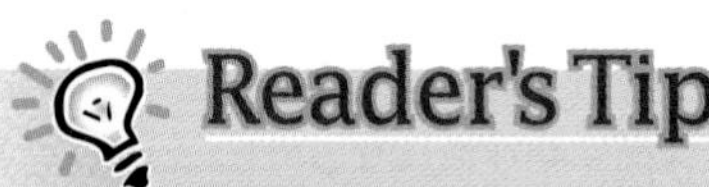

Preparing for a Test

Professors report that students gain awareness before content exams from truthfully writing answers to questions like the following:

* **How will the test look?** How many parts to the test? What kind of questions will be asked? How will points be counted?
* **What material will be covered?** What textbook pages are covered? What lecture notes are included? Is outside reading significant?
* **How will you study?** Have you made a checklist or study guide? Have you read all the material? Will you study notes or annotations from your textbook? Will you write down answers to potential essay questions? Will you include time to study with a classmate?
* **When will you study?** What is your schedule the week before the test? How long will you need to study? How much of the material do you plan to cover each day? What are your projected study hours?
* **What grade are you honestly working to achieve?** Are you willing to work for an A, or are you actually trying to earn a B or C?

Read and Follow Directions. Find out what you are supposed to do by reading the directions. On a multiple-choice test, perhaps more than one answer is needed. Perhaps on an essay exam you are to respond to only three of five questions. Find out what to do, and then do it.

Schedule Your Time. Wear a watch and plan to use it. When you receive your copy of the test, look it over, size up the task, and allocate your time. Determine the number of sections to be covered and organize your time accordingly. As you work through the test, periodically check to see if you are meeting your time goals.

On teacher-made tests, the number of points for each item may vary. Do the easy items first, but spend the most time on the items that will yield the most points.

Work Rapidly. Every minute counts. Do not waste the time that you may need later by pondering at length over an especially difficult item. Mark the item with a check or a dot and move on to the rest of the test. If you have a few minutes at the end of the test, return to the marked items for further study.

Think. Use knowledge, logic, and common sense in responding to the items. Be aggressive and alert in moving through the test.

If you are unsure, use a process of elimination to narrow down the options. Double-check your paper to make sure you have answered every item.

Don't Be Intimidated by Students Who Finish Early. Early departures draw attention and can create anxiety for those still working, but calm yourself with knowing that students who finish early do not necessarily make the highest scores. Even though some students work more rapidly than others, fast workers do not necessarily work more accurately. If you have time, review areas of the test where you felt a weakness. If your careful rethinking indicates another response, change your answer to agree with your new thoughts. Research shows that scores can be improved by making such changes.[5]

After the Test

Analyze Your Preparation. Question yourself after the test, and learn from the experience. Did you study the right material? Do you wish you had spent more time studying any particular topic? Were you mentally and physically alert enough to function at your full capacity?

Analyze the Test. Decide if the test was what you expected. If not, what was unexpected? Did the professor describe the test accurately or were there a few surprises? Why were you surprised? Use your memory of the test to predict the patterns of future tests.

Analyze Your Performance. Most standardized tests are not returned, but you do receive scores and subscores. What do these scores tell you about your strengths and weaknesses? What can you do to improve?

Content area exams are usually returned and reviewed in class. Ask questions and seek a clear understanding of your errors. Find out why any weak responses that were not wrong did not receive full credit. Do you see any patterns in your performance? What are your strengths and weaknesses? Plan to use what you learn to make an even higher grade on the perpetual "next test."

Meet with your professor if you are confused or disappointed. Ask the professor to analyze your performance and suggest means of improvement. Find out if tutorial sessions or study groups are available for you to join. Ask to see an "A" paper. Formulate a plan with your professor for improved performance on the next test.

Strategies for Standardized Reading Tests

Read to Comprehend the Passage as a Whole

While discussing test-taking strategies, a student will usually ask, "Should I read the questions first and then read the passage?" Although the answer to this is subject to some debate, most reading experts would advise reading the passage first and then answering the questions. The reasoning behind this position is convincingly logical. Examining the questions first arms the reader with

[5] F. K. Berrien, "Are Scores Increased on Objective Tests by Changing the Initial Decision?" *Journal of Educational Psychology* 31 (1940): 64–67.

a confusing collection of key words and phrases. Rather than reading to comprehend the author's message, the reader instead searches for many bits of information. Reading becomes fragmented and lacks focus. Few people are capable of reading with five or six purposes in mind. Not only is this method confusing, but it is also detail-oriented and does not prepare the reader for more general questions concerning the main idea and implied meanings.

Too many students muddle through test passages with only the high hopes that they will later be able to recognize answers. In other words, they passively watch the words go by with their fingers crossed for good luck. Avoid this by being aggressive. Attack the passage to get the message. Predict the topic and activate your schema. Interact with the material as you read, and use the thinking strategies of good readers. Monitor and self-correct. Function on a metacognitive level and expect success. Apply what you already know about the reading process to each test passage.

Read to understand the passage as a whole. Each passage has a central theme. Find it. If you understand the central theme or main idea, the rest of the ideas fall into place. The central theme may have several divisions that are developed in the different paragraphs. Attempt to understand what each paragraph contributes to the central theme. Don't worry about the details, other than understanding how they contribute to the central theme. If you find later that a minor detail is needed to answer a question, you can quickly use a key word to locate and reread for accuracy the sentence in which it appears.

Anticipate What Is Coming Next

Most test passages are untitled and thus offer no initial clue for content. Before reading, glance at the passage for a repeated word, name, or date. In other words, look for any quick clue to let you know whether the passage is about Queen Victoria, pit bulls, or chromosome reproduction.

Do not rush through the first sentence. The first sentence further activates your computer chip and sets the stage for what is to come. In some cases, the first sentence may give an overview or even state the central theme. Other times, it may simply pique your curiosity or stimulate your imagination. In any case, the first sentence starts you thinking, wondering, and anticipating. You begin to guess what will come next and how it will be stated.

Anticipating and guessing continue throughout the passage. Some guesses are proven correct and others are proven wrong. When necessary, glance back in the passage to double-check a date, fact, or event that emerges differently than expected. Looking back does not signal a weak memory but instead indicates skill in monitoring one's own comprehension.

Read Rapidly, but Don't Allow Yourself to Feel Rushed

Use your pen as a pacer to direct your attention both mentally and physically to the printed page. Using your pen will help you focus your attention, particularly at the times during the test when you feel more rushed.

That uneasy, rushed feeling tends to be with you at the beginning of the test when you have not yet fixed your concentration and become mentally involved with the work. During the middle of the test, you may feel anxious again if you look at your watch and discover you are only half finished and half of your time is gone (which is where you should be). Toward the end of the test, when the first person finishes, you will again feel rushed if you have not yet finished. Check your time, keep your cool, and use your pen as a pacer. Continue working with control and confidence.

Read with Involvement to Learn and Enjoy

Reading a passage to answer five or six questions is reading with an artificial purpose. Usually you read to learn and enjoy, not for the sole purpose of quickly answering questions. Most test passages can be fairly interesting to a receptive reader. Try changing your attitude about reading the passages. Use the thinking strategies of a good reader to become involved in the material. Picture what you read and relate the ideas to what you already know. Think, learn, and enjoy—or at least, fake it.

Self-Test for the Main Idea

Pull it together before pulling it apart. At the end of a passage, self-test for the main idea. This is a final monitoring step that should be seen as part of the reading process. Work efficiently, with purpose and determination. Actively seek meaning rather than waiting for the questions to prod you. Take perhaps ten or fifteen seconds to pinpoint the focus of the passage and to review the point that the author is trying to make. Again, if you understand the main point, the rest of the passage will fall into place.

Pretend that the passage on the next page is part of a reading comprehension test. Read it using the above suggestions. Note the handwritten reminders to make you aware of a few aspects of your thinking.

Certainly your reading of the passage contained many more thoughts than those indicated on the page. The gossip at the beginning of the passage humanizes the empress and makes it easier for the reader to relate emotionally to the historic figure. Did you anticipate Peter's downfall and Catherine's subsequent relationships? Did you note the shift from gossip to accomplishments, both national and then international? The shift signals the alert reader to a change in style, purpose, and structure.

Take a few seconds to regroup and think about what you have read before proceeding to the questions that follow a passage. Self-test by pulling the material together before you tear it apart. Think about the focus of the passage and then proceed to the questions.

Recognizing the Major Question Types

Learn to recognize the types of questions asked on reading comprehension tests. Although the phraseology may vary slightly, most tests will include one or more of each of the following types of comprehension questions.

No title, so glance for key words. Dates? Names?

Practice Passage A

Great image

In January 1744 a coach from Berlin bumped its way eastward over ditches and mud toward Russia. It carried Sophia, a young German princess, on a bridal journey. At the Russian border she was met with pomp, appropriate for one chosen to be married to Peter, heir to the Russian throne. The wedding was celebrated in August 1745 with gaiety and ceremony.

Why wait 1½ years?

Surprise!

Will he be tsar?

What is she planning?

For Sophia the marriage was anything but happy because the seventeen-year-old heir was "physically less than a man and mentally little more than a child." The "moronic booby" played with dolls and toy soldiers in his leisure time. He neglected his wife and was constantly in a drunken stupor. Moreover, Peter was strongly pro-German and made no secret of his contempt for the Russian people, intensifying the unhappiness of his ambitious young wife. This dreary period lasted for seventeen years, but Sophia used the time wisely. She set about "russifying" herself. She mastered the Russian language and avidly embraced the Russian faith; on joining the Orthodox church, she was renamed Catherine. She devoted herself to study, reading widely the works of Montesquieu, Voltaire, and other Western intellectuals.

What is that? How?

Did she kill him?

Ironic, since she's not Russian

When Peter became tsar in January 1762, Catherine immediately began plotting his downfall. Supported by the army, she seized power in July 1762 and tacitly consented to Peter's murder. It was announced that he died of "hemorrhoidal colic." Quickly taking over the conduct of governmental affairs, Catherine reveled in her new power. For the next thirty-four years the Russian people were dazzled by their ruler's political skill and cunning and her superb conduct of tortuous diplomacy. Perhaps even more, they were intrigued by gossip concerning her private life.

What gossip? Lovers?

Unusual term

Did she kill them?

Long before she became empress, Catherine was involved with a number of male favorites referred to as her house pets. At first her affairs were clandestine, but soon she displayed her lovers as French kings paraded their mistresses. Once a young man was chosen, he was showered with lavish gifts; when the empress tired of him, he was given a lavish going-away present.

Now moving from personal info to accomplishments

Double check years—not long

So, she did little toward human progress

Catherine is usually regarded as an enlightened despot. She formed the Imperial Academy of Art, began the first college of pharmacy, and imported foreign physicians. Her interest in architecture led to the construction of a number of fine palaces, villas, and public buildings and the first part of the Hermitage in Saint Petersburg. Attracted to Western culture, she carried on correspondence with the French *philosophes* and sought their flattery by seeming to champion liberal causes. The empress played especially on Voltaire's vanity, sending him copious praise about his literary endeavors. In turn this *philosophe* became her most ardent admirer. Yet while Catherine discussed liberty and equality before the law, her liberalism and dalliance with the Enlightenment was largely a pose—eloquent in theory, lacking in practice. The lot of serfs actually worsened, leading to a bloody uprising in 1773. This revolt brought an end to all talk of reform. And after the French Revolution, strict censorship was imposed.

Changes to foreign policy accomplishments

In her conduct of foreign policy, the empress was ruthless and successful. She annexed a large part of Poland and, realizing that Turkey was in decline, waged two wars against this ailing power. As a result of force and diplomacy, Russian frontiers reached the Black Sea, the Caspian, and the Baltic. Well could this shrewd practitioner of power tell her adopted people, "I came to Russia a poor girl. Russia has dowered me richly, but I have paid her back with Azov, the Crimea, and Poland."

What was the point?

T. Walter Wallbank et al., *Civilization Past and Present*

Main Idea

Main idea questions test your ability to find the central theme, central focus, gist, controlling idea, main point, or thesis. The terms are largely interchangeable in asking the reader to identify the main point of the passage. Main idea items are stated in any of the following forms:

The best statement of the main idea is . . .

The best title for this passage is . . .

The author is primarily concerned with . . .

The central theme of the passage is . . .

Incorrect responses to main idea items tend to fall into two categories. Some responses will be too general and express more ideas than are actually included in the passage. Other incorrect items will be details within the passage that support the main idea. The details may be attention-getting and interesting, but they do not describe the central focus of the passage. If you are having difficulty with the main idea, reread the first and last sentences of the passage. Sometimes, though not always, one of the two sentences will give you an overview or focus.

The following main idea items apply to the passage on Catherine the Great. Notice the remarks in parentheses reflecting the thinking involved in judging a correct or incorrect response.

__________ The best statement of the main idea of this passage is

a. Peter lost his country through ignorance and drink. (Important detail, but focus is on her)
b. gossip of Catherine's affairs intrigued the Russian people. (Very interesting, but a detail)
c. progress for the Russian people was slow to come. (Too broad and general, or not really covered)
d. Catherine came to Russia as a poor girl but emerged as a powerful empress and a shrewd politician. (Yes, sounds great)

__________ The best title for this passage is

a. Catherine Changes Her Name. (Detail)
b. Peter Against Catherine. (Only part of the story, so detail)
c. Catherine the Great, Empress of Russia. (Sounds best)
d. Success of Women in Russia. (Too broad—this is only about one woman)

Details

Detail questions check your ability to locate and understand explicitly stated material. Such items can frequently be answered correctly without a thorough understanding of the passage. To find the answer to such an item, note a key word in the question and then scan the passage for the word or a synonym. When you locate the term, reread the sentence to double-check your answer. Stems for detail questions fall into the following patterns:

The author states that . . .

According to the author . . .

According to the passage . . .

All of the following are true except . . .

A person, term, or place is . . .

Incorrect answers to detail questions tend to be false statements. Sometimes the test maker will trick the unsophisticated reader by using a pompous or catchy phrase from the passage as a distractor. The phrase may indeed appear in the passage and sound authoritative, but on close inspection it means nothing. Read the detail question on Catherine the Great and note the remarks in parentheses.

________ Catherine changed all of the following except (Look for the only false item as the answer.)

a. her religion. (True, she joined the Orthodox church)
b. her name. (True, from Sophia to Catherine)
c. Russia's borders. (True, she gained seaports)
d. the poverty of the serfs. (The serfs were worse off, but still in poverty, so this is the best answer.)

Implied Meaning

Questions concerning implied meaning test your ability to look beyond what is directly stated and your understanding of the suggested meaning.

Items testing implied meaning deal with attitudes and feelings, sarcastic comments, snide remarks, the motivation of characters, favorable and unfavorable descriptions, and a host of other hints, clues, and ultimate assumptions. Stems for such items include the following:

The author believes (or feels or implies) . . .

It can be inferred from the passage . . .

The passage or author suggests . . .

It can be concluded from the passage that . . .

To answer inference items correctly, look for clues to help you develop logical assumptions. Base your conclusions on what is known and what is suggested. Incorrect inference items tend to be false statements. Study the following question.

________ The author implies that Catherine

a. did not practice the enlightenment she professed. (Yes, "eloquent in theory but lacking practice")
b. preferred French over Russian architecture. (not suggested)
c. took Voltaire as her lover. (not suggested)
d. came to Russia knowing her marriage would be unhappy. (not suggested)

Purpose

The purpose of a reading passage is not usually stated; it is implied. In a sense, the purpose is part of the main idea; you probably need to understand the main idea to understand the purpose. Generally, however, reading comprehension tests include three basic types of passages, and each type tends to dictate its own purpose. Study the following three types.

1. **Factual**
   Identification: Gives the facts about science, history, or other subjects
   Strategy: If complex, do not try to understand each detail before going to the questions. Remember, you can look back.
   Example: Textbook
   Purposes: To inform, to explain, to describe, or to enlighten
2. **Opinion**
   Identification: Puts forth a particular point of view
   Strategy: The author states opinions and then refutes them. Sort out the opinions of the author and the opinions of the opposition.
   Example: Newspaper editorial
   Purposes: To argue, to persuade, to condemn, or to ridicule
3. **Fiction**
   Identification: Tells a story
   Strategy: Read slowly to understand the motivation and interrelationships of characters.
   Example: Novel or short story
   Purposes: To entertain, to narrate, to describe, or to shock

_________ The purpose of the passage on Catherine is
a. to argue. (No side is taken)
b. to explain. (Yes, because it is factual material)
c. to condemn. (Not judgmental)
d. to persuade. (No opinion is pushed)

Vocabulary

Vocabulary items test your general word knowledge as well as your ability to use context to figure out word meaning. The stem of most vocabulary items on reading comprehension tests is as follows:

As used in the passage, the best definition of ______ is ______.

Note that both word knowledge and context are necessary for a correct response. The item is qualified by "As used in the passage," and thus you must go back and reread the sentence (context) in which the word appears to be sure you are not misled by a multiple meaning. To illustrate, the word *sports* means *athletics* as well as *offshoots from trees.* As a test taker you would need to double-check the context to see which meaning appears in your test passage.

In addition, if you knew only one definition of the word *sport,* rereading the sentence would perhaps suggest the alternate meaning to you and help you get the item correct. Note the following example.

________ As used in the passage, the best definition of *dreary* is (2nd paragraph)
a. sad. (Yes, unhappiness is used in the previous sentence)
b. commonplace. (Possible, but not right in the sentence)
c. stupid. (Not right in the sentence)
d. neglected. (True, but not the definition of the word)

Strategies for Multiple-Choice Items

Consider All Alternatives Before Choosing an Answer

Read all the options. Do not rush to record an answer without considering all the alternatives. Be careful, not careless, in considering each option. Multiple-choice test items usually ask for the best choice for an answer, not any choice that is reasonable.

________ Peter was most likely called a "moronic booby" because
a. he neglected Catherine.
b. he drank too much.
c. he disliked German customs.
d. he played with dolls and toys.

Although the first three answers are true and reasonable, the last answer seems to be most directly related to that particular name.

Anticipate the Answer and Look for Something Close to It

As you read the beginning of a multiple-choice item, anticipate what you would write for a correct response. Develop an answer in your mind before you read the options, and then look for a response that corroborates your thinking.

________ The author suggests that Catherine probably converted to the Russian Orthodox church because . . . she wanted to rule the country and wanted the people to think of her as Russian, rather than German.
a. she was a very religious person.
b. Peter wanted her to convert.
c. she was no longer in Germany.
d. she wanted to appear thoroughly Russian to the Russian people.

The last answer most closely matches the kind of answer you were anticipating.

Avoid Answers with 100 Percent Words

All and *never* mean 100 percent, without exceptions. A response containing either word is seldom correct. Rarely can a statement be so definitely inclusive or exclusive. Here are some other 100 percent words to avoid:

no	none	only
every	always	must

_________ Catherine the Great was beloved by all the Russian people.

Answer with *true* or *false. All* means 100 percent and thus is too inclusive. Surely one or two Russians did not like Catherine, so the answer must be false.

Consider Answers with Qualifying Words

Words like *sometimes* and *seldom* suggest frequency but do not go so far as to say *all* or *none.* Such qualifying words can mean more than *none* and less than *all.* By being so indefinite, the words are difficult to dispute. Therefore, qualifiers are more likely to be included in a correct response. Here are some other qualifiers:

few	much	often	may
many	some	perhaps	generally

_________ Catherine was beloved by many of the Russian people.

Answer with *true* or *false.* The statement is difficult to dispute, given Catherine's popularity. An uprising against her occurred, but it was put down, and she maintained the support of many of the Russian people. Thus the answer would be *true.*

Choose the Intended Answer Without Overanalyzing

Try to follow logically the thinking of the test writer rather than overanalyzing minute points. Don't make the question harder than it is. Use your common sense and answer what you think was intended. Answer with *true* or *false.*

_________ Catherine was responsible for Peter's murder.

This is false in that Catherine did not personally murder Peter. On the other hand, she did "tacitly consent" to his murder, which suggests responsibility. After seizing power, it was certainly in her best interest to get rid of Peter permanently. Perhaps without Catherine, Peter would still be playing with his toys, so the intended answer is *true.*

True Statements Must Be True Without Exception

A statement is either totally true or it is incorrect. Adding an incorrect *and, but,* or *because* phrase to a true statement makes the statement false and thus an unacceptable answer. If a statement is half true and half false, mark it false.

__________ Catherine was an enlightened despot who did her best to improve the lot of all her people.

Answer with *true* or *false.* It is true that Catherine was considered an enlightened despot, but she did very little to improve the lot of the serfs. In fact, conditions for the serfs worsened. The statement is half true and half false, so it must be answered *false.*

If Two Options Are Synonymous, Eliminate Both

If *both* is not a possible answer and two items say basically the same thing, then neither can be correct. Eliminate the two and spend your time on the others.

__________ The purpose of this passage is
a. to argue.
b. to persuade.
c. to inform.
d. to entertain.

Because *argue* and *persuade* are basically synonymous, you can eliminate both and move to the other options.

Study Similar Options to Determine the Differences

If two similar options appear, frequently one of them will be correct. Study the options to see the subtle difference intended by the test maker.

__________ Catherine was
a. unpopular during her reign.
b. beloved by all of the Russian people.
c. beloved by many of the Russian people.
d. considered selfish and arrogant by the Russians.

The first and last answers are untrue. Close inspection shows that the 100 percent *all* is the difference between the second and third answers that makes the second answer untrue. Thus, the third answer with the qualifying word is the correct response.

Use Logical Reasoning If Two Answers Are Correct

Some tests include the options *all of the above* and *none of the above.* If you see that two of the options are correct and you are unsure about a third choice, then *all of the above* would be a logical response.

__________ Catherine started
a. the Imperial Academy of Art.
b. the first college of pharmacy.
c. the Hermitage.
d. all of the above.

If you remembered that Catherine started the first two but were not sure about the Hermitage, *all of the above* would be your logical option because you know that two of the above *are* correct.

Look Suspiciously at Directly Quoted Pompous Phrases

In searching for distractors, test makers sometimes quote a pompous phrase from the passage that doesn't make much sense. Students read the phrase and think, "Oh yes, I saw that in the passage. It sounds good, so it must be right." Beware of such repetitions and make sure they make sense before choosing them.

_________ In her country Catherine enacted

a. few of the progressive ideas she championed.
b. the liberalism of the Enlightenment.
c. laws for liberty and equality.
d. the liberal areas of the philosophers.

The first response is correct because Catherine talked about progress but did little about it. The other three answers sound impressive and are quoted from the text, but are totally incorrect.

Simplify Double Negatives by Canceling Out Both

Double negatives are confusing to unravel and, in addition, time consuming to think through. Simplify a double negative statement by first canceling out both negatives. Then reread the statement without the confusion of the two negatives, which at this point have canceled each other out, and decide on the accuracy of the statement. Answer the following with *true* or *false*.

_________ Catherine's view of herself was not that of an unenlightened ruler.

Cancel out the two negatives, the *not* and the *un* in the word *unenlightened*. Reread the sentence without the negatives and decide on its accuracy: Catherine's view of herself was that of an enlightened ruler. The statement is correct so the answer is *true*.

Use Can't-Tell Responses If Clues Are Insufficient

Mark an item *can't tell* only if you are not given clues on which to base an assumption. In other words, there is no evidence to indicate the statement is either true or false.

_________ Catherine the Great had no children.

From the information in this passage, which is the information on which your reading test is based, you do not have any clues to indicate whether she did or did not have children. Thus, the answer must be *can't tell*.

Validate True Responses on "All of the Following Except"

In this type of question, you must recognize several responses as correct and find the one that is incorrect. Corroborate each response and, by the process of elimination, find the one that does not fit.

Note Oversights on Hastily Constructed Tests

Reading tests developed by professional test writers are usually well constructed and do not contain obvious clues to the correct answers. However, some teacher-made tests are hastily constructed and contain errors in test making that can help a student find the correct answer. Do not, however, rely on these flaws to make a big difference in your score because they should not occur in a well-constructed test.

Grammar. Eliminate responses that do not have subject-verb agreement. The tense of the verb as well as modifiers such as *a* or *an* can also give clues to the correct response.

__________ Because of his described habits, it is possible that Peter was an
a. hemophiliac.
b. alcoholic.
c. Catholic.
d. barbarian.

The *an* suggests an answer that starts with a vowel. Thus *alcoholic* is the only possibility.

Clues from Other Parts of the Test. If a test has been hastily constructed, information in one part of the test may help you with an uncertain answer.

__________ Not only was Peter childlike and neglectful, but he was also frequently
a. abusive.
b. drunk.
c. dangerous.
d. out of the country.

The previous question gives this answer away by stating that he was possibly an alcoholic.

Length. On poorly constructed tests, longer answers are more frequently correct.

__________ The word *cunning* used in describing Catherine suggests that she was
a. evil
b. dishonest.
c. untrustworthy.
d. crafty and sly in managing affairs.

In an effort to be totally correct without question, the test maker has made the last answer so complete that its length gives it away.

Absurd Ideas and Emotional Words. Avoid distractors with absurd ideas or emotional words. The test maker probably got tired of thinking of distractors and in a moment of weakness included nonsense.

________ As used in the passage, the term *house pets* refers to

a. Peter's toys.
b. Catherine's favorite lovers.
c. the dogs and cats in the palace.
d. trained seals that performed for the empress.

Yes, the test maker has, indeed, become weary. The question itself has very little depth, and the last two answers are particularly flippant.

Exercise 12.1 Reading with Understanding

Pretend that the following selection is a passage on a reading comprehension test. Use what you have learned to read with understanding and answer the questions.

It seems odd that one of the most famous figures of antiquity—the founder of a philosophical movement—was a vagrant with a criminal record. Diogenes the Cynic began life as the son of a rich banker. This fact may not seem so strange when one remembers the rebellious young people of the late 1960s in America, many of whom also came from affluent families.

The turning point in Diogenes' life came when his father, Hikesios, treasurer of the flourishing Greek commercial city of Sinope in Asia Minor, was found guilty of "altering the currency." Since Hikesios was a sound money man concerned about maintaining the high quality of the Sinopean coinage, this was obviously a miscarriage of justice. The Persian governor of nearby Cappadocia had issued inferior imitations of the Sinopean currency, and Hikesios, who realized that this currency was undermining the credit of Sinope, ordered the false coins to be defaced in order to put them out of circulation. But a faction of Sinopean citizens—it is not clear whether for economic or political reasons—successfully prosecuted Hikesios. Hikesios was imprisoned, and Diogenes, who was his father's assistant, was exiled. He eventually settled in Athens.

The shock of this experience caused Diogenes to become a rebel against society—to continue "altering the currency," but in a different way. He decided to stop the circulation of all false values, customs, and conventions. To achieve this goal, he adopted the tactics that made him notorious—complete freedom in speaking out on any subject and a type of outrageous behavior that he called "shamelessness."

Diogenes called free speech "the most beautiful thing in the world" because it was so effective a weapon. He shocked his contemporaries with such statements as "Most men are so nearly mad that a finger's breadth would make the difference." He advocated free love, "recognizing no other union than that of the man who persuades with the woman who consents." He insisted that "the love of money is the mother of all evils"; when some temple officials caught someone stealing a bowl from a temple, he said, "The great thieves are leading away the little thief." He liked to point out that truly valuable things cost little, and vice versa. "A statue sells for three thousand drachmas, while a quart of flour is sold for two copper coins." And when he was asked what was the right time to marry, he replied, "For a young man not yet; for an old man never at all."

Diogenes' "shamelessness"—his eccentric behavior—was his second weapon against the artificiality of conventional behavior as well as his means of promoting what he called "life in accordance with nature," or self-sufficiency. He believed that gods are truly self-sufficient and that people should emulate them: "It is the privilege of the gods to want nothing, and of men who are most like gods to want but little." It was said that he "discovered the means of adapting himself to circumstances through watching a mouse running about, not looking for a place to lie down, not afraid of the dark, not seeking any of the things that are considered dainties." And he got the idea for living in a large pottery jar—his most famous exploit—from seeing a snail carrying its own shell. Above all, Diogenes admired and emulated the life-style of dogs because of their habit of "doing everything in public." For this reason he was called *Kynos*, "the Dog," and his disciples were called Cynics.

"We live in perfect peace," one Cynic wrote, "having been made free from every evil by the Sinopean Diogenes." Eventually the citizens of Sinope also came to honor their eccentric exile with an inscription in bronze:

> Even bronze grows old with time, but your fame, Diogenes, not all eternity shall take away. For you alone did point out to mortals the lesson of self-sufficiency, and the easiest path of life.

T. Walter Wallbank et al., *Civilization Past and Present*

Identify each question type and answer with *a, b, c,* or *d*. Explain what is wrong with the incorrect distractors.

_______ 1. What is the best statement of the main idea of this passage?

(Question type ____________________) (Explain errors)

a. The turning point in the life of Diogenes was the imprisonment of his father. _______

b. The eccentric Diogenes founded a philosophy and promoted self-sufficiency. _______

c. Diogenes became famous for living the life of a dog. _______

d. The Greek way of life and thought changed under the influence of Diogenes. _______

_______ 2. The best title for this passage is
(Question type _______________) (Explain errors)
a. "Diogenes Shocks Athens." _______
b. "Great Greek Philosophers." _______
c. "The Eccentric Behavior of a Philosopher." _______
d. "Diogenes, the Self-Sufficient Cynic." _______

_______ 3. Diogenes' father
(Question type _______________) (Explain errors)
a. was exiled from Athens. _______
b. destroyed counterfeit money. _______
c. stole from the treasury. _______
d. was treasurer of Sinope and Cappadocia. _______

_______ 4. The author believes that Diogenes was all of the following except
(Question type _______________) (Explain errors)
a. uninhibited by tradition. _______
b. insincere in not practicing what he preached. _______
c. angered by his father's persecution. _______
d. vocal in advocating free speech. _______

_______ 5. The author's purpose is to
(Question type _______________) (Explain errors)
a. argue. _______
b. inform. _______
c. ridicule. _______
d. persuade. _______

_______ 6. As used in the passage, the best definition of *affluent* is
(Question type _______________) (Explain errors)
a. wealthy. _______
b. close-knit. _______
c. loving. _______
d. politically prominent. _______

Strategies for Content Area Exams

Almost all professors would say that the number one strategy for scoring high on content exams is to study the material. Although this advice is certainly on target, there are other suggestions that can help you gain an edge.

Multiple-Choice Items

Multiple-choice, true-false, or matching items on content area exams are written to evaluate the following three categories: factual knowledge, conceptual comprehension, and application skill. Factual questions tap your knowledge of names, definitions, dates, events, and theories. Conceptual comprehension questions evaluate your ability to see relationships, notice similarities and differences, and combine information from different parts of a chapter. Application questions provide the opportunity to generalize from a theory to a real-life illustration, and they are particularly popular in psychology and sociology. The following is an example of an application question from psychology.

__________ An illustration of obsessive-compulsive behavior is

a. Maria goes to the movies most Friday nights.
b. Leon washes his hands over a hundred times a day.
c. Pepe wants to buy a car.
d. Sue eats more fish than red meat.

The second response is obviously correct, but such questions can be tricky if you have not prepared for them. To study for a multiple-choice test, make lists of key terms, facts, and concepts. Quiz yourself on recognition and general knowledge. Make connections and be sure you know similarities and differences. Lastly, invent scenarios that depict principles and concepts. Use your own knowledge, plus the previous suggestions for multiple-choice tests, to separate answers from distractors.

Short-Answer Items

Professors ask short-answer questions because they want you to use your own words to describe or identify. For such questions, be sure that you understand exactly what the professor is asking you to say. You do not want to waste time writing more than is needed, but on the other hand, you do not want to lose points for not writing enough. Study for short-answer items by making lists and self-testing, just as you do when studying for multiple-choice items.

Essay Questions

Essay answers demand more effort and energy from the test taker than multiple-choice items. Rather than simply recognizing correct answers, you must recall, create, and organize. On a multiple-choice test, all the correct answers are somewhere before you. On an essay exam, however, the only thing in front of you is a question and a blank sheet of paper. This blank sheet of paper can be intimidating to many students. Your job is to recall appropriate ideas for a response and pull them together under the central theme designated in the question. The following suggestions can help you respond effectively.

Translate the Question. Frequently the "question" is not a question at all. It may be a statement that you must first turn into a question. Read and reread this statement that is called a *question*. Be sure you understand it and then reword it into a question. Even if you begin with a question, translate it into your own words. Simplify the question into straight terms that you can understand. Break the question into its parts.

Convert the translated parts of the question into the approach that you will need to use to answer each part. Will you define, describe, explain, or compare? State what you will do to answer. In a sense, this is a behavioral statement. The following example demonstrates the process.

- **Statement to Support:** It is both appropriate and ironic to refer to Catherine as one of the great rulers of Russia.
- **Question:** Why is it both appropriate and ironic to refer to Catherine as one of the great rulers of Russia?
- **Translation:** The question has two parts:
  1. What did Catherine do that was really great?
  2. What did she do that was the opposite of what you would expect (irony) of a great Russian ruler?
- **Response Approach:** List what Catherine did that was great and list what she did that was the opposite of what you would expect of a great Russian ruler. Relate her actions to the question. (See page 502.)

Answer the Question. Your answer should be in response to the question that is asked and not a summary of everything you know about a particular subject. Write with purpose so that the reader can understand your views and relate your points to the subject. Padding your answer by repeating the same idea or including irrelevant information is obvious to graders and seldom appreciated.

EXAMPLE

The following is an inappropriate answer to the question "Why is it both appropriate and ironic to refer to Catherine as one of the great rulers of Russia?"

> Catherine was born in Germany and came to Russia as a young girl to marry Peter. It was an unhappy marriage that lasted seventeen years. She . . .

(This response does not answer the question: it is a summary.)

Organize Your Response. Do not write the first thing to pop into your head. Take a few minutes to brainstorm and jot down ideas. Number the ideas in the order that you wish to present them and use the plan at the top of page 516 as your outline for writing.

In your first sentence, establish the purpose and direction of your response. Then list specific details that support, explain, prove, and develop your point. Reemphasize the points in a concluding sentence and restate your purpose. Whenever possible, use numbers or subheadings to simplify your message for the reader. If time runs short, use an outline or a diagram to express your remaining ideas.

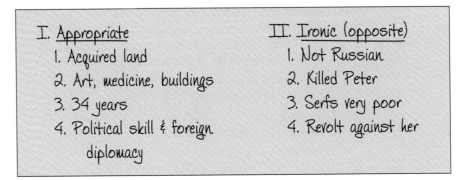

I. Appropriate
1. Acquired land
2. Art, medicine, buildings
3. 34 years
4. Political skill & foreign diplomacy

II. Ironic (opposite)
1. Not Russian
2. Killed Peter
3. Serfs very poor
4. Revolt against her

EXAMPLE To answer the previous question, think about the selection on Catherine and jot down the ideas that you would include in a response.

Use an Appropriate Style. Your audience for this response is not your best friend or buckaroo but your learned professor who is going to give you a grade. Be respectful. Do not use slang. Do not use phrases like "as you know" or "well." They may be appropriate in conversation, but they are not appropriate in formal writing.

Avoid empty words and thoughts. Words like *good, interesting,* and *nice* say very little. Be more direct and descriptive in your writing.

State your thesis, supply proof, and use transitional phrases to tie your ideas together. Words like *first, second,* and *finally* help to organize enumerations. Terms like *however* and *on the other hand* show a shift in thought. Remember, you are pulling ideas together, so use phrases and words to help the reader see relationships.

Study the following response to the question for organization, transition, and style.

Catherine was a very good ruler of Russia. She tried to be Russian but she was from Germany. Catherine was a good politician and got Russia seaports on the Baltic, Caspian, and Black Sea. She had many boyfriends and there was gossip about her. She did very little for the Serfs because they remained very poor for a long time. She built nice buildings and got doctors to help people. She was not as awesome as she pretended to be.

(Note the total lack of organization, the weak language, inappropriate phrases, and the failure to use traditional words.)

Be Aware of Appearance. Research has shown that, on the average, essays written in a clear, legible hand receive a grade level higher score than essays written somewhat illegibly.[6] Be particular about appearance and considerate of the reader. Proofread for correct grammar, punctuation, and spelling.

Predict and Practice. Predict possible essay items by using the table of contents and subheadings of your text to form questions. Practice brainstorming to answer these questions. Review old exams for an insight both into the questions and the kinds of answers that received good marks. Outline answers to possible exam questions. Do as much thinking as possible to prepare yourself to take the test before you sit down to begin writing.

View Your Response Objectively for Evaluation Points. Respond to get points. Some students feel that filling up the page deserves a passing grade. They do not understand how a whole page written on the subject of Catherine could receive no points.

Although essay exams seem totally subjective, they cannot be. Students need to know that a professor who gives an essay exam grades answers according to an objective scoring system. The professor examines the paper for certain relevant points that should be made. The student's grade reflects the quantity, quality, and clarity of these relevant points.

Unfortunately, essay exams are shrouded in mystery. The hardest part of answering an item is to figure out what the professor wants. Ask yourself, "What do I need to say to get enough points to pass or to make an *A*?"

Do not add personal experiences or extraneous examples unless they are requested. You may be wasting your time by including information that will give you no points. Stick to the subject and the material. Demonstrate to the professor that you know the material by selectively using it in your response.

The professor scoring the response to the question about Catherine used the following checklist for evaluation.

Appropriate	Ironic
1. Acquired land	1. Not Russian
2. Art, medicine, buildings	2. Killed Peter
3. 34 years	3. Serfs very poor
4. Political skill and foreign diplomacy	4. Revolt against her

The professor determined that an *A* paper should contain all of the items. In order to pass, a student should give five of the eight categories covered. Listing and explaining less than five would not produce enough points to pass. Naturally, the professor would expect clarity and elaboration in each category.

[6]H. W. James, "The Effect of Handwriting upon Grading," *English Journal* 16 (1927): 180–85.

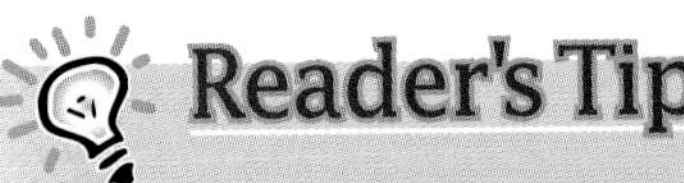

Key Words in Essay Questions

The following key words of instruction appear in essay questions.

* **Compare:** List the similarities between things.
* **Contrast:** Note the differences between things.
* **Criticize:** State your opinion and stress the weaknesses.
* **Define:** State the meaning so that the term is understood, and use examples.
* **Describe:** State the characteristics so that the image is vivid.
* **Diagram:** Make a drawing that demonstrates relationships.
* **Discuss:** Define the issue and elaborate on the advantages and disadvantages.
* **Evaluate:** State positive and negative views and make a judgment.
* **Explain:** Show cause and effect and give reasons.
* **Illustrate:** Provide examples.
* **Interpret:** Explain your own understanding of a topic that includes your opinions.
* **Justify:** Give proof or reasons to support an opinion.
* **List:** Record a series of numbered items.
* **Outline:** Sketch out the main points with their significant supporting details.
* **Prove:** Use facts as evidence in support of an opinion.
* **Relate:** Connect items and show how one influences another.
* **Review:** Write an overview with a summary.
* **Summarize:** Retell the main points.
* **Trace:** Move sequentially from one event to another.

After the Test, Read an *A* Paper. Maybe the *A* paper will be yours. If so, share it with others. If not, ask to read an *A* paper so that you will have a model from which to learn. Ask your classmates or ask the professor. You can learn a lot from reading a good paper; you can see what you could have done.

When your professor returns a multiple-choice exam, you can reread items and analyze your mistakes to figure out what you did wrong. However, you cannot review essay exams so easily. You may get back a C paper with only a word or two of comment and never know what you should have done. Ideally, essay exams should be returned with an example of what would have been a perfect *A* response so that students can study and learn from a perfect model and not make the same mistakes on the next test, but this is seldom, if ever, done. Your best bet is to ask to see an *A* paper.

Study the following response to the previous question. The paper received an *A*.

> To call Catherine one of the great rulers of Russia is both appropriate and ironic. It is appropriate because she expanded the borders of Russia.. Through her cunning, Russia annexed part of Poland and expanded the frontier to the Black, Caspian, and Baltic seas. Catherine professed to be enlightened and formed an art academy and a college of pharmacy, and she imported foreign physicians. She built many architecturally significant buildings, including the Hermitage. For thirty-four years she amazed the Russian people with her political skill and diplomacy.
>
> On the other hand, Catherine was not a great Russian, nor was she an enlightened leader of all the people. First, she was not Russian; she was German, but she had worked hard to "russify" herself during the early years of her unhappy marriage. Second, and ironically, she murdered the legitimate ruler of Russia. When she seized power, she made sure the tsar quickly died of "hemorrhoidal colic." Third, she did nothing to improve the lot of the poor serfs and after a bloody uprising in 1773, she became even more despotic. Yet, Catherine was an engaging character who, through her cunning and intellect, has become known to the world in history books as "Catherine the Great."

(Note the organization, logical thinking, and use of transitions in this response.)

Locus of Control

Have you ever heard students say, "I do better when I don't study," or "No matter how much I study, I still get a C"? According to Julian Rotter, a learning theory psychologist who believes that people develop attitudes about control of their lives, such comments reflect an external locus of control regarding test taking.[7] Such "externalizers" feel that fate, luck, or others control what happens to them. Since they feel they can do little to avoid what befalls them, they do not face matters directly and thus do not take responsibility for failure or credit for success.

People who have an internal locus of control, on the other hand, feel that they, rather than "fate," have control over what happens to them. Such students

[7]Julian Rotter, "External Control and Internal Control," *Psychology Today*, 5(1) (1971): 37–42.

might evaluate test performance by saying, "I didn't study enough" or "I should have spent more time organizing my essay response." "Internalizers" feel their rewards are due to their own actions, and thus they take steps to be sure they receive those rewards. When it comes to test taking, be an "internalizer," take control, and accept the credit for your success.

Summary Points

- **Can testwiseness help?**

  Test taking is a serious part of the business of being a college student. Preparation and practice—testwiseness—can lead to improved scores on both standardized reading tests and content area exams.

- **How should you prepare before a test?**

  Study according to the type of test you are taking. Plan your study times so that you are not cramming. Arrive rested and alert.

- **What should you notice during a test?**

  Read the directions and keep up with the time.

- **What strategies should you use to read a comprehension passage?**

  Items on standardized reading tests tend to follow a predictable pattern and include five major question types. Learn to recognize these types and the skills needed for answering each.

- **What are the major question types?**

  They are (1) main idea, (2) details, (3) inference, (4) purpose, and (5) vocabulary.

- **What hints help with multiple-choice items?**

  Be careful, not careless; consider all options; notice key words; and use logical reasoning.

- **How do you answer an essay question?**

  Be sure you understand the question, brainstorm your response, organize your thoughts, and write in paragraphs with specific examples.

READER'S JOURNAL

Name ______________________ Date __________

CHAPTER 12

Answer the following questions to learn about your own learning and reflect on your progress. Use the perforations to tear the assignment out for your instructor.

1. How were you or were you not physically prepared for your last test?
2. How did you divide your time on the last test?
3. In what subjects do you have test anxiety? Why?
4. Are you anxious about public speaking? Why or why not?
5. Review your correct and incorrect responses to the comprehension questions in this text. What type of question seems to be most difficult for you?
6. What type of question do you usually get correct?
7. How would you diagnose your problems on multiple-choice tests?
8. How would you describe the difference in your preparation for a multiple-choice or an essay exam in history?
9. Do you score higher on multiple-choice or essay exams? Why?

Appendix 1

Ten Weekly Vocabulary Lessons

Expand your vocabulary by linking new words with familiar word parts. Learn more than 200 words in the following ten vocabulary lessons using a "word family" approach. Plan to master one lesson each week. All weekly lessons follow the same format except for slight variations in Lesson 3 on doctors and Lesson 10 on foreign terms.

Directions:

- Begin by learning the word parts and definitions listed at the beginning of each lesson.
- Brainstorm any words that you already know using the listed prefixes, suffixes, or roots.
- Read the initial sentence for each section and underline the word that uses a related word part.
- At the end of each list, fill in the blank with an additional word that fits the definition and uses the highlighted prefix, suffix, or root.
- Study the bulleted "family" words and the sentences in which they are used.
- Complete the review exercises to quiz yourself and reinforce your learning. Be flexible in adding suffix variations to the bulleted words.
- Continue to study the new words in short intervals throughout the week to reinforce learning. Prepare for a 20-item multiple-choice quiz to review your progress.

Lesson 1: Over, Under, Around, and Through

Prefixes

sur-: over, above, more
amb-, ambi-: around, about, both
sub-: under, beneath
dia-: through

Words with *sur-:* over, above, or more

The fugitive surrendered himself to the police when he could no longer avoid capture.

- ***surcharge:*** an additional charge, tax, or cost
  The *surcharge* on items such as cigarettes or alcohol is sometimes called a "sin tax" since these items are considered by some to be vices rather than necessities.
- ***surface:*** uppermost or outermost area; top layer
  When the deep-sea diver reached the *surface,* he saw that he had drifted far from his boat.
- ***surfeit:*** overindulgence in eating or drinking, an excessive amount
  Thanksgiving dinner usually means a *surfeit* of foods far beyond the usual amount served for an everyday meal.
- ***surmise:*** to guess, to infer without certain evidence
  At the point that Cindy and Gary were thirty minutes late to the ball game, I *surmised* that they probably were not coming.
- ***surveillance:*** a watch kept over someone or something
  The United States flies *surveillance* missions all over the world to collect information vital to our security.
- _______: an amount greater than needed
  The government had collected more taxes than it needed, so there was a ____________ to be returned to the taxpayers.

Words with *sub-:* under, beneath

Jorge's subconscious belief that he wasn't a good enough athlete probably contributed to his poor performance during basketball tryouts.

- ***subsequent:*** occurring later, following
  Ill health is usually a *subsequent* occurrence after long periods of ignoring good nutrition and getting little sleep.
- ***subservient:*** excessively submissive
  Victorian husbands expected their wives to be *subservient.*
- ***subsidiary:*** subordinate or secondary
  The food products corporation decided to sell its *subsidiary* clothing company and remain focused on foods.
- ***substantiate:*** to establish by proof
  A witness was able to *substantiate* Linda's story that the auto accident was not her fault.
- ***subvert:*** to overthrow something, such as a government; to cause the ruin of
  Castro's regime in Cuba came into power by *subverting* Batista's presidency.
- __________: a means of supporting life
  Her small ____________ check from the government was all the octogenarian had for living expenses after her husband died.

Words with *amb-, ambi-:* around, about, both

The horse's gait was kept to an amble as the jockey slowly walked him into the winner's circle.

- ***ambiance*** or ***ambience:*** the mood or atmosphere of a place or situation
  The day spa's low lighting, comfortable furnishings, and quiet music produced an *ambience* of soothing relaxation.
- ***ambidextrous:*** able to use both hands equally well; unusually skillful
  Being *ambidextrous* allows Keisha to write for long periods of time by switching hands when one gets tired.
- ***ambiguous:*** having two or more possible meanings
  Rosa was *ambiguous* when she said she fell on the skiing trip. We expected to see a cast on her leg, not a new boyfriend on her arm.
- ***ambivalent:*** fluctuating between two choices; having opposing feelings
  Jealousy and tremendous familial pride were the two *ambivalent* feelings Juan was experiencing over his brother's acceptance at a prestigious school.
- ***ambulatory:*** capable of walking
  Doctors didn't think Nora would be *ambulatory* again after the accident damaged her spinal cord.
- _______: strong desire for fame or power
  His ____________ to climb the corporate ladder drove Jim to work long hours to accomplish his goal.

Words with *dia-:* through

If you know the diameter of a circle, it is easy to find the circumference.

- ***diagnosis:*** a determination of the cause of medical symptoms; analysis of the cause of a situation
  The doctor's *diagnosis* of strep throat was proved correct when the lab report came back.
- ***dialogue:*** conversation between two or more persons
  The three actors practiced the scenes in which they had a humorous *dialogue* together.
- ***diametrical:*** pertaining to a diameter; at opposite extremes
  Susan was pro-life and *diametrically* opposed to any pro-choice legislation in Congress.
- ***diatribe:*** a bitter, abusive criticism
  After listening to a *diatribe* from her possessive boyfriend because she spent time with her girlfriends, Angelina decided to end the unhealthy relationship.
- ***dialect:*** a distinct variety of a language that differs from the standard
  Parts of rural England have *dialects* that differ from the English spoken in London.
- _______: an oblique or slanting line connecting opposite corners or angles
  Rather than being laid square, the floor tiles were laid on the ____________ for an additional decorative effect.

Review

Part I

Choose the best word from the box to complete the sentences below.

ambience	ambulatory	diagnosis	dialect	diametric	subsequent
	subsidiaries	surface	surfeit	surveillance	

1. Even though the patient was ________________, the hospital required her to leave the facility in a wheelchair.
2. ________________ to receiving his college degree, Jose secured job interviews with four companies he had been unable to interview with before.
3. The literary ________________ of Shakespeare's time differs from the ordinary language in word order and vocabulary.
4. The ________________ created by the candlelight, flowers, and violins made the restaurant dinner especially romantic.
5. Jordan's speedy ________________ of the computer problem in the office got everyone back online quickly and prevented a significant delay in the work schedule.
6. For many people, freckles show up on the ________________ of the skin after exposure to the sun.
7. Many large companies are diversified and own ________________ that are secondary to their main area of business.
8. The sick feeling I had when I woke up this morning was a result of the ________________ of food and drink at the party the night before.
9. Feelings of love and hate are at ________________ ends of the spectrum.
10. The murder suspect was under ________________ by police who were hoping to catch him with new evidence.

Part II

Choose the best synonym from the boxed list for each of the words below.

confirm	conversation	corrupt	excess	presume	skillful
	stroll	subordinate	tirade	vague	

11. surmise ________________
12. ambidextrous ________________
13. surplus ________________
14. dialogue ________________
15. subvert ________________
16. substantiate ________________
17. amble ________________
18. diatribe ________________
19. ambiguous ________________
20. subservient ________________

Lesson 2: The Good, the Bad, and the Ugly

Prefixes

bene-: well, good
mal-: bad, evil
eu-: good
kakos- (caco-): harsh, bad, ugly

Words with *bene-:* well, good

During the benediction, the minister blessed the infant and called for all family members to be positive influences in the child's life.

- ***benefaction:*** a charitable donation
  The anonymous *benefaction* came just in time to prevent the foreclosure on the school for the deaf.
- ***beneficial:*** producing a benefit; helpful
  The week away from work proved *beneficial* to Miguel, and he returned refreshed and cheerful.
- ***beneficiary:*** a person or group who receives advantages; one named to receive funds or property in a will
  The lawyer's call telling Rosa she was named as a *beneficiary* in a will came as a complete surprise to her.
- ***benefit:*** something that causes improvement or an advantage; a public event to raise money for a charitable cause
  As a prospective new father, Charles was relieved when he became eligible for medical *benefits* at work.
- ***benevolent:*** expressing goodwill or kindness; charitable; set up to do charitable works
  The *Benevolent* Women's Society set a priority of addressing the needs of the elderly in the community.
- ________: person who gives a benefit
  The wealthy ____________ achieved great satisfaction from donating money to the charity.

Words with *eu-:* good

The eulogy delivered at the funeral was full of praise, befitting the benevolent character of the deceased.

- ***euphony:*** a pleasant sounding combination of words
  The poem had a lilting rhythm and a harmonious *euphony* that fell like music on the ears.
- ***euphoria:*** a feeling of well-being, confidence, or happiness
  After winning the State Salsa Championship, Jose and his dancing partner experienced a *euphoria* that lasted for days.
- ***euphemism:*** a substitution of a milder word or expression for a more blunt or offensive one
  Barry expressed his condolences to the widow at the funeral by using the *euphemism* "passed away" rather than expressing sorrow that her loved one had committed suicide.
- ***euthanasia:*** putting to death painlessly or allowing to die; mercy killing
  Dr. Jack Kevorkian is well known as an advocate of *euthanasia* for patients who are terminally ill and request his services.
- ______: an exclamation of triumph at a discovery, meaning, "I have found it!"
  Archimedes exclaimed, "____________!" when he discovered a test for the purity of gold.

Words with *mal-:* bad, evil

After being confronted, Marie realized the pain she had caused Janice by continuing to malign her in public about a previous boyfriend.

- ***maladroit:*** lacking resourcefulness; awkward; not skillful in using the hands or body
  Because of his *maladroit* sawing and hammering, Jules wasn't going to sign up for the furniture-making class.
- ***malady:*** a sickness or disorder of the body; an unhealthy condition
  Some of the volunteers working in the impoverished country had come down with an unidentified *malady*.
- ***malaise:*** general weakness or discomfort usually before the onset of a disease
  Emily canceled her long-anticipated trip due to her general feelings of *malaise* for the past several days.
- ***malapropism:*** an amusing misuse of words that produces an inappropriate meaning
  After asking the waiter to bring the soap du jour, John was embarrassed to have made such a *malapropism*.
- ***malcontent:*** someone unsatisfied with current conditions
  Numerous *malcontents* were protesting outside the school about the hiring of the famous professor.
- ***malevolent:*** wishing evil or harm to others; injurious
  Georgia had *malevolent* feelings toward the girls on the newly selected cheerleading squad and wished one of them would break a leg.
- ***malfeasance:*** misconduct or wrongdoing, especially by a public official
  Some voters feel that Bill Clinton committed the greatest *malfeasance* in office of any elected official—lying to the American people; others feel he committed a crime—lying under oath.
- __________: fail to function properly
  Although it worked well at the store, the computer ____________ when we got it home and set it up.

Words with *kakos- (caco-):* harsh, bad, ugly

- ***cacophony:*** a harsh, jarring sound; a discordant and meaningless mixture of sound
  The toddler's attempt to play an improvised drum set of pots, pans, and spoons created such a *cacophony* that her father required earplugs.
- __________: bad handwriting; poor spelling
  His sister's beautiful calligraphy was in stark contrast to Mark's messy ____________.

Review

Part I

Indicate whether the underlined word in each of the following sentences is used correctly (C) or incorrectly (I).

_________ 1. The unexplained *cacophony* of shrieks, banging, and irritating musical sounds that frequently woke the Williamsons in the early morning made them think their house was haunted.

_________ 2. Marguerite's prescription proved *beneficial*, and she was over her symptoms of bronchitis in a few days.

_________ 3. "*Eureka!*" shrieked Marielle as she lost her ring down the sink drain.

_________ 4. The *beneficiary* of a will is entrusted with the duties of carrying out the wishes of the deceased and receives nothing for performing these duties.

_________ 5. The new play was an experimental performance that was made possible by a patron of the arts, a *benefactor* who funded the production.

_________ 6. The new car that Manuel received as a graduation present gave him such a feeling of *eulogy* that he didn't even feel bad when his girlfriend broke up with him.

_________ 7. Jeanette's *malaise* had given her so much energy she just wanted to stay out dancing all night.

_________ 8. The harsh criticisms of the drill instructor were *euphonious* to the ears of the overworked recruits.

_________ 9. Film buffs know Clint Eastwood's character in *The Good, the Bad, and the Ugly* as a man of few words; those few words, however, weren't wasted on *euphemisms*—he just said it like it was.

_________ 10. Benito learned how *maladroit* he was after the audition for the new *Survivor* show revealed his lack of skill and resourcefulness in the wild.

Part II

Choose the best synonym from the boxed list for the words below.

ailment	blessing	clumsy	discord	elation
misconduct	gift	libel	mercy killing	rebellious

11. euphoria _________________
12. cacophony _________________
13. malign _________________
14. euthanasia _________________
15. malfeasance _________________
16. maladroit _________________
17. benediction _________________
18. benefaction _________________
19. malcontent _________________
20. malady _________________

Lesson 3: Who's Who in Medicine?

Suffixes

-ist, - ician: one who

-ologist: one who studies

- ***dermatologist:*** skin doctor (*derma:* skin)
  Dermatologists remove skin cancers.
- ***internist:*** medical doctor for internal organs (*internus:* inside)
  The *internist* will administer a series of tests to determine the cause of Ben's mysterious pain.
- ***intern:*** a medical school graduate serving an apprenticeship at a hospital
  The *interns* work under the close supervision of doctors on the staff.
- ***gynecologist:*** doctor for reproductive systems of women (*gyne:* women)
  The *gynecologist* recommended a Pap smear to check for cervical cancer.
- ***obstetrician:*** doctor who delivers babies (*obstetrix:* midwife)
  Many *obstetricians* are also gynecologists.
- ***pediatrician:*** doctor for children (*paidos:* children)
  Pediatricians use antibiotics to treat sore throats and earaches.
- ***ophthalmologist*** or ***oculist:*** doctor who performs eye surgery
  The *ophthalmologist* performed the cataract surgery on the woman.
- ***optometrist:*** specialist for measuring vision
  An *optometrist* tests eyesight and fits glasses and contact lenses.
- ***optician:*** specialist who makes visual correction lenses for eyeglasses and contact lenses
  Opticians are usually working behind the scene, often at an optometrist's office.
- ***orthopedist:*** doctor who corrects abnormalities in bones and joints (*orthos:* straight or correct)
  The *orthopedist* set up his practice near a ski area.
- ***orthodontist:*** dentist for straightening teeth
  Her braces had to be adjusted every six weeks by the *orthodontist.*
- ***cardiologist:*** heart doctor (*cardio:* heart)
  Cardiologists treat patients who have had heart attacks.
- ***psychiatrist:*** doctor for treating mental disorders (*psycho:* mind)
  The *psychiatrist* prescribed drugs for the treatment of depression.
- ***psychologist:*** counselor for treating mental disorders
  The *psychologist* administered tests to determine the cause of the child's behavior.
- ***neurologist:*** doctor for disorders of the brain, spinal cord, and nervous system (*neuron:* nerve)
  Neurologists are searching for new treatments for patients who have suffered a spinal cord injury.
- ***oncologist:*** doctor for treating cancer and tumors (*onkos:* mass)
  The *oncologist* recommended various methods for dealing with the cancerous tumor.
- ***urologist:*** doctor specializing in the urinary tract (*ouro:* urine)
  The *urologist* was treating several patients for impotence.
- ***podiatrist:*** specialist in the care and treatment of the foot (*pod:* foot)
  The *podiatrist* knew the best way to deal with blisters, corns, and bunions.
- ***anesthesiologist:*** doctor who administers anesthesia to patients undergoing surgery (*anesthesia:* insensibility)
  Usually a patient will meet the *anesthesiologist* just prior to surgery.
- ***hematologist:*** doctor who studies the blood and blood-forming organs (*hemat:* blood)
  A hematoma is treated by a *hematologist.*
- ***radiologist:*** doctor using radiant energy for diagnostic and therapeutic purposes (*radio:* radiant waves)
  After the removal of a cancerous tumor, further treatment by a *radiologist* is usually recommended.

Review

Part I

Indicate whether the following sentences are true (T) or false (F).

_______ 1. A hematologist puts patients to sleep for operations.

_______ 2. Dermatologists treat acne.

_______ 3. An internist investigates stomach pain.

_______ 4. An optometrist can fit eyeglasses.

_______ 5. A pediatrician operates primarily on the feet.

_______ 6. A psychologist is a medical doctor.

_______ 7. An obstetrician treats cancer.

_______ 8. Optometrists and oculists are two terms for doctors who do eye surgery.

_______ 9. An anesthesiologist attends to a patient in the days after an operation.

_______ 10. Neurologists treat patients who have a family history of breast cancer.

Part II

Choose the doctor from the boxed list that best fits the job description.

gynecologist	radiologist	intern	optician	cardiologist
orthodontist	urologist	orthopedist	psychiatrist	oncologist

11. Treats mental disorders with drugs _______________
12. Medical student still in training _______________
13. Doctor for women's reproductive systems _______________
14. Sets broken arms and legs _______________
15. Makes the lenses for eyeglasses _______________
16. Straightens teeth _______________
17. Operates on urinary tract _______________
18. Specialist for treating cancer _______________
19. Performs surgery on the heart _______________
20. Uses radiation to diagnose and treat cancer _______________

Lesson 4: What's In, What's Out? What's Hot, What's Not?

Prefixes		Root
en-, em-: in *non-:* not	*e-, ec-, ef-, ex-:* out	*calor:* heat

Words with *en-, em-:* in

Jackson was able to employ several of his friends as tech reps for his Internet software company.

- ***encapsulate:*** to place in a capsule; to condense or summarize
  Drug manufacturers *encapsulate* some medications so that they are easier to swallow.
- ***enclave:*** any small, distinct area or group within a larger one
  Before the Berlin Wall came down, West Berlin was a democratic *enclave* surrounded by communist East Germany.
- ***enmesh:*** to catch in a net; entangle
  Animal rights groups are against the use of nets in tuna fishing because dolphins become *enmeshed* in the nets and die.
- ***ensemble:*** all parts of a thing considered only as the whole, not separately, such as an entire costume or a group of musicians, singers, dancers, or actors.
  The cast of NBC's sitcom *Friends* is an *ensemble* of six actors.
- ***embed:*** to fix or place firmly in a surrounding mass; to insert, as a clause in a sentence
  The senator knew that to get his controversial proposal passed by Congress, he had to *embed* it in a more popular bill.
- ***embroiled:*** to be involved in conflict or confusion
  The twins were *embroiled* in a wrestling match when their father finally had to separate them.
- ***embellish:*** to beautify with ornamental or elaborate details
  The speech writer's goal was to enhance but not overly *embellish* the governor's speeches.
- _____: to register or become a member of a group
  Jenny needed to ____________ in the Psychology 101 class before it became filled.

Words with *e-, ec-, ef-, ex-:* out

It's best to renew your driver's license before it expires to avoid having to take the driving test again.

- ***eclipse:*** any obscuring of light (darkening) especially of planets; to surpass by comparison
  To protect your eyes during a solar *eclipse,* wear sunglasses and look at the sun only through a pinhole in a piece of paper.
- ***emaciate:*** to make abnormally thin; a gradual wasting away
  Tanica had lost so much weight on her fad diet that she looked *emaciated.*
- ***eccentric:*** peculiar or odd; not having the same center
  The neighbor on the corner is an *eccentric* man who wears pajamas to the grocery store.
- ***effervescent:*** bubbling; lively or enthusiastic
  The bottled spring water was so *effervescent* that they let it set awhile so the bubbles of gas could escape.
- ***exalt:*** raise or elevate in rank or character; praise highly
  In his opening remarks, the club president *exalted* the literary talent and accomplishments of the guest speaker.
- __________: to stretch the limits of the truth or overstate
  John always ____________ the size of the fish he claims he almost caught.

Words with *non-:* not

Military personnel such as surgeons or chaplains who are not fighters are considered noncombatants.

- ***nonchalant:*** coolly indifferent, unconcerned, unexcited
  Tonia's *nonchalant* way of accepting dates makes it seem as though she just has nothing better to do.
- ***nondescript:*** undistinguished or dull, a person or thing of no specific type or kind; not easy to describe
  Since the dorm rooms were extremely *nondescript,* students used imagination and money to decorate the space to reflect their own personalities.
- ***nonpartisan:*** an objective person; not controlled by any established political party
  It is almost a necessity to have *nonpartisan* politics when the government is split evenly between two parties.
- ***nonplussed:*** completely puzzled, totally perplexed so as to become unable to continue
  The stand-up comedian was inexperienced and became totally *nonplussed* by the hecklers in the audience.
- ____________: someone who refuses to act in accordance with established customs
  A ____________ would not be a good candidate for a private school where uniforms are worn.

Words with *calor-:* heat

When capitalized, the word Calorie refers to Kilocalorie (1,000 small calories) and is used to measure the amount of energy produced by food when oxidized in the body.

- ***calorie:*** a specific unit of heat (cal.) in physics; a unit expressing the energy value of food (Cal.) in nutrition
  Judy always tries to eat low-*calorie* meals including salads, fish, lots of vegetables, and few desserts to maintain a healthy weight.
- ***caloric:*** of or pertaining to calories or heat; high in calories
  Eating highly *caloric* meals makes it necessary to exercise more often just to maintain your current weight.
- ***scald:*** to burn with hot liquid or steam; to bring to a temperature just short of the boiling point
  Some recipes require the cook to *scald* milk before adding it to the other ingredients.
- ***caldera:*** a basinlike depression or collapsed area caused by the explosion of the center of a volcano
  The scientists were injured by hot lava when they got too close to the edge of the *caldera* of a still active volcano.
- _______: a large kettle for boiling
  Shakespeare's *Macbeth* includes a scene with witches stirring their boiling mixture in a ____________.

Review

Part I

Indicate whether the following sentences are true (T) or false (F).

_________ 1. An encapsulated version of a book is a shortened or condensed version.

_________ 2. Nonplussed is a mathematical term for omitting addition.

_________ 3. Starvation causes the body to become emaciated.

_________ 4. A person with an effervescent personality would probably be dull and uninteresting.

_________ 5. Embroiled describes a healthy way to have meats cooked.

_________ 6. A red BMW convertible would most likely be considered a nondescript vehicle.

_________ 7. Caldera is the lava that spills from a volcano.

_________ 8. An ensemble can be a group of people or things.

_________ 9. A Kilocalorie is equivalent to one hundred small calories.

_________ 10. A person who does not like parties or celebrations is known as a nonpartisan.

Part II

Choose the best antonym from the boxed list for the words below.

brighten compliant chill dislodge fatten
interested minimized undecorated untangled usual

11. eccentric _________________

12. embellished _________________

13. eclipse _________________

14. exaggerated _________________

15. emaciate _________________

16. enmeshed _________________

17. embed _________________

18. nonchalant _________________

19. scald _________________

20. nonconformist _________________

Lesson 5: The Sun, the Moon, and the Stars

Roots
sol, helio: sun
aster, astro: star
luna: moon

Words with *sol, helio:* sun

A sundial is a primitive example of a solar chronometer, a device indicating the time by means of the sun.

- ***solar:*** of or pertaining to the sun; proceeding from the sun; operating on energy from the sun
  Solar panels on rooftops to heat water for homes have become a popular way to conserve energy.
- ***solarium:*** a glass-enclosed room that is exposed to the sun's rays
  A *solarium* in a home usually becomes the favorite spot in winter because it is naturally warmed by the sun.
- ***solstice:*** either of two times a year when the sun is farthest from the equator
  The summer *solstice,* the longest day in the Northern Hemisphere, occurs around June 21 or 22 when the sun is farthest north of the equator.
- ***heliotherapy:*** treatment of disease by exposure to sunlight
  Heliotherapy is prescribed sunbathing for certain illnesses such as tuberculosis or rickets.
- ***heliotropic:*** turning or growing toward the light or sun
  Without frequent turning, some *heliotropic* houseplants would grow only in one direction—toward the sunlight.
- ____: an inert gaseous element present in the sun's atmosphere and in natural gas
  Since ________ is a chemically inactive gas, it is used as a substitute for flammable gases in dirigibles (blimps).

Words with *luna:* moon

The small demilune table was just the right size for the narrow foyer since its half-moon shape did not extend far into the room.

- ***lunar:*** of or pertaining to the moon; round or crescent-shaped; measured by the moon's revolutions
  A *lunar* month is equal to one revolution of the moon around the earth, approximately 29½ days.
- ***lunatic:*** an insane or recklessly foolish person
  The old gentleman was labeled a *lunatic* and unable to handle his legal affairs responsibly.
- ***lunatic fringe:*** members on the edges of a group, such as a political or religious group, who hold extreme views
  Members of the *lunatic fringe* of some environmentalist movements have destroyed property to protest further building in certain areas.
- ***lunar eclipse:*** an obscuring of the light of the moon when the earth is positioned between the moon and the sun
  During a *lunar eclipse* the earth casts its shadow on the moon.
- ________: a division of time equal to twelve lunar months
  In a ___________ the moon orbits the earth twelve times.

Words with *aster, astro:* star

An aster is a daisylike flower with colored petals radiating around a yellow disk.

- ***asterisk:*** a small, starlike symbol (*) used in writing and printing to refer to footnotes or omissions
  An *asterisk* can be used to refer readers to an explanation of an item in the written material.
- ***asteroid:*** a small, solid body orbiting the sun between Mars and Jupiter
  Scientists believe that *asteroids* collided with earth in the past and predict they will do so again.
- ***astronomy:*** the science that deals with the universe beyond the earth's atmosphere
  Astronomy involves studying the motion, position, and size of celestial bodies.
- ***astronomical:*** pertaining to astronomy; extremely large or enormous
  Projected costs for the new hospital wing were so *astronomical* that the board decided to postpone the project.
- ***astrology:*** the study that attempts to foretell the future by interpreting the influence of the stars on human lives
  Most people don't believe in *astrology;* they believe they are responsible for what happens in their future.
- ________: a person trained for space flight
  The ___________ all went to bed early the night before their scheduled space shuttle mission.

Review

Part I

Choose the word from the boxed list that best completes each of the sentences below.

asterisks	asteroids	heliotherapy	helium
lunar	lunatic fringe	solar	solstice

1. In *Stopping by Woods on a Snowy Evening,* Robert Frost refers to "The darkest evening of the year"—the winter ________________ or shortest day of the year.
2. When reading advertisements, it's wise to look for ________________ that might refer the reader to fine print that further explains pertinent conditions.
3. A ________________ eclipse occurs when the moon comes between the sun and a point on the earth causing the sun to appear darkened from that point.
4. Ocean tides are affected by ________________ attraction of the moon.
5. Another term for orbiting ________________ is *space junk.*
6. Too much ________________ can lead to sunstroke.
7. To accomplish their goal of saving lives, some of the ________________ of the Pro-Life Movement have taken extreme contradictory measures such as bombing abortion clinics and killing doctors who perform abortions.
8. Besides enabling blimps to fly, ________________ makes balloons float.

Part II

Indicate whether the underlined word in the following sentences in used correctly (C) or incorrectly (I).

__________ 9. Kelly wants to study *astronomy* so that she knows the signs of the zodiac and can set up shop as a fortune-teller.

__________ 10. The *asters* blossomed across the backyard planting beds in colorful drifts of pink and white.

__________ 11. The *demilune* table that the Eriksons bought was too square and boxy for the round foyer.

__________ 12. The dermatologist told Angela that aging of the skin is attributed to exposure to *solar* rays.

__________ 13. Sue made sure to buy only *heliotropic* furniture so it would not be damaged if left in the sun.

__________ 14. Bill's friends all thought it was sheer *lunacy* for Bill to ski the expert slope on his first day of skiing.

__________ 15. One controversial theory about the extinction of the dinosaurs is that an *asteroid* hit the earth, destroying their food supply.

Lesson 6: Can I Get That in Writing?

Roots

graph: write

scrib, scrip: write

Words with *graph:* write

Tests that use computer-readable answer sheets require that a No. 2 graphite pencil be used for marking the answers.

- ***graph:*** something written; a diagram or chart; a network of lines connecting points
  The calculus homework required a written solution and a corresponding *graph* for each problem.
- ***graphic:*** described in realistic detail; vivid; pertaining to any of the graphic arts such as painting, drawing, and engraving
  The movie had too much *graphic* violence to get anything other than an R rating.
- ***phonograph:*** a machine for reproducing sound from records in the form of cylinders or spiral-grooved revolving disks
  The early *phonograph* had a tuba-looking device that transmitted the sound.
- ***cinematography:*** the art or technique of motion-picture photography
  The movie that won Best Picture at the Academy Awards also won for *cinematography.*
- ***polygraph:*** a lie detector
  A *polygraph* records changes in such things as a pulse rate or respiration to determine if a person is telling the truth.
- ***geography:*** the science dealing with differences between areas of the earth's surface, such as climate, population, elevation, vegetation or land use
  Interactions between populations may be explained by *geography*—such as whether mountains or rivers separate them or whether they are in close proximity.
- _______: a system for sending distant messages or signals between two electric devices connected by wire
  The telephone and e-mail on the Internet have largely replaced the __________ as a means of communicating.

Words with *scrib, scrip:* write

The bride and groom had an inscription engraved inside each of their wedding rings.

- ***scribble:*** to write hastily or carelessly; to cover with meaningless marks
  Before running to catch my bus, I quickly *scribbled* a note to my roommate that I would not be home for dinner.
- ***transcribe:*** to make a written or typed copy of spoken material; to translate into another language
  Saundra loved her job at the U.N. where she *transcribed* multilingual meetings into English.
- ***transcript:*** a written, typewritten, or printed copy of something
  An official *transcript* of your college records is required when you transfer to another school.
- ***ascribe:*** to assign or attribute to a particular cause or source
  Stephen *ascribes* his good looks to his father's genes.
- ***subscription:*** a sum of money pledged as a contribution; the right to receive a magazine or other service for a sum; the act of appending one's signature to a document
  Public television relies on *subscriptions* pledged during their annual fund-raising drives.
- ***prescription:*** a written direction from a doctor for the preparation and use of a medicine
  Pharmacists read and fill *prescriptions* and usually warn about possible side effects of the prescribed drugs.
- ***circumscribe:*** to draw a circle around; to enclose within bounds or confine
  Since Emilio had just started to drive, he had a *circumscribed* area out of which he was not allowed to take the family car.
- ***script:*** handwriting; written text of a play, movie, or television program
  The *script* of the play went through some changes when the screenwriters started work on the movie version of the story.
- ***postscript:*** an addition to a concluded and signed letter; a supplement appended to a book
  I forgot to tell my Mom about my promotion until after I had signed the letter, so I added a *postscript* telling her about my new position.
- _______: a representation of something in words or pictures; a sort or variety of thing
  The witness to the robbery gave the police sketch artist a good __________ of the suspect.

Review

Part I

Choose the best synonym from the boxed list for the words below.

attribute	diagram	homonym	lie detector	message
official copy	scrawl	translate	vivid	written instruction

1. scribble ______________________
2. homophone______________________
3. ascribe ______________________
4. prescription ______________________
5. transcribe ______________________
6. graphic ______________________
7. transcript ______________________
8. graph ______________________
9. inscription ______________________
10. polygraph ______________________

Part II

From the boxed list, choose the word that best completes each of the sentences below.

cinematography	circumscribed	description	geography	inscription
phonograph	postscript	telegraph	subscription	unscripted

11. In the nineteenth century, the ______________________ was one of the fastest means of communication.
12. Marla's ______________________ to *People* magazine did not start to arrive within the six-week time period that had been promised by the sales promotion.
13. ______________________ includes the study of the earth's surface, as well as its people.
14. Since many tax laws changed after the accounting textbook was written, a ______________________ of supplemental tax information was appended to the end.
15. The two comedy writers hoped to sell their ______________________ idea for a TV pilot to the television executives.
16. In film noir, the ______________________, or the overall look and feel of a movie, is starkly shadowed to create a harsh look or evoke a gloomy feeling.
17. The book was a gift and had an ______________________ on the flyleaf from the author to his friend.
18. A turntable or ______________________ is handy if you still own vinyl records.
19. Leonardo da Vinci's pen and ink drawing of the Vitruvian Man is enclosed within a square ______________________ within a circle illustrating man's anatomical proportions.
20. The breeds at the AKC dog show fit almost every possible ______________________.

Lesson 7: Say, What?

Roots

dic, dict: say
lingu: tongue
locu, loqui: speak

Words with *dic, dict:* say

Each morning Rose used a word processor to transcribe dictation from a recording machine on which her boss had recorded letters and memos the previous day.

- ***dictate:*** to say or read aloud for transcription; to command with authority
  Sarena's parents *dictated* the nonnegotiable conditions of her upcoming slumber party: no boys, no alcohol.
- ***dictator:*** a ruler using absolute power without hereditary right or consent of the people
  Fidel Castro, who staged a coup to oust former President Batista of Cuba, is a *dictator* who has remained in power for many years.
- ***diction:*** that aspect of speaking or writing dependent upon the correct choice of words; the voice quality of a speaker or singer
  Listening to public speakers with fine *diction* is much easier than trying to decipher the words of those whose speech is not clear and distinct.
- ***contradict:*** to state the opposite of or deny; to imply denial with actions
  Mark's wild lifestyle seems to *contradict* his claim of being the quiet, studious type.
- ***indict:*** to charge with a crime; to seriously criticize or blame
  The grand jury *indicted* the alleged computer hacker for breaking into banking system computers to illegally move funds electronically.
- ***predict:*** to declare in advance or foretell the future
  Meteorologists *predict* the weather based upon facts, experience, and complex meteorological instrument systems.
- _______: a reference book of alphabetically arranged words and their meanings
  Word-processing computer programs usually contain a __________ in order to run a spelling check on typed documents.

Words with *locu, loqui:* speak

The defendant's attorney was skilled in fluent, forceful, and persuasive speech, so it came as no surprise that his closing statement was eloquent enough to convince the jury of his client's innocence.

- ***elocution:*** the study and practice of public speaking; a style of speaking or reading aloud
  Julianne was taking speech classes for all of her electives, hoping that the *elocution* practice would help in the frequent presentations required in her chosen career of public relations.
- ***locution:*** a word or phrase as used by a particular person or group
  In the late sixties and early seventies the *locution* of hippies included words like "groovy" or "way out, man."
- ***colloquial:*** characteristic of informal speech or writing; conversational
  Choosing the word "nope" instead of "no" is an example of using a *colloquial* expression.
- ***soliloquy:*** the act of speaking to oneself; a speech in a drama in which a character reveals innermost thoughts
  Aspiring actors often use *soliloquies* from Shakespeare's plays as audition monologues.
- ***loquacious:*** tending to talk too much or too freely; garrulous
  When meeting new people, Nadia often becomes nervous and *loquacious,* and tends to chatter on and on about unimportant things.
- __________: a roundabout or indirect way of speaking; using more words than necessary
  After all the __________ in Sydney's story, such as what she was wearing, what she had to eat, and what time they left, we finally got to hear whether or not she liked her blind date.

Words with *lingu:* tongue

When you visit the doctor it is customary for the nurse to take your sublingual temperature and your blood pressure.

- ***linguistics:*** the study of language
  Phonetics is a branch of *linguistics* involving the study of the production of and written symbols representing speech sounds.
- ________: able to speak several languages with some ease
  Some public schools in the United States are experiencing a need for __________ teachers due to the influx of immigrants who do not yet speak English.

Review

Part I

Choose the best antonym from the boxed list for each of the words below.

acquit or discharge	confirm	dialogue	directness	
elected ruler	formal speech	obey	recall	silent	unconvincing

1. contradict ____________________
2. circumlocution ____________________
3. dictate ____________________
4. predict ____________________
5. loquacious ____________________
6. dictator ____________________
7. indict ____________________
8. eloquent ____________________
9. soliloquy ____________________
10. colloquial ____________________

Part II

From the boxed list, choose the word that best completes each of the sentences below.

contradiction	Dictaphone	dictatorship	diction	elocution
linguistics	multilingual	predict	soliloquy	sublingual

11. The ____________________ of Joseph Stalin in the Soviet Union was a government of harsh and oppressive tyranny.
12. The heavily accented sounds of Charo's Spanish singing voice and her comical destruction of the English language make it impossible to mistake her ____________________ for anyone else's.
13. Jose's continual ____________________ or denial of everything Juan said was getting on Juan's nerves.
14. ____________________ is a brand name for a type of dictating machine.
15. If you are taking a European tour of several countries, it might be helpful to take along a ____________________ pocket dictionary.
16. Political candidates need to have finely sharpened ____________________ skills due to all the speeches they have to make in public.
17. Sean studied three languages and majored in____________________.
18. Hamlet's famous ____________________ starting with the words "To be, or not to be" is one of the most well-known speeches from Shakespeare.
19. Digital thermometers read ____________________ temperatures in seconds.
20. It is difficult to ____________________ how someone will react when criticized.

Lesson 8: Lights, Camera, Action!

Roots
luc, lum: light
act, ag: to do
photo: light

Words with *luc, lum:* light

Mexican Christmas lanterns called luminarias—bags with sand and a lit candle inside—line streets and driveways, not only in the Southwest but all over America at Christmastime.

- ***lucid:*** clear; glowing with light; easily understood; sane
  The patient's statements were not *lucid* when she was brought into the psychiatric treatment center.
- ***luminescence:*** the giving off of light without heat
  A fluorescent lightbulb or tube is a *luminescent* fixture that gives off light but remains cool when the mercury vapor inside the tube is acted upon by electrons.
- ***luminous:*** radiating or reflecting light; well-lighted; intellectually brilliant
  Due to neon lighting on most of the buildings, Las Vegas is one of the most *luminous* cities in the United States at night.
- ***luminary:*** a celestial body; a person who is a shining example in a profession
  Muhammad Ali is still a *luminary* in the boxing world.
- ***illuminate:*** to supply with light; light up; to make lucid or clarify
  Let me *illuminate* the facts for you before you take misinformed action.
- ***elucidate:*** to make lucid or clear; explain
  Mario had to successfully *elucidate* details about his new invention to investors in order to get funding.
- ________: allowing light to pass through without being transparent
  The Martinez family chose a __________ frosted glass that would provide privacy for the renovated bathroom.

Words with *photo:* light

The wrinkles and discolored skin on Brooke's face and hands were signs of photoaging from spending years in the sun without sunscreen protection.

- ***photogenic:*** having features that look attractive in a photograph
  The supermodel was extremely *photogenic,* and she could also act.
- ***photography:*** a process of producing images on sensitized surfaces by the chemical action of light or other forms of radiant energy
  Sensitized film in a camera receiving sunlight or flash lighting by opening the camera's aperture or eye is a form of *photography.*
- ***photogrammetry:*** the process of making surveys and maps through the use of aerial photographs
  The surveying firm had its own small airplane for taking aerial photos to use in the *photogrammetry* project for the National Park Service.
- ***photosensitivity:*** quality of being photosensitive; abnormal sensitivity of the skin to ultraviolet light
  Some prescription drugs can cause *photosensitivity* requiring avoidance of the sun or use of a sunscreen.
- ***telephoto lens:*** a camera lens that produces a large image of distant or small objects
  George's *telephoto lens* made it possible to get close-up pictures of the inaccessible waterfall.
- ________: a duplicate of a document or print made on specialized copying equipment
  Xerox, the name of the first and most well-known __________ machine manufacturer, is the word commonly used to mean "copy."

Words with *act, ag:* to do

The actors and actresses were waiting offstage for their cues to go onstage during Act Three of the play.

- ***act:*** anything done, being done, or to be done; a formal decision, law, or statute; a main division of a play
  A clown performing a magic *act* entertained the children at the six-year-old's birthday party.
- ***activate:*** to make active; to place a military unit on active status

A new credit card has to be *activated* before using it by calling a telephone number to notify the company that you have received the card.

- ***activism:*** the practice of achieving political or other goals through actions of protest or demonstration
  During the 1960s, *activism* was used to protest the Vietnam War and civil rights injustice in the United States.
- ***agent:*** a representative working on behalf of another
  Toby's *agent* promised to get him a film role before the end of the year.
- ***agency:*** an organization that provides a particular service; the place of business of an agent
  The FBI is an *agency* of the U.S. government.
- ***agenda:*** a list or outline of things to be done or matters to be acted or voted upon
  A vote for a new accounting firm to represent the company was on the *agenda* for the annual stockholders' meeting.
- ____: serving as a temporary substitute during another's absence; the art of performing in plays, films, etc.
  While the city mayor was out on maternity leave, one of the council members served as ________ mayor.

Review

Part I

Indicate whether the following statements are true (T) or false (F).

________ 1. The sun is the brightest luminary in our solar system.

________ 2. Photogrammetry makes use of pictures taken from above.

________ 3. An agent works for the benefit of someone else.

________ 4. Luminescence requires heat.

________ 5. Photography requires the use of an airplane.

________ 6. People with photosensitivity do not like to have their picture taken.

________ 7. Activists are usually politically passive.

________ 8. The speaker who elucidates the details of a project will be the most effective.

________ 9. In times of civil emergency, the state or federal government can activate the National Guard.

________ 10. The agenda of a meeting lists items to be addressed.

Part II

Choose an antonym from the boxed list for each of the words below.

blocking light	confuse	darken	demobilize	glowing with heat
insane	not pretending	original	stupid	unattractive

11. photogenic ________
12. translucent ________
13. illuminate ________
14. luminous ________
15. photocopy ________
16. lucid ________
17. acting ________
18. activate ________
19. elucidate ________
20. luminescent ________

Lesson 9: Play It Again, Sam

Prefix	Root
re-: back, again	*lud, lus:* to play

Words with *re-:* back, again

Although Humphrey Bogart never said the line "Play it again, Sam" in the movie *Casablanca*, it has been repeatedly attributed to his character, Rick.

- ***reconcile:*** to cause to become friendly or peaceable again; to cause one to accept something not desired
  The purpose of the peace conference was to get the opposing sides to *reconcile* their differences and find a way to coexist in the region.
- ***reconstruct:*** to rebuild; to re-create in the mind from available information
  The witness to the auto accident was asked by the police officer to *reconstruct* from memory the events leading up to the crash.
- ***recriminate:*** to bring a countercharge against an accuser
  Melissa feared that legally accusing her ex-husband of being an unfit father would cause him to *recriminate* against her as an unfit mother.
- ***refrain:*** to keep oneself from doing something
  I had to *refrain* from laughing when the professor walked into class wearing bedroom slippers.
- ***regress:*** to revert to an earlier or less advanced state
  The paralyzed patient had been making progress in physical therapy, but suddenly she *regressed* to being unable to walk a single step.
- ***reiterate:*** to say or do repeatedly
  The infomercial *reiterated* the cleaning product's claims until I became annoyed at hearing over and over how white my shirts could be.
- ***rejuvenate:*** to make young again; to make new again
  The facial product line was promoted as being able to *rejuvenate* a user's skin by reducing wrinkles and uneven skin tones within two weeks with a money back guarantee.
- ***renege:*** to go back on one's word
  Daniel had to *renege* on his promise to drive his friends to the football game after his father refused to lend him the car.
- ***repel:*** to push away by force; to fail to mix with; to resist absorption; to cause distaste in
  Oil and water do not mix; rather, they *repel* each other.
- ***repercussion:*** an effect of some previous action; recoil after impact; reverberation
  Excessive running on pavement can have serious *repercussions* on your health such as wearing out the knee joints from the constant impact.
- ***retract:*** to withdraw a statement or opinion, etc. as inaccurate; to withdraw a promise
  Celebrities often sue magazines or newspapers asking for a *retraction* of inaccurate statements printed about them.
- _____: to inflict pain or harm in return for a wrong received; to get even or get satisfaction
  Cindy's __________ for Sonia's lies was not inviting Sonia to the best party of the year.

Words with *lud, lus:* to play

The prelude or introductory piece of music to an opera is called an overture.

- ***ludicrous:*** causing laughter because of absurdity; ridiculous
  Durwood looked *ludicrous* in the extremely short haircut that made his ears stick out.
- ***allude:*** to refer casually or indirectly to
  He will *allude* to his days as a football star whenever the guys start discussing sports.
- ***allusion:*** a casual or passing reference to something, either direct or implied
  A casual *allusion* to Shakespeare would be to call him the Bard.
- ***interlude:*** any intermediate performance or entertainment such as between the acts of a play
  The instrumental *interlude* between the verses of the song had a melancholy sound.
- ***delude:*** to mislead the mind or judgment of
  Jonathan felt silly when he realized the two con artists who tricked him out of his money had *deluded* him.
- ***elude:*** to avoid capture; to escape perception or comprehension of
  The reason for her popularity *eludes* me; I just don't get it.
- _____: an unreal or misleading appearance or image
  Faux finishes like marbleizing a column with paint create an inexpensive __________ in home decorating.

Review

Part I

Indicate whether the underlined words are used correctly (C) or incorrectly (I) in the sentences.

_________ 1. It is best to reconcile oneself to the fact that college requires a certain amount of studying.

_________ 2. Trying to refrain from smoking is difficult for many people who have become addicted to nicotine.

_________ 3. Trompe l'oeil, literally meaning "fool the eye" in French, is a form of painting that creates an allusion that appears to be real.

_________ 4. Martin is extremely naive and easy to delude by playing upon his trusting nature.

_________ 5. The twins knew that missing their curfew again would cause serious repercussions from their parents.

_________ 6. Denise regressed on her promise to lend her new dress to her sister for an important date.

_________ 7. The newspaper issued a formal retraction of the previous day's incorrect story about the mayor accepting a bribe in exchange for awarding a contract for services.

_________ 8. The escaped convict managed to allude capture until after dark.

_________ 9. The organist performed a prelude as the church filled before the christening ceremony.

_________ 10. The witness was able to recriminate the robbery suspect from a police lineup.

Part II

Indicate whether the following statements are true (T) or false (F).

_________ 11. To reconstruct is to rebuild.

_________ 12. Reiterate is another word for repeat.

_________ 13. A neighbor who feels mistreated might possibly seek revenge.

_________ 14. If sensitive people engage in ludicrous behavior, they risk having their feelings hurt when others laugh at them.

_________ 15. An interlude comes at the beginning of a song.

_________ 16. A soaking wet raincoat is one that has failed to repel the rain.

_________ 17. To rejuvenate a piece of furniture is to antique it to make it look old.

_________ 18. A message that is completely understood is a message that has eluded everyone.

_________ 19. You can be easily trusted if you can be relied on to renege on your word.

_________ 20. Having an illusion about a friend's true character is not seeing him for what he really is.

Lesson 10: Foreign Terms

- ***bon vivant:*** a lover of good living; a gourmet
  While living in Paris with plenty of money, he enjoyed the lifestyle of a *bon vivant.*
- ***avant-garde:*** advance guard, pioneers, offbeat
  The radical ideas of the sociology professor may be too avant-garde for the conservative freshmen.
- ***carte blanche:*** "white paper," unlimited authority, blanket permission
  The new company gave her *carte blanche* to entertain the top three customers at the convention.
- ***magnum opus:*** great work
  After seven years of work, the novel was recognized as the author's *magnum opus.*
- ***de rigueur:*** strict etiquette, very formal, in good taste at the moment
  A jacket and necktie are *de rigueur* for the occasion.
- ***deja vu:*** already seen
  The feeling of *deja vu* became more intense as the same people seemed to be saying the same things as in 1997.
- ***double entendre:*** allowing two interpretations with one usually being off color
  As soon as the sentence was uttered, the speaker realized the *double entendre* and laughed knowingly.
- ***faux pas:*** "false step," or mistake
  I realized the *faux pas* when I saw my friends giggling in the background.
- ***joie de vivre:*** "joy for living"
  The guide's *joie de vivre* was contagious, and thus we all enjoyed the trip.
- ***esprit de corps:*** group spirit of pride
  Through shared experiences, the marines build a strong *esprit de corps.*
- ***coup d'etat:*** sudden stroke that overturns the government
  The foreign diplomats sought to leave before the predicted *coup d'etat.*
- ***raison d'etre:*** "reason for being," justification
  For the last three years, raising my child has been my *raison d'etre.*
- ***potpourri:*** mixture
  A *potpourri* of ideas was presented for the group to consider.
- ***nouveau riche:*** newly rich, suggesting poor taste
  Have you seen the pillow that says, "Better to be *nouveau riche* than not rich at all"?
- ***nom de plume:*** pen name, pseudonym
  Samuel Clemens used Mark Twain as his *nom de plume.*
- ***junta:*** group of political plotters
  By gaining control of the military, the *junta* overthrew the existing government.
- ***sotto voce:*** "under the voice," whisper
  The criticism was overheard even though it was said *sotto voce.*
- ***vendetta:*** blood feud
  Because of the assault, the gang continued the *vendetta.*
- ***alfresco:*** "in the fresh air," outdoors
  During the summer months, the restaurant offered *alfresco* dining.
- ***fait accompli:*** finished action
  Submit your comments to the dean before the decision becomes a *fait accompli.*

Review

Part I

Indicate whether the following sentences are true (T) or false (F).

__________ 1. A *vendetta* is an agreement between two countries.

__________ 2. A *double entendre* often includes a sexual twist.

__________ 3. An artist's *magnum opus* could be a painting or a sculpture.

__________ 4. A *junta* will plot against the existing government but seldom try to sieze power.

__________ 5. A *potpourri* of guests can be a mixture of friends, relatives, and coworkers.

__________ 6. A *nom de plume* can also be the real name of the writer.

__________ 7. A *bon vivant* usually does not like wine and food.

__________ 8. As a client, you would usually welcome *carte blanche* treatment.

__________ 9. *Deja vu* is like a replay from the past.

__________ 10. In a *coup d'etat* the existing government remains the same.

__________ 11. A *raison d'etre* is a central driving force.

__________ 12. Winning sports teams usually lack *esprit de corps*.

Part II

Choose the word from the boxed list that means the opposite of the words below.

joie de vivre	*faux pas*	*de rigueur*	*nouveau riche*
sotto voce	*fait accompli*	*avant-garde*	*alfresco*

13. incomplete __________

14. informal, without rules __________

15. indoors __________

16. loud __________

17. behind the times __________

18. unhappy outlook __________

19. poor __________

20. correct action __________

Frequently Used Word Parts

Prefixes	Meaning	Example
a-, an-	without, not	atypical, anarchy
ab-	away, from	absent, abnormal
ad-	toward	advance, administer
ambi-, amphi-	both, around	ambiguous, amphibious
anna, anno	year	annual
anti, contra-, ob-	against	antisocial, contradict
bene-, eu-	well, good	benefactor, eulogy
bi-, du-, di-	two or twice	bicycle, duet, dichotomy
cata-, cath-	down, downward	catacombs
cent-	hundred	centipede
con-, com-, syn-	with, together	congregate, synthesis
de-	down, from	depose, detract
dec-, deca-	ten	decade
demi-, hemi-, semi-	half	hemisphere, semicircle
dia-	through	diameter, diagram
dis-, un-	not, opposite of	dislike, unnatural
dys-	ill, hard	dystrophy
ex-	out, from	exhale, expel
extra-	beyond, outside	extralegal
hyper-	above, excessive	hyperactive
hypo-	under	hypodermic
il-, im-, in-	not	illogical, impossible
in-	in, into	inside, insert, invade
infra-	lower	infrared
inter-	between	intercede, interrupt
intra-	within	intramural
juxta-	next to	juxtaposition
mal-, mis-	wrong, ill	malformed, mislead
mill-	thousand	milligram
non-	not	nonconformity
nove-, non-	nine	novena, nonagon
oct-, octo-	eight	octopus
omni-, pan-	all	omnipotent, pantheist
per-	through	perennial, pervade
peri-, circum-	around	perimeter, circumvent
poly-, multi-	many	polygamy, multiply
post-	after	postscript
pre-, ante-	before	prepared, antebellum
pro-	before, for	prologue, promoter
proto-	first	prototype

Prefixes	Meaning	Example
quad-, quatra-, tetra-	four	quadrilateral, tetrad
quint-, penta-	five	quintuplet, pentathlon
re-	back, again	review, reply
retro-	backward	retrogress, retrospect
sequ-	follow	sequence
sex-, hexa-	six	sextet, hexagram
sub-	under	submarine, subway
super-	above, over	supervise
temp-, tempo-, chrono-	time	temporal, chronological
trans-	across	translate, transcontinental
tri-	three	triangle
uni-, mono-	one	unicorn, monocle
vice-	in place of	viceroy

Roots	Meaning	Example
alter, hap	to change	alteration, mishap
ama, philo	to love	amiable, philosophy
anima	breath, spirit	animate
aqua	water	aquarium, aqualung
aster, astro	star	disaster, astronomy
aud	to hear	audible, auditory
auto, ego	self	autonomy, egotist
bio	life	biology
cap	head	caption, capitulate
cap, capt	to take	capture
card, cor, cord	heart	cardiac, core, cordial
cosmo	order, universe	cosmonaut
cresc	to grow, increase	crescendo
cryp	secret, hidden	cryptogram
dent	teeth	dental
derma	skin	dermatologist
duc, duct	to lead	reduce, conduct
equ, iso	equal	equivocal, isometric
err, errat	to wander	erratic
ethno	race, tribe	ethnic
fac, fact	to do, make	manufacture
fract	to break	fracture
frater	brother	fraternity
gene	race, kind, sex	genetics, gender
grad, gres	to go, take steps	graduation, digress
gyn	woman	gynecologist
hab, habi	to have, hold	inhabit, habitual
helio, photo	sun, light	heliotrope, photograph

Roots	Meaning	Example
hom, homo	human, man	hominid
lic, list, liqu	to leave behind	derelict, relinquish
lith	stone	monolith
loc	place	location, local
log	speech, science	logic, dialogue
loquor	to speak	loquacious, colloquial
lum	light	illuminate
macro	large	macrocosm
manu	hand	manual, manuscript
mater	mother	maternity
med	middle	mediate
meter	to measure	barometer
micro	small	microscope
miss, mit	to send, let go	admit, permission
morph	form	morphology
mort	to die	immortalize
mut, muta	to change	mutation
nat	to be born	natal, native
neg, negat	to say no, deny	negative, renege
nym, nomen	name	synonym, nomenclature
ocul	eye	oculist, monocle
ortho	right, straight	orthodox, orthodontist
osteo	bone	osteopath
pater	father	paternal
path	disease, feeling	pathology, antipathy
phag	to eat	esophagus, phagocyte
phobia	fear	claustrophobia
phon, phono	sound	symphony, phonics
plic	to fold	duplicate, implicate
pneuma	wind, air	pneumatic
pod, ped	foot	tripod, pedestrian
pon, pos	to place	depose, position
port	to carry	porter, portable
pseudo	false	pseudonym
psych	mind	psychology
pyr	fire	pyromaniac
quir	to ask	inquire, acquire
rog	to question	interrogate
scrib, graph	to write	prescribe, autograph
sect, seg	to cut	dissect, segment
sol	alone	solitude
soma	body	somatology, psychosomatic
somnia	sleep	insomnia
soph	wise	sophomore, philosophy

Roots	Meaning	Example
soror	sister	sorority
spect	to look at	inspect, spectacle
spir	to breathe	inspiration, conspire
tact, tang	to touch	tactile, tangible
tele	distant	telephone
ten, tent	to hold	tenant, intent
tend, tens	to stretch	extend, extension
the, theo	God	atheism, theology
therma	heat	thermometer
tort	twist	torture, extort
ven, vent	to go, arrive	convention, advent
verbum	word	verbosity, verbal

Suffixes	Meaning	Example
-able, -ible	capable of	durable, visible
-acy, -ance, -ency, -ity	quality or state of	privacy, competence, acidity
-age	act of, state of	breakage
-al	pertaining to	rental
-ana	saying, writing	Americana
-ant	quality of, one who	reliant, servant
-ard, -art	person who	wizard, braggart
-arium, -orium	place for	auditorium
-ate	cause to be	activate
-ation	action, state of	creation, condition
-chrome	color	verichrome
-cide	killing	homicide
-er, -or	person who, thing which	generator
-esque	like in manner	picturesque
-fic	making, causing	scientific
-form	in the shape of	cuneiform
-ful, -ose, -ous	full of	careful, verbose
-fy, -ify, -ize	to make, cause to be	fortify, magnify, modify
-hood, -osis	condition or state of	childhood, hypnosis
-ics	art, science	mathematics
-ism	quality or doctrine of	conservatism
-itis	inflammation of	appendicitis
-ive	quality of, that which	creative
-latry	worship of	idolatry
-less	without	homeless
-oid	in the form of	tabloid
-tude	quality or degree of	solitude
-ward	in a direction	backward
-wise	way, position	clockwise

Appendix 2

ESL: Making Sense of Figurative Language and Idioms

What Is ESL?

How many languages can you speak? Are you a native English speaker who has learned Spanish or are you a native Farsi speaker who has learned English? If you have acquired skill in a second or third language, you know that it takes many years and plenty of patience to master the intricacies of a language. Not only must you learn new words, but you must also learn new grammatical constructions. For example, the articles that are habitually used in English such as *a, an,* or *the* do not appear in Russian, Chinese, Japanese, Thai, or Farsi. In Spanish and Arabic, personal pronouns restate the subject, as in *My sister she goes to college.* In Spanish, Greek, French, Vietnamese, and Portuguese, "to-words" are used rather than "ing-words," as in *I enjoy to play soccer.* These complexities, which are innately understood by native speakers, make direct translation from one language to another difficult. The English language, especially, has many unusual phrases and grammatical constructions that defy direct translation.

To assist students with these complexities, most colleges offer courses in ESL, which stands for English as a Second Language. These courses are designed to teach language skills to non-native speakers of English. If you are an ESL student, you may have been recruited through an international exchange program with another college, you may be a newly arrived immigrant, or you may be a citizen with a bilingual background. You bring a multicultural perspective to classroom discussions and campus life that will broaden the insights of others. Not only are some obvious things like holidays different from those of others, but your sense of family life, work, and responsibility may also be different. Share your thoughts and ideas with native English speakers as they share the irregularities of the language with you.

What Is Figurative Language?

One aspect of the English language that defies direct translation and confuses non-native speakers, and sometimes even native speakers, is **figurative language**. This is the manipulation of the language to create images, add interest, and draw comparisons by using figures of speech (see Chapter 7 on Inference). The two most commonly used figures of speech are *similes* and *metaphors:*

Simile: a stated comparison using *like* or *as*

The baby swims like a duck.

Metaphor: an implied comparison

The baby is a duck in water.

Many figurative expressions are common in English. As in the previous metaphor, the *baby* is not actually a *baby duck*, but the implication is that *the baby swims very well.* However, neither direct translation nor a dictionary will unlock that meaning. When you encounter a figure of speech, look for clues within the sentence to help you guess the meaning.

Directions

The following practice exercises contain figurative language. Read each dialogue passage for meaning and then use the context clues to match the number of the bold-faced figure of speech with the letter of the appropriate definition. To narrow your choices, the answers to 1–5 are listed within a–e and the answers to 6–10 are listed within f–j.

Exercise 1

Angelina: You're (1) **as busy as a bee**. What are you working on?

Ginger: I'm working (2) **like gangbusters** on plans for Tony's twenty-first birthday party. Tony has been (3) **a fish out of water** since he moved here, so I'm hoping that the party helps him to get (4) **in the swim** of things.

Angelina: Can I (5) **give you a hand** so the party (6) **gets off the ground** smoothly?

Ginger: Sure. You can help me (7) **dig up** some of Tony's old pals who have been living (8) **like nomads** since high school.

Angelina: I'll be (9) **at your beck and call** whenever you need me.

Ginger: Terrific! Just remember, it's a surprise, so (10) **keep it under your hat**.

________	1. as busy as a bee	a. a person in a strange environment
________	2. like gangbusters	b. involved in many activities
________	3. a fish out of water	c. buzzing with activity
________	4. in the swim	d. help you
________	5. give you a hand	e. with energetic speed
________	6. gets off the ground	f. wandering from place to place
________	7. dig up	g. into action; gets started
________	8. like nomads	h. keep it secret
________	9. at your beck and call	i. find; locate
________	10. keep it under your hat	j. always ready to do as ordered

Exercise 2

Julio: I wish everyone would (1) **get off my case**.

Renae: You're as (2) **tight as a snare drum**. What's wrong?

Julio: My professor (3) **caught me off guard** yesterday when she wanted a quick answer to a difficult question, and I couldn't (4) **pull it out of a hat**. I thought she (5) **made a monkey out of me**. Next, I (6) **got behind the eight ball** with my boss when I arrived late for work. (7) **The final straw** came when my folks got (8) **up in arms** last night because I'm behind in my schoolwork.

Renae: I'm glad I could listen while you (9) **let off some steam.**

Julio: Thanks for listening. Now I need to (10) **get my act together.**

________	1. get off my case	a. produce as if by magic
________	2. tight as a snare drum	b. caused to look foolish
________	3. caught me off guard	c. stop nagging or criticizing
________	4. pull it out of a hat	d. visibly tense
________	5. made a monkey out of me	e. surprised me
________	6. got behind the eight ball	f. release tension by talking unrestrainedly
________	7. the final straw	g. got in an unfavorable position
________	8. up in arms	h. to behave responsibly and efficiently
________	9. let off some steam	i. the last insult one can endure
________	10. get my act together	j. angered; feeling displeasure

Exercise 3

Rodney: This car I bought is (1) **a lemon**. It (2) **rides like a stagecoach**. Next time I buy a used car, I'm going to have a mechanic (3) **go over** it (4) **with a fine-toothed comb.**

Jamal: My brother is a mechanic. He is busy, but if you need (5) an **ace in the hole**, I'll ask him to help you. He is certainly (6) **on the up and up**.

Rodney: Great! I'm going to (7) **bite the bullet** and (8) **dump** this car for parts and get a decent (9) **set of wheels.**

Jamal: From the sounds of your car, you better do it (10) **like greased lightning.**

________	1. a lemon	a. resource in reserve
________	2. rides like a stagecoach	b. very carefully
________	3. go over	c. merchandise that is defective
________	4. with a fine-toothed comb	d. examine
________	5. ace in the hole	e. drives rough and bumpy
________	6. on the up and up	f. accept the unpleasant reality
________	7. bite the bullet	g. extremely fast
________	8. dump	h. get rid of
________	9. set of wheels	i. honest; trustworthy
________	10. like greased lightning	j. a car

What Are Common English Idioms?

An **idiom** is an expression with a special meaning that cannot be understood by directly translating each individual word. Because of years of exposure to the language, idioms are usually understood by native speakers but they are confusing if you are learning English as a second language.

Idioms are more common in spoken and informal language than in formal writing. In fact, most idiomatic expressions can usually be replaced by a single formal word. To add to the confusion, some idioms have more than one meaning, and many idioms are grammatically irregular.

EXAMPLE What does the idiomatic expression *go over* mean in the following sentences?

(a) How did my speech ***go over***?

(b) I want to ***go over*** the exam paper with the professor.

EXPLANATION In both sentences, the use of the idiom is informal. A more formal version of each would be:

(a) *How was my speech* ***received*** *by the audience?*

(b) *I want to* ***review*** *the exam paper with the professor.*

Notice the grammatical irregularity in the first sentence. *Over* is not followed by a noun (name of a person, place, or thing) as a preposition (connecting words like *in, out,* and *at*) normally would be according to the rules of grammar. Instead, *over* becomes part of the verb phrase (words showing action). Thus the translation requires a change in wording, whereas the second use of the idiom is grammatically correct and can be directly translated by the single word *review*.

No one will argue that understanding idioms is easy. If you go to a bookstore, you will see that entire books have been written about categorizing, recognizing, and translating thousands of them. To help clear up the confusion, some books group idioms according to families like root words, and others categorize them according to grammatical constructions. Either way, understanding idiomatic expressions depends more on using context clues to deduce meaning and familiarity with the informal, spoken language than with learning rules.

In the following practice exercises, use the context clues within each sentence to write the meaning of the boldfaced idiom in the blank provided.

Exercise 4

1. Margaret's new job pays very well, so she intends to save her money and be **in the chips** very soon. ______________________
2. When Marcy stopped him in the hall, Jim was **in a rush** because his math class had already begun. ______________________
3. Tom hadn't been notified that the party was formal and he looked **out of place** in his jeans. ______________________
4. Juanita had a **heart-to-heart** talk about boys and dating with her younger sister. ______________________
5. His channel surfing and the constant clicking of the TV remote control are getting **on my nerves.** ______________________
6. Miguel is going to backpack through Europe after he graduates, but it will have to be **on a shoestring**, since he hasn't been able to save much money. ______________________
7. Denise didn't study for the exam she is taking; she decided to **wing it** and hope for the best. ______________________
8. I can't **get over** how much my blind date last night looked like Brad Pitt. ______________________

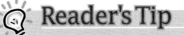

Reader's Tip

Categorizing Idioms

Idioms are sometimes categorized into the following groups:

* Word families: grouping around a similar individual word

  Down as in *step down, take down, pipe down, narrow down, nail down, run down, tear down, knock down, let down, die down, cut down*, etc.

* Verb + preposition: action word plus a connecting word

  Hammer away means *persists, stand for* means *represents*, and *roll back* means *reduce.*

* Preposition + noun: connecting word plus the name of a person, place, or thing

  On foot means *walking, by heart* means *memorized*, and *off guard* means *surprised.*

* Verb + adjective: action word plus a descriptive word

  Think twice means *consider carefully, hang loose* means *be calm*, and *play fair* means *deal equally.*

* Pairs of nouns: two words naming a person, place, or thing

  Flesh and blood means *kin, part and parcel* means *total*, and *pins and needles* means *nervous.*

* Pairs of adjectives: two descriptive words

  Cut and dried means *obvious, fair and square* means *honest, short and sweet* means *brief.*

9. My computer monitor is **on the fritz** so I can't send any e-mail until I get it fixed.
   ____

10. Being assigned to the new project at work will finally give me a chance to **pull out all the stops** and show them what I'm really worth. ____________________

Exercise 5

1. I try to do my homework every night because I feel anxious if it starts to **pile up** and I get behind schedule. ____________________
2. I'm feeling **on top of the world** with my new laptop computer.
   ____
3. Shaundra tries **to shrug off** the fact that she doesn't have a date for the spring dance, but it's obvious that she is bothered. ____________________

4. Let's **put our heads together** and see if we can grill hamburgers without buying more charcoal. ____________________

5. When you go on the job interview, don't **sell yourself short** by being too modest about your skills. ____________________

6. A job interview is definitely the time **to toot your own horn** and explain your skills and accomplishments. ____________________

7. Now Melinda and Tonya aren't speaking, and Melinda expects all of their mutual friends **to side with her** in the argument. ____________________

8. Mandy's little brother is too much of a **live wire** for me to baby-sit. ____________________

9. We might as well go in and **face the music** for breaking Dad's tool that we weren't supposed to be using. ____________________

10. I don't know how Eduardo can afford to buy every electronic gadget that comes on the market and still **make ends meet**. ____________________

Exercise 6

1. I'm **in seventh heaven** when I have a plateful of chocolate chip cookies still warm from the oven. ____________________

2. Her mother must have **nerves of steel** to be able to stay in a house full of screaming children and still remain sane. ____________________

3. Wanda has been walking around in a daze with her **head in the clouds** ever since she started dating Jose. ____________________

4. I've **had it** with Bill borrowing money and never paying it back. No more! ____________________

5. My little brother is **a pain in the neck** when he'd rather annoy my friends than stay in his room. ____________________

6. Tina is **playing with fire** by accepting rides from total strangers. ____________________

7. I just got paid, and I'm finally going to **shell out** for the new DVD player I've wanted to buy. ____________________

8. His boss is going to **can him** if John keeps making personal phone calls on his shift. ____________________

9. Roberto was **flying high** after he got accepted at the college of his first choice. ____________________

10. With 67 percent correct, I passed the math test **by the skin of my teeth**. ____________________

Glossary

acronym An abbreviation pronounced as a word and contrived to simplify a lengthy name and gain quick recognition for an organization or agency. For example, *UNICEF* is the acronym for the United Nations International Children's Emergency Fund.

analogy A comparison showing connections with and similarities to previous experiences.

annotating A method of using symbols and notations to highlight textbook material for future study.

argument Assertions that support a conclusion with the intention of persuading.

assertion A declarative statement.

attention Uninterrupted mental focus.

bar graph An arrangement of horizontal or vertical bars in which the length of each represents an amount or number.

believability Support that is not suspicious but is believable.

bias An opinion or position on a subject recognized through facts slanted toward an author's personal beliefs.

bookmarking On the Internet, a save-the-site technique that lets you automatically return to the designated Website with just one or two mouse clicks.

browser The software that searches to find information on the Internet.

cause and effect A pattern of organization in which one item is shown as having produced another.

chronological order A pattern of organization in which items are listed in time order or sequence.

cognitive psychology A body of knowledge that describes how the mind works or is believed to work.

comparison-contrast A pattern of organization in which similarities and differences are presented.

concentration The focusing of full attention on a task.

conclusion Interpretation based on evidence and suggested meaning.

connotation The feeling associated with the definition of a word.

consistency Support that holds together and does not contradict itself.

context clues Hints within a sentence that help unlock the meaning of an unknown word.

Cornell Method A system of notetaking that involves writing sentence summaries on the right side of the page with key words and topics indicated on the left.

creative thinking Generating many possible solutions to a problem.

critical thinking Deliberating in a purposeful, organized manner to assess the value of information or argument.

cumulative bar graph A bar graph that shows a cumulative effect in which all the bar's segments add up to a total. Rather than having multiple bars or lines, the groups are stacked on top of each other to dramatically show differences.

databases Computer-based indexes to assist research. A single article may be listed under several topics and may appear in several different indexes.

deductive reasoning Thinking that starts with a previously learned conclusion and applies it to a new situation.

definition A pattern of organization devoted to defining an idea and further explaining it with examples.

denotation The dictionary definition of a word.

description A pattern of organization, listing characteristics of a person, place, or thing, as in a simple listing.

details Information that supports, describes, and explains the main idea.

diagram A drawing of an object showing labeled parts.

domain name A name registered by a Website owner.

domain type The category to which a Website owner belongs; for example, *edu* is the domain type for colleges and universities.

download A method of transferring a file from the Internet to a particular computer.

emoticons In e-mail communication, symbols such as smiley faces :) used to represent emotions in a lighthearted way. They are not appropriate for formal correspondence but are frequently used in informal contexts.

etymology The study of word origins involving the tracing of words back to their earliest recorded appearance.

external distractors Temptations of the physical world that divert the attention from a task.

fact A statement that can be proved true.

fallacy An inference that first appears reasonable but closer inspection proves to be unrelated, unreliable, or illogical.

figurative language Words used to create images that take on a new meaning.

fixation A stop the eyes make while reading.

flaming Offensive e-mails that make personal attacks.

flowchart A diagram showing how ideas are related, with boxes and arrows indicating levels of importance and movement.

habit A repetitious act almost unconsciously performed.

home page The entry point to a Website through which other pages on the site can be reached.

humorous Comical, funny, or amusing.

hypertext links In Web technology, phrases that appear as bold blue or underlined text. Clicking on them will not only move you from one page to another within the Website, but can also send you to other related Websites. The words chosen and underlined as the link describe the information you are likely to find at that destination.

idiom A figurative expression that does not make literal sense but communicates a generally accepted meaning.

imagery Mental pictures created by figurative language.

implied meaning Suggested rather than directly stated meaning.

inductive reasoning Thinking based on the collection of data and the formulation of a conclusion based on it.

inference Subtle suggestions expressed without direct statement.

intent A reason or purpose for writing, which is usually to inform, persuade, or entertain.

internal distractions Concerns that come repeatedly to mind and disturb concentration.

Internet An electronic system of more than 25,000 computer networks using a common language that connects millions of users around the world. The Internet is the networked system that allows the World Wide Web to function.

irony A twist in meaning or a surprise ending that is the opposite of what is expected and may involve a humorous undertone.

knowledge network A cluster of knowledge about a subject; a schema.

lateral thinking A way of creatively thinking around a problem or redefining it to seek new solutions.

learning style A preference for a particular manner of presenting material to be learned.

line graph A frequency distribution in which the horizontal scale measures time and the vertical scale measures amount.

main idea A statement of the primary focus of the topic in a passage.

map A graphic designation or distribution.

mapping A method of graphically displaying material to show relationships and importance for later study.

metacognition Knowledge of how to read as well as the ability to regulate and direct the process.

metaphor A figure of speech that directly compares two unlike things (without using the words *like* or *as*).

mnemonic A technique using images, numbers, rhymes, or letters to improve memory.

multiple meanings The defining of a word in several ways. For example, the dictionary lists over thirty meanings for the word *run*.

notetaking A method of writing down short phrases and summaries to record textbook material for future study.

opinion A statement of a personal view or judgment.

outlining A method of using indentations, Roman numerals, numbers, and letters to organize a topic for future study.

pattern of organization The structure or framework for presenting the details in a passage.

personification Attributing human characteristics to nonhuman things.

pie graph A circular graph divided into wedge-shaped segments to show portions totaling 100 percent.

point of view A position or opinion on a subject.

prefix A group of letters added to the beginning of a word and causing a change of meaning.

premise The thesis or main point of an argument.

previewing A method of glancing over a reading passage to predict what the passage is about and thus predict to assess your prior knowledge and needed skills.

prior knowledge Previous learning about a subject.

propaganda A systematic and deliberate attempt to persuade others to a particular doctrine or point of view and to undermine any opposition.

purpose A writer's underlying reason or intent for writing.

rate Reading pace calculated according to the number of words read in one minute.

recall Reviewing what was included and learned after reading a passage.

regression Rereading material because of a lack of understanding or concentration.

relevance The degree to which related material supports a topic or conclusion.

root The stem or basic part of a word; in English, roots are derived primarily from Latin and Greek.

sarcasm A tone or language that expresses biting humor, usually meaning the opposite of what is said, with the purpose of undermining or ridiculing someone.

scanning Searching reading material quickly to locate specific points of information.

schema A skeleton or network of knowledge about a subject.

simile A comparison of two things using the words *like* or *as.*

simple listing A pattern of organization that lists items in a series.

skimming A technique for selectively reading for the gist or main idea.

study system A plan for working through stages to read and learn textbook material.

subvocalization The inaudible inner voice that is part of the reading process.

suffix A group of letters added to the end of a word and causing a change in meaning as well as the way the word can be used in the sentence.

summary A concise statement of the main idea and significant supporting details.

table A listing of facts and figures in columns for quick reference.

tone A writer's attitude toward a subject.

topic A word or phrase that labels the subject of a paragraph.

topic sentence A sentence that condenses the thoughts and details of a passage into a general, all-inclusive statement of the author's message.

transition A signal word that connects the parts of a sentence and leads readers to anticipate a continuation or a change in the writer's thoughts.

Uniform Resource Locator (URL) The address for finding a specific site on the World Wide Web, just as an address and zip code are required to mail a letter. A URL is similar to an e-mail address, except that it routes you to a source of information called a *Web page* or *Website* rather than to the mailbox of an individual person.

vertical thinking A straightforward and logical way of thinking that searches for a solution to the stated problem.

Web directory A type of search engine that organizes hypertext links into categories similar to the way in which libraries organize books into categories.

Web pages The formal presentation of information provided by individual people, businesses, educational institutions, or other organizations on the Internet.

World Wide Web (WWW) An electronic information network that is similar to an enormous library, with Websites being like books and Web pages being like the pages in the books.

Credits

Adams, Pam. From "Why Looks Matter," *Peoria Journal Star*, June 27, 1999. Reprinted by permission.

Alden, John R. "Breakfast at the FDA Cafe as appeared in *The Wall Street Journal*, 1991. Reprinted by permission of the author.

Associated Press. From "Hackers Flaunt Dignitaries' Credit Card Data," *The Atlanta Journal-Constitution*, February 6, 2001. Reprinted with permission of The Associated Press.

Avery, Sarah. From "Duke Expands Cord Blood Bank," *The News & Observer*, February 11, 2001. Reprinted by permission.

Barnet, Sylvan. From *A Short Guide to Writing About Art*, Fifth Edition. Copyright © 1997 by Sylvan Barnet. Reprinted by permission of Pearson Education, Inc.

Bari, Judi. "The Feminization of Earth First!" *Ms.* Magazine, 1992.

Block, Sandra. From "50 Not So Nifty for Baby Boomers," *USA Today*, September 20, 2000. Copyright © 2000, USA Today. Reprinted with permission.

Bovée, Courtland L. and John V. Thill. From *Business Communication Today*, Sixth Edition. Copyright © 2000 by Bovée and Thill LLC. Reprinted by permission of Pearson Education, Inc., Upper Saddle River, NJ.

Brehm, Barbara. From *Stress Management: Increasing Your Stress Resistance*. Copyright © 1998 by Barbara Brehm. Reprinted by permission of Allyn and Bacon.

Byer, Curtis O. and Louis W. Shainberg. From *Living Well: Health in Your Hands*, Second Edition. Copyright © 1995: Jones and Bartlett Publishers, Sudbury, MA. (http://www.jbpub.com). Reprinted with permission.

Capron, H. L. From *Computers: Tools for an Information Age*, Sixth Edition. Copyright © 2000 by Prentice-Hall, Inc. Reprinted by permission of Pearson Education, Inc., Upper Saddle River, NJ.

Certo, Samuel C. From *Modern Management*, Eighth Edition. Copyright © 2000 by Prentice-Hall, Inc. Reprinted by permission of Pearson Education, Inc., Upper Saddle River, NJ.

Cooper, Sheila and Rosemary Patton. *Writing Logically, Thinking Critically with Readings*. New York: Longman, 2001.

Cunningham, Amy. "Why Women Smile," *Lears*, March 1993.

Daily Record—Scotland. "Dolphin Saves Boy's Life; Boy Pushed Back to his Boat After Fall," *Daily Record—Scotland*, August 30, 2000. Reprinted by permission of the Trinity Mirror.

DeVito, Joseph A. From *The Elements of Public Speaking*, Seventh Edition. Copyright © 2000 by Addison Wesley Longman, Inc. Reprinted by permission of Allyn and Bacon.

Ebert, Ronald J. and Ricky W. Griffin. From *Business Essentials*, Second Edition. Copyright © 1998 by Prentice-Hall, Inc. Reprinted by permission of Pearson Education, Inc., Upper Saddle River, NJ.

Elowsky, Jackie. From "Destination: The World—Consider Working in the Global Marketplace," *Resource*, August 2000. Reprinted by permission of the American Society for Agricultural Engineers.

Fox, Justin. From "The Triumph of English," *Fortune*, September 18, 2000. Reprinted by permission.

Fuller, Geoff and Pamelyn Casto. From "A Short Course in Short-Short Fiction," *Writer's Digest*, February 2001. Reprinted by permission of the authors.

Garraty, John A. and Mark C. Carnes. From *The American Nation*, Tenth Edition. Copyright © 2000 by John A Garraty. Reprinted by permission of Pearson Education, Inc.

Gavlak, Dale. From "In Sudan, Childhoods of Slavery," first published in *The Christian Science Monitor*, August 22, 2000. Reprinted by permission of the author.

Gerow, Josh R. From *Psychology: An Introduction*, Second Edition. Copyright © 1989 Scott, Foresman and Company. Reprinted by permission.

Gerow, Josh R. Diagram, "The Major Structures of the Human Ear" from *Psychology: An In Introduction*, Fifth Edition. Copyright © 1997 by Addison-Wesley Educational Publishers, Inc. Reprinted by permission of Pearson Education, Inc., Upper Saddle River, NJ.

Good, Owen S. From "Ramseys Sue Ex-cop for Libel, Slander," *Rocky Mountain News*, March 30, 2001. Reprinted with permission of Rocky Mountain News.

Greulach, Victor A. and Vincent J. Chiappetta. From *Biology: The Science of Life*. Copyright © 1977 by Scott, Foresman and Company. Reprinted by permission of Pearson Education, Inc.

Hamilton, Eva May Nunnelley et al. From *Nutrition: Concepts and Controversies*, Fifth Edition, by Hamilton, Whitney, and Sizer. © 1991. Reprinted with permission of Wadsworth, an imprint of Wadsworth Group, a division of Thomson Learning.

Harari, Oren. "Leading People," *Executive Excellence*, June 2000.

Harvard Business Review. Reprinted by permission of *Harvard Business Review* from "How Entrepreneurs Craft Strategies that Work" in *Harvard Business Review*, March-April 1994. Copyright © 1994 by Harvard Business School Publishing Corporation; all rights reserved.

Henslin, James M. From *Sociology: A Down-To-Earth Approach*, Fifth Edition. Copyright © 2001 by James M. Henslin. Reprinted by permission of Allyn and Bacon.

Herbert, Robert. From an essay on Millet's *The Gleaners* as appeared in exhibition catalog *Man and His World: International Fine Arts Exhibition*, Montreal, 1967. Reprinted by permission of Robert Herbert.

Johnson, Kirk. From "Today's Kids Are, Like, Killing the English Language," *The New York Times*, August 9, 1998. Copyright © 1998 by The New York Times Co. Reprinted by permission.

Katz, Sidney. From "The Importance of Being Beautiful," originally published in *Today*, July 24, 1982. Copyright © 1982 by Sidney Katz. Reprinted by permission of the author.

Kemp, Michael. From "Listening Skill Saves Time, Increase Effectiveness," *The American Salesman*, September 2000. Reprinted by permission of © National Research Bureau, P.O. Box 1, Burlington, Iowa, 52601-0001.

Kettmann, Steve. From "Bush's Secret Weapon," *Salon.com*, March 20, 2000. Reprinted by permission of Salon.com.

Koehler, Carol F. "Mending The Body By Lending An Ear: The Healing Power Of Listening" from address delivered to the International Listening Association Business Conference, Kansas City, Missouri, March 19, 1998. Reprinted by permission of the author.

Lasky, Jane. From "Make the Right Gesture on a Trip to Asia," *The Secured Lender*, November/December 2000. Reprinted by permission of the author.

Light, Donald Jr. and Suzanne Keller. "Unity in Diversity" from *Sociology*, Fourth Edition. Copyright © 1986 by McGraw-Hill, Inc. Reproduced with permission of The McGraw-Hill Companies.

Maugham, W. Somerset. "The Ant and the Grasshopper" from *Cosmopolitans*. Copyright 1924 by W. Somerset Maugham. Reprinted by permission of the heirs of W. Somerset Maugham.

McAfee, Robert E. "Regulation Won't Work: Ban Boxing" as appeared in *USA Today*, December 20, 1990. Reprinted by permission of the author.

McConnell, James V. "Imprinting" and "Monkey Love" from *Understanding Human Behavior: An Introduction to Psychology*, First Edition. © 1974. Reprinted with permission of Wadsworth, an imprint of the Wadsworth Group, a division of Thomson Learning.

McDonald, Daniel. "Tracking the Werewolf," *Skeptical Inquirer*, Summer 1993. Used by permission of Skeptical Inquirer, PO Box 703, Amherst, NY 14226. (www.csicop.org).

McGinn, Daniel. From "Scouting a Dry Campus," *Newsweek*, November 27, 2000. © 2000 Newsweek, Inc. All rights reserved. Reprinted by permission.

Merriam-Webster, Inc. Material reprinted by permission from *Merriam-Webster's Collegiate® Dictionary*, Tenth Edition. © 2001 by Merriam-Webster, Incorporated.

Michaels, James W. From "Practicing What He Preaches," *Forbes*, October 20, 2000. Reprinted by permission of Forbes Magazine. © 2001 Forbes, Inc.

Miller, Roger LeRoy, Daniel K. Benjamin, and Douglass C. North. From *The Economics of Public Issues*, Twelfth Edition. Copyright © 2001 by Addison Wesley Longman, Inc. Reprinted by Permission of Pearson Education, Inc.

Neuwirth, Robert. Excerpt from "Letter from Brazil" by Robert Neuwirth reprinted by permission from the June 10, 2000 issue of *The Nation*.

New York Times Editorial Desk. From "Life by Design: Fertility for Sale," *The New York Times*, March 4, 1998. Copyright © 1998 by The New York Times Co. Reprinted by permission.

Peterson, Thane. From "A Blue Period for Art Buyers." Reprinted from the December 25, 2000 issue of *Business Week* by special permission. Copyright © 2000 by The McGraw-Hill Companies, Inc.

Phu, Ta Thuc. "Elderly Parents: A Cultural Duty" from "Vietnamese: A Lifetime Commitment," *Orlando Sentinel*, May 2, 1998. Copyright © 1998. Reprinted by permission of Ta Thuc Phu.

Pitt, Leonard. From *We Americans*. Copyright © 1987 Kendall/Hunt Publishing Company. Reprinted with permission.

Powell, Colin L. Specific quotes from *My American Journey* by Colin L. Powell appearing in Oren Harari's "Leading People" are reprinted by permission of International Creative Management as agent for General Colin L. Powell.

Powell, Colin L. From *My American Journey* by Colin Powell with Joseph E. Persico. Copyright © 1995 by Colin L. Powell. Used by permission of Random House, Inc.

Reeve, Lloyd Eric. "Caged" from "Practical English," *Household Magazine*, March 2, 1960.

Roget's 21st Century Thesaurus. Published by Dell Publishing, A Division of Random House. Copyright © 1992, 1993, 1999 by The Philip Lief Group, Inc. Reprinted by permission.

Schontzler, Gail. From "In the Name of Research," *Bozeman Daily Chronicle*, December 3, 2000. Reprinted by permission.

Sowell, Thomas. "Students Led to Believe Opinions More Important than Knowledge" as appeared in *Arizona Republic*, August 18, 1998. Reprinted by permission of Thomas Sowell and Creators Syndicate, Inc.

Thomas, Lewis. "Notes on Punctuation." Copyright © 1979 by Lewis Thomas, from *The Medusa and the Snail* by Lewis Thomas. Used by permission of Viking Penguin, a division of Penguin Putnam, Inc.

Time Magazine. From "Numbers," *Time*, April 30, 2001; March 12, 2001; January 29, 2001. © 2001 Time Inc. Reprinted by permission

Wallace, Robert. From *Biology: The World of Life*, Fifth Edition. Copyright © 1990 by Scott, Foresman and Company. Reprinted by permission of Pearson Education, Inc.

Yeoman, Barry. From "Dangerous Food: The Shocking Truth that Puts Your Family at Risk," *Redbook*, August 2000. Reprinted by permission of the author.

Zucker, Martin. From "Food and Stress," *Better Nutrition Magazine*, May 2000. Copyright © 2000 Better Nutrition Magazine (www.betternutrition.com). Reprinted by permission.

Index of Concept Prep Terms

Index